I0043161

Economic Organization of the British Coal Industry

Economic Organization of the British Coal Industry (1934) is a study that shows on the one hand the organization of the coal industry in Britain in the 1930s in conjunction with the economic forces working behind the industry, and on the other hand shows the influence of political, authoritarian thought on its structure.

Economic Organization of the British Coal Industry

Andrew Martin Beuman

Routledge
Taylor & Francis Group

First published in 1934
by George Routledge & Sons, Ltd.

This edition first published in 2025 by Routledge
4 Park Square, Milton Park, Abingdon, Oxon, OX14 4RN

and by Routledge
605 Third Avenue, New York, NY 10017

Routledge is an imprint of the Taylor & Francis Group, an informa business

Publisher's Note
The publisher has gone to great lengths to ensure the quality of this reprint but points
out that some imperfections in the original copies may be apparent.

Disclaimer
The publisher has made every effort to trace copyright holders and welcomes
correspondence from those they have been unable to contact.

A Library of Congress record exists under LCCN a 34001254

ISBN: 978-1-032-90547-1 (hbk)
ISBN: 978-1-003-55854-5 (ebk)
ISBN: 978-1-032-90553-2 (pbk)

Book DOI 10.4324/9781003558545

ECONOMIC ORGANIZATION
OF THE
BRITISH COAL INDUSTRY

By

ANDREW MARTIN NEUMAN
LL.M. (*Warsaw*) ; B.Sc. (Econ.) ; Ph.D. (*London*)

With a Foreword by

THE RIGHT HON. SIR HERBERT SAMUEL
G.C.B., G.B.E., M.P.
Chairman of the Royal Commission on the Coal Industry, 1925

London
GEORGE ROUTLEDGE & SONS, LTD.
Broadway House : 68–74 Carter Lane, E.C.
1934

The Senate of the University of London awarded to the author of this book a grant towards its publication.

PRINTED IN GREAT BRITAIN BY
STEPHEN AUSTIN AND SONS, LTD., HERTFORD

TO MY PARENTS

CONTENTS

LIST OF TABLES

LIST OF DIAGRAMS

LIST OF APPENDICES

FOREWORD

By the Rt. Hon. Sir HERBERT SAMUEL, G.C.B., G.B.E., M.P.
(*Chairman of the Royal Commission on the Coal Industry*, 1925.)

Nature has endowed Great Britain with an equable climate, a fertile soil, many fine harbours, and one vast source of mineral wealth—the extensive deposits of high-quality coal. The working of those deposits and the development of industries based upon them has been the chief factor in the industrial growth and power of Britain. Between three and four millions of our population have been directly dependent for their livelihood upon coal-mining. Coal has provided four-fifths, in bulk, of the outward cargoes of our shipping. The annual value of the product has been in the neighbourhood of £250,000,000. But the coal industry has fallen upon very hard times since the War. For generations it had been the unhappy theatre of disputes between employers and employed, and the depression has increased the friction. At the same time it has brought out very clearly the imperative need for the highest industrial organization in the production of coal and the greatest scientific efficiency in its use. Inevitably these questions have occupied the close attention of Parliament and have become matters of keen political discussion.

Mr. Neuman in this book presents a lucid survey of the course of events in recent years and a clear picture of the present situation. He describes the economic factors that have been at work and the political factors; he traces their interaction and deals with their occasional conflict. Finally, he gives a careful analysis of the marketing schemes under the Act of 1930, and their working.

While I cannot endorse every passage in the book, nor even concur in some of its conclusions, I can commend it as a whole as a thorough and comprehensive study. The writer disentangles the threads of a complicated subject and offers a simple account for the ordinary reader. He has rendered a useful service, both to those engaged in the coal industry itself, and to the wider public who realize its importance to the nation and earnestly desire to promote the restoration of its prosperity.

HERBERT SAMUEL.

3rd January, 1934.

INTRODUCTION

Motto : " Quand le charbon ne va pas, rien ne va "—(Delattre)

The present economic difficulties of the coal industry, in Great Britain as in all coal-producing countries, cannot be analysed in complete isolation from those of other industries. It is impossible to consider the coal industry in a water-tight compartment, faced with economic problems peculiar to itself alone. In fact, the opposite is the truth. There is no such thing as economics of coal industry. Coal, of course, enters into economic equations—it may play there an important rôle, according as its significance in the processes of production and consumption is greater or smaller; it may have some special problems of its own which are chiefly of a technical nature, but economically it is always linked with more general problems and interdependences between the means and the ends which are at our disposal. In this respect one is inclined to agree with two American writers that " to deal with the coal industry in isolation is like trying to cure a plant disease without reference to the soil of its environment ".[1]

Coal is an article which enters the economic structure in all stages of production. It participates in the highest stages, producing goods for the use of other producers. It participates in the lowest stages by helping to produce consumers' goods. Finally, it constitutes a consumers' good itself in its raw or its manufactured form, which is capable of providing immediate satisfaction of human needs for heat, power, light, etc. Being, therefore, in such a broad way a participant in human economic activity, coal is affected immediately, though in various degrees, by any change in the trade cycle. This ubiquity of coal means that the different sections of the industry producing coal for

[1] I. Lubin and H. Everett, *British Coal Dilemma*, New York, 1927.

various uses participate in the trade cycle in very different ways ; each of them according to the characteristics displayed by the demands for their respective products.

As the term " British Coal " covers varying products used in many different ways, it is very difficult for any single section of the industry to alter so as to meet fresh demands. Hence, each producing unit must participate more or less in supplying its respective demand. As Professor Ohlin would probably say, the monopoly of each section of the industry is affected by the nature of its respective demand.[1] Thus the demand for industrial coal for constructional industries was affected by a fall of investments in the earlier stages of production. Several reasons contributed to this decline, by far the most important being a diminution in voluntary savings in Europe [2] especially in the period just following the War, which was marked by general monetary instability. World production of coal grew very little as compared with the average for 1909–1913 ; this rise was probably not much larger than the increase of the population.

During the greater part of the post-War period the main World coal producers, together with other industries, felt the depression in the higher stages of production, but those sections of the industry which cater for the consumers and those industries which are nearer to the consumers were in relative prosperity. But of all factors which determine the development of our industry, the most important is the state of the higher stages of production and that of exports. For this reason, the depression in the British coal industry is closely connected with that in other industries producing capital-goods.

In order to throw more light on the position of British coal mining and its particular problems viewed against the screen of other industries, it is necessary to realize that it is largely an exporting industry. Hence, problems arise which are common to all exporting industries

---

[1] Cf. *The Course and Phases of the World Economic Depression*, Report, presented to the Assembly of the League of Nations, Geneva, 1931, p. 249.
[2] Cf. A. Loveday, *Britain and World Trade*, London, 1931, p. 19.

having to compete in the world's scramble for markets. When the world is reconstructing its capital equipment, these industries are booming and prosperous. On the other hand, in times of recession they have to reduce both prices and quantities shipped. In addition, the exporting industries of Britain suffer from " weak selling " due to cheaper competition from countries with a lower standard of life and a more flexible, or a less capitalistic cost structure, which allow them to adjust themselves quicker to fluctuations.

British coal, which constitutes a very large part of all coal entering international trade, shares all the advantages and disadvantages arising from it : while in periods of falling international trade there is a glut of coal and some pressure on the home market, on the other hand any revival immediately benefits most of the British coalfields. This is one of the chief problems of the industry.

A coal problem seems to have existed in Great Britain from the very beginning of her mining. In all centuries, economists and politicians were busy discussing the coal dilemma of their day. This dilemma has undergone a long and interesting evolution, and its constituents have varied from time to time in the different periods of history. Now Great Britain is again facing a dilemma, but one very remote from the 1865 prophecies of Jevons, whom M. André Siegfried calls the English Cassandra of his time. The difficulty is now a plethora of coal and the problem is to find a means of reducing this abundance. Jevons greatly feared a shortage.[1]

How strange to-day sound the statements of this famous economist about coal, which he thought could never be too abundant ! Jevons feared that coal must become expensive because of its scarcity and the possibility of its exhaustion, while recently there have been attempts to make it artificially scarce and dearer precisely on account of its plenty. What a remarkable change ! According to

[1] W. Stanley Jevons. *The Coal Question*, 3rd ed., London, 1906, p. 369 : ". . . the pre-eminent usefulness of iron places it beside coal and corn as a material of which there cannot be too much—which itself excites and supports population, offering it the means of constant multiplication."

the earlier view,[1] expensiveness was the result of the ultimate working of natural economic forces, according to the latter it is to come as a result of an artificial restriction scheme, stemming the excessively wide stream of coal supplies.

All these recent attempts to introduce some degree of " planned economy " into the fabric of the British coal industry have emphasized the significance of its organization. The structure of the industry comes into special prominence now, when under the marketing clauses of the Coal Mines Act, 1930, the coal-owners are not completely free to conduct their undertakings as they did in the past. This gives scope for a fuller review of the existing forms of organization, and so it must justify our attempt to produce this sketch on the architecture of the coal industry.

The long-continued coal depression, which recently developed into a crisis, has acutely accentuated some of the economic processes in the industry, which in normal times are regulated spontaneously by natural adjustments. Thus the present depression has engendered two major maladjustments : on the one hand disparity between the productive capacity and the actual demand ; on the other disparity between market prices and the costs of production. These two disparities are so considerable that many people have been led to doubt whether they could be equalized by the ordinary economic processes of equilibration without artificial assistance from outside. Thus opinion directed attention to the alleged lack of co-ordination in the industry, and the problem of organization became of general importance.

In the British coal industry, perhaps more than elsewhere, one can witness a close race between the forces of

[1] In the evidence before the House of Commons Committee on Coal in 1829, various authorities opposed exports on the ground of the exhaustion of national mines. Thus, the learned Professor Sidgwick " expressed himself as not being prepared to answer the question as to the expediency of exporting coal ". But Dr. Buckland of Oxford went much further against the policy of permitting the exportation of coal, which is " permitting foreigners to consume the vitals of our own posterity. I consider coals the stamina upon which the manufacturing prosperity of the country primarily depends, and I think it our duty not to spare one ounce of coals to any person but ourselves " (see " The History and Description of Fossil Fuel ", *The Collieries and Coal Trade of Great Britain*, London, 1835, pp. 455–6).

disruption and of integration. These two streams, representing respectively individualism and organization, have always met and contended in all industrial economic activity connected with coal mining. The first of these principles finds its explanation in the policy of the maximization of profits, in the desire to produce the largest tonnage at the highest possible rate of capacity of the mines, in the tendency towards the reduction of costs. The second aims at bringing some degree of economic equalization, at the widest distribution of risk, higher prices of produce leading to higher wages, indirectly at restriction of output, and finally towards mutual assistance in achieving ends common to all.

Here we may point out that in the coal industry the technically optimum size of the producing unit alters as time goes on. Each unit exists first of all in itself, possessing its own individual economic features, ends, and environment, and it enters into larger groups as a member, only when in community it can better satisfy its needs. Thus each colliery undertaking becomes first a part of a large combine, next a participant in its district organization, then probably a member of the area association, and finally it takes its part in national organization. Each of these stages is looser and wider in its scope than the previous one ; again we encounter the warring ideas of disruption and integration. Thus one combine competes with another, one district undercuts another's prices, one area contends with another. Carrying this idea further, the same two tendencies of organization are observable even between one country and another. In Great Britain the centrifugal tendency was always strong on account of the very uneven conditions in which her mining was carried on. But the propensity towards integration was well defined and the coal-owners have always met many of their common problems collectively. Moreover the importance of organization was ardently stressed by the labour employed in the British coal industry.

At all times in its past history the forms of organization in the British coal industry were strictly bound up with its economic development. Economic considerations constituted the origin of the actual organization, which was evolved naturally and spontaneously by otherwise independent contractors. This endogenous activity of the coal-owners was the best guarantee that all partners would reap benefits from organization in conformity with economic laws. To put this in economic terms, the factors of production were free to distribute themselves throughout the coal industry so as to yield the maximum total net product. In such an organization there was no room for coercion from outside, and political forces foreign to the industry were not allowed to perform vivisection on the organism of the coal industry. After the War, however, when the coal depression became prominent and coal ceased to sell itself, as it had done previously, political pressure began gradually to interfere with economic theory. The time was propitious for schemes of reorganization of the British coal industry. " Every decade produces new students of the coal problem, with a panacea, which to them is new but which to the industry is old," [1] said Mr. Raynes, and in no one period was this observation more true than in the post-War era, when the industry, in addition to economic difficulties, was continually troubled with political interference and threatened with State intervention. The well-established truth that whenever economics was in opposition to politics the latter always hampered natural progress, could not find a better example than in the British coal industry. Political reorganization proved always to be either a complete failure whenever it was divorced from actual reality or harmful in the long run to the welfare of the industry.

It was freely said after the War that economic forces had ceased to operate, and economics had no connection with reality. The coal industry provides the best example for the repudiation of these fallacies, most of which are simply based on inadequate analysis, or insufficient knowledge of data. In no industry has it been more clearly shown that any attempt to interfere with the normal processes

[1] J. R. Raynes, *Coal and Its Conflict*, London, 1928.

are completely futile. Interference leads only to still further interference which either frustrates the effect of the first laws, or brings the industry further into confusion.

In this study we attempt to show on the one hand the existing organization of the coal industry in Britain in conjunction with the economic forces working behind the industry, and on the other hand we show the influence of political, authoritarian thought on its present structure. After dealing in Part I with the economic factor, we proceed in Part II to stress the significance and extent of the political factor, including a special chapter on the attitudes of the leading political parties on the coal problem.

Finally, in Part III we investigate the clash between the two aspects of organization and evaluate the recent structure of the British coal industry under the Coal Mines Act, 1930.

LONDON,
November, 1933.

PART I

THE ECONOMIC FACTOR

CHAPTER I

THE ECONOMIC SITUATION OF THE COAL INDUSTRY AFTER THE WAR [1]

§ 1. THE GENERAL POSITION

Having stated in the introduction the problem of our inquiry into the organization of the British coal industry, we must now proceed to outline as briefly as possible the economic background against which the organizing process in the industry was going on. A candid picture of the actual position of our industry will provide us with a clue to the explanation of current opinions and landmarks in reorganization. We thus find it incumbent to show the intertwined relations between the progress of the coal crisis and the advancement of the organization movement. The two ways of looking at the industry, i.e. from the purely economic point of view and from its antithesis, the political, become much clearer when they are related to the surroundings which in due course gave rise to them.

If we compare the economic conditions prevailing in the coal trade before the War with those which arose after, we are struck immediately with growth of irregularity and abnormality. Here we do not agree with those views which are inclined to over-stress, in the post-War period, the importance of structural deficiencies. Certainly, the War had a detrimental effect on the technical progress of the industry, both by slowing down the rate of new investments and by speeding up the march of capital consumption ; but, on the other hand, it scarcely can be argued that it constituted a drawback to the capital or commercial organization of the industry. Neither do we think that the War can give any explanation of the existence

[1] In the course of writing this chapter the author received the most valuable support and help from Professor Lionel Robbins.

3

of the excessive productive capacity or of a large number of small and poorly planned collieries, the lack of the so-called co-operative spirit among the masters, or of the striking differences between the marginal and the best mines in the country, except in so far as it created a short period of apparent prosperity.   We feel equally reluctant to agree that the process of external substitution,[1] i.e. the replacement of coal by other commodities, has such a prominent bearing on the future prospects of our industry.   It is often over-emphasized that oil, water-power, electricity, etc., are chiefly responsible for the development of the coal crisis. In our opinion, the process of substitution is continually going on and continually advancing, simultaneously with the advancement of economic progress.   In normal times, however, the readjustment goes on much more smoothly, and while coal is being displaced in one process of the industrial structure it is immediately absorbed in another. In coal, it is the very economy of its use which leads to its extensive consumption.   It has been so in the past and will be so in the future.[2]   Even now it has been stated during the debates of the 3rd World Power Conference that the development of motor traction has created a new demand for coal in all the motor constructing industries.   Thus it appears that, generally speaking, coal and its substitutes display more features of complementarity than is generally assumed.   It is certainly not through a primitive " back to coal movement " and through the artificial " death knelling " of progress [3] that coal will be restored to its previous position.

In discussing the difficulties of the coal industry, which are common to all raw material producing industries, or, as they are often termed, the industries of the higher stages of production,[4] we are taking the view that all those defective elements which have come out at the time of the present industrial and financial depression existed a long time before the War, though partly concealed under the surface.

[1] See Part I, Chap. II, § 2.
[2] W. Stanley Jevons, *The Coal Question*, 3rd ed., p. 141.
[3] *Vide* Capt. Bernard Acworth, *Back to the Coal Standard*, London, 1932.
[4] Cf. F. v. Hayek, *Prices and Production*, London, 1931.

We agree with Messrs. Lubin and Everett[1] that " during the decades when coal was coming into the height of its power, its problems were those of a successful industry carrying on its back the other industries of a prosperous people, employing an increasing number of workers, mining abundant and accessible coal for a market where there was no problem of substitutes and little serious competition ". Hence we do not propose to embark upon the customary gloomy description of the notorious deficiencies of the industry, but we intend to stress those changes which after the War brought the previously prosperous industry to a state of despair.

It has already been mentioned above that coal, together with several other industries engaged in the production of producers' goods, suffered severely throughout nearly the whole period after the War, and especially later in the great depression 1930–33. This was clearly reflected in relatively much higher unemployment in these industries than in the industries of the later stages of production.[2]

At this point it will perhaps be appropriate to observe that even in any prosperous branch of industry we can always find out some units which are antiquated, or which are inefficient in comparision with the actual state of technique, or in relation to something like the representative firms (in the Marshallian sense) [3] in this branch of industry. But such units in normal times are either eliminated in due course, or they quickly adapt themselves by a process of reconstruction to the general level. Hence, at a time when trade is going on an even keel, such inefficiency does not constitute any important difficulty for the industry as a whole.

This automatic adjustment to the necessities of

---

[1] Isador Lubin and Helen Everett, *The British Coal Dilemma*, London 1927, p. 5.
[2] See Addendum to this Chapter—No. I.
[3] Cf. Alfred Marshall, *Industry and Trade*, London, 1919, p. 509 : " These tendencies [technical progress] have constantly increased the size of the representative business unit, that is of the unit whose costs of production exercise so great an influence on the amount that will be forthcoming to meet any given market demand, that they play a prominent part in the regulation of price under competitive conditions."

economic life seems to have worked much more smoothly before the War than after, when conditions are changing with much greater rapidity, and on the other hand the industry itself is less fitted to meet these changes. Moreover, it seems that the very fact of the break in this automatic adjustment which existed during the pre-War period, when it was only necessary for the captains of industry to keep ready for an increasing demand for fuel, will give an adequate explanation of the reorganization movement in the coal industry. That pre-War automatic adjustment rendered the question of organization much less conspicuous than after the War. Many proposals and plans for a new industrial architecture arose just out of the creed that something is fundamentally wrong with the industry, that not merely ordinary economic reorganization, but radical political changes must be brought about. And here we face an important problem which has already been so much stressed in post-War years. A large section of the community is led to believe that coal is facing a purely structural crisis, arising out of complete mismanagement by the leaders of the industry. It is often argued that the difficulties of the industry arose entirely from the " structural formation ", that is from the forms of ownership and methods of management existing in the industry. The great difficulties confronting coal mining strengthen those sections of reformers who would like to see political pressure applied as a cure. While in normal conditions automatic adjustment as well as the process of reorganization arise, as Professor Macgregor [1] would probably say, from the needs of the representative firms, so in time of abnormal pressure, or abnormal adjustment of supply to demand, the self-adjusting forces are to a great extent paralysed.

At this juncture it will perhaps be appropriate to mention that we appraise the whole position in the coal industry as having its root in the general economic depression which in various phases was developed since the War. Those views which try to explain all the troubles by merely quoting

[1] Cf. D. H. Macgregor, *Industrial Combination*, London, 1906.

examples of the faults of organization, and of other intrinsic defects in the industry itself, certainly underrate the significance and the degree of the general crisis. Never after the War did the short spells of economic revival last long enough to stimulate a strong wave of new investment in this basic industry, or to evoke a process of internal reorganization. All the time the coal industry felt the hard blows of the deflationary tendencies and unstable monetary conditions, all the time it had to think about reducing prices, especially in the export markets, although confronted at the same time by the difficulties of an extremely rigid wage system, a high pitch of elasticity of demand for a fall,[1] depressed conditions of those basic industries which formerly were its best customers, and throughout bearing the millstone of excess capacity round its neck. A relatively large reduction in ocean freight-rates has facilitated the export of coal for other countries, even if they have had no return cargo like Britain to carry back home.[2]

The chronic coal depression is deeply intertwined with the general trade cycle. One could therefore hardly argue that it arises only from structural causes, without taking into account the conjunctural causes. The inadequacies of reorganization and modernization of the coal industry as a whole have their roots in the fact that a large degree

[1] See Part I, Chap. II, § 2.
[2] Interesting figures concerning the reduction in freight-rates are published by the Economic Intelligence Service of the League of Nations in the *World Economic Survey, 1931–2*, Geneva, 1932, p. 19.

TABLE No. 1

INDEX NUMBERS OF OCEAN FREIGHT-RATES AND WHOLESALE PRICES, 1913–1931

Year.	United Kingdom.		United States.		Germany.	
	Freight Index.	Wholesale Prices.	Freight Index.	Wholesale Prices.	Freight Index.	Wholesale Prices.
1913	100	100	100	100	100	100
1924	127	165	106	141	106	137
1928	110	142	97	139	102	140
1930	82	113	85	124	92	125
1931	85	98	85	105	84	111

United Kingdom, *The Statist*; United States of America, *U.S. Dept. of Commerce*; Germany, *Wirtschaft und Statistik*.

of capital investment, so badly needed especially at present, can usually only take place in an expanding industry with prospects for increased sales and profits, while the static rationalization with which we shall deal later,[1] is extremely unpopular. But in addition to all these purely economic reasons, political interference, which has chosen the coal industry as its favourite domain, has undoubtedly in our view prevented all sound reconstruction work, because the leading owners had to exert all their energy in defending the status of their industry. Though the competing foreign coal industries, especially in Germany, Poland, and Belgium, contended in the first post-War years against all sorts of political interference, the industry in these countries was left free much sooner than in Britain, where operation has been in more or less normal political conditions only since 1927. Thus political interference lasted here much longer than abroad, accentuating the state of uncertainty. In telescoping our preliminary remarks, we want to make it quite clear that we consider the British coal crisis as being greatly affected by the general crisis throughout the whole post-War period, and that we do not accept as a sufficient explanation for the coal troubles the lack of organization, or, as it is most often described, the failure on the part of the coal owners to follow technical progress.

The grave situation of the British coal industry which arose after the War and continues at the present moment springs both from *internal* and from *external* conditions. Since the former remained within the control of the industry itself, they could be altered by concerted action of the owners or with some assistance from the State. This assistance first took place in 1926, through the provisions for amalgamations of mines, and again in 1930 through the formation of a planned marketing system and the promotion of concentration of undertakings. The latter, however, were completely heteronomous, and were closely correlated with the phases of the world economic depression.

We shall deal first with these *external* events, which remained outside the control of the industry itself,

[1] See Part III, Chap. III, § 3.

since in our opinion they directly influenced the internal organization. These occurrences were common to the home situation and to the international world. The enormous economic readjustment which took place all over the world after the War affected Britain's basic industry to a great extent. German reparations [1] ; the occupation of the Ruhr in 1923, and the consequent reduction in German output of coal, which left that usually exporting country with a net import of more than 18 million metric tons of coal (mostly from England) ; the tariff war [2] from 1925 between Poland and Germany, which, on the one hand, led to an artificial development of the German lignite industry, and of the German Silesian coalfields [3] and, on the other, forced Polish coal to find an outlet in Scandinavia ; and finally the revalorization of the pound sterling. Mr. Keynes [4] considers the coal industry " as being above all others a victim of our monetary policy ". As that state of depression in the industry is ultimately reflected in the miners' standard of life he concludes that :—

> " they represent in flesh the ' fundamental adjustments ' engineered by the Treasury and the Bank of England to satisfy the impatience of the City fathers to bridge the moderate gap between \$4.40 and \$4.86."

[1] Under the clauses of the Dawes Plan which was signed in April, 1924, Germany was allowed to pay part of her reparations in kind. Amongst these deliveries, coal was the main item.

[2] In accordance with the provisions of the Polish-German Agreement of 15th May, 1922, the so-called Geneva Convention, regulating for a transition period the relations between the German and the Polish parts of Silesia, the Reich was obliged to accept a delivery of Polish coal from Upper Silesia. The amount was fixed for each year at about 6 million tons, or 500,000 tons per month. The Polish Republic on the other hand was bound to secure smooth deliveries in order to prevent any eventual shortage of coal in Eastern Germany ; in 1923, during the occupation of the Ruhr coal district, the amount so delivered actually surpassed the fixed quota. In the first half of 1925, Poland was exporting on an average about 450,000 tons of coal monthly to Germany. These deliveries were suddenly stopped in the middle of 1925 by the German embargo on Polish coal, which gave rise to the economic war between the two countries.

[3] The present German section of Upper Silesia produced before the War in 1913 about 11 million tons. In 1925, when the economic war with Poland began, this section produced 14·2 million tons. The production rose further to 22 million tons in 1929, then fell to 18 million tons in 1930, and to 16·8 million tons in 1931. On the other hand, Polish Upper Silesia did not, except in 1929, exceed its pre-war output.

[4] J. M. Keynes, *The Economic Consequences of Mr. Churchill*, London, 1925, pp. 22 and 23.

This appreciation of the £ exercised the strongest influence in the export districts in South Wales, since it coincided with the devalorization of the French franc. Further external factors operating outside the control of the British coal industry were, the abnormal monetary conditions in the majority of countries in Europe, and other parts of the world ; the import quotas and restrictions imposed on British coal by France, Germany, Belgium, the Irish Free State, and other countries ; and the depressed conditions of the iron and steel and other basic industries. Though for a short time the depreciation of the £ in 1931 clearly helped the exporting branches, recent events in America and elsewhere again affected the industry which has now to compete, for instance, with cheaper American anthracite in Canada.

At the beginning of this section we stressed the fact that after the War our industry had to face a much larger degree of abnormality than before. Now, we shall devote some space to prove this proposition, since on the assumption that those irregularities are to be blamed for the introduction of the disorganization and chaos in the normal expansion and normal organization of the industry our argument stands or falls. All the economic irregularities which beset the coal industry after the War from outside may be telescoped into three headings, since they all came from three different sources : (1) Irregularities in the demand for coal ; (2) Irregularities in the trend of prices ; (3) Irregularities in the trend of profits.

(1) *Irregularities in the Demand for Coal*

Probably the enormous jumps in the demand for coal provide the ultimate explanation of the behaviour of points (2) and (3), and for this reason we shall analyse this point first. If we take the pre-War conditions and investigate the volume of production, we shall notice that, though on several occasions the figures of output fluctuated very substantially, they tended practically always to rise, while the downward movements were relatively insignificant, and never lasted more than one or two years, after which production again exceeded the previous records. Exactly the same observation applies to the quantities of British coal shipped abroad, either as exports or as bunker in foreign and home marine in service of foreign trade. Turning now to the post-War conditions, we find a completely reversed picture of the whole situation, which reveals the abnormal tendencies exhibited by the demand. A table has been constructed in order to show the enormous fluctuations in demand, both total and foreign, in the years following the War.[1]

We notice continuously repeated swings downward and upward in the total output of coal. The maximum fall in production is extremely serious, being, in round figures, 67 million tons ; the falls from year to year are also very considerable, being 66 million tons in the strike year 1921, and 24 million both in 1925 and 1931, i.e. about 10 per cent of the output. Such enormous oscillation, which did not exist before the War, raises the difficulty of defining the actual volume of existing redundant capacity, and so hinders any constructive economic planning. Obviously judging by the volume of output in any selected year one would obtain an entirely different estimate of the over-capacity from that reached in another year where the production has either risen or fallen. Thus the most sagacious computations based on one period are completely upset by these irregular fluctuations.

Professor Allen tried recently to define the volume of over-capacity of the coal industry, in his study on the organization of British industries.[2] In his view, whenever additional tonnage could be produced without increasing fixed costs, over-capacity exists ; this over-capacity is equal to the difference between actual output and that output which could be produced without additional fixed capital. Besides several drawbacks of this formulation,

---

[1] See Addendum to this Chapter—No. II.
[2] G. C. Allen, *British Industries and their Organization*, London, 1933. The passage reads as follows : " The development of these additional coal-producing resources, accompanied as it has been by a very slow growth in demand, has resulted in a large surplus of capacity in the industry. This surplus may be defined as the difference between the tonnage which the existing mines could produce without additional fixed capital and the actual production." (p. 37.)

it is a purely static definition of over-capacity, and it would mean that as actual production even in equilibrium may vary from day to day, from year to year, from hour to hour— the excess capacity is never the same.   In our view, physical over-capacity should not be linked with the intricate problem of full employment or consumption of either kind of capital.   Physical excess capacity in our view is that portion of mining investments which is above the needs of the existing structure of production if the latter were set in full motion.   Or to express it in economic jargon—any amount which is above what is required to keep the existing length of the average period of production, i.e. which does not cause less capitalistic methods of production.   This problem of over-capacity must be kept well in mind, because it forms the point attacked for the most part by those who often do not realize that the volume of over-capacity cannot and must not be arbitrarily determined.   For instance, what in 1928 could be regarded as over-capacity, say under the Scottish Marketing Scheme of 1928,[1] might in 1929, owing to the revival of foreign trade, be considered as a good working unit.   Hence a complete removal of over-capacity remains a very problematic proposition.[2]   But we cannot at this stage expatiate any longer on this question, and we must now direct our attention to the export trade.

Here, those tendencies already noticeable in the total volume of output are magnified and still more visible. The difference in volume exported between the maximum and minimum years is expressed in the index by 146·4 and 52·1, i.e. by 94·3 points.[3]   Even in the last six years (1927–1932) the amplitudes are as large as 21·2 points. All the fluctuations in the exporting sections are both much more prominent and more irregular than those either in the total volume of output, or even more in the volume of coal available for home consumption, which on the whole appears to be steady.   In 1924 and 1931 the quantities exported on both occasions dropped approximately by 20 per cent, while at the same time the total output dropped

---

[1] See Part I, Chap. II, § 2.
[2] Cf. Part II, Chap. II, § 3.
[3] On all this *vide* Appendix to this Chapter.

in the first instance by just short of 4 per cent, and in the second by about 8 per cent. All this is due of course to the fairly steady home demand where no such vehement fluctuations take place.

At this juncture we may perhaps be allowed to revert for a moment to the problem of excess capacity, to which passing reference has already been made. Owing to more rapid movements in the exporting sections, we must not be astonished to find a greater potential capacity in these districts than in those supplying home trade.[1] Any proposals for the reorganization of the industry which are not prepared to allow for this excess are bound to fail on purely economic grounds. The organization of exporting districts, besides the reasons for greater elasticity of demand for coal with which we shall deal in a later place,[2] must also have more looseness than that of districts supplying home requirements, as the variations in demand are so much greater. This necessity for reserve capacity in the exporting branch is undoubtedly one of the reasons explaining why the exporting areas like Fifeshire, Northumberland, Durham, and part of South Wales found themselves, on the whole, reluctant to evolve their own schemes for restriction of output, and were in most cases strongly opposed to the compulsory reorganization brought forward by the Coal Mines Act, 1930.

Passing now to the proportion of coal used at home and that exported, we can easily notice that there is a marked propensity for the percentage of coal shipped abroad to fall from 1924 onwards.[3] A larger proportion of output than before is placed at home, thus increasing the significance of the home market. This growing importance of home sales was emphasized by the combination both of the declining percentage of tonnage shipped abroad and of the relative fall of prices in the export markets. To this latter tendency we are going to devote now a few words.

[1] Cf. on the excess capacity in the exporting district of the north-east coast the Industrial Survey of the North-East Area of England, prepared for the Board of Trade by Armstrong College, Newcastle-upon-Tyne (H.M. Stationery Office, 1932, August).

[2] See Part I, Chap. II, § 2.

[3] *Vide* Addendum to this Chapter—No. II.

(2) *Irregularities in the Trend of Prices* [1]

In addition to enormous abnormalities in the volume of output and in the relation between export and home consumption, we observe after the War a strong downward trend in export prices. While all countries displayed the tendency to develop their own resources of power and fuel to the utmost, the volume of international trade at the same time tended to become smaller. This led to a gradual displacement of British coal by other supplies of fuel, and is illustrated clearly in the Addendum to this Chapter.[2] The increase of foreign consumption of coal is not accompanied by a pro-rata increase of British exports. On the contrary, the world market for British coal inclines to shrink, since the absolute figures of tons exported show a sharp decrease, not only when compared with the peak year 1913, but also when compared with the average exports between 1909 and 1913. The share of British coal in the total world consumption (Great Britain excluded) has substantially diminished. In 1929, this decrease amounted to nearly 30 per cent when compared with the pre-War ratio.

As this decline in the total volume exported was not accompanied even by a gradual increase in the home consumption of coal, the evil of over-capacity in the exporting areas came to be clearly recognized as aggravating the whole British coal question. Hence the disposal of a large tonnage, even at reduced prices, on the foreign markets was of great importance. The price of export-coal was gradually approaching the price of coal at pit. The value of export was falling. The margin which had always existed between the average selling value of coal at the pit-head and the average declared value f.o.b. per ton of coal exported rapidly diminished after the War. In the British coal trade, export had become less remunerative even before the War and the home market tended to be the only profitable one. But this pre-War trend, which was

---

[1] *Vide* Addendum to this Chapter—No. III.

[2] The author would like to acknowledge here the assistance of Professor A. J. Sargent, whose suggestions helped substantially to clarify the main argument of this section.

of a rather moderate nature, and was partly due to economies on transport costs, became very violent and pronounced after the War, when the margin fell rapidly.[1] This was due particularly to the enormous competition with other coal exporting countries, but partly also to the desire to prevent the existing elasticity of demand for a fall [2] from diminishing the demand for coal, and to the effort to check the tendency to shift the demand toward substitutes. Such inclination of the export prices towards the prices at the pit reveals clearly the growing relative unremunerativeness of the overseas trade, and shows that the whole production as far as price is concerned is balanced rather by home consumption than by the export of coal.[3] The home consumer begins to have an ever-increasing importance in the commercial policy of the industry. The trend of export prices downward toward pit-head prices could be observed long before the War,[4] but after the removal of Government control it became simply cataclysmic.

The average margin for the whole of the last decade fell much lower than even the yearly margin in any single year before 1914. Here is a proof of the falling remunerativeness of British export of coal, which accentuates at the same time the growing importance of the inland sales of coal. Such a time is the most suitable for floating restriction schemes of output and sales in the home market. As practically all the producers will, during the falling margin of export prices, be inclined to pay an ever-increasing attention to the home market,[5] the necessity arises for some

[1] Cf. Addendum to this Chapter—No. IV.
[2] Cf. Part I, Chap. II, § 2.
[3] In the recent trade agreements concluded with the Scandinavian countries and with Denmark, which prescribed the percentages of the total coal imports into those countries which should be shipped from this country, the maximum prices of coal have been fixed on a very low level.
[4] A certain part of the fall in the margin could be expected *a priori* over a long time owing to the diminishing proportionate costs of services per ton of coal exported, which enter as items of the f.o.b. prices. This fall, however, was far less rapid than the fall in the post-War trend of the margin. Neither does it explain the violent yearly fluctuations which we witnessed during the period analysed.
[5] The insufficient attention paid by the trade to the home market has been always very prominent. Foreign trade, though really often of less dimension and importance, seemed to be more favoured than the internal market. This is well pointed out by Mr. G. D. H. Cole in the following way : " At present, in this country, the home market is commonly the

extensive arrangements among the coal owners to avoid
ruinous competition.   It would be a very illuminating
study to compare the history of the attempts to restrict
the output and sales of coal with the periods of falling
margins between home and export prices, and to discover
a large degree of correlation between the two.[1]   Any fall in
the margin renders the home consumption of relatively
greater importance to the industry, since the average
price of coal at the pit-head represents the combined prices
of coal at pit both for home use and intended for export.

last to receive the attention of either economists or statesmen. We have
lived so long under the spell of international trade that most of us still
find it difficult to think in other terms. Even now, the remedies proposed
for our troubles in capitalist circles are conceived almost wholly in terms
of our trade overseas." (*The Next Ten Years in British Social Economic
Policy*, London, 1929, p. 38.)

[1] Here we point out only some of the attempts to cartelise the coal
industry. As far back as the early eighties of the last century, John
Nixon, a well-known business man in Welsh steam coal, advocated the
formation of an association for the regulation of output. See *John Nixon,
Pioneer of the Steam Coal Trade in South Wales*, by J. E. Vincent, London,
1900, and George R. Carter, *The Tendency Towards Industrial Combination*,
London, 1913, p. 238. In 1891, Sir George Elliott launched a scheme for the
regulation of production and reorganization of sales by means of a syndicate.
The scheme received wide publicity in 1893, and was discussed in *The Times*
on 20th September, 1893.

According to J. R. Raynes, the districts of Yorkshire, Derbyshire,
Lancashire, and Staffordshire were ready to co-operate (*Coal and its
Conflict*, London, 1928, p. 48).

In 1894, there were in existence some forms of cartels to regulate prices :
The Durham Coal Sales Association, which co-operated with Northumber-
land (see the *Colliery Guardian* of 23rd February, 1894, and Henry W.
Macrosty, *The Trust Movement in British Industry*, London, 1907, p. 30).

In 1894, the Price Association in Fifeshire, and an Association in
Lancashire and Cheshire.

In 1896, the scheme of Lord Rhondda for the regulation of production
was widely discussed. It was subjected to severe criticism in the *Journal
of the Royal Statistical Society*, in 1896, p. 669.

In March, 1897, the coal-owners of South Wales met together in order
to discuss a scheme for co-ordinating production, but it failed to command
the required majority of 90 per cent (see Raynes, op. cit., p. 88).

In 1901, many coal owners urged the necessity for the creation of a
coal cartel.

Co-ordinating tendencies were clearly distinguishable in 1904, when
a small coal combine was proposed (see *The South Wales Coal Annual*,
1905, p. 33).

Other Schemes followed :—

1912 and 1913, the famous E. Lewy scheme advocated a complete
international control of the coal industry.

1919 the scheme of Sir A. Duckham.

1926 Lord Melchett's scheme for the formation of an export syndicate
(see *The Accountant*, 26th June, 1926, pp. 876–8).

1928, the regional cartels in Scotland, South Wales, and in the Midlands.

The drop, therefore, of one of the two items accentuates the significance of the other. This fact is all the more important since the home market presents different features, as regards possibilities of restriction, from the world market, where various nations' commercial habits and costs of production find their reflection in the competitive struggle. In times of falling margin, therefore, such as those during the last decade, there is the endeavour on behalf of the exporting districts to secure as far as possible a large share in the home markets. This leads to a fight for territory in the home markets, which is reflected in a general reduction of prices, since the home demand for coal remains as a whole little elastic for a rise, and cannot take up the total loss in tonnage incurred abroad.

The whole problem seems to be concentrated in the question of over-production of coal for foreign use.[1] Such over-production caused a large fall of the price margin. This fall emphasized the relative dearness of coal in Great Britain in comparison with its price in importing countries. This occurred for the first time soon after the completely reverse situation, i.e. after the period of control when home prices were unduly low in relation to the actual costs of production, and the prices for export coal swelled enormously. Whereas then Great Britain enjoyed very cheap coal, the importing nations had to pay exorbitantly in order, partly, to make good the low level of prices at home.

[1] The difference between the price mechanism of coal for export and that for home use was stressed by Professor Aftalion, and the relatively stronger home prices for coal are explained on the ground that at home in the beginning of the depression coal was used chiefly for consumption purposes, or for goods of the later stage of production. He states that " au moins pour les marchés intérieurs, les prix du charbon ne baissent pas aussitôt après la crise générale, mais souvent haussent encore la première année de la dépression. Cette continuation de la hausse s'explique-t-elle entièrement par la pratique des contrats de longue durée ? Ne peut-elle pas être due, au moins pour partie, à ce que malgré la crise la demande de charbon reste encore considérable de la part des industries productrices de biens de consommation dont l'outillage vient de s'accroitre grandement ? N'est elle pas un indice de la production accrue de biens de consommation dans les premiers temps de la dépréssion ? "   In this passage the author rightly stresses that coal used in the later stages of production can be nearly proof from fall in prices, but this is scarcely true of all kinds of coal, which are more dependent on industrial revival at home or abroad than on consumers' demand. (See Albert Aftalion, *Les Crises Periodiques de Surproduction*, vol. ii, p. 158.)

It was the export trade which to a great extent subsidized home prices, disturbing, therefore, the right balance in the calculation of prices both for home use and for export. One section of the trade had to pay more than would otherwise be justified if the home price machinery were left free to operate. This position was the more dangerous since it was perfectly obvious that sooner or later the coal hunger abroad would give way to normal supplies from other sources and that the inflated prices for export coal based on false apportionment of revenues between this country and abroad would contribute to future difficulties. So long as export paid, this country would adopt optimistically cheap prices of coal at home, but as soon as the export failed, British coal was unable to make both ends meet, having unreasonably cheap prices at home, and a declining export trade, with a rapidly falling margin between the two sets of prices. In 1919 the margin rose to 73 per cent and in 1920 attained the unprecedented height of 131 per cent, making the f.o.b. export prices substantially more than double the price of coal at pit.[1] Moreover, the price for the home market being restricted, the rise could not find any expression similar to that of the world price. It has been expressed clearly enough by Sir Richard Redmayne [2] in his study on State control of the coal industry. Hitherto the process of adjustment of home prices of coal to the actual costs of production had been partly cancelled ; the only channel which remained under this system free for

---

[1] Cf. Addendum to this Chapter—No. IV.

[2] Sir Richard Redmayne, who took an active part in the work and proceedings of the governmental control of the industry, pointed this out in the following words :—

"Speaking of control generally, apart from financial control, it did in fact secure a fair distribution of coal to the British public and to the Allies, and did prevent prices soaring to extravagant heights. From the very high prices which characterized coal supplies to neutral nations during and subsequent to the War, it is evident that had the Government not instituted prices in respect of coal for home consumption, the cost of coal for industrial and household purposes would have been far in excess of the supply, and in place of a rise in respect of household coal, of 19s. which was the extent of the rise reached to about May, 1920, it is not improbable that the advance would have been in the neighbourhood of 40s. or even 60s. per ton ; and wages would have advanced far beyond the height to which they attained under control." (*The British Coal Mining Industry during the War*, Oxford, 1923, p. 265.)

extensive exploitation was export to neutral countries. It was the foreign importer who had to pay for the consequences of the Price of Coal (Limitation) Act.[1] Unfortunately for the industry, even long after the cessation of hostilities the conditions thus created remained in force : unreasonably high prices for exports and demoralizingly low prices at home. This abnormal situation contained in itself the roots of the future coal crisis in Britain ; it could exist only until the British coal supplies were to a great extent supplanted either by those of other countries, or by native coal, or by substitutes for coal. The 1920 boom, which accentuated the inflated prices exclusively on the foreign market, compared with restricted prices at home, was in itself a harbinger of the inevitably approaching crash, and of the collapse of the whole conception of keeping the coal industry going only by export prices. Such an expedient was too far from any sound commercial and economic principle to yield a successful result.

Here we are in complete agreement with the pertinent remarks of Professor Allen who deprecated equally the policy of over-charging foreign buyers and the policy of subsidizing the industry to enable it to export.[2] The collapse in fact came in 1921, and was reflected in a colossal fall of prices abroad. The position became fatal. England with her cheap coal at home could not now expect her exports to bridge the gulf between actual price and cost. The foreigner as a subsidizer of home prices suddenly disappeared. The situation was the more serious as not only did export prices cease to be remunerative, but the price level at home was now too low to make production pay. The coal industry after the sudden decontrol, lost the remunerative foreign trade, while the home market could not meet the actual costs. Attempts were made to reduce labour costs and a

[1] The Price of Coal (Limitation) Act, 1915, operated from the end of July, 1915, until the cessation of the Control at the end of March, 1921.

[2] Professor G. C. Allen says that : " During the post-War boom it [the Government] permitted coal to be sold at exorbitant prices to the foreigner, with the result that the development of alternative sources of power was stimulated. In 1925, it adopted the opposite policy of subsidizing the industry, so that the foreigner could be provided with coal cheaply at the expense of the taxpayer." (British Industries and their Organization, London, 1933, p. 45.)

critical deadlock arose ; the gap between costs of production and prices had to be filled up by State grants to the tune of ten million pounds. Subsidies were designed to cover the difference in wages between the amount agreed upon in the terms of the settlement ending the strike of 1921 and the amount adopted during the period of transition to the lower wage scale. This way of reducing wages was the first serious attempt to decrease the costs of production and to adjust the whole industry to the world situation. Artificial tying up of the prices of coal at home had, doubtless, greatly retarded the natural process of adjusting the costs of production to prices, and vice versa. It was not until the margin between the export and home prices had catastrophically decreased that some attempts were made to widen it by lowering the only factor under the control of the industry, i.e. the prices of coal at the pit. Control over the export prices had been lost to a great extent, since the costs alone at home were now higher than the prices in the world coal markets. The erroneous price policy of British coal export in the years immediately following the War, which based the main calculation on foreign shipments, could in the long run bring only one result—the stimulation of an excessive coal production abroad, as well as the galvanization of all the possible substitutes for coal as power and fuel.

The breakdown of the foreign export market was the more painful because, when the whole world began to work on cheap coal, Great Britain had to pay proportionately much higher prices. An illustration of this may be found in a comparison of the prices of two coal districts in England, one exporting coal and the other producing coal for home use only, before and after the collapse of prices in the world market.[1]

We notice in the prices of coal for export an enormous

[1] We choose for this purpose the price of South Wales Large Steam for export (f.o.b.) as representative of export coal and the Lancashire Best House (on wagon at pit) as representative of coal for home consumption. South Wales coal was quoted, in 1921, as follows : For 7th January it was sold at 67s. 6d. to 70s., on 28th July the price slumped suddenly to the level of 42s. to 43s. per ton, and on 29th December, the price was as low as 23s. to 24s. During 1922 and 1923 the price oscillated round the level of 27s.

and continuous fall during the whole of 1921. After a slight rise during 1922 and 1923, the prices continued to drop further, but not so sharply. When we turn to the prices of coal for home use, e.g. in Lancashire, we notice a different feature. While the export prices dependent on external factors outside the control of e.g. the Welsh coal industry have dropped during the year by more than 66 per cent, the prices paid by the British consumer for Lancashire coal have practically remained unchanged.[1] It may perhaps furnish a good illustration of the essential change in the significance of the price movement, if we remark that while at the beginning of 1921 the Welsh Large Steam coal for export (f.o.b.) was nearly twice as expensive as the Lancashire Best Coal (on wagon at pit), at the end of the year the reverse position occurred and the Lancashire coal was about 60 per cent more expensive than the Welsh Large Steam for export. This expensiveness of coal can be better grasped if one remembers that the general price level was substantially falling. The gradual drop in prices of coal at home means, therefore, a relative rise in comparison with the position at the beginning af 1921. The index numbers of wholesale prices as published in the Board of Trade Journal merely shows the tendency of prices in general. The yearly average for all articles was 307·3 (Prices in 1913, 100) in 1920 ; this figure dropped in the next two years to 197·2 and 158·8 respectively. The price of Lancashire coal did not exhibit any similar feature and remained practically stable. The excessive protection of the consumers during the control, which did not allow prices to find their natural level, had been paid for by relatively high prices at home afterwards. This essential truth, that "Coal, like water, has the forceful habit of finding its level ",[2] seems to have been forgotten entirely.

[1] On 7th January, 1921, a ton of coal was valued here at from 37s. 6d. to 39s. 8d. ; on 28th July, of the same year, the price was still 37s. 8d., and at the end of the year coal was sold at 36s. 6d. and 38s. 6d. During the two subsequent years 1922 and 1923, the price of this grade of coal fell very gently to the average level of 35s. per ton on wagon at pit. These facts reveal a very interesting change which took place in the mutual relations of home and export prices.
[2] J. R. Raynes, *Coal and its Conflicts*, London, 1928, p. 49.

All that we have said about the ill-success of the attempt to protect the consumer in the post-War years does not at all mean that we do not approve of the policy of low prices of coal at home. On the contrary, the real meaning is that in a coal exporting country such as Britain the margin between the export prices and the inland prices ought to be kept as stable as possible. The stability of the margin cannot be effected if one set of prices is tied up and so gives an additional stimulus towards the overgrowth of the set which is left free. Excessive disequilibrium between the two prices created the danger that any coal, which could not find an outlet under changed conditions abroad, would be suddenly diverted towards the home market. In fact, the additional quantities of coal available at home disorganized the market still more. The industry, which was already working under low prices at home and being assisted by foreign exports, had not only to overcome the loss of the subsidy, but was also obliged to combat the enormous additional pressure of coal formerly designed for export and now no longer wanted. The result of this is obvious. The prices, which were already low, fell to a still lower level. Competition at home became more violent, developing into acute underselling, and with the exception of 1923 only, margins between export and home prices kept falling.

However, the impossibility of a sudden adequate lowering of costs of production to the new level of prices finally induced the industry to take up a fresh position—to turn from subsidizing the consumer to subsidizing export. Home markets, being easier to conquer, gradually became the subject of some arrangement between the producers, and the situation became entirely reversed. This process, however, necessarily took a certain time, and in reality the first movement in that direction is not noticeable in this country until early in 1926.

Export prices during the whole post-War period, except for the time of coal famine in 1920 and 1923-4, were generally much lower than home prices. The lowest quotations were from Northumberland, Durham, and Scotland, all exporting districts, which had to compete at the prices of

German and Polish coal in the Baltic markets and in
Northern Europe.[1]   South Wales, another important
exporter, obtained however, much higher prices for her
coal.   Thus the cheapest coal was shipped from Newcastle,
Grangemouth, Kirkcaldy, and Methil, while the costs of
production were also the lowest both in Northumberland
and in Scotland.

3. Irregularities in the Trend of Profits

The big fluctuations discussed in the previous two headings
exerted their effect on the trend of profits in the industry.
Irregularities in demand as well as in prices caused the
profitability of the industry to vary very substantially.
We are in a fortunate position in that all the figures of profits
and losses in the coal industry are officially ascertained every
quarter since 1920 individually for each coal district of the
country.   The biggest profits and the heaviest losses appear
in our industry between 1920 and 1926, afterwards the movements are much smaller.[2]   The whole year 1920 is a period of
big profits, which are especially noticeable in all the exporting
districts with the exception of Scotland, which worked
actually with small losses, and of Lancashire.   The
highest profits above 18s. in the first quarter of the
year were reaped by Northumberland and South Wales,
next came Durham.   In all these areas profits substantially
exceeded the average for the whole of Great Britain.   A
similar situation was repeated in 1923, when again all
the exporting coalfields, this time including also Scotland,
exceeded the average profits of Great Britain.   In 1922,
1924, 1925, 1926, 1927, 1931, and 1932 the converse was
the case, and the exporting districts obtained results
inferior to the average for Great Britain.   Generally speaking
the exporting districts yielded much poorer results than
the other districts, though Lancashire with her old and
small mines, half of which employ less than 50 men, is in
some years an exception; this is probably attributable to the
depressed conditions in the cotton industry, which is the

---

[1] *Vide Eleventh Annual of the Secretary for Mines*, p. 7.
[2] *Vide* Addendum to this Chapter—No. V.

most important consumer of Lancashire steam coal.[1] The proceeds of the coal industry are of course very much dependent on seasonal fluctuations, the second and third quarters of the year are usually the leanest. But every time we take this into consideration and discount these usual movements, we can notice substantial changes as from year to year in the profitability of the industry. Gradually as time went on the amplitudes of balances between proceeds and costs tended to be smaller in all the districts, and the gulf between the average balance for Great Britain and the balances of individual districts diminished. This points towards the important fact that the process of equalization of profits in the British coal industry was continually advancing from the post-War discrepancies among the districts. This was most important, since with enormous differences in profits as between district and district, as well as between colliery and colliery, it was almost impossible to achieve any degree of amalgamation. We develop in another place the point that the lack of competitive equality among the units and districts must be considered as a factor working against the amalgamation and reorganization of the industry.[2]

Taking the country's average balances between proceeds and costs of production in the British coal industry, we shall see that during the whole period after decontrol they were generally on the credit side, but they were considerably lower than before the War. Sir Josiah Stamp's computation presented to the Royal Commission on Coal of 1919, and hitherto unchallenged, gives the average return on capital in the coal industry as something between 8 and 9 per cent. Taking the traditional figure of 15 shillings as the capital outlay for each ton of coal produced,[3] this profit would represent $15s. \times \dfrac{8}{100} = 1s.\ 2\frac{1}{4}d.$ per ton of coal produced.

[1] *Vide Industrial Survey of the Lancashire Area (excluding Merseyside),* made for the Board of Trade, by the University of Manchester, H.M. Stationery Office, 1932.

[2] Cf. Part I, Chap. II, § 1.

[3] Cf. G. R. Carter, *Tendency Towards Industrial Combination,* London, 1913, p. 282—After the War it was accepted to reckon £1 of capital per ton of product: See Lord Aberconway, *The Basic Industries of Great Britain,* London, 1927 ; and The Royal Commission on the Coal Industry, 1925, *Report,* vol. ii, B., p. 548 evidence No. 10164.

Our calculation corresponds very closely with the calculations suggested in the report of the Royal Commission [1] of 1925, where the result was obtained by comparing the average profits in different periods recalculated at the prices of coal in 1909–1913. After the War the profitability of the industry fell very substantially. Between 1922–1925 it represented only 0·64 shillings per ton measured at prices of coal of 1909–1913, while during 1927–1932 there was no profit at all, and on the whole, losses and profits counterbalanced each other. The heaviest losses appeared in 1928. Later however the industry was yielding about 2·5 to 3 per cent on capital, which compares with 8 to 9 before the War.

Such a substantial reduction in the profitability of the industry constitutes an abnormality, especially if we compare it with the relatively high yield on capital invested in enterprises belonging to lower stages of production, i.e. those nearer consumption. After 1929, however, the general trend of profits went down, and the low rate in the coal industry ceased to be in striking contrast to the rest of the country's economic activities. What has been said so far applies to the profits of the whole coal industry, but it must be observed that since the end of 1927, there is a marked propensity for the individual districts to follow each other closely. The striking disparity existing previously between the profits of different districts has now partially disappeared. It is probably the most important fact in all the question of profits and, as we noted, paves the way towards spontaneous reorganization of the industry, since the most important basis for capital integration—namely the profit per tonnage of output—is now more equal all over the country.

Here we may perhaps note that all attempts to check this natural tendency towards the equalization of profits in the coal industry are in the long run harmful to the industry and only lead to more trouble. It is a well established economic law that all units of capital invested

---

[1] *Vide The Report of the Royal Commission on the Coal Industry* (1925), vol. i, Cmd. 2600, p. 218, etc. : " The mean profit per ton of the five periods from 1889 to 1913 is exactly a shilling at actual prices ; at the prices of 1909–1913 the mean profit is 1·12s."

in coal companies should tend to yield equal profit if freed from all outside restrictions. But when we artificially stop the self-adjusting processes by introducing subsidies for the industry, which we cannot maintain permanently, it is quite obvious that as soon as the subsidies disappear, the disparities between the various sections of industry will again become apparent and the whole problem will be reopened. The only effect of a temporary subsidy is that instead of accelerating the process of equalization it retards it, and therefore prevents the integrating movement from developing. For these reasons we feel that both the subsidy in 1921 and that of 1925–6 had a harmful influence on the development of the coal organization. Similarly the period of control, which survived two years after the War, caused many difficulties to the industry.

Having shortly discussed the external difficulties of the coal industry in the fields of demand, prices, and profits, we shall pass now to its *internal* troubles, and see the attempts made to cope with them. All internal difficulties are to be found in the organization of production and distribution. The elements which needed to be reconditioned in order to bring the industry up to date were analysed by the Royal Commission, 1925, which found grave defects in its efficiency and organization. The former embrace the problems of increasing output per man-shift worked, of further mechanization of all productive processes, of a more careful treatment of coal, of improved conveyance of mineral, etc. The latter refer to the shortcomings in the organization of the individual companies, collieries, and pits, as well as to the structure of the industry as a whole. It seems, however, that the difficulties arising out of the insufficient progress in the efficiency of the industry cannot be treated and cured separately, since they are actually mingled with its organization. There exists a large degree of correlation between existing organization, on the one hand, and output per unit of capital engaged in the industry, on the other. Moreover, in large undertakings, the possibility of working to full capacity, the planning of production in advance, without depending on the capricious changes of the trade cycle, are all elements which contribute towards the intensification of output, and ultimately result in reducing costs of production.

The competitive power of Britain was particularly injured by the progress of the coal industries in other coal producing countries, whence her position grew relatively worse than it was in pre-War times. This lack of adequate progress of the British coal industry in comparison with other countries finds good illustration in the League of Nations' Report on Coal,[1] where we read :—

> " Not only have the actual sales from certain districts rapidly mounted, but in Europe generally the efficiency of the industry has been very materially improved. Thus the French mines in the Pas-de-Calais and in the Nord have been completely reorganized. In the latter district 70 per cent of the coal to-day is hewn with the aid of mechanical power. According to the evidence we heard, the proportion so hewn in the Ruhr was 2 per cent in 1913 and 83 per cent in 1927. Throughout Europe this so-called ' rationalization ' of industry has proceeded."

We should do, however, less than justice to the leaders of the British coal industry, if we refused to acknowledge that much has been done here by the industry to meet its difficulties, which for the most part boil down to the question of excessive costs of production. As soon as the spectre of political experiments in the structure of the industry propagated by various sections of the community, gave way to systematic economic administration, the industry made a great advance along the path of technical rationalization ; especially after the national dispute of 1926 came to an end. The movement towards reducing costs of production has been visible all through the industry. And this does not apply, as some would have it, only to the reduction of labour costs, either by lengthening hours of work, or by reducing the scales of wages directly, but also to all items entering into the production-costs sheet. Certainly, when costs greatly exceeded the natural, or world prices,

---

[1] League of Nations, *Economic Organization : The Problem of the Coal Industry.* Interim Report on its International Aspects by the Economic Committee of the League of Nations, Geneva, 1929, p. 9.

the industry attempted to reduce wages costs, which are by far the heaviest item in the sheet, but also considerable progress has been achieved in the reorganization of the methods of production. It suffices now to travel to the main coalfields in this country to discover that in all districts technical progress has made great advances in all directions. Scotland, South Yorkshire, and the small districts of Kent are leaders in this direction. Here a new Sulzer Deep Well pumping scheme electrically driven, the largest of its type in the world, there an aerial ropeway the greatest in Europe, in one colliery a complete mechanization of the underground haulage system, or an extensive application of steel arches and pit props in another, a better and more modern treatment and preparation of coal for the market, and the introduction in the terminal points of antibreak-appliances unknown before—all are obvious signs of advancing technique to anybody visiting the numerous coal areas and ports.[1]

A sum between £10 million and £20 million has been spent in the decade 1923–1933 by the coalowners on the provision of new equipment for preparing coal for the market.[2] But to evaluate the real significance of all the technical advances in the British coal industry is much more the job of a technician and engineer than of an economist. Assuming that all the technical improvements were necessary, and that they yielded economies in production, or secured better prices for the product, it must be inferred that a reduction of costs did ensue. This reduction could be made still greater if the rate of employment of the industry could be increased, or otherwise if it could work at the fullest capacity possible.

After the War there was a marked tendency to concentrate production on a smaller number of mines and to increase slightly the mean output in each mine. In 1913 there were 3,289 coal mines at work, which number gradually diminished to 2,419 in 1929 and finally fell to 2,158 in 1932.[3] We must, however, remember that though certainly there

[1] *Vide* Addendum to this Chapter—No. VI.
[2] The Commercial (*Manchester Guardian*), 29th April, 1933.
[3] Cf. Addendum to this Chapter—No. VII.

was a drift to close down the mines, some of them may be reopened as soon as trade revives. Passing now to the average tonnage of output per mine, we cannot freely compare the yearly figures of production, since at various times the mines were producing at various lengths of shifts. We think it, therefore, appropriate to bring our figures to a common denominator by comparing the yearly outputs of a one hour shift. Having reduced them to an hourly basis,[1] we notice that the pre-War output of 10,900 tons has risen to 13,100 tons in 1931. Such a rise in the size of mines is also visible in a greater average employment per mine. While before the War the average number of workers employed below and above was 340, the figure has increased to 400 in 1930, when the same number of hours were involved. In 1931, in spite of a half-hour reduction in the length of the shift the figure has slightly dropped by 9 workers.

The tendency towards the reduction of costs and towards increasing efficiency can be noticed in the results obtained per person employed in the industry. Though, as Dr. Rhodes [2]

[1] This is only a rough calculation. We must bear in mind that changes in the length of the shift effect output more than proportionally since some time is actually spent on winding the miners down the shaft and a further time is spent by the hewers before they get to the coal face. Denoting all this time by Z and the time of the shift by X, we get the actual time spent at work $X - Z$, and therefore one hour of the shift corresponds only to $\frac{X - Z}{X}$ hour of actual work. It is on this basis that changes in tonnage must be calculated. Hence denoting the output of the X hour shift as P, and the actual lengthening or shortening of the time as Q, we shall get the formula for output reduced to an hourly basis $P \frac{(X - Z) \pm Q}{X \pm Q}$. The proportion, therefore, of the former value of a one hour shift to the latter will be :—

$$Y = \frac{P \dfrac{X - Z}{X}}{P \dfrac{(X - Z) \pm Q}{X \pm Q}} = \frac{(X - Z)\ (X \pm Q)}{X[(X - Z) \pm Q]}.$$

[2] E. C. Rhodes, " Labour and Output in the Coal Mining Industry in Great Britain," *Journal of the Royal Statistical Society*, vol. xciv, part iv, 1931, p. 486. In the Midlands " the improvement in working results is due mainly to the lengthening of hours after the 1926 stoppage . . . " however " there has definitely been an improvement in working results due to more efficient working, or to more efficient mines only producing " (p. 522). In the case of Durham, Dr. Rhodes says, " the improvement in working results since the stoppage elsewhere below ground and on the

suggested in his paper before the Royal Statistical Society, some of the changes must be attributed to the changes in time of employment ; nevertheless, we notice even on an hourly basis a rise in the yearly output per man below, as well as above the ground. This is not a sign of inefficiency of management, but shows on the contrary that owners and managers were taking advantage of improved methods, whenever such improvement proved profitable in the existing conditions. We notice that whereas in 1914 the yearly output per man below ground, reduced to an hourly basis, was 39·2 tons, in 1931 this figure rose to 42·3 tons, which is nearly a 10 per cent improvement. Similar improvement can be seen in the output of all the workers, which rose from 31·6 tons, measured on an hourly basis, to 34·9 tons between 1914 and 1931. Such improved results per worker are in direct relation to the advancing rationalization. So far, full advantage of this rationalization could not be obtained, since the industry, from 1929, had again to decrease the output of coal, this time perhaps not so much because of its excessive prices, as owing to the intensification of the financial and industrial depression, which reached its climax in the years 1932–3.

We see, therefore, that besides the adjusting of costs of production to prices, the coal owners had to solve somehow the especially difficult problem of over-capacity, which was not a purely British one, but related to the whole world. This was clearly enough summarized by the recent report of the League of Nations,[1] which says : " This improvement, which was very definite in 1929, has unfortunately not continued. The discrepancy between the production and consumption of coal has since then been aggravated despite the very considerable reduction in the extraction of coal in the

surface is probably entirely accounted for by the lengthening of time, but the improvement at the coal face of about 13½ per cent is much more than would be expected, due to a lengthening of the shift by half-an-hour, and we must conclude that part of the improvement is due to definite improvement in efficiency generally, or to the more efficient mines being used for production " (p. 523).

[1] League of Nations, Economic Committee, *The Coal Problem*, Geneva, May, 1932, p. 5.

majority of countries. Consumption is diminishing more rapidly then production, and this decline cannot be kept pace with. Markets are more congested than ever, and all are affected simultaneously. Stocks are accumulating. Chaotic price-cutting by producers, being powerless to stimulate demand, simply increases the losses of different undertakings . . ." There is, however, one important aspect of the coal problem which finds no consideration in the Report, viz., the discrepancy between the world prices of coal and the prices charged at home by the main producing countries. Germany, Great Britain, and Poland all charge disproportionately higher prices at home than for export.[1] If one can speak about the phenomenon of dumping in international trade, certainly coal will provide the most classical example. Hence, when one is arguing about the disproportion between supply and demand for coal, it is always legitimate to observe that it applies only to export, where owing to an excessive competition prices are low and the elasticity of demand for a rise [2] works up to the maximum limit of satiation. In the coal-producing countries coal is comparatively very expensive ; the indices of its prices are much above those of wholesale prices, foodstuffs, and raw materials. If there exists, and in our view there does exist, a high degree of elasticity of demand for a rise for certain kinds of coal, this potential market is closed by high quotations. Hence an abnormal situation, that instead of attempting to stimulate the demand where a large potential capacity exists, the whole industry reduces prices for export, where at present *rebus sic stantibus* there is no chance of placing more coal. This need for having cheaper fuel is, however, strongly appreciated by the leading and far-seeing captains of industry, who seek permanently to reduce the costs of production by other ways than mere wage cuts. As the dead weight of potential over-capacity is aggravating the position, they also attempt to do away with it. We shall discuss later the attempts of the industry to dispose of redundant mines in our chapter

[1] In spring, 1933, the Polish Government forced the coal-owners sub-stantially to reduce their home prices.
[2] Cf. Part I, Chap. II, § 2.

on integration. Here we make only a passing reference to it in connection with the abnormal conditions under which coal mining was carried on after the War.

In concluding our review of different aspects of the coal industry, we must apologize to the reader for not dealing in greater detail with the problem of labour. This subject in itself is so vast and so important that there is no possibility in a study of the organization of the coal industry of dealing with it adequately, and only passing references will be made throughout this volume to labour problems, whenever they have any direct bearing on the structure of the industry. On the whole the writer of this work does not consider that the price of labour in coal mines constituted any abnormal hindrance to the development of the industry, considering the fact that wages in the coal industry were on the whole lower than in other industries, though probably their rigidity added to the difficulty of certain sections. The difficulties coming from the side of labour were rather of a political nature, and these, with other facts, undoubtedly retarded the progress of the industry in the first post-War period. On the other hand, recent restrictions of output, which prevent the most productive mines working at fullest possible capacity, have in our view undoubtedly the effect of depressing wages to a level lower than that necessary if the production could be concentrated on the most efficient units.[1]

Now that we have reviewed these post-War abnormalities in the fields of home and foreign demand for coal, together with the problem of surplus capacity, the abnormal trend of prices, and the fluctuations of profits which retarded the introduction of a more suitable organization, we shall attempt to show the coal industry after the War and the general economic conditions of the country in perspective.

[1] Compare our remarks on the problem of full capacity in Part III, Chap. I, § 2.

STATISTICAL ADDENDUM TO CHAPTER I[1]

CONTENTS

No. I. Distribution of Unemployment Through Various Stages of Production

In an article in the *Westminster Bank Review*, sixteen industries with the highest degree of unemployment and sixteen industries with the lowest degree of unemployment have been compared. Among the former is the coal industry. The tables which have been based on published data in *The Ministry of Labour Gazette* for 26th September, 1932, are as follows :—

TABLE No. 2A

SIXTEEN INDUSTRIES WITH HIGHEST UNEMPLOYMENT PERCENTAGES

Industry.	Percentage of insured workers unemployed (over one year).
Shipbuilding and Ship Repairing	59·5
Lead, Tin, and Copper Mining	56·6
Marine Engineering, etc.	50·8
Iron Ore and Ironstone Mining . . .	49·4
Steel Melting, Iron, and Steel Rolling . .	46·6
Tin Plates	45·5
Public Works Contracting	45·0
Iron and Steel Tubes.	41·9
Pig Iron (Blast Furnaces)	41·1

[1] Official sources have been used in this and other chapters of this work with the kind permission of the Controller of H.M. Stationery Office.

D

TABLE No. 2A (*Continued*)

Industry.	Percentage of insured workers unemployed (over one year).
Jute	39·1
Coal Mining	38·7
Constructional Engineering	37·3
Miscellaneous Unspecified	36·9
Hand Tools, Cutlery, Saws, Files	35·5
Dock, Harbour, River, and Canal Service	34·9
Coke Ovens and By-product Works	34·5

TABLE No. 2B

SIXTEEN INDUSTRIES WITH LOWEST UNEMPLOYMENT PERCENTAGES

Industry.	Percentage of Insured workers unemployed (over one year).
Commerce, Banking, Insurance, and Finance	5·6
Tramway and Omnibus Service	6·0
Professional Services	6·4
Tobacco, Cigars, Cigarettes, and Snuff	7·4
Cardboard, Boxes, Paper Bags, and Stationery	8·9
Dressmaking and Millinery	8·9
Laundries, Dyeing, and Dry Cleaning	9·0
Stationery and Typewriting Requisites (not paper)	9·4
Printing, Publishing, and Bookbinding	10·3
Wallpaper Making	10·3
Paint, Varnish, Red and White Leads	10·4
Dress Industries (not separately specified)	10·5
Grain Milling	10·6
Carpets	11·1
Explosives	11·1
Gas, Water, and Electricity Supply Industries	11·2
Average for all Industries in United Kingdom	22·9

The conclusions in the article on the varying effects of the depression are very similar to our views expressed above. We read thus what follows :—

" Broadly it will be seen that the most depressed industries in the country, which have from one-third to over one-half of their labour forces standing idle, comprise the shipbuilding, mining, constructional, docking, metallurgical, and heavy trades, i.e. all those which are interested mainly in the production of capital goods, or of services connected with international trade. With scarcely a single exception, the industries which have best maintained their activity and employment capacity produce consumption goods and services whose field of demand is practically co-extensive with the entire population of the country."—[" Saving and Spending," an article in *The Westminster Bank Review*, November, 1932.]

No. II. Production ; Exports and Home Consumption

Fluctuations in the demand for coal, both total and foreign, in the years following the War are seen in the table on page 36.

We have chosen the year 1925 as the base in computing our index numbers, since it was probably the most representative average year of the whole period under consideration, being neither affected by the short-lived " boomlet " of 1923–4 caused by the occupation of the Ruhr basin, nor yet by the export-trade depression of 1927–8.

The inferences from the last two columns of the table are merely illustrations of what has been said before about fluctuations in export and home trade. These two columns show the existing relation between the two branches of trade, as well as the wide swings in their mutual proportion. Taking the relation between the volumes of export trade and home trade in 1925 as equal to 100, we notice that this relation rises as high as 148 in 1923 and falls to 92 in 1932. After the War the relation seems to move on the whole in favour of coal used for home consumption. This can be seen better from Table No. 4, which is constructed to show the relation between these two branches of the trade.

TABLE No. 4

PERCENTAGE OF COAL SHIPPED ABROAD AND THAT AVAILABLE FOR HOME CONSUMPTION BETWEEN 1913–1932

Year.	Total quantity of coal shipped abroad.	Coal available for Home Consumption for all purposes.	Total output of coal.
	%	%	%
1909–13, approx. av.	32·7	67·3	100·0
1913	34·1	65·9	100·0
1922	34·9	65·1	100·0
1923	37·6	62·4	100·0
1924	31·4	68·6	100·0
1925	29·2	70·8	100·0
1926	23·8	76·2	100·0
1927	28.6	71·4	100·0
1928	29·9	70·1	100·0
1929	31·3	68·7	100·0
1930	30·0	70·0	100·0
1931	28·0	72·0	100·0
1932	28·3	71·7	100·0

Computed from official sources.

TABLE No. 3

FLUCTUATIONS IN THE QUANTITIES OF COAL

(1) Produced ; (2) exported ; (3) available for Home Consumption and in the proportion of Coal Exported to that consumed at Home from 1913 to 1932

Year	Total Output of Coal		Total Quantity of Coal shipped abroad [1]		Coal available for Home Consumption for all Purposes		Quantity of Coal Exported expressed as a proportion of the Quantity Available for Home Consumption	
	Tonnage	Index Nos.	Tonnage	Index Nos.	Tonnage	Index Nos.	Percentage	Index Nos. The proportion of 1925 = 100
	1,000,000 tons	1925 = 100	1,000,000 tons	1925 = 100	1,000,000 tons	1925 = 100	%	1925 = 100
1913	287	118·1	98	138·0	183	108	53·5	128
1920	229	94·2	43	60·5	180	106	23·8	57
1921	163	67·0	37	52·1	127	75	29·1	69
1922	249	102·4	87	122·5	157	92	55·4	133
1923	276	113·5	104	146·4	168	99	61·9	148
1924	267	109·8	84	118·3	180	106	46·6	112
1925	243	100·0	71	100·0	169	100	41·6	100
1927	251	103·2	72	101·4	179	105	40·2	96
1928	237	97·5	71	100·2	163	96	43·5	104
1929	258	106·1	82	115·4	173	101	47·6	114
1930	244	100·4	75	105·6	166	98	45·1	108
1931	219	90·5	61	85·9	156	92	39·1	93
1932	209	81·9	57	80·2	150	88	38·0	92

[1] Including some portion of the coal supplied to vessels of the Navy and to auxiliary vessels employed on Admiralty account. Allowance has been made for the fuel imported and retained for Home Consumption from 1921, and the necessary adjustments made in respect of shipments to Northern Ireland.

Page 36.]

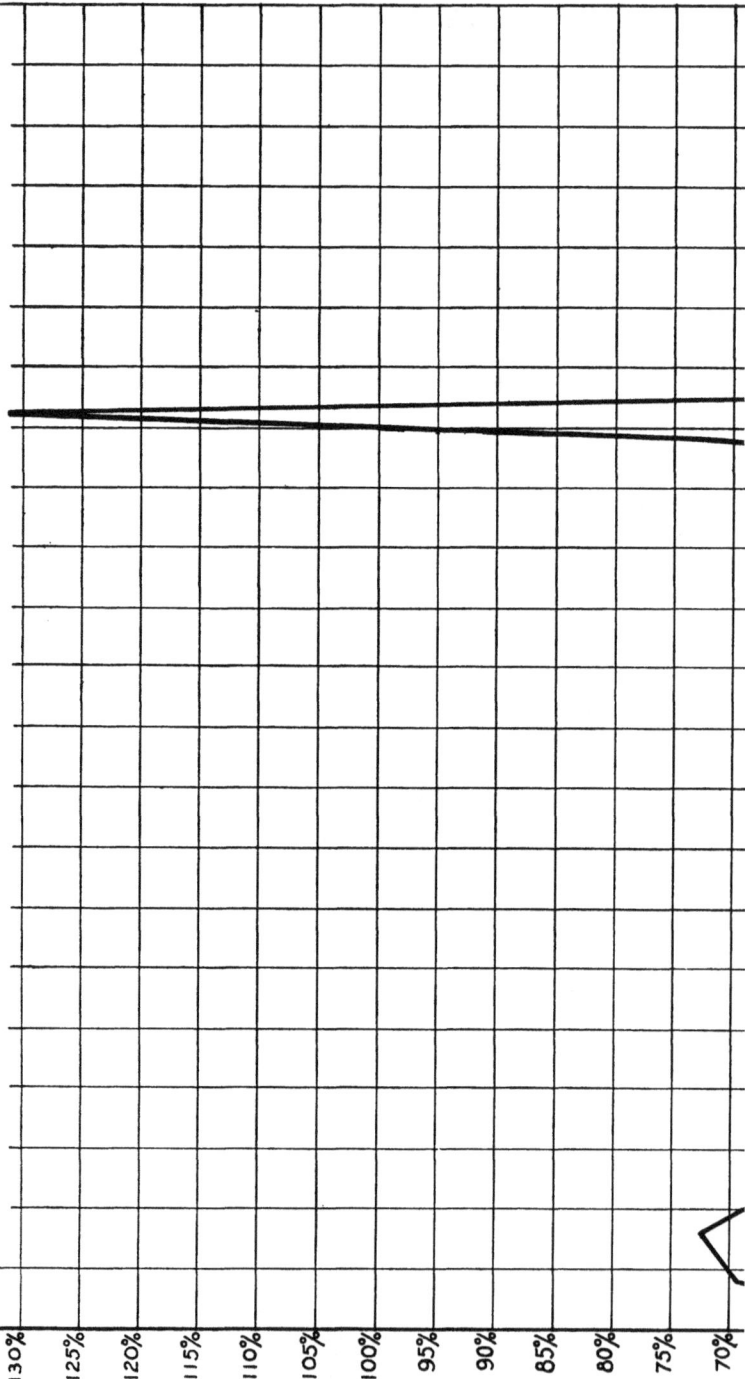

DIAGRAM ILLUSTRATING THE MOVEMENTS OF THE MARGIN OF DIFFERENCE BETWEEN THE AVERAGE DECLARED VALUE (F.O.B) PER TON OF COAL EXPORTED FROM UNITED KINGDOM AND THE AVERAGE SELLING VALUE PER TON OF COAL RAISED AT PIT FROM 1882 TO 1932 MEASURED AS PERCENTAGES OF THE AVERAGE SELLING VALUE PER TON OF COAL RAISED AT THE PIT EACH YEAR.

130%
125%
120%
115%
110%
105%
100%
95%
90%
85%
80%
75%
70%

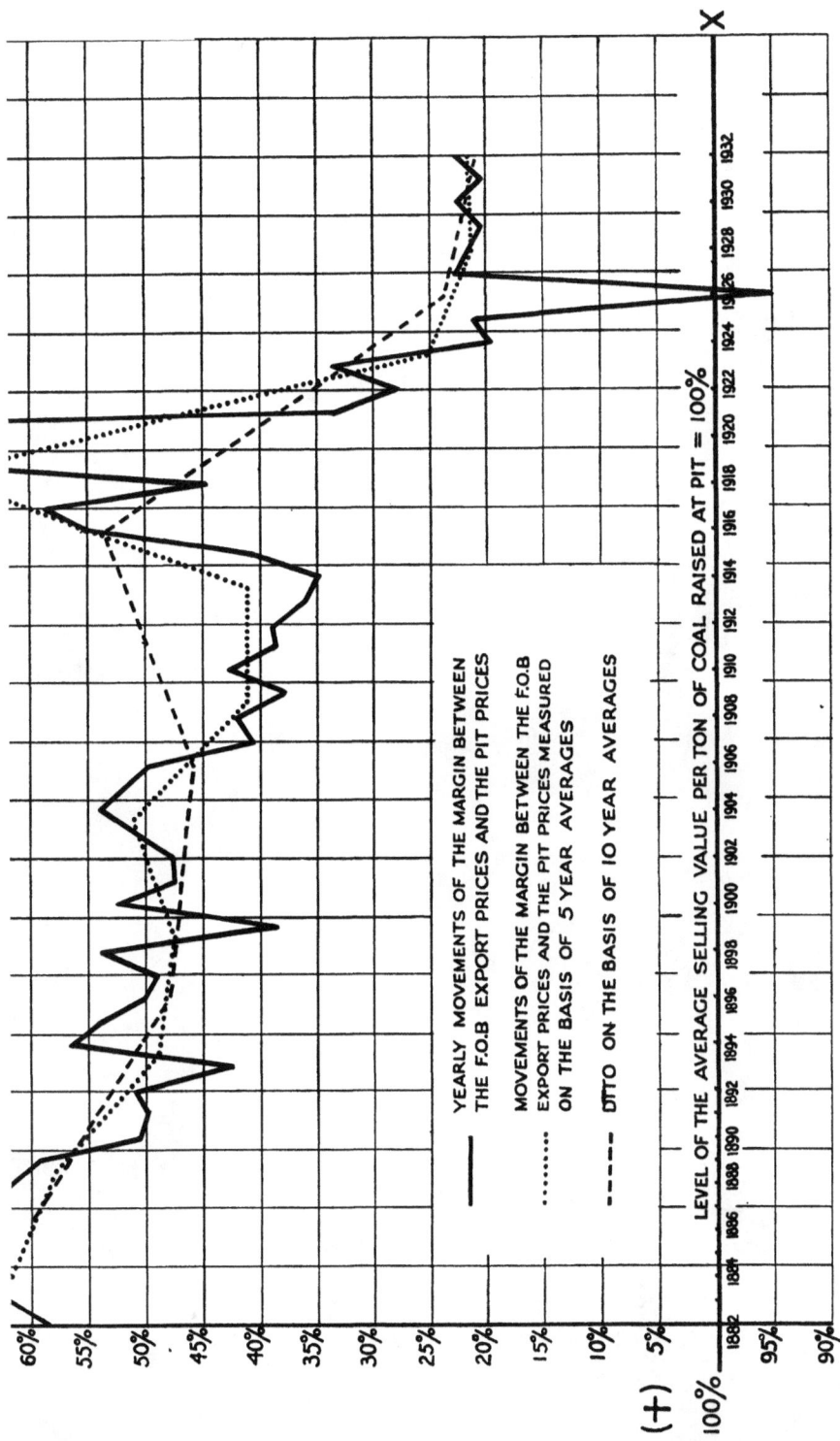

YEARLY MOVEMENTS OF THE MARGIN BETWEEN THE F.O.B EXPORT PRICES AND THE PIT PRICES

MOVEMENTS OF THE MARGIN BETWEEN THE F.O.B EXPORT PRICES AND THE PIT PRICES MEASURED ON THE BASIS OF 5 YEAR AVERAGES

DITTO ON THE BASIS OF 10 YEAR AVERAGES

LEVEL OF THE AVERAGE SELLING VALUE PER TON OF COAL RAISED AT PIT = 100%

(+)

100% 95% 90%

5% 10% 15% 20% 25% 30% 35% 40% 45% 50% 55% 60%

1882 1884 1886 1888 1890 1892 1894 1896 1898 1900 1902 1904 1906 1908 1910 1912 1914 1916 1918 1920 1922 1924 1926 1928 1930 1932

X

[To face page 36.

No. III. DISPLACEMENT OF BRITISH COAL BY FOREIGN COAL IN THE WORLD MARKETS

The gradual displacement of British coal by other supplies of fuel may be illustrated by contrasting the total world consumption of coal with the trend in the net British exports of coal, including foreign bunkers. This is shown in the table on page 38.

No. IV. MOVEMENT OF COAL PRICES IN THE HOME MARKETS AND IN EXPORT MARKETS

Table No. 6 serves to show the fluctuations in prices of coal at pit and of coal exported from the United Kingdom. In all the years between 1882 and 1930 there was a substantial margin between the two prices in favour of the f.o.b. prices of coal exported, the only exception being the year 1926, when the average price of coal at pit, owing to the stoppage, was greater than the export prices. Such margins were derived by deducting the value of coal at pit from the export price. In order to be able to compare the margins thus calculated, we represent each of them as percentages of the pit-head prices of coal. By adding therefore 100 to each of the percentages thus computed, we obtain the figures which represent the f.o.b. export prices expressed in terms of percentages of the pit-head prices.

The diagram facing this page based on Table No. 6 shows the oscillation of the margins for each year since 1882. Any point on the diagram lying on the intersection with the abscissa represents the level of the average selling value per ton of coal raised at pit in a single year. This value, being selected as a basis for calculating the margin, is taken for each year as 100 per cent. The distance between any point on the continuous line and the (X) axis represents the margin between the export prices and pit-head prices. The margin is expressed in terms of percentages of the pit prices. When the export prices are higher than the pit-head prices the continuous line lies above the (X) axis ; and vice versa.

TABLE No. 5

Consumption of British Coal at Home and Abroad Compared with the Total World Consumption of Coal

Year	1909–13 Average	1913	1922	1923	1924	1925	1927	1928	1929	1930	1931	1932
Home Consumption	176	184	158 [1]	169 [1]	180 [1]	170 [1]	180 [1]	164 [1]	173 [1]	167	156	150
Production abroad	821	923	791	923	917	940	1,022	1,006	1,066	968	849 [2]	0
Net British Export and Foreign Bunkers	89	100	89	104	83	70	70	70	81	73	60	57 [2]
Total Consumption abroad	910	1,022	880	1,027	1,000	1,010	1,090	1,076	1,146	1,041	909 [2]	0
Percentage of British Coal in the total consumption abroad	9·9%	9·7%	10·1%	11·2%	8·3%	6·9%	6·4%	6·5%	7·0%	7·0%	6·6%	0

(Home Consumption expressed in MILLION TONS. Production abroad and Total Consumption abroad expressed in MILLION METRIC TONS (2,204 lb.).)

Computed from the *Colliery Year Book and Coal Trades Directory*.

[1] Allowance has been made for the fuel imported and retained for home consumption from 1922, and the necessary adjustments made in respect of shipments to Northern Ireland.
[2] Provisional figures.

Page 38.]

TABLE No. 6

MARGIN OF DIFFERENCES BETWEEN THE AVERAGE DECLARED VALUE (F.O.B.) PER TON OF COAL EXPORTED AND THE AVERAGE SELLING VALUE PER TON OF COAL RAISED AT PIT IN THE UNITED KINGDOM FROM 1882 TO 1932

(This margin is represented as a percentage of the Average Selling Value per ton of Coal raised at Pit during each year from 1882–1932)

Year.	Average Selling Value per ton of Coal raised at Pit.	Average Declared Value (f.o.b.) per ton of Coal Exported.	Margin of Difference between the Pit-head Value per ton of coal and the f.o.b. Value per ton of Coal Exported.	Margin of Difference between Export Prices and Pit Prices per ton of Coal represented as a Percentage of the Pit-head Prices.	Year.
1.	2.	3.	4.	5.	6.
	s. d.	s. d.	s. d.		
1882	5 8	9 0	3 4	58·8	1882
1883	5 8	9 2	3 6	61·7	1883
1884	5 5	9 2	3 9	69·2	1884
1885	5 2	8 10	3 8	70·9	1885
1886	4 10	8 4	3 6	72·4	1886
1887	4 10	8 2	3 4	68·9	1887
1888	5 1	8 3	3 2	62·2	1888
1889	6 4	10 1	3 9	59·2	1889
1890	8 3	12 5	4 2	50·5	1890
1891	8 0	12 0	4 0	50·0	1891
1892	7 3	10 11	3 8	50·5	1892
1893	6 10	9 9	2 11	42·6	1893
1894	6 7	10 4	3 9	56·9	1894
1895	6 0	9 3	3 3	54·1	1895
1896	5 10	8 9	2 11	50·0	1896
1897	5 11	8 10	2 11	49·2	1897
1898	6 4	9 9	3 5	53·9	1898
1899	7 7	10 6	2 11	38·4	1899
1900	10 10	16 6	5 8	52·3	1900
1901	9 4	13 9	4 5	47·4	1901
1902	8 3	12 2	3 11	51·0	1902
1903	7 8	11 7	3 11	54·0	1903
1904	7 3	11 0	3 9	51·8	1904
1905	6 11	10 6	3 7	49·4	1905
1906	7 3	10 10	3 7	40·7	1906
1907	9 0	12 8	3 8	42·0	1907
1908	8 11	12 8	3 9	38·1	1908
1909	8 1	11 2	3 1	42·8	1909
1910	8 2	11 8	3 6	38·7	1910
1911	8 2	11 4	3 2	38·7	1911
1912	9 1	12 7	3 6	38·5	1912
1913	10 2	13 10	3 8	36·0	1913
1914	10 0	13 6	3 6	35·0	1914
1915	12 6	16 9	4 3	40·4	1915
1916	15 7	24 2	8 7	55·0	1916
1917	16 9	26 7	9 10	58·7	1917
1918	20 11	30 3	9 4	44·6	1918
1919	27 4	47 3	19 11	72·8	1919
1920	34 7	79 11	45 4	131·0	1920
1921	26 2	34 10	8 8	33·1	1921
1922	17 8	22 7	4 11	27·8	1922
1923	18 10	25 2	6 4	33·6	1923
1924	18 10	23 5	4 7	24·3	1924
1925	16 4	19 10	3 6	21·4	1925
1926 [1]	19 7	18 7	−1 0	−5·1	1926
1927	14 7	17 10	3 3	22·2	1927
1928	12 10	15 7	2 9	21·4	1928
1929	13 5	16 2	2 9	20·4	1929
1930	13 7	16 8	3 1	22·7	1930
1931	13 6	16 3	2 9	20·3	1931
1932	13 3	16 3	3 0	22·6	1932

[1] Abnormal year of the coal strike, when there was a large import of coal into the United Kingdom. Computed from the *Annual Reports* of the Secretary for Mines and H.M. Chief Inspector of Mines ; the Board of Trade *Report on Wholesale and Retail Prices*, and the *Annual Statement of Trade*.

TABLE No. 7

Profit and Losses per Ton of Coal Disposable Commercially in various districts in Great Britain for each Quarter from 1920 to 1932

Quarter Ending	Scotland. Per Ton.	Northumberland. Per Ton.	Durham. Per Ton.	South Wales & Monmouth. Per Ton.	Yorkshire. Per Ton.	Lancashire. Per Ton.	Great Britain. Per Ton.
1920							
31st March	− 2·17d.	+ 18s. 5·21d.	+ 8s. 4·85d.	+ 18s. 7·67d.	+ 10·26d.	− 4s. 7·92d.	+ 5s. 1·97d.
30th June	− 9·85d.	+ 15s. 10·65d.	+ 5s. 9·82d.	+ 10s. 5·89d.	+ 1s. 1·73d.	− 4s. 8·9d.	+ 3s. 0·32d.
30th Sept.	− 4·84d.	+ 12s. 3·32d.	+ 7s. 0·84d.	+ 11s. 7·45d.	+ 4s. 2·67d.	− 3s. 6·02d.	+ 4s. 10·33d.
31st December.	− 3s. 8·79d.	+ 5s. 9·13d.	+ 3s. 2·32d.	+ 2s. 5·83d.	− 0·40d.	− 7s. 10·89d.	− 6·19d.
1921							
March	− 7s. 7·09d.	− 9s. 7·25d.	− 4s. 2·4d.	− 19s. 9·26d.	− 6·49d.	− 9s. 3·19d.	− 6s. 11·8d.
June [1]							
September	+ 5·70d.	+ 2s. 4·81d.	+ 1s. 1·5d.	+ 1s. 11·5d.	+ 3s. 5·9d.	+ 3s. 3·23d.	+ 2s. 3·76d.
December [2]	+ 1·13d.	− 1s. 2·95d.	− 1s. 4·36d.	− 9·79d.	+ 1s. 8·84d.	+ 1s. 5·85d.	+ 3·47d.
1922							
March	+ 10·70d.	+ 1s. 9d.	+ 1s. 1·25d.	+ 4·5d.	+ 1s. 8d.	+ 1s. 5·44d.	+ 1s. 1·62d.
June	+ 1s. 5·03d.	+ 8·18d.	+ 1s. 1·41d.	+ 4·13d.	− 1s. 3·65d.	− 8·78d.	− 0·17d.
September	+ 0·10d.	+ 2s. 3·13d.	+ 1s. 7·05d.	+ 7·25d.	+ 1s. 9·56d.	− 8·96d.	+ 1s. 1d.
December	+ 2s. 5·05d.	+ 2s. 1·58d.	+ 1s. 10·83d.	+ 6·95d.	+ 2s. 1·8d.	+ 0·34d.	+ 6·89d.
1923							
March	+ 3s. 2·96d.	+ 3s. 2d.	+ 2s. 11·88d.	+ 2s. 2·92d.	+ 2s. 7·30d.	+ 11·01d.	+ 2s. 5·32d.
June	+ 4s. 7·05d.	+ 4s. 11·89d.	+ 4s. 1·39d.	+ 3s. 9·91d.	+ 2s. 8·41d.	+ 9·20d.	+ 3s. 2·64d.
September	+ 4·15d.	+ 1s. 11·56d.	+ 2s. 0·87d.	+ 1s. 2·45d.	+ 1s. 3·10d.	− 10·43d.	+ 1s. 0·22d.
December	+ 2s. 5·70d.	+ 1s. 2·32d.	+ 1s. 9·83d.	+ 1s. 1·88d.	+ 2s. 9·62d.	+ 1s. 3·56d.	+ 1s. 11·53d.
1924							
March	+ 2s. 7·62d.	+ 1s. 11·57d.	+ 2s. 4·55d.	+ 2s. 2·24d.	+ 3s. 9·32d.	+ 2s. 6·05d.	+ 2s. 9·63d.
June	+ 1s. 8·45d.	+ 6·82d.	+ 1s. 2·46d.	+ 6·45d.	+ 1s. 8·26d.	+ 1s. 6·23d.	+ 1s. 0·40d.
September	+ 2·71d.	− 7·44d.	+ 7·51d.	− 8·80d.	+ 10·08d.	− 1s. 0·56d.	+ 0·29d.
December	+ 0·74d.	− 3·78d.	+ 3·10d.	− 6·28d.	+ 2s. 0·01d.	+ 0·94d.	+ 7·61d.
1925							
March	− 1s. 1·41d.	− 9·44d.	− 2·67d.	− 3·97d.	+ 1s. 7·55d.	+ 1s. 8·14d.	+ 6·13d.
June	− 3·36d.	− 1s. 9·51d.	− 1s. 5·10d.	− 3·67d.	+ 3·27d.	− 2·74d.	− 11·81d.
September	− 2·84d.	− 9·77d.	+ 7·07d.	− 4·5d.	+ 7·05d.	+ 6·78d.	− 2·82d.
December [2]	+ 1s. 6·12d.	+ 10·25d.	+ 8·24d.	+ 4·27d.	+ 1s. 9·51d.	+ 2s. 8·75d.	+ 1s. 6·70d.

[1] National Dispute. [2] Include Government subsidy.

TABLE No. 7 (Continued)

Quarter Ending	Scotland. Per Ton.	Northumberland. Per Ton.	Durham. Per Ton.	South Wales & Monmouth. Per Ton.	Yorkshire. Per Ton.	Lancashire. Per Ton.	Great Britain. Per Ton.
1926 [1]							
March	+ 1s. 3·46d.	+ 1s. 2·23d.	+ 10·49d.	+ 1s. 4·28d.	+ 1s. 8·77d.	+ 1s. 3·47d.	+ 1s. 4·99d.
December [2]	+ 9·91d.	+ 6·50d.	+ 9·30d.	+ 1s. 1·21d.	+ 5·18d.	+ 1s. 3·57d.	+ 9·23d.
1927							
March	− 1s. 2·58d.	+ 9·81d.	+ 3·80d.	− 4·88d.	+ 2s. 0·20d.[3]	+ 1s. 7·36d.	+ 1s. 2·41d.
June	− 1s. 3·79d.	− 1s. 2·23d.	+ 8·75d.	− 1s. 1·74d.	− 3·81d.	− 1s. 4·87d.	− 1s. 0·65d.
September	− 1s. 4·93d.	− 1s. 1·70d.	− 1s. 3·87d.	− 1s. 5·25d.	− 7·71d.	− 1s. 7·22d.	− 1s. 2d.
December	− 10·55d.	− 1s. 2·84d.	− 1s. 1·31d.	− 1s. 7·87d.	− 10·36d.	− 1s. 0·32d.	− 1s. 0·43d.
1928							
March	− 8d.	− 10·2d.	− 10·2d.	− 1s. 5·7d.	− 6·2d.	− 10·2d.	− 9·34d.
June	− 1s. 1·7d.	− 1s. 4·5d.	− 7·7d.	− 1s. 8·7d.	− 1s. 9d.	− 2s. 0·5d.	− 5·02d.
September	− 1s. 1·5d.	− 1s. 4d.	− 1s. 1·7d.	− 1s. 8·7d.	− 1s. 4d.	− 2s. 7·7d.	− 1s. 4·11d.
December	− 1·88d.	− 6·27d.	− 7·95d.	− 6·88d.	− 2·12d.	− 5·30d.	− 2·87d.
1929							
March	+ 10d.	+ 9·5d.	+ 8d.	+ 1·74d.	+ 1s. 3·5d.	+ 9·5d.	+ 9·15d.
June	− 4·42d.	+ 4·82d.	+ 1·07d.	− 4·43d.	+ 1·99d.	− 10·89d.	− 3·43d.
September	− 2·45d.	+ 6·04d.	+ 4·17d.	− 2·66d.	+ 1·82d.	− 1s. 1·90d.	− 0·22d.
December	+ 9·15d.	+ 9·62d.	+ 9·12d.	+ 10·92d.	+ 1s. 3·59d.	+ 7·42d.	+ 11·29d.
1930							
March	+ 7·19d.	+ 3·6d.	+ 10·95d.	+ 7·87d.	+ 1s. 7·31d.	+ 1s. 1·44d.	+ 1·37d.
June	− 6·50d.	+ 4·33d.	+ 3·24d.	+ 0·78d.	− 0·39d.	− 10·72d.	− 1·94d.
September	− 8·20d.	+ 1·70d.	+ 1·10d.	+ 3·94d.	− 2·7d.	− 1s. 3·68d.	− 2·4d.
December	+ 2·74d.	+ 9·44d.	− 3·47d.	− 6·06d.	+ 10·31d.	+ 6·94d.	+ 6·2d.
1931							
March	+ 5·87d.	+ 7·95d.	+ 4·80d.	− 2·59d.	+ 9·83d.	+ 1s. 1·01d.	+ 9·04d.
June	− 7·34d.	− 2·93d.	− 4·10d.	− 0·92d.	+ 1·22d.	− 6·13d.	− 1·34d.
September	− 9·52d.	− 6·36d.	− 4·94d.	− 1·70d.	+ 0·51d.	− 1s. 0·79d.	− 2·05d.
December	+ 1·09d.	+ 3·73d.	+ 0·14d.	+ 0·77d.	+ 10·42d.	+ 10·57d.	+ 7·06d.
1932							
March	− 1·81d.	+ 0·50d.	− 3·19d.	− 2·82d.	+ 9·60d.	+ 11·20d.	+ 6·46d.
June	− 9·45d.	− 7·63d.	− 5·0d.	− 2·46d.[4]	+ 2·24d.	+ 0·06d.	− 1·91d.
September	− 1s. 1·07d.	− 1s. 1·74d.	− 10·11d.	− 4·28d.	− 6·88d.	− 4·31d.	− 7·55d.
December	+ 3·75d.	− ·77d.	− 0·84d.	+ 5·74d.	+ 1s. 3·05d.	+ 1s. 8·17d.	+ 8·87d.

[1] Includes Government subsidy.

[2] May to December—National Dispute in the Coal Mining Industry; figures cover month ended 30th April, 1926, together with such particulars as were available for the last eight months of the year 1926.

[3] Up to 1927 includes figures for Yorkshire, Notts, Derbyshire, Leicestershire, Cannock Chase, and Warwickshire; after 1927 only Yorkshire.

[4] May, June, July.

This diagram furnishes the most concise illustration of the situation which arose in the British coal export trade after the War ; it shows a disastrous fall of margin between export prices and the pit-head prices. The black dotted line on the diagram, representing the trend, was sloping downwards long before the War ; the rapidity expressed by the angle of the curve, however, was quite different in the pre-War period from what it became after de-control.

In 1921 our diagram shows an unprecedented, nearly vertical, fall of export prices to a level of just over 30 per cent above the pit-head prices.

No. V. Trend of Profits and Losses in Various Districts

We can have recourse to the official statistics in order to investigate the behaviour of profits and losses in Great Britain as a whole and in the various districts separately.

A table comparing profits and losses per ton of coal is given on pages 40 and 41.

In reading the data we must remember certain facts which operate to dim the clarity of the whole table, and up to 1927 render interpretation most difficult. First State subsidies on wages introduced in 1921, and even more those in the December quarter of 1925 and the March quarter of 1926, work to show profits in industry where, in fact, heavy losses existed. Without the subsidy all districts in 1925–6 would have worked with debit balances. Secondly, the relatively high profits in the third quarter of 1921 and in the first quarter of 1927 are merely the result of prolonged suspension of work during the preceding national disputes, and so they only reflect the replenishment of depleted stocks. Presumably in normal conditions those profits would not appear, or they would be greatly reduced. So much for the explanation of the true value of our figures, from which it appears that only since 1927 are they fully representative of the real trend of profits.

Table No. 7 provides us with a good comparison of various types of district : Scotland, Northumberland, Durham, and

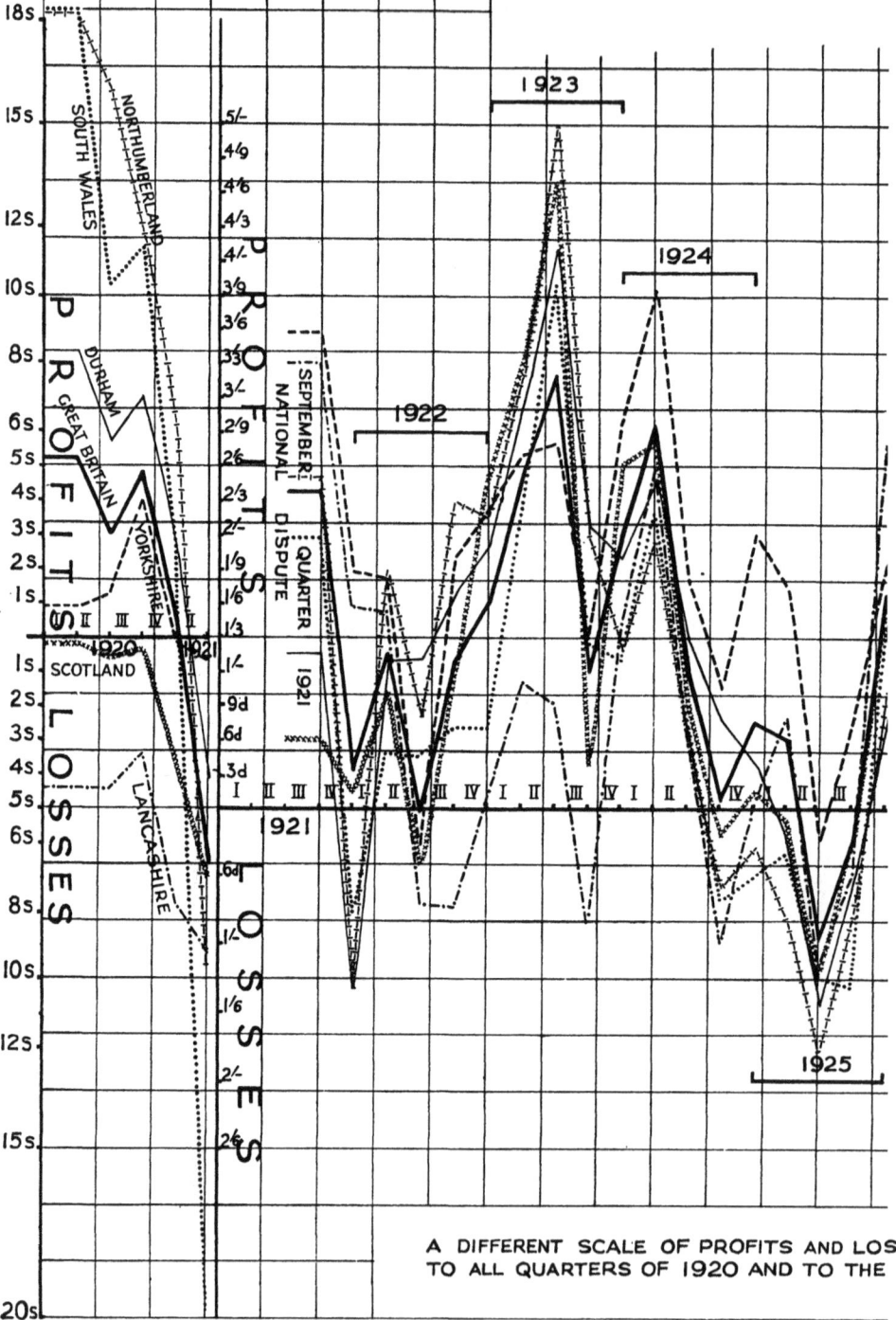

DIAGRAM OF PROFITS AND LOSS

PROFITS

LOSSES

PROFITS

LOSSES

18s
15s
12s
10s
8s
6s
5s
4s
3s
2s
1s

1s
2s
3s
4s
5s
6s
8s
10s
12s

15s

20s

5/-
4/9
4/6
4/3
4/-
3/9
3/6
3/3
3/-
2/9
2/6
2/3
2/-
1/9
1/6
1/3
1/-
9d
6d
3d

.6d
1/-
1/6
2/-
2/6

SOUTH WALES
NORTHUMBERLAND
DURHAM
GREAT BRITAIN
YORKSHIRE
SCOTLAND
LANCASHIRE

SEPTEMBER NATIONAL DISPUTE QUARTER 1921

1920   1921

1921

1922

1923

1924

1925

I II III IV I II III IV I II III IV I II III IV I II III

A DIFFERENT SCALE OF PROFITS AND LOS
TO ALL QUARTERS OF 1920 AND TO THE

THE BRITISH COAL INDUSTRY FOR EACH QUARTER FROM 1920 TO 1932
(PER TON)

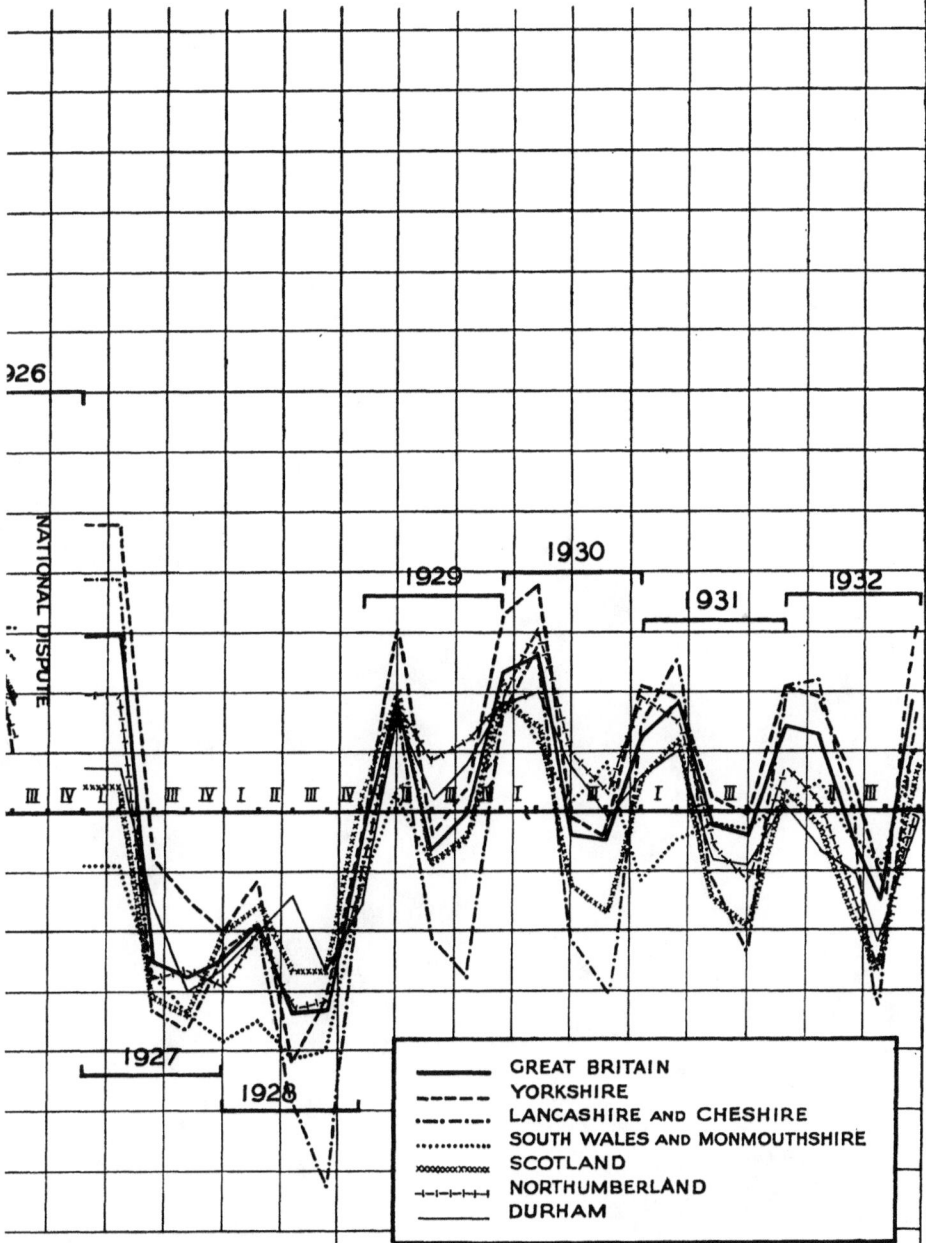

)26

NATIONAL DISPUTE

1929 1930 1931 1932

III IV I II III IV I II III IV I II III IV I II III IV I III IV I III

1927

1928

	GREAT BRITAIN
-----	YORKSHIRE
·—·—·—·	LANCASHIRE AND CHESHIRE
············	SOUTH WALES AND MONMOUTHSHIRE
xxxxxxxxxxxxx	SCOTLAND
+-+-+-+-+	NORTHUMBERLAND
	DURHAM

HAS BEEN APPLIED
T QUARTER OF 1921

[To face page 42.

South Wales are examples of exporting regions ; Lancashire and Yorkshire produce chiefly for home consumption. But, while Lancashire [1] represents an old and declining coalfield with antiquated methods and collieries, Yorkshire is a developing area.

Our diagram facing this page brings out the question of profit in the districts.

No. VI. TECHNICAL PROGRESS IN THE BRITISH COAL INDUSTRY 1913–1932

We shall now allow the statistics to speak for themselves and show the advances achieved in the fields of technical rationalization.

TABLE No. 8

COAL CUTTING MACHINES

| | Total Nos. in Use driven by : | | Coal cut by Machines. | |
Year.	Compressed Air.	Electricity.	Tonnage (Million).	Percentage Proportion of Total Output. %
1913 .	1,590	1,305	24	8
1921 .	3,002	2,257	23	14
1925 .	3,516	3,134	48	20
1928 .	3,545	3,586	61	26
1930 .	3,597	4,040	76	31
1931 .	3,345	4,026	77	35
1932 .	3,167	3,970	80	38

TABLE No. 9

MECHANICAL CONVEYANCE IN USE BELOW GROUND

Year.	At Coal Face.	Elsewhere.	Tonnage of Coal Conveyed. (million tons)	Percentage Proportion of Total Output. %
1913 .	359	Not available	Not available	—
1927 .	2,078	,, ,,	,, ,,	—
1928 .	2,203	653	28	12
1929 .	2,598	620	37	14
1930 .	2,991	756	42	17
1931 .	3,137	816	47	21
1932 .	3,265	855	53	25

[1] *Vide Industrial Survey of the Lancashire Area (excluding Merseyside).* Made for the Board of Trade by the University of Manchester, H.M. Stationery Office, 1932.

TABLE No. 10

ELECTRICITY USED IN BRITISH COAL MINES. AGGREGATE HORSE-POWER INSTALLED

Year.	Below Ground. h.p.	Above Ground. h.p.
1913 .	371,000	256,000
1921 .	644,000	503,000
1925 .	840,000	715,000
1929 .	918,000	835,000
1930 .	955,000	862,000
1931 .	961,000	873,000
1932 .	970,000	885,000

TABLE No. 11

COAL-WASHING OR CLEANING

Year.	Number of Plants in Use.			Coal Treated.	
	Washeries.	Dry Cleaning Plants.	Froth Flotation.	Tonnage. (million tons)	Percentage Proportion of Total Output.[1]
1927 .	505	27	6	51	20·5
1928 .	527	53	5	60	25·4
1929 .	562	74	6	71	27·6
1930 .	583	91	6	73	30·0
1931 .	570	109	6	67	30·0
1932[1] .	594	128	6	72	34·0

[1] In relation to the output of coal which is generally suitable for washing or cleaning, i.e. fine or small coal, the proportion actually so treated is, in general, considerably higher than is indicated above by the percentage of the total output of coal.

A perusal of the above tables provides a summary of progress in the field of mechanization of the British coal industry since the War. Where possible, 1913 figures have been included, and the progress which has been made is at once obvious. It is also interesting to note that development has been particularly rapid since the stoppage of 1926.

Our figures show that whereas in 1913 only 8 per cent of the output was cut by machinery, in 1925 20 per cent was machine cut, while in 1931 the figure went up to 35 per cent. Equally great progress was achieved in the use of electricity in the mines, which rose from 256,000 aggregate horse-power installed in 1913 to 885,000 in 1932. Mechanical conveyors in use below ground are now applied extensively; from 12 per cent of the country's output handled in 1928 their use extended to cover 21 per cent in 1931, which corresponds to 47 million tons. Coal-washing and cleaning plants which in 1927 turned over 20 per cent of the national production, increased this figure up to 30 per cent in 1931. Particularly large is the growth of dry cleaning plants, the number in use increased from 27 in 1927 to 128 in 1932.

Simultaneously with the increased use of machinery underground, especially of mechanical conveyors, the number of horses and ponies employed in the mines has been reduced. The reduction is quite substantial since 1920, and it is proceeding continually.

TABLE No. 12

NUMBER OF PONIES EMPLOYED BELOW GROUND

Year.	Number.
1920	68,000
1921	66,000
1926	57,000
1929	50,000
1930	49,000
1931	44,000
1932	41,500

Better methods of mining are also responsible for a decrease in the rate of fatal accidents in the industry. While in 1914, 1921, and 1925, one million tons of coal meant 4·7 human lives lost in accidents; between 1928 and 1930 the figure slightly decreased to 4·2, and continued to drop to 3·8 in 1931, but rose again to 4·1 in 1932. Such an advance in the safety of the mining industry is due presumably to more modernized methods which are constantly being introduced.

No. VII. PHYSICAL PRODUCTIVITY OF MINES IN THE BRITISH COAL INDUSTRY 1913–1932

The development in the productivity of the British coal industry, both in reference to output per mine and per men in mine, is represented below. In order to facilitate a common basis for comparison an hourly basis has been introduced. This makes it possible to overcome the difficulty arising out of changes in working time.

TABLE No. 13

NUMBER OF COAL MINES AT WORK AND YEARLY AVERAGE OF OUTPUT
AND MEN EMPLOYED PER MINE IN GREAT BRITAIN (1913–1932)

Year	Number of Coal-mines at work	Yearly Average per Mine			
		Tonnage of Output		Number of Men employed	
		000 omitted	Reduced to hourly basis	Below ground	Below and above ground
1913 [2]. .	3,289	87	10·9	270	340
1921 [3] .	3,045	53	7·7	290	370
1924 [3] .	2,855	94	13·4	340	420
1928 [2] .	2,539	90	11·3	290	370
1929 [2] .	2,419	106	13·3	310	390
1930 [2] .	2,328	105	13·3	315	400
1931 [4] .	2,243	98	13·1	310	391
1932 [4] .	2,158[1]	97	13·0	299	374

No. VIII. PHYSICAL PRODUCTIVITY OF LABOUR IN THE BRITISH COAL INDUSTRY

TABLE No. 14

TONNAGE OF COAL RAISED PER PERSON AND NUMBER OF PERSONS
EMPLOYED

Year	Yearly output per man below ground		Below and above ground			Total number of men employed
	Total	Reduced to hourly basis	Yearly output per man		Output per man-shift	
			Total	Reduced to hourly basis		
	Tons	Tons	Tons	Tons	Cwt.	000 omitted
1914 [2]	314	39·2	253	31·6	20·32	1,006
1922 [3]	271	38·7	217	31·0	18·02	1,158
1923 [3]	286	40·8	229	32·9	17·83	1,213
1925 [3]	277	39·6	221	31·5	18·02	1,112
1927 [2]	309	38·6	245	30·6	20·61	1,032
1930 [2]	330	41·2	262	32·7	21·62	939
1931 [4]	317	42·3	262	34·9	21·61	873
1932 [4]	323	43·1	262	34·9	21·99	803

[1] Provisional.　　[2] 8 hour shift.　　[3] 7 hour shift.　　[4] 7½ hour shift.

CHAPTER II

DISINTEGRATING FORCES IN THE BRITISH COAL INDUSTRY

§ I. CAUSES OF DISINTEGRATION

The depressed state of the British coal industry after the War soon attracted attention of political thought. It was believed possible to rid the industry from difficulties by reorganizing its structure. Gradually, more and more Government regulations were imposed, most of which proved a dismal failure whenever they were not a product of the industry itself. Several of these external enactments were entirely self-frustrating. As is always the case with State interference, *l'appétit vient en mangeant* and some of the Government measures immediately brought others into existence. But no magical abracadabra performed by the Government could successfully impose a fresh network of organization unless this was the product of industry's genuine economic development. So, in order to gauge the measure of success achieved by Government interference designed to uplift the industry, we must first study the economic forces which were at work within the industry in the years following the War. This chapter is devoted to a consideration of disruptive forces which were tending to split the industry, and the following chapter discusses the integrating forces working in a reverse direction.

As the chief cause of the low degree of co-operation in the industry, it became fashionable, particularly after the War, to over-emphasize the element of individualism to be found among coal-owners, and very often to ascribe to this egocentricity all the existing troubles of the industry. From a whole range of publications dealing with the economics of coal production, one might easily gather the impression that the psychological factor alone was of

47

importance, that it proved able to retard the sound development of the whole industry. Many of these works convey the idea that, granted only a change in the attitude of owners towards each other, the coal trade could recapture its previous glory and sound position. Lack of so-called " co-operative feeling," was held responsible for the recent failures. Hence, of course, in many circles this belief led to the advocacy of political action and compulsion to force the hand of the recalcitrants. The habit of representing the leaders of the coal companies in this way can be observed in a vast amount of literature on the subject.[1]

The fame of the British colliery owner has even spread outside this country. The following description is taken from *The American Encyclopædia of the Social Sciences*.[2]

"The Coal Owners of Great Britain have always been highly individualistic. Such formal relations as they have had with each other have been in the nature of organizations for mutual protection against labour unions and social legislation rather than for the co-ordination of activities in the conduct of their industry. The steady growth of the industry following the constantly increasing demand for its product both at home and abroad gave no occasion for modifying existing practices, and attempts to change managerial or marketing methods have always been opposed as unnecessary."

[1] We quote below a few examples of this view :—
Mr. Allan Greenwell, editor of the *Colliery Guardian*, explained the reasons operating in Britain against any concerted movement : " These reasons may also be summed up in the word ' insularity ', a characteristic of the people . . . An attempt to promote an understanding as to output and prices throughout the country . . . is foredoomed to failure under existing conditions." (*The Economic Position of the Coal Industry of the United Kingdom, Lectures on British Commerce*, London, 1912, p. 236.)
Mr. R. C. Smart drew a comparison between the mine-workers and the entrepreneurs, from which he inferred that both the miners and owners are highly self-centred, narrow in their outlook, muddling through their petty local affairs without any large grasp of the real requirements of the situation ("The State and the Mining Industry," *Fortnightly Review*, 2nd March, 1931, p. 389).
Even in English literature they are often represented in a very unfavourable light. Thus, for instance, Mr. H. G. Wells says in his *World of William Clissold*, that : " The typical British mine-owner still belongs very generally to the horse-headed class ; the equestrian tradition still dominates mine-owning. Economically he is an antiquated nuisance " (Book IV, p. 508).
[2] *The Encyclopædia of the Social Sciences*, New York, 1930, vol. iii, p. 588 ; *Coal Industry*, by Isador Lubin.

Professor Floris Delattre,[1] the French author of a sketch of British social psychology, which he bases on the events leading up to and occurring during the General Strike, depicts the mentality of the coal-owner in a similar way. According to the author's description, the British coal-owner is a stubborn conservative and traditionalist, sticking to the old established ways and practices just like a " tortoise, which instinctively clings tightly to the ground from fear of being turned on to its back ".

The coal-owners were accused of being incapable of producing any reforms appropriate for the industry as a whole. Those writers who attributed the position of the industry to the peculiar psychology of the colliery owners, paid generally little or no attention to the various industrial causes responsible for the lack of co-operative spirit. It was so much easier for them to account for the phenomena on this simplified assumption than to attempt by economic analysis to throw a search light upon the intricacies of the coal industry. Simply by casting the whole responsibility for the difficult situation on the shoulders of the management, by imputing to it the lack of some necessary moral and mental qualification, these authors imagined that they had explained the whole situation. But, in reality, this line

[1] Floris Delattre. Professeur à l'Université de Lille. *L'Angleterre d'Après-Guerre et le Conflit Houiller*, 1919–1926. In chapter vii, p. 92, we read about the owners of mines as follows : " Les [coal-owners] représentent en effet la classe la plus traditionaliste, peut-être même la plus rétrograde du royaume, et leur mentalité générale repose toute sur la notion du conservatisme insulaire le plus rigidement fermé au mouvement du monde. Ce conservatisme est non seulement pareil à l'instinct avec lequel une tortue s'aggrippe au sol avec ses griffes de peur qu'on ne la renverse sur le dos, comme le remarquait Emerson il y a plus d'un demi-siècle ; il semble encore le plus obstinément ' buté ' qui se puisse imaginer . . ."

Professor Robert Liefmann gives four reasons for the slow development of monopolistic tendencies in English industries, and lays great emphasis upon the individualistic outlook of British business men and upon the prevalent economic doctrines of unrestricted competition . . . " die individualistischen Anschauungen des englischen Unternehmertums, die in Zusammenhang mit der englischen Volkswirtschaftslehre von jeher die freie Konkurrenz als den einzigen natürlichen Zustand des Wirtschaftslebens ansahen. Diese Anschauungen wirkten auch dann hemmend auf die Bildung monopolistischer Organisationen, wenn sie nur von einem Teile der Unternehmer vertreten wurden, ein anderer Teil aber monopolfreundlich war." (Professor Robert Liefmann, *Kartelle, Konzerne und Trusts*, Stuttgart, 1927, p. 200.)

E

of attack hardly elucidates anything whatsoever about the forms of British coal organization. On the contrary, the assumption of a "non-gregarious complex" in the British colliery owners does not explain in the least the continuous process of integration which has been taking place in the industry.

For those commentators whose investigation of the structure does not go deeper than a brief statement about the mentality of the owners, State interference in the affairs of the industry seems simply a useful method of overriding the ignorant obstinacy which blocks the way of progress. They are inclined to represent any statutory regulations as necessary and essential impositions on the industry. Moreover, whatever their judgment on the measure itself, they always regard it as an outside invention. Parliamentary measures always appear to be new openings for industrial development. The Coal Mines Act, 1930, with its marketing clauses, represents for these people a *Deus ex machina* of the State, which suddenly forces on an unprepared industry a perfected organization which had never before been tried.

It is perfectly true that the process of creating a structural scheme was rather slow in the British coal industry, but besides the individualism which has been so much overstressed, there were very strong reasons for this reluctance to initiate changes in organization [1]—reasons, some of which we shall enumerate.

[1] Mr. George Carter has made a short investigation into the reasons which operated against the tendency towards industrial co-operation. His remarks are based on the pre-War conditions. There are six main causes, according to Carter, which hamper integration of the coal industry. First the natural conditions " militate against the formation of effective combinations " ; the diversity and variations between the enterprises and the districts render a common feeling and collaboration difficult. The author points out the danger of inter-district competition, which is likely to check all the attempts within the boundaries of one producing area. Secondly, the excessive number of the existing collieries, which retards the development even of local combination. The industry lacked concentration into a smaller number of units. The third reason is closely connected with the first, namely the collieries vary greatly in size, efficiency, and methods of producing and distributing. Fourthly, there is the suspiciousness of the public concerning any manipulation of prices and quantities. The integrating movement has to break the ice of public prejudice. The fifth difficulty comes from the distributing section, which,

There is the well-known fact that the British coalfields are widely dispersed over the country, forming several important coal basins, none of which, however, preponderates greatly over any other,[1] so that hardly any could be regarded as Britain's leading coal-field. Any one basin produces various grades of coal from highly different seams, mined in unlike technical and natural conditions, and commanding separate markets. This is clearly a great obstacle to spontaneous combination.

as Émile Lewy said (*International Regulation of the Coal Trade*, London, 1896, pp. 26–7), " will always oppose any project which has for its object the restraint of the abuses they practise, and by which they profit." Finally, the special economic feature of coal mining, which tends to reduce overhead charges by producing larger quantities of coal, is not the least important factor impeding co-ordination of production (*The Tendency Towards Industrial Combination*, London, 1913, pp. 227–235).

Mr. Patrick Fitzgerald attempted to explain " How did so many of them [coal producers] come to be created, and why have they so stubbornly resisted the general tendency towards combination ? The chief reasons would appear to be, first, that the English coal industry was established at a relatively early stage of modern capitalism ; secondly, that the terms under which the original leases were granted, the diversity of geological conditions, the special ease with which coal could be mined, and the phenomenal growth of consumption made for the creation and continued existence of many enterprises ; and finally, that given equally good seams, a moderately-sized colliery concern can, generally speaking, work as efficiently as a large one. For these reasons the creation of a trust in the industry appears to be quite impracticable, however desirable it may be in the interest of producers whose mutual rivalry is one of the main causes of their present deplorable condition " (*Industrial Combination in England*, London, 1927, p. 35). Mr. D. J. Williams in a very sketchy and rather inadequate review of the obstacles to concentration does not consider national psychology as an obstacle. His reasons for the lack of amalgamation are : (1) the geographical disparity, which in his opinion does not exist in Germany ; (2) the difficulty of valuation ; (3) the different degrees of productivity of the mines, which he links with different profitability ; and (4) finally special marketing and transport facilities. In our view, however, points (1), (2), and (4) can be applied to any coal industry and do not constitute, as represented by the author, a specially British characteristic (*Capitalist Combination in the Coal Industry*, London, 1924, pp. 73 et seq.).

[1] Miss G. M. Colman emphasizes the geographical factor as being partly responsible for the slow rate of advancement of combinations : " One influence of importance is, of course, geographical ; it is easier for firms in the same locality to co-operate with each other than for those which are widely separated. The fact that the British coal mines are less closely grouped than the German partly explains why combination between mining interests has gone ahead much more rapidly in Germany than in Great Britain " (*Capitalist Combines*, London, 1927, p. 15). Report of the Balfour Committee refers to the coal industry as below . . . " The scattered nature of the British coalfields and the diversity of the markets which they supply have hitherto prevented the establishment of unified control of either pit-head prices, output, or distribution " (*Report*, part i, p. 77).

Apart from these obvious causes, other very important factors must be taken into account. The varying demand both in amount and elasticity for different kinds of coal, coupled with the enormous variety of grades of coal produced, makes any form of restriction much more difficult than it would be if the demand for all coals were inelastic, or at least of similar elasticity.[1] In fact, however, some of the qualities only display elasticity of demand for a fall, i.e. they react only in the case of rising prices by causing a decrease in the demand ; some of them display the opposite feature, i.e. elasticity of demand for a rise ; and some are elastic in the positive as well as in the negative sense.— All this makes the co-operation of producers of those various types of coal very difficult.

One of the obstacles to integration is to be found in the differences of productivity of the various mines and mining districts, which are not counterbalanced by other advantages tending to reduce the costs of production or aiding in the search for high prices, for instance a special local market. Such differences in the physical productivity of the mines are to a great extent connected with the various ages of the mines, causing in the older mines a gradual exhaustion of the easily-worked coal, and also with the natural conditions of the seams. As a typical example of an old and gradually decaying coalfield we can quote Lancashire,[2] whose share in British output gradually diminishes, and where the output per man is much lower than the average for Great Britain, while costs per ton are much higher. On the other hand new districts equipped with the most modern appliances, such as those in South Yorkshire or Kent, represent a good productivity and lower costs of production than the average for the whole country. But even within one area it is easy to find great differences in productivity, caused either by natural differences between the mines, or more often by the various degrees of rationalization applied in neighbouring

[1] Cf. § 2 below.
[2] *Vide An Industrial Survey of the Lancashire Area.* Made for the Board of Trade by the University of Manchester, 1932. H.M. Stationery Office, 51–196, Appendix No. 6.

groups. On the whole, the disparities between the mines in one area are not so conspicuous as disparities between areas themselves.

Besides the difference in productivity, the various units also differ widely in size and in financial strength. Hence, to some of the collieries integration meant great potential economies arising out of the unification of output and control, to others it did not represent any notable savings. Apart from that, combination or cartellization alone did not mean any increase of their efficiency ; what they needed was a large outlay of fresh capital for new equipment, and not merely an increase in size. For those collieries, using Professor Macgregor's phrase, combination only to a very small degree was a " representative method of industrial enterprise ".[1] and did not present an equal attraction to all.

With the problem of varying types of demand for coal, which has been already stressed, was closely associated the tendency of the British colliery owners to aim at cheap production. The history of the coal industry provides several instances showing that they were, with few exceptions, champions of cheap production and cheap selling. After the collapse of the combination called the Newcastle Vend, in the forties of the last century,[2] this practice was prevalent amongst the coal-owners The expanding industry could always find an outlet, provided the price was not too high. " British coal sells itself " was the saying of the day. Production was steadily growing from year to year and, except in 1901, 1908, and 1912, the annual output in Great Britain was always considerably higher than that of each previous year. This expansion had sometimes to be effected by sharp adjustment of prices, but this could easily be achieved. The competitive desire to keep the prices and costs of British coal as low as possible militated against any attempt at artificial restriction of prices or output. Besides the general cause that a large proportion of the national output depended on foreign demand for coal in all its forms, which was on the

---

[1] D. H. Macgregor, *Industrial Combination*, London, 1906, p. 16.
[2] *Vide* Appendix.

whole of high elasticity for a rise,[1] the small degree of vertical combination acted as a deterrent against keeping up prices by means of restriction. One can quite easily conceive that those producers who are connected with iron, steel, or other plants, after having supplied their own plants very cheaply with coal, might be tempted to bolster up the prices for the rest of their coal output. But pure coal undertakings have every inducement to keep prices low and to work at full capacity. This was one of the most important aims of the British coal industry. It tried to preserve its complete freedom of action in order to take all possible advantage from such working. Moreover, by spreading high overhead charges over a maximum tonnage, this method permitted the lowest obtainable cost per ton of coal. Here we may add that overheads in this country are higher per ton of output than in most of the competing countries.

Even the enormous fall in the general output in Great Britain, which occurred in 1908, was unable to affect the principle of working at full capacity. While in 1907 the industry produced 267·8 million tons, the following year the figure was reduced to 261·5 million tons, or by about 2·5 per cent. This fall, however, was much more than offset by the subsequent reduction of the working day to eight hours, which was at that time voted and passed by Parliament, and came into force in 1909. The principle of working full capacity could thus be preserved. Further, it must be remembered that, as we have already explained,[2] while the principle of full capacity applied to the whole industry, many sections, especially those exporting, had to maintain a greater margin of over-capacity than others, owing to a more irregular demand. But notwithstanding this margin the industry tried as a first essential to keep production as near as possible to its potential maximum. It is worth noticing as one of the reasons against restriction that in the pre-War period, when the general volume of production was shrinking, the maximum shrinkage which occurred—it took place in 1912—did not reduce the output of the previous

---

[1] See next section.   [2] *Vide* Part I, Chap. I, § 1.

year by more than 11 million tons or 3·7 per cent. After the War, however, the curve of production shows a much greater irregularity ; in fact, the yearly difference reached in 1925 the figure of nearly 24 million tons. The fluctuation in the volume of output became much more apparent after the War, bringing the question of productive over-capacity in the industry into special prominence. Clearly in the exporting districts those fluctuations were much more considerable than in the areas producing for home consumption. Thus, whereas in 1925 the exporting districts of South Wales and Durham reduced their output below the level of 1924 by about 15 per cent, Yorkshire, Derbyshire, Nottinghamshire, and Leicestershire needed only to reduce their production to between 2 and 6 per cent below that of the previous year. The same holds good if we analyse periodical outputs in corresponding quarters of two years.

TABLE No. 15

TONNAGE OF SALEABLE COAL RAISED IN GREAT BRITAIN DURING THE QUARTERS ENDING 30TH SEPTEMBER, IN 1930, 1931, AND 1932.

District	September, 1930	September, 1931	September, 1932	Decrease in 1931 over the figures of the corresponding quarter in 1930		Decrease in 1932 over the figures of the corresponding quarter in 1931	
	Tons	Tons	Tons	Tons	Per Cent	Tons	Per Cent
Northumber- land	2,924,200	2,817,100	2,686,000	107,100	3·6	131,000	4·6
Durham .	8,237,500	6,845,800	6,239,000	1,391,700	16·8	606,000	8·8
Yorkshire .	10,246,700	9,543,000	8,124,000	703,700	6·8	1,419,000	14·8
Lancs, Cheshire, & N. Wales	4,012,900	3,869,500	3,400,000	143,400	3·5	469,000	12·1
Derby, Notts, & Leicester .	7,653,400	7,348,400	6,124,000	305,000	3·9	1,224,400	16·6
Staffs, Salop, Worcs, & Warwick .	4,078,600	3,905,400	3,855,000	173,200	4·2	50,400	1·3
S. Wales & Monmouth .	10,694,800	9,348,100	8,308,000	1,346,700	12·58	1,040,100	11·1
Scotland .	7,182,000	6,363,500	6,487,000	818,500	11·38	123,500[2]	1·8[2]
Great Britain [1]	55,030,100	50,040,800	46,431,000	4,989,300	9·06	3,609,800	7·2

[1] Includes also Cumberland, Westmorland, Gloucester, Somerset, and Kent. Computed from the *Board of Trade Journal* for 10th December, 1931, and 24th November, 1932.
[2] A Rise.

Note.—In the two issues of the *Board of Trade Journal* the figures for the September quarter, 1931, do not exactly correspond with one another.

For instance, the decrease of output in the September quarter of 1931, compared with that of the same quarter in the preceding year, is much more pronounced in the exporting districts than in the others. This is, however, not true of the September quarter of 1932, with the only exception of South Wales. The general principle can be easily perceived from the Table No. 15, by simple comparison of the percentage decrease in the exporting districts of South Wales, Durham, and Scotland with that of the other areas.

In the case of an expanding market, as in the year 1929, again the greatest difference in the tonnage is borne by the exporting districts. It is interesting to note here that the areas producing chiefly for the home market are exposed to even greater fluctuation in their exports than the remaining districts. Thus, e.g. the Midland Collieries reduced in the year ending June 30, 1932, their coal exports from the Humber ports by 28 per cent, while for the whole of Great Britain coal exports fell off by 13 per cent. On the whole, the exporting markets display a higher degree of irregularity than the home markets in both directions. It is, therefore, much more difficult to adjust the supply of coal in the exporting districts than in those producing for domestic consumption. This difficulty has been well experienced by the Central Council under the Coal Marketing Scheme, which has to ascertain the allowed maximum production in the districts. It is also referred to in a report on the working of the Central and District Schemes.[1]

Large variations in demand are a considerable hindrance to co-operation at any time. This disintegrating motive works with redoubled force in the coal industry, as this

[1] Mines Department, Coal Mines Act, 1930 ; Report by the Board of Trade under Section 7 of the Act on the Working of Scheme under Part I of the Act during the June and September Quarters, 1931, Cmd. 3982, p. 5.
" It is easier to forecast the home demand for coal than that for export. That being so, the output in the districts supplying inland needs should approximate more closely to allocation than in the case of the exporting districts. The inland districts are practically all included in group . . . where the allocation was slightly below or slightly in excess of the output. The exporting districts of Scotland, Durham, and South Wales, on the other hand, appear in the group of districts where the allocations were considerably in excess of demand."

widely fluctuating demand applies to the exporting sections only. By reducing prices at home and by attempting to preserve a good footing in the national markets, the exporting districts succeeded in creating strong price competition and thus impeded co-operation. In this connection we may apply the American conception of " competitive equality " which initially aimed at adjusting different items constituting the costs of production, chiefly labour costs, to the competitive conditions in the coal-market. This conception was, in fact, an application of Adam Smith's law of equalization of profits to the particular industry. According to Mr. Suffern :—

> " Although this principle [competitive equality] was never given precise formulation, it was apparently conceived as a means of putting all employers upon a substantially equal competitive basis. To do this it would have been necessary to offset the advantages which certain operators might possess because of richer seams of coal, nearness to market, and so on, by the payment of higher wages and higher transportation charges. . . . The agreement on the principle of ' competitive equality ' was the outgrowth of competition in an over-developed industry." [1]

At a time of difficult selling in foreign markets the British coal industry offers many instances of aggressive excursion from the exporting areas into the territory of the other districts.

The different firms attempted to overcome the natural difficulties acting as a drawback towards equalizing their profits. J. S. Mill mentioned this possibility.[2] Normally exporting districts wish to share in the remunerative home trade, and thus balance the losses incurred abroad, One can in this respect extend the conception of competitive equality beyond labour items and say that the exporting areas aim at securing a competitive equality abroad by destroying

[1] Arthur E. Suffern, *The Coal Miners' Struggle for Industrial Status : A Study of the Evolution of Organized Relations and Industrial Principle in the Coal Industry*, New York, 1926, p. 319.

[2] J. S. Mill formulated the law of equalization of profits in the following way : " After due allowance is made for these various causes of inequality, namely differences in the risk or agreeableness of different employments, and natural or artificial monopolies, the rate of profit on capital in all employments tends to an equality " (*Principles*, book ii, ch. xv, § 4.)

at the same time the existing order at home. This quasi-competitive equality certainly acts as a highly disintegrating element upon organization. It was just the tendency towards levelling costs and the desire for foreign competitive equality which produced individualism in the British coal industry and separated the different units according to their special characteristics. Hence one can draw the conclusion that the individualism of those colliery undertakings which are either technically inefficient or have unfavourable markets is derived from an attempt to alter the existing competitive equality. As a logical consequence this tendency has brought about the principle of ascertaining wages on a district, as opposed to a national, basis.

All these causes, which prevent the introduction of uniform conditions for the whole of the industry, had a more or less disintegrating effect and prevented the process of concentration, or co-operation. Here we may make a passing reference to two facts, which had a strong influence especially in the past, viz. the diffusion of transport and the widely dispersed system of royalties.

Starting first with transport, we note that the relatively large number of separate railway companies created a possibility of transport alternatives. Very often in one small coal-field there existed several railway lines mutually competing, and granting different terms to the coal concerns. Even to-day, in such districts as the Lothians, Yorkshire (Houghton Main Colliery, Co.), or Lancashire, there are companies using the services both of the L.M.S. Railway, and of the L.N.E. Railway. This dispersion in the transport system and costs was certainly the cause of the introduction of wide disparities in colliery costs. Before the Railways Act, 1921, amalgamating the railways into four groups, a large number of companies gave various terms for transport of coal ; and though, since the Rates and Charges Confirmation Act, 1892, the maximum charges were limited by the State, the railways were always free to reduce their charges through various rebates.

In the course of years dozens of small railways had been amalgamated, but the differences in costs of transport still remained. Presumably the railway pooling schemes of 1933 will act to some extent as integrating factors in the coal industry. In countries like Germany, where the transport system was unified in the hands of the Government, transport costs before the War did not vary as in the United Kingdom, and they were practically computed on the mileage principle, thus facilitating the division of the markets into well defined uncontested areas. These fell chiefly under the sphere of influence of the Rheinish-Westphalian Coal Comptoir and the Upper-Silesian Coal Convention, operating since 1898 together with the Lower Silesian Coal Cartel. The contested area of Berlin, which was of enormous importance to the coal-fields, was divided between the competing cartels in an agreed proportion. But this form of protection afforded by freights, which existed in Germany and favoured the application of an extensive zoning scheme, was substantially diminished in Britain by the competitive efforts of the many railway lines.

Even in recent years, rail transport conditions in this country are still a disruptive rather than an integrating force. In Germany, for example, large coal syndicates can obtain greatly reduced rates for a guaranteed minimum of traffic ; but in this country, the Railways Act, 1921, itself prohibits any benefits of this sort to large combines.[1]

Other factors facilitated the differentiation of costs. The system of privately owned wagons is largely used in this country, especially for the conveyance of coal. At the beginning of 1932, out of the 650,000 private wagons in this country, 520,000 were employed in the coal trade. By using their own trucks, or those belonging to the associated companies, collieries can make substantial economies, and certainly have an advantage over those which do not possess their own wagons.

Apart from the competition among railways, however, Great Britain's coal-fields are in a position to enjoy the advantage of competition between rail, sea, and, to some extent, canals ; this in fact has assisted them enormously

[1] Interpretation of the Act by L. J. Scrutton, in Court of Appeal, concerning appeal of G.W.R. against the decision of Railway Rates Tribunal, June, 1933.

and helped to differentiate the costs of transport. In the history of coal organization in England, this last named competition caused the destruction of the biggest of all hitherto known cartels in this country, viz. the Newcastle Coal Vend, which supplied the London area with coal from the North Eastern Coast.[1]

The influence of the system of coal royalties in England on organization is similar to the land transport factor. In all countries, where the leasing power reposes in the hands of a State minister, we witness a greater degree of uniformity of both conditions, rules, and prices paid. In this country, where the number of royalty owners exceeds three thousand, naturally there must exist a great variety of provisions. This in turn leads to cost disparities, and so provides a further disintregating force.

We pass now to a very important group of reasons for the lack of co-ordination in British coal mining ; these are to be found on the side of capital, and especially in the difference between the British and foreign banking systems.[2]

The essential dissimilarity between the continental methods of financing enterprises and those in this country have an historic foundation. British bankers always believed that " a banker should never become industrialist " and that

---

[1] This historical cartel of the eighteenth and nineteenth centuries is described in the Appendix B.

[2] Allan Greenwell, in a lecture delivered at the London School of Economics in 1911, on the Economic Position of the Coal Industry of the United Kingdom, gave such reasons for the failure of voluntary cartel schemes : " . . . on two occasions have such schemes been launched in the North of England, but the more successful of the two, that known as ' Limitation of the Vend ', did not survive the prolonged test of experience. In South Wales, again, two similar attempts have been made, but neither reached the stage of actuality. In Yorkshire and other places associations have been formed amongst the collieries producing particular qualities of coal with the object of maintaining prices, but with no conspicuous success. In their failure may be found the causes of all such failures in the British coal trade. It must be remembered that coal mining enterprise in Great Britain has been much more of a " family business " than elsewhere ; concerns have thriven or withstood the stress of bad times, through several generations on capital to which the subscribers have been few in number. But it must not be inferred that the banks have played the same role in such enterprises here that these useful institutions have played in Germany, for instance." (See *Lectures on British Commerce, including insurance, business, and industry*, London, p. 237.)

the debtor and creditor should be independent, while the continental banks closely collaborated with the industry and influenced its organization.[1]

The pure coal company in Britain on the whole did not take much advantage even of the open money market, and very few issues were made before the War on their behalf. The following figures show the amount of those issues, which is extremely low.

TABLE No. 16

ISSUES MADE ON BEHALF OF PURE COLLIERY COMPANIES, 1899–1913 [2]

Year.			£ million.
1899	.	.	Nil.
1900	.	.	2·5
1901	.	.	·5
1902	.	.	·6
1903	.	.	1·1
1904	.	.	·3
1905	.	.	·7
1906	.	.	·1
1907	.	.	·1
1908	.	.	·6
1909	.	.	·2
1910	.	.	1·0
1911	.	.	·9
1912	.	.	·6
1913	.	.	1·0

As a result of this difference between the two methods, the industrial units in Britain are freer to adopt such forms of organization as they think best for themselves, whereas the Continental units, often strictly supervised by the banks, follow more general lines of development, and so amalgamation is easier. In addition, the Continental banks, being

[1] Such pressure of the continental banks on their customers has been well described in *The Statist*. " They saw, before we did, that the future lay with the bigger unit and the bankers for their part played a decisive role in determining the general outlines of the combinations that have taken place during recent years in such countries as Germany and Belgium. The leadership of the banks was one of the factors which enabled this movement to proceed along lines of truly national co-ordinated policy, and which brought to the fore the individuals most competent to manage the rationalized industries. These lessons of the possibility of closer co-operation between finance and industry are undoubtedly now being learned in this country." Vol. cxv, p. 1029, *Banks and Industrial Reorganization*.

[2] These figures have been collected by Mr. G. L. Ayres, owing to whose kindness the author has been able to secure them.

much more closely connected with the different enterprises, tend to provide them more readily with long-term loans necessary for reorganization or amalgamation, and having achieved financial control over several productive units they pave the way to concentration for their industrial clients through amalgamation or absorption.[1]

Only very recently in this country have some of the banks taken a greater interest in the fundamental reorganization of coal mining. Mr. Thomas [2] quotes as an illustration of financing by the joint-stock banks the fusions between the concerns of Dorman Long and Bolckow-Vaughan and that between Guest, Keen and Nettlefolds and Baldwins, who operate their coal interests under the name of Welsh Associated Collieries, Ltd. ; and instances the Securities Management Trust, an offspring of the Bank of England, as financing an important amalgamation of coal-mining and distributing interests in Lancashire known as the Wigan Coal Company.[3] Penetration by the joint-stock banks and the merchant banking houses into the financing of reorganization of the coal industry and its by-products has lately made a

[1] The British banks have been sometimes criticized for not forcing the industry to organize, or for maintaining the moribund mines. Sir Arthur Salter considered that in this respect the banks were not sufficiently dictatorial. (See *The Banker*, January, 1931, p. 30). The Balfour Report refers to these views : " It has been suggested that in many cases their (banks) support has been not too niggardly but too lavish, and that injury has been done to the permanent interests of the British industry and trade by the nursing of weak undertakings by the banks in the vain hope of an early recovery. These critics urge that it would have been much better to let the weaker concerns go into liquidation and to concentrate production in the hands of the stronger, or at least the more efficiently equipped and managed, undertakings . . ." (*Final Report of the Committee on Industry and Trade*, Cmd. 3282, 1929, p. 51). Mr. P. Barrett Whale, in his admirably clear book on German banking, pointed out that before the War a firm of moderate size was largely dependent on the dictation of its banker. " If it happened to fall upon bad times, it was likely to lose this freedom entirely and be compelled to accept any scheme of reconstruction or fusion which the bank might choose to dictate." He described the interesting case of the Hibernia Mining Co., in which the banks prevented the Prussian Government from interfering with the structure of the Rheinish Westphalian Coal Syndicate (*Joint Stock Banking in Germany : A Study of the German Creditbanks before and after the War*, London, 1930, pp. 55–64).

[2] S. Evelyn Thomas, *British Banks and the Finance of Industry*, London, 1931, p. 143.

[3] Op. cit., p. 150.

substantial advance. Sir Eric Hambro may be cited as a merchant banker interested in financing, through the Smokeless Fuel Concessions Co., Ltd., and the Coal Petroleum Co., Ltd., formed recently as a private company, to acquire any patent relating to the carbonization, distillation or other treatment of carbonaceous materials, and the development of new processes of low temperature carbonization likely to affect several colliery districts in the country.[1] Patents of high temperature carbonization are acquired by a special international concern associated with the Imperial Chemical Industries, Ltd.

The relative lack of mutual dependence between the banks and the coal companies had undoubtedly some effect on the preservation in Britain of a great number of private family concerns, operating as a rule the small and middle size collieries. On the North-East Coast, in the Lancashire and Cheshire area, in Scotland, and in some of the smaller coal-fields the number of such private companies is very considerable, and they are very often reluctant to amalgamate.[2]

It is particularly noticeable that private firms do not often combine successfully with joint-stock companies, especially when they are efficient and they do not anticipate further economies of production from amalgamation. This point has been often emphasized in Northumberland and Durham as an argument against the general and Draconian suggestions of the Coal Reorganization Commission acting under the Coal Mines Act, 1930. The dislike of private concerns for amalgamation with joint-stock companies is based partly on psychological grounds (goodwill, personality of the concern, etc.). But the chief practical obstacle is the difficulty of valuation of the joint-stock companies' assets, as they have often been much inflated at the time when the coal trade paid well. Such watering of capital, which was not followed by a corresponding increase

[1] *The Times*, 21st December, 1931, and 27th September, 1932; and the *Colliery Guardian*, vol. cxlv, p. 604, September, 1932.
[2] Cf. Industrial Survey of the North-East Coast Area, made for the Board of Trade by Armstrong College (University of Durham), H.M. Stationery Office, 51–194, 1932, *Memorandum on the Coal Mining Industry*.

in profits, acted as a deterrent for the small units run on conservative methods. We have taken the capitals of a few of the big companies [1] in various districts to show how much they were increased between 1913 and 1924, when the deflationary wave had already reduced their profits.

This increase of capital in relation to profits, which we may add is often much exaggerated by the critics of the joint-stock companies, is connected with the method of financing the industry. Not until recently did the banks request the coal companies to reduce their capital to a profitable basis. As an instance of such a reduction of capital can be given the Ebbw Vale Steel, Iron and Coal Co., Ltd., which in 1932, on the request of its bankers, reduced the capital from £3·7 million to £250,000; or the small company the Moira Colliery Co., Ltd., where a reduction of capital from £650,000 to £320,000 recently took place. Similar reduction of capital has been approved by the court in reference to Pease and Partners, Ltd., where with the approval of Barclays Bank and of the Royal Exchange Assurance Co., the capital of the firm has been cut down from £3,000,000 to £1,500,000.[2]

Severe writing down of capital took place in Dorman Long and Co., a well-known concern of the North-East Coast, which in 1933 merged its assets with the South Durham Steel and Iron Co., Ltd. The bankers, who were much interested in the two companies, fostered the scheme which was an alternative to receivership, while new finance to the amount of £2·5 million was promised from a private syndicate,[3] owing to intervention of the Bankers' Industrial Development Company.

In some other companies less drastic measures have been taken, while certain companies have had recourse to a high depreciation ratio which they continually write off each year, e.g. the Yorkshire Amalgamated Collieries, Ltd., in the course of the last five years, 1927–1931, has written off on account of its subsidiaries a sum of £500,000 of capital.

[1] See Table 17 on the following page.
[2] *Vide The Times*, 24th January, 1933.
[3] The syndicate was headed by Messrs. N. M. Rothschild and Sons.

TABLE No. 17

CAPITAL RESERVES AND CARRIED FORWARD (INCLUDES DEBENTURE CAPITAL), 1913–1924.

End of Year.	Baldwins, Ltd.	Dorman Long & Co., Ltd.	Ebbw Vale Steel Coal & Iron Co.	Guest, Keen & Nettlefolds, Ltd.	Horden, Collieries, Ltd.	Pearson & Knowles Coal & Iron Co., Ltd.	Powell Duffryn Steam Coal Co., Ltd.	Sheepbridge Coal & Iron Co.
	£	£	£	£	£	£	£	£
1913	1,728,000	2,079,000	—	6,476,000	829,341	—	2,316,000	—
1914	—	—	—	—	—	—	—	1,345,000
1917	—	—	1,572,000	—	—	—	—	—
1918	3,816,000	4,085,000	1,840,000	6,953,000	—	—	2,816,000	1,524,000
1919	5,576,000	5,531,000	5,504,000	7,966,000	1,366,000	—	2,916,000	1,600,000
1920	6,609,000	7,519,000	9,914,000	14,977,000	1,847,000	2,059,000	3,911,000	1,657,000
1921	9,605,000	8,915,000	—	15,926,000	1,859,000	2,041,000	4,081,000	1,574,000
1922	9,679,000	9,130,000	—	16,131,000	1,911,000 [1]	2,945,000	5,493,000	1,810,000
1923	10,016,000	12,619,000	9,348,000	16,186,000	1,987,000 [1]	2,969,000	5,604,000	1,783,000
1924	10,095,000	—	9,478,000	17,062,000	2,058,000 [1]	3,060,000	5,628,000	2,112,000

OWN COLLIERIES, PLANT, ETC.

End of Year.	Baldwins, Ltd.	Dorman Long & Co., Ltd.	Ebbw Vale Steel Coal & Iron Co.	Guest, Keen & Nettlefolds, Ltd.	Horden, Collieries, Ltd.	Pearson & Knowles Coal & Iron Co., Ltd.	Powell Duffryn Steam Coal Co., Ltd.	Sheepbridge Coal & Iron Co.
	£	£	£	£	£	£	£	£
1913	957,000	871,000	—	2,821,000	1,315,000	—	1,938,000	—
1914	—	—	—	—	—	—	—	994,000
1917	—	—	1,348,000	—	—	—	—	—
1918	1,619,000	1,902,000	2,018,000	2,821,000	—	—	1,977,000	1,085,000
1919	2,205,000	2,534,000	5,479,000	2,921,000	1,585,000	—	2,115,000	1,254,000
1920	2,885,000	3,127,000	6,510,000	2,895,000	1,750,000	747,000	2,413,000	1,291,000
1921	3,406,000	3,491,000	—	3,006,000	1,958,000	854,000	2,929,000	1,402,000
1922	3,625,000	3,377,000	—	3,082,000	1,870,000	869,000	3,402,000	1,502,000
1923	3,559,000	9,462,000	7,072,000	3,111,000	1,954,000	850,000	3,663,000	1,592,000
1924	3,512,000	—	7,143,000	3,115,000	2,687,000	866,000	3,810,000	1,745,000

INTERESTS IN OTHER COMPANIES

End of Year.	Baldwins, Ltd.	Dorman Long & Co., Ltd.	Ebbw Vale Steel Coal & Iron Co.	Guest, Keen & Nettlefolds, Ltd.	Horden, Collieries, Ltd.	Pearson & Knowles Coal & Iron Co., Ltd.	Powell Duffryn Steam Coal Co., Ltd.	Sheepbridge Coal & Iron Co. [2]
	£	£	£	£	£	£	£	£
1913	208,000	695,000	—	2,677,000	—	—	32,000	—
1914	—	—	—	—	—	—	—	—
1917	—	—	409,000	—	—	—	—	—
1918	1,153,000	2,406,000	408,000	3,260,000	—	—	166,000	—
1919	1,783,000	2,610,000	—	4,172,000	—	—	523,000	—
1920	2,299,000	3,619,000	2,803,000	11,689,000	—	519,000	1,098,900	—
1921	3,813,000	4,601,000	—	12,742,000	—	522,000	1,315,000	—
1922	4,123,000	5,022,000	—	13,287,500	79,000	1,773,000	1,575,000	—
1923	4,250,000	776,000	2,805,000	13,591,000	221,000	1,770,000	1,666,000	—
1924	4,234,000	—	2,805,000	13,338,000	200,000	1,835,000	1,342,000	—

[1] Debenture capital included.
[2] Interest in allied firms included in fixed assets.

Source: *The Statist*, *The Stock Exchange Year Book*; *The Stock Exchange Gazette*.

The big concern, Welsh Associated Collieries, Ltd., formed in 1930 with a potential output of 10 million tons, has put on depreciation account £100,000 in 1931, against nil in 1930. A similar effect was obtained in some cases by the reduction of interest on companies' debentures. This process was greatly stimulated by the cheap money policy of the Government and the Bank of England, which facilitated the obtaining of low interest loans for the purpose of redeeming old debentures.[1] The reconstruction of capital took in some companies the form of cancelling all arrears of dividend on preference stocks, thus relieving the firms from heavy liabilities. In April, 1933, the Amalgamated Anthracite Collieries, Ltd., asked its preference shareholders to cancel all arrears of dividend.[2] In certain extreme cases the banker demanded the liquidation or the receivership of the companies, which were usually sold on fair valuation. Thus, for instance, Lloyds Bank, which is in possession of a large number of debentures of the Nautgwin Anthracite Colliery (1927), Ltd., with an output of about 70,000 tons, asked for the appointment of a receiver of this company.[3]

But as already pointed out, all these measures to reduce the capital of the coal companies are only a relatively new movement. Ultimately it should have some effect in facilitating a further degree of integration.

§2. THE DEMAND FOR COAL [4]

The special character of the demand for British coal stands as a definite cause in itself among the various

[1] Cf. Part II, Chap. I, § 3.

[2] The scheme provided for the complete cancellation of all arrears of dividend to preference shareholders amounting gross to £686,203, instead of that they were credited with a sum of £514,652, for which amount they received funding certificates bearing interest at $4\frac{1}{2}$ per cent per annum and having a cumulative sinking fund of $2\frac{1}{2}$ per cent (Report of the Company, published on 11th April, 1933).

[3] The *Iron and Coal Trades Review*, 7th July, 1932, p. 109.

[4] A summary of this section was read by the author before the Royal Statistical Society's Study Group on 9th February, 1932.

After this chapter had been written, I had the privilege of discussing with Professor Henry Schultz certain problems connected with the elasticity of demand.

disintegrating factors operating in the industry. Probably in no other industry is the demand less homogenous either as regards quality, quantity, distribution through time, the geographical localization, or in respect to the type of consumers requiring fuel. The demand comes from the producers of producers' goods, from the producers of consumers' goods, and finally it comes directly from the consumer. This very fact exercises its influence against the uniform consolidation of the British coal industry. But there are further factors, either working independently or connected with those already mentioned, which are responsible for the introduction of a great degree of irregularity in the demand for coal. First of all the principle of substitution, which operates with varying intensity according to the price of coal and technical considerations in relation to the different consumers of coal, affects the producers of coal in an unequal degree. Further, this links us with the problem of coal prices, about which Professor Jevons so aptly said when discussing the economics of coal : " The point of central interest—the pivot of economic forces—is the price of coal . . . " [1] Here again wide variations in the degree of importance which coal exhibits in different productive processes work against any uniformity of demand, especially in view of the fact that changes in the price of coal do not affect the demand in an equal way. Here we approach the problem of elasticity of demand for British coal. The existence of a great general elasticity of demand, or the co-existence of various degrees of elasticities of demand according to different sections of the coal trade, are naturally an obstacle to cartellization and amalgamation of collieries. These problems must be attacked in an analysis of the causes preventing integration.

The British coal industry, scattered all over the country, producing a very wide range of coal, finds itself in a position much less suitable for natural integration than industries the demand for whose products is equally elastic or inelastic. This is so because the schemes for the artificial

[1] H. Stanley Jevons, *The British Coal Trade*, London, 1915, p. 257.

regulation of prices affect the demand from the numerous sections of the coal industry in a very uneven way [1] and, while they prove beneficial to some of them, they are prejudicial to the others. In this section we shall investigate the problem of disintegration along the lines of demand, with chief consideration to the influence of prices on demand and to internal substitution within the coal industry. We do not so much propose, however, to make computations aiming at precise numerical estimates of the weight of the component forces affecting the demand. Our real objective is to elucidate their particular influence upon the progress of organization in the industry. " We do not need to give numerical values to the law of demand to be in a position to use it for deducing important consequences." [2] For our purpose of weighing the causes of disintegration, a study attempting to give statistical magnitudes would be completely misleading. Besides the fact that, as Professor Pigou,[3] observed, such precise numeric computations would be but of very doubtful value owing to the lack of sufficiently accurate data, they would necessarily apply only to a specified period, thus giving us an answer valuable exclusively from the viewpoint of static economics, but actually useless in dynamic economic phenomena, and, as Professor Robbins [4] brilliantly shows, of importance only to history. What we aim at is the explanation of a purely dynamic process continuing in time space, and not confined to a single moment. For all these reasons, in this study we concentrate actually more on

[1] Cf. Professor Henry Louis in an article, " Exports of British Coal," British Industries number of *The Times*, 1st November, 1932, says ". . . it is even doubtful whether it is right to speak of the British coal industry as one entity, seeing that the coals produced by the different coalfields, the objects for which these are produced, and the markets which they supply, are all so widely different that it is perfectly possible that anything that may be in the advantage of one field may well be to the detriment of another."

[2] Lionel Robbins, *An Essay on the Nature and Significance of Economic Science*, London, 1932, p. 65.

[3] " We can, indeed, by a careful study of all relevant facts, learn something about the elasticities of demand and supply for a good number of things, but we cannot ascertain their magnitude with any degree of exactness " (A. C. Pigou, *The Economics of Welfare*, 4th ed., p. 10).

[4] Loc. cit., p. 101.

the tendencies and changes in demand than on their valuations.

There are three main forces which may influence the shape of the coal-demand curve in a definite market, or markets. All three have a distinct bearing upon the price or quantity disposed of in the market, though actually in practical life their activity is mutually entwined. These are : competition of buyers, substitution of goods,[1] and elasticity of demand. Imagining, therefore, a definite market for British coal, one can detect all three factors working from the demand side, either separately or more probably jointly. The first two, though influencing the shape of the demand curve of our particular product, do not cause any diminution in the satisfaction of accumulated wants ; whereas the last can bring about alterations in both directions, i.e. either relative abstinence or extension of the amount of fuel required.

In numerous studies of the factors determining the demand for coal, both competition and external substitution in all their varieties have received close attention, and have been subjected to careful investigations by national experts as well as by international inquiries. The four reports of the League of Nations (I & II vol., 1927, 1929, 1932), the Congresses on Power and Fuel, the Royal Coal Commissions, the British Association, and many other bodies and experts have analysed them from various angles and emphasized their significance for the industry. Of course competition of buyers is of prime importance in connection with the state of supply, but the problem of external substitution comes from the demand side spontaneously either as a result of technical considerations or of economies in use. In this way oil has successfully competed with coal in many fields, and in many cases has supplanted it altogether ; particularly in the Royal Navy, which consumed in 1913–14 about 1·7 million tons of coal valued at £2,000,000, but used in 1930 only 180,000 tons, and about 110,000 in 1932. Also in the Mercantile Marine the number and gross tonnage of steamers

---

[1] On the theoretical aspect of substitution and complementarity, see Dr. P. N. Rosenstein-Rodan's article on marginal utility in the *Handwörterbuch der Staatswissenschaften*, 4th Edition.

fitted for burning oil fuel and of motorships has substantially increased since the War, for the whole world to about 25,000,000 tons, which is equal to 40 per cent of all tonnage.[1] For Great Britain and Ireland the tonnage figure of oil-using vessels is 7,000,000, which represents 35 per cent of the total British tonnage. These figures were often misread by many writers, since they did not make any allowance, in their computations, for the newly constructed vessels. Taking the whole world, the total increase of tonnage since 1913–1930 is equal to more than 20,000,000 tons, while in the same period the tonnage of oil-using ships has risen by about 23,000,000. In other words, one can roughly state that the newly constructed tonnage is nearly equal to the total tonnage of the oil-using ships, which amounts to saying that the coal-using vessels were very little eliminated from transport and that to a great extent oil is supplying ships actually representing the newly constructed tonnage, while a tonnage equal to the pre-War figure is still carried on coal power. The chief cause of the reduction in the demand for coal for the Marine is thus not only oil but the economic depression, the fall in international trade, and the relatively high price of British coal.

In other fields than shipping, even including heating, oil has proved its ability to compete with coal. To-day the national shrines, Westminster Cathedral and Canterbury Cathedral, the Bank of England, the offices of the Federation of British Industries, and many hospitals, schools, public buildings, and hotels, are heated by oil fuel central heating.[2]

London hospitals alone use at present 12,500 tons of fuel oil yearly. In many industries, oil is widely used ; for instance, it is the chief fuel for the manufacture of high quality aluminium alloy forgings and castings ; for the jute industry ; and about 100,000 tons of oil are used yearly by the glass manufacturers.[3]

[1] Figures taken from Lloyd's *Register of Shipping*, vol. ii, Statistical Tables Nos. 3 and 4.
[2] Cf. *The Compendium of Commerce*, vol. xviii, No. 1, p. 3, 5th February, 1933.
[3] See *The Compendium of Commerce*, vol. xviii, No. 5, p. 152.

It must be remembered, however, that benzol can be produced from coal ; price, however, is the main deciding factor in favour of oil.[1] On the other hand, the technique of burning coal in all its forms has been greatly advanced. It can now generate greater power and be used more cleanly and conveniently. Recently attempts were made by the Cunard line to use in one of its steamers a " colloidal " fuel, which is a mixture of 60 per cent of oil and 40 per cent of pulverized coal.[2]

Electricity is, to some extent, another rival of coal, particularly as a means of generating power and heat. But in this respect, especially as far as home demand is concerned, there is a large degree of complementarity between the two. This applies less to those countries where, as in Sweden, Italy, or recently in Russia, hydro-electric generating power stations have been installed.

The displacement of coal by the generation of water power has been enormously exaggerated ; accurate figures as to the amount of this displacement are not easily available. The report of the League of Nations [3] quotes only one instance, Italy, where the increase of hydro-electric power is equal yearly to a consumption of coal of about 9 million tons ; but the bulk of this goes into new uses. Mr. Morgan [4] took for the whole of Europe the figure of 28 million tons of coal as the quantity represented by water power, which is a very insignificant item when one remembers that the production of coal in Europe was equal when this estimate was made to about 600 million tons. And even out of these 28 million tons only a very small portion went to displace coal ; the rest was absorbed in entirely new industrial developments or consumptive uses.

Actual derivatives from coal, such as gas, coke, patent fuel, etc., are often regarded as competitive substitutes ;

[1] See letter of Professor Tizard in *The Times*, 10th December, 1932.
[2] For details see Professor J. S. S. Brame, a paper, " Colloidal or Coal-oil Fuel," *Iron and Coal Trades Review*, 21st October, 1932.
[3] *The Problem of the Coal Industry*. Interim Report on its International Aspects by the Economic Committee of the League of Nations, Geneva, 1929.
[4] Alfred Morgan, " Coal Problem as seen by a Colliery Official," *The Economic Journal*, December, 1926, p. 574.

but in our view those articles which are derived from a more rational consumption of coal must rank equally with all those devices which are the outcome of the more economical use of coal and increased value of each of its units. All these more economical uses of coal after some time help to increase the general demand. In this respect the remark of Jevons,[1] that " It is wholly a confusion of ideas to suppose that the economical use of fuel is equivalent to a diminished consumption " is equally true at the present day. A cheap supply of power, fuel, and light will ultimately benefit coal, though perhaps in a more or less roundabout way. One must, moreover, remember that even those substitutes which took the place of coal in a rather revolutionary way also require a technical equipment, which in a large degree depends on coal and is a cause of its increased demand.[2] Thus, for instance, the motor traffic, which may be said at one stage to displace coal used by railways, also provides a new and most considerable demand for coal by expanding the manufacture of steel.[3]

Though of course the demand for new commodities cannot in the short run compensate for the fall in demand for coal, in our view the whole problem of competition between coal and its substitutes is not so much dangerous in itself, as it is rather serious in view of the general economic depression which in the higher stages of production, supplying the producers' goods, has existed since 1920 with varying intensity. Finally we must also remark that

[1] W. Stanley Jevons, *The Coal Question*, 3rd ed., p. 140.

[2] The same fact has been stressed during the debates of the Chemistry Section of the British Association in London in 1931. In the symposium Mr. H. T. Tizard " suggested that (in diminishing home consumption of coal) the competition of oil had played, and would play, no great part, because oil-using motors had created an entirely new demand for coal, which was required on a large scale in all processes of their production. Export, including shipping, showed a different state of affairs."—Mr. H. T. Tizard, " The British Fuel Problem," quoted from *The Times*, 29th September, 1931.

[3] Owing to the kindness of Mr. Leon F. Duval, head of Statistical Dept. of the Society of Motor Manufacturers and Traders, Ltd., it was possible to obtain the figures hitherto unpublished of British steel used by the motor car trade. This figure amounts to about 300,000 tons yearly ; for the production of that amount of steel about 1,500,000 tons of British coal is used per annum.

in certain cases the substitution must be regarded as a fact already accomplished with the change of technique. Indeed raw coal no longer is a substitute—it has been relegated from this stage of production altogether and may be considered as a raw material entering industry through a higher stage in the whole structure of production.

Passing now to substitution which took place in foreign demand, we must reckon to some extent with hydro-electric developments, as well as with the growth of foreign mining. In the latter we must include the quickly rising lignite industry, especially in Germany, Czechoslovakia, and in the Danubian valley. Germany alone, with her production of 133 million tons of lignite, was responsible for more than 80 per cent of the total European output. The rise of lignite production, though certainly an important factor, has very often been overrated in certain circles. We must remember first that already in 1913 about 90 million tons of lignite were produced in Germany alone, and secondly, that the calorific content of lignite as compared with coal is very low (about 1 : 5), which renders it in many cases non-competitive with higher classes of imported coals.

To sum up shortly our views on external substitution, we must say that during a general depression any new source of economy, or any new supply of power, heat or light, certainly adds to the difficulties of the coal industry. Further, we may add that as not all coals are equally substitutable, this external substitution affects the various sections of the coal industry in different ways and thus prevents to some extent the progress of integration. But in the long run, external substitution does not seem to be contrary to the interests of the coal industry, since in many cases coal is used in higher stages of production to provide the necessary appliances for the use of external substitutes. The problems of internal substitution will be dealt with a little later.

Among the causes of disintegration in the industry, the elasticity of demand for coal and the problem of internal substitution have not been treated adequately in the studies of the existing situation in coal mining, though undoubtedly their existence should be taken into account in correlation with other factors. The omission of the elasticity of demand for coal from scientific investigations can probably be attributed to total incredulity among some economists as to its existence. In fact the whole matter has been simplified to a generalization that coal is an article of inelastic demand, since the demand is determined by factors other than price. Such a vague statement, which in times like the present depression is quite common, implies two things. First, the belief that dear coal has no effect on demand, and second, that the prices of coal are irrelevant to economic life as a whole, except perhaps to the exporting sections. But both of these assumptions are obviously erroneous. Moreover, a generalization about the elasticity of demand for coal does not take into account short and long periods ; the demand may be inelastic in the short run, but elastic in the long run, or in exceptional cases vice versa. In order to explain the fluctuations in demand some economists look for causes outside the province of prices. For instance, they find in the state of the weather the main cause determining the demand for domestic coal, while that for other sorts of coal, e.g. for industrial coal, is said to be solely defined by the position of the individual industry, even without regard to the function of coal in that industry. The same plausible argument is applied to transport, bunker coal, etc. The demand for gas coal is said to depend exclusively on forces analogous with those determining the demand for household coal. Similar reasoning is often extended to the nature of demand for coal in the foreign market.

But the assumption of an inelastic demand, and of a complete lack of correlation between the price of coal and the strength of demand, certainly does not explain definite cases of increasing output and falling prices of coal in non-competitive conditions, and further does not elucidate adequately the movements of coal prices. Even in the case of a sudden fall in demand or a sudden rise of supply, it would be wiser on this reasoning for the owners to embark upon schemes of artificial restriction than to compete and cut down prices. If this is not practicable, it is to some extent due to the existence of elasticity of demand in general, and particularly to the uneven degree of elasticity in various sections of the market. Otherwise, what logical sequence would lead the seller of coal who has not to fear competition to reduce his prices, if he knew that demand was affected by forces existing beyond his control, and not by price ? And those writers who reject altogether the bearing of the elasticity of demand for coal on the problem of integration have recourse to the ever doubtful explanation on psychological grounds as lying at the back of the whole difficulty. On an earlier page we have already rejected this motive as a major cause for the lack of amalgamation, cartellization, and co-operation, and we shall show later that at certain moments the industry evolved, without any pressure from outside, its own temporary schemes for regulating production or sales. The question of disintegration in the industry would be inexplicable if we assumed a total inelasticity [1] of demand for coal, both in the short as well as in the long run.

Before embarking upon a further analysis of our problem we must define the conditions in which the two elasticities of demand, i.e. for a rise and for a fall, may exist—those

---

[1] Some economists consider the demand as inelastic when the co-efficient of elasticity is less than 1·0, e.g. Professor Henry Schultz classifies elasticity as follows : " In mathematical symbols the co-efficient of elasticity of demand y is :—

$$y = \frac{dx}{x} \Big/ \frac{dy}{y} = \frac{d \log x}{d \log y} = \frac{dx}{dy} \cdot \frac{y}{x}$$

where x is the quantity demanded, and y the price per unit. If this is numerically equal to 1·0 for all values of x the demand is neither elastic nor inelastic. If this is numerically greater than 1·0 the demand is said to be elastic. If it is numerically less than 1·0 the demand is said to be inelastic. The size of the co-efficient measures the degree of elasticity." (See Henry Schultz, *Statistical Laws of Demand and Supply*, Chicago, 1928, pp. 4–5.)

Alfred Marshall speaks about great or small elasticity : ". . . we may say generally ; the elasticity (or responsiveness) of demand in a market is great or small according as the amount demanded increases much or little for a given fall in price, and diminishes much or little for a given rise in price."—(*Principles of Economies*, 8th edition, London, p. 102.)

Marshall does not accept the point that when the coefficient of elasticity is less than 1·0 then the demand is inelastic—he probably would say small elasticity.

Thus there seems to be an important difference as to the conception of inelasticity of demand, a fact which perhaps has not been sufficiently emphasized in the analysis of the elasticity of demand for coal; it is important to stress this difference in order to avoid confused thinking.

in which inelasticity may exist, and those cases where there is never any direct causal relation between prices and demand. By *elasticity of demand for a rise* is to be understood an increase of quantity actually demanded as a reaction to lower prices, by *elasticity for a fall* a decrease in quantity demanded in response to increased prices. As, however, the two processes cannot in reality happen at the same time, that is to say, prices cannot in the same moment rise and fall, the two elasticities cannot be represented on the same curve of demand. This could be only done on a hypothetical curve of demand, which in practical life we cannot statistically devise.[1]

---

[1] The author would like to acknowledge here the help and suggestions of Professor Lionel Robbins, Dr. P. N. Rosenstein-Rodan, Dr. Marschak, and Mr. A. Lerner.

The historical demand curves for coal, the data for which have been obtained, at different times, from the actual transactions taking place in the market at different prices, by their nature can only be valid for illustrating changes of the price/quantity system in one direction. It may conceivably be that owing to some changes in data the function is of an irreversible nature. Hence the justification for the distinction between the elasticity for a rise and the elasticity for a fall. Of all these changes in data the most important is the velocity of price changes, which affects the quantity of commodities sold in the market. The concept has been introduced by Professor Griffith C. Evans, who says : " Whether the price is going up or down is itself an important factor in the demand for the quantity. In actual cases the demand is often not merely a function of the price alone, but is stimulated or depressed by the mere fact that price is rising or falling." (*Mathematical Introduction to Economics*, London–New York, 1930, pp. 36–49.) While according to previous doctrines the quantity was equal to a function of price $q = f(p)$; now we can say that $q = f\left(p ; \dfrac{dp}{dt}\right)$

(t = time element), where ratio $\dfrac{dp}{dt}$ measures the velocity of price changes

In a period of boom, $\dfrac{dp}{dt} > 0$, in a period of depression $\dfrac{dp}{dt} < 0$; consequently in the first case there will be a tendency towards larger elasticity for a rise, in the second towards larger elasticity for a fall of demand for coal. But the demand for coal must not only be an irreversible function when understood as a historical curve. It applies also to ordinary demand curves. Moreover, the elasticities of demand for a rise and for a fall can be different both when the demand curve is continuous as well as when it is discontinuous. Here also the introduction of the notion of elasticity for a rise and for a fall helps substantially to deal with the problem of demand when the time element is introduced. Elasticity of demand, which was noticed by Cournot as early as 1838, and expressed by him as $pF(p)$, which corresponds in our example to (price per unit) × quantity, was given its actual definition by Marshall. But this great economist assumed that the change in prices in both directions must act identically. There is, however, no explanation in his example why " if a fall in price from

Prices as well as demand can follow three courses : Either
they can increase, decrease, or remain stable. Hence there

say 16*d*. to 15*d*. per lb. of tea would much increase his purchases, then a
rise in price from 15*d*. to 16*d*. would much diminish them." This statement
refers probably only to point elasticity, but not to arc elasticity, whereas
generally it is considered valid also in the latter case. It will be more
convenient to use for our purpose the specified notion of double elasticity.

Those two notions of elasticity were introduced by Dr. H. Dalton in
Some Aspects of the Inequality of Incomes in Modern Communities, London,
1929, pp. 192–7, where he demonstrated that in the case of " constant
outlay " curves arc, elasticity is never equal to unity, and that it must be
always different in the case of elasticity for a rise from the case of
elasticity for a fall over the same range of the curve.

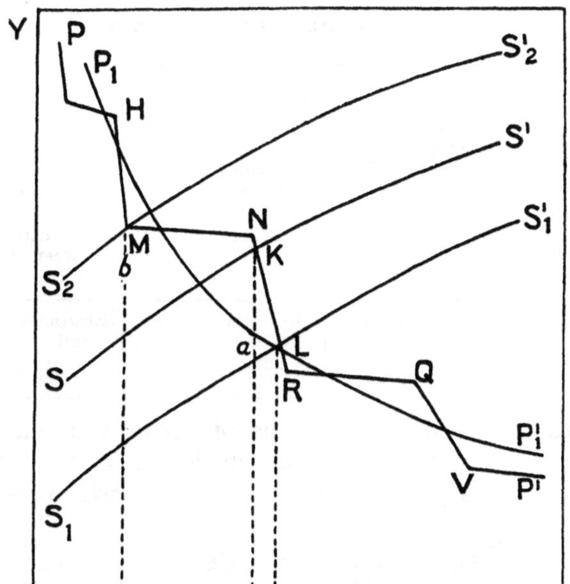

Fig. 1.

For our purpose it will be more convenient to use the specified notion
of double elasticity of demand. In the case of a discontinuous demand
curve the introduction of double elasticity helps to overcome another
complication, which arises in the case of a reduction of prices, when
the elasticity for a rise reacts differently from the elasticity for a fall.
Let us illustrate this by use of simple diagrammatical representation.
PP' represent the discontinuous demand curve, and *SS'* the supply

follow nine different combinations between movements of prices and demand. In two of these combinations elasticity of demand can occur [1] either as rising demand during a period of falling prices, and then we shall speak of elasticity of demand for a rise, or, as falling demand during a period of increasing prices, which is called elasticity of demand for a fall. Again, inelasticity of demand may be found during rising or falling prices and during stable demand. All this can be represented in the following tabular way :—

TABLE No. 18

Movements of Price	Movements in the Demand		
	Stable demand	Rising demand	Falling demand
Stable price .	Static equilibrium	No relation between price and demand	No relation between price and demand
Falling price .	Inelasticity	Elasticity for a rise	No relation between price and demand
Rising price .	Inelasticity	No relation between price and demand	Elasticity for a fall

In Table 18 all combinations of prices and quantities demanded provide two cases in which elasticity can occur. But there are a good many circumstances which work to

curve. Now let us assume that the supply curve moves downwards to $S_1 S_1{}^1$. The fall of prices equals then Ka and this causes the demand to rise from K to L, i.e. by the amount $K'L'$. Now when the supply curve moves from SS' to $S_2 S_2{}'$, or by an amount bM smaller than Ka, then the quantity demanded falls by an amount $K'M'$, which is several times greater than $K'L'$. Especially at the points of inflection H, M, N, R, etc., the elasticity for a rise and the elasticity for a fall are quite different. In the case of continuous curves $P_1 P_1{}^1$, point elasticities differ much less from one another, while they are exactly equal when the demand curve adopts the shape of a rectangular hyperbola. A somewhat similar curve for the purpose of measuring elasticity of demand for credit has been used by M. Victor Bloch in a note entitled " Zur Frage der Ankurbelung durch Kreditpolitik," in *Zeitschrift für Nationalökonomie*, vol. iv, No. 3, pp. 404–8.

[1] We use the words "can occur" because in these combinations the price-quantity relationship may possibly be only what Professor Ragnar Frisch calls a historical trend connection. (*Pitfalls in the Statistical Construction of Demand and Supply Curves*, Leipsig, 1933, p. 10.)

conceal its existence. Professor Schultz, in his standard work on elasticity, names only some of them, and calls them the " disturbing factors ".

First of all, in the study of demand for coal, consideration must be given to cyclical and seasonal fluctuations. The demand for certain types of coal is substantially affected by the winter or summer seasons. Further, in the long term fluctuations, it might be appropriate to compare the movements of prices of coal with general purchasing power of money in the form of a price index, and then to ascertain the relative position of coal on the background of other commodities. This method involves the additional difficulty of computing the real value of coal on the basis of index numbers, namely that in such an index not all the consumers are equally affected at the same time ; thus, e.g. in a trade depression the position of shipping transport will tend to be affected sooner than the gas works.

A further complication in the study of the elasticity of demand for coal is the difficulty of deciding at what point to submit the data to analysis and where to measure the elasticity : at the pit as it is felt by the producers, or as it reaches the ultimate consumer. Theoretically it is quite possible that the two demands might be different, when there exists a margin between the demand from the producers and the demand from the middlemen. Fortunately, in practice, however, the two demands follow each other very closely in the case of coal, owing to the difficulty of keeping high stocks, and owing to the higher value of freshly hewn coal. For this reason in our investigation we have adopted the measurement of demand as it affects the collieries. Speaking technically, one could compare the two demand curves to the general demand curve and the pure demand curve.[1]

Another disturbing factor in the detection of elasticity of demand for coal is to be found in the methods and quantities of sales. The more perfect and flexible is the supply, the greater use can be made of the existing but concealed elasticity. Sometimes a fraction might be added

[1] See Schultz, op. cit., p. 22.

to the total order which is never actually achieved owing to the methods, or inadequate divisibility of the supply. In the case of the coal trade this difficulty possibly applies only to certain types of household coal consumers in the poorer districts, but in general its significance is almost negligible owing to the bulky character of the article. Gas and electricity, the supply of which can be very strictly regulated, have therefore a greater elasticity of demand than coal used for the same purpose.

With the problem discussed above is strictly connected one more disturbing factor, which works to obscure the elasticity of demand. While the previous disturbing factors relate to quantities supplied in such a way that they could be absorbed by the consumer, this, on the other hand, refers to the operation of prices within so small a range as to be indifferent to the consumer. It is difficult to detect the elasticity of demand when the price has not fallen low enough, or not risen high enough, to galvanize the increase in demand into activity. In this respect what Wicksteed called *minimum sensibile* [1] has not yet been reached, and the dormant though existing elasticity not revealed. Hence it is impossible to make a judicial statement as to the elasticity below and above the amplitude of prices actually attained, though in fact it may be very high.

Also, as already mentioned, the responsiveness of demand to variations of prices is not the same in coal during all seasons of the year. Thus, e.g. winter favours and stimulates the elasticity of demand for domestic coal, while summer and autumn increase that for bunker coal. It has been pointed out by Professor Schultz [2] that such seasonal

[1] *Vide*, Philip H. Wicksteed, *The Common Sense of Political Economy, including a study of the Human Basis of Economic Law*, London, 1933, vol. ii, p. 406.

[2] Henry Schultz, *Statistical Laws of Demand and Supply*, Chicago, 1928, pp. 15–16: ". . . But as Cournot pointed out, both the price and the law of demand of a commodity may vary considerably during the year. This raises some interesting questions: Is it possible for a commodity to have an elastic demand during one season and an inelastic demand during another? Suppose that monthly data of consumption (or production) and prices yield an elastic (or inelastic) demand. Would annual averages derived from the same data also yield an inelastic (or elastic) demand? It is to be hoped that statistical data will be forthcoming which will enable one to derive specific answers to these questions."

changes in the elasticity of demand often completely disappear when the yearly averages are taken into consideration, and though they affect the demand they would thus be partly or completely ruled out. The well-known practice of the British coal trade to reduce the prices of household brands in summer by 2s. to 4s. per ton is based on the seasonal changes in the elasticity of demand for a rise.

In the study of demand neither the Royal Commission on the Coal Industry, 1925, nor the Report of the Lewis Committee ignored the existence of the elasticity of demand for coal ; but they only approached it very generally. Thus we read in the Report of the Royal Commission : " It is certain, in any case, that in order to dispose of, say, 250,000,000 tons of coal the collieries must, on an average, take a lower price per ton than they can get for 220,000,000. This holds true on general grounds, whatever the course of the market . . ." [1] This remark refers to the elasticity of demand for coal for a rise, while on the elasticity of demand for a fall we find a quotation from the Minority Report of the Lewis Committee which reads : " The inference to be drawn . . . is that any attempt artificially to raise the general level of coal prices would have defeated its own object by limiting demand." [2]

While in the two Reports no distinction is made between the short and long term elasticity of demand, this division can be found in a brief study on the coal industry written by Sir Herbert Samuel.[3] He does not think that in the short run there is enough elasticity to cause demand to expand in response to cheap prices, but at the same time he maintains that cheap prices in the long run will considerably stimulate the demand coming from industry.

A vigorous plea for cheap prices of coal based on the operation of the elasticities of demand for a rise and for a fall is made in a letter by Sir Richard Redmayne, who

[1] *Report of the Royal Commission on the Coal Industry* (1925), vol. i, Cmd. 2600, 1926, p. 173.
[2] *Report of the Minority of the Committee on Co-operative Selling of Coal*, Cmd. 2770, 1926, p. 42, No. 8.
[3] The Rt. Hon. Sir Herbert Samuel, *Problem of the Coal Mines*, London, 1927.

G

emphatically states that " demand for coal is governed by price . . . cheaper coal would mean an increased home demand and increased export, and increased production means reduction in working cost ".[1]

The question of demand for coal, however, cannot be discussed as a whole. Any study of the matter must proceed to some more detailed investigation in order to avoid the mistakes which have been made by certain students of the problem.

Though, for instance, in certain cases the demand for British coal in general may tend to be inelastic in the short run, in the long run it may be highly elastic, and again, while the demand for the whole supply may not be very elastic, nevertheless the demand of a special type of consumer or the demand for a particular class of coal may display features of high elasticity. Further, coal, although one in name, embraces a vast galaxy of different articles, which from the point of species, quality, and economic destination must be considered as very different goods. Any analysis of demand for coal must distinguish between those various sorts of coal ; they all are characterized by their own particular commercial features. Though often similar in quality, they may fluctuate in very different directions.

While the desirability of articles other than coal is determined more by quality and kind, in the coal trade it is more the purpose for which it is used that defines the larger or smaller changes in the demand for coal as well as prices. For instance, the quantity of best steam coal used by railways for heating the boilers will be very little affected by a reduction of prices in the other qualities of coal. The railway companies, which had to use inferior qualities of coal in the trunk lines during the War, found that this led to largely increased expenses on maintenance of engines, and since the War have reverted to only the highest grades of steam coal. It would be impracticable for them to return suddenly to the lower classes of coal, however cheap they might be.

On the other hand, those industries which are not so dependent on the quality of coal used can more easily shift

[1] *The Times*, 23rd October, 1929.

from one type to another. In these industries the price of different qualities of coal is an indicator for their buying policy. They watch the coal market with the greatest care, and compare the quotations of prices of all different qualities which are substitutable for one another in their industries. If the low quotation overbalances the inconveniences of using an inferior quality of coal, the former would probably be the decisive factor. In fact, such a situation has arisen quite often in the history of the British coal trade. During nearly the whole of 1932 and 1933, small coal was in exceptionally strong demand in all the coalfields.

In the Midlands, owing to depressed conditions in the industry, many firms turned to the cheapest sorts of coal, even if this meant some physical consumption of their fixed assets, so long as they reduced their prime costs.[1] In South Wales, for instance, most of this small coal was washed and adapted for bunkering and other industrial purposes, where it was used in place of the more valuable kinds of coal. Cases of mechanical artificial breaking of large coal were reported in order to satisfy the demand. Obviously, in the majority of cases it was not an economically sound proposition. Similar situations of acute demand for small varieties were experienced in Scotland and several other coalfields, where the general trend towards cheaper fuel was noticeable. This demand tended to alter the existing balance of prices. But in addition to those short term movements from one kind to another merely on account of the difference in prices, we can notice in Britain a long term shifting from expensive fuel towards the cheaper sorts, giving the maximum number of B.T.U.s (British Thermal Units) per £1 spent. Thus, while before the great crisis in 1929 only seventeen undertakings in the metallurgical industry were using pulverized coal,[2] this figure grew to thirty-nine in 1931, and is still further rising, with the result that many collieries, especially in the Scottish

[1] This finds a good confirmation in the Report by the Board of Trade on the Working of Schemes under Part I of the Coal Mines Act, 1930, during the year 1932, Cmd. 4224, 1932, f. 11.

[2] Cf. Commander H. D. Tollemache, " The Marketing of Pulverized Coal in Great Britain," and the Twelfth Report of the Secretary for Mines, p. 17, *The Iron and Coal Trades Review*, 21st October, 1932.

basins and in South Wales, have installed pulverizing plants at the mines. Moreover, a considerable tonnage of pulverized coal is used at present in the mercantile marine. There again the elasticity of demand for small and large coal may vary enormously.[1]

This brings us to the question of internal substitution, which we have purposely omitted when external substitution was being discussed. As we know, substitution or shifting in the demand for coal can be twofold : external and internal. The former turns the demand for coal towards some other goods or energy capable of performing the same industrial function as coal ; the latter operates within the various types and grades of coal, thus bringing one of them into demand instead of anthracite, or patent fuel, etc. Again, in the case of internal substitution there are instances of demand shifting towards higher grades of coal from the lower, where prices are not correctly scaled.   In such cases, it appears that the demand skips the lower grades, the prices of which are not adequately adjusted to the prices of better varieties.

Similar disequilibrium between the prices of different sorts of coal may be easily observed in the home market. When, during the working of the newly-instituted compulsory cartel, under the Coal Mines Act, 1930, all prices of high grades of coal under the fixed minimum

---

[1] Cf. J. H. Jones, " Organized Marketing in the Coal Industry," *Economic Journal*, vol. xxxix, June, 1929, p. 158 ; " There are many classes of coal, and each supplies its own market. Since the various classes are partial substitutes, the demand for each is moderately elastic, and its price moves in sympathy with the prices of other classes. I understand that the coal obtained in the area lying between Leeds and Sheffield is more suitable for gas production than that which is obtained farther east, where the mines produce largely for export, but a fall in the relative price of the latter in recent years has resulted in an increase in demand, at the expense of the former, from gas-producing undertakings. Again, the demand from a particular geographical area for any class of British coal may be highly elastic on account of the competition of supplies from a rival coal industry or section of the industry. . . . If, however, we regard coal as a single product the demand under normal conditions is highly inelastic."

Unfortunately, Professor Jones does not explain what he understands by " under normal conditions ", and the reader is left to guess whether they include only short term elasticity or whether they embrace also the long term changes.

price system had been established too low in comparison with those of the inferior grades—we witnessed a replacement of the bad qualities of coal by higher grades. This phenomenon, which we called uneconomic substitution of coal, tends to increase the demand for better coal at the expense of poorer grades, which will begin to accumulate at the pits. As the demand for cheap good coal increases, the stocks of bad coal will have to rise, since any increase in the production of large coal must stimulate the production of small and duff.[1] This is specially the case in those districts, like Scotland, where the mechanization of production has been accomplished to a large extent. In these districts, the percentage of small coal may on some occasions increase as a result of technical considerations, e.g. owing to the working of undercutters, which crush a certain amount of bottom coal. This fact will doubtless lead in the next period of price regulation to drastic reorganization in the coal minimum price stabilization schedules of the compulsory Marketing Scheme. One of the following alternatives will be then applied : either

(1) the price of small coal will be substantially reduced ;
(2) the price of large coal will be raised ; or
(3) the lower grades of coal will have to be improved and manufactured into some higher product, e.g. briquettes.

In order to speed up the adjustment of prices and production all the three alternatives may be simultaneously applied. The transitional period, however, must be very difficult for those consumers using better grades, as they will have either to pay higher prices for coal or revert to inferior qualities of fuel. In either case they will have to suffer inconvenience. Such uneconomic substitution must be distinguished from economic substitution, which results in transforming the cheap and less valuable types of coal into better manufactured products, and consequently fosters a demand for lower grades. In this way, for instance, over 3,500,000 tons of pulverized coal were used in this country

---

[1] In South Wales the proportion of the former to the latter is about 3 to 1.

in 1932, chiefly for steam raising in the electric works and for heating in cement kilns.[1]

The demand for large coal is of quite a different nature from that for small coal. The price apparatus of the two sorts of coal works in a very different way. Normally, large coal is an article which is on the whole desired, and the sale of which does not present any great difficulties even in the middle of a depression, provided that prices are not too high, as in the case already discussed. Small coals, duff and dry smalls, on the other hand, have to adjust their prices much more to the sensitiveness of the market. Moreover, it is outside the powers of the collieries to curtail the tonnage of small coal raised without reducing the output of large coal, because they constitute a joint product which must be produced together in different but fixed proportions in the various districts and collieries. An increase in the output of large coal must be accompanied by a *pro rata* increase in the supplies of small coal, which is one of the products of mining. But whereas it is very difficult to convert the small descriptions into another type of fuel, it is on the other hand nearly always possible to convert large coal into smaller sorts whenever such a breaking proves to be a paying proposition. In certain cases large dry steam coal, such as the Welsh " Admiralty " coal, is at present being broken and used for household purposes, where it can be substituted for anthracite.[2] For instance, such household brands as " The Radawn ", used in closed stoves and in cookers, are the product of transforming large dry steam coal into smaller grades. Hence those districts where the proportion of small coal is considerable tend to take more radical steps to solve this problem than areas where the percentage of small coal is lower. This feature naturally acts as a strongly disintegrating element against any sort of common price policy. Small coal, being unable to adjust its quantity independently of large, must regulate its sale by the medium of price policy. By selling

[1] See Debates, House of Commons, 5th July, 1932, and Twelfth Annual Report of the Secretary for Mines, for year 1932.
[2] Cf. *Large Coal* v. *Sized Coal*. An article in the *Iron and Coal Trades Review*, 18th August, 1933.

small coal cheaper when the price of large coal has a downward tendency, and selling it dearer when large coal is rising, it is possible to exercise a certain amount of control over the market, where the demand for small coal displays generally an elasticity for a fall.

We find that the earlier the period of history, and the more primitive the preparation of coal for use as well as technique of its using, the less small coal was desired and the more its sales had to be adjusted by price manipulation. Thus the Newcastle Vend of the eighteenth and nineteenth century found difficulty in regulating the prices of small coal for the London market. Jevons [1] tells us that the Vend in the eighteenth century could only exercise any large degree of control over the better kinds of coal. Very often it was nearly impossible to find an outlet for the small coal, and therefore " a considerable portion of the coal raised at the beginning of the nineteenth century used to be separated out and burnt as waste, the whole cost of raising the coal being loaded on the price of the large coal sold ".[2] On some occasions this powerful combination forced small coal into the market by admixing it with better brands.[3]

Owing to the operation of the Marketing Scheme, exactly the opposite happened in 1932–3, when the buyer was forced to take a certain proportion of large coal together with his order for small and sized.

Slowly but steadily, with the progress of technique, small coal, both in its raw and its manufactured form, came to secure purchasers, but this in turn depended on keeping the price low when either the demand for large coal was slack or its prices were reduced. Again, at any time when the home demand for large coal rose for one cause or another, the price of small coal was substantially

---

[1] W. Stanley Jevons, *The Coal Question*, 3rd ed., p. 86.
[2] Jevons, loc. cit.
[3] *Vide* the evidence of Nathaniel Clayton, the Town Clerk of Newcastle before the Committee on the Coal Trade, 1800 : " Does it occur to you that the Coal-owners possessed any other means of raising the price of coal than those which you have already described ? . . . It occurs to me that the depressed prices being almost entirely on the inferior sorts of coal, those prices were raised by the assistance given to them in the increased quantity they worked in consequence of the agreement. (Limitation of the Vend.) " (*Report*, p. 544.)

increased in the market. The price of small coal was subject to much wider oscillations than that of the other qualities. The prices of small coal must always adjust themselves in such a way as not to induce uneconomic internal substitution. For this reason we find a great reluctance in this part of the trade to be subject to price regulations and Government tampering with price systems. A margin of a flexible character is always kept between the prices of small and large grades, and the demand for small coal is on the whole much more elastic for a fall than the demand for large.

It is interesting to notice in Great Britain that in 1931, after the introduction of an artificial restriction scheme based on compulsory cartellization, the minimum prices of different sorts of coal in the districts were very carefully scaled and adjusted to each other, so as to avoid any disequilibrium between the sales of different sizes of coal produced. But even with the most cautious elaboration of the relative scales, it was not feasible to avoid rigidity and to check the possibility of the adjustment of demand through price. Thus, we observe at the outset, as soon as the coal marketing schemes were put in full swing there was for some time great difficulty in dealing with excessive supplies of small coal. Whereas the commercial outlook for the best qualities remained moderately steady, and in a favourable position, the small steam coal maintained throughout a very dull and weak appearance. The price of small varieties fluctuated considerably more than that of other coals, touching in most districts the official minimum price fixed by the local colliery owners' organizations.

In some districts even, the minimum had to be lowered in order to solve the difficulty. South Wales provides a good example of the effect of lowering prices on the quantity of small coal demanded. Thus in December, 1931, when the stocks of small coal began to rise unduly high, the South Wales Marketing Association's Executive decided that small coal lying on the pit banks might be sold at a reduction of 2s. per ton, provided that it did not displace freshly wrought coal and was not included in quantities for which licences are required in France. Moreover, it made, in July, 1932, a concession of 5s. per ton to patent fuel makers, which lasted till September of the same year. Of course, in the absence of compulsory regulation, such adjustments are carried out spontaneously by the industry, very often even anticipating the changes in demand. As an instance of the amplitude of fluctuations in the prices of small and large coals, we may cite the price quotations from Newcastle for two different kinds of coal of the large and small sorts. The samples of prices are taken during two successive representative weeks of the year 1931, and merely illustrate the phenomenon. While large sorts hardly declined in price, small coals had to move sharply down in order to find an outlet.

TABLE No. 19

PRICES OF COAL IN NEWCASTLE OF BOTH LARGE AND SMALL SORTS OF BEST BLYTH AND TYNE PRIME DURING TWO SUCCESSIVE WEEKS OF MAY, 1931

Date.	Best Blyth.		Tyne Prime.	
	Large.	Small.	Large.	Small.
2nd May	13s. 6d. to 13s. 9d.	10s.	12s. 9d.	10s. 6d.
9th May	13s. 6d.	7s. 6d.	12s. 9d.	8s.
Fall in price	1½d.	2s. 6d.	—	2s. 6d.
Per cent fall in price	1·0%	25·0%	0·0%	24%

The typical variations in the prices of coal shown above are representative of similar movements in the prices of small and large coal of different kinds in different parts of the country, and in various seasons of the year. Table No. 19 serves as an illustration that whereas the prices of large coal have remained nearly stable, the small coal, in order to control demand, were reduced in price by 25 per cent and 24·0 per cent respectively. Small sorts of coal are much more susceptible than large ones to any changes in the potentialities of the market. Any shrinkage in the willing-ness of buyers to absorb more coal leads immediately to drastic changes in prices so as to maintain sales.

But it would be quite erroneous to imagine that the price of small coal requires to be especially flexible only in the downward direction. This is not always the case. When the price of large coal was fixed too high there was a general shift towards small coal. In purely competitive conditions, where processes of price adjustments could easily take place in all directions, this quantitative change in demand was not so conspicuous, but in conditions of monopolistic competition prevailing under the Coal Mines Act, 1930, the scarcity of certain brands appears at once. We can thus observe a rather paradoxical situation of a glut of large best steam coal existing at the same time and in the same market as a famine of washed small coal and other smaller brands. This situation is possible owing to the joint mining of small and large coals, which as we noted form joint products in a proportion defined by technical considerations. As the amount of small coal, and still less the amount of large, could hardly be increased without adding to the supply of the conjoint coal, therefore in a regime of fixed prices, shortages must always occur. In fact, the last five months of 1932 and nearly all 1933 witnessed in several districts, especially in South Wales, Durham, and Scotland, a considerable shortage of small steam coal and excessive stocks of large without buyers, since prices of large coal were prevented from falling by restrictions, while at the same time small steam and bituminous coal commanded a price considerably above the minimum fixed under the Marketing Scheme. In South Wales dry cobbles and dry nuts commanded a premium of 10s. above the minimum schedules in October, 1932. Towards the end of 1932 the position became so serious and stocks of large coal grew so rapidly, that the Cardiff colliery salesmen have had to insist on buyers taking a definite proportion of large coals with small and dried. In autumn, 1933, cases were reported from the Humber of ships unable to receive suitable bunker and consequently being unable to accept contracts.

So far we have been analysing the demand for coals which are more or less substitutable for one another, and we have called attention to the extent to which this possibility exerted its influence upon prices and their fluctuation. This in turn constituted an argument against integration, and especially against any artificial regulation of prices, which would diminish the possibility of adjustments. All this referred only to the interdependence and interchangeability of one quality of coal for another. There was one sort of coal which could be used instead of another, or the product of one mining district which could come to the market in place of another, the whole amount of coal measured by some common denominator, [e.g. by quantity of heat, or power generated] remaining unchanged. It was only within this general demand for coal that some shifting would have been executed. What was added to one quality of coal was taken away from another, and the total demand for coal for the period remained the same.

We shall now say a few words about the demand for coal, attacking the question from the point of view of elasticity of demand for different kinds of coal and of different types of consumers, which again is one of the highly disintegrating forces in the industry. Naturally the possibility of substitution will have some effect on elasticity of demand, and clearly enough cannot be completely isolated from other forces influencing the demand. We shall start our study with anthracite, which is one of the least substitutable kinds of fuel. The demand for British anthracite, which is shipped from Swansea and Llanelly in South Wales, and in smaller quantities from the county of Ayrshire, is quite different from that of other types of coal. Welsh anthracite, containing up to 95 per cent of fixed carbon,[1] has no rival for its quality in the whole world. Comparing the demand for anthracite with that for other coal, one can easily notice its much greater stability from year to year. In addition, while the demand for all coal

[1]

TABLE No. 20

COMPOSITION OF ANTHRACITE IN GREAT BRITAIN

Coalfield.	Fixed Carbon. %	Volatile Matter. %	Ash. %	Moisture. %	Total. %
Wales—Carmarthen Stan- llyd Vein (Blaina) . .	93·76	5·09	1·15	—	100
Scotland—Caprington (Ayr)	83·9	11·1	3·2	1·8	100

Source : Anthracite in the *Encyclopædia Britannica*, xivth ed.

has the tendency to diminish since the War, that for anthracite is gradually increasing.

This process can be seen clearly from the table below, which shows the special position of Welsh anthracite in the total demand for Welsh coal.

TABLE No. 21

COMPARISON OF THE OUTPUT OF ANTHRACITE AND OTHER KINDS OF COAL
IN SOUTH WALES FROM 1913 TO 1930

Year.	Output of all Coal.	Output of Anthracite.	Output of all Coal other than Anthracite.
	1924 = 100	1924 = 100	1924 = 100
1913 .	111	97	113
1920 .	91	85	91
1923 .	106	98	107
1924 .	100	100	100
1925 .	87	112	85
1926 .	40	51	38
1927 .	91	116	88
1928 .	85	98	83
1929 .	94	113	92
1930 [1]	88	112	85

Source : *Industrial Survey of South Wales*, H.M. Stationery Office, 1932.

[1] Computed.

The demand for British anthracite, of which about 90 per cent is produced in South Wales and the rest in Scotland, comes chiefly from foreign countries. More than 60 per cent, i.e. about 4,000,000 tons is exported at fairly steady prices. The elasticity of demand for a fall seems not to effect anthracite to an appreciable degree, in contrast to many other kinds of coal. If, from those features of the demand side for anthracite which are most favourable for integration, one turns towards its organization, it is not astonishing to find there a very large degree of concentration. In South Wales two combines responsible in 1931 for 5,043,000 tons were controlling practically the whole output of anthracite, i.e. the Amalgamated Anthracite Collieries, Ltd., and the Welsh Anthracite Collieries, Ltd. The former of these has an annual output of about 4,000,000 tons, and in many ways co-operates with the latter, being bound to it by extensive interlocking directorates. At present the anthracite section of the industry represents a highly integrated structure, being in many ways connected with others, especially the chemical industry.

Passing now to the home demand for kinds of coal other than anthracite, it would be misleading to treat the whole of it as being of one kind, without drawing any distinction between the various grades and the different purposes for which it is used. This differentiation has a very great significance in the determination of the nature of the demand and its influence on the organization of the industry. Thus, the more we advance from those industries where coal is a very small item, and turn towards those consumers of coal who use it in a lower stage of production,[1] the more extensive is the influence which its price exerts on the demand. In a lower stage of production, which is not distant from that ultimate product and the ultimate consumer, coal plays an active part in satisfying final wants. The form in which coal can be consumed is probably a still more important determinant of the elasticity of demand. Thus, the demand for household coal is less elastic than the demand for gas or the demand for electricity used for similar purposes. In the industrial demand this latter consideration does not occur. The iron and steel industries, which are very considerable consumers of coal and coke, are to a great extent dependent on the price of coal. It has been shown by Mr. G. A. Mitchell[2] how far the price of coal is reflected in the costs of pig iron and steel. He quotes figures to show that coal as such, or in the form of coke, represents over one-third of the total cost of iron and steel products. An increase of one shilling per ton of coal, according to Mr. Mitchell, may represent 2s. per ton on the cost of pig iron, and about 3s. or 4s. per ton on the cost of steel. In these industries the price has not only the tendency to transfer the demand for coal from one quality to another, in a state of affairs which creates an opportunity to use a different coal owing to its price—but it affects also the whole

[1] Cf. F. von Hayek, *Prices and Production*, London, 1931, Lecture II, p. 29.
[2] George A. Mitchell, Chairman, Lochgelly Iron and Coal Co., Ltd., Glasgow, " Interdependence of the Basic Industries," Mining Supplement of the *Daily Telegraph*, 16th September, 1930.

quantity used by the industry, as it is directly reflected in the price of the manufactured product. Since, on the other hand, the manufactured product possesses in the market an elasticity of demand of its own, a reduction in its price will cause a rising demand, and ultimately it will benefit coal. It is no longer a question of reduction of costs by using cheap fuel, though it is of lower quality, but a question of larger purchases of coal.

Marshall [1] demonstrated that the upward direction in the movement of prices has the effect of reducing the demand for certain kinds of coal. He argued that industry uses as a measure of retrenchment against high prices of coal several means by which it reduces its demand. One of these consists in " economies " in the use of coal, which are very useful as direct promoters of economic progress. It appears, moreover, that by " economies " Marshall understands a contraction in the total amount of coal purchased. The immediate consequence of the high price of coal will probably be a reduction in quantity used, unless the demand for those articles where coal enters as only a small item is at the same time rapidly increasing.

The tendencies towards a larger or smaller reduction in sales of coal in view of price changes do not only depend on the amount of the increase in price, but are to a great extent determined by the users of coal and by the relative importance of coal to them. The curve illustrating the total demand for coal must therefore be composed of different sections, each representing the demand of different types of consumers. Marshall [2] pointed out that ". . . the general demand curve for a commodity cannot be drawn with confidence except in the immediate neighbourhood of the current price until we are able to piece it together out of the fragmentary demand curves of different classes of society ". Applying his argument to the coal demand

---

[1] Alfred Marshall, *Principles of Economics*, London, 8th ed., book iii, chap. iv, " The Elasticity of Wants," p. 111. ". . . when in recent years the price of coal became very high, a great stimulus was given to the invention of economies in its use, especially in the production of iron and steam ; but few of these inventions bore much practical fruit till after the high price had passed away."

[2] Op. cit., p. 114.

curve, it would be better to include reference to home consumers of different types of coal, as well as different classes of society, because their position after an alteration in any direction in the price of coal is not always changed in the same manner. This phenomenon explains a sharper or milder reaction of various types of consumers to the movement of prices of those qualities of coal of which they are the users.

Indeed, the prices of different descriptions of coal do not all move in the same manner, and their producers, in a greater or less degree, are interested in being free to fix their own prices in a manner to take into account the particularities of the demand. A few years after De-control the various movements in the price of coal for different classes of consumers were specially investigated in the Report of the Advisory Committee for Coal and the Coal Industry, 1923, which in its final conclusions advocated increasing industrial demand for coal through the lowering of all costs, and ultimately prices.[1] The comparison of different price movements is of the utmost interest for our argument, since it shows how little uniformity there is among them, and the extent to which the characteristics of demand affect those changes in prices. The Report reveals the wide fluctuations which took place in the pit-head prices of coal for various purposes. It may serve as an example of how differently prices were scaled according to the destination of coal.[2] All these variations show a considerable degree of coincidence with what one should expect *a priori* from a deduction based on the elasticity of demand; the less elastic coals both in the short and in the long run displayed

[1] Report: " It is in the main to increased industrial demand that we must look for a reduction in the costs of production and in the financial position of the coal trade."

[2] Thus, in August, 1922, the average cost of producing a ton of coal at the pit was 16s. 10$\frac{1}{4}$d., as compared with an average of 9s. 4d. in 1913, a rise of 79 per cent. The analysis of the average increases in the pit-head prices of the chief qualities of coal as compared with the pre-War period gave the following result: Household coal showed increases for the higher grades from 110–120 per cent; for medium qualities 80–120 per cent; for lower 70–100 per cent. Gas coal rose from 75–90 per cent; locomotive coal 50–86 per cent. Bunker coal showed increases ranging from 55–95 per cent for best qualities, and from 75–110 per cent for smalls. Other industrial coal moved 30–50 per cent.

a greater rise in prices than the more elastic ones. Locomotive coal, although it is on the whole little dependent
on price, is an exception ; it suffered a relatively small
rise. This strange phenomenon can be explained however
first of all by the fact that in the period in question the
British railways were concentrated in a small number of
units, and so could more freely bargain on the market for
their purchases of coal against a smaller number of competitors in these particular sorts, and secondly by the fact
that after the War, as we have already mentioned, the type of
coal used for the locomotives was changed, and the process
of reversion to the pre-War qualities was not completed
by 1923.

From the comparison of the figures just quoted, we see
that the price of industrial coal was the least changed,
which must be explained by the fact that its elasticity is in
the long run considerable ; the same applies to the elasticity
for a fall in the best bunker, i.e. that purchased by steamers
which are the most likely to turn towards other substitutes,
whereas small bunkers used by smaller units or in coastal
traffic showed less elasticity for a fall, and consequently
a greater rise in price. Comparing our figures of household
coal and gas coal we notice that the latter did not rise so
much, and also that the disparity between the two limits (the
maximum and the minimum range of rise) was smaller. This
is so because those types of consumers who could satisfy
their need for coal more easily and more economically in a
direct way present a more elastic demand. Hence the
price of coal for gas works has a considerable influence on
the quantity of gas sold, and therefore on the amount of
coal bought by gas companies. The close dependence
between the price of coal, on the one side, and the amount
of gas sold and gas used, on the other, has been stressed by
the leaders of the gas industry over and over again.[1] This

[1] Dr. E. W. Smith, Chairman of the Council of the Society of British
Gas Industries, pointed out during the general meeting of the Society in
1931, the attempt of the gas producers to stimulate sales by means of
lowering prices. He said in respect of this problem : " Gas undertakings,
municipally owned, in desiring to extend their business were forced by
economic circumstances and competition to aim at the highest efficiency
and the production of satisfactory gas at the lowest cost, profits being taboo.

works both in the short and in the long run. A similar argument holds good in the case of coal supplied for electric works. This demand, which in 1913 absorbed only 5 million tons, or 2·7 per cent of the total consumption, had risen in 1932 to 9·7 million tons, or 5·8 per cent of the total (consult Table). We may perhaps be allowed a small digression, and note that in this industry, which provides people with a most convenient form of power, light, and heat, the increase of coal consumption has been the largest of all. Of course, the number of units generated was still higher. In 1922 about 4·9 thousand million[1] units were consumed, rising to 13·6 thousand million in 1932.

The fluctuations in the prices of household coal are of the utmost interest, and confirm our suggestion that the demand for this fuel in the poorer dwellings is considerably more elastic than the demand for the best and medium grades. Thus, the percentage difference in the rise of the lower limits of prices in the best and the worst classes of coal is equal to 40 per cent, and that of the upper limits equals 20 per cent ; while the same figures for the medium and best grades are 30 and 0. We append a table on p. 98 which gives some idea as to how the total home consumption of coal is distributed.

It is interesting to notice that the official statistics, though supposed to provide figures of consumption of coal by its different users, leave in fact the bulk of the national consumption, about 60 per cent, unclassified under the vague heading of " general manufactures and all other purposes ". The figure is only a residuary figure, and in fact it does not even give any idea as to the amount of stocks held by the collieries and their consumers, which of course must be deducted for the right ascertainment of consumption. It is generally assumed that the amount of coal used yearly for household purposes in its crude form amounts to 40,000,000 tons, and that this consumption of domestic coal has been stable since the War. However reliable this

Company-owned undertakings had the extra incentive that the lower the price of gas the greater the dividends would be ".—(*The Times*, 20th November, 1931.)

[1] This figure refers to the year ending 31st March, 1922.

H

TABLE No. 22

CONSUMPTION OF COAL IN 1869, 1887, 1903, 1913, AND FROM 1920. DISTINGUISHING THE PRINCIPAL PURPOSES FOR WHICH USED.

(Based upon the information supplied to the Commissioners " appointed to inquire into the several matters relating to Coal in the United Kingdom" 1871; the Royal Commission on Coal Supplies (1905); and the Coal Conservation Committee of the Ministry of Reconstruction; "The Coal Question", a paper read by Mr. Richard Price-Williams, M.Inst.C.E., before the Royal Statistical Society in 1889; and the Annual Reports of the Secretary for Mines.)

Great Britain and Ireland.

Purpose for which used.	Quantity of Coal Consumed. (Million Tons.)				
	1869.	1887.	1903.	1913.	1920.
Gas Works	6·3		15·0	15·0	18·6
Electric Works		1·5	3·0	5·0	7·4
Rlys. for Locomotive use	2·8	6·2	12·0	13·6	13·8
Coasting steamers (bunker for)	1·2	1·5	2·0	2·5	1·7
Coal Mines	6·7	10·9	15·0	18·0	17·3
Pig Iron Manf.	14·0	15·3	18·0	21·2	17·2
Iron & Steel Wks. (except pig iron)[5]	[1]	[1]	[1]	[1]	
Domestic[4]	18·5	28·3	32·0	35·0	36·5
Miners' Coal				5·8	6·6
General Manf. & all other purposes[4]	44·9	58·7	70·0	70·0	66·7
Total	**94·4**	**130·4**	**167·0**	**189·1**	**185·8**

Great Britain.

Purpose for which used.	Quantity of Coal Consumed. (Million Tons.)													
	1913.	1920.	1921.	1922.	1923.	1924.	1925.	1926.	1927.	1928.	1929.	1930.	1931.	1932.
Gas Works	16·7	16·88	15·6	15·18	15·38	16·66	16·45	16·47	16·97	16·83	16·75	17·00	16·69	16·37
Electric Works	4·9	7·36	6·3	6·54	7·24	7·70	8·08	8·29	8·96	9·27	9·89	9·68	9·61	9·81
Rlys. for Locomotive use	13·2	13·42	10·5	12·19	13·33	13·51	13·36	11·43	13·58	13·05	13·41	12·87	12·27	11·70
Coasting steamers (bunker for)	1·9	1·28	0·9	1·18	1·16	1·27	1·16	0·74	1·18	1·24	1·37	1·28	1·19	1·19
Coal Mines	18·0	17·20	13·7	16·25	16·85	16·57	15·42	*[2]	14·55	13·50	13·69	13·51	12·61	12·04
Pig Iron Manf.	21·2	18·80	6·3	9·51	14·41	14·23	12·03	4·69	13·45	12·17	14·18	11·69	7·11	6·56*
Iron & Steel Wks. (except pig iron)[5]	10·2	11·82	4·0	8·00	11·29	10·34	9·26	{ 86 to 91 }	9·25	8·37	9·11*	7·10	5·50	5·37*
Domestic[4]	} 40·0	40·0	35·0	40·0	40·0	40·0	40·0	(86 to 91 — see above)	40·0	40·0	40·0	40·0	40·0	40·0
Miners' Coal	(included with Domestic)		{ 33·5 to 35·5											
General Manf. & all other purposes[4]	57·7	53·96	33·5 to 35·5	48·91	49·10	60·08	53·81	(86 to 91 — see above)	61·60	49·43	55·10	53·15	50·70	46·46
Total	**183·8**	**180·72**	**126–128**	**157·76**	**168·76**	**180·36**	**169·57**	**128–133**	**179·54**	**163·86**	**173·50**	**166·58**	**155·68**	**149·50**

[1] Available for Great Britain from 1913 when the particulars shown above relate only to coal, or its equivalent as coke, used in the manufacture of products coming within the purview of the National Federation of Iron and Steel Manufacturers. For the earlier period the consumption of coal in the industry, including coal (or its equivalent as coke) used for making pig-iron, was approximately as follows: 1869, 32,450,000 tons; 1887, 26,700,000 tons; 1903, 28,000,000 tons.

[2] Provisional figure.

[3] Included with "General Manufacturers, etc." From the *Colliery Year Book & Coal Trades Directory*, 1931, and from the Tenth, Eleventh, and Twelfth *Annual Reports of the Secretary for Mines* and the *Annual Report of H.M. Chief Inspector of Mines* for the years 1930, 1931, and 1932.

[4] These residuary figures are subject to the changes in the stocks of coal held by producers and consumers, as to which information is not available generally. The same considerations apply to the consumption figures. The consumption of coal for domestic purposes in private houses, public buildings, and institutions, including coal for domestic industries and miners' coal was estimated after the war at 40,000,000 tons a year.
Information as to Domestic Consumption in more recent years is not available.

[5] These figures cover only the coal, or its equivalent in coke, used in the manufacture of products coming within the purview of the National Federation of Iron and Steel Manufacturers.

estimate may seem, it must be remembered that since 1913 the number of houses, and consequently of fire-places, stoves, kitchens, etc., has immensely increased. In spite of all the pulling down of many old dwellings and slum clearance, the net increase of houses was considerable.

Jevons [1] measured in his treatise the use of domestic coal per head of population, but in the present situation, when housing conditions are changing rapidly in the middle and working classes of the population, it would be better to measure the use of domestic coal not only per head of population, or even per family, but per room heated. As the number of persons per room gradually falls, the requirement of heat and fuel tends to rise proportionally, not only to the increase of population, but also in direct relation to the number of rooms and houses. And so the consumption of fuel per head for domestic purposes must be continually growing. Since the Jevons's estimate, in 1865, home consumption has increased by about 30 per cent, or a rate of about 0·65 per cent per year. But the bulk of this rise occurred before the War. On the other hand, since the War the number of houses has increased enormously. A statement supplied by the Ministry of Health to the National Housing and Town Planning Council shows the large increase in the number of houses built in Great Britain between 1919–1931, under the various State-assisted schemes, and of those completed by private enterprise without State assistance,[2] equal together to about 1,750,000. The bulk of those houses (more than one million) was subsidized, and they belong to the type of coal consumers who have a demand which tends to be elastic for a rise. Moreover, one must realize that the cubic capacity of these new houses is, basing our estimate on representative samples, about 20 to 30 per cent bigger per person than in the old houses, therefore the requirement for heat is presumably respectively higher. The population itself has also increased since 1913 by 10 per cent, i.e. by 4·5 millions. This growth

[1] W. Stanley Jevons, *Coal Question*, 3rd ed., p. 138.
[2] *Vide* John C. Martin, " The Present Housing Situation in England and Wales," Thirty-first Annual Report of the National Housing and Town Planning Council for the financial year ending 31st March, 1931, p. 8.

was very remarkable, especially in the case of England and Wales.

Leaving this question for a moment, we shall examine the figures of coal for the general manufacturers and all other purposes in which domestic coal is included. First of all we subtract the tonnage of stocks held usually in this country at pit and at the disposal of the distributing section, relative to the heading of general manufactures and other purposes. These stocks are estimated at 8–12 million tons,[1] and are subject to wide fluctuations. Hence, allowing for the stocks which are carried over from year to year, we shall notice that the whole position regarding coal for general manufactures and other purposes fluctuates relatively little around 80 million tons, which means that either all its constituents are stable in position, or else that some of them follow the opposite course to others, and counterbalance each other. This latter possibility, however, has no foundation, since it is quite improbable that in times of depression, when the position of general manufactures deteriorates, the consumption of domestic coal should rise in the reverse proportion, especially in the absence of any inducement from the price mechanism. Therefore, for the reasons just expounded, we adhere to the first alternative, i.e. that there was no appreciable rise in the demand for domestic coal, in spite of all the changes in the conditions.

In view of a complete lack of statistics, it is extremely difficult to solve the British household coal mystery and to give accurate figures and conclusions. The author has had to have recourse on several occasions to private inquiries and to samples. On the whole, the demand for lower qualities of coal, and the demand coming from poorer districts both

---

[1] We arrived at these figures by studying the behaviour of the market in times of extensive replenishment of stocks, caused either by strikes, or by unusually heavy demand in a particular year. And thus, for instance, in 1927, after the complete deplenishment of stocks, the market absorbed nearly 8 million tons more than it used to in an economically similar year of 1925 or 1922. Again, in 1924, after the excessively strong demand of 1923, which was stimulated by the foreign shipments, and the general deplenishment of stocks caused by a high level of coal prices, the demand in these sections rose from 89 million tons to 100 million tons, i.e. by 11 million tons, which, in our view, must be greatly attributed to the reconstruction of stocks.

in London and in the whole country, seems to be fairly elastic. This view was also confirmed by the coal dealers with whom the author came into contact.[1]

In order to gain a clearer idea about the demand for domestic heat, and about the degree of satiation reached, we must mention other methods of heating. Though the consumption of gas has risen, it has not proved able to supersede coal on a large scale. The national consumption of gas,[2] amounting in 1920 to some 250,000,000,000 cubic feet, has risen in 1930 to nearly 330,000,000,000 cubic feet. This rise, however, of 80 million does not represent the degree to which coal as a domestic fuel has been superseded by gas. At present some 3,000 trades are using gas for an average of seven processes in each.[3] A large proportion, therefore, of the increased gas consumed went to industry. Moreover, the increase of the total consumption of gas during the decade 1920–1930 was 26·9 per cent, which is a considerably lower rate of increase than in the previous decade 1910–1920. After making an adequate allowance for gas used for purposes other than heating, and after subtracting gas used for industry, the rise in the amount of gas consumed will not account for all the increase in heating. The statistics given by Mr. George Everett [4] show an increase in the home consumption of gas during 1910–1920 of 31·3 per cent, an increase of 58,185,000,000 feet. The comparison of the relative figures for the decade ending 1920 with those for the decade ending 1930 shows that there was no higher development in the rate of using gas, the rate being even lower than in the former decade, though much more cooking is being done now by gas. As during the last

[1] An interesting illustration of the extent to which the trade works in the dark in respect of the question of elasticity of demand occurred during one of our investigations in a coal distributors' firm in Barnet, where one director emphatically maintained that the demand of their customers is elastic, while another took quite the opposite view.

[2] Sir Francis Goodenough, *Gas Service in Home and Industry*, a paper contributed to the British Commercial Association at Galashiels on 30th April, 1930.

[3] The Gas Light and Coke Company, Ltd., alone supplied, during the year 1931, 14,400 factories with gas for various industrial purposes.

[4] George Everett, *The Administration and Finance of Gas Undertakings*, London, 1922, p. 2.

decade there were no important changes in the very method of burning gas as a fuel and in the amount of heat obtained from one cubic foot of gas, we omit these changes from our considerations as being of a purely technical character, and not affecting on a large scale the thermal value of a unit of gas.   Only very recently attempts were made to render the radiation of gas fires more pleasant by the emission of short infra-red rays, which will recall the open grate fire so deeply rooted in English tradition.

A certain amount of gas which was formerly used for lighting has been supplanted by electricity, and has thus been freed. Of course, this is not necessarily used for heating, because a major part of it has been absorbed partly for lighting the newly constructed housing areas, partly for better lighting in general, and partly for cooking.[1]   It is true also that the electricity works have doubled their consumption of coal, and several times increased their production— but electric current is mostly used in Great Britain as a means of providing light and power.   In spite of campaigns to encourage the use of electricity, it is still expensive, and not widely used as domestic fuel. Even in competition with gas, electricity in many cases cannot compete successfully at home in most of the processes.[2] Much depends here on the price, and undoubtedly there is a great future before electricity, both on account of its cleanliness and its easy handling. Of course, in an indirect way, coal will ultimately also benefit from such a demand for electricity ; but at present electricity plays a relatively unimportant part as a means of heating.[3]

Again, the economies obtained by the convection of heat from central-heating installations are not a factor of importance in reducing the absolute quantity of coal or coke consumed,

[1] Many of the leading gas companies reported an increase of demand for street lighting and similar purposes. Thus, in 1933, we meet references to increased sales on that account in the reports of the South Metropolitan Gas Company, the Gas Light and Coke Co., South Suburban Gas Co., etc.

[2] *Vide* Gas *v.* Electricity in the home. Extract from Minutes of the London County Council of 24th February, 1915.

[3] Cf. Margaret Fishenden, in chapter v, *The Utilisation of Coal-Domestic Heating ; the Preparation, Selections, and Distribution of Coal*, published under the auspices of the Coal Trade Luncheon Club and the Institute of Fuel, London, 1931, p. 103.

because central heating at the same time increases the amount of heat distributed on the average in a single building. The consequent reduction of the demand for coal in this way is probably without great significance, while the advance of progress and personal comfort is considerable.

At present some distributing companies are making attempts to popularize in place of household coal the use of coke, of certain grades of steam coal, and of patent fuel, mostly " Coalite ", " Cleanglow ", " Metro-coalite ", "Consett ", or semi-coke, "Gloco" the product of low temperature carbonization. This effort has only met with limited success as yet, since the difference in volatility and ash necessitates the introduction of new types of stove. It is important to remember that a large amount of these products, sold for domestic purposes, went to the heating of water in boilers which gained popularity in large towns,[1] and so did not entirely displace coal from its former uses.

A small displacement of coal for domestic purposes by external substitution took place in cooking. Here we refer to oil, which is to some extent used for cooking. But though an important substitute, its use since the War has not increased to any considerable extent in spite of the lower price of oil. On the other hand, one can recently notice a process of reversion from oil to coal in cooking, owing to the introduction of highly improved cookers, such as the " Aga " cooker, insulated with asbestos, burning solid fuel (coke or anthracite), and supplying an efficiency figure about four times as great as that of an ordinary solid fuel range.

Now, in spite of the growing population, and of the existence of a larger number of houses to be heated and provided with fuel, the quantity of coal used for this purpose is said to remain practically stable. As we already pointed out, all the internal substitutes for coal and better methods of utilizing coal do not provide the necessary balance in the supply of heat. On the other hand it must be supposed most unlikely that the English public is changing its habits as regards its caloric requirements, nor was there a

[1] *Vide* address of Dr. Charles Carpenter to the General Meeting of the South Metropolitan Gas Company, on 11th February, 1932.

noticeable change in the weather conditions of this country which could overbalance the fall in caloric units required for the individual households. It is clear, therefore, that either a certain potential demand, especially from the smaller households, is being restricted by general abstention, or the demand for coal for household purposes is not stable. In our view both these suggestions hold true. We may infer that in respect to such consumers of coal there is always some abstention and a certain large margin of potential increase in purchase of coal or other fuels, which always ultimately benefit coal—provided that the price is sufficiently attractive. There is constantly in existence an elasticity of demand for a rise for gas, electricity, manufactured fuel, and anthracite used in domestic stoves, while elasticity for a fall of coal in its raw form checks the demand of the middle and poorer classes. And on the other hand, in view of a complete lack of official information we suppose that the stationary figures of household consumption could be subject to drastic revision.

From the point of view of the producer, in whom we are here chiefly interested, these characteristics of demand are extremely important—they contribute substantially towards the explanation of the disintegrating motives. As in Britain, unlike in other European countries, the collieries are more strictly connected with particular markets, and even with the particular types of consumers, the various lines of the demand they are meeting require different adjustments. For this reason the producers of household coal, and other coal products used in the home, must naturally follow a different price policy such as would take account of the elasticity of demand, which is not homogenous throughout the whole British Isles.

As domestic coal, gas coal and coal used for electric works form together approximately 40 per cent of the home consumption of coal, the existence of a potential elasticity of demand for coal under these headings is certainly not a negligible item. The price of coal is one of the main factors which impede a large development in sales for these purposes. Hitherto the downward swings of fluctuations in the price of coal have not proved sufficiently wide or lasting to induce the buyers to appear, especially in view of the fact that very often the reduction of prices at pit did not reach the consumer at all.

In turn we pass now to the home demand as a whole, and compare the connection between prices and actual demand. In considering this demand for coal for all purposes, one can find several instances where the reduced price of coal was coupled with larger sales. These instances are not confined to one occasion. The tendency is perfectly obvious : both the reduction in prices and the increase in sales were considerable, even in the difficult post-War years.

The following table gives the average selling values per ton of coal raised at pit, and the quantities of coal available for home consumption for all purposes :—

TABLE No. 23

AVERAGE PIT-HEAD PRICES OF COAL AND QUANTITIES OF COAL AVAILABLE FOR HOME CONSUMPTION IN GREAT BRITAIN FOR 1920-1932

Based upon the Annual Reports of the Secretary for Mines and the Annual Reports of H.M. Chief Inspector of Mines, the Board of Trade *Report on Wholesale and Retail Prices*, and the Annual Statement of Trade.

Year.	Average selling value per ton of Coal raised at pit.		Quantity of Coal available for Home Consumption for all Purposes.[1]
	s.	d.	Tons.
1920 . .	34	7	180,720,000
1921 . .	26	2	127,000,000
1922 . .	17	8	157,760,000
1923 . .	18	10	168,760,000
1924 . .	18	10	180,360,000
1925 . .	16	4	169,570,000
1926 [2] . .	19	7	—[3]
1927 . .	14	7	179,580,000
1928 . .	12	10	163,860,000
1929 . .	13	5	173,500,000
1930 . .	13	7	166,500,000
1931 . .	13	6	155,700,000
1932 . .	13	3	150,200,000

A few words preliminary to our figures first. We must notice that we are not analysing the average selling value

[1] These particulars relate to Great Britain only, the necessary adjustments having been made in respect of shipments to and from Ireland.

[2] Prices were much affected by the prolonged Coal Strike.

[3] Estimate approximately in 1926 from 128 to 133 million tons available that year.—Partly from the *Colliery Yearbook and Coal Trades Directory,* 1931.

at pit per ton of coal designed only for home consumption. It would be almost impossible to get accurate data on this subject, as there are no special statistics of the average prices of coal at pit available for the home market. On the other hand, it would be misleading to compare changes in the general quantity of coal available for home consumption with the movement of prices of a special quality of coal, or even of a series of prices of different qualities. Those different kinds of coal, as already demonstrated, might fluctuate in price in a way which would not be representative for the whole volume of coal sold in the home market. In the absence of suitable statistics of average home prices, we take into consideration the average selling value per ton of coal raised at pit. By taking those prices we are liable to a certain error, namely, that the price mentioned includes also the coal exported—but, on the other hand, the quantity of coal for home consumption is much larger than that exported, and the movement of the price of coal exported does not, in the absence of cartels, differ very widely at pit from the pit price of coal for the home market. We therefore assume, with a certain admitted degree of error, that the yearly fluctuations of the average pit price are representative of the pit price of coal for home consumption.

Nor is the quantity of coal available for home consumption for all purposes identical with the quantities sold in the market. But here we can assume that the movements from year to year in the coal consumed at home are to a very great extent similar to the movements of coal disposable for the home market. The British coal owners are always anxious to follow the actual demand as closely as possible, and they dislike keeping large stocks of coal. It is impossible that an increase in the stores of coal would not immediately affect the current output of the mines owing to the lack of suitable railway sidings, suitable arrangements for storing coal, and because of the deterioration of coal.[1] The effect of growing stores would

[1] Cf. W. Benton Jones, ex-Chairman Central Collieries Commercial Association, " Quota, Production, and Minimum Prices," *Daily Telegraph*

be, either a reduction in prices in order to dispose of the surplus or else a diminution in the rate of output in accordance with the actual demand, or both. Hence, when we consider changes in the actual extraction of coal year by year, the trend is practically the same as that of consumption. This explains how the figures representing the quantity of coal available for home usage can be analysed together with the prices of coal at pit.

After this preliminary explanation we can now investigate the relation between prices and quantities. The table drawn below indicates rises and falls in the average value per ton of coal raised at pit, and in the quantity of coal available for home consumption, converted into a percentage of the respective figures for the preceding year. The column of the selling values of coal shows the increase (plus), or decrease (minus), over the previous year expressed as a percentage of the figures of that year, e.g. the year 1924 plus is based on 1923. The column of quantities of coal available for home consumption is calculated on the same lines. The year 1927, has been measured in a different way. As it was practically impossible to base any comparison on 1926 figures, the quantity for home consumption in 1927 has been compared with that of 1925. In order to show the movement in prices we have used for the year 1927 a double comparison both with the 1925 level of prices and with the 1926 level of prices. All other figures are based exclusively on the data of the previous year. In using this method of percentage link relatives, one can avoid the necessity for comparing the fluctuations of two different elements with a standard year taken as a basis. Our method renders all the changes of

Coal Supplement, 16th September, 1930. "It is obvious that if coal must be dispatched at the same rate as it is produced a fall in demand immediately exerts on the management of coal mines a great pressure to sell, since failure to sell quickly puts a stop to production."

Further, he says: "If coal cannot be stored, and it has been shown that this is impracticable, it is obvious that actual output with only a very short lag is controlled by demand . . ."

Also *vide* Report of the Royal Commission on the Coal Industry (1925), vol. ii, part B, *Memorandum of Evidence by the Mining Association* (No. 2), Annex D, No. 19, p. 949.

both prices and quantities more conspicuous and clear, especially if they are applied in a diagrammatic form.[1]

TABLE No. 24

RISES AND FALLS IN (1) the AVERAGE SELLING VALUE PER TON OF COAL RAISED AT PIT AND (2) THE QUANTITY OF COAL AVAILABLE FOR HOME CONSUMPTION IN GREAT BRITAIN FROM 1920, EXPRESSED AS PERCENTAGES OF THE PRECEDING YEAR'S OUTPUT.

Period.	Average Selling Value per ton of Coal raised at Pit. (Link relative of selling value over previous year.)		Coal Available for Home Consumption [2] for all purposes. (Link relative of consumption over previous year.)	
Yearly average.	Plus.	Minus.	Plus.	Minus.
1920	—	—	—	—
1921	—	24·3	—	29·1
1922	—	32·4	24·1	—
1923	6·6	—	6·9	—
1924	0·0	0·0	6·9	—
1925	—	13·2	—	5·9
1926 [3] . . .	19·6	—	—	—
1927 (based on 1925) .	—	10·7	5·9	—
(based on 1926) .	—	25·5	—	—
1928	—	12·0	—	8·7
1929	4·5	—	5·8	—
1930	1·2	—	—	4·0
1931	—	0·6	—	6·4
1932	—	1·8	—	3·5

From a first glance at the diagram, it is obvious that, during the whole period under consideration, up to the introduction of compulsory restriction schemes in 1930, the relative percentage falls in prices were always considerably higher than the falls in consumption, the only exception being the year 1921, where the margin between prices and actual demand was rather small. The fall in the price curve being quicker than that in the quantities curve demonstrates clearly that it was the price of coal that constituted the

[1] A similar method of comparing the growth of consumption of coal from year to year was adopted by Jevons. He calculated the average ratio or rate per cent of increase and compared the consumption of coal for every year between 1854 and 1863 with that of the previous year.— (W. Stanley Jevons, *The Coal Question*, 3rd ed., p. 268.)

[2] Allowance has been made for the fuel imported and retained for home consumption from 1921 and the necessary adjustments made in respect of shipments to Northern Ireland.

[3] Prices were largely affected by the Coal Strike.

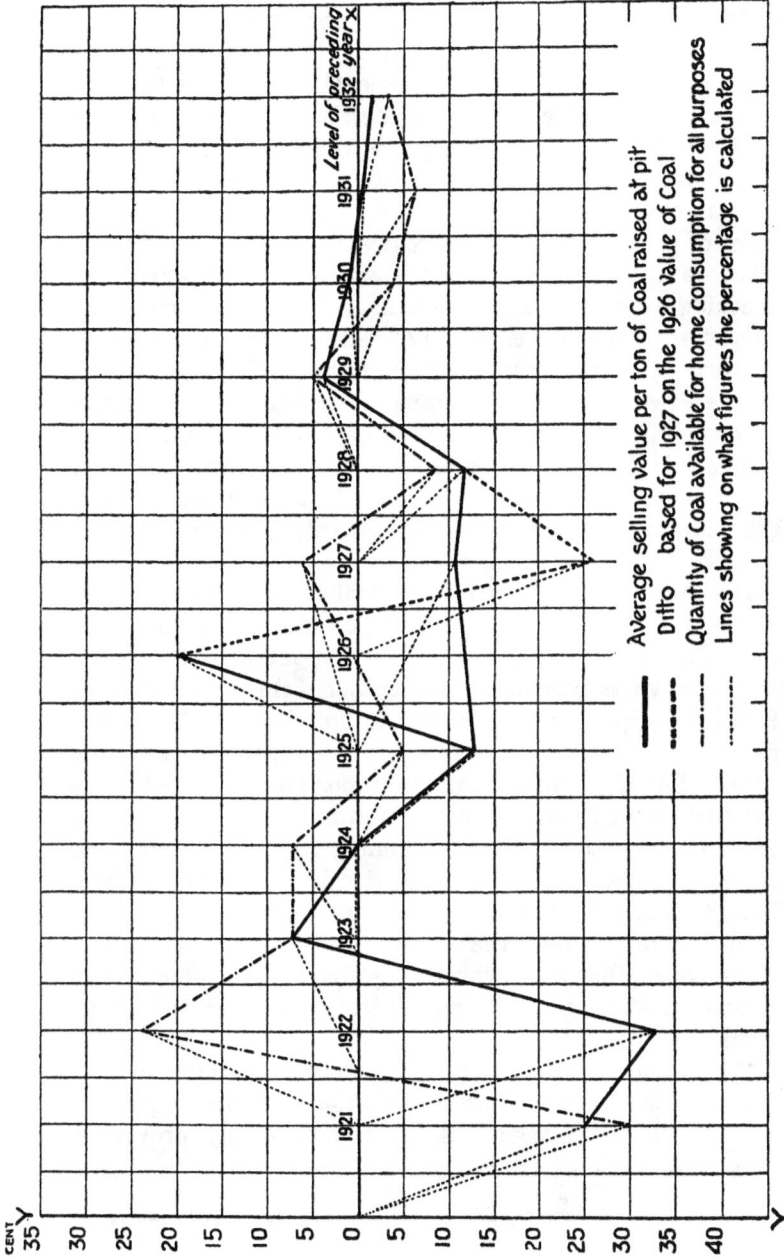

Average selling value per ton of Coal raised at pit

Ditto   based for 1927 on the 1926 value of Coal

Quantity of Coal available for home consumption for all purposes

Lines showing on what figures the percentage is calculated

DIAGRAM 3. SHOWING THE RELATIVE RISES AND FALLS IN PRICE AND QUANTITY OF COAL AVAILABLE FOR HOME CONSUMPTION IN GREAT BRITAIN FROM 1920, EXPRESSED AS A PERCENTAGE OF THOSE OF THE PRECEDING YEAR.

moveable item, in spite of fairly inflexible costs. It was by adjusting prices to different situations that the quantity was kept at a much more stable level. The amplitudes of the price fluctuations were considerably greater than those of demand. This is especially the case when the quantity curve was on the downward trend. The movement was to a great extent counterbalanced by the much larger movement of price. The prices of coal were therefore the flexible factor, and it is the price policy which was instrumental in checking the fall in quantities. The same moveable character of prices has been pointed out for the nineteenth century conditions by Jevons,[1] in his admirable chapter on the Price of Coal. He compared the movement of prices of coal with the general trend of wholesale prices, and concluded that " the movement in coal prices has been more violent in the extent of its fluctuations than that of the average of wholesale commodities represented in Sauerbeck's index number ".

One must realize how far the coal industry is interested in keeping the production at a certain level, and how important it is not to sink below that level, to be able to realize why the price of coal is considered the preponderating factor of adjustment to economic conditions. The whole problem of economy in working at full capacity is involved here.[2] For these reasons much importance is attached by the coal owner to a free price determination ; for instance, when in June, 1915, the Coal-mining Reorganization Committee discussed the question of the desirability of fixing a limit to the selling price of coal, in the first stage of the investigations before the Committee a prominent representative of the coal owners suggested the introduction of limitation of profits, but no control of prices,[3] and so no regulation of sales.

We may note here that the first coal cartel in the Midlands, the so-called Five Counties Marketing Scheme, supplying widely different markets, did not include any provisions

[1] W. Stanley Jevons, *The Coal Question*, 3rd ed., London, 1906, p. 92.
[2] Cf. Part III, Chap. I, § 2.
[3] Sir R. A. S. Redmayne, *The British Coal-Mining Industry during the War*, Oxford, 1923.

for the regulation of prices, though its output-restricting machinery was highly elaborated. The regulation of prices was initially attempted in the voluntary Welsh Coal Marketing Scheme, but even there the scheme had to be soon altered, as it proved to be unworkable. The price had to be free in order to adjust itself to the demand and to induce the market to absorb a larger quantity of coal. This holds especially true in the case of internal substitution, when a lower quality of coal is under consideration. In analysing home prices of coal it would be, however, practically impossible to distinguish the degree to which they are affected by the structure of the supply and demand schedules. Thus the only certain statement which can be made here is that the fall or rise of prices is not due to foreign competition, and that the conditions abroad do not directly and immediately affect the determination of the price of coal in the home market.

Observing *a posteriori* the behaviour of prices and quantities of coal demanded, especially in the first years after the War, we have detected cases in which elasticity of demand for a rise could occur, while the behaviour of prices of lower grades of coal would point to a still greater degree of elasticity for a fall.[1] The examination of the diagram shows two situations where there exists a set of conditions which are necessary for the elasticity for a rise of demand. In 1922, a fall in the price of coal of 32·4 per cent on the basis of 1921 prices is coupled with a rise in demand of 24·1 per cent over 1921. In 1927 a rise in demand of 5·9 per cent is caused by a fall in price of 10·7 per cent over the 1925 year basis, or of 25·5 per cent over the 1926 year basis.

There is no doubt that lower prices had their explanation in the reduced costs of production, especially in 1927, after the introduction of the eight-hour working day. This reduction of costs facilitated the lowering of prices, but on the other hand the lower prices induced the market to absorb

---

[1] The mere coincidence of movements in the two series (the price and quantity series) is not yet a sufficient proof of any kind of elasticity of demand.

a great amount of coal. It would be more justifiable to say that the low prices were introduced, not because of the low costs, but owing to the desire to sell more coal, that the lower costs made it possible to do so, and that this method has proved effective. It is rather of secondary importance to ask whether the reduced prices were a result of competition, calculation, or any other causes ; what is relevant here is that the demand for coal reacted to the lowering of prices, and that the market by absorbing more coal proved elastic. The introduction of compulsory marketing schemes which restricted quantities and regulated prices does not make it possible to analyse the changes with the same accuracy as those which occurred before 1930.

It is essential to our inquiry into the nature of the demand for coal to remember that what has been said hitherto refers to the home market as a whole, without making any distinction between the different kinds of coal and different purposes for which it may be used. The facts above demonstrate the existence of conditions during the decade 1920–1930, in which elasticity for a rise of demand has been working, and when we analysed the different kinds of coal the existence of elasticity of demand for a rise was even more patent.

Already in the foregoing discussions it has been clearly emphasized that both prices and tonnage of coal exported were extremely changeable.[1] In fact, it is towards the foreign demand that one must look as one of the chief disintegrating factors in the British coal industry. The striking difference between the conditions of the exporting sections and the home sections of the industry strongly militated against any general understanding or co-operation. In the foreign demand there is a very large elasticity of demand for coal, and a still stronger elasticity of demand for British coal, if treated separately, which elasticity has always been in existence. Even some of those writers who deny its existence at home admit its validity abroad. Professor Jones writes that " under present conditions " elasticity occurs, and he

[1] Cf. Part I, Chap. I.

looks for a remedy in concluding an international agreement.[1] It would, however, be a mistake to assume that the elasticity of demand for coal on the foreign markets arises only " under the present conditions ", since there are many other instances where similar elasticity could exist in the past history of the coal trade.[2] Already the Newcastle Vend in the eighteenth century had on many occasions had recourse to dumping, whenever the foreign market was shrinking on account of high prices. But glancing at the more recent history of the seventies of the past century, we find that in 1873 the average f.o.b. price of coal exported was at a very high quotation, touching 20s. 6d. per ton, a price which was never reached again except during the period 1916–1924. The exports at that average price during the year 1873 amounted to some 16 million tons. During the following year an unprecedently large reduction of prices took place, and it is interesting to note that six years later the quantity of coal exported had increased by some 5 million tons, while the price of coal exported was a little more than half the 1873 level. It is also very important to remember that this reduction of prices was not caused by the existence of a large surplus of coal in the home market. The actual rise in the total output of coal in the United Kingdom was equal only to the increased volume of the export trade : something near 5 million tons. This expansion in sales on the foreign markets, coupled with a stationary home consumption, was absorbing the total

[1] " To use technical terms, the demand for coal in general is inelastic, but under present conditions the foreign demand for British coal is highly elastic. The immediate need is to reduce such elasticity of foreign demand for British coal, and this can only be achieved by international agreement."—(J. H. Jones, " The Coal Dilemma," in *The Accountant*, 27th July, 1929, p. 109.)

[2] A noteworthy example of elasticity of demand for a fall in coal exports is quoted in an old book on the coal trade by an anonymous author of 1835, who modestly signed himself as " the author of Treatise on manufactures in metal ", presumably John Holland. He writes : " Lord North thought it a good reason for proposing an increase of duty on the foreign trade during his administration, that our enemies ought not to be allowed to burn our coal as cheaply as ourselves ; but that reason ceased to influence the Cabinet the moment that the Minister was convinced by the coal owners that such a course, instead of increasing, would diminish the revenue."—" (The History and Description of Fossil Fuel," *The Collieries and Coal Trade of Great Britain*, London, 1835, p. 438.)

additional increase in the general output of coal. The fall in prices was not the result of a combination of factors working outside the existing price policy of British owners, and was not caused by any external suppliers of coal, as the world exporters of those times were England, Scotland, and Wales. W. Stanley Jevons, who published his *Coal Question* at this time (1865), considered foreign competition as being absolutely negligible. The possibility of competition on a large scale between British and foreign coal in the overseas markets did not arise in his mind.[1]

In Great Britain, home consumption of coal was stationary in the years 1873–9, and the general production of coal was not expanding more rapidly than that of the expansion of exports. The industry suffered, as it does to-day, from the existence of a large over-capacity.[2] This enlargement of capacity came as a result of previous very remunerative prices of coal, and was undoubtedly the main stimulus then pressing the industry to dispose of more coal in the market at a much lower price. Thus it was greatly interested during this period in increasing its sales abroad through price reductions. The elasticity of demand for a rise for coal in the foreign markets had responded, and the exports were increasing at a fairly steady rate. From this time the price policy based on the use of the elasticity of

---

[1] " So long as the current of trade and navigation continue in their present general course, there are no coalfields capable of competing with and reducing the demand for our coal in regard to the oversea coal trade. The only other way in which a foreign coalfield could affect the prosperity of our coal-consuming industry would be by nourishing abroad great systems of manufacturing industry capable of withdrawing from us a part of the custom of the world, which we have enjoyed, as regards coal-made articles, almost to the extent of a monopoly."—(W. Stanley Jevons, *The Coal Question*, London, 3rd ed., p. 332.)

[2] The high prices in 1873 " stimulated the efforts of coal owners in every direction, and as a consequence the number of collieries at work was increased from 2,760 in 1871 to 4,933 in 1875—an increase of about 80 per cent within four years. The number of men and boys employed in and about the collieries of the United Kingdom advanced in the same four years from 371,000 to 538,000—an increase of 167,000 or about 45 per cent. In the quantity of coal raised during this interval there was, however, no corresponding advance. The output of 1871 was 117,000,000—while that of 1875 was 131,000,000, being an increase of 14,000,000 tons, or only about 12 per cent, and as a matter of fact the average annual output per employee fell from 316 tons in 1871 to 246 tons in 1875, being an average decline of about 70 tons."—(Extracted from *The Times*, 18th October, 1888.)

demand became more and more ingrained in the minds of the captains of industry. It had been put to the test at a time when the home market had proved unable to absorb further quantities of coal, and when it had been stationary for some time.

In the history of the coal export trade, we can find similar examples of the existence of elasticities of demand for a rise and for a fall. They are, however, neither so prominent nor of such a decided character as those described above during the 1873–9 period. On the other hand, the nearer we approach our own times the more difficult is it to exclude from the general play of forces the question of foreign competition, which gradually became more and more acute. Elasticity for a rise of demand for coal could be postulated in 1896, when the price dropped from 9s. 3d. (average f.o.b. per ton) to 8s. 9d. and the total quantity of coal exported rose from 42·9 million tons to 44·6 million tons. Similar phenomena can be observed in the years 1901–5, when the corresponding data for exports [1] in million tons were 57·8, 60·4, 63·8, 65·8, 67·1, and the figures for prices 13s. 9d., 12s. 2d., 11s. 7d., 11s., 10s. 6d. We notice here a steady decline in prices, which over the whole five years amounts to 3s. 3d., and in consequence a substantial increase in tonnage exported, amounting to 9·3 million tons. In 1927, again, a fall in prices from the 1925 level was coupled with an increase in exports.

A case of elasticity for a fall of demand may be well postulated in the United Kingdom in 1910, when the price rose by 6d., and this was bound together with a fall in exports of 1·5 million tons. Again, in 1930, a similar rise in price was accompanied by a fall in British export of 7 million tons.

All these instances of the two types of elasticity of foreign demand for coal need very careful consideration, because there is a fundamental difference between the conditions prevailing in later periods and those in the seventies and eighties of the nineteenth century, when, as already

[1] Presumably the exports would be still greater had the Government not imposed export duties on coal in 1901.

demonstrated, Great Britain was practically the only coal exporter, and could conduct an independent price and quantity policy.[1] Latterly the export trade, though still carried on by Britain on a very large scale, has been no longer totally regulated by her own decision. It is, therefore, much more difficult to ascribe a certain adjustment between price and quantity exported exclusively to the working of elasticity of demand. Foreign competition is of first importance here. Judging, however, only from the British point of view, one cannot refrain from inferring that a substantial reduction of prices has secured much larger sales abroad, and that a rise in prices has been followed by a fall in sales. When we observe a reduction of prices and a rise in sales, not during a short period, but over a rather longer time, like that of the years 1901–5, then we must admit that seasonal disturbing factors cannot exert a preponderant effect on the whole argument. We can then safely draw conclusions as to the whole trend, even on the basis of such rough figures as the yearly averages.

Hitherto we have been discussing the export trade as a whole, and have discovered some years in which the existence of elasticity of demand for coal has been clearly visible. Taking now the demand for different qualities of coal exported, one finds that they display somewhat similar features to those ruling in the home market. The prices of different qualities and of various sizes of coal tend to swing in very diverse ways. As we have already demonstrated, prices of coals for which the demand is fairly steady are subject to smaller variations from year to year than those which are obliged by a very elastic demand to regulate their sales by means of price.

In order to discuss the demand for British coal in the international market, we take two different kinds of coal, each of a different commercial nature, viz. anthracite and steam coal. Moreover, we shall consider the prices of small and large coals for each of these kinds. The export prices of anthracite and steam coal, which are compared during

[1] *Vide* Henry Louis, " The Coal Industry," *Reconstruction*, 7th May, 1932, p. xxviii (publ. by *The Times Trade and Engineering Supplement*).

the period after the War, represent different commodities from the point of view of demand. Anthracite, on the one hand, is one of those qualities of coal the export of which is monopolized to a great extent by definite coalfields in comparatively few countries—U.S.A., Great Britain, Indo-China, and Russia. But steam coal producers have to compete both with foreign exporters and with other home producers.

We quote below the f.o.b. prices of small and large anthracite and those of small and large steam coal for the years 1920–1932.

TABLE No. 25

AVERAGE DECLARED VALUE PER TON (F.O.B.) OF EACH PRINCIPAL KIND OF COAL EXPORTED FROM 1920 TO 1932

(Based upon the Annual Reports of the Secretary for Mines and the Trade and Navigation Accounts)

Period	ANTHRACITE				STEAM			
	Small	Sized and Small	Sized	Large	Small	Sized and Small	Sized	Large
Yearly Average		*s. d.*		*s. d.*		*s. d.*		*s. d.*
1920		51 3		81 4		69 2		89 6
1921		39 0		61 3		22 9		38 11
1922		28 2		45 6		17 10		24 9
1923		25 0		41 0		20 7		27 5
1924		26 1		41 8		18 7		25 4
1925		25 6		40 3		14 9		21 11
	s. d.		*s. d.*		*s. d.*		*s. d.*	
1926	9 5		43 6	86 0	11 9		17 4	20 4
1927	10 0		38 8	33 4	12 9		16 8	19 6
1928	8 4		31 11	28 5	11 3		14 6	16 11
1929	8 10		31 2	30 4	11 9		15 4	17 6
1930	10 2		32 8	31 7	12 8		14 9	17 8
1931	8 7		32 4	31 5	11 8		14 1	17 6
1932	8 2		32 2	32 0	11 1		13 10	17 1

From *The Colliery Year Book and Coal Trades Directory.*

Those prices shown in Table No. 25 vary substantially from year to year. To bring these variations to a common denominator we have used the link-relative method of calculating the percentage changes over each preceding year. This method, which we consider the best for this purpose, allows us to see at the first glance all the price reactions of different kinds and sorts of coal over the previous year.

　　　THE ECONOMIC FACTOR

TABLE No. 26

RISES AND FALLS IN THE AVERAGE DECLARED VALUE PER TON (F.O.B.)
OF DIFFERENT KINDS OF COAL EXPORTED FROM GREAT BRITAIN AND
NORTHERN IRELAND FROM 1920 TO 1932, EXPRESSED AS A PERCENTAGE,
ABOVE OR BELOW THAT OF THE PRECEDING YEAR.

(Based upon the Annual Report of the Secretary for Mines and the Trade
and Navigation Accounts)

PERIOD	ANTHRACITE				STEAM COAL				PERIOD
	Small [1]		Large		Small [1]		Large		
Yearly Average	Plus	Minus	Plus	Minus	Plus	Minus	Plus	Minus	Yearly Average
	%	%	%	%	%	%	%	%	
1920	—	—	—	—	—	—	—	—	1920
1921	—	25·0	—	25·0	—	68·0	—	56·0	1921
1922	—	28·0	—	26·0	—	22·0	—	36·8	1922
1923	—	11·0	—	10·0	16·3	—	6·8	—	1923
1924	4·5	—	1·8	—	—	9·0	—	7·6	1924
1925	—	2·0	—	3·4	—	27·2	—	13·1	1925
1926 [2]	4·0	—	—	10·0	—	2·3	—	6·5	1926
1927	6·0	—	—	7·4	8·4	—	—	4·9	1927
1928	—	16·7	—	15·0	—	11·8	—	13·2	1928
1929	6·0	—	12·6	—	4·4	—	3·4	—	1929
1930	15·0	—	4·0	—	7·8	—	0·9	—	1930
1931 [3]	—	3·9	—	0·5	—	6·0	—	0·9	1931
1932	—	4·8	1·8	—	—	5·0	—	2·4	1932

From Table 26 we can now draw a diagram showing the
fluctuations of f.o.b. prices of different kinds and sorts of
coal. These fluctuations measured in percentages over the
previous year will be very different in each case.

The abscissa measures the time on yearly averages, the
ordinate indicates the percentage swings of prices. Any
point on the abscissa represents the coal price level of the
previous year. Above the X axis we measure the rise of
prices over the previous year, below the X axis the fall in
prices. The diagram represents the price fluctuations both
of small and large anthracite and steam coal. We can see
from the small anthracite curve that the largest fall of
prices in one single year was 28 per cent over the previous

[1] Up to 1925 the movement of the average (f.o.b.) values of small and
sized coal (anthracite, steam) have been considered as representative for
small coal.

[2] The quotations of values f.o.b. are not the average of the whole year
1926, owing to the prolonged strike, and the subsequent cessation of
exports. These figures are arrived at by comparing the arithmetical
average of the (f.o.b.) export values of small and sized coal (anthracite,
steam) in 1925 with the f.o.b. export value of small coal (anthracite, steam)
in 1926.

[3] First year of price regulations.

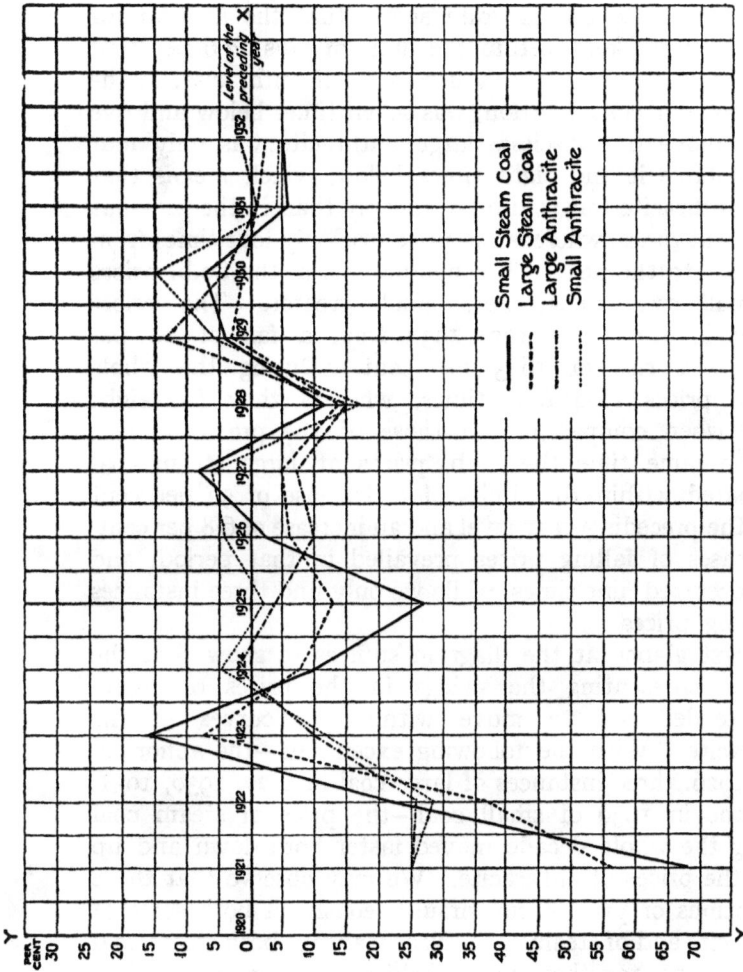

DIAGRAM 4. COMPARISON OF THE RELATIVE MOVEMENTS IN EXPORT VALUES OF FOUR TYPES OF COAL

Rises and Falls in the Average declared Value per ton (f.o.b.) of small Anthracite, large Anthracite, small Steam and large Steam Coal, exported from Great Britain and Northern Ireland from 1920-1932, expressed in each case as a percentage above or below that of the preceding year.

one, and the largest annual rise in price during the whole period 1921–1932 was 15 per cent. It follows therefore that the f.o.b. prices of small anthracite fluctuated between minus 28 and plus 15 per cent from year to year. In the case of large anthracite the diagram shows that the fluctuations of prices were kept within the limit of plus 12·6 per cent and minus 26 per cent. Whereas small anthracite, in the period under consideration, was seven times below and five times above the abscissa, large anthracite was only four times above it and eight times below, which means that large anthracite was sold more cheaply than in the previous year eight times, whereas the price rose only four times from one year to the next. The fluctuations in the f.o.b. prices of small steam coal were much greater. The prices swung in the years 1921–1932 from a fall of 68 per cent to a rise of 16·3 per cent. During the whole period prices rose four times, whereas they fell eight times when compared with those of the previous year. At the same time the f.o.b. prices of large steam coal fluctuated within the limits of a decrease of 56 per cent over the preceding year level and an increase of 6·8 per cent. The cases of falling prices prevailed in that period, and they occurred nine times, while we only find three instances of rising prices.

A first glance at the diagram suffices to show that the curves representing the swings in the prices of steam coal tended not to move within the curves of the anthracite. With the following exceptions—the abnormal year 1926, three instances of large coal in 1927, 1930, 1931, and one in 1930 of small coal—the price of steam coal during the whole decade moved faster both down and up than the prices of anthracite. We may observe that those oscillations of price occur simultaneously in both sorts of anthracite and of steam coal. Nearly always both steam coal curves kept together either below or above anthracite, showing that steam coal followed in a similar direction ; the only exception besides those already mentioned was the year 1922, when the curve showing large steam coal lay below the anthracite curves, and the small steam curve was above.

From the observation of these facts it can be inferred that the sensitiveness [1] of anthracite prices is on the whole less than that of steam coal. This would not necessarily be the case unless the respective curves illustrating the fluctuations of steam and anthracite coal moved in the same direction with the difference only in intensity. One could easily imagine a case where both anthracite lines would lie outside the steam coal lines, but each set moving in a different direction, e.g. one falling, the other one rising. This fact would not mean that one kind of coal is more sensitive than another. It might simply mean that whereas one kind of coal has adopted high prices, the other kinds have reduced theirs. In our case, however, both sets of curves had the tendency to follow the same path, though occasionally the changes in price of anthracite showed a time-lag behind the movement of steam coal. This occurred several times between 1922–8. From 1928 the prices moved in a closer connection. After having noted the fact of the same general direction in the price fluctuations of both anthracite and steam coal, we are now entitled to compare those variations and the length of the amplitude of the swings. Up to 1927 the relative swings were always larger in the case of steam coal than those of anthracite. The distance between the abscissa and the coal curves is longer in both directions than that of the anthracite curves. From 1927 to 1930 the situation altered and it was the anthracite which swung more in price than steam coal. In 1930 the price of small steam swung more than the f.o.b. price of large anthracite, but less than that of small anthracite. From 1930 the operation of the compulsory marketing schemes prevented prices from moving freely. On the whole, however, anthracite has during the decade 1921–1932 fluctuated less in f.o.b. prices than steam coal.

This fact only confirms what has already been said about the nature of demand for coal and about the price apparatus. Anthracite, being much more concentrated, and nearly monopolized by a few districts in a small number

[1] Cf. with our earlier discussion on the "minimum sensibile" in this section.

of countries, was less subjected to price changes with the object of increasing sales. Having under its control the quantitative supply of anthracite, the exporting industry did not need price manipulation in order to increase the sales. On the other hand the world, being also much more dependent on the supply of British anthracite than on steam coal, had to buy it at a less fluctuating price. Putting it in another way, the demand for British anthracite had a lower elasticity for a fall than steam coal in times of depression, and a higher one in times of boom. The demand for British steam coal, being enormously elastic, caused sweeping movements in prices. For this reason the yearly amplitudes in the price swings were much wider in the case of steam coal than of anthracite. This clearly shows a much greater reaction to demand on the part of steam coal than on that of anthracite. But the most pronounced difference in the movement of export prices is in the period 1931–2, and is to be found in the relative swings of small and large steam coal, as contrasted with small and large anthracite. With a very few exceptions the margin between the two steam coal curves is much wider than that between the two anthracite curves. The two sorts of anthracite fluctuated in a closer relation than the two sorts of steam coal. The widest fluctuations are shown by small steam coal, which in order to become saleable had to vary rapidly in price; hence, the black continuous line illustrating small steam coal is always first to fall and first to rise. Our diagram shows that, whereas both sorts of anthracite were saleable at a very similar rate, and had to quote prices with parallel alterations over a course of years, the two sorts of steam coal moved very dissimilarly, causing therefore a much larger margin. In the Strike year 1926, in 1929, 1930, and 1932, the relative fluctuations were larger in anthracite. In 1930, however, the difference was very small, whereas all the margins between the prices of steam coal were essentially wider in 1921, 1922, 1923, and 1925 than the margin between the changes in prices of anthracite, small and large.

This confirms the fact that while the demand for anthracite, being steady and less dependent on price, holds the price movements of its different sorts more closely together, the demand for steam coal is of a very different character; there exists a much greater elasticity for a fall in the case of small steam than in the case of the large. Consequently the quotations of the former are forced to diverge more widely and to move more frequently than those of the latter. These price differences between the small and the large are the more striking when we consider the proportion of the two sorts of coal sold in the foreign markets. The table below shows the amount of small and large coal sold abroad.

TABLE No. 27

QUANTITY OF COAL EXPORTED FROM GREAT BRITAIN AND NORTHERN IRELAND DURING THE PERIOD 1924–1932, DISTINGUISHING CERTAIN KINDS AND QUALITIES OF THE COAL EXPORTED

(Based upon the Annual Reports of the Secretary for Mines, and the Annual Reports of H.M. Chief Inspector of Mines)

Period	Anthracite		Steam		Total export of Coal [1]
	Small	Large	Small	Large	
	Tons	Tons	Tons	Tons	Tons
1924 .	1,703,856	1,379,055	13,637,169	26,029,708	61,651,273
1925 .	1,760,494	1,253,294	11,392,280	21,532,210	50,817,118
1926 .	406,459	351,005	3,087,741	8,636,464	20,596,372
1927 .	1,148,848	1,025,423	7,396,604	20,636,532	51,149,193
1928 .	946,458	879,846	6,416,414	18,568,298	50,051,195
1929 .	1,299,082	1,101,841	7,160,040	20,630,343	60,266,618
1930 .	1,042,897	1,131,257	6,007,887	18,008,243	54,874,065
1931 .	629,172	1,033,311	5,160,288	13,663,362	42,749,740
1932 .	551,290	1,072,661	4,239,665	12,272,477	38,898,800

As is shown in Table 26, the tonnage of large steam coal exported is much greater than that of small steam coal. The two qualities of anthracite exported do not show such wide divergence in quantity. Having shown that the amount of small disposed of abroad is considerably less than that of large steam coal, and having reason to believe that it is a less marketable commodity, we must conclude that price adjustment is adopted by the industry in order to keep

[1] Includes also other kinds of coal not set out separately.

up the sale. In this way the existing elasticity of demand is met, and any sharp fall in sales prevented. The elasticity of demand for small is much more pronounced than that for large coal.

In our considerations of the demand in export markets we did not adopt the same method as in the case of home demand. The rising and falling prices have not been correlated with relative movements in the demand for British coal only, because whereas in Great Britain all coal consumed at home was of British origin and there were no foreign supplies, in the case of overseas countries the sources of their supplies were manifold. While the demand for British coal might seem inelastic, the general demand could prove highly elastic for a rise in the case of those exporting countries which were able to reduce prices below the British level.

The seasonal disturbing factor is very pronounced in the exporting section both in prices and in quantities ; thus in 1930, for instance, there was an exceptionally brisk seasonal demand in the first quarter of the year. Prices and tonnage sold reached a considerably higher level than in 1929, though, after all, the latter year was generally much better. But when we take into consideration a whole series of years these differences operate with less force, and the fluctuations are bound to be smoothed out over time. Analogously varying features of demand may occur, not only in the time space, but also in respect to its geographical distribution. Some regions prove to be more elastic than others ; in some districts the price may influence the sales to a higher degree than in others. It would be, however, difficult and outside the scope of our investigations to measure the elasticity of demand in different regions and for different sorts of coal. It is quite enough to prove that on the whole the foreign demand is much less regular than the home demand, while on the other hand in this section the prices are more erratic and changeable owing to the great elasticity of demand in both directions both in the short and in the long run. Competition adds its share to the other factors operating abroad, and must be met either by means of price adjustment or by tolerating a reduction in shipments. *Tertium non datur.*

From what has been already said one can infer that, taking the whole exporting section of the British coal industry, we shall see on the demand side powerful disintegrating factors. One must therefore recognize on this side of the industry a strong force working against integration, and an opposition to devices restricting the freedom of price movement. This opposition will probably not be equally strong in all exporting districts, because they do not supply exactly the same geographical regions nor the same product. Hence we witnessed on many occasions varying degrees of opposition to integration, according to the particular features of their respective demands, both in the short as in the long time space. Thus, e.g. South Wales, where the demand of their foreign customers was less elastic and less determined by the alteration in prices, was more in favour of restriction schemes than Northumberland or Durham, which had to cope with an entirely different demand.

We have dealt with the demand side at a somewhat greater length than with the other disintegrating motives in the British coal industry, as we believe that demand is certainly one of the most important factors which have in the past determined its organization. In this province the strongest disruptive factor consisted in the fact that each district, and very often each unit, has been accustomed to satisfy a demand dissimilar to the rest of the industry. Moreover, the different degrees of internal and external substitution for the many brands of coal, the changes in elasticity of demand both seasonal and long period, the various degrees of economizing fuel, the uneven demand of the different types of consumers, and finally movements in demand even within different classes of society, must all be quoted as potent reasons for disintegration. In foreign trade it is true that international agreements might perhaps put an end to ruinous competition, but nobody could guarantee that they would not lead to the shrinkage of the foreign market unless the rise in prices was kept below the level at which elasticity of demand for a fall begins to operate.

This is our reply to those who attempted to explain the lack of co-operation in the British coal industry on the simplified assumption of abnormal individualism among the coal-owners—all protagonists of the doctrine " each for himself and the Devil take the hindmost ".

CHAPTER III

INTEGRATING FORCES

§1. MOTIVES FOR INTEGRATION IN THE INDUSTRY

The disintegrating forces in the coal industry mentioned in previous sections were bound to be stemmed sooner or later. Even before the War, pressure towards reorganization began to make itself felt inside the industry. Various factors, differing much in intensity, and working sometimes together, sometimes separately, contributed towards the combination movement. It is most misleading to argue—as has sometimes been done—that the industry owes its present status to the authoritative will of Parliament, and to political conceptions which have abruptly shunted the whole development of the industry into a new organization. During many years strong forces were streaming in and round the industry, preparing the way for a final imposition of organization by law. Beginning with opposition to the growing power of organized labour, and with co-ordination of efforts to resist the greedy enlargement of State penetration into the industry, co-operation developed for commercial and industrial purposes, for the strengthening of export markets, for the regulation and standardization of technical processes and scientific research.

The scope, however, of the early organizations in the coal industry was not very wide, and it was restricted chiefly to the regulation of labour problems. So these organizations became the representative bodies of the coal-owners. In this way the Mining Association of Great Britain, which dates back to 1854, had primarily for its object the settlement of the principles determining the payment of wages and the regulation of other questions connected with conditions of employment.[1] It was then

---

[1] For fuller details see : W. A. Lee, " History of Organization in the Coal Industry," in the *Historical Review of Coal Mining*, London, 1924, p. 351.

preponderantly an employers' organization to which individual coal-owners could become a party. Up to this time it had not yet acquired the character of a central association co-ordinating the work of the district bodies. This status was given to the Mining Association in 1920, when its membership was restricted exclusively to the district associations of coal-owners. In the course of years, as Government interference became more extensive, the Association began to play the part of mouthpiece for the majority of the industry. This development was clearly shown, for example, in matters relating to legislation, since it often acted as the attorney of the coal industry. At present the Mining Association serves chiefly in this latter character, while labour problems have been transferred to the districts. It is composed of nearly all the districts except Kent, and represents more than 90 per cent of the whole industry.

The early district associations and other working agreements between owners had aims similar to the national association ; for example the regulation of labour problems was undertaken on a large scale. Thus, an early agreement of the masters of the North-East Coast decided that no coal-owner should hire another's men unless " they produced a certificate of leave from their master ", which, as Mr. Sidney Webb [1] says, was usually refused. This hindered the mobility of labour, and so helped to maintain low wages. The South Wales and Monmouthshire Coal Owners' Association, which was formed in 1890, was very active in assisting the owners in the event of strikes. They developed a system of indemnity payments to cover losses from strikes or lock-outs.

Co-operation for industrial and commercial purposes developed later, but the forms of combination enumerated by the Balfour Report [2] were nearly all evolved, in the

[1] Sidney Webb, *The Story of the Durham Miners* (1662–1921), London, 1921.

[2] In this class of industrial activity the Balfour Report distinguishes in general thirteen varieties of organizations for limiting competition, namely : (1) Informal understanding or " gentlemen's agreements " ; (2) associations for regulating prices ; (3) associations for regulating output ; (4) pooling associations ; (5) associations for allocating contracts ; (6) the selling agency ; (7) the participating cartel with selling syndicate ; (8) variations of the participating cartel with selling syndicate ; (9) financial community of interests (Interessengemeinschaft) ; (10) the " voting "

course of time, as the result of strong integrating motives bringing the diffused interests together. Deficient organization and lack of co-operation on the commercial side of the industry were subjected to frequent attacks from different quarters. The first criticism came from the coal-owners themselves. The producers began to realize that " cut-throat " competition,[1] deficiently organized export, dumping, lack of full-capacity working, out-of-date methods of production, the mixture of small and large units in the same industry, the co-existence of modern and antiquated mines, perpetual labour troubles and demands for reform, constituted dangerous obstacles to the rehabilitation of the industry. The necessity for strengthening the fighting power of the British coal trade against substitutes which were supplanting coal in the home and foreign markets, the increased costs of production per ton of coal, the growing consolidation and concentration of labour, both in national and international spheres, the equalizing activity of the International Labour Office in matters referring to working conditions, the modernization of the coal industry in foreign countries, the appearance of new or more formidable competitors in the World markets (Germany, Poland, Holland), the steps taken by the League of Nations to appease the fuel war, the influence of Socialism, the rising tendency to combination and cartellization in other British industries, the growing capital concentration, and the greater dependence on borrowed capital by the industry—these are only some of the factors which fostered a greater desire for integration among the owners. To them

trust ; (11) exchange of shares ; (12) holding companies ; (13) consolidations or mergers (Committee on Industry and Trade, *Factors in Industrial and Commercial Efficiency*, being part i of a Survey of Industries, 1927, p. 71).

[1] Mr. John Hilton quotes the desire to limit competition as the only reason for the advance of combination. We do not entirely agree, especially in the case of the coal industry, with his argument, which runs: " Neither should it be supposed that the movement towards association and consolidation has been primarily animated by the thought of the great economic possibilities which combination opens out. The reasons given for the formation of particular combinations almost always turn upon the desire to limit competition or, as it is more usually expressed, ' to prevent cut-throat competition,' with the object of securing higher prices and larger profits " (*Report of Committee on Trusts*, 1919, Cmd. 9236, p. 16).

we may add the slow advance towards uniformity in methods of mining and preparing coal, accompanied by increasing mechanization, which tended to raise output to the maximum possible per man-shift per hour, and on the other hand to minimize the natural differences between the coal-fields. With the development of the science of mining, and with the advance of technique in the production and treatment of coal,[1] larger units were bound to emerge. Penetration into deeper and often irregular seams required a large capital investment which could be more easily secured by big companies, or combines.

Another impulse to combination came from the distributing side, which gradually improved its organization beyond that of the producing section, upon which, in consequence, it exerted a strong influence. Coal agencies control a large amount of coal. Such agents very often act as the only distributing centres of a number of collieries, and sell all their output, virtually allotting to them the amount of production which the agents feel able to dispose of in the market. In this capacity they perform the function of a cartel,[2] allotting productive quotas to its members. The size of these agencies may be gathered when we say that one of them, William Cory & Son, Ltd., shows a yearly sale of over 6 million tons,[3] which is substantially more than the output of many of the largest individual colliery undertakings. Such enormous units, which have considerable control over the market, are doubtless able to a great extent to ascertain future demand, and further

[1] As a good example of a complete union of interests in the coal by-product section, we may quote the formation of British Briquettes, Ltd., in which all the South Wales makers of patent fuel pooled their works and resources.

[2] In some cases even with the existence of coal cartels the distributing organization may perform the function of a cartel. An interesting example can be quoted from German practice. In 1897 the competition between the Rhenish-Westphalian Syndicate and the Upper Silesian Syndicate in the Berlin market became very pronounced. Thus the following way out was devised. The sales of Westphalian coal were entrusted to the well-known firm, Cæsar Wollheim, Ltd., which was distributing Silesian coal in the Berlin area, with the condition that it would allocate to both producing coal-fields the agreed proportions of coal. The arrangement was functioning up to the outbreak of the War.

[3] *The Times*, 28th May, 1931.

to equalize production by allowing their customer collieries to work at an even rate, as far as possible approaching their full capacity. We have already noted how anxious the colliery companies have always been to be able to work at an even rate. An example of this occurs in one of the South Wales coal export contracts.[1] One clause in the delivery section reads as follows : " The purchasers will provide tonnage to take delivery of the coal between the . . . and the . . . in as nearly as possible equal proportions per calendar month. Such delivery shall be f.o.b. at one of the following docks . . . as ordered by the Vendor before the ship's arrival." The variation of prices for household coal in winter and summer has the same end in view, viz : the spreading of purchases over the whole year, thus allowing the production of coal at a more even rate.

The coal industry owes its present organization to a whole complex of forces and causes, operating within different periods and with varying strength. We may distinguish here between those which prepared the way for the new structure imposed later by the State (in 1930), and those which gave the final impetus to its introduction. We shall first deal with spontaneous forces paving the way for reorganization. Under this head our classification is, however, different from that which has been adopted by some other authors [2] and which we consider inadequate for the purpose of our investigation.

---

[1] *The South Wales Coal Annual*, edited by A. P. Barnett and T. J. Beynon, Cardiff, 1933, p. 40.

[2] e.g. Mr. H. A. Marquand. The author explains the forces bringing about industrial integration by saying : " The chief motives which have led to the formation of combinations may, then, be classified as techno-logical and administrative ; commercial or strategic ; financial ; and personal " (*The Dynamics of Industrial Combination*, London, 1931).

Mr. W. J. Williams notices the following forces making for local or national unification of the coal industry. He puts in the first place the development of transport, and proceeds to say that " without a highly developed transport system a modern capitalist combine, with its wide and extending interests, could never function ". But in the opinion of this author (and rightly), the development of transport " generally leads to intense competition ". But Mr. Williams infers from this that " the only way the coal-owners can save themselves from the rigours of the price-cutting which ensues is by some form of agreement." This argument, however, seems erroneous. We cannot agree that the same reason can be working for disintegration and concentration at the same time. It is clearly illogical to quote the development of transport, which certainly

Integrating motives in the coal industry are to be found in different spheres, and may be divided into certain groups :—

(1) *Labour*, which was becoming better and better organized, not only on the national, but also on the international basis, influenced the industry's fabric to a very great extent. The influence of growing labour power was a strong incentive towards a higher degree of co-operation.[1]

The activity of the miners in all districts galvanized co-operation among the coal-owners, already associated for the purpose of wage bargaining. Such co-operation

was one of the forces destroying the combination of the Newcastle Vend, as assisting combination. That the later development of competitive price-cutting led to co-operation is a different matter. Competition of this sort is not the outcome only of the development of the transport system and the railways in particular. The further argument about the extension of the interest of great combines in the new railway system can be maintained. In our survey we have considered the development of transport together with the rise of competition, but can hardly agree to treat it as a force assisting unification, since what it does is to strengthen the centrifugal tendencies in the whole industry of the country.

As other influences working towards aggregation of collieries, Mr. Williams quotes " the present capitalist method of working the coal ", and the desire to save the " immense waste of resources caused by working different collieries under separate control . . .", though the author finds it necessary to add that " there is no need to emphasize, of course, that no capitalist combination is formed to save this coal for the nation because ", as he tells us, " capital's object is, not the conservation of national resources, but the accumulation of profits."

Other reasons given for concentration are : The " importance of foreign trade to the coal industry ", which may lead to the establishment of selling agencies for overseas trade ; next, the desire to secure economies possible under a large scale production and unified control. " But the real, vital force making for combination "—says the author—" is the possibility of influencing and controlling prices." Finally " a most potent cause of combination amongst capitalists in all industries is the necessity of resisting the demands of organized labour " (*Capitalist Combination in the Coal Industry*, London, 1924, pp. 75–82).

Mr. Arthur Robert Burns considers that " the most important forces making for the concentration of control are : (1) the desire to profit from the exploitation of improved methods of products involving operation on a large scale ; and (2) the desire to profit from the control of market prices . . . Of these two stimuli, the first . . . has increased in importance during the process of industrialization " [" The Process of Industrial Concentration," *Quarterly Journal of Economics*, vol. xlvii, No. 2, p. 277]. This division, in our view, though substantially right, seems however to be too broad for a critical examination of the different causes of integratory movement.

[1] *Vide* George R. Carter, *The Tendency towards Industrial Combination*, London, 1913, pp. 14 and 298.

tended to bring about a further degree of organization extending also to other purposes.[1] Generally the demand for higher wages and shorter hours stimulates to some extent a closer organization of the industry, provided that the increases of wages are uniform throughout the whole country, or throughout a sufficiently wide area. But in British coal, labour was not co-ordinated, and the haphazard demands here or there for higher wages probably had for a long time the reverse effect. But when the organization of the miners became consolidated, the owners were forced to combine. Professor J. B. Clark already noted that " a trust has this power of making larger concessions than competing employers, because it can make the public pay the bills." [2] Clark's view has been lately supported by Mr. Rowe in a somewhat changed form ; he considers that " modern trade unionism can probably control the supply price of labour for periods sufficiently long to produce a direct effect on the technique and organization of industry . . ." [3] It must be, however, made quite clear that in this respect organized labour can have some effect on organization, but only and exclusively when markets are expanding and the elasticity of demand for a fall operates very slowly. In the case of shrinking markets, neither Professor Clark's nor Mr. Rowe's proposition would hold good, because the elasticity of demand for a fall is the cause of the inelasticity of the substitution of capital for labour.

The miners themselves often realized that combination and monopoly could help them to get better wages. Thus on many occasions they demanded restriction of output and

[1] Professor D. H. Macgregor noted in his standard work about combination that " the process of formation is easier if there have been already opportunities for communication between the parties which combine. Such opportunities are furnished by Chambers of Commerce, by associations of masters with reference to the demands of labour . . ." (*Industrial Combination*, London, 1906, p. 123).

[2] John Bates Clark, *The Problem of Monopoly*, New York, 1904, pp. 65–6.

[3] J. W. F. Rowe, *Wages in Practice and Theory*, London, 1928. Referring to coal mining, the author says : " The rise in wages in the pre-War period was of course partly the result of the improved technique and the expansion in demand, but it also seems likely that in part the rise in wages was an active cause, and not merely a passive result, of the improved technique " (p. 218).

regulation of prices.   However, it is a notable illustration of the enormous division existing in the English coal industry that miners from export districts strongly opposed such proposals.[1]

In our view it is not only through high wages that the industry can be forced by labour to reorganize.   In the past such influence was achieved through the Joint Committees for the regulation of wages and employment, such as were set up in the second half of the last century,[2] in nearly all the districts.   These brought the owners into contact with each other, which often led to the formation of price regulation associations, or associations for the sharing of accident risks and payments of damages, and compensation under the Employers' Liability Acts.   Thus, soon after the passing of the Workmen's Compensation Act, 1897, the industry organized throughout the coal-fields Mutual Indemnity Associations, which occupy the place of insurance companies, leaving their profits in the hands of the industry.   In Yorkshire a successful institution of this kind is well known under the name of Yorkshire Coalowners' Mutual Indemnity Company.   At present, in every district except Lancashire such associations are in existence, and insure the owners against their liabilities under the Act, excepting only payments due in disablement cases in respect of the first six months.

(2) *Science* and the development of mining technique ; methods of utilizing, preparing, grading, screening coal, together with a larger and more scientific use of its by-products ; all the consequences of scientific management, rationalization, etc., a better use of the results of coal

[1] For details, see J. R. Raynes, *Coal and its Crisis*, London, 1928, pp. 46 and 72.

[2] A statement of one of such associations formed in the North-Eastern Coast in 1877, gives the following object for its activity : " That the object of the Joint Committee shall be to discuss all questions (except such as may be termed county questions, or questions affecting the general trade) relating to matters of wages, practices of working, or any other subject which may arise from time to time at any particular colliery, and which shall be referred to the consideration of the Committee by the parties concerned.   The Committee shall discuss all disputes and hear evidence, and their decision shall be final." (Extracted from the *Joint Committee Rules*, Steam Collieries Defence Association, March, 1877, Newcastle-upon-Tyne, reprinted, 1888.)

research ; the exchange of successful experiments between individuals ; the need for carrying on the work of common research institutes, stations, and coal laboratories ; the rising importance of public scientific congresses and meetings—must be all accounted as vitally contributing towards reorganization. Two aspects need particular consideration. First, simultaneously with the exhaustion of the easily accessible seams, and parallel with the progress of technique, the size of the working industrial unit must be gradually increased. The optimum size of the unit is being continuously raised, and a maximum limit has not yet been reached in the majority of cases. Hence arises the propensity towards concentration upon a lesser number of large and efficient collieries. Secondly, with the advance of efficiency and rationalization the significance of working the mines at fullest potential capacity becomes more pertinent. The heavy overhead charges must be kept low per unit of product to make a more advanced method of production worth while. Consequently, the tendency towards full capacity employment is greater in the new and well equipped districts like South Yorkshire than in the old ones. Analogously the districts with mixed mines, new and old, show a determination to work towards excluding the inefficient unit by means of combinations and subsequent closure, as has been done in some Scottish and Welsh coal-fields.

Modern progress in the methods of using coal and in the development of new appliances, enabling it to maintain its foothold in spite of extreme competition from substitutes, have led the coal-owners to co-operate closely in research and propaganda work. Recently created from inside the industry, the Coal Utilization Council is carrying out such research as is not undertaken by the Fuel Research Board.[1]

(3) *State activity* has been penetrating gradually deeper with its administrative machinery into practically all the functions of the coal industry and it was a strong stimulus to industrial consolidation. Statutory regulations intimately

[1] The first publication of the Coal Utilization Council, issued in May, 1933, dealt with practical suggestions for meeting competition from fuel oil for central heating.

controlling nearly all the vital activities of the industry ; the determination of the conditions in which the productive processes must be carried on and those which must be maintained in regard to employment ; assistance from Government authorities in securing competitive superiority in the export markets, and in official investigation of marketing possibilities for British coal in foreign countries ; [1] the direct assistance of the industry by State credit subsidies, or special bounties, were all factors of great importance in forwarding equalization within the industry and the extirpation of economic individualism.[2]

(4) A further incentive to concentration came from the *international side*. The Continental coal industries, enormous nationally organized units, were in keen competition with the scattered and unco-ordinated British industry in markets already shrinking. Again, Geneva had a certain influence. The International Labour Office, and the inquiries of the Economic Section of the League urging an international solution, plainly called attention to the lack of a national organization as a hindrance to further co-operation.

Moreover, large units are better able to obtain benefits from bargaining with other countries than small and competing companies. Since the War the direct supply of materials has become of considerable importance, and can only be handled on a satisfactory scale by large units. This applies to both purchases and sales ; for example, the Welsh colliery combinations purchased recently large supplies of timber directly from Portugal, Russia, France, and Newfoundland, securing considerable economies in their timbering costs.

(5) Next we may quote a whole series of forces working for a new order and originating this time from the side of *capital*. The growing concentration of capital, coupled with a greater dependence of the industry on capital borrowed from the banks, substantially assisted the movement. The productive processes, in time, need a greater

[1] In September, 1930, a British delegation of coal-owners and exporters, headed by the Secretary for Mines (Mr. Shinwell), studied the possibilities of enlarging the sales in Sweden, Norway, and Denmark.
[2] Cf. Pt. II, Chap. I, § 3.

amount of fixed capital in comparison with working capital, and therefore the proportion of the industry's own investments to those from external sources is smaller, and the amount of control by external capital over the organization is larger than before. On the other hand, during the depression part of the capital lent by the banks became " frozen assets " owing to the inability of many companies to meet their banking debts, which were gradually soaring from year to year. In this way the banks were willy-nilly forced, in order to save their money, to co-operate more closely with the industry, and to stimulate reorganization along the lines of efficient production.[1]

Strong banking interests urged the writing down of capital by the coal companies; this assisted combination and co-operation by bringing the nominal values of the individual units to their real basis, i.e. that which is able to secure a profit-taking close to the market rate of interest. Such a real basis, uniform for a whole section of the industry, is of great assistance in amalgamation.[2] Recently the banks forced some of the companies drastically to cut down their capital and debentures. So the Ebbw Vale Steel, Iron and Coal Company, Ltd., the largest bituminous concern in South Wales, wrote down its assets in 1932 to a considerable extent. A little later Pease and Partners, Ltd., a Durham company, reconstructed its capital; similarly the Scottish combine, the Lochgelly Iron and Coal Company, Ltd., owning all shares of the Kinneil Cannel and Coking Co., the Plean Colliery Co., and also controlling the Robert Forrester Co., Ltd., decided to deflate its capital in the same way.[3]

New investors would probably refuse to put money into

[1] Cf. " Banks and Industrial Reorganization," *The Statist*, vol. cxv, p. 1029, 31st May, 1930.
[2] Professor D. H. Macgregor holds a similar opinion when he says: " combination in its initial stages requires the help of capital; and the availability of capital strongly influences the facility of combination, especially when this is of the trust form. It is of less importance for cartels which maintain the ' pure ' structure, that is, in which the syndicate is entirely composed of the producers themselves; but becomes of importance to cartels also in proportion as they depart from this type and approximate to the trusts " (*Industrial Combination*, London, 1906, p. 124).
[3] Information from the *Manchester Guardian Commercial Supplement*, vol. xxv, 10th September, 1932.

an undertaking whose methods were inefficient or which was engaged in a dangerous competitive struggle. This capital inter-dependence helps penetration and intermixture of the interests of one district with those of another. Capital concentration breaks down the walls between areas and assists the interweaving of collieries of different districts in horizontal combination. The vertical combination was well established long before the War.[1] And so South Wales penetrated into Kent, Yorkshire into Leicester, South Yorkshire into North Wales, etc.

Capital concentration took place also in the form of holding company, though this kind of control of working, treating, and disposing of coal is not yet widely spread in this country.[2]

Capital concentration in other industries has also a bearing on the organization of the coal industry, since any increase in the size of the buying concern affects the seller. The larger and stronger the purchasers appearing on the market, the greater their power of dictating the terms of transactions.

(6) *Competition* between the different producers, accompanied by the certainty that they will be, in fact, unable to place all the potential supply of coal, must be looked upon as another powerful stimulus to reorganization, leading especially to cartellization. This competition forces the coal-owners to combine as a safeguard against the inroads of other owners, and usually results, in times of economic depression, in a headlong reduction of prices. This is carried on without consideration of the variations

[1] A good instance of such a firm whose interests were vertically combined long before the War is presented by the combine of John Brown & Co., Ltd. Originally established at Sheffield for the manufacturing of rolled and heavy steel products in the nineties of last century, it amalgamated with large engineering and shipbuilding interests in the Clyde Valley. It was then said about this Company that it was capable of undertaking processes " right from the extraction of raw materials to the construction of finished-vessels " (G. Carter).

[2] Lately a private holding company, the Bedlington and Associated Collieries (Holding Company), Ltd., has been formed with the capital of £100 for the purpose of acquiring the shares of the Bedlington Coal Co., Ltd., the Seghill Colliery, Ltd., and such other colliery undertakings as will vest in the company their control and management, with a view to the more economical and efficient working, treating, and disposal of coal (January, 1933).

in the elasticity of demand, but simply with the aim of capturing the available tenders. Forces tending to reorganization found therefore a good field for action in eliminating " ruinous competition " and introducing " more rational " methods of marketing.

(7) We have already referred to the existence of a higher degree of concentration in *distribution* of coal than in production, especially among the coal agents. This can be regarded as another reason for the progress of concentration in the production of coal. Indeed the industry tends to secure for itself any advantages which might be lost by disintegration. This does not mean that there is any attempt to eliminate middlemen, or to reorganize the basis of the coal trade, but simply that the industry aims at strengthening its own bargaining position in face of the coal merchants. The large profits of the distributing section are always looked upon with an envious gaze by the producers, who at the same time are often bearing heavy losses on their own economic activity.

The British colliery-owners had been brought up in a regime which always impressed upon them that the business of the producer is to extract and not to dispose of coal. But in the course of time they observed that those collieries which possessed their own selling agencies, as did a group [1] of Doncaster mines, operating under the name of Doncaster Collieries Association, were having better financial results. The commercial interests of several companies of South Yorkshire and Wales were similarly represented by the Carlton Collieries Association.[2] The Rotherham and District

[1] The following five collieries are members of the Doncaster Collieries Association : the Brodsworth, the Bullcroft, the Hickleton, the Markham Main, and the Yorkshire Main.

[2] The Carlton Collieries Association acts as the agent for three colliery companies of South Yorkshire, namely the Carlton Main Colliery Co., Ltd., the Hatfield Main Colliery Co., Ltd., the Hodroyd Coal Co., Ltd., and also for Llay Main Collieries, Ltd., of North Wales. The first of these companies, which was formed in 1872 as the Yorkshire and Derbyshire Coal and Iron Co., Ltd., owns directly three collieries in South Yorkshire : the Grimethorpe, the Frickley, and the South Elmsall. It controls also the Hodroyd Coal Co., through the ownership of its entire share capital ; the latter company operates two collieries—the Brierley and the Ferrymore. Moreover, the company possesses a large portion of the capital of the Llay Main Collieries, Ltd. In this way, as one can see, there is a

Collieries Association, Ltd., is based on similar lines. It is responsible for the distribution of over 5·6 million tons of coal yearly.[1] A vast number of large concerns have at the present moment their own selling departments and are independent of coal agents. Other combines possess a large share in the selling agencies disposing of their own coal and even have connections abroad. For instance, Guest, Keen, and Nettlefolds, Ltd., now forming part of the Welsh Associated Collieries, Ltd., have controlled since 1921 a coal exporting agency known as Gueret, Llewellyn, and Merrett, Ltd.; [2] the Powell Duffryn Company took over the old established firm of coal merchants, Stephenson, Clarke and Co., Ltd., in order to co-ordinate its selling policy.[3] In certain other large groups part of the output is sold by the colliery offices, and part is distributed through agents in London ; e.g. the Fife Coal Co., Ltd., the largest combine in Scotland, uses this method of selling a large part of its output through the office of William Cory and Sons, Ltd.

In addition to interests held in distributing agencies, the colliery companies are often largely interested in wagon

very close connection between all the companies forming the Association. Together the Association disposes of coal from seven collieries, to the amount of about 4·5 million tons, mined by 13,500 miners.

[1] The Rotherham and District Collieries Association, Ltd., represents the following companies : (1) John Brown and Co., Ltd. (Aldwarke and Rotherham Main Collieries) ; (2) the Dalton Main Collieries, Ltd. (Silverwood Colliery) ; (3) Stewart and Lloyds, Ltd. (Kilnhurst Collieries) ; (4) the Tinsley Park Colliery Co., Ltd. The Association represents also (5) the Rother Vale Collieries, a commercial branch of the United Steel Co., Ltd., embracing its coal undertakings with approximately 2 million tons of yearly output coming from the Treeton, Orgreave, and Thurncroft Main Collieries and (6) Samuel Fox and Co., Ltd., an associated company with the United Steel Co.

[2] Messrs. Gueret, Llewellyn, and Merrett, Ltd., are associated with the coal combine of Messrs. F. Haniel, of the Ruhr. In this connection it is interesting to point out that when the Irish Free State, under the leadership of Mr. de Valera, imposed restrictions upon British coal, German shipments were sent to Ireland by Messrs. Haniel, while after all part of the profits came indirectly to the Welsh Associated Collieries.

[3] In order to centralize and co-ordinate their sales of South Wales coal, the two distributing firms, William Cory and Son, Ltd., and Stephenson Clarke and Associated Companies, Ltd., formed a new company, Coal Distributors (South Wales), Ltd. From July, 1933, the new company acts as the sole selling agent of the Powell Duffryn group of mines. Moreover, it took over all South Wales and Monmouth coal trade which hitherto was carried on separately by the two firms. The capital of the new company, amounting to £50,000, is held in equal shares by each of the companies (16th June, 1933).

hiring companies, or wagon repairing companies, since wagon costs are an important item in marketing expenses.[1] This financial dependence is secured either by actual control of shares, or by interlocking directorates.

Since the small collieries cannot for obvious reasons afford to form on their own anything corresponding to a sales department, there arises the desire to pool the efforts of several collieries, or to increase the size of the units. This again is a direct incentive to aggregation.

Having now reviewed the forces making for spontaneous combination, we notice that, though numerous and powerful, they succeeded only very slowly and gradually in over-balancing the disintegrating elements. The first achievement was co-operation on a local basis. The movement soon spread to districts, and finally reached national dimensions in the critical year of 1928. Hence, we shall, in later sections, follow the integrating movement first in the district. We shall then trace its growth from one district to another, until units are seen to cover certain defined geograpical areas. Later, units reach from one end of the country to the other, and co-operation is seen on a national scale. Finally, forces making for international co-operation are discussed, and the economic forces governing the industry are seen to be nearly as powerful in this wider sphere as in the limited national field.

§ 2. THE DEVELOPMENT OF INTEGRATION

Gradually the integrating motives operating in the coal industry made it more advantageous for the individual

[1] e.g. John Brown and Co., Ltd., controls the majority of shares in Craven's Railway Carriage and Wagon Co., Ltd. (the *Stock Exchange Official Intelligence*, 1931, p. 1507). The shares of Wagon Repairs, Ltd., are in possession of different wagon companies, some of which again are controlled by colliery companies. It is accepted that all wagons owned by finance companies, collieries, hiring companies, etc., are worth about £40,000,000 (from *Iron and Coal Trades' Review*, 16th December, 1932).

producer to combine for certain purposes with others, and to carry on his productive activities on a collective basis than to work alone.   Such combinations of producers may be quite loose, embracing only the achievement of some selected common ends, but they may also be very close, binding the individuals very firmly, sometimes even to the extent of endangering their individuality altogether.   At one extreme we have the association of owners, at the other is the complete merger of two or more companies into a new combine.

The different degrees of mutual dependence of one unit upon another are determined by the purpose for which they combine.   Reviewing combination in the coal industry from this standpoint, we can find cases in which integration was the outcome of various economic aims.   Thus, to quote only a few examples, the coal-owners may be led by the desire for better financial results, expressed in the profits paid by the combination ;   or they may wish to serve their commercial ends more efficiently by having a large control over prices and output or over common purchases of materials ;   further, they may join together for the better achievement of technical possibilities, for instance common drainage schemes ;   or again they may be induced to combine in order to defend their professional rights, for instance against the excessive interference by the State, or local authorities.   Amongst further incentives we may notice the social motive, which leads the employers to oppose the demands of organized labour ;   the scientific motive, which pools together the efforts of the industrialists in the service of the improvement of the mining technique, or of the progress of safety.   However, it is often impossible in practice to draw a definite line of division between the aims of collective bodies of the coal-owners.   Usually, some or all of the above motives are at work.

Now that we have mentioned the existence of different ends for which integrations may occur in the coal industry, we must in turn call attention to the forms of organization in which these individual ends may be satisfied.   Beginning first with the more limited organization and proceeding towards the more comprehensive, we register first the joint stock company, leading to combines embracing some or all of the possible varieties : amalgamations, absorptions, trusts, etc. There are either sectional, district, and area organizations, or national organizations, which in certain cases participate in arrangements comprising more than the territory of the British Isles. We propose to discuss organizations according to their ramifications throughout the country and to deal in this section only with those combinations which do not exceed the boundaries of one mining area.

Only a few words need to be said about the joint stock limited companies, which have greatly increased in number and size since the beginning of this century.[1] In its origin British coal mining was developed by private enterprise, and for many centuries it remained in the hands of individuals or of family concerns.[2] Thus, for instance, the well known Newbattle Collieries of Midlothian remained in the hands of the Lothian family for 330 years without interruption until its conversion into a joint stock company in 1800.

In the first half of the nineteenth century, however, a

[1] The extensive development of joint stock companies in all fields of industrial enterprise is a feature of the twentieth century. The coal industry has naturally also participated in this movement. Attention has been called to it in *Britain's Industrial Future* in the following terms : " It is not always recognized how recent a development the joint stock company is as the dominant and characteristic type of business organization. The whole system is less than a hundred years old, and its present all-embracing growth has been an affair of the last twenty years consequent on the new legislation of 1908 " (*Britain's Industrial Future*, London, 1928, chap. vii, p. 84).

[2] Professor J. V. Nef, of Chicago, whose enormous and well-documented treatise on the early history of the British coal industry has recently appeared, refers to this subject in the following terms : " Of joint stock enterprise in our restricted sense, there are, we repeat, few cases in connection with the early coal industry . . . the circumstances under which they do appear suggest why it was that this particular form of association spread less rapidly through the English than through the French coalfields, which began to be exploited much later. We have found no record of joint stock enterprise in connection with the British collieries until the very end of the seventeenth century ; and then this form of ownership was adopted chiefly as a means of financing the carriage of coal from newly exploited mines in competition with the output of districts which had hitherto monopolized the market. The first joint stock company of which we have a record was organized in London between 1688 and 1692, under the title of the ' Blyth Coal Company ' " (*The Rise of the British Coal Industry*, London, 1932, vol. ii, p. 45).

new process began to develop, that is the gradual admission of a large number of partners, a process which led ultimately to the rise of joint stock companies in the British coal industry. As mining operations increased in size and significance, more capital was required, and the actual coal-owners had to enlarge the circle of people through whom they financed production. This led to the development of extensive partnership in the industry, which was beginning to grow rapidly in the second half of the nineteenth century. After the passing of the Companies Act of 1856, the progress of the limited liability companies was also rapid. This change in the structure of coal companies in this country is of importance since it is one of the necessary preliminaries to amalgamation. Moreover, this form of undertaking facilitated the access of the industry to the best source of fresh external capital necessary for investment.

The advance of the joint stock company in the coal industry is best illustrated in the following table.

TABLE No. 28 [1]

COAL AND IRON MINES COMPANIES REGISTERED, 1856–1880

Years.			"Effective."		"Abortive."
1856–1859 [2]	.	.	40 ⎫		
1860–1862	.	.	25 ⎬ 161		64
1863–1865	.	.	96 ⎭		
1866–1868	.	.	69 ⎫		
1869–1871	.	.	60 ⎬ 400		90
1872–1874	.	.	271 ⎭		
1875–1877	.	.	81 ⎫ 114		39 [3]
1878–1880	.	.	33 ⎭		

At the present moment the great majority of large and modern collieries are already concentrated in the hands of joint stock limited companies.

From what has been said so far we may conclude that, to-day, the division between the private companies and the joint stock companies is of historical and formal interest

[1] Table 28 contains figures from the official registers at Somerset House so far unpublished. They have been provided owing to the kindness of Mr. H. A. Shannon.
[2] From July, 1856.
[3] In addition to 114 companies *publicly* formed and effective, 55 *private* companies were effectively formed.

rather than economic in so far as the concentration movement is concerned. The chief difference is in the formation of the private company which does not look outside for capital, while the public company requires external financing; hence in a private company there is to some extent a tendency to undervaluation of assets, and in a public company towards watering the capital.

For our purpose we can already assume that the joint stock company is the lowest unit in the structure of industry; we can treat it for practical purposes on an equal footing with other companies which form the substratum of combinations of higher order. Thus, we may now proceed straight forward to the discussion of the concentration movement in the coal industry.

Concentration was going on continually in the British coal industry. It took place in two ways; first of all, the average size of the unit increased as time went on, and secondly, production came under the control of a smaller number of units. In 1875, the number of collieries equalled 4,933, producing together 131,000,000 tons of coal, whereas, in 1930, only 2,382 mines at work produced 244,000,000 tons. Generally speaking, the average output per mine rose during these 55 years about four times. But this process is continually going on,[1] and seems far from ultimate completion. In Britain the optimum size of mines is at present still much larger than the actual size.[2] For a shorter period, figures illustrating the physical concentration of production are included in the North-East Coast Industrial Survey. They indicate that whereas, in 1913, the number of mines at work was 433, with an average output of 130,000 tons each, in 1930 there were only 345 mines, each producing 142,000 tons. If one considers that generally in 1913 the whole industry was working at a greater rate of capacity than in 1930, the figures just quoted are even more expressive, A similar intensification of output was taking place also in the other leading coal-fields in the country. Thus, for instance, in South Wales and Monmouthshire

[1] *Vide* Part I, Chap. I.
[2] *Report of the Royal Commission on the Coal Industry* (1925), vol. i, Cmd. 2600, chap. v.

the number of collieries amounted in 1894 to 537, while in 1927 it fell to 470 and, in the same period, output rose by 30 per cent.

The inevitable nexus between the physical expansion of the producing unit and the demand for fresh capital investments meant naturally a vast expansion of the latter.[1] Moreover, the growing significance of coal for all industrial processes, which was permanently rising during the whole course of the past century, encouraged capital to take a new interest in coal-mining. All the three causes mentioned, viz. the growth of the mines, new investment, and the interest of other industries in coal resulted in quickening the concentration of the coal industry in fewer hands.

It is almost impossible to say whether horizontal or vertical integration developed first, for while the horizontal combine was less conspicuous, and continually spreading, the vertical type was much more striking to the eye, because it was carried through between units which were already very considerable, and desired to control the prices of their raw materials. Thus we cannot agree with Mr. Williams,[2] who seems to argue that in the coal industry the main concentrative tendency was in a horizontal direction, and that "there is no great incentive for a colliery amalgamation to develop along vertical lines ". But Mr. Williams necessarily contradicts himself only a few pages later, when he gives the history of the origin of the main combines in the industry, from which one sees that the great majority of the oldest combines involving coal were of the vertical type.

Let us quote a few examples. The Ebbw Vale Steel, Iron, and Coal, Co., the largest bituminous coal concern in South Wales, was established in 1864. It was a mixed concern for the production of pig-iron and finished iron,

---

[1] Mr. D. J. Williams rightly called attention to the increasing dependence between the new methods of mining and the requirement for fresh capital. " A revolution in the technical structure of any industry calls forth a corresponding revolution in its economic organization. This was the case in the coal industry in the nineteenth century. The new mechanical devices cost a great deal of money ; and the successful pursuit of coal mining required ever-increasing amounts of capital " (*Capitalist Combination in the Coal Industry*, London, 1924, p. 91).

[2] Op. cit., p. 93.

steel, and coal, and purchased the properties of one of the members of the well-known Coalbrookdale family. There were also the Tredegar Iron and Coal Co., Ltd., and many others.[1]

[1] The Tredegar Iron and Coal Co., Ltd., was established in 1873 in Monmouthshire, and constituted a well-developed vertical concern. The history of the origin of the company is sketched in the following words by Lord Aberconway, its present chairman : " The Tredegar Works were started at the end of the eighteenth century by Samuel Homfray (of Liverpool) and W. Forman, who built the first furnace in the Sirhowy Valley and ran a coal level in 1799 ; but there are records of work by a level in 1750, which was restruck in 1796. Pits were sunk there in 1806, and at various periods during the last century. The Tytrist Colliery, sunk in 1841, and the Bedwelty, sunk in 1850, are still at work. Trevethick built a high-pressure steam locomotive in 1801, which was worked over the Tredegar tramway for more than half a century. In 1873, the present Tredegar Iron and Coal Co. bought the ironworks and mineral property, reorganizing both the mines and the iron works. The Pochin pits, named after Henry Davies Pochin, one of the founders of the Company, were sunk in 1880. . . . The Company established before the War the McLaren, the Oakdale, and the Markham Collieries, and has recently sunk the Wyll Colliery at the lower end of the valley. The capital was in each case found by the parent company from its reserves " (The Rt. Hon. Lord Aberconway, *The Basic Industries of Great Britain*, London, 1927, p. 271).

Some other examples of vertical combinations : The Sheepbridge Coal and Iron Co. presided over to-day also by Lord Aberconway, provides another example of an early vertical combination operating collieries in Derbyshire, Notts, South Yorkshire, and taking its ironstone supplies from Northamptonshire and Rutland. The Sheepbridge Ironworks include blast furnaces, foundries, and a forge (op. cit., p. 39). The present group was formed into a limited company in 1864 by the same capitalists who controlled the Staveley property. The Sheepbridge Coal and Iron Co. is interested to-day in the Rossington Main Colliery Co., which was promoted jointly with John Brown and Co., and constitutes, at present, part of the newly-formed group of Yorkshire Amalgamated Collieries, Ltd. Another example of an early and very extensive combine is John Brown and Co., Ltd., founded in 1864, originally of Sheffield ; since the War it has expanded, and is also under the chairmanship of Lord Aberconway. By 1890 the combine had begun to purchase vast interests in different stages of production, including iron-ore in Lincolnshire and Northamptonshire and in Spain, as well as several collieries. Before the War, Mr. George Carter wrote that the firm of John Brown and Co. was " in a position to build and equip throughout, without the assistance of outside firms, the largest battleship or the fastest liner ". The firm is amalgamated and connected with a large number of subsidiary undertakings (*The Tendency towards Industrial Combination*, London, 1912, p. 82).

In Durham, amongst other early vertical concerns connected with coal, a prominent position is occupied by Pease and Partners, Ltd. The founders of the firm were of great influence in the development of the British railway system. One of them, Edward Pease, formed in 1824, together with George and Robert Stephenson and Michael Longridge, a company to build locomotives. In 1898, the combine was considerably enlarged, and became interested in coal, coke, ironstone, and limestone. Later, important additions both in size and in scope were made by this firm.

As an early example of a vertical combination stands the Redbourn

The old manufacturing district of Lancashire provides several examples of early vertical combination of coal, iron, and steel undertakings.[1] Some of the present pure colliery concerns started their history as mixed undertakings, vertically combining various stages of production. Thus, for instance, North's Navigation Collieries (1889), Ltd., were started originally as a vertical combine, formed in 1872 under the name of Llynvi Tondu and Ogmore Coal and Iron Co.

These few examples, which certainly do not exhaust the long list of capital concentration in combines including coal, are sufficient to show that the early vertical concentration was just as prominent, (if not even more pronounced), as the horizontal combination illustrated by such firms as the Fife Coal Co., Ltd., of Scotland established in 1872, or the Powell Duffryn Steam Coal Co. of South Wales started in 1864, which has remained throughout a pure horizontal combine, and has retained this character even after the War. To-day the latter is one of the largest units in the country capable of producing 5–6 million tons of steam and other coal. It is at present out of " the big Five " of South Wales, together with the Welsh Associated Collieries, Ltd., the Amalgamated Anthracite Collieries, Ltd., the Ocean Coal Co., Ltd., and the Ebbw Vale Steel, Iron, and Coal Co. On the North-East Coast a significant horizontal combine was controlled by the Joicey family (which was in 1886 transformed into a limited company under the name of James Joicey & Co., Ltd.). Later the

Hill Iron and Coal Co., created in 1872 in Lincolnshire to produce steel. The company had substantially increased in size until after the War it was absorbed by Richard Thomas and Co., of South Wales, the largest tinplate makers in this country.

[1] Among these was the Wigan Coal and Iron Co., which dates back to 1865, i.e. when the properties of John Lancaster were combined with the interests of Lord Lindsay, the owner of the Haigh Colliery (cf. Lord Aberconway, op. cit., p. 113).

Another noteworthy vertical concern in Lancashire is the Pearson and Knowles Coal and Iron Co., formed in 1874 near Wigan. The company acquired first two private concerns ; those of George Pearson and of Thomas Knowles. Later, important additions and development work were carried on. Recently the trading of the coal department of this firm has been merged with the Wigan Coal and Iron Co., Ltd., to form the Wigan Coal Corporation, Ltd., with a potential annual output of 3 million tons.

company was associated with the Lambton Collieries, Ltd., responsible to-day for about 5 milion tons of potential output. This company is one of the best examples of amalgamation in that period.

All this early movement towards the reconstruction and enlargement of capital, some illustrations of which we have quoted above, was clearly developing both vertically and horizontally. Moreover, it is important to notice that this first wave of capitalist combination in the British coal industry, which was chiefly developing between the years 1864 and 1873, was taking place chiefly during the end of a period when prices were generally rising, and coal prices in particular went up. These circumstances greatly facilitated the formation of new companies and the amalgamation of the existing ones.[1] This was frequently done at the expense of highly inflated assets, as the projects of the promotors seemed profitable in times of rising prices. The beginning of the crisis, which as usual started first in the higher stages of production, stopped the amalgamation movement for nearly fifteen years. In this respect the situation was somewhat parallel to the post-War position when, during the period of high prices of coal, i.e. up to 1921, many amalgamations were carried on and subsequently the process was stopped for several years.[2]

The early amalgamations developed at first within the boundaries of one valley or one district. Initially the tendency was to expand in the immediate neighbourhood. Groups of collieries are formed and they embrace the nearest mines, where local and technical conditions are similar. Especially in South Wales and Scotland this is a well-defined tendency. In this way the district became an extremely important stage in the development of integration. It combined similar interests which could easily be opposed

[1] Between 1870–4, owing to cheap money supplies and other circumstances, a record number of new coal companies were formed (cf. Willand Long Thorp, *Business Annals*, New York, 1926, p. 167). However, a certain number of joint stock companies formed in this period did not represent any progress of integration, but merely a change in the legal form of their undertakings, which facilitated the transfer of shares and reduced the liability of the owners.

[2] Cf. *Business Annals*, pp. 167–171.

to the interests of other districts.   The *district* as a unit was an important step in the national organization of the industry.

To-day nearly all the districts have formed their *district associations* to co-operate in matters common to all, or to oppose the demands of labour, which was also becoming rapidly organized on a district basis. It would be outside the scope of this work to describe the history of each individual coal-owners' association in the country. These number twenty-five, and are concentrated to-day in the Mining Association of Great Britain. In the majority of the districts these organizations were formed in the seventies of the last century. The Midland Counties Colliery Owners' Association was formed in 1874 by the owners of Derbyshire and Nottinghamshire ; the Durham Coal Owners' Association was established to deal with wages in 1871 ; in Northumberland an organization called The Steam Collieries Association goes back to 1852 and dealt with both prices and wages, but the present Northumberland Coal-owners' Association was formed in 1871. In Scotland, also, most of these organizations were established in the seventies.[1]

The formation of the District Association has facilitated a further advancement of mutual co-operation among the coal-owners in the district, and helped to create some kind of *esprit de corps.* On several occasions the Association has rendered great services to its members by providing them with opportunities of discussing technical matters and commercial problems, and not seldom of making arrangements as to prices.

The second great wave of concentration came about at the end of the nineteenth century and at the very beginning of the twentieth, when several considerable amalgamations and combinations were carried through. This period witnessed the birth of United Collieries, Ltd., in Scotland, the powerful Welsh combine known as the Cambrian Group, headed by Lord Rhondda, another Welsh consolidation,

[1] Information from W. A. Lee, " History of Organization in the Coal Industry," in the *Historical Review of Coal Mining*, London, 1924, and J. R. Richardson, *Industrial Relations in Great Britain*, Geneva (International Labour Office), 1933.

Baldwins, Ltd., Guest, Keen, and Nettlefolds Co., Ltd., of South Staffordshire associated since 1930 with Welsh Associated Collieries, Ltd., and many others. But even in this second period of concentration there was still a strong tendency towards the combination of undertakings within the same district. Although in some cases the interests of the concern outgrew the boundaries of a district, these were the exception rather than the rule. Just before the War came another short spell of amalgamation progress. The chief result was the consolidation of already existing units, and the further absorption of small companies by the larger. Amalgamation of giants came at a later stage. Gradually, however, the financial concentration of undertakings was growing beyond the district limits. First it concentrated on a geographically larger unit embracing the neighbouring districts, and now we find units which reach from one end of the country to the other.

The War witnessed an enormous expansion of the capital of many colliery undertakings, a fact which later acted as a deterrent to amalgamation. Owing to strict control during the War, and to the fixed profits of the entrepreneurs, there was not any special incentive to carry out extensive amalgamations. But immediately after the War, when prices, and chiefly export prices, began to soar higher and higher, many concentrations took place in the industry. These were proceeding steadily up to 1921, i.e. to the moment when prices suddenly collapsed. From this time the concentration movement has been greatly retarded.[1] Except two consolidations in the Welsh anthracite coalfield, the Amalgamated Anthracite Collieries, controlling at present 75 per cent of the output, and the United Anthracite Collieries, Ltd., formed in 1923 under the chairmanship of Sir F. A. Szarvasy, who is the present Chairman of the reconstructed Amalgamated Anthracite Collieries, Ltd., concentration advanced very little. The Powell Duffryn Co., Ltd., absorbed the Windsor Coal Co., while Pearson

[1] Cf. *Report of the Royal Commission of the Coal Industry* (1925), Minutes of Evidence, p. 972, Q. 15896.

and Dorman Long, Ltd., made some advance in Kent, where a treasury guarantee of £2 million granted in February, 1926, under the Trade Facilities Act, assisted them in the development of this new coal-field.

In addition to this amalgamation movement, certain groups of collieries in Yorkshire began to pool their interests together for the purpose of forming selling agencies. The best example of such co-operation is the Markham Group of collieries, operating under the name of Doncaster Associated Collieries, Ltd.

A new wave of concentration came again a few years later between 1927–1930. This was partly due to the great emphasis laid upon amalgamation by the Royal Commission on Coal, 1925, which regarded this expedient as a means of reducing the costs of production, a desideratum extremely important in a period of acute depression and severe competition for markets. The integration, however, which was proceeding during this latest period was of a different type from the previous ones. It was not a series of absorptions of smaller undertakings, or an enlargement of the already existing units, but rather a consolidation of existing interests aiming at a more scientific management of the whole industry. The spontaneous movement was to some extent, though not very considerably, stimulated by State assistance in the form of amalgamation clauses in the Mining Industry Act, 1926. But of the great majority which were carried through, only a few needed to be submitted to the Railway and Canal Commission, which was empowered by the Act to assist the whole procedure connected with amalgamations carried out under authority of the Government.[1] This went to show that only voluntary arrangements were of lasting value and that they alone could change the structure of the industry.

Between 1920 and 1928, a considerable increase in the size of the units was noticeable. They covered in the period as much as 172 pits normally employing 126,000 workpeople and comprised 17 separate schemes, subsequently further reduced to 14 by the amalgamation of the South Wales

[1] *Vide* Part II, Chap. I, para. 3.

Anthracite groups.[1] Of all these schemes only three were submitted to the Railway and Canal Commission for approval. Among the new concerns formed in this period are the Powell Duffryn Colliery Co., Ltd.[2] The new company secured in all 36 pits employing 25,100 workmen. The next largest amalgamations were Ocean Coal and Wilson's, Ltd., the Carlton Collieries Association, the Yorkshire Amalgamated Collieries, Ltd., both in South Yorkshire, and the Amalgamated Anthracite Collieries, Ltd., in the Swansea Area. As we can see, all these new big amalgamations were kept within the boundaries of one area, and combined the local coal interests. The last named anthracite group was formed out of the Amalgamated Anthracite Collieries, Ltd., and the United Anthracite Collieries, Ltd.; it controls 80 per cent of the output in South Wales. The amalgamation movement in 1927–8 was chiefly confined to South Yorkshire and South Wales. During the more prosperous year 1929 fewer amalgamations took place. They comprised, however, six schemes affecting sixty-one pits normally employing 43,760 workers.[3] By far the most important of these is the Manchester Collieries, Ltd., comprising ten independent colliery companies of Lancashire owning together twenty-two pits with 19,000 workpeople. The capital of the combine amounts to over £5,000,000.

At the end of the year 1929 and in 1930 two very important regroupings took place, the vertical combines resulting in the disconnection of coal mining from other interests. Thus, in South Wales the coal interests of Guest, Keen, and Nettlefolds, Ltd., were merged with the Welsh Associated Collieries, while at the same time all other plants of Guest, Keen, and Nettlefolds, Ltd., were combined with Baldwins, Ltd., into the British (Guest, Keen, Baldwins) Iron and Steel Co. In this way the Welsh Associated Collieries, Ltd., control at present sixty pits

[1] *Report of the Board of Trade*, § 12, on the Working of the Act, 1928, Cmd. 3214.
[2] The new concern united the Powell Duffryn Steam Coal Co., the Great Western Colliery Co., the Lewis Merthyr Consolidated Colliery Co., the Cardiff Collieries Co., the Taff Rhondda Navigation Steam Coal Co.
[3] Cmd. 3454/1929.

employing normally 32,000 men,[1] and are capable of producing 9 million tons of coal. Moreover, this concern, controls the sales and export agency, Gueret, Llewellyn, and Merrett, Ltd., and in addition it owns about 25,000 wagons.

A similar reorganization of coal, iron, and steel interests took place in Lancashire, where under the title of the Wigan Coal Corporation, Ltd., the coal mines of the Wigan Coal and Iron Co., Ltd., of Pearson and Knowles Coal and Iron, Ltd., of Moss Hall Coal Co., Ltd., and of the Wigan Junction Colliery, Ltd., were fused,[2] while the separated iron and steel undertakings were voluntarily combined into the Lancashire Steel Corporation, Ltd., which in turn is connected with Armstrong's. All this regrouping was carried out under the patronage of the Bank of England, which, through its subsidiary, the Securities Management Trust, Ltd., in co-operation with the " City ", financed the reorganization to the amount of £2,000,000. The directors of the concern, which is the subsidiary of the Lancashire Steel Corporation, Ltd., are nominated by the Governor of the Bank of England. The Wigan Coal Corporation possesses seventeen pits employing normally 10,000 workmen, and has a capital of about £750,000. Together with Manchester Collieries, Ltd., and the three smaller amalgamations all formed after 1929,[3] approximately half of the output of the district is in their hands. This rapid concentration led some people to consider a complete merger of all the undertakings in the Lancashire and Cheshire district into one. But this somewhat artificial plan, leaving out of consideration economic realities, failed owing to the substantial differences between the undertakings, which are mostly small, and number over 100 in all.[4] Also some of these concerns are bound vertically

[1] Cmd. 3743/1930.
[2] In 1933, it has been decided by the Pearson and Knowles Coal and Iron Co. to liquidate its subsidiaries, the Moss Hall Coal Co. and the Wigan Junction Coal Co., whose assets consisted of investments in the shares of the Lancashire Steel Corporation and the Wigan Coal Corporation (*The Times*, 1st April, 1933).
[3] *An Industrial Survey of the Lancashire Area (excluding Merseyside)*, London, 1932, p. 162.
[4] Ibid., p. 170.

with iron and steel interests, and thus possess a market of their own.

Altogether in 1930 only three amalgamations were effected. In addition to the two already mentioned, a smaller amalgamation was carried out in South Yorkshire combining the interests of Newton Chambers and Co., Ltd., with those of Hoyland Silkstone Coal and Coke, Ltd.

During the three years 1931, 1932 and 1933 very few amalgamations were carried out, in spite of strong pressure from the Coal Mines Reorganization Commission, which advocated large concentrations involving all the undertakings in any one district.[1] The most important of all the new combines formed in 1931 is the Bairds and Dalmelington Co., Ltd., composed of two Ayrshire companies possessing together twenty-four pits employing about 7,000 workmen. A significant attempt to combine all the companies in the Fifeshire coal-field, in Cannock Chase, North Wales, and other districts, was undertaken by the Reorganization Commission towards the end of 1932 and in 1933. Under the Coal Mines Act, 1930, all the companies in Fifeshire were officially invited to submit a scheme of amalgamation to the Board of Trade.[2] Such enormous concentration was endorsed by Mr. A. Carlow, the managing director of the Fife Coal Co., who, in an address to the Mining Institute of Scotland, explained the expected advantages accruing from an extensive grouping of all the collieries within one natural coal-field.[3]

From this very short *aperçu* of the concentration movement in the British coal industry, we notice that even in later years the district is still the dominant boundary for amalgamation, and is only exceeded in exceptional circumstances. In all districts, leading companies control a large proportion of the total output, but usually these leading units have few interests in other coal-fields. On the other hand, the biggest concerns in the various areas are often connected together by means of interlocking

[1] *Vide* Coal Mines Reorganization Commission, *Memorandum on Colliery Amalgamations*, London, 1931, p. 22.
[2] *The Times*, 21st November, 1932.
[3] *Edinburgh Evening Dispatch*, 1st September, 1932.

directorates, which is usually the effect of the penetration of capital coming from one source into several coal-fields.

The great significance which the district had acquired, even before the War, as a stage in the organization of the industry has been still further magnified during and after the War. During the period of Control the district constituted a unit in itself, which was endowed with important administrative duties in the industry. Moreover, the zoning of sales by means of the Railway Traffic Scheme during the War emphasized the significance of the district as a separate unit. After the War three events accentuated still further the district principle of organization.

First, the method of paying wages, brought about in spring, 1921, and developed in 1924, which introduced uniform wage advances for the whole country, was revised after 1926, and the district method restored. Moreover, the principle that in profit-sharing schemes for labour in the district the results of all collieries are taken into account, has to some extent the effect of equalizing the disparities between the collieries in the district, since this system of wage calculation gradually affects the marginal collieries, i.e. those showing lower profits or greater losses than the average. The effect of this equalization can be best seen in a period when the average firm in the industry shows profits. This leads to an increase in wages, leaving the inefficient units in a comparatively worse position.

Secondly, the district principle of organization has been emphasized by the way in which the Government paid subsidies to the industry. This again was through an organization somewhat similar to the machinery of district wage ascertainment. It must be remembered that the subsidy paid to cover the losses of the industry was not granted to each undertaking separately, but the total was paid over to the district. The Fifth Report of the Secretary for Mines [1] gives a short account of this method of paying the subsidy, where we read : " It will be seen, therefore, that within each district all collieries were treated alike. Their

[1] *Fifth Annual Report of Secretary for Mines for year ended* 31st *December,* 1925, p. 10.

relative economic positions remained undisturbed. In this respect each district was treated as a single unit, and no question arose as to the actual trading results of any individual concern. Since the measure of Subvention in every case depended upon the trading results of the district as a whole, and upon the results of a previous period, it was impossible for any particular colliery to reduce its prices at the expense of the Exchequer."

Thirdly, a most conspicuous illustration of the district principle of organization occurred after the War, in the voluntary district schemes for the regulation of production.[1]

When the crisis in the higher stages of production began to be noticeable, i.e. since 1923, attempts were made to regulate output. But only when faced by greater difficulties

---

[1] Since the collapse of the Vend, no temporary agreements covering production had been heard of in Great Britain. Apart from some few attempts or some short-lived schemes, there were no important cartels of coal-owners which had any influence on the development of the industry. Yet numerous attempts were undertaken in the past, either by influential entrepreneurs like Elliot, Lord Rhondda, and others, or by the representatives of the workers. These efforts usually coincided with lean times in the industry. Here we may add that already the well-known Limitation of Vend operating in the eighteenth and nineteenth centuries on the North-East Coast applied the district principle to the combination of coal-owners.

The principles on which the Vend was founded were explained before the Committee on the Coal Trade, 1800, by Nathaniel Clayton, Town Clerk of Newcastle. (Question) : " In addition to those causes, did you ever hear of any agreement subsisting among the Coal-owners, calculated to preclude the natural effect of the difference of the circumstances and situation of the collieries upon the Tyne ? (Questions of new and old mines)—I have not only heard, but I am certain that from time to time there has existed an agreement among the Coal-owners (which they call regulations), but I am not able to judge whether such agreement is an additional cause or has the effect alluded to in the question : I will state as much as I know of that agreement : I understand that the Coal-owners and Coal-workers meet together and take an account of the general Vend of coals for a stated time, generally for a year ; they add to this quantity a large quantity, probably one-half, probably more ; they then divide this aggregate quantity amongst all the collieries upon the river, allotting to each colliery a certain proportion of that aggregate quantity, according to the powers of working and other circumstances attendant upon each respective colliery. The actual vend of the stated period, when ascertained, is distributed amongst the collieries in like manner, each part of the actual vend bearing the same proportion to the actual vend as the allotted part bore to the original quantity taken as a basis of the vend. I understand that those collieries which have in the course of the year sold more than their allotted quantities, pay to those collieries who have sold less a certain allowance per chaldron, but what it is I do not know." (Committee on the Coal Trade, 1800 ; evidence 19° die Martii 1800.)

were district schemes finally realized in the critical year 1928. Early in 1926, Mr. Frank Hodges, the Secretary of the Miners' International Federation, pleaded before the Royal Commission for the introduction of a co-ordinating selling scheme on the lines of the ten German syndicates with the central Reichskohlenverband in command.   During April, 1926, a new scheme of coal export syndicates was launched by the late Sir Alfred Mond (Lord Melchett), to which the *Economist* [1] refers in the following terms :—

> "During the past week, the Hodges proposal has been revived by Sir Alfred Mond. He has been advocating the creation both of a national selling agency and area selling agencies. He has expressed the view that what is practicable in the Ruhr is practicable also in the United Kingdom. He has urged that the exporting districts should take the matter immediately in hand, and has expressed the view that a workable scheme could be arranged within a few months.   In coal trade circles the Mond scheme has not received serious consideration, and Sir Alfred's intervention is resented more than it is appreciated. . . . Still it is admitted there are brief periods under conditions of depressed trade when there is undercutting of prices between colliery salesmen and middlemen. The brunt of this competition in recent years has been borne by the colliery companies. . . . From time to time efforts have been made to eliminate this inter-competition. In the South Wales coal-field, for instance, schedules of prices have been arranged, and also weekly consultative meetings of colliery salesmen have been held, with the object of maintaining minimum prices, but these schemes have all failed in their purpose."

South Wales was the first district to produce a workable scheme for the stabilization of prices and later for the regulation of output. This district produced three schemes, of which only two were ever actually in operation. In the spring of 1927 the Welsh coal-owners had realized that further competition at home and abroad meant an over-proportionate fall of prices. This led some industrialists to open conversations as to the introduction of a workable scheme, but enormous difficulties were encountered in securing sufficient support.

[1] "Central Coal Selling Agencies," the *Economist*, 24th April, 1926, p. 822.

The first of these schemes was started in November, 1927. By a majority of 80 per cent the colliery owners formed a *South Wales Coal Marketing Association*, with the object of "steadying the market and stabilizing prices". All collieries belonging to the Association were classified into groups, according to the description and grading of coal produced. Then minimum price schedules were drafted, below which members were forbidden to quote, finally a levy of 3*d.* per ton of coal produced was charged to the general pool to compensate those producers who were losing trade through observing the minimum prices, as was the case in the steam coal trade. The scheme did not come into operation till April, 1928. According to the statutes of the Association, all owners were eligible for membership except (*a*) the collieries employing less than fifty men ; (*b*) any colliery which had not raised coal since December, 1927, until coal is raised for at least four weeks and sold ; (*c*) any colliery permanently closed down. The purpose of this exclusion was to discourage the small and inefficient mines from starting production on account of the Association, which paid compensation for any loss of trade out of the common fund. But in no case was compensation to be paid for loss of trade caused by strikes, lockouts, disputes, accidents, breakage of machinery, etc. This provision resembles very closely a section of the new compulsory Welsh scheme. The amount of compensation depended on the size of the compensation fund derived from levies on output. This fund was periodically divided between the so-called compensatable tonnage. For the purpose of fixing prices, the collieries were divided into groups according to the description of coal produced, and Group Committees were formed to recommend minimum prices to the Executive Committee. The recommendations that the minimum prices should not be so high as to reduce the volume of trade, and that the gross proceeds from such prices should not exceed average cost, was of great significance. That again was an advanced clause aiming at the exclusion of extramarginal mines. Selling below minima was penalized at 2*s.* per defaulted ton. The effect of this first Welsh scheme was somewhat to steady the price, but, in view of the competition from other districts and from the unassociated owners, the scheme had soon to be remodelled to include regulation of output and methods of dealing with dissentient owners.

After January, 1929, the South Wales Coal Marketing Association decided to change its methods and restrict the output by means of quotas, and a scheme was launched. But this second scheme never commanded a sufficient majority of the owners to be carried through. In the meantime the scheme in force could not be fully operated, and since the beginning of May, 1929, minimum prices were observed for steam coal only.

Finally, in the autumn of 1929 a third scheme was drafted. The objects were as follows :—

1. " To regulate output according to the demand for coal." [1]

[1] The scheme regulated the output in the following manner : Each company was entitled to choose any of the six quarters preceding 30th June, 1929, or the month of March, 1929, adjusted to a quarterly basis, for the purpose of ascertaining the conventional output. The newly-opened collieries, as well as those which were extending production before 1929 by development of their mines, together with those collieries which, owing to technical difficulties during the period aforesaid, or other breaks, or stoppages, were working below normal, were all subject to special provisions in ascertaining past production.

In regulating the output, the Executive Committee of the S.W.C.M.A. had to fix, according to the state of the market for each class of members and of coal produced, a percentage of their total conventional output, to be known as the total annual quota, equal for all the members of the same class and the same description of coal. This total annual quota was equally divided into the four quarters of the year, and formed a sort of minimum guaranteed output allocated to the collieries for the whole year. Moreover, the scheme provided for additional correctives to the quarterly outputs of the collieries, in any case when the estimated quarterly demand might exceed one-quarter of the total annual quota in all or some class or classes of coal. These corrective quotas, called period quotas, were granted at the discretion of the Executive Board to all or some classes of coal, the demand for which during the coming quarter might seem to exceed the allowed production, " after making allowance for (1) each quarter's quota ; (2) the maximum additional quantities allowed to single collieries ; (3) amounts necessary to provide for any increase in the Members annual quota due to increase of the conventional output ; (4) any amounts allocated to any separate body of members or classes of coal as may be decided upon ; and (5) any deficiencies estimated or liable to be brought forward from the preceding quarter." Together, the total quarter quota and period quota were to be called members' quarterly allocation, and four of these allocations total allocation. In addition to its quarterly allocation each colliery was entitled to produce in any quarter an additional

2. " To fix and regulate the minimum prices for any class or description of coal, and for this purpose to settle groups and to allocate collieries or classes of coal thereto." [1]

3. " To compensate members for loss of output." [2]

4. " To co-operate or form any working arrangement or association with any similar organization."

The coming into operation of this plan was made dependent on the approval of colliery owners representing at least 70 per cent of the output in the quarter ending June, 1929.

Experience has thus proved that the Welsh cartel could not work without fixing both the supply and the prices. By adopting this scheme South Wales attracted much interest in other districts, which were at the time busy in framing their own organizations, sometimes without noticeable success.

The Midland counties, Lancashire and Cheshire, were parties to the *Central Collieries Commercial Association*, better known as the Five Counties Scheme, an organization which regulated output and paid a subsidy to exporters. This enormous cartel, including producers controlling nearly 100 million tons yearly output,[3] was founded in

tonnage, which might not, however, exceed one-fourth part of the difference between the conventional output and the quarterly allocation. This tonnage was not transferable from one quarter to another, whereas any deficiency in the quarterly allocation could be transferred by individual collieries from one quarter to another within the same year ; they might be, with the permission of the Executive Committee, transferred to another colliery undertaking. A penalty of 2s. 6d. was provided for exceeding the allowed tonnage.

[1] All collieries were to be grouped and classified for the purpose of fixing minimum f.o.b. prices per ton for their coal, and minimum prices at pit-head for coal other than that intended for shipment. The minimum prices could not be lowered under a penalty of 2s. 6d. per ton. The grouping of collieries and classification of their coal was to be carried out by committees, composed of representatives of each colliery in the district.

[2] Members of the S.W.C.M.A. could claim compensation at a rate of 2s. per ton for the amount by which they fell short of their total allocation, provided that this shortage was not caused by strikes, accidents, or breakages of machinery. In this way compensation might be paid on each ton of coal not produced below the total allocation ; the maximum tonnage on which compensation was paid could not exceed 10 per cent of the total allocation.

[3] The actual output of the members of the C.C.C.A. for the year ended 31st March, 1929, was 91,000,000 tons ; whereas the permitted output was 94,000,000 tons, i.e. about 90 per cent of the total production of the area.

M

December, 1927, when the coal-owners of Yorkshire, Nottingham, and Derbyshire met for the first time in Leeds to discuss a scheme for the regulation of production. Soon after, the Lancashire and Cheshire Coal-owners' Association joined the scheme, but North Wales remained outside. Cannock Chase, Leicestershire, North Staffordshire, and Warwickshire also joined the cartel, which was actually in operation from 1st April, 1928. The scheme had two chief objects, first to increase the export of coal and second to regulate output by means of quotas allocated to each colliery. All members had to pay to the common fund a contribution not exceeding 3d. for each ton of coal raised. From this fund subsidies on export were to be drawn. These subsidies varied in time from 1s. 6d. to 4s.

Production was regulated in the following way : first a basic tonnage was fixed for each mine by the Basic Tonnage Committee ; this amount was based on the actual output of the mines in any one year selected by each owner from the last fifteen years. A quota, or percentage of the basic tonnage, was fixed for each month by the Quota Committee, equal for all the mines. Special provisions were made to meet the claims of developing mines. Moreover, a pool of unraised quotas was instituted, from which those desirous of increasing their own quotas could purchase an additional amount subject to the approval of the Quota Committee, which in this way became seller and buyer of the available quotas of " unraised shortages ". A penalty of 3s. per ton was imposed on any member exceeding his quota by more than 1 per cent.

All penalties and other contributions went to the Central Fund, out of which assistance was paid to the exporters. The amount of the assistance was decided by a special Export Committee. Arrangements were made with coal exporters by which they were remunerated for their services on the basis of a commission fixed per f.o.b. ton. This was necessary to prevent them from taking the amount of the subsidy without reducing their prices on the foreign market. In addition to all this complicated machinery, the C.C.C.A. established a Shipping Bureau to watch the members' interests abroad and to provide necessary information ; in this were included the Port Committees of the Mersey and the Humber exporters.

The next question was the actual operation of the C.C.C.A. First, we must observe that its full working was confined only to about eighteen months from the time it was put into action in April, 1928. Afterwards Lancashire and Cheshire left the scheme, and created an independent organization. The chief drawbacks of the scheme were that it did not regulate prices, thus allowing the members to undercut each other ; moreover, the computation of basic tonnages was unsatisfactory. In this last respect the third South Wales Coal Marketing Scheme of 1929, described above, was greatly superior to the Central Collieries Commercial Association (Five Counties Scheme) in its method of solving the problem of estimating basic tonnage for developing collieries. While in the C.C.C.A. scheme members were allowed to select any one of the fifteen years preceding the introduction of the plan as a basis for their yearly agreed output, under the South Wales Scheme the members had only the choice of one out of the six quarters immediately preceding 30th June, 1928, or the month of March multiplied by an agreed multiplier, to arrive at a quarterly tonnage. The Welsh method of computing the quarterly output allowed much consideration for expanding collieries. Even in Yorkshire, where there is much more uniformity among the collieries than in South Wales, the long-term method of computing the basis of tonnage was prejudicial to the growing and developing mines. Owing to the imperfect method of arriving at standard tonnage in the Five Counties Scheme, the aggregate area tonnage was much higher than the yearly output, because each colliery chose for its basic tonnage the output of its best year. Naturally for this reason the Quota Committee had to fix a very restricted percentage from the very beginning. Thus for 1928 the quotas were as follows :—For April, 65 per cent ; for May, $67\frac{1}{2}$; June, 60 ; July, 60 ; August, 56 ; September, 65 ; October, 60 ; November, 65 ; December, 60 ; January (1929), $62\frac{1}{2}$; February, 80 ; March, 80. About 10 per cent of coal-owners remained outside the scheme and were free to increase their output by working at full capacity. This had to be taken into consideration in fixing quotas. Moreover, the existing stocks had to be cleared, and a considerable reduction of output was found imperative. Actually, after the first year of the operation of the scheme stocks were reduced by nearly 1,000,000 tons, but in our view this was due much more to the revival of trade in the winter of 1928-9 than to the policy of the C.C.C.A. The actual tonnage raised was 3,000,000 tons, or 3 per cent less than the allowed tonnage, which left much room for price-cutting, especially as all attempts to co-ordinate sales were fruitless. On the whole, there were only a few cases of output exceeding permitted tonnage—equivalent together to an insignificant tonnage of 0·05 per cent of the permitted aggregate output. This was subject to penalties, which later, as a matter of grace, were partly refunded.

The most important achievements of the C.C.C.A. were in the export section, where it succeeded with the assistance of the subsidy which operated until September, 1930, in making some advance in the foreign markets, chiefly at the expense of other British exporting districts. During the first year of its operation, the C.C.C.A. stimulated sales abroad up to nearly 5 million tons, which compares favourably with the previous year, when only 2·2 million tons were sold.[1] Much resentment was expressed on this account by the North-East Coast coal-fields and by Scotland, which lost trade to the C.C.C.A. No practical export agreement between the districts could be arranged, owing to the different economic structure of each district and to the different distribution of their home and foreign markets.

Early in 1930, when trade seemed to be improving, the C.C.C.A. came *de facto* to its end. The first sign of this was the secession of Lancashire and Cheshire, and the second the suspension of the subsidy. New proposals for regulating prices did not find sufficient support.

In relation to the study of the organization in the industry, the Five Counties Scheme provided an extremely important

---

[1] Cf. *First Report on the Working of the Five Counties Scheme* during the twelve months ended 31st March, 1929.

and interesting illustration. In the first place, it was an association which for the first time in the history of the British coal industry embraced a whole area, including neighbouring districts. It thus emphasized the significance of the area as a wider unit than the district. Secondly, together with the Welsh Scheme and the Scottish Scheme, with which we shall deal below, it proved that the industry was able to create a temporary form of organization which was effective in preventing an excessive capital consumption during a transition period to new conditions of equilibrium. Thirdly, the importance of the scheme lay in its voluntary nature, which goes to prove that all the talk about the inability of the owners to co-operate when co-operation is really expedient is not based on facts. Voluntary action is the best guarantee of economic justification that any new scheme could have, since it can be terminated at any moment if it seems likely to prevent progress.

Apart from these two schemes a plan for organization was brought about in Scotland, where the coal-owners co-operated in the *Scottish Coal Marketing Scheme* for the purposes of keeping the inefficient collieries idle, allowing the others to work at fuller capacity, and of raising the price of coal for certain types of consumers.[1] The construction of the scheme, which was put into operation on 6th March, 1928, was perfectly simple and its economic consequences were for the time considerable. The scheme, which was supported by a majority of more than 90 per cent of all owners in the district, was financed by a levy on all coal for home consumption not exceeding 6*d*. a ton. Export coal, bunker coal, and coal sold to ancillary or associated undertakings was tax-free. Further, coals designed for certain sections of consumers could be charged with a special levy, if the administrative committee was of opinion that the demand could bear this additional increase. Only in the case of household coal the special levy had to be approved by a majority of 80 per cent of all members of the scheme. As the

[1] For a good account of the working of the " Scheme for dealing with the abnormal position of the Coal Industry in Scotland ", see *The Commercial Manchester Guardian*, xvii, 661, " Scottish Plan to Stop Coal Trade Losses."

export prices were at that time falling, the economic effect of the levies was to increase the price of coal at home, without increasing export prices at the same time, which was tantamount to making home trade more attractive and so reducing the pressure on the exporting section.

All money derived from these two levies had to be paid into a common pool, out of which the small and inefficient collieries received agreed payments for keeping their pits, or parts of them, closed during a determined period. By this means it was intended to curtail the output of the industry and for some time to reduce the potential capacity of the Scottish coal industry, and at the same time to allow the efficient units to be more fully employed. The whole scheme was administered by an Executive Committee composed of representatives of the coal-owners' associations, twelve from Lanarkshire, six from Fife and Clackmannan, four from the Lothians, and four from Ayrshire.

Passing now to the actual operation of the scheme, we must note that it left the undertakings complete freedom to operate at any rate of capacity they desired, and no restrictions in general terms were imposed. A special levy of 1s. 6d. was imposed on certain types of coal, the demand for which was only of small elasticity for a fall. This levy affected public utility companies and the railways ; but soon, owing to outside competition, the increase in prices could not be entirely shifted on the buyer, and it was partly borne by the coal-owner. However, owing to the policy of the merchants of playing one district, and one owner, against another, an agreement made between Scotland, Lancashire, and Cumberland to raise prices on the Irish market was much less successful. The scheme as a whole achieved a certain amount of temporary success in its endeavour to close the inefficient pits, but they reopened again after a few months. This occurred principally in the home section, while the exporting districts tried to sell as much coal as possible at home in order to cover their losses from foreign sales, and in order to reduce expenses by working at the fullest capacity possible. The price charged by the collieries for standing idle was on the whole high, with the result that the plan proved to be very expensive : and the industry could not afford to keep it going for long. As the slightest hope of an improvement in trade immediately caused owners to advance claims for reopening their mines at once, it was difficult for the scheme to achieve its object of permanently reducing the capacity of the district. But during the worst part of the period of depression the whole scheme had its effect in stiffening up the market, chiefly in the home section.

The critics of the scheme drew attention to the paradoxical situation that any owner of several pits was in a position to draw benefit from keeping one of his pits closed, while at the same time he could increase the output of his others without any restriction. Moreover, the home sections of the trade, particularly Lanarkshire, criticized the scheme as favouring the exporting collieries indirectly, since they found new markets at home at the expense of the levies paid by them to keep as many mines closed as possible. When the scheme came to an end in March, 1929, many new proposals for increasing its scope were put forward. These included a plan to fix output quotas for each mine, to co-ordinate prices, and to pay a subsidy to the exporting collieries out of a fund derived from contributions made by collieries whose proceeds from inland selling exceeded the " standard difference ". This " standard difference " consisted in the excess between the average selling price at home and that for export.[1] Owing to the opposition of Lanarkshire, which objected to such favourable treatment of the exporting sections, no fresh scheme commanded a sufficient majority. Thus, since the extinction of the first Scottish scheme, no common organization has been called into existence.

In Northumberland and Durham the coal-owners have been bound by no formal scheme, but they operated nevertheless some agreement on price policy which was carried out under the ægis of the local Associations.

Thus we see by the schemes emanating from the industry, designed to overcome that most difficult period 1927–8, that each district solved the problem in its special

---

[1] Cf. Statistical Addendum to Chap. I, No. 4.

way, having consideration to its local economic conditions. In all the schemes the district principle was very strongly accentuated ; the district has thus proved to be a national unit in the British coal industry, capable of spontaneous solution of its own difficulties in times of distress.

In other sections of this work we deal with the growing tendency towards co-operation for technical purposes, of which the most outstanding are the drainage schemes, covering in some cases a whole district. We have also dealt with the development of common selling organizations, which mark a definite progress of the integrating movement since 1925.

Finally we must draw attention to the *area* which constitutes a distinct form in the organization of the British coal industry. Naturally the area is less strictly defined, but roughly speaking one can distinguish at present in Britain four such divisions : the South, the Central Coal-field, the North-east, and Scotland. In a few cases the area has actually found its expression in the organization of the industry. For instance, the so-called Federated Area included the Yorkshire and the Midland Counties for the purpose of collective wage bargaining through a Joint Conciliation Board. This area organization existed long before the twentieth century.[1] When the Minimum Wages Act, 1912, introduced District Wages Boards, the Federated Area had only one Board for representing all the coal-owners and all the miners.

Another instance of a clear realization of the significance of the area is to be found in the Mining Industry Act, 1920.[2] Besides pit, district and national committees composed of owners and miners, this Statute provided for the creation of seven Area Committees for Scotland, Northumberland, Durham, Midlands, South England, South Wales, and Ireland. Although Part II of the Act never came into operation owing to the opposition of both parties, it is nevertheless significant that Parliament saw the necessity for

[1] The Federated Area included Yorkshire, Notts and Derbyshire, Staffordshire, Warwickshire, Leicestershire, North Wales, and Lancashire.
[2] 10 and 11 Geo. 5, Ch. 50, Mining Industry Act, 1920, pt. ii.

separating the interests of an area, as being of higher and different nature from those of the district.

It is clear from what has been said that the gradual progress of the spontaneous integration movement was forming a network of varying forms of organization on different levels in the industry.   The next section will describe the recent attempts of the British coal industry to evolve in turn a national form of co-ordination.

§3. NATIONAL ORGANIZATION OF INDUSTRY

We have now reviewed the elementary forces working for unification in the industry over a long period, and their effect in the districts.   We must note that in recent years these motives operated more powerfully.   Together they succeeded in over-riding the disintegrating tendencies, and the industry was rapidly becoming prepared for national development.   This marks the economic preparation for the final stage—the imposition of national organization by the State in 1930.   It was the coincidence of motives already long in existence in the coal industry with the direct impetus of the depression that really produced this national organization.   This final stage was thus the result of the following three events :—

(1) the rapid development on a national basis of the integration movement within the coal industry, noticeable especially after the year 1928 ;

(2) the intensification of international competition, and the possibility of international control of export markets ; and lastly

(3) the coming to power of the Labour Government in 1929, with a coal programme bound by political pledges given to its adherents during the electoral campaign.

The political ground was already well prepared for a national reform of the structure of the coal industry and the Government only took the initiative in the final stage.   For the

Labour Party, the coal organization was only the prelude of a whole system of reorganization of all the connected industries, coal, power, transport, etc.[1]

The first two of these factors leading to national unification are economic in their nature, and caused a spontaneous reorganization of forms in the coal industry, the third involved the political weapon of compulsion. Before we proceed to discuss the new organization imposed by Statute on the coal industry, we must first examine the natural forms of organization produced by the industry itself, in order to be able to judge later to what extent the political influences were capable of altering the economic forces. It is not our purpose to analyse here the numerous and varied schemes for integration which have been launched in the past, with or without success. We confine our attention only to the integrating movement of the second half of 1928, which led to the elaboration of fundamental principles for national co-operation. This was a vigorous attempt to co-ordinate the British coal industry, in order to increase its internal strength and to regain the losses incurred after the strike of 1926.

The year 1928 was one of the most disappointing in the records of the coal trade [2]; the output of the whole country fell to the very low level of 237 million tons, which was $5\frac{1}{2}$ per cent less than the production in 1927 and 2 per cent less than in 1925. Prices went down, and the total selling value of coal in pounds sterling was the lowest reached since the beginning of the War ; unemployment was at its height ; and the proceeds of undertakings fell considerably. After a rise in 1927, which was chiefly the result of the replenishment of stocks depleted during the stoppage, home consumption fell sharply in 1928, by nearly 15 million tons, and compared with 1925 by nearly $5\frac{1}{2}$ million tons—the lowest home demand since 1922. In addition to this home situation, one must add a drastic cut in prices of, on the average, two shillings and three pence per ton on the foreign markets, and a slight decrease in the quantity of coal

---

[1] Cf. *Coal and Commonsense*, p. 15.
[2] Cf. the Calendar of Events in the Appendix.

exported, as compared with 1927. This disappointing commercial situation was revealed in the first three quarters of the year, and was in clear connection with the crisis already perceptible in the industries of higher stages of production, engaged in manufacturing producers' goods. All the districts in the country worked[1] with debit balances, which in some cases (e.g. Lancashire in the September quarter) amounted to 2s. 7d. per ton commercially disposable. Not a single district made profits during these nine months. Such difficult times compelled the captains of the industry to reorganize on a national basis, which would allow the harmonious utilization of all available resources and, in particular, the elimination of excessive competition.[2] The existing elasticity of demand for a rise for coal, which would operate provided that prices could be lowered, was only available at a level so low as to be unattainable by the producers owing to their high costs. In such circumstances they were driven to attempt the method of price-regulation, and of co-ordination of production on a wide national basis.

At the time, as we have seen, district schemes covering several important areas were already in existence, operating on various principles by restricting either prices or output, or both. In 1928, those schemes included about 80 per cent [3] of the whole output ; but they were not nationally co-ordinated and price cutting continued fiercely between them. It became urgent to solve the dilemma, so ably formulated by Mr. Smart.[4] " How was it possible to fit in the old individualistic regime by ruthless cutting of costs into the new orientation of industrial grouping and control

[1] See Statistical Summary of Output and of the Costs of Production, Proceeds and Profits of the Coal Mining Industry for the Quarters ending 31st March, 30th June, and 30th September, 1928 ; Cmd. 3129 ; Cmd. 3210 ; Cmd. 3256.

[2] The position was similar in other raw-material producing industries. Compare an article by Mr. J. W. F. Rowe, " The Artificial Control of Raw Material Supplies," *Economic Journal*, vol. xl, No. 159, where the author maintains after having studied several of the industries that excessive supply is always the ultimate cause of restriction.

[3] According to our information from the Mining Association of Great Britain, the existing schemes controlled 82 per cent of the output ; another source quotes the figure 79 per cent.

[4] R. C. Smart, *The Economics of the Coal Industry*, London, 1930, p. 231.

evidenced in other industries . . . ? " Co-ordination and organization on a national basis was one of the important preliminaries.

The initiative for developing the three schemes already in force, in South Wales, Scotland, and in the Midlands, and for bringing the whole industry under one general structure, originated from the exporting districts, which were suffering both from foreign and home competition. Exports had substantially decreased, and trade was being lost, particularly in the Scandinavian markets, to foreign competitors, who were able to supply coal much more cheaply. In other markets foreign restrictions prevented the enlargement of sales. The table below provides an illustration of the monthly exports in 1928 compared with 1927 :—

TABLE No. 29

MONTHLY EXPORTS OF COAL FROM GREAT BRITAIN DURING SIX MONTHS ENDING 30TH JUNE, 1928, COMPARED WITH 1927 AND 1913

Month.	1928.	1927.	1913.
	Tons.	Tons.	Tons.
January	3,904,000	4,092,000	6,070,000
February	4,007,000	4,172,000	5,569,000
March	4,110,000	4,819,000	5,598,000
April	3,722,000	4,117,000	6,350,000
May	4,487,000	4,802,000	5,929,000
June	4,345,000	4,312,000	6,006,000
Total	24,577,000	26,318,000	35,526,000
Average per month	4,096,000	4,386,000	5,921,000

The quantity of coal and coke shipped abroad had substantially decreased by 1928, particularly in the Scandinavian and Baltic regions, where there was a corresponding increase in imports from Poland. "This free import market forms the centre of the competitive coal trade." [1] In certain cases the fall of exports in the first six months of 1928 amounted to nearly fifty per cent. For instance, Sweden, which took in 1927 (six months) more than 1 million tons of British coal, bought in the corresponding period in 1928 only 550,000 tons. Similar conditions prevailed in Finland, Denmark, and Norway.

[1] *Vide* League of Nations Economic Committee, *The Coal Problem*, Geneva, 1932, p. 18.

Not only was there a fall in the quantities exported from Britain in the first half of the year, but prices also dropped substantially in all foreign markets. On the average, prices fell by about 15 per cent during the first half of 1928 as compared with the previous years. Below we append a table giving a comparison of export prices in six successive months of 1928 with 1927 and 1930.

TABLE No. 30

AVERAGE MONTHLY F.O.B. PRICES OF BRITISH COAL DURING SIX MONTHS ENDING 30TH JUNE, 1928, COMPARED WITH 1927 AND 1913

Month.	1928.	1927.	1913.
	s. d.	£ s. d.	s. d.
January	15 8	1 0 11	13 5
February	15 8	19 0	13 4
March	15 9	18 5	13 7
April	15 9	18 6	13 11
May	15 7	18 4	13 9
June	15 7	17 10	14 0
Average Price	15 8	18 10	13 8

Extracted from *The Iron and Coal Trades Review*, 20th July, 1928.

The steady fall of export prices was felt most by the exporters from the North-Eastern Coast, from Scotland, and from the Humber. But as the Midlands succeeded in constructing the Five Counties Scheme, including a subsidy derived from a 3d. levy upon every ton of coal produced, they were able actually to improve their foreign sales by considerably more than 1 million tons. The counties vitally concerned in export trade, whose interests were threatened by this subsidy, were Durham, Northumberland, and, to some extent, the East of Scotland. The two North-eastern counties together export, on the average, more than 45 per cent of their total output. These two exporting districts, as we noted, had during the greater part of 1928 a loose agreement as to the minimum price schedule for export of coal to Scandinavian and Baltic markets. But there was no strong organization binding the districts. As the subsidies on exports of the C.C.C.A. allowed a certain degree of price cutting, Northumberland and Durham could in these conditions scarcely adhere to their own price restrictions abroad. On the other hand, while the Midland and Yorkshire districts, having a large home sale, could easily afford to subsidize exports, the North-Eastern district could not so easily put a levy on the home consumer for this purpose, because the leviable tonnage was too small. It is not surprising, therefore, that, being attacked on the one hand by foreign competitors and the shrinking demand, and on the other hand by the competition of better organized English districts, they offered a suggestion for the settlement of competitive conditions. Thus early in July, when trade was very bad and Northumberland experienced for the quarter ending 30th June a general debit balance of 1s. 4½d. and Durham of 7½d., they took the lead in entering into an arrangement with the other competing districts to stop undercutting of prices in the contested markets.

As all districts were faced by heavy losses in their overseas shipments, the initiative taken by the coal-owners from the Tyne, Blyth, Wear, and Tees, met with sympathetic approval all over the country. The first conversations, however, dealt exclusively with the regulation of foreign trade, and left home affairs untouched. At this early stage, the movement came to the notice of the Mining Association, and this representative body of coal-owners was entrusted with the task of carrying the process of co-ordination further. Thus the whole co-ordinating movement was centred in London, and the preparatory work started without delay. Already in the second half of July a meeting of delegates of all exporting districts was summoned to London to discuss the possibilities of formulating a scheme to regulate export trade and competition. It was first attempted to remedy certain defects resulting from the district organizations which, " in the absence of co-ordination, have somewhat disturbed the former equilibrium in the foreign trade of the coal exporting districts." [1] The districts were represented by chosen members of their respective Coal Marketing Associations.

As the chief result of the conference, a Central Marketing Committee of the Mining Association was established

[1] *Vide The Iron and Coal Trades Review*, 13th July, 1928.

with the object of preparing a general marketing scheme for the whole country. The three district schemes then in existence were to serve as a substratum for the elaboration of a general plan. Like other committees of the Mining Association, the Marketing Committee was composed of delegates of district associations represented on a tonnage basis. As the district associations embrace approximately 95 per cent of the industry, practically the whole industry took part indirectly in the debates. Soon after its constitution the Committee tried to arrange an inter-district exchange of views on the question of organization, but not a single district sent any constructive reply. In the course of unofficial discussions, which lasted the whole autumn, all the existing British coal schemes in force were analysed, and the statutes of some foreign coal cartels, especially the German and the Polish, were also considered.

Between July, 1928, and January, 1929, nothing was agreed or even drafted ; attention was directed almost exclusively towards securing a sufficient majority to support the proposals. The initiators of co-ordination wanted to obtain the approval of owners representing at least 90 per cent of the whole country's output and, as no State intervention nor any form of compulsion was proposed, it took a very long time to probe opinion throughout the industry. Gradually, however, with the advance of negotiations, it became evident that it was not practicable to restrict the co-operative plans only to export concerns and to leave home competition entirely unregulated. Mr. A. W. Archer,[1] an ardent advocate of closer organization in the British coal industry, drew attention to the existing competition between sea-borne Tyne coal and Midland coal sent by rail to the South of England ; this was due to the insufficiency of mere district schemes, and he inferred that these schemes, though a very useful step towards controlling conditions in one area, are inadequate for the whole country. He concluded that so long as some markets are common to more than one district, the full benefit of regulation of

[1] Mr. A. W. Archer, speaking in the Leeds Luncheon Club on 18th March, 1929 (*The Commercial*, 21st March, 1929, p. 339).

output, from the national point of view, is not obtained, and whilst the districts concerned may derive benefit sufficient to justify their own schemes, the position cannot be considered as entirely satisfactory.

By January, 1929, a plan comprising the main purposes of the organizations was already sketched. This comprised :—

(1) provisions for the allotment of district quotas, but without proposals as to the quotas of individual collieries ;

(2) provision for increasing the share of the exporting districts in the home market at the expense of non-exporting districts ;

(3) the district quotas to be based on three years' arithmetical mean production, namely those of 1925, 1927, and 1928.

There was in the scheme no reference to any profit pools, or any sort of general subsidy, there was no question of regulation of prices, no compulsion for non-conforming outsiders, no plan for a selling organization, no penalties for exceeding the quotas. Obviously the scheme was a mere outline not yet well elaborated. The most interesting of its provisions was the second ; the differential treatment in the home market for the exporting districts. The proposal was that simultaneously with the expansion of trade, especially of exports, those districts should regain the percentage in the total output of the country which they had had in 1913, i.e. they would appropriate the whole amount of the increase, with a view to restoring the pre-War percentage of output in each district. This principle can perhaps be better illustrated by the following fictitious example.

Let us assume two exporting districts in the country, X and Y, which produced the percentages shown in Fig. 2 (p. 177) of the whole country's output.

As we see now from our example, the whole production of the country has decreased by 47 million tons in 1928. According to the proposals made in the scheme in the case of expanding trade, these 47 million tons were to go wholly to benefit districts X and Y, till their proportions of the country's output should be again 15 per cent and

10 per cent. All other districts, which in 1913 contributed 75 per cent, produced in 1928 82 per cent, and thus they were not entitled to share in the expanding markets till the " equilibrium "—15 per cent and 10 per cent for the two exporting regions—were regained. We may easily observe that, while the actual amount of tonnage produced by different districts has substantially changed, the relation of one district to another has been altered still more, since the whole change between the districts occurred during

District	In 1913		of the whole country's output	In 1928	
	Tons million	%		Tons million	%
X produced	43	15		24	10
Y ,,	29	10		20	8
all others	215	75		196	82
Total ..	287	100		240	100

FIG. 2.

a general fall in output, which, according to our example, principally affected the exporting districts.[1]

[1] In order to represent graphically what the Coal Co-ordination Scheme actually proposed, we shall show as percentages the participation the participation of different districts in the whole country's production. We assume the existence of two different fictitious districts M and N, of which the latter is an exporting district. In 1913 district M produced, say, 25 per cent of the whole country's output, whereas district N produced the rest, i.e. 75 per cent. In 1928 the proportion has changed, while the whole output of the country has decreased. The situation is as represented by Fig. 3 (p. 178).

Along the ordinate we measure the quantities of coal produced, and along the abscissa the time.

By hypothesis $OA = AB = BC = BC = CD = \dfrac{OD}{4}$

The curve $DB''C'$ represents the total output of the country composed for the sake of simplification of only two producing districts M and N The curve $AA''A'$ represents the production of district M. Hence the difference between the curve $DB''C'$ and $AA''A'$ shows the actual production in district N.

As we see, the output of district N substantially decreased, whereas that of district M was only slightly fluctuating. While in 1913 the

N

This is how the national coal scheme was intended to work. It is significant to note that it was constructed to benefit especially the exporting districts. Probably the idea behind the proposed restriction was that as the greatest fall in quantity and in prices had actually taken place in foreign trade, the exporting districts should be permitted

proportion of district M to the whole country's production was $\frac{AO}{OD} =$ 25 per cent and district N was thus responsible for the remaining 75 per cent, in 1928 the proportion of district M to the whole output was $\frac{KA''}{KB''}$ or 50 per cent and for N only 50 per cent was left. What is represented here, is the position before the introduction of the proposed scheme of

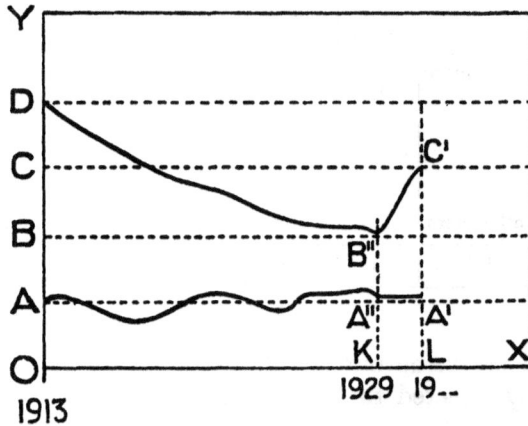

FIG. 3.

restriction. But now let us assume that the scheme has been in operation since the beginning of 1929. What will be the position? *Pari passu* with the improvement of trade, on which the principle was based, the whole volume of production will increase, but the two districts will not share equally in the rise. It will accrue only to district N until the percentage of district N in the whole national output is restored to 75 per cent, which will ultimately happen either when production rises to the level of OD or if district M produces less than the amount OA.

The moment of introduction of the restriction scheme is marked by the line $KA''B''$. Henceforward the output of district M is stabilized, and therefore represented by a straight line $A''A'$, whereas the whole additional output goes to the benefit of district N. In these circumstances, as trade expands, the participation percentage of district M diminishes, while that of N increases. And in some year 19 . . . as presented on the curve, district M will produce $\frac{LA'}{LC'}$ or $33\frac{1}{3}$ per cent of the whole output and district Y the remaining share of $66\frac{2}{3}$ per cent, etc., till it reaches finally the former 75 per cent.

to retain their remunerative uncontested " Hinterland " market intact while they were fighting to regain their pre-War equilibrium in foreign markets.

The whole scheme for reorganization of the coal industry as here presented was hotly discussed during the successive meetings of the Coal Marketing Committee in January, 1929. Further enlargements of the proposed plan followed. By the middle of January the conversations were already so far advanced that Sir Adam Nimmo,[1] in reviewing the position, referred to the co-ordinating efforts as follows :—

> " The discussions have tended to show that there is much common ground existing between the districts, and what is of special significance, there is a genuine disposition to recognize and face the obvious difficulties of the situation and a serious desire upon a broad basis to deal with the problems of the industry that are common to all."

Later in the winter the scheme underwent several refinements, and finally, as it stood in March, 1929, it contained the following suggestions :—

(1) The tonnage of coal produced in the country was to be fixed.

(2) Provisions controlling inland prices for the whole country were to be included, but it was not yet definitely decided what sort of control it should be.

(3) Special district machinery to administer the scheme was provided in each area, but there was no formal national machinery. An agreement of the individual districts, which were to co-operate in determining the national quota and in co-ordinating prices, but without fixing their actual amounts, was to be regarded as a sort of central scheme. But while there was a considerable measure of accord as to district co-operation on a national scale, the way of defining and adopting the principle of collaboration within the district bristled with difficulties. Northumberland, Durham, and Scotland, in particular demurred.

[1] Sir Adam Nimmo, " Review of the British Coal Industry in 1928," *Iron and Coal Trades Review*, 25th January, 1929, p. 108.

(4) Penalties of 2s. 6d. per ton for exceeding the allotted quotas of production were provided, but there were to be no penalties for the lowering of prices, as they were not to be definitely fixed.

(5) An export pool was proposed to help foreign trade by means of the deduction of a certain agreed proportion of the excess of home over world prices when home prices were higher. This was designed to allow the exporting districts to share in the benefits of the more remunerative home trade.

These were the general outlines of the improved proposals put forward. Comparing them with the scheme of two months before, we see that though the main idea of giving compensation from the home markets to the exporting districts remained, the whole scheme has been substantially altered and enlarged. The most interesting feature was the lack of co-operation between the districts in reference to prices, a difficulty which was also experienced under the compulsory marketing scheme in 1930. The scheme was in fact not feasible, because it was constructed in such a way as to combine all sorts of provisions, some of which conflicted with the others. Each coal-owner found some different section with which he disagreed, and so was unable to accept the scheme as a whole.

The scheme never progressed beyond that point of development. In the meantime, the general situation in the coal trade during the first quarter of 1929 changed considerably, and the future outlook became for the time being much brighter. Owing to an exceptionally hard winter the demand for coal became very brisk, and trade revived.[1] So the enthusiasm for the proposed scheme melted, many colliery owners simply considering it unnecessary in the changed conditions of the markets. The work of the drafting committee, therefore, had to be suspended, especially in view of the fact that not a single district sent its criticisms of the scheme. Thus once more

[1] *Vide* Mines Department, Coal Industry : Statistical Summary of output and of the costs of production, proceeds and profits of the coal mining industry for the quarter ended 31st March, 1929. Cmd. 3358.

the well-known proverb found illustration : " When the Devil was ill, the Devil a saint would be ; when the Devil was well, the Devil a Saint was he."

The first national co-operative project in the coal industry was, however, far advanced, and undoubtedly had a chance of realization. It was a measure of outstanding importance, and we have little hesitation in saying that it was one of the most direct incentives to the introduction of compulsory organization into the coal industry. The Labour Government, which came into power only a very few months later, submitted the proposals of the Central Coal Marketing Committee to careful investigation. But probably even more important was the fact that the conversations within the industry, lasting for more than half a year, supplied its representatives with material and points for criticism which were of invaluable service later. Moreover, they provided a proof that in cases of real emergency the industry was perfectly capable of discussing its common difficulties and of devising a national co-operative plan which, provided the circumstances which called it to existence were sufficiently lasting, would be effected without any pressure from politics. In fact, it was always politics which took constructive ideas from economics. The scheme showed the new Government the way in which industrial develop-ment was tending, and thus lent colour to the idea of energizing this development by State authority. It provided the Government with an explanation of how the industry could bear the fresh burdens arising from a proposed shorter working time underground by adopting the method of national planning—reducing output and raising prices where possible. In concluding, we must note, however, that in a scheme so conceived there was little room for rationalization. No incentive was provided to stimulate the introduction of improved methods and more efficient working. Its only merit would be in facilitating the transition period. In fact, it was merely a short term device.

§4. INTERNATIONAL COAL PROSPECTS AND THEIR EFFECT ON ORGANIZATION IN THE BRITISH COAL INDUSTRY

The spontaneous movement in the coal industry which produced district co-operation in the critical year 1928, and a judicious scheme for national regulation, went so far as to touch all European producing countries. Thus a powerful stimulus to concentration and industrial integration in British mining was given by the vision of an international settlement of the coal question. Competition, and difficulties connected with the disposal in the world market of all coal produced, led to a recognition that the situation could not be handled successfully on a national scale. The Economic Committee of the League of Nations gave strong expression to this conviction in their 1929 Report.[1] The urgent economic problem was to dispose of potential over-production by restricting output and maintaining a stable level of prices. The average costs of the British collieries were too high, and they allowed competitors to capture a large proportion of their former markets. Apparently, to solve the problem of excess capacity by reducing prices and selling more coal was a difficult matter for Britain, because the reductions could not go further than those of the Continental competitors, and on the other hand the demand for coal was not sufficiently elastic in the short run to absorb both the aggregate output of British collieries plus the former supplies from the Continent.

The British miners were the first to recognize the international element of the coal question, especially in so far as co-ordination of supply was concerned. The cheap prices policy, in the opinion of the miners, was naturally reflected immediately in their wages, since these constituted on the whole about 70 per cent of all the costs of producing coal. Competition of individual companies between districts as well as nations was held responsible for the serious conditions of the workers. At the time the miners' leaders, headed by the late Mr. A. J. Cook, definitely denied the existence

[1] League of Nations Economic Organization : *The Problem of the Coal Industry*. Interim Report on its International Aspects, by the Economic Committee of the League of Nations, Geneva, 1929, p. 13.

of elasticity of demand for coal.[1] In this policy, the miners proved themselves to be once more strong protagonists of high prices. In the past, at the time when wages were regulated according to prices of coal by means of sliding scales, they advocated fair prices of coal, on the principle that these should be determined by labour costs and not vice-versa. On this ground they attacked the sliding scales. Their contention refers particularly to the districts producing for inland consumption.[2] Though between 1888 and 1914 the sliding scale system of wages gradually disappeared in the districts, nevertheless the demand for high prices of coal was repeated on several occasions.

Proposals for bolstering up prices by means of an international arrangement were launched even before the War. In 1893 a scheme put forward by Émile Lewy, a French coal-owner, for the regulation of output in Western Europe attracted much attention in the miners' circles. This " simply aimed at regulating production and distributing supply more regularly over every part of the year, according to the requirements of the consumptive demand, and with due regard to whatever circumstances may necessitate the putting of coal in stock. An important object is to reduce the number of pits temporarily forced to close, and the periods of shortness of employment so injurious to the industry ".[3] This plan was submitted to the successive Congresses of the Miners' International.

[1] Replying to Sir Richard Redmayne's views on low prices of fuel, Cook exclaimed : " It is remarkable to think that after the experience of the last eighteen months any man should be fool enough to believe that further reductions of prices will either gain markets or solve problems we are faced with . . ." (A. J. Cook, " Sir Richard Redmayne's Remedy," *The Miner*, 7th July, 1928.)

[2] F. W. F. Rowe, *Wages in the Coal Industry*, London, 1923, p. 39 : " There was in 1888 a complete cleavage in opinion and practice regarding the regulation of wages by sliding scales. Roughly speaking, miners in Yorkshire, Lancashire, and throughout the Midlands were determined that wages should never again be arbitrarily regulated by sliding scales, and openly declared that wages must control prices, and not vice versa. These coalfields were at that time producing almost exclusively for home production, and were not affected by conditions in the export markets. On the other hand, the miners in the north-eastern coalfield and South Wales could not blind themselves to the fact that it was impossible to control export prices, whatever might be done in the home trade."

[3] Émile Lewy, *A Scheme for the Regulation of the Output of Coal by International Agreement. The eight hours' day. The minimum wage ; profit sharing*. London, 1896.

In 1894, Lewy's scheme was summarized by M. Alfred Defuisseaux, a representative of the Belgian miners, in *The Labour Tribune*,[1] before the meeting of the yearly Congress which was to be held in Berlin. M. Defuisseaux, however, could not personally attend the Congress, having been deported from Germany by the Government at the request of the Belgian authorities, and therefore the scheme was not adequately defended. M. Defuisseaux, in recommending the Lewy Scheme, suggested, as a practical means of securing international regulation of production, the all round adoption of an eight hours' day on four days a week—the men to be paid five days' wages for four shifts—a plan closely resembling President Roosevelt's experiment in America. By this uniform reduction of time worked in all the countries concerned, output could be effectively restricted. The plan provided for the formation of an International Committee of Production composed of representatives of workers, of coal-owners and experts having special qualifications and possessing commercial, financial, and administrative experience.

The Committee, which would be in reality an " International Ministry of Mines ", should have power to supervise and regulate the output according to the demand. In this capacity it would be able to authorize one or other of the four countries to increase its production, provided that " the increased output was not used to undersell the others, as is now being done ". The Committee would permit, " according to circumstances, certain collieries to augment the number of their working days, more particularly when such collieries are giving manifest proof of their sympathy with the men ". Only in exceptional cases could the eight hours' day be exceeded.

The miners fought truculently for an international organization of production. Next year, in 1895, at Paris, the scheme was once more submitted to the International Miners' Congress, and was strongly supported by the French and Belgian workers. Opposition, however, from

---

[1] The then organ of the Federation of Miners of Great Britain, published at West Bromwich, near Birmingham.

certain British miners' circles proved so strong that the French and Belgian delegates actually thought of leaving the Congress. " But rather than offend the laws of hospitality and strike a deadly blow at the bonds of international brotherhood," they decided to swallow the insult. "After all, the Britishers as a body were not responsible for the disgraceful attitude adopted by one of their friends (John Wilson, M.P., Durham), though they might have made some sort of protest." [1]

After the Paris Congress, which made no decision on the plan, the Belgian Miners' Federation continued to place the Lewy proposal every year on the agenda of the Miners' International, but without any success. In 1912 the scheme revived again. It was coloured now by certain pacifist ideals, and aimed at scattering the " German War Cloud " by the establishment of international control by the workers over coal, which is the " bread of Peace and War ".[2]

After the War, in the time of slackening coal trade and growing competition, the British miners' leaders in their turn devised an international coal policy that was to solve the difficulty. They suggested an agreement between the different coal-producing countries to promote, in the first place, better organization of labour conditions throughout the industry, and as a more remote plan, the improvement of trade by restriction of production. The International Miners' Federation, which has existed for more than forty years, established for the first time in the summer of 1925 a permanent secretariat, co-ordinating work of international importance. In the same year, at the annual World Conference, the Miners passed a resolution setting forth the policy of international co-ordination, and requested the International Labour Office and the Economic Committee of the League of Nations to call a World Conference of the coal-producing countries, and the International Committee of the mine-workers to prepare a case. The Brussels resolutions, passed by the Committee of the

[1] *International Regulation of Output of Coal in Western Europe. The Lewy Scheme. Miners' Wages. The German War Cloud.*—Paris: Giard and Brière, 1912–13, p. 2.
[2] Ibid., p. 12.

International Miners' Federation in April, 1925,[1] recommended the reorganization of the coal-mining industry on an international scale, and the investigation of the whole question of wages, hours of work, etc.[2] In 1928 both the Congresses of the International Miners' Federation at Nîmes and of the Christian Miners' Union at Munich advocated a shorter working day in the coal mines on an international scale. The International Miners' Federation's Congress in Cracow in 1930 and in London in 1932 insisted strongly upon the expediency of concluding a general agreement between the competing countries.[3]

From the International Miners' Federation,[4] of which Mr. Herbert Smith of the Miners' Federation was President, and where British influences were of great weight, the initiative for international action passed to the international bodies in Geneva. The International Labour Office

[1] *Vide International Labour Review*, vol. xxiv, No. 5, p. 509.

[2] The passage of the Brussels resolution here referred to reads : " The Committee decides that efforts should be made to secure the standardization of working conditions of miners on an international basis."

" Since the Committee desires to be fully informed before it formulates definite and concrete proposals, it decides to organize, in agreement with the National Miners' Federations, an international investigation in the principal coal-producing countries. This investigation shall deal with hours of work, annual holidays, and wages paid by employers to the various categories of mining workers."

" In order that the proposed investigation should be as thorough as possible and that the inquiry may be completed with the least possible delay, the Committee also decided to appeal to the International Labour Office for assistance and the co-operation of the means of investigation at its disposal." (International Labour Office, Studies and Reports, Series D. No. 18, *Wages and Hours of Work in the Coal Mining Industry*, Geneva, 1928.)

[3] Cf. Agenda and Reports of the Thirtieth International Congress of Miners' International Federation in London, September, 1932.

[4] In May, 1928, the Economic Consultative Committee of the League of Nations passed the following resolution : " Impressed with the serious position of the coal industry and the importance of the international factors involved in this problem : (it) recommends, in the interest of the consumers and the producers alike, that the Council shall invite the economic organization of the League to take up the inquiries that have been started in relation to the coal problem and to supplement them as soon as possible by obtaining such advices as it may deem appropriate and in the manner suggested by the Economic Conference. A report should be submitted to the Council in order that the latter may be able to judge whether concerted international action could further the solution of this problem." (League of Nations, Economic Organization, *The Problem of the Coal Industry*, Interim Report on its International Aspects by the Economic Committee of the League of Nations, Geneva, 1929, Annex 11, p. 44.)

undertook, in 1925, an inquiry into the wages and hours of work in the coal industry, while the Economic Committee of the League of Nations took up the productive side. The latter advised the Council in 1928 to undertake an investigation into the practicability of extensive action in the coal industry.

British delegates played a conspicuous part in the work of the Committee. Professor R. H. Tawney, and the late Mr. A. J. Cook, who accompanied him as an expert adviser, gave their views concerning the drafting of the Report. Sir John Hindley, a prominent mine-owner, represented the employers' interests of this country.

The experts put before the Committee several suggestions involving international action.[1] These may be classed in the following four groups :—

(1) International agreements of producers concerning output, markets, and prices.

(2) The appointment of an international committee representing all interests, viz. : Governments, employers, miners, merchants, and consumers.

(3) Assimilation, and possibly equalization, of wages, hours, and social conditions of labour in all the coal-fields.

(4) Abolition of artificial restrictions to trade and of artificial stimulations to production.

The first of the above proposals gained the largest support both from the owners' and from the miners' side. In view of the severe depression in the coal industry in practically all producing countries, there was an increasing body of opinion ready to look for the solution of the over-supply difficulty by means of an understanding either as to output, export, prices, or markets. The Interim Report called attention, however, to the importance of leaving the initiative in convening the international coal conference to the owners interested, and recommended that the League should undertake no official action beyond the supplying of information and statistical data.[2] Other proposals

---

[1] Ibid., p. 13.
[2] Ibid., p. 17, and in the League of Nations, Economic Committee. *The Coal Problem*, Geneva, 1932, pp. 8 and 29.

concerned with international regulation of social reforms and working time, advocated mainly by the miners, were assigned expressly to the I.L.O. The initiative in the solving of international coal questions was divided between two different institutions.

While the international bodies deliberated on the general European aspect of the coal crisis, the British coal-owners were experiencing a most difficult period in trade, especially in the exporting sections. The first three quarters of 1928 especially were, as we have seen, extremely disappointing. They slowly grew convinced of the possible expediency of international action in settling the whole question of rivalry between nations.

Two factors preventing the development of the British coal industry were clearly revealed in 1928. First, there was an increasing surplus capacity continuously threatening the British producers. Secondly, British coal was on the whole more expensive than foreign coal and in order to increase exports prices would have to be further depressed. These two facts became evident to many enlightened owners, who began earnestly to reconsider all the possibilities of concluding some international arrangement. They realized that the demand for coal was only elastic at a price level too low to be reached by British producers, owing to the rigidity of costs of production. At this juncture many coal-owners, especially in those districts working for a market with a demand less elastic for a rise than for a fall,[1] e.g. the Midlands, embarked upon a policy of restrictions and control of prices. The Midlands, whose shipments abroad amounted to about 9 per cent of their whole output, were much keener to enter into an international agreement than Northumberland or—in particular—Durham, which relied to a far greater extent upon foreign trade. Whereas e.g. a 10 per cent cut in foreign shipments would mean to Yorkshire a decrease of 1 per cent or so in its aggregate production, exactly the same percentage decrease would mean to Durham and Northumberland about 5 per cent of their total production, which is relatively a much greater sacrifice and

[1] See Pt. I, Chap. II, § 2.

entails working at further decreased capacity and a consequent rise in costs.[1]

As at that time foreign exporters, especially Poland, had been continually expanding their Scandinavian and Baltic trade, any possible agreement could only be based on a further decrease in the proportion of world trade held by Britain. For this reason the exporting districts, though actually initiating an understanding between the different home areas as to the export markets, were not keen to consider the possibility of concluding international understandings.

On the other hand, the Midland owners were on the whole willing to initiate some form of co-operation with their foreign competitors. Mr. Archer, one of the leading figures in the Midlands coalfield, was a strong advocate of an understanding between coal-exporting nations. Having spent some time in the Continental coal-fields, he paid much attention to the possibilities of making arrangements for a *modus vivendi*. After his return to England he tried to impress upon the leading coal industrialists the advisability of opening discussions on coal export between the countries concerned. In a special article which was published in *The Yorkshire Post* in the middle of August, 1928,[2] he explained the reasons why Polish coal, though mined far from the sea, could successfully find outlet in the contested northern markets. In this way Mr. Archer tried to disperse the false opinions persistently maintained about the potentialities of the Polish industry by the Germans, who, in their technical Press, led by the *Deutsche Bergwerks Zeitung* of Düsseldorf, propagated the view that it would be undesirable to conclude any understanding with Poland because, as it was alleged,

[1] In 1932 South Wales exported 56 per cent of its output, Northumberland and Durham 39 per cent, Scotland 26 per cent, and Yorkshire 15 per cent.

[2] Mr. Archer summarized his observations on Britain's European competitors. He " was much impressed with what he saw in Poland . . . it would be a mistake for us to underestimate Poland's potentialities as a competitor, and to attempt to console ourselves for the difficulties created by her incursion into the Scandinavian markets with the reflection that this is a mere spasmodic effort, and one which we have the power to overcome . . . the position achieved by Poland . . . is not one which she will lightly relinquish " (quoted from the *Iron and Coal Trades Review*, 17th August, 1928).

that country was " threatened by a financial crisis due to her dumping policy ".[1] The purpose of such misrepresentation by one of the potential members of the international coal agreement was perfectly clear, if we remember that Germany was opposed to an arrangement which would restrict her production of lignite, an aim always kept in view by the Polish producers. The latter argued, not without justice, that a coal settlement must also embrace lignite, of which Germany is the chief producer, since that fuel could successfully compete with certain grades of coal which would henceforward be restricted. In fact, the difficulties of arriving at an understanding with the Germans proved still greater and more complex than with the Poles.

Pari passu, however, with the stagnation of trade and the disastrous commercial results in all districts, there grew a strong demand for more pertinent international initiative. Already the Coal Commission of 1925 had pointed out certain fields where collaboration with foreign countries might prove of great value. It [2] suggested, namely, the possibility of establishing an approved public authority, whose duty it should be to sample the coal cargoes at the ports by methods internationally agreed. Further, the Report continued that if Britain's foreign customers approved this idea, Great Britain, as the principal coal producer, should summon an international technical conference to eliminate the double sampling and analysis in the exporting and importing ports.

As the economic position in 1928 became more difficult,

---

[1] The relevant passage in the *Deutsche Bergwerks Zeitung* which we extracted in the English version from the *Iron and Coal Trades Review*, 31st August, 1928, and which tries to impress upon the reader the false idea of some abnormal conditions in the Polish coal industry, reads as follows : " When certain experienced English mining directors recently visited the Ruhr the possibilities of international agreements were naturally discussed, and the visitors are reported to have been obviously depressed by the comparison of English and German mining conditions. In Poland certain definite proposals for an agreement appear to have crystallized from their conversations. In England, however, these negotiations by no means excited general satisfaction, for it is thought there that Poland is on the eve of a grave financial crisis. It is considered undesirable, therefore, to conclude any sort of agreement with Poland, as that country will herself soon see the error of her price-cutting policy on the coal market."

[2] *Report of the Royal Commission on the Coal Industry* (1925), vol. i, Cmd. 2600, p. 95.

the responsible mine-owners began to look abroad for some way of warding off catastrophe. In July, 1928, a party of British coal-owners went to Poland and Germany to discuss the possibility of concluding some form of agreement which would stop " cut-throat competition ". They held a number of conferences with the Polish coal-owners, with whom they discussed in detail the manifold aspects of Anglo-Polish coal competition on the Baltic and in Scandinavia. A visit to London was arranged [1] for the Polish colliery owners' delegates. The British owners next went to the second most important competitor, Germany. Although the conversations with the Ruhr colliery representatives covered a vast field, it became clear that, though the latter favoured such proposals in principle, fundamental difficulties existed in the way of an international understanding.

After the return of the British coal-owners from their Continental tour, a vigorous movement was launched for a large European coal agreement, which would eliminate both the lamentable competition of British exporting districts with one another and the rivalry between the coal-producing countries. Proposals put forward to frame an international covenant included Great Britain, Germany, Poland, Belgium, France, and Holland, which countries are responsible in Europe for more than 90 per cent of the output of bituminous coal and about 85 per cent of bituminous and lignite together. Mr. Archer was one of the chief protagonists of this joint European action, and he found numerous followers amongst the colliery-owners and economists. Controversy, however, arose as to whether the United Kingdom could afford to surrender something of the volume of her pre-War export in return for coal peace. While many coal-owners maintained that England could not consent to anything less than her pre-War volume of foreign trade, Mr. Archer was of opinion that some sacrifices would have to be made. Various projects appeared.

Professor Bellerby [2] propounded a plan somewhat on the lines of the Lewy scheme for regulation of hours of work in

---

[1] Reuter-Warsaw, 2nd August, 1928.
[2] J. R. Bellerby, *Coal Mining : A European Remedy*, London, 1928, p. 45.

the mines by an International Mining Board, composed of representatives of mine-owners and mine-workers from all European countries, under the chairmanship of an independent president. The same body would have additional powers to regulate the changes of wages ; though the author did not assume that wages would be equal in all the countries. Professor Bellerby tackled also the possibility of a European effort to reduce production. Starting from the assumption that the demand for coal is exceptionally inelastic, he showed that for this reason considerable advantages could be gained by international regulation of output.[1]

Similarly also Professor Jones pleaded for international control on the familiar ground of inelasticity, which he said was revealed on the side of demand, and to a certain extent on the side of supply.[2] Such rigidity of demand and supply should effectively facilitate the drafting of an international scheme. In an address delivered to the Royal Statistical Society in November, 1929, Professor Jones recommended an international regulation of coal prices.[3]

The possibilities of reaching an agreement for concerted action between the chief coal-producing nations roused some hope in many circles, both in this country and abroad. The prospects for the control of ruinous competition were carefully watched on both sides of the Channel, and many leading coal-owners were prepared to enter into official negotiations with the competing countries. Amongst the coal-owners in this country Lord Melchett had been a prominent protagonist of national and international reorganization.[4] In the Jubilee number of *The Statist* of 1926,[5] Lord Melchett strongly emphasized the need for world industrial organization, on the ground that markets

[1] Ibid., p. 68 : " In general it may be said that whenever this particular condition, an inelastic market, exists, there are exceptional advantages to be gained for the industry, and certain disadvantages to be averted, through international organization for regulating output."

[2] *Vide The Accountant*, 27th July, 1929, p. 108, and *The Accountant*, 29th September, 1929, p. 324.

[3] " The Present Position of the British Coal Trade," *Journal of the Royal Statistical Society*, vol. xciii, part i.

[4] The Mond Scheme for National and Area Coal Selling Agencies, see *The Economist*, vol. cii, 24th April, 1926, p. 822.

[5] Rt. Hon. Lord Melchett, " The Rise of the Modern Industrial Organization," *The Statist*, 30th June, 1928, Jubilee Section, p. 21.

to-day form one unit where everybody can trade, and modern means of transport have neutralized geographical differences. As production can be infinitely increased in modern industry, the necessity arises for regulation of output to avoid a catastrophic collapse of prices. Finally, he called attention to an essential point, namely that a national structure must be erected as a preliminary to international organization to figure as representative of the country's industry. Without adequate organization of its own, the British industry could not participate in nor draw benefits from co-operation on a large scale.

Lord Melchett's plea for the organization of the coal industry had a considerable effect upon the advance of the whole integrating movement. An agreement of all important coal-producing countries became the topic of discussion and general interest, as the last recourse for the strained industry. Even Mr. Lee, the Secretary of the Mining Association of Great Britain, though rather sceptical as to the possibilities of solving the European coal problem, nevertheless admitted that : " nothing is to be lost, and enormous benefits may be secured by the direction of our attention towards the possibility of thus stabilizing the European coal supply on an equitable basis." [1] Sir Samuel Instone, the chairman of colliery companies in Yorkshire and South Wales, was among those who pleaded for the establishment of a voluntary scheme whereby useless cut-throat competition between nation and nation could be stopped and an economic price agreed for the sale of their products. [2]

At this stage, in conformity with the colliery owners, the miners and the public strongly favoured concerted international action in the coal industry. Largely owing to the personal influence of Mr. Herbert Smith, the late President of the British Miners' Federation, the International Miners' Federation, at its annual conference in Paris in 1928, agreed that in view of the situation joint action had become

[1] A. W. Lee, "The Future of the Coal Industry," *The Statist*, 30th June, 1928, p. 80.
[2] Information from Horace B. Pointing, *A Survey of the Coal Problem*, London, 1929, p. 15.

necessary. As recently as February of that year, however, the British miners had opposed a plan of organization of production and distribution through international agreement, submitted by M. Delattre (Belgium), Secretary of the International Miners' Federation. British delegates argued that this course of action would involve support of rationalization in the interests of the employers against the miners. The resolution was nevertheless carried against the votes of British representatives.[1]

After a very short time, however, parallel with the growing depression in the industry, the problem of international agreements of producers came to be recognized by the official body of the mine workers, and we very soon find the whole question included in their party programme.[2]

Some time after this, the late Mr. A. J. Cook ably defended the European arrangement before the Trades Unions Congress :—

> "It is no good," he exclaimed, "protesting about cheap Polish coal when British coal is sold in Paris at 4s. or 5s. a ton less than it cost to produce. Surpluses lead to dumping, dumping to tariffs, tariffs to price cuts, price cuts to chaos. The solution is international agreements."

During the discussion convened by the League of Nations at Geneva in January, 1929, on the desirability of concerted action, experts representing eleven chief European producing countries unanimously agreed that the coal problem was essentially an international one. Following a temporary revival of trade which occurred in the winter, 1928–9, the new wave of depression began to be felt, and at Geneva, in September, 1929, the British Labour Government came forward once more with their plan for international action in close understanding with the League of Nations. The late William Graham, President of the Board of Trade, and Dr. H. Dalton, Under-Secretary of Foreign Affairs, took

[1] Information from *The Daily Herald*, 25th February, 1928.
[2] *The Mining Situation : An Immediate Programme.* Issued under the joint auspices of The Trades Union Congress, The Labour Party, The Miners' Federation of Great Britain (Labour Publications Department, London, p. 17).

the lead in urging the collaboration of national coal industries.[1]

Further conversations between the interested parties were continued during the meeting of the coal delegation of the Economic Committee of the League of Nations in October, 1929, working under the chairmanship of Dr. Trendelenburg (Germany). The delegation heard evidence from twenty-two experts representing employers' and workers' organizations both in producing and consuming countries. At these meetings a fact of great significance for international co-operation was officially notified by the Chairman, namely, that two countries, Great Britain and Belgium, being almost without any organizations representative of their entire coal industries, were now on the way to creating them. It was doubtless a very momentous achievement, facilitating the way to World organization.[2] Even the coal-importing countries proceeded to build up centralization schemes. Spain, by a Government decree of 10th January, 1928, grouped all her colliery companies into syndicates controlled by a federation of those syndicates, whose orders were to be observed under penalties. France followed suit in the summer of 1932 by a voluntary agreement between the districts of Pas de Calais, Nord, Central, Sud, Lorraine, and Saar. Under this recent agreement each district received productive quotas and the right of exclusive selling in determined areas.

The agreements between coal producers soon outgrew even the national boundaries, and thus a commercial agreement was concluded between the Polish Coal Convention and the German Upper Silesian Coal Syndicate, apportioning all their exports to Austria and Hungary in proportions fixed at 86·52 per cent for Poland and 13·48 for German Silesia. Poland was to take charge of the actual sales. Another international coal agreement was in operation between Germany and Belgium during the whole of 1931 and at the beginning of 1932. This agreement

[1] Dr. Dalton summarized the situation in an interview in *The New Leader*, 30th August, 1929.
[2] *Vide, The Coal Problem*, Geneva, 1932, p. 6.

referred to the sales of coal in the territory of the contracting countries.

So long as Great Britain had no organ which could directly represent the interests of her coal industry in the international cartel, she could not participate in the international coal negotiations.   The Mining Association of Great Britain was unable to control national production, and on this account could not be considered.   Some controlling apparatus was rendered necessary.   The possibility in 1929 of an international coal cartel gave, therefore, a strong stimulus to the creation within the British coal industry of a national organization which would enable it to enter as a regular participant into the European coal system.   It was quite obvious that the formation of some national control scheme would only be an introductory step. Henceforward, as the prospect of a European coal settlement improved, the desirability of a national form of restriction in coal production came to be more widely recognized.

Discussions began in Europe without the participation of Great Britain, and the first meetings considered the restriction of the large over-supply of coal in the foreign markets. Owing to the severe crisis, Poland and Germany, at the beginning of 1928, began negotiations for the joint regulation of the marketing of exports.

District schemes, which in the early spring covered the greater number of British coal areas, were at the time just in process of formation.   Undoubtedly anxiety among the British coal-owners to take part as an organized unit in the preliminary conversations abroad was one of the important stimulants to a speedy consolidation.   In fact, the Five Counties Scheme, assisting the Humber exports by means of subsidies and severe restrictions of output, came into operation in March, 1928.   At this time a scheme had already been in force in South Wales since November, 1927, for the regulation of minimum price schedules, and for the compensation of producers losing their trade through the existence of the minimum price arrangements.

Naturally it was impossible to make marketing agreements

in the export trade excluding some of the main competitors. The promoters of the European coal cartel realized that Britain's participation was a *sine qua non* of its successful operation. But, on the other hand, it was scarcely conceivable to make an arrangement with all the separate and unco-ordinated undertakings of this country. Students of the coal industry in England, as well as the leaders within the trade, clearly realized to what an extent the lack of organization was a hindrance to effective international regulation of marketing. Everyone admitted that the European control of an industry like coal could not be successfully achieved without adequate national and district organization. To this difficulty Professor Bellerby [1] referred in the chapter of his work on the international remedy for the coal dilemma. Similarly, Mr. Archer [2] clearly revealed the relative lack of organization in this country. He laid emphasis on the need for regulating output, controlling prices, and creating a centrally directed marketing plan. " Apparently," he said, " the Five Counties Scheme, too, will have to be altered before all the schemes can be dovetailed together. Can it be that Scotland refuses to swallow the pill of quota output ? " [3]

[1] J. R. Bellerby, *Coalmining : A European Remedy*, London, 1928, p. 59 : ". . . the possibility of setting up some system for regulating the entire output of European coal mines depends essentially on the degree to which control has been developed already on a national basis in the several countries. Organization necessarily begins at the bottom ; as small groups coalesce into larger groups, and large groups into still larger ones, the whole country may become widely enough organized to be brought under one central administration. Only when the national organization has reached this pitch of development will it be possible to consider the application of an international system to the control of output."

[2] A. W. Archer, " Some Aspects of the International Coal Situation," paper read to the Huddersfield Rotary Club on 17th December, 1928.

[3] After the passing of the Coal Mines Act, 1930, Mr. Archer called attention to the significance of co-operation between coal producers. In a paper entitled " Re-organization of the Coal Industry " (kindly lent by Mr. Archer) we read : " After we established co-operative activity between British districts, the next step in organization should be, I think, international co-operation. We are a long way from that mark yet, but our faces are set in that direction. The alternative to competition is co-operation—the recognition by the coal industries concerned of their common interest in common markets, and the conclusion of an International Agreement relating to prices and, perhaps, sales quotas in those markets. This was recognized by those responsible for the administration of the C.C.C.A., who contemporaneously with their adoption of an export

Foreign producers of coal watched with the keenest attention the progress of the integrating movement in Great Britain. A discussion with individuals was merely beating the air, and could not achieve anything positive; so the competing countries tried to impress upon English leaders in the industry the real significance of bringing the whole national production into some sort of scheme. The Germans especially, whose exports of coal contracted enormously after the coal stoppage in 1926, emphasized at every opportunity how much importance they attached to the organization of the British trade. These views were well expressed by Dr. Pinkerneil,[1] of Berlin, in the Section on the Rhineland in *The Commercial*. Discussing exports of coal in the contested areas, he finished his survey by saying: " The question of an agreement with Britain, and of its scope, depends on the extent to which organization can be carried in Britain, where at present no body similar to the German coal syndicates exists." But this was not the opinion of German coal circles alone. The Report of the Economic Committee of the League of Nations, 1929,[2] made a definite allusion to the lack of national structure in the British coal industry as being an obvious stumbling-block in the

subsidy, were exploring, by informal conversations with coal producers abroad, the possibility of co-operative action. The difficulties attendant upon such an agreement are considerable. Before the passing of the Coal Mines Act they were insuperable. Now, however, there is in existence for the first time a central body which is representative of the whole of the British Coal Industry."

[1] Dr. Fr. A. Pinkerneil, Berlin, " Coal," *The Commercial*, 19th July, 1928, Rhineland, p. x.

[2] League of Nations, Economic Organization, *The Problem of the Coal Industry*, Interim Report on Its International Aspects by the Economic Committee of the League of Nations, Geneva, 1929, pp. 14-15: " We were informed . . . that the only central employers' organization in the United Kingdom is the Mining Association, which has no power to deal with coal prices or the distribution of orders and can only negotiate concerning hours, wages, or conditions of work, with the express consent of the district associations which it represents. . . . But there is no national representative body with power to negotiate on all the subjects which might be covered by an international agreement. . . . The Miners' experts were anxious that, if competition were checked at one point it should not be deflected so as to act with still greater force against their interests. They urged, moreover, that there are employers' organizations in all countries adequate for the immediate undertaking of such negotiations." *Vide* also, League of Nations, Econ. Committee, *The Coal Problem*, Geneva, 1932, p. 6.

way of an international cartel.[1] Such a moment was favourable for a comprehensive arrangement at home.

After a short spell of improvement in trade during the first months of 1929, due to severe weather conditions, trade slackened again, and the prospects for a definite international settlement of markets revived. The Five Counties Scheme took the lead in foreign negotiations, and in the autumn of 1929 held several conferences with their competitors, among whom were included both foreign and home coal districts. By the end of August, 1929, the Central Collieries Commercial Association sent a delegation of its representatives to the Continent, with the object of studying and discussing the relevant points of the international agreement. In September the delegation met the representatives of the Polish Coal Convention (Central Organization) in Berlin to consider the possibilities of concluding an understanding, but these attempts were only undertaken by one large organization of Midlands colliery owners. Clearly they could not successfully make arrangements with a vast well-organized foreign coal-field. Full success could not be attained by such negotiations unless they embraced all competing areas, national as well as foreign. Mr. Benton Jones, Chairman of the Central Collieries Commercial Association and of the South Yorkshire Coal Owners' Association,[2] included among the chief exporters the four producing districts of Great Britain, the Ruhr, and Poland, all of which would have to be considered.

The discussions in Geneva in October, 1929, during the Preparatory Technical Coal Conference between the nine European coal-producing countries on conditions of work in coal-mines did not in the end yield any positive result, owing chiefly to the difference in the interpretation of the hours of work, and to the lack of agreement as to the time by which hours should be shortened. The difference in methods of computing the hours of work in the mines accounted to a large extent for the failure of the Conference.

[1] Cf. *Mines Department, Eighth Annual Report of the Secretary for Mines* for the year ending 31st December, 1928, p. 5.
[2] *The Times*, 22nd November, 1929.

The British Government was represented by Sir Sydney Chapman, who actively endeavoured to standardize hours as well as labour conditions on an international basis. Another international conversation took place in London in January, 1930, between the representatives of the Five Counties Scheme and the delegates of all the Polish colliery owners, in which representatives of South Wales, Northumberland, and Durham were also invited to participate informally. This meeting was held with the purpose of bringing some measure of co-operation into the exporting markets, and led to the signing of heads of agreement, which, however, in fact never came into force.

This was later followed by a conference in London in September, 1931, in which seven countries participated, and by a conference at Geneva in January, 1932, discussing the possibility of shortening hours as a remedy against over-production of coal. In December, 1932, private negotiations were carried on in Brussels between the makers of coal briquettes in Great Britain, Germany, France, Holland, and Belgium. Though all these conferences proved to be fruitless, nevertheless the natural tendency of the industry to integrate owing to internal competition and expansion thus received definite encouragement through the hope of an international order.

The Labour Government, which introduced the compulsory organization scheme for the whole British industry, was actuated—apart from several motives with which we shall deal below—by a keen realization of the international possibilities, and of the necessity for national integration if their hopes were in fact to be realized. The late William Graham, who so skilfully piloted the Coal Mines Bill through the rough seas of Parliamentary discussion, in outlining the means by which the new organization would benefit the whole coal industry, alluded in particular to the dawning European coal settlement and the necessity of having a national organization to take part in it.[1] For some time artificial control of prices and

[1] Official Report, Parliamentary Debates, House of Commons, vol. 233, No. 58, 17th December, 1929, Coal Mines Bill Motion of Second Reading, cols. 1259–1260. The President of the Board of Trade (Mr. William Graham):

production of coal, conducted on a World basis, or at least extending over European coal-producing countries, appeared to be practical politics. The gradual fall of prices of coal in the exporting districts, the acrimonious fight for markets, together with the so-called " dumping " in the contested areas at the expense of the home consumers, especially those whose demand did not exhibit signs of elasticity for a fall, led the interested countries to look for an international arrangement. A vast section of British owners was and is interested in carrying this through, if the problem of national organization could be settled.

We have thus little hesitation in considering the prospect of building a European coal cartel as one of the direct incentives towards spontaneous national organization. This,

" Only within recent times has there been a discussion between the representatives of the Five County Scheme and German and Polish producers. There are some proposals for the allocation of the European markets which are not acceptable to many of the coal producers in Europe. There are other proposals which seek to arrive at some kind of price agreement in order that those countries may make up their minds not to undersell one another, nor to offer coal at a loss in what is practically a suicidal competition."

" What is the difficulty of making progress along those lines ? If we take Poland and Germany to-day we shall find that a very large part of their export trade is concentrated. In this country it is very largely scattered, and it is plain, from an analysis of these detailed discussions, that until we have some kind of organization enabling us to present a united front in Great Britain to German, Polish, French, and other Continental coal competition, we have little or no chance of getting an effective place in international agreements. The owners have said in the plainest terms in the Five County Scheme they do not like this so-called subsidy any more than we do. My own belief—and I quite realize the difficulties of the so-called retaliatory argument—would be that the very presence of the power to use it would make it certain that it was never used and that, in fact, the ability to enter into those discussions in terms of this co-ordination on something like lines of reasonable equality would strengthen the hands of these pioneers—because they are pioneers, in British industry—who have conducted those discussions and widened them to include in our representation the representatives of the Mining Association itself."

" I am not going to say here, having lived with this subject for five or six months, that the path of international agreement is easy. I should absolutely mislead the House if I said anything of the kind. But I say that, in absence of some plan of this kind, the difficulties are very greatly increased, and already there are signs that the moment a plan of this kind is practical politics and is accepted in Great Britain there will be a movement of those European countries of a very valuable character to Great Britain, because they have been impressed by the aggregate static demand for European coal in terms of that 650,000,000 metric tons to which I alluded earlier in my speech."

and the natural integrating movement, have contributed most to the formation of the present British coal structure. The Labour Government's coal laws have only reinforced the pressure of the home sections of the industry upon the recalcitrant exporting interests. Of course, it must be realized that the exporting sections had a very fair case. Having to depend on World markets, they rightly realized that the reasons for declining trade must be sought, first in the ravaging effect of the depression in the constructional industries of the higher stages of production,[1] and secondly in the high prices of coal, which supported a high cost fabric, characterized by the lack of static rationalization of the industry. Those considerations led them to fight for a free hand in determining prices independently of the home sections ; a principle which had to be recognized even by the Government.

In summing up our discussion in this section and in the whole of Part I, we must not suppose that the structure of the industry was static and impervious to economic change. The opposite is the case : when expedient, and when economically justified, the industry proved quite able to evolve district organizations, to sketch a national scheme, and finally to take an active part in international collaboration. All these steps were taken without any Government compulsion, and were purely spontaneous.

The next part of this work will describe how the political struggle between compulsory integration by means of nationalization and national disintegrating forces was gradually directed towards the much more delicate problem of actual forms of organization. Politics now enters the field, and the battle continues in the guise of nationalization versus private ownership.

[1] See Pt. I, Chap. I, § 1.

PART II

THE POLITICAL FACTOR

CHAPTER I

POLITICAL SITUATION OF THE INDUSTRY AFTER THE WAR

§ 1. NATIONALIZATION AND POLITICAL INTERFERENCE VERSUS INDUSTRIAL REORGANIZATION

The extremely uneven line of development of the coal industry, its high costs of production, the existence of unemployed resources and of unemployed labour on a scale unknown before the War—all these symptoms of trade depression attracted considerable attention to the problem of organization; more than the public had been accustomed to pay hitherto. The British coal industry, which suffered two serious national stoppages in the five years after decontrol, had necessarily to subject its organization to a very thorough scrutiny. It is in the field of organization that the fate of the coal industry was in fact decided.

The necessity for the introduction of some measures of organization in the coal-mining industry was recognized even before the War.[1] There were then two main schools of thought. The first wanted to achieve a radical change in the structure of production and conceived the ideal reform of coal-mining as some hazy kind of nationalization of mines, as a sort of social reformation, and desired to see the reform introduced by State compulsion. The second school did not believe in compulsion, but it objected in the main to unorganized production, and wanted to counteract the tendency to over-production. The reformers of the former group wished to achieve an alteration in the field of property and administration. While having chiefly in view some form of social administration of mines and minerals, they did not primarily desire to obtain economic ends. The latter school took as their main objective the ex-pediency of economic reorganization, unfettered by the

[1] On the subject of Government interference before the War, see Appendix C.

notion of public administration. When they advocated the need of co-operation between the coal units, it was only in order to counteract economic forces, chiefly over-production and excessive competition. As a good example of the views of this school we can quote G. R. Carter, who published his book before the War,[1] urging the need for an organized movement among the coal-owners in order to check unrestricted competition. He wanted to achieve a particular economic end, i.e. the removal of an existing over-capacity by means of industrial combination, but this was to be brought about without State action of any kind. If any rationalization was necessary, it was to be carried out by the coal-owners themselves.

Before the War any interference from the Government would have been regarded as tantamount to nationalization of the industry. But while saying this we wish to make it quite clear that the nationalization movement was then very feeble, and confined exclusively to the rank and file of the miners. Indeed the question could not arise on any national scale, and hardly any Government Department could be conceived as interfering with the structure of the industry. The prosperous state of the coal industry did not invite public attention to matters of its organization. Reorganization, as separated from nationalization, practically did not exist at all. Hence we may venture the statement that, while different social motives may have given rise to a demand for compulsory reorganization, purely economic thinking never resorted to public pressure and force. So the struggle was between political and social ends, on the one hand, and economic ends on the other. Even among the miners, who were the chief advocates of nationalization, there always

[1] George R. Carter, *The Tendency Towards Industrial Combination*, London, 1913, p. 225. Basing some of his arguments on such an authority as Lord Rhondda (D. A. Thomas), he wrote : " Combinations of colliery firms to restrict prices would seem highly desirable. It is also a question of national importance, since it has been said that at times we are exporting large quantities of coal at less than cost price . . . giving away to the foreigners, with insane prodigality, our mineral wealth—wealth that is by no means inexhaustible and that cannot be replaced. Over-supply and the competition of home collieries are constantly cited as causes of depression and loss in the coal industry."

existed, as we shall show later, an oscillation between the political and economic sections. Generally speaking, the economic wing considered questions of production, distribution, efficiency, cost of production, etc., while the political side paid chief consideration to problems of ownership and power. The fight between the two was another example of private versus public ownership.

After the War, however, new problems opened before the coal industry, which together with other basic industries participated in the crisis longer than the industries of the so-called lower stages of production, i.e. those nearer to the ultimate consumer. Coal ceased now to be an expanding industry with problems of dynamic rationalization and natural adjustments before it. In the short run, the new demand for coal, at the price at which it could be offered by the British coal-owners, proved much lower than the industry could normally supply. Maladjustments between demand and supply, between costs of production and World prices, between prices of coal and prices of other wholesale articles, placed new questions before the British coal industry and other basic industries. Two new points arose from purely economic conditions. First, there was a growing recognition of the necessity for introducing new forms of organization in the coal industry, and for altering the size as well as the number of individual producing units and increasing the efficiency of the industry as a whole. This understanding was achieved as the result both of general reports on industry, which revealed new tendencies, and of special inquiries into coal mining. The *opinio communis* of economists, shared also by some of the leading coal-owners, was in favour of adopting a cheaper and possibly a more up-to-date system of production. Secondly, an important change appeared in the views of some circles on the duties of the State in the reconditioning of the mining industry.

The Committee on Trusts, which presented its Report [1] to the Ministry of Reconstruction in 1919, followed with satisfaction the rapid growth of trade associations and

[1] Report of Committee on Trusts, Ministry of Reconstruction, 1919; Cmd. 9236.

combines. In order, however, to safeguard the public from abuses at their hands, the Report recommended the institution of special machinery, which would investigate their operation. In contrast, however, with such purely economic motives of the Report stood the views of the minority group, contained in an Addendum signed by Messrs. Ernest Bevin, J. A. Hobson, W. H. Watkins, and Sidney Webb. The Addendum, on the ground of protecting the consumers, argued that though combinations are economically desirable, nevertheless nationalization was the only alternative to the " evils of monopoly ".[1]

The great struggle between nationalization and private administration was waged before the Coal Industry Commission, 1919, presided over by Sir John Sankey.[2] By this time the movement for nationalization had reached its climax and the Commission was entrusted with the subtle duty of analysing the various claims for public ownership and framing a programme for the organization of the industry after the end of the War control system. In fact, the Commission proved to be the buffer between the two irreconcilable points of view : private ownership and public control. Out of the seven reports published by the Sankey Commission, three[3] were of a preliminary nature, and referred only to problems connected with the pending dispute on

[1] Ibid. Addendum : In those trades " where the product enters into practically universal consumption, we see no alternative to State Ownership. But State Ownership does not necessarily imply State Management ". The coal industry would certainly be included under this last heading.

[2] Professor D. H. Macgregor, " The Coal Bill and the Cartel," *The Economic Journal*, vol. xl, March, 1930, p. 45 : " The Sankey Commission debated in its evidence, especially that of Sir Richard Redmayne, the issue between what one side implied to be the ' Giant Sloth of Nationalization ' and what were called by the other side the ' Black Tigers ' or capitalist combinations. Even if the tigers were to have their claws cut, as Redmayne thought possible, by the provision of controls over producers' amalgamations or associations, the debate went against this solution, and even against the Duckham scheme for controlling the profits of large producers' unions."

[3] Coal Industry Commission, 1919, vol. i, Cmd. 359.

(a) Interim Report by the Hon. Mr. Justice Sankey, Mr. Arthur Balfour, Sir Arthur Duckham, and Sir Thomas Royden.

(b) Interim Report by Messrs. R. Smillie, Frank Hodges, and Herbert Smith, Sir Leo Chiozza Money, Messrs. R. H. Tawney, and Sidney Webb.

(c) Interim Report by Messrs. Cooper, Forgie, and Evan Williams.

wages and hours of work. The other four reports [1] reveal
the striking contrast between the nationalization outlook
and the individual outlook. Sir John Sankey's Report,
which presumably was influenced by German coal legislation
at that time, advocated the nationalization of mines and
minerals after a period of three years of further State control.
He proposed three stages in the whole organization : a
National Mining Council, District Councils, and Local Mining
Councils at each mine. All the emphasis in this scheme
was laid on District Councils, which were to administer
the operation of the districts, while the National Council
was to be purely consultative. Over the whole structure
was the Minister of Mines, responsible to Parliament ; he
was to preside over the National Mining Council and to
supervise the functioning of the industry. The short
Report of the Labour group, which endorsed the views of
Sir John Sankey on nationalization differed however in
certain points. They wanted to place greater responsibility
upon the National Council and to secure for the miners a
stronger influence in the determination of policy. Sir John's
scheme had left this largely to representatives of various
groups of society. In principle they endorsed the
Nationalization Bill submitted by the Miners' Federation to
the Commission. Sir Arthur Duckham's scheme stood
on the side of private property, but he wished to achieve a
complete amalgamation of all collieries within each area
into a Statutory Company (District Coal Board), whose
profits would be divided in a prescribed manner ; [2] part
of them going to reduce the price of coal to consumers.

---

[1] Coal Industry Commission, 1919, vol. ii. Cmd. 360.
(1) Report by the Hon. Mr. Justice Sankey.
(2) Report by Mr. Frank Hodges, Sir Leo Chiozza Money, Mr. Robert
Smillie, Mr. Herbert Smith, Mr. R. H. Tawney, and Mr. Sidney Webb.
(3) Report by Messrs. Arthur Balfour, R. W. Cooper, Sir Adam Nimmo,
Sir Allan M. Smith, and Mr. Evan Williams.
(4) Report by Sir Arthur Duckham.
[2] Report, loc. cit., § 29 c : " Profits in excess of those necessary to
pay the 4 per cent dividend and usual depreciation may be utilized :—
(1) To form such reserve funds as may be approved by the Minister of
Mines ;
(2) to pay a further 2 per cent dividend. Of the remaining profits one-
third may be utilized for paying further dividend on shares, but the
other two-thirds must be used to reduce the price of coal."

P

His plan of reform was, however, very unpopular and was opposed both by the owners and the miners.

In extreme opposition to these views were the owners, who denied the State any right to interfere with the management of the industry. Lord Gainford, speaking before the Commission as a witness for the coal-owners, forcibly stated that they could not accept any compromise which would remain on the border line of public control and private administration. The Report of the owners as a whole rejected the counsels of nationalization and compulsory reorganization. At the same time it proposed to establish a network of joint pit committees, district councils, and a national council for common discussions of current problems. But while disagreeing on practically all major questions, the four reports all agreed that mining royalties should be nationalized. Moreover, they all asked for the almagamation of the different administrative offices, scattered among several departments, into one body, with the Secretary of Mines at its head. The motives underlying these recommendations, however, differed much from one another. The main motive of the Chairman's Report, and of the Labour Group's additional Report, was the creation of a central agent responsible to Parliament for the administration of a nationalized industry. He was to be assisted by a Standing Committee of eighteen members elected from and by the National Mining Council, a body representing the District Mining Councils, and was to superintend the operation of the District Mining Councils and to preside over the National Mining Council. In addition to those functions strictly connected with nationalization of mines, he was to be responsible for the supervision of safety in mines and the superintendence of health regulations. A research section was to be attached to the Ministry of Mines for the purpose of carrying out research into safety and health conditions, and also into the economic conditions affecting the industry. The motives of the Owners' Report in suggesting the formation of a Mines Department had nothing to do with nationalization of mines. The Department should administer only the ownership of minerals and combine other functions scattered among various depart-ments.[1]

After the publication of the Sankey Reports the Government showed no signs of undertaking any reorganization of the industry, so, after a short educational campaign by the miners in favour of nationalization, this movement gradually faded from the public eye, and only remained as part of the general labour movement.   Mean-while, conditions in the industry greatly improved, so the chief attention of the miners was paid to securing an adequate share in the profits, especially in view of the rising prices. Thus, the chief problems centred round the question of wages.   The decision was between a national pool and national wage regulation, and the latter was finally achieved by the miners in successive agreements with the owners in 1921 and 1924.   In the meantime the industry was changing its internal structure, and in all coal-fields the colliery companies greatly increased their size and substantially inflated their capital.   This process can be seen in the following representative sample.

TABLE No. 31

INCREASE OF CAPITAL OF COAL, IRON, STEEL, AND ENGINEERING COMPANIES
BETWEEN 1919–1925

	31st December, 1919.	28th February, 1925.
	£	£
Coal and Pig Iron Companies [2]	5,326,000	6,451,000
Coal, Iron, and Steel Companies [3]	29,481,000	42,431,000
Iron, Steel, and Engineering Companies [4]	26,137,000	35,930,000

Source : The National Federation of Iron and Steel Manufacturers.

[1] Report by Messrs. Arthur Balfour, R. W. Cooper, Sir Adam Nimmo, Sir Allan M. Smith, and Mr. Evan Williams, dated 20th June, 1919, § 43 : " This department should exercise the function of State so far as regards the ownership of coal. . . . It should also have administrative functions including the functions which are at present exercised by a Mines Depart-ment at the Home Office and it should have jurisdiction over all questions relating to the coal mines except the adjustment of labour disputes and wages, which are appropriate subjects for the jurisdiction of the Minister of Labour.   For example, it should deal with questions of safety and technique ; should collect and publish statistics relative to accidents, output, export, and consumption ; it should be a record office for data relating to the coal industry, and should deal with questions affecting new coal-fields and the development of existing ones."
[2] Seven Companies.
[3] Nineteen Companies.
[4] Eight Companies.

Several mergers and amalgamations took place in the relatively prosperous period 1919–1924. These mergers on the whole did not effect economies either in production or distribution, but they swelled the capital of the industrial units. Moreover, the very speed of the movement appeared to show that the industry was spontaneously reorganizing, and therefore nationalization or political pressure were not necessary. We can say that the movement towards industrial combination substantially blunted the influence of political pressure, and brought the industrial arguments once again to the fore. *Coal and Power*, [1] a Liberal Report published under the ægis of Mr. Lloyd George, is the best example of this attitude. In this report amalgamation and concentration in the most progressive mines formed the gist of all proposed reforms. [2] Political transfer of the ownership of mines is placed in the background and economic reorganization is considered all important. In 1925, by reason of a strong depression which had settled on the coal industry, the controversy turned once more to the dilemma of public versus private ownership of mines. This was bound up with a renewed struggle over hours, wages, and other labour problems. The most interesting phases in the wrestling of the two mutually inconsistent systems took place before the Royal Commission on the Coal Industry, 1925.

It is difficult to find much relation between the conclusions reached by the Sankey Commission in 1919, the Samuel Commission in 1925, and the reforms in organization brought about later. Let us consider first the report of the Sankey Commission. They were analysing the grievances of the industry during State Control. The problem was then not how the industry was to be conducted, but who was to be its owner—the private individual or the nation ? No *aurea mediocritas* was practicable. The situation required clear-cut decisions on questions concerned with the defence or rejection of the public ownership of mines. During this period labour difficulties remained essentially the chief

---

[1] *Coal and Power*, the Report of an Inquiry presided over by the Rt. Hon. D. Lloyd George, London, 1924.
[2] For further details, consult Pt. II, Chap. II, § 2.

problem.[1] The movement for the nationalization of mines was then at its zenith, both in Great Britain and abroad. Any measures of State compulsion were therefore interpreted as a triumph for the protagonists of expropriation, and were strongly opposed on the same ground.

Like the Sankey Commission, the Royal Commission on the Coal Industry, 1925, was faced by the spectre of labour troubles. It confined its chief attention to the relations between employers and employed. Hence, social problems were widely dealt with, and occupied more than 100 pages of the Report ; but only one aspect of the structure of the industry was discussed at all—the problem of amalgamation, dealt with in nineteen pages. Eleven pages only were devoted to questions of distribution. The Report contained a final condemnation of the programme of nationalization of mines, but it prescribed that :—

> " The mineral should be acquired by the State—by purchase where it has a market value, by a declaration of State owner-ship in the case of unproved coal or coal at deep levels which has now no market value." [2]

Among the few recommendations of the Commission dealing with organization, no room was left for compulsion, which then was still associated with socialization of mines. Somewhat indecisively the Report declared itself in favour

[1] Sir Richard Redmayne gives us a vivid picture of the conditions prevailing in the year 1919, when the Sankey Commission was busy endeavouring to find the way out for the Coal Industry : " The year 1919 will probably go down in history as the most memorable one in the annals of the coal-mining industry of the United Kingdom. The year opened gloomily, for, although the total output of coal showed an upward tendency, this was owing to the augmentation of the labour employed in the mines by the return of a considerable number of ex-miners demobilized from the Army, and not to increased output per person employed ; the home demand was in excess of the supply available to meet it, and our obligations to our Allies imposed certain limits to the restriction of export. The horizon was overcast with great and imminent labour troubles ; working costs, due to the rise in wages (principally the result of the increased cost of living) and the unprecedented increase in the price of materials used in mining, had attained a figure hitherto unknown in the history of the industry, and the inadequacy of the transport facilities, both by sea and land, prevented the amount of ' Clearance ' at the collieries and the ports requisite to meet the possible output." (Sir R. A. S. Redmayne, *The British Coalmining Industry during the War*, Oxford, 1923, p. 215.)
[2] *Report of the Royal Commission on the Coal Industry* (1925), vol. i, p. 233.

of larger units, but rejected the method of compulsory amalgamation.[1]

A certain distrust of Government action was manifested in the Report, when it recommended the rejection of any general measure for the compulsory grouping of coal mines. In the opinion of the Commission, State compulsion should only be used where " one or more undertakings in an area desired to effect an amalgamation, but (if) others, whose co-operation was necessary, refused, or demanded unreasonable terms " ; " in this case there must be power in the public interest to over-ride such opposition." When we analyse this recommendation, which should be considered in close connection with the opinion of the Commissioners that a certain number of years ought to elapse after the passing of the Act before Government compulsion should be applied, we cannot resist the impression that the State is considered here rather as a passive observer who would give his authority only to supplement the will of the majority. This is a very different outlook from that of the previous Commission, who regarded the State as a possible leader in reorganization. The Samuel Report laid down that only on the request of mine-owners could the Government be called in to assist certain auxiliary measures in the general movement towards amalgamation. Even this convincing warrant that the State would act only and exclusively when invited did not seem to the Royal Commission a sufficient guarantee that interference would not be excessive. They wished to allow the whole movement to be utterly and completely self-determining. The State should only come forward later to give legal sanction to schemes already decided.[2] Its function was rather to persuade reluctant members to conform to the

---

[1] " Even if there be a balance of advantage in favour of the large unit, when purely economic calculations of a general kind are alone taken into account, this would be more than neutralized if individual colliery companies were forced by some outside authority to amalgamate against their will." Ibid., p. 51.

[2] Ibid., p. 61. " On the whole, we recommend that the legislation that would be needed to give effect to these proposals in general should include a provision of the character described ; but that this provision should not come into effect upon the passing of the Act, but at a specified later date, perhaps after three years ; and then only if a statement is

economic structure chosen by the majority of the industry than to create an independent programme of organization. Authority ought to be used, not in order to compel those units already following the general trend of the industry to join an elaborate scheme of reorganization, but rather in order to bring a dissentient minority into the accepted framework.

Among other recommendations affecting the organization of the industry, the Report advised the promotion of closer co-operation of mining with the allied industries and State support in research work. Further, a hint was made in connection with the establishing of selling agencies attached to several colliery companies, which used to sell their coal, buy materials, etc. Such agencies were common in South Yorkshire and in South Wales. The Report suggested that municipal retail trading in coal should be authorized.[1] Some of the recommendations dealing with the labour problems affected organization. Among them were the Joint Pit Committees, which were to be formed in the industry, and the obligatory profit-sharing schemes, which constituted the only section in the whole field of proposed reorganization which required statutory compulsion.[2]

At this juncture the old controversy between public and private administration took on a new aspect. No longer did discussion centre on whether it was necessary to reorganize or not. The only problem outstanding was the method by which reorganization could be secured, i.e. with or without State interference. Though at the time of the Sankey Commission in 1919 and of the de-control of mines in 1921 we can still witness strong remnants of the old controversy, large-scale production versus small independent units, nevertheless, as already noted, all attention is gradually focused on the dilemma of rationalization with or without Government interference. Finally, in later years

made by the Mines Department that it is satisfied that it is necessary in the public interest to bring it into operation. During the interval the situation will have become clearer, and it will be seen whether the application of this somewhat drastic provision is really required."
[1] Ibid., p. 93.
[2] Ibid., pp. 234–5.

this controversy became crystallized into a struggle between individual and co-operative efforts.

While the need for reconstruction was recognized, there was strong resistance against using any statutory action to assist the industry towards amalgamation or co-operation. Many industrialists, while in favour of new forms of organization, flatly objected to State interference.[1] Those who were in stout opposition to nationalization at that time did not reserve any part whatever for State action within the industrial structure. Such opinion was emphatically voiced before the Royal Commission in 1925, in the evidence of Mr. C. P. Markham,[2] Chairman and Managing Director of some of the best and most efficient collieries and iron and steel companies in the Midlands. In his memorandum he advised the freeing of the industry from any restrictions :—

" Any Government interference would stifle all initiative, and the colliery industry would be placed in a far worse position if ruled by permanent officials than it is at the present time. The head men in the industry have invariably risen

[1] Lord Gainford, Chairman of Pease and Partners, Ltd., etc., " I believe in the right of both owners and workmen to combine, but not in compelling either of them to do so by law."
The Marquis of Londonderry, " British Mining and its Revival," Mining Supplement of The Daily Telegraph, 16th September, 1930 : " The present Government, however, came forward with proposals for further interference, for which there was no justification whatever in the national interest. And yet the history of the coal industry affords convincing proof that the position of Great Britain as the premier coal-producing country in Europe and coal-exporting centre of the world is due to the initiative, courage, and enterprise of individuals." (" Colliery Development in the Future," ibid.)

[2] Report of the Royal Commission on the Coal Industry (1925), vol. 2 (Part B), Minutes of Evidence, Memorandum of Evidence of Mr. Charles Paxton Markham, D.L., J.P., p. 538.
Mr. C. P. Markham was Chairman and Managing Director of the following Companies : The Staveley Coal and Iron Co., Ltd. ; the Parkgate Iron and Steel Co., Ltd. ; the Markham Main Collieries, Ltd. ; the Newstead Colliery Co., Ltd. ; the Yorkshire Main Colliery, Ltd. ; the British Soda Company, Ltd. ; the Doncaster Collieries Association, Ltd. ; the Midland Ironstone Company ; the Burton Ironstone Co., Ltd. ; the Cranford Ironstone Co., Ltd. ; the Loddington Ironstone Co., Ltd. ; the Eastwell Iron Ore Co. ; Markham and Co. (1925), Ltd.
He was Joint Managing Director of the Brodsworth Main Colliery Co., Ltd.
He was also Director of the following companies : The Ramscroft Colliery Co., Ltd. ; the Hickleton Main Colliery Co., Ltd. ; the Firbeck Main Collieries, Ltd. ; the Industrial Housing Association, Ltd. ; the Chesterfield Housing Co., Ltd. ; the Chesterfield Housing Association, Ltd.

from the ranks and obtained their positions by hard work and merit. . . . I think that interference with the Coal Industry by the Government would lead to chaotic disaster in the coal trade."

Simultaneously, however, with the fading prospects of nationalization, the intransigent view of many owners and other sections of the community underwent a rapid change in the direction of using the power of the State as an organ of rationalization. The duty of such an organ, as Mr. Hobson described it very appropriately, would be " pumping into the conduct of the economic system as an organic whole a sufficient quantity of reason to eliminate the waste of friction and conflict from which it has hitherto been suffering ".[1] As from 1923, the difficulties of the coal industry grew worse, opiinon came more into line with the recommendations of the Commissions and those representatives of the industry who were in favour of co-operation. This change was especially noticeable after 1926, when economic thinking ousted political thinking, and when, owing to enormous losses in all the coal-fields, the industry itself spontaneously began to pay more consideration to integration. If at that stage any considerations arose of the use of Government authority in industry, it was now no longer understood as signifying nationalization, but as speeding up the reorganization originated by the industry itself. This change came, however, very slowly, and we can watch in the various successive official reports a gradual waning of general interest in the political problem and a turn towards economic problems.

Immediately after the publication of the Report of the Samuel Commission in 1926, the question of coal-mining organization began to develop further. The Commission's emphasis on the existence of an excessive number of mines, on over-capacity, and on the necessity for amalgamation, its passing reference to selling agencies such as the Doncaster Collieries Association, all stimulated new suggestions and " pick-me-ups " for the industry, drugged under the chloroform of State subsidies.

[1] J. A. Hobson, " The State as an Organ of Rationalization," *Political Quarterly*, vol. ii, No. 1.

Part of the criticism of the Samuel Report was focused on the problem of the elimination of old and inefficient collieries which were alleged to hamper sound development. Subsequent analysis revealed the inadequacy with which the Royal Commission had dealt with this important subject of organization. New criticisms and views, which came to light in connection with this Report, led to fresh suggestions for meeting the existing state of affairs.

Gradually, the concept of State interference in the coal industry took on a new aspect. When in the early post-War years the State was discussed as an agent intervening in the affairs of the coal-mining industry, it was then conceived as a prospective owner which would occupy the place of private enterprise. Later, however, the development of public opinion brought about a new conception of Government interference. The stage at which the State was regarded as being in opposition to privately owned and conducted industry had passed away. Now political influence was conceived as a useful champion for the reorganization of the coal industry, forcing the hand of recalcitrant sections which might hamper the progress of integration. Simultaneously with the increasing remoteness of all prospects for nationalization of mines, especially after the stoppage of 1926, the idea of State ownership ceased to be attached to intervention.

Meanwhile the views of many of the leading mine owners had also rapidly altered. This was clearly shown amongst others by the late Lord Melchett, one of the leading industrialists in this country, who discriminated between the old meaning of rationalization and the new. He emphasized the necessity for carefully distinguishing between two completely different notions, so as not to confuse the reorganization of industry with " the old political and economic nostrum of the Socialists ".[1] As he considered the nationalization movement dead, he pressed the more strongly for the adoption of a programme of speedy reorganization of the coal-mining industry. The day after the Government introduced in the House of Commons the

[1] Sir Alfred Mond, *Industry and Politics*, London, 1927, p. 210.

Mining Industry Bill, 1926, which contained clauses dealing with amalgamation and a modicum of compulsion by the State, but which left the initiative to the industry, Lord Melchett criticized the measure as not going far enough.[1]

Indeed, State assistance was now generally loudly demanded for the rationalization of the coal industry. Even the protagonists of nationalization were now turning most of their attention to the problem of organization. In this view, nationalization was to be merely a means of attaining similar ends under public control. Both were aiming in the first place at cheapening the costs of production. It was generally held that the number of producing units was too large, that some units were on the whole inefficient, and finally that there existed a lack of co-operation between individual producers, which depressed prices and exhausted the strength of the industry. But great differences of opinion existed as to the way in which inefficiency could best be eliminated. Those who thought that through the natural process of competition the marginal units would in time be removed opposed any extraneous action directed towards reorganization. Those who believed in some sort of intervention were themselves divided ; some thought that amalgamation of the undertakings into a smaller number would finally pave the way to co-operation, while others thought that to begin with schemes of co-operation would lead to amalgamation within the network of a cartel system. The former opinion was held by those who, like Professor Levy,[2] considered the amalgamation of individual undertakings as being the " foundation stone of English cartels and trusts " or, like Professor Macgregor,[3]

---

[1] Ibid., p. 196.

[2] Professor Hermann Levy, *Monopolies, Cartels and Trusts in British Industry*, 2nd ed., London, 1927, p. 313: " Concentration of works and undertakings is the foundation-stone of English Cartels and Trusts. The conditions which made monopoly possible in other countries, even where concentration was but slightly, if at all, developed, being wanted in England, until the recent growth of concentration it was inconceivable."

[3] Professor D. H. Macgregor, " The Coal Bill and the Cartel," *Economic Journal*, March, 1930, vol. xl, p. 39 : " In this country, the organization may come out to the same result by whichever method we start. Amalgamations prepare the way for Cartel agreements ; history shows that Cartels with movable quotas tend to create fusions of interests."

who maintained that the movements for amalgamation and co-operation are to some extent interdependent. Either concentration may speed up cartelization, or the converse may happen, i.e. a fusion of interest arises through the movable output quotas involved in the cartel scheme. Especially in the case of the coal industry, he thought that it might be more rational to start by creating amalgamations and proceed later with restriction schemes. The latter opinion was often expressed by those who thought that the primary remedy for the industry was in reducing output and the existing over-capacity of mines by some form of agreement, and that concentration on the more efficient mines and amalgamation of the smaller undertakings was only to be pushed forward at a later stage.

At this stage some of the students of the British coal industry, who were following closely the developments in the industry and the tendency towards integration, laid great stress on the necessity for organization. Their proposals suggested several lines along which reconstruction could develop. Here also it is noticeable that the farther we move from the critical years of 1926 the less important is the part reserved for the direct interference of the Government. A typical compromise between the two solutions of State ownership of mines and complete individualism is to be found in an article by Professor Jones,[1] written soon after the publication of the Samuel Report in which he advocated that the Government should engage in a purely industrial activity as an entrepreneur, so that it would accelerate reorganization by competing with private owners. We must bear in mind that the project was not new in detail, but the emphasis was now on the combination of State action on the one side, with industrial reform on the other. A little later,

---

[1] J. H. Jones, " The Coal Report, *The Accountant*, 3rd April, 1926, vol. lxxiv, p. 502. Professor Jones saw no special difficulties in realizing this bold and far-reaching experiment : " The Commission advocates the transfer to the State of property rights in unmined coal. As mineral owner it might embark upon mining, and by experiment seek the most efficient unit of business control and the most efficient method of mining. Those who have greatest faith in private enterprise would be the last to fear such competition on the part of State mines, provided it were conducted on equal terms."

different and more complete proposals were put forward by Professor Jones.[1]

Among other writers, Mr. J. W. F. Rowe [2] stressed the importance of reorganization on grounds of efficiency. In a comparative study of American and English mining, he pointed out the different conditions of the two industries. In his view, while in the former country, the whole difficulty consisted in preventing the opening of new mines, in England " our problem is how to ensure that old and inefficient mines close down sufficiently rapidly ". Mr. Rowe doubted whether the working of economic forces alone would scrap badly organized mines within a short time, as Mr. Gowers had maintained in the evidence before the Samuel Commission. " The tenacity of life," he says, " displayed by the British mines is extraordinary," and he therefore would like the Commission to have devoted more attention directly to the problem of closing down some of the pits as well as to the phenomenon of over-capacity.

The American students of the " British Coal Dilemma," [3] in their analysis, came to the conclusion that a proper regulation of production is essential to the well-being of the industry. Such regulation must be carried out by some central body representing the interests of the whole industry. This, in the opinion of the authors, was not tantamount to nationalization, but they preferred a reform involving some form of public coercion, considering

[1] *Vide* J. H. Jones, " The Coal Situation, *The Accountant*, 12th June, 1926, p. 810.

" The industry is still so deeply entrenched in nineteenth century traditions that we cannot hope for the creation of associations for controlling output and thereby relieving the market and raising prices. It is for that reason that I suggested a few weeks ago the adoption of the principle of a statutory minimum price," and J. H. Jones, " The Marketing of Coal," *Journal of the Institute of Bankers*, May, 1929, vol. i, part v, p. 258, in which he suggests regional and national associations to control prices, output, and marketing syndicates along the German lines.

[2] J. W. F. Rowe, " The Coal Mining Industry in Great Britain and the United States," *Economica*, June, 1926, p. 205.

[3] Isador Lubin and Helen Everett, with the aid of the Council and Staff of the Institute of Economics, U.S.A., *The British Coal Dilemma*, London, 1927 : " Between private enterprise as now carried on and nationalization there are many different kinds of public co-ordination and control which might conceivably be adopted to achieve the ends of an efficient industry."

that the owners by themselves were unable to adjust the output of coal to the actual demand of the market. The menace of foreign cut-throat competition forced upon the mine-owners problems which did not exist in the days when their primary concern was to enlarge output.

In his historical study on *Coal and its Conflicts*,[1] Mr. Raynes traced the evolution of different forms of producers' organizations, and went on to make some forecasts concerning future development, which probably represent his views on the reforms of which the industry stood in need. " Holding up a periscope to peep into the future, one sees prophetically the gradual cohesion of the coal marketing scheme of South Wales, the Five Counties, and Scotland into one co-ordinated whole, possibly acting in concert with similar marketing schemes in France, Germany, Belgium, Poland, and other countries of Europe. Output will be transferred to those undertakings that can produce it most economically and will be regulated according to market requirements. Losses on production will cease for the owners, and privations of standards of life will cease for the miners." Such changes seemed to Mr. Raynes likely to come as a result of a natural process of evolution. There is no reference in this vision of the future coal industry to Parliamentary interference as a stimulant to reconstruction.

Before proceeding further with our discussion of the development of ideas concerning State interference and reorganization, it behoves us to say a few words about certain recommendations contained in the Reports of the Departmental Committee on Co-operative Selling in the Coal Mining Industry, working under the chairmanship of Sir Frederick W. Lewis, Bart.[2] As the recommendations of the Samuel Commission dealing with marketing schemes were only vague, and for the most part referred to the export trade, a Committee was set up in order to put forward more detailed and practical proposals. This Committee was appointed by the Government on 22nd July, 1926, to inquire into the desirability of developing co-operative selling in the

---

[1] J. R. Raynes, *Coal and its Conflicts*, London, 1928.
[2] Reports of the Departmental Committee on Co-operative Selling in the Coal Mining Industry, 1926, Cmd. 2770.

coal industry. Its interesting findings threw new light on the question of State interference, and advanced the idea of Parliamentary action one step further. Though the recommendations on the question of compulsion were as yet weak, and they refused to "contemplate anything in the nature of general compulsion ", nevertheless they advised a substantial enlargement of statutory activity in the field of organization.

The starting point of the whole Report was the assumption of the existence of an over-production of coal and of consequent cut-throat competition. The Committee judged it desirable to develop organized marketing in order to avoid excessive competition, to effect economies and improvements in the marketing of coal, and to help to stabilize the industry. Hence the importance of a speedy progress of consolidation into a smaller number of units was strongly emphasized.[1] In fact the Committee confined their attention rather to local arrangements, more particularly to selling pools and to district organization, than to any national unification. The expediency of some form of national organization was entirely neglected.[2] Indeed, if competition between individual producers were abolished, it might, on the other hand, merely give way to rivalry between district organizations. This absence of any national outlook is typical ; for throughout the Report the emphasis is only on district and local arrangements.

The merit of first pointing out the importance of national co-ordination must be conceded to the Report of the coalowners sitting on the Committee. In opposition to the main Report, they made the striking declaration that neither district nor local schemes could work successfully without national co-ordination.[3]

[1] Ibid. : " We are convinced that the full development and benefits of organized marketing within the industry cannot be realized unless the industry can be consolidated by amalgamations into a much smaller number of units."

[2] Ibid. : " The co-ordination of the district associations will be ultimately a desirable development, but can only be justified to the community by the industry effecting and sharing with the consumer economies not only in the marketing of coal but in all phases of its production and transport."

[3] *Vide* ibid. : " Interpenetration of coals from various districts among the various markets, both in this country and abroad, takes place to such an extent that it would be impossible to establish water-tight compartments or to set up a scheme for the control of selling arrangements on

This statement pointed towards a danger which was in fact soon to be experienced by the voluntary district schemes such as the Five Counties Scheme. From the start they had felt in the home markets the competition of the non-cartelized districts from the North-East Coast and Scotland. Any scheme of regulation must at least embrace the whole output of those kinds of coal which are interchangeable with each other in the market, or which might be easily substituted for one another. On the whole, however, the owners' Report was opposed to the policy of co-operative selling.

The main Report reserved an important rôle for statutory enactments in the formation of district marketing organization and wished to support a progressive majority by enabling them to compel a dissentient minority to conform to the lines of the proposed district arrangement. But at the same time it carefully laid down that the initiative in forming such schemes should be left to the industry itself.

The whole Committee was of the opinion that Parliament ought to pass legislation which would apply to the formation of the district schemes similar principles to those embodied in Part I of the Mining Industry Act, 1926, dealing with amalgamations. Under this Act two or more coal-owners could apply for amalgamation or absorption, in spite of the disapproval of an undefined number of opposing persons, whereas in the case of district marketing schemes the Report recommended that compulsion should only be applied where the minority does not exceed 25 per cent. The scheme was to be made compulsory by the Railway and Canal Commission on condition that it would lead to more efficient marketing of coal, that it would be dictated by national interest, and finally that it should prove fair to all its members.

The Miners' Memorandum attached to the Report greatly favoured the idea of general compulsion and recommended that the principle of voluntary amalgamation with legislative

any basis which did not embrace the whole coal production of the country."
(Report signed by Sir David Llewellyn and Messrs. J. R. D. Bell, and A. K. McCosh, p. 44.)

assistance should be given a full trial over a period of two years. Should, however, the owners fail to make substantial progress towards the co-ordination of the industry, then

" the Board of Trade should have power to propose a scheme which when settled, after full investigation and consultation with the industry, should be imposed on all concerned."

On the point of organization an interesting change took place in the attitude of the miners. Nationalization had been relegated to a position of lesser importance, and attention was now directed towards a reduction in the surplus capacity of the producing units. As the prospects of nationalization faded away, the miners therefore, more in sorrow than in anger, turned towards an immediate programme of rationalization for the industry. Nationalization was not mentioned, but they were in general agreement with the other members of the Committee in holding that the industry required reorganization. After this change of opinion, reorganization was placed in the forefront of their programme : nationalization, though not completely lost to sight, had to take a back seat. Henceforward the miners became staunch supporters of the movement for restricting production and for raising prices.

To sum up now the views of the main Report of the Lewis Committee, we must notice two fresh ideas involved in it. First, the official recognition of the desirability of cartelizing the industry, and second the demand that this process should be assisted by State compulsion. The Report gave its blessing to the policy of restricting production and regulating prices. The apparatus proposed, though imperfect, yet formed the basis on which further and improved projects were to be founded.

The immediate result of its publication was an exuberant crop of projects for the restriction of the free play of supply and demand in the industry. To the personal influence of Lord Melchett, one of the most active members of the Committee, the whole movement for reorganization owes a very great debt. The effect of his personality can hardly be disregarded, since he was one of the first protagonists of reorganization in industry as a whole, and in the coal industry particularly. An ardent believer in methods of co-operation, both in the relations between labour and capital and in the relations between industrialists themselves, Lord Melchett actively promoted the idea of industrial reorganization. This he interpreted as "an attempt to adjust the means of production to the probable means of consumption, and so to regulate prices that instead of curves rising and falling like the contour of the Alps there should be a fairly level roadway of prices along which trade and commerce could move".[1] As an advocate of the adoption of some form of coal-selling organization, more or less along the lines of the Rhenish-Westphalian Coal Syndicate, he initiated a propaganda campaign for the introduction of similar methods in the British Coal Industry. Lord Melchett drew up a full scheme for separate district organizations to sell coal on a co-operative basis and for a liaison organization to dovetail the various local schemes. The business of his central selling institution was to be mainly the determination of district quotas, adjudication of disputes, and regulation of exports. So thoroughly organized an industry would be in a position to make arrangements with other exporting countries for the better exploitation of foreign markets. In his plan, Lord Melchett[2] thus desired to produce a closely organized coal industry in place of the state of complete individualism pervading all the districts. Perhaps the great significance of his scheme lay in the fact that it was one of the earliest demands for general concentration, based on private ownership, coming from one of the leaders of the industry. After the strong demands for concentration arising in political centres, the voice of a practical industrialist was now heard urging reorganization.

Such a far-reaching innovation as that could not at once

---

[1] Sir Alfred Mond, Bart., *Industry and Politics*, London, 1927, p. 211.
[2] See Presidential Address to the Society of British Gas Industries on the 23rd of June, 1926, where he described his attempts to secure improved methods of organization. "I (Lord Melchett) have for several months, with increasing energy, been impressing upon mine owners, miners, and Ministers the value which would accrue to all concerned from the establishment of coal-selling organizations in this country. Some months ago I invited two of the leading directors of the Rhenish-Westphalian Coal Syndicate to come across to inform me of the methods and administration of coal-selling syndicates in Germany" (ibid. p. 199).

materialize without opposition from the mine owners, whose general attitude to intervention had not been improved by the recent nationalization propaganda. To political fears, however, one must add very strong economic motives which militated against integration. The disparities between various firms were, especially at the expiry of the subsidy, greatly accentuated, and the process of concentration had not yet advanced very far. On the other hand the depleted stocks after the stoppage created the appearance of a steady demand which would be maintained. The use of compulsion to force reorganization was therefore still condemned, both by a very large body of the leaders of the industry and by the Mining Association of Great Britain.[1]

But as the economic condition of the industry grew worse, it came to be realized that excess capacity could only be checked by some form of artificial control, and many economists as well as coal experts demanded more and more energetic measures on the part of the State. Works which have appeared in the last few years on the coal industry have not been able to pass by such a momentous problem in silence. The question of co-ordination in the industry and of the scrapping of excess capacity have therefore occupied a more prominent place.

In the meantime one district after another evolved its own scheme of co-ordination of production designed to assist the industry to withstand the pressure from increasing competition parallel with the deepening of the depression. The year 1928 witnessed the birth of the Five Counties Scheme, covering nearly all the Midlands as well as the old coal-field of Lancashire and Cheshire ; of the South Wales Marketing Scheme regulating prices and output ; of the Scottish Coal Scheme designed to eliminate the high costs of collieries, and of an arrangement as to export prices in the North-East Coast basins. These schemes together

[1] Mining Association of Great Britain, 1926 : " The owners must accordingly urge that a truer perspective be observed in these matters, and in particular that it be realized that the theory that the industry can be coerced into prosperity by restrictive action from outside is unsound and is foreign to the tradition of free and open competition on which the success of British industry has been built up under private enterprise in the past." (Quoted by R. C. Smart, *The Economics of the Coal Industry*, London, 1930, p. 206.)

controlled more than 80 per cent of the national output. In the same year a substantial amount of amalgamation and absorption was carried through, both vertical and horizontal, covering a considerable proportion of district outputs, e.g. the amalgamation known as the Manchester Collieries, Ltd., which was created at this time, covered 25 per cent of the whole output of the Lancashire coal-field. Apart from integration, exporting coal-fields made substantial inroads into the markets of those producing for home consumption. This led to much resentment and to the demand for a speedy division of markets, or for some other sort of regulations. At this juncture, the Liberal Industrial Report of 1928 [1] appeared, marking a further stage in the discussion of the problems of compulsory reorganization. The adoption by an official publication of the Liberal Party of the idea of using Parliamentary powers to stimulate the introduction of selling agencies and to accelerate the process of amalgamation among the individual undertakings, constituted a new inducement, for people who were not in favour of nationalization, to move towards the view that the industry must be granted powers by the State for use against some of the excessively individualistic members of the community. But the proposals in the Liberal Report, while they endorsed the majority findings of the Lewis Committee, went one step further, for they favoured the use of legislative compulsion, even without the initiative of the owners. This was, however, regarded as a drastic expedient, to be used only after the prescribed period of two years if the industry had proved unable to reorganize on its own accord.

Also in the official Reports, organization was very strongly urged. The Report of the Balfour Committee considered the question of reorganization to be the first step towards the re-establishment of industrial health. In 1929, in concluding their final Report,[2] they say :—

" the first step towards putting British industries in a position to compete successfully in overseas markets, is to subject

[1] *Britain's Industrial Future*, being the Report of the Liberal Industrial Inquiry, London, 1928.
[2] *Final Report of the Committee on Industry and Trade*, Balfour Committee, March, 1929, Cmd. 3282, p. 297.

their organization and equipment to a thorough process of reconditioning.   To carry through this process successfully, two pre-requisites must be fulfilled.   In the first place there must be an active will to reorganize, based on real insight into the changing conditions and needs of the national and international economic situation.   In the second place there must be the power to reorganize, based on adequate means of access to the financial and technical resources necessary for material equipment, together with the whole-hearted co-operation of all the human factors to ensure that the best results shall be obtained from the transformation."

These findings of the Balfour Committee referred to the whole field of industry, but they had in mind first and foremost those staple industries which were, and are, particularly affected by the prevailing depression and by a lack of internal co-ordination.   The Report unfortunately did not state explicitly with what sort of powers the parties should be equipped ; nor who should grant these powers. Nevertheless the desirability of some kind of compulsion was clearly recognized and strongly underlined.

We see, then, that the notion of compulsion as applied to the economics of coal began to find its way to one section of the community after another ; Parliamentary aid was now sought not for nationalization, but in order to adjust industrial life to the changed conditions of the market.   In the light of the advanced technique, especially in the treatment of coal, in Germany and Polish Upper Silesia, the owners were now strongly advised to pursue a policy of " rationalization ", adopting compulsion as a tool to this end where incumbent. It was argued that the tendency to-day in other spheres of life is towards co-operation, and that the same spirit ought to be allowed to permeate the whole coal industry.   All obstacles were to be removed by force, and some form of national organization for the industry to be found.   Political discussion is now centred on the advisability of compulsion as an aid to reorganization.   The necessity of reorganization in itself is no longer disputed, and nationalization as a political aim has faded into the background.   Economic discussion followed the same lines.   The want of organization, the dispersion of production between good and bad units, the lack of co-ordination, the costly methods of winning, screening, grading, transporting, and marketing coal, the hindrances arising from over-capacity, sometimes over-capitalization—difficulties both in home and foreign markets, danger from substitutes for coal, the more economic use of coal without adequate economies in its production, and finally a whole sea of labour problems—such were the economic questions which centred around the political dilemma of public control.

The plans for reorganization were various. The coal industry has always perhaps been the most striking example of *quot capita, tot sententiae*. Just as before nationalization was viewed differently by each of the numerous sections advocating it, now there was no agreement as to the best way of reorganizing. While the uncompromizing attitude so typically expressed by the late Mr. C. P. Markham, a representative of the Yorkshire Colliery Owners, before the Royal Commission, 1925, underwent a radical change, the Socialist panacea for the coal industry passed through an important metamorphosis from nationalization to State intervention. This was precisely the point at which the sectional remedies met and agreed as to the future conduct of the industry. The necessity for a certain degree of compulsion was understood by some of the owners them-selves. Those who had tested the advantageous results of the voluntary restriction schemes in three of the largest coal-producing districts advocated a modicum of compulsion, which would bring the dissentient owners under the scheme. Whereas in 1925 the late Mr. C. P. Markham rejected, in his evidence before the Royal Commission, all Parliamentary interference with the coal industry, in 1931 Lord Aberconway, another distinguished representative of the industry, and several other captains of industry spoke in favour of the compulsory coal marketing scheme. During the general meetings of the shareholders of Yorkshire Amalgamated Collieries, Ltd. [1]—a very large company—and later of the John Brown Co., Ltd.,[2] held in June, 1931, Lord Aberconway

[1] *The Times*, 30th June, 1931, Company Meetings.
[2] Ibid., 2nd July, 1931.

commented upon the significance of the Coal Mines Act, 1930, as follows : " I am of opinion that had there been no Act of Parliament there would have been such unrestricted outputs that prices would have fallen away and our position would then have been worse than it is at the present time." Other districts, especially those devoted to exports, hoped for the best from the largest possible home sales. Areas where coal-mines are in close vertical combination with other industries, were naturally inimical to political interference, which would force them to regulate prices and output.[1]

This concludes our general survey of the development of political thought since the War, as it affected the organization of the coal industry. We have seen how the conflict of nationalization versus small independent units, which was waged in early years, gradually merged into present-day thought. The necessity for reorganization and co-operation became recognized by all sections of the industry.

[1] In South Wales political interference in the coal-mining industry was condemned by the representatives of the owners. During the meeting of the Amalgamated Anthracite Collieries, Ltd., Mr. F. A. Szarvasy, Chairman of this merger, said in connection with the Coal Mines Act, 1930 : " Legislative interference with business gives encouragement to lethargy rather than stimulation to individual enterprise and courage, which alone will in the end bring about a better set of circumstances and which, as we all know, have in the past proved the stimulating factors in any recovery and success achieved by this company." (*The Times*, 29th April, 1931.)

Colonel Sir W. Charles Wright, Chairman of Baldwins Limited, a large composite concern in South Wales, criticized State interference on the following ground : " With regard to the coal trade, when I addressed you in April of last year (1930), the Coal Mines Bill was looming ahead, and I then stated what a catastrophe it was that the coal industry should again be threatened with political interference which was brought about by a rash election pledge. The Bill received the Royal Assent and became law on 1st August, despite grave warnings both in Parliament and throughout the country. . . . As far as the provisions of Part 1 of the Act are concerned, we have failed to derive any comfort from the fact that by paying our own collieries higher prices for that proportion of their output that we consume, and which amounts to over 50 per cent, we are helping to compensate for the increased cost of production they incur under Part 3. The Act as framed obviously entails hardships on composite concerns which consume a large proportion of their own collieries' production, as we do, while, in addition, the absence of any international arrangement to support the price of that proportion of the output which we export, coupled with the fact that the restriction of our colliery output under the district regulations is below the rate at which we have been able to dispose of the coal in the past, by themselves enhance materially the cost of production, altogether apart from the reduction in hours. The politician must leave trade alone; otherwise, in my opinion, there will be little peace or prosperity for this nation." (*The Times*, 4th April, 1931.)

At the same time the conception of nationalization itself suffered a change and became concerned less with expropriation than with unification, a step which would make possible the payment of equal wages throughout the whole country and the obtaining of higher rewards for the miners' toil.   Mr. Frank Hodges, one of the authorities on the nationalization movement, admitted now that unification was quite compatible with private enterprise, and that the chief objective of nationalization would be to keep the public safe from the mighty tentacles of that enormous " octopus ", the capitalist coal monopoly.[1]   In this scheme State ownership was conceived more as a supervisory precaution than as a real assistance towards organization.

At this stage the struggle between the State ownership of mines and economic reorganization had been decided in favour of the latter.   Public opinion began to realize that in order to bring about a better organization of the industry it was not necessary to resort to change in actual ownership or administration.

In the next section we pass on to consider the various forms which Government interference could take, and we turn later to the actual development of Government interference in the coal industry before the Act of 1930.

§ 2. METHODS OF GOVERNMENT INTERFERENCE

We have already seen how all shades of political thought had gradually become more and more interested in the structure of the coal industry.   Undoubtedly in the long run it was chiefly economic reasons which had determined

---

[1] Frank Hodges, " Nationalization of Industry," *The Mines Book of the Labour Party*, edited by Herbert Tracey, London, vol. ii, p. 13 : " Voluntary unification of the industry into one national unit would certainly solve many anomalies in the present form of production and distribution within the industry, and such unification is quite in keeping with private enterprise . . ."

the actual framework in which individual industrial units remained linked to one another, but political thinking exerted its influence from time to time and often affected the industry in manifold ways.   The most important of the political elements which influence the conduct of the industry is the Government, and all the factors which determine its policy. This includes public opinion, the programme of the political party actually in power, the current ideas in political science, etc.   History showed that before the War the growing degree of Governmental interference, starting from fragmentary regulations protecting the consumers, and having for its purpose the raising of money by taxation, finally came to embrace the industry's most complicated internal functions.[1]

Before the War this interference was completely outside the field of internal organization and the relation of one industrial unit to another.   The State was only gradually grasping control in other branches of industrial activity and had not yet shown initiative in bringing about any particular organization among the coal-producing units.   All the institutions erected by the industry, whether coal-owners' associations, trade combinations, amalgamations, or selling agencies were exclusively an endogenous product.   During the War, however, and later, State agencies came forward to give a fillip to reorganization in the coal industry and to regulate the industrial relations between enterprises.   In this way State interference, from its earliest form appertaining only to taxation, protection of the consumer and of the miner, was to become a factor in actual organization.

By influencing an industry, or otherwise by *interfering*, we understand such an action of the Government which causes the industry to distribute its available resources in a different way from what it would choose if it were left completely to itself.   Of course an action of the Government can possess widely different effects.   In some cases it can bring about only minor readjustments, irrelevant from the point of view of equilibrium both in the long and in the short run.   In

[1] See Appendix C.

some other cases it can disequilibrate the whole industry, or stabilize it at the cost of upsetting the equilibrium of the whole economic system. In its arsenal of interference the State has always several possible alternatives. It can interfere either by public ownership and public administration of a branch of industry, or by other methods. Thus, as an example of the first, the Government can place itself in the same position as private individuals and carry on an industry, or a whole branch of an industry, on a commercial basis, e.g. the British Government is the owner and monopolist of the telephones and telegraphs. The other methods of Government action include activities which affect the industry indirectly, or else regulation of industrial affairs by authoritarian means usually confined to the realm of public life. Often in this last capacity the Government is called upon to perform the function of a reorganizer of industry.

By either method the Government can take the responsibility for the management. We can term these three methods of interference : *commercial*, *indirect*, and *regulative* respectively.[1] In Britain the first and last of these methods were, until lately, little known and little discussed. In Continental countries, however, especially in Germany and the Southern and Eastern European countries, the problem of State activity in industry was widely ventilated. Two respective terms have been coined. " Etatismus " for commercial, and " Interventionismus " for regulative interference. Professor Mises [2] of Vienna rightly defined the nature of " Interventionismus " as standing half way between the maintenance of private property and the nationalization of means of production and forming a sort of limited capitalist system.

In Britain this attitude of the State towards industry is a novelty which is now developing with an amazing

[1] In this work we use the term " State interference " to denote any Government activity of whatever kind in the widest sense which has an influence on the conduct of the industry ; while by " intervention " is meant direct authoritarian regulation of the very process of production.
[2] Ludwig Mises, *Liberalismus*, Jena, 1927, p. 67.

rapidity.[1] Hitherto, no Government had imposed any line of organization on the coal industry.   Except for the War years of Control, the industry was at liberty to adopt such forms as were evolved naturally during the course of its development. Every mine-owner was perfectly free to appear in the organization in any form he liked.   Nobody was forced to organize, and integration was progressing only on the basis of purely private understanding.   For this reason State interference was always conceived as either nationalization of mines and exploitation by public bodies ; or otherwise as those legal enactments which affected the management of the industry, but did not infringe on the forms of organization.[2]

Since 1926, however, a new meaning was added to State interference.   The State began to influence the reorganization of the coal industry by encouraging amalgamation ; which further developed in 1930 into compulsory regulation of output and prices. The organization of the owners then received the mark of publicity.   It was gradually realized that, as Clark [3] noted in 1904, any highly developed form of industrial organization usually contains certain elements which go beyond private activity, and which concern public life.   This holds good particularly in an organization of producers which is imposed by Statute and made compulsory for all.   The activity of such a large and powerful body in the basic industries is a matter of public concern, since it may greatly influence the economic life of the country, completely checking certain social and economic forces, e.g. the normal working of competition and the price apparatus,

[1] Professor J. H. Richardson presented a Memorandum on *State Intervention in Private Economic Enterprise* to the Second International Conference on the State and Economic Life held in London in May and June, 1933.   He enumerated the following methods of intervention: (1) Full public ownership and management by a Government Department or Local Authority; (2) Partial public ownership by the method of shareholding with varying degrees of control; (3) Subsidies to a private industry; (4) Control by a public corporation; (5) Establishment of statutory conditions to which private industry is required to conform; and finally (6) Tariff protection import quotas.

[2] *Vide* Appendix on the rise of Government interference in the coal industry.

[3] John Bates Clark, *The Problem of Monopoly*, New York, 1904, " a monopoly that controls the supply of fuel performs a public function and the people have something to say about every discontinuance of it," p. 68.

especially in certain kinds of coal, for which the demand proves less elastic than for others. It also creates new methods of tackling social problems by altering the existing relations in wage-bargaining ; it abolishes the power to regulate the level of production, by changing the supply of certain types of coal in favour of others, etc. The nature of the industry is also a matter of some consequence, since the more basic the industry whose product is being organized, the greater will be the part played by that industry in the structure of production, and so in the sequence of booms and depressions. Therefore, its organization becomes a matter of general concern. For this reason the formation of a national compulsory scheme for producers in one of the staple industries opens many public questions connected with the nature of this organization.

To quote an instance, one of the main questions asked was whether a cartel should be regarded as being of a public or private character. It was the subject of much discussion at the Thirty-fifth Annual Conference of German Lawyers held in Salzburg in September, 1928.[1] In the resolutions dealing with economic and financial law, it was pointed out that the cartels have two legal aspects : the public and the private. As to their public activity, the State ought on the one hand to grant necessary powers and help where needed, and, on the other hand, to stop their undesirable action where necessary. The Government must have power to control the cartel through the Minister of Economy (Wirtschaftsminister) assisted by an independent Committee, and in cases of special importance, it must also have the authority to dissolve it, and to alter it, or to form a new one by compulsion. Similar opinions on the distinction between the private and public nature of cartel law were also expressed by the majority of witnesses before the German Committee of Inquiry into the Cartels, in 1930.[2]

[1] 35th Juristentag—*Verhandlungen des Fünfunddreissigsten Deutschen Juristentages* (Salzburg), 2nd vol., 2nd number, 1929, pp. 712, et seq. and 850, et seq. Discussions of Section 4 of the Conference.
[2] Ausschuss zur Untersuchung der Erzeugungs—und Absatzbedingungen der deutschen Wirtschaft : Verhandlungen und Berichte des Unterausschusses für allgemeine Wirtschaftsstruktur.—3 Arbeitsgruppe—Wandlungen in den wirtschaftlichen Organisationsformen—Vierter Teil—

The deliberations of the German experts are illuminating in considering the nature of recent British forms of organization in the coal industry, as regulated by the Coal Mines Act, 1930. Certainly the national scheme under the Act contains elements of a public character, and the attitude of the Government to such a national organization is and must indeed be different to that adopted when the industry remained completely disintegrated.

To revert now to the methods of State interference, we have noted three different groups : first State ownership and management of the industry, next direct State intervention into the structural problems of the industry, and finally Government activity which indirectly affects the development and forms of the industry. The first of these was never applied in practice, the two remaining methods gradually developed.

Strange as it may seem, indirect interference dates back very far.[1] Many steps affecting the coal industry have been taken by the British Government at various times in the past. Some were exclusively directed to coal mining, e.g regulations pertaining to safety in mines, or to limitation of profits during the period of control. Others had only an indirect influence upon it, such as the promotion of scientific research. Since its infancy, the industry has paid taxes, has borne various State duties, and has been subject to many limitations and rules. It depended, on one

Kartellpolitik—Zweiter Abschnitt 1930. The majority of witnesses representing different economic activities, lawyers, professors, professional economists, etc., were in favour of separating the private functions of cartels from the public ones, and of amending the law in this way. As one of the witnesses, Herr O. Bernstein expressed it : " All those cases where a private individual stands against a private individual have to be dealt with by ordinary Courts, all those cases which arise out of § 4 [of the Cartel Law] belong to the Administrative Courts."

The names of those who were in favour of the amendments of the existing law on these lines included among others : Messrs. A. Frowein, O. Bernstein, H. Grunfeld, Dr. Metzner, Dr. J. Weisbart, Professor Dr. E. Lederer, Professor Dr. Vershofen.

The minority : Professor Dr. Caro, Professor Dr. Passow, and others, were in favour of leaving the principle of the cartel legislation as it stood i.e. the fusion of public and private law in a single whole.

[1] In Appendix C, the growth of indirect interference is sketched in detail, and it is shown how the expanding importance of the industry brought it more and more into the indirect control of the State.

side, on certain legal activities of the Government, such
as the concluding of commercial treaties, arranging for export, diplomatic action in case of restriction on imports to
foreign countries, etc.   On the other side, the industry
naturally came up against the Government in activities
such as the building of roads, canals, ports, etc. It was
also very extensively controlled both on labour questions
and on the technical methods of mining coal. As time
went on, the field of State activity increased, especially
after the War, with the result that to-day the coal-mining
industry is working within a dense net of Governmental
regulations. The nature, however, of this State interference
has gradually changed from a very vague to a developed
system of intervention.

§3. RELATION BETWEEN THE STATE AND THE COAL
INDUSTRY

Government influence upon the organization of the industry
gradually became more direct. The War greatly speeded up
State penetration into the conduct of the industry. During
the period of Control of mines introduced by the Lloyd George
Government, the industry was, broadly speaking, led and
directed from Whitehall. The Government then guaranteed
wages and profits—it regulated the distribution as well as the
transport of coal. This control, which was at first opposed
by the miners on the ground that it might reduce their
standard of living, regulated nearly all industrial functions
in coal mining. But though it was only temporary, and
introduced to meet the stringencies of the War, it left its
mark on the organization of the industry, especially as it
accustomed the owners to guaranteed profits which were
independent of the state of efficiency and the volume
of trade.

After decontrol, which came in March, 1921, at a time

of severe depression, the organization of the industry was left to private enterprise. But that did not mean a reversion to the same conditions as before the War, since the State henceforward collaborated with the industry much more closely than before. This occurred in two different ways : first it assisted the mining industry directly by granting various kinds of subsidies [1] out of the Exchequer, or by facilitating the acquisition of mineral rights. Secondly, and later, the State appeared in its regulative character of organizer of the industry.

The development of closer relations between the State and the coal industry was facilitated by the formation of the Mines Department by the Mining Industry Act, 1920.[2] This was the result of the recommendations of all the reports of the Sankey Commission,[3] of an earlier Report of the Coal Conservation Committee, 1916–18 [4], and of the Acquisition and Valuation of Land Committee, 1919. The newly-formed Mines Department, headed by a Secretary of Mines subordinate to the Parliamentary Secretary of the Board of Trade, amalgamated the mining functions of the Home Office with certain of the duties of the Coal Controller. Powers of other Departments [5] could be similarly transferred to the Mines Department. No such powers have as yet been transferred to the Department. Section I, Part I of the Act [6] which defined the principal aim of the newly-created Department as :—

> " . . . securing the most effective development and utilization of the mineral resources of the United Kingdom and the safety and welfare of those engaged in the mining industry. . . ."

[1] In this work we adopt the following definition : *State subsidy* consists of any such action of the State which by monetary advantages given to industry, or any branch of industry, causes a different distribution of resources from that which would otherwise exist, and at the same time results in a reduction of State revenues.

[2] 10 and 11 Geo. V, Cap. 50.

[3] *Coal Industry Commission*, vol. ii, Reports dated 20th June, 1919, on the Second Stage of the Inquiry.

[4] *Vide* Report of the Mining Sub-Committee.

[5] Under part i, section 2 (2) of the Act.

[6] A. S. Comyns Carr and Wilfred Fordham, *Recent Mining Legislation, including the Coal Mines Act*, 1930, London, 1931, p. 2.

Among other duties, the Mines Department has to "undertake the collection, preparation, and publication of information and statistics relating to the mining industry, and it shall co-operate with such Committees of the Privy Council as are formed for the purpose, and any other Government departments concerned, in the initiation and direction of research in relation to matters conected with the powers and duties of the Board of Trade ".[1]

Under this section the Board of Trade publishes a long list of valuable statistics referring to production, numbers of men employed, days worked and wages, cost of production, proceeds, profits, distribution, consumption, prices, plants, accidents, etc.[2] An important part of the work of the Mines Department is devoted to the development of mining science through the " Safety in Mines " Research Board, and to conferences on safety in mines organized by the Department and other bodies carrying out scientific investigations. The Mining Industry Act, 1920, thus prepared the ground for an intensive interference in mining affairs which was soon to follow. It mobilized all the State administrative powers and transferred them to one office ; after this, the State was completely fitted to launch a forward movement in the reorganization of the industry along the lines foreshadowed by Royal Commissions, by economic science, and by foreign experience.

The same Mining Industry Act, 1920, which created the Mines Department substantially assisted the reorganization of mines by promoting schemes of drainage between groups of mines, to be imposed by the Board of Trade. Several drainage schemes were inaugurated in accordance with the procedure here laid down, chiefly in the Midlands. A scheme covering almost a complete area was set up in August, 1929, in South Yorkshire to provide for the carrying on of co-operative pumping and drainage operations. Another drainage scheme was instituted in the Old Hill district of Staffordshire.

[1] Cf. Pt. 1, Sec. 3, of the Mining Industry Act, 1920.
[2] These statistics are collected under Section 21 of the Act, which requires the owners, agents, and managers of any mine to furnish to the Board of Trade all necessary information.

Other new developments which the Act desired to evolve for the industry included the establishment of a Welfare Fund for the miners, towards which the owners were obliged to pay a levy of 1*d*. per ton produced, and the establishment of a system of joint committees between labour and capital. The last provision, however, was never realized owing to the hostile attitude of the Miners' Federation towards such mixed institutions.

All these aspects of Government interference into the industry were the result of the state of public opinion and of labour difficulties. But very soon the economic depression, especially acute in all the industries responsible for the supply of producers' goods, encouraged the Government to widen its activities in order to assist the industry during the time of difficulties. Among these new measures were the pure *subsidies*, and reductions of rates and *rebates* on transport freights. Such payments from public money to the industry constituted a novelty in the attitude of the Government. The subsidies paid from the Exchequer were perhaps the most striking example of State assistance to the industry. According to our definition of interference, which embraces all Government action affecting the industry in any particular way, subsidies must be treated as a method of interference. All those measures, whether operating temporarily, like the subsidies, or for a longer period, like the rebates on transport or the de-rating privileges and other taxation advantages, exerted a striking influence on the organization of the industry. Certainly they did not constitute the kind of interference by which the Government becomes an organ of rationalization, since the alleviation of burdens, which the weaker units could not fully bear at the time, visibly retarded that process of adjustment, which was especially desirable in the disorganized coal industry. The subsidy, it is true, was paid not according to the individual results of each of the fourteen hundred companies in Britain, but on the basis of the average district results. But even then, the district adjustments were by no means free, and the efficient areas could not compete with the inefficient on an equal basis, or even force the inefficient to reduce their costs to the level of the market price. In fact, the result of the temporary assistance of this nature was the retardation of the process of equalization of costs throughout the whole country, in the absence of which no voluntary integration is possible. Apart from the profits guaranteed by the State during the period of Control, subsidies were tried twice after the War, in 1921 and in 1925–6.

The settlement of 1st July, 1921, ending a three months' strike, provided a grant from the Treasury amounting to £10,000,000 in subvention of wages.[1] This grant was offered on behalf of the Government by Sir Robert Horne (Chancellor of the Exchequer); the offer first amounted to £7½ millions,[2] and was increased on the 28th April to £10 millions.

In a like manner, the subsidy of 1925–6 was paid to smooth over sharp disparities between costs of production and current prices; it also was instituted for a limited period, and similarly had to cope with special difficulties.

It began to operate on 1st August, 1925, for a prescribed period of nine months, so as to allow the decision on wage reduction to be postponed till the issue of the recommendations of the Royal Commission then in conference. The subsidy was intended to bridge the gulf between the minimum wages actually paid on the basis of the 1924 working agreement and the current proceeds of the industry in any month. The subsidy paid between 1st August, 1925, and 30th April, 1926, cost the Exchequer £23,350,000. Out of this sum £11,000,000 were spent in 1925.

[1] Paragraph 11 (d and e) of the Coal Settlement Terms of 1st July, 1921, explained the purpose and working of the subsidy, which was meant to smooth the gradual reduction of wages. The relevant clauses read:
" Sect. (11d). The Government will give a grant not exceeding £10,000,000 in subvention of wages."
" Sect. (11e). This subvention shall be available for making such increases to the wages otherwise payable in any district as may be necessary to prevent the reductions below the March rates of wages being greater than the following amounts:
" During July, 2s. a shift for persons of 16 years of age and upward, and 1s. a shift for persons under 16. During August, 2s. 6d. and 1s. 3d. respectively.
" During September, 3s. and 1s. 6d. respectively, provided that the balance of the subvention is sufficient for this purpose."
[2] Sir R. A. S. Redmayne, *The British Coal Mining Industry during the War*, Oxford, 1923, p. 250.

After the crisis in May, 1926, another subsidy of £3,000,000 was offered.   The immediate purpose of this subsidy was stated in the proposals of the Prime Minister, presented on the 14th May to both parties to the Mining Dispute, and containing the declaration that :—

" For a period not exceeding . . . weeks :—

(1) The miners will accept a reduction of . . . per cent in minimum wages (other than subsistence rates) in all districts.

(2) The owners will bear wages equivalent to 100 per cent of ascertained net proceeds (in January–March) so far as necessary to maintain those wages."

The proposed subsidy was never granted to the industry because the terms of the settlement [1] suggested by the Prime Minister were rejected by the mine-owners as well as by the workers.

Besides pure subsidies which were instituted for precisely determined periods, the Government extended further *financial assistance* to the coal industry, e.g. under the Trade Facilities Acts 1921–6.[2]   In our view the chief economic difference between the former and the latter measures consists in the determinateness of the period for which they were instituted.   The transitory period of subsidy was strictly defined,[3] while other types of grants were bound to remain available for a fairly long time.

By means of financial assistance, however, the Government

---

[1] On the night of 1st June, 1926, the Prime Minister summarized in the House of Commons his negotiations with the parties to the dispute.   He took his stand on the Government proposals of 14th May, and dealt with the initial point of wages.

Vide Parliamentary Debates, Official Report, House of Commons, 1st June, 1926, cols. 669, etc.

[2] An example of this type of aid was the Treasury guarantee of £2,000,000 under the Trades Facilities Acts to Messrs. Pearson and Dorman Long, Ltd., in February, 1926.   This was to be used for the development of the Kentish Coal-fields, and it is interesting to note the indirect assistance of the Government to development work of this kind.

[3] The Report of the Balfour Committee refers to the transitory nature of these subsidies in a chapter on State measures for meeting post-War difficulties of industry : ". . . a large sum of money was expended as a subsidy to the coal-mining industry during the financial year 1925–6, but this, like the Coal Subvention of 1921–2, was a purely temporary measure." (Committee on Industry and Trade, *Factors in Industrial and Commercial Efficiency*, 1927, p. 385.)

did not directly interfere with the conduct of industry, since such measures could always be withdrawn as soon as they were considered to be no longer necessary. The exemption from excise duties of the by-products resulting from scientific treatment of British coal (benzol, liquid fuel, etc.), as well as of Scottish shale oil is an example of another type of State interference. Since all light hydrocarbon oils, whether imported or derived from imported materials, have to pay custom-duties,[1] this form of preference given by the State to the by-products of British coal was designed to stimulate new uses of coal in the modern scientific processes of extracting oil. The formation of the British Benzol and Coal Distillation Company, Ltd., with a capital of £250,000 was probably partly the result of the duties. This company, which extracts oil from coal by means of hydrogenation,[2] has already placed orders for four million tons of Welsh coal to be delivered during fifteen years at the rate of 750 tons daily. At the same time the development of low temperature carbonization made a definite advance, thus increasing the consumption of coal. From the Report of the Fuel Research Board [3] for the year ending in March,

[1] Originally, in April, 1928, the duty amounted to 4d. per gallon, raised later in the 1931 Budget to 6d. and increased again in September, 1931, to 8d.

[2] The other processes of extracting oil from coal and high temperature carbonization, and hydrogenation, have been concentrated in the hands of Imperial Chemical Industries, Ltd., which erected an experimental plant at Billingham capable of transforming daily 15 tons of coal into synthetic oil at a price which is nearly competitive with natural oil. The company concluded in April, 1931, an agreement with the Royal Dutch Shell Trust, with the Standard Oil Co. of New Jersey, and the I.G. Farbenindustrie, A. G., by which all four combines agreed to collaborate and eventually exchange the results of research work on hydrogenation through the formation of the International Hydrogenation Patents Company. (Vide Reports, General Meeting of Imperial Chemical Industries, Ltd., 14th April, 1932, The Times, 15th April, 1932.)

[3] Department of Scientific and Industrial Research, Report of the Fuel Research Board for the year ending 31st March, 1929, with Report of the Director of Fuel Research, London, 1929.

On p. 4 we read as follows : " Among the plants now (1929) working is that erected by the Gas Light and Coke Company at the Richmond (Surrey) Gas Works, to the general design developed at the Fuel Research Station. Companies with a total nominal capital of some £5,500,000 have been formed to develop some twenty-six different processes ; some of these are now (1929) working, and others should be producing in the near future. It is unlikely that all will prove successful, and some have unfortunately been launched without that careful trial of full-size unit plant which is so essential.

1929, when the preference already operated, it can be gathered that new commercial plants had been or were being erected to work, on different systems, a good many processes which might prove profitable. The Report, however, does not embark upon predictions on the number of commercially successful processes ; moreover, it gives warning of possible disappointments.

Among the leading firms working the low temperature process is Low Temperature Carbonization, Ltd., producing petrol and smokeless fuel in its plants at Barugh near Barnsley, at Askern near Doncaster, and at Greenwich. From its formation in 1928 up till 1933, the company carbonized about one million tons of coal. At this embryonic stage, however, of the new oil industry, which is entirely dependent on Government subsidy, it would scarcely be possible to demonstrate how much of its development is due to the duty imposed on foreign oil in 1928 and how much to other factors. We may add that in July, 1930, the leading firms engaged in carbonization and distillation of coal by low temperature processes formed the Low Temperature Coal Distillers' Association of Great Britain, a representative organization to defend the interests of the industry.

A further step in the field of assisting the uneconomic home production of oil from British raw materials (coal, shale peat, or derivatives thereof) was made in July, 1933, when the Government committed themselves to maintaining for a long period the preference for domestically produced light hydrocarbon oils. The commitment consisted of a guarantee to maintain a preference of at least 4d. a gallon for ten years, from 1st April, 1934, or a larger preference for a shorter period, so that if a tax of 8d. per gallon were imposed the preference would last them 4½ years. A figure of 3s. has been taken as the total amount of preference for the whole period. This expensive method of assisting the coal industry will cost the Treasury several million pounds. As *The Economist*[1] has pertinently pointed out, " the scheme will give employment to 1,000 extra miners—

[1] *The Economist*, 22nd July, 1933, vol. cxvii, p. 175.

at a cost to the Treasury, under present conditions, of £1,000
per miner—and all for the purpose of producing an extra
supply of a commodity which is not necessary." The
immediate effect of this new guarantee was the announcement of Imperial Chemical Industries, Ltd., of their
plan to erect a large plant capable of turning over 400 tons
of coal daily.

About the same time the coal industry received still
more assistance from the Government, by the imposition of
a tax on foreign heavy oil, one of its competitors. Home
produced oil was exempted from the tax. Under the Finance
Act, 1933, a specific duty of 1d. per gallon has been imposed
on hydrocarbon oils, with the exception of oils used for
coastal traffic. This meant a 30 per cent increase in the
price of fuel oil. In the discussion which criticized this
step, it was shown clearly that such a specific duty
would hit chiefly those industries using exclusively oil
fuel, and therefore the tax amounted to an attempt
to force coal down the throats of industrial users. It was
pointed out that a simple *ad valorem* duty of say 10 per cent,
would raise the same revenue, as the burden would fall
more heavily on lubricating oils, which are used generally
throughout industry. But a " specific " tax was merely an
attempt to protect coal. The protective intentions
of this measure were clearly revealed in the decision to
exempt fuel oil used by coastwise shipping from the duty.
Moreover, it was argued that as shipping was unprotected
and open to considerable foreign competition, it must not be in
any way hindered ; coal was only to benefit from prosperous
industries. And so shipping was allowed to have its supply
of oil free of duty. Under the influence of all these financial
inducements several schemes for the production of oil
from coal emerged in various coalfields. In the middle of
September the South Wales Industrial Development Council
had under consideration an extensive plan for the erection
of one hydrogenation plant and ten low temperature
carbonization installations capable of treating about 4,000,000
tons of coal. At the same time in North Wales a scheme
for low temperature carbonization was under consideration.

A further kind of assistance easing in the field of transport and rates the financial burdens encumbering the coal industry, and designed to strengthen its competitive power against foreign rivalry, was granted by the State in the form of the Railway Freight Rebates Scheme and of the De-Rating Scheme operating as from December, 1928. Necessary funds were provided in the first year by the already mentioned tax on foreign oils. As other countries (France, Germany, Holland, Belgium, Poland, Spain, America) gave railway rebates on the transport of coal, the advantages arising from the situation of British exporting coal-fields near the sea shore [1] were partly nullified. By the Railway Freight Rebates Scheme, therefore, British coal benefited from cheaper freights, which were reduced in 1929, on the average, by $7\frac{1}{2}d.$ per ton of coal exported, including also coal used for bunkering of ships engaged in foreign trade, while in the case of coal required by iron and steel works the reduction amounted to an average of $9\frac{3}{4}d.$ per ton. A further important reduction of freights, equal to 10 per cent, was granted to the collieries on the transport of timber, iron, and steel props used as mines' supports. Since the introduction of the railway scheme the rebates have been further considerably increased.

The Railway Freight Rebates Scheme provided for the year ending September, 1930, a sum of £2,955,411, which was used as rebates on certain classes of coal, coke, and patent fuel. In view, however, of the declining tendency of coal traffic, the rate of rebates has constantly been raised as follows :—

TABLE NO. 32

BOUNTY ON TRANSPORT OF COAL IN GREAT BRITAIN

Coal, Coke, and Patent Fuel.	Prior to December, 1930.	From 1st December, 1930.	From 1st December, 1931.	From 1st December, 1932.	From 1st December, 1933.
Exported	25% plus $1\frac{1}{2}d.$ per ton flat rate.	$27\frac{1}{2}$% plus $1\frac{1}{2}d.$ per ton flat rate.	30% plus $1\frac{1}{2}d.$ per ton flat rate.	$41\frac{1}{2}$% plus $1\frac{1}{2}d.$ per ton flat rate.	36% plus $1\frac{1}{2}d.$ per ton flat rate.
Delivered to Iron and Steel Works	10%	15%	$17\frac{1}{2}$%	25%	21%

[1] In the North-East Coast basis the average distance from pit to port is only 10 miles.

A somewhat similar scheme developed later in rather an interesting direction. It has been shown conclusively that the most efficient and economical method of transporting coal is in 20-ton wagons. Owing to the large quantity of old rolling stock in use, the average capacity of wagons is at present below 12 tons, so the Great Western Railway Co. decided to give additional rebates on 20-ton wagons, thus increasing the benefits of their use. At the same time the Government stepped in by giving guarantees under the Development Act, 1929, which allowed the G.W.R. to build 5,000 of these new wagons and hire them out at very favourable terms.[1]

Closely connected with the Freight Rebates Scheme stood the De-Rating Scheme of 1928,[2] by which the collieries and other depressed industries, including railways, docks, canals, etc., and agriculture, were relieved of three-quarters of their rate burdens, which henceforward would be paid from the Exchequer to the Local Governments. These direct reliefs were of great significance to the coal-mining industry, materially reducing certain items in the costs of production and distribution. The Chairman of a very large Welsh concern, the Powell Duffryn Steam Coal Company, Ltd., estimated that at the 1930 level the charges for railway and dock services had increased by approximately 90 per cent as compared with pre-War rates, but thanks to the working of rebates the increase was reduced to 50 per cent.[3]

We must mention here the benefits which accrued to the coal industry, among others, from the financial policy of the Government during 1932 and 1933. By a deliberate and somewhat artificial cheapening of money by means of embargo on capital exports, the Government prepared the way not only for its own conversion schemes, but also for the conversion

---

[1] Wagons to be hired for ten years, with an option of purchase for a nominal figure at the end of the period. Financial assistance given by the Government to be passed on in full to the collieries. It is a condition of hire that colliery companies shall break up obsolete wagons of a total tonnage capacity of not less than the new 20-ton wagon.

[2] The Rating and Valuation (Apportionment) Act, 1928, 18 and 19 Geo. V, Ch. 44.

[3] See the speech of Mr. Edmund Hann, Chairman and Managing Director of Powell Duffryn Steam Co., Ltd., during the annual general meeting of the shareholders on 26th March, 1931, referred to in *The Times*, 27th March, 1931.

to a lower rate of interest of industrial capital generally. The coal industry made a certain amount of use of these facilities [1] either by converting debentures or by repaying banking overdrafts, but new capital issues were very limited.[2]

From May 1933 the Government helped the coal industry in still another direction. Reciprocal *trade agreements* were made with several European countries, and in all cases benefits were obtained for British coal exporters. The most important agreement was that concluded with Germany in April, 1933. It was agreed that the coal quota taken by Germany [3] from England shall be in no case less than 180,000 tons a month, and whenever consumption exceeds 7½ million tons per month the total quota of English coal shall increase in proportion. Of course, this did not mean that Germany would take 180,000 tons a month, but only that she would give permission for that quantity to be imported. Commercial agreements were concluded about the same time with Norway, Sweden, Denmark, Iceland,[4] and in September 1933 with Argentina,[5] and Finland [6] also involving benefits to the coal industry.

In addition to the purely financial assistance of the industry by means which have been just discussed, the

[1] The following are typical examples of conversion operations in the coal industry during 1932–3 :—
Sheepbridge Coal and Iron, Ltd., increased its debentures by £103,000 in thus borrowing money from the market in order to pay off its more expensive debts.
Powell Duffryn Steam Coal Co., Ltd., £1,169,000 7% debenture stock, and £1,350,000 6% Redeemable Notes converted to a 5¼% basis.
Shipley Collieries, Ltd., existing 6½% Debenture Stock replaced by a 5½% issue.
[2] *Vide The Economist*, vol. cxvii. p. 616, 30th September, 1933.
[3] In exchange for this, duties on imports of toys, gramophones, clocks, and other small manufactured articles were lowered.
[4] *Norway*. Amount of coal imported from United Kingdom is to be at least 70 per cent of total coal imports.
Sweden. Amount of coal imported from United Kingdom to be at least 47 per cent of total coal imports.
Iceland. Amount of coal imported from United Kingdom to be at least 70 per cent of total coal imports.
Denmark. Amount of coal imported from United Kingdom to be at least 80 per cent of total coal imports.
[5] *Argentina* granted a preferential treatment to British coal and coke by allowing them free entry.
[6] *Finland*. Amount of coal imported from United Kingdom to be at least 75 per cent of total coal imports.

Government interfered with the relations between the entrepreneurs and the mineral owners, with the object of removing certain difficulties which were likely to be encountered in this field.

On the whole there are very few freehold mines in Britain. Figures produced before the Royal Commission in 1925 estimated that only 4·2 per cent were freehold, while practically all others were working on leases. Hence, the legislation changing the terms of granting the leases affected the whole industry. Following the policy of assisting the industry, the Government gave to it valuable new privileges referring to *mineral rights*. Under the Mines (Working Facilities) Act, 1923, and the Mining Industry Act, 1926, the colliery owners received : (1) a right to work minerals, (2) rights ancillary to that right, (3) a right to support, and (4) a right to search for coal in cases where they might be prevented by the royalty owners. By " working " minerals the Act of 1923 means " working, carrying away, treating, and converting minerals ".[1] As ancillary rights the Act includes [2] :

(a) a right to let down the surface ;
(b) a right to air-way, shaft-way, or surface or underground way-leave, or other right for the purpose of access to or conveyance of minerals, or the ventilation or drainage of the mines ;
(c) a right to use or occupy the surface for the erection of washeries, coke ovens, railways, by-product works, brick-making or other works, or of dwellings for persons employed in connection with the working of the minerals, or with any such works ;
(d) a right to obtain a supply of water or other substances in connection with the working of minerals ;
(e) a right to dispose of water or other liquid matter obtained from mines or any by-product works and other rights not enumerated.

A novel right to search for coal was given by the Mining Industry Act, 1926, Part II, S. 13, to " any person who is desirous of searching for it or working, either by himself or through a lessee ". Such a person may apply for this

[1] 13 and 14 Geo. V, Ch. 20, Pt. i, S. 1 (2).
[2] Ibid., Part I, S. 3 (2).

right to the Railway and Canal Commission. The right to support, vertical or lateral, is given [1] by the Act of 1923 to anybody who does not possess this right but is vitally interested in obtaining it for the purpose of protecting his buildings or works. But an important reservation is made by the law of 1923 [2] in favour of the colliery owner. Namely, the support must be secured only in cases when the Railway and Canal Commission [3] is satisfied that the sacrifice borne by the colliery undertaking in not working coal will be more than the value of the building or the damage caused by subsidence, in which case only compensation is paid. Thus it cannot be prevented from working its mine by anyone whose interest might be endangered by its operations, without consideration of sacrifice borne. Large use has been made by the coal-owners of this legislation. [4]

In some cases " where the working of any coal in the most efficient and most economical manner is impeded by any restrictions, terms or conditions contained in mining

[1] Section 8 (1) of the Mines (Working Facilities and Support) Act, 1923, reads : " If any person having an interest in any land is not entitled to support or sufficient support, whether vertical or lateral, for any buildings or works whether on or below surface, erected or constructed, or intended to be erected or constructed, on or below the surface, and alleges that it is not reasonably practicable to obtain a right to such support by private arrangement for any of the reasons mentioned in section four of this Act, he may send to the Board of Trade an application that such restrictions may be imposed on the working of the minerals under that land and the land adjacent thereto as he may consider necessary to secure sufficient support to the buildings or works."

[2] Ibid. Section 8 (7) : " In determining whether restrictions should be imposed the Commission shall have regard to the value of the buildings or works or the cost of repairing damage likely to be caused thereto by subsidence, as compared with the value of the minerals, or to the importance in the national interest of the erection or preservation of the buildings or works, as compared with the importance in the national interest of the working of the minerals."

[3] The Railway and Canal Commission was established by the Railway and Canal Traffic Act in 1888. In 1921 most of their functions, in particular those referring to rates and charges, were transferred to the Railway Rates Tribunal. The Commission retained, however, the questions of facilities.

By the end of July a Bill abolishing the Railway and Canal Commission and transferring all its functions in the coal industry to the Chancery Division received a second reading in the House of Lords.

[4] In December, 1932, the Railway and Canal Commission Court empowered Messrs. Crawshaw and Warburton, Ltd., colliery owners, to work two seams of coal, scattered over an area of 300 acres, and actually in possession of about 300 smallholders. (*The Iron and Coal Trades Review*, 23rd December, 1933.)

lease " the lessee may apply to the Railway and Canal Commission for new terms or complete release from such hindrances. This fresh provision of the 1926 Act [1] has certainly very great significance in cases where unreasonable terms of leases may stop the producers in their activities. Messrs. A. S. Comyns Carr and Wilfred Fordham [2] maintain the view that the section even " extends to revising the royalties or other payments reserved, if those make it economically impossible to work the coal except at a loss, or even without a reasonable profit ". This argument, plausible as it may seem, cannot, however, be upheld if one takes into consideration the whole nature of the Act and its purpose. It is an Act to facilitate the working of collieries and to override certain hindrances offered by the royalty owners to the normal physical development of productive processes. It does not attempt any alterations which would affect the financial, economic, or capital structure of the industry. The agreed amount of royalties is inherent in freedom of production, it constitutes the price paid for a particular right—the right of mining coal. The seller of the royalty is not responsible either for the miscalculation of the entrepreneurs, or for the fluctuations in prices or costs of production which are reflected in their profits or losses. The Act is not intended to guarantee a profit to entrepreneurs ; what it does is to facilitate the more rational and physically more economical exploitation of coal resources.

By all these enactments, State interference advanced a big step further towards bringing the hitherto private relations between mineral owners and coal-owners under statutory regulations. Though the State machinery, already discussed, affected the coal-mining industry in manifold ways, it was not directly responsible for the organization among the owners themselves, or between the owners and the distribution section. It constituted only an indirect interference, and did not disturb the individualism which had always reigned in the industry. But at the same time as the industry was being helped by the various kinds of

[1] 16 and 17 Geo. V, Ch. 28, S. 13 (2).
[2] A. S. Comyns Carr and Wilfred Fordham, *Recent Mining Legislation, including the Coal Mines Act*, 1930, London, 1931, pp. 16 and 100.

indirect Government aid discussed above, the State was gradually preparing to take over actual organization and control.   Already in 1926, we notice an important advance in State *intervention* directly affecting the structure of the industry.

The provisions of Part I of the Mining Industry Act, 1926, constitute the first attempt by the State to accelerate the process of reorganization and to use compulsion in order to bring the dissentient minorities into schemes approved by the majority of the industry.   For the first time the legal term " national interest " [1] was officially introduced into the conduct of an industry in Great Britain.   The legislation refers, however, to only one aspect of reorganization :   for it confines itself to stimulating concentration.   All that it does is to give the sanction of the State to the will of the majority of owners who consider an amalgamation necessary.   Nevertheless, it is the harbinger of approaching Governmental intervention on a larger scale, embracing a vast field and directed towards compulsory reorganization.

So the Mining Industry Act, 1926, constitutes an attempt to regulate the internal structure of the British coal industry by Act of Parliament.   For the first time the State lends its power to the majority of the owners in order to help them to secure reorganization more easily.   Compulsory powers could only be invoked under certain prescribed conditions, and an application on the part of the owners was required before any steps could be undertaken under the Act.   Furthermore, the whole initiative in reorganizing remained in the hands of the leaders of the industry, and the rôle of the State is limited to helping the majority to carry out their proposals.   Compulsion may be used in order to bring the dissentient owners into line with the amalgamation schemes, or to enforce schemes already agreed by coal undertakings but being held up by other

[1] Section 7 (2) of the Mining Industry Act, 1926, allows the Railway and Canal Commission to confirm a scheme of amalgamation or absorption " if satisfied that it would be in the national interest to do so, and that the terms of the scheme are fair and equitable to all persons affected thereby ".

interested parties, e.g. royalty owners. Thus, under Part I of the Act, the owners of two or more undertakings, who decide to amalgamate either wholly or partially "with a view to the more economical and efficient working, treating or disposing of coal", are entitled to prepare and submit to the Board of Trade the necessary schemes. Similarly, they may submit plans of total or partial absorption, when it is expedient for the success of the whole scheme prepared by the willing undertakings that "one or more other such undertakings, the owners of which are unwilling to agree to the proposed terms of amalgamation, should be absorbed". The Act prescribes a certain procedure before the Board of Trade, which afterwards refers cases to the Railway and Canal Commission. After confirmation by this Commission the scheme becomes binding on all parties concerned. The Commission shall confirm a scheme "if satisfied that it would be in the national interest to do so, and that the terms of the scheme are fair and equitable to all persons affected thereby". By these provisions any owner may be obliged to abide by the will of those of his fellow-owners who are anxious to integrate by means of amalgamation. The principle of compulsion involved in the Act is significant, because it underlines the importance of the State as an organ of rationalization. Thus the only sphere in the whole of the coal-mining industry which had hitherto remained untouched by the State, namely, the organization of the individual producing units and their mutual relations, had now at last been entered.[1]

In the Coal Mines Act, 1930, we see the real entry of the State into the actual organization of the industry. The tendencies shown in 1926 developed into full-blooded State intervention. This Act forms an important part of this book, and is fully discussed in Part III below, so we do not intend to explain it here. We have shown how State interference

[1] Under the provisions of the Mining Industry Act, 1926, a scheme for close co-operation of all mines in West Yorkshire was submitted in September, 1933. This scheme proposed to secure co-operation of owners for better marketing arrangements, and for the closing of a certain number of mines. It came, however, soon to an end owing to lack of support by a sufficient majority.

spread gradually from one field to another, until from indirect interference it finally became definite intervention, and reached directly the actual structure and working of the industry.   At this stage it becomes incumbent to discuss the development of political thought on the subject.   After all, Governments are composed of politicians, and we should expect to find some explanation of the rapid growth of State interference in the programmes of the political parties.

CHAPTER II

POLITICAL PARTIES AND COAL [1]

§ 1. THE LABOUR PARTY'S COAL PROGRAMME

The problem of the mines became very prominent soon
after the War and began to occupy an ever larger space in
the official pronouncements of the Parliamentary parties
and other social organizations. Political, religious, charitable,
even philosophical bodies considered themselves authorized
to express their views on the economics of the coal industry,
on its internal relations, and on its structural problems.
The industry became a favourite plaything of public
discussion, engaging a vast circle of people often entirely 1920
outside the scope of its activity. This great interest in the
coal industry arose especially after the 1920, 1921 and 1926
stoppages.   These two occasions caused a cloudburst of
pamphlets, studies, novels, leaflets, etc., dealing with widely
different sides of the industry and touching the subject
from all possible points of view. A whole army of new coal
students appeared suddenly on the horizon.   The coal
industry became then *à la mode.*

In such circumstances the political parties could not avoid
adopting a definite position towards the coal question.
It was much too important a propagandist weapon
in electoral campaigns to be left aside without a
careful inquiry. It was no longer a matter of adopting
a hand-to-mouth attitude to this or that Act of Parliament pertaining to a definite difficulty affecting the coal
industry. The moment required from them the formation
of a complete coal policy—a policy involving a constructive

[1] In the course of writing the whole of Chapter II, the author has been
greatly assisted by Dr. Herman Finer, whose kind help and excellent
suggestions we should like to acknowledge here.
In the course of preparing this chapter hundreds of articles, booklets, and
political pamphlets and leaflets had to be carefully read and sifted, but
only the most representative are quoted in the footnotes.

plan for the economic administration of the industry. Such tactics could not relate only to a special aspect of the whole, or attempt to solve only one set of difficulties particularly interesting the party followers, for instance, social struggles between capital and labour, or the problem of transport costs ; the party's manifesto had to provide a total remedy.

The Labour Party was the first to incorporate in its official programme a policy designed to deal with the coal problem, though at first it touched only a very small part of the whole. Nationalization of mines was merely the stimulant of a social policy. During the whole nineteenth century it remained a purely theoretic and academic, not yet a constructive, plan. The Labour Party, while declaring for some sort of social change which would be brought about under a regime of nationalized collieries, did not yet pay sufficient attention to the difficulties of organization, as the formal dilemma of property at that time eclipsed all other subjects. Nationalization arose in the nineteenth century on the ground of social needs, and, therefore, it is not surprising that round these interests centred the early Labour projects and that it constituted one of " the most popular planks in the Labour Party's programme ".[1]

The mechanism, however, through which socialization could be carried into effect was not elaborated at all. It can be gathered from an early resolution passed in 1886 by the Trades Union Congress held in Hull how little interest was attached to the actual administration of mines. The motives underlying the resolution were as follows : in the first place, the need for higher wages and a higher standard of life for the miner, and secondly, some moral consideration such as the greatest good of the greatest number. Such early schemes of nationalization adhered to the idea of bureaucratic administration of mines which emanated from the concept of State Socialism.

From this early rudimentary stage of development the mining programme of the Labour group passed into newer

[1] Cf. Frank Hodges, " Nationalization of Industry : the Mines," in *The Book of the Labour Party : its History, Growth, Policy, and Leaders*, ed. by H. Tracey, vol. xi.

garb after the War. How high the desire for nationalization
ran, not only in England but also in other countries, can
be judged from the decisions of the Miners' International
Federation.   At the first Miners' International gathering
after the War, held in Geneva in August, 1920, it was
decided that only those national unions could be affiliated
which undertook to pursue a programme of nationalization
in their respective countries by every means at their
disposal, strikes and direct action not excluded.[1]

In Britain the movement for nationalization had reached
its zenith at the time of the Sankey Commission in 1919.
Then the political and the economic aspects were both at
issue. Questions of ethics, organization, and administration
were fully ventilated.   State control of mines kept the
miners persuaded of the practicability of nationalization.
Before the Commission Mr. Straker, on behalf of the miners,
outlined the future constitution of the industry under
national ownership.   In the debate, however, the question
of proprietorship often overshadowed the real needs of
reorganization.[2]

The believers in socialization of mines thought that it
would : (1) rectify certain social injustices (moral aspect),
(2) help to raise the standard of life of the miners (social
aspect), and (3) introduce better organization and more
rational methods into the industry (economic aspect).   All
these three aspects of the Labour plan overlapped each other
and were mutually interdependent. We notice, however, that
the economic side of these schemes is much more recent,
and less fully developed than the ethical and social aspects.
In our study we must concentrate chiefly on the Labour plan
for economic reorganization.

One of the chief and fundamental assumptions underlying
the whole nationalization scheme was the idea of *unification*.
This was perhaps the main girder supporting the future
structure of the mining industry under a Socialist regime.
Social unification of all the coal-fields in the country (and

---

[1] Information from *The Mining Crisis, its History and Meaning to all
Workers*, by W. Livesay, London, 1921.

[2] Cf. Coal Industry Commission, vol. ii, Reports and Minutes of Evidence
on the Second Stage of the Inquiry, Cmd. 260, 1919, Q. 11,404.

in the remote future in all the coal-producing lands) involving such aims as the levelling up of labour conditions, working time, and wages, constituted a goal which, on the other hand, was to be attained through economic unification.

Economic unification has two distinct aspects, one following on the other, on the one hand technical unification, and on the other the unification of control. The former requires the application of all possible rational and scientific methods to the conduct of the industry; the latter makes this application feasible by concentrating all the economic resources under one control. The economic advantages of technical integration have been enumerated by one of the highest miners' authorities [1] as follows :—

" Technically voluntary or compulsory unification would :—

(1) Eliminate multiplicity and overlapping of control and ownership of the minerals themselves. In the last ten years royalty owners have taken £60,000,000 out of the industry and have given nothing in return. Any further rents or compensation would be the subject of decision by a specially constituted tribunal of assessors.

(2) Abolish an endless source of waste of precious coal by the removal of the need for leaving unmoved ' barriers ' of coal, which are merely left in the mine to delimit the holdings of the various mineral owners who are leasing, or who have leased, their coal to colliery owners. Some 4,000 million tons have already been thus left and are irrecoverable.

(3) Unify the task of providing power for existing collieries from central generating plants in appropriate areas, and thus enable the scrapping of obsolete steam-raising plant, and the consequential waste of coal, wherever the life of the colliery would justify such scrapping.

(4) Save the waste of small coal by installing bigger and more efficient plant for separating small coal from rubbish and refuse . . . Small colliery companies cannot afford to instal such plant for lack of capital.

(5) Save the enormous waste of small coal left in the mine because of the poor price secured in the

[1] Frank Hodges, " Nationalization of Industry: the Mines," *The Book of the Labour Party*, vol. ii, p. 14.

market for small or slack. . . . The coal-owners have never shown a willingness to expend the capital necessary for the recovery of the chemical constituent of small coal. It would be a large sum but a unified industry could stand it.

(6) Avoid the loss of such a large volume of coal used in raising steam at the collieries themselves. In a modern plant the percentage of coal used to raise steam and produce power is considered too extravagant if it exceeds $1\frac{1}{2}$ per cent of the output."

In the last resort, technical unification is dependent on unified control, which in the mind of the Labour Party can work successfully and smoothly only under a regime of nationalization, which in this way became the keystone of the Socialist construction.

Public opinion, however, has removed this keystone by rejecting the issue of nationalization. Is the labour coal programme to collapse and the idea of unification to be abandoned ? If integration could be brought about by individual private units, it would result in the same economies and improvement.[1] It is only because the Socialists disbelieved in the possibility of the mine-owners effecting any sort of concentration on their own accord and disliked the " octopus " of capitalist coal monopoly, that they devised nationalization as an alternative. From a purely technical and economic point of view, nationalization was suggested not as an end in itself, but only as the sole alternative to the inefficiency and lethargy of the present proprietors. Provided, however, that a sufficient under-standing of the situation, and the necessary energy, existed on the part of the colliery owners, the economic reason for nationalization would to a very great extent, or even altogether, disappear. This reasoning was endorsed by the miners' leaders, who admitted that for nationalization " there is the same argument technically as for trustification ". The difference, however, between the two courses adopted

[1] Cf. Frank Hodges, op. cit., p. 75 : " . . . It would be foolish indeed to deny that the costs of production could be reduced under private ownership if such private ownership were reduced to a few unified under-takings. All the economies that characterize combines, monopolies, or trusts could characterize the mining industry in similar circumstances . . ."

was enormous : whereas the former hit the foundation of capitalism and produced some sort of public ownership, the latter perpetuated private control. Though economically the two unifications may effect similar results, socially they could never be reconciled.

Mr. Frank Hodges [1] makes it clear in his book that, as the " social outlook " of the miners is against capitalistic amalgamations, they " will not work for trusts or combines in such a manner as to render effective the economies of unification ". The last objection, however, is in our view not implicit in a rationalized capitalistic organization of the industry. It is neither an intrinsic evil nor a defect in the actual working of the whole machinery. The reluctance on the part of the labour element engaged in production to work effectively under that regime, though improved and efficient as it might be in the future, may be considered only as a temporary psychological factor which must soon vanish when the benefits arising out of the better working of coal were realized. The political threat of " ca'canny working " is an anticipation of only very questionable value. But even assuming the validity of this argument, it would seem impossible to refrain from the impression that the fault is not inherent in the industry itself, but that it arises from a defective organization of labour. If the inefficiency of the coal mines were really due, not to the maladaptation of the industry to the demands of modern society, but to the determined and premeditated opposition of the workers, then it would surely be quite fair to think of rationalizing labour rather than the industry. Should labour refuse to co-operate under any other system than that of nationaliza-tion, the coal-owners could by *reductio ad absurdum* with a similar degree of logic claim the " nationalization " of coal labour on exactly the same grounds, i.e. that the community suffers a waste of coal and has to pay exorbitant prices because of the reluctance of labour under the present organization to work for the benefit of the nation.

All the social and political ideas involved in nationalization were based only on certain beliefs or feelings. Probably the

[1] Frank Hodges, op. cit., p. 83.

first accidental improvement in trade and the consequent increase of wages, or any other event, would, as it often did before the War, bring a sudden change in the attitude of the workers, leading to the adoption of a new social programme. For such proposals there is not room in a flourishing trade. The miners deny that they desire to take over the mines and exploit them for their own benefit. All their arguments point out the advantages which would accrue to the community as a whole from nationalization. These advantages arise from unification and are economic in nature.

In this examination we refrain entirely from giving any sort of valuation to the moral significance of the miners' claim to command the industry. We cannot, however, consider their demands in any other than a political light, as a fight for power between two groups in the community. From the community's point of view, economically there is no special advantage in either system, provided that the industry is run in the best way possible. We must leave out entirely political or class ideas and discount those motives underlying the nationalization schemes which have their origin in social grounds, e.g. the tendency towards social equalization throughout all the coal-fields, expressed in equal wages and conditions for all, and turn towards the reorganization scheme for production, treatment, and distribution of coal under the suggested socialization.

Unification was the magic economic panacea in all the Labour schemes for curing the depressed industry. Mr. Rowe[1] has expressed the view in his book that the principle of unification constitutes the fundamental difference between the Labour and non-Labour schemes. As to the genus nationalization and the genus individual ownership, it seems to us that the chief distinction between them must be found in the sphere of ownership rather than, as Mr. Rowe suggested, in unification. But we think Mr. Rowe is justified in his remark which points to unification as the primary object of all the contrivances of nationalization. It would perhaps be misleading to set out in a generalization of this sort the

[1] J. W. F. Rowe, *Wages in the Coal Industry*, London, 1923, p. 130.

different motives underlying the particular schemes of socialization of mines. It is much safer to indicate their object.

All the authoritative Labour publications and pamphlets brought unification into special prominence.[1] The official manifesto of the Labour Party,[2] which had an enormous influence on the future of the coal industry, instituted an energetic claim for unification :—

> " The only effective course, the Labour Party holds, is to unify the coal industry under public ownership, and to rescue it from the ever-deepening chaos into which it has fallen by converting it into an efficient and honourable public service, to develop coal treatment on scientific lines as an integral part of the industry, to reorganize the distributive processes under public control, and to administer the industry with due regard both to the requirements of the community and to the claim of the mine-workers for civilized standards of life and work."

There is a slight difference of degree in the demands brought forward by Mr. Hodges in 1920, and the Labour Manifesto issued several years later, after the struggle for nationalization had passed its high watermark. In Mr. Hodges' scheme, unification seems to be not the chief desire of the Party but only the first effect of nationalization. There emerges in his reasoning a certain doctrinaire tone, so characteristic of the early post-War socialization movement, and which a few years later the same author was eager to discard completely from his argument.[3]

If we now turn our attention to the " Labour and the Nation " coal programme of 1927–8, we see in the forefront the desire for better organization and for unification of the industry as things valuable in themselves, but which can only be effected under public ownership. Nationalization, of course, did not lose any of its sacred insignia for the Socialists, and remained always the striking feature of their coal programmes, repeated in practically all the publications. But faced with economic and political reality, the

[1] Frank Hodges, *Nationalization of the Mines*, London, 1920, p. 92.
[2] *Labour and the Nation*, 2nd ed., p. 25.
[3] See Frank Hodges, " Nationalization of Industry: the Mines," in *The Book of the Labour Party*, vol. ii.

Labour Party was forced to build up an immediate plan feasible under the existing circumstances.

Before we proceed to trace further the development of Labour ideas on unification and the results which followed from them, we must refer to a cleavage of views, which took place in the coal programme of the miners after the War, especially following the 1921 stoppage. This difference of beliefs has given rise to a constructive policy.

Nationalization has always had two different aspects for the miners : first and foremost it represented for them a regime where their conditions would improve and their standard of life be raised ; secondly, they linked with it a more rational and economic production of coal, conceived *sui generis* as a public service. These two sides of socialization, i.e. the economic interest of the miners as a class on the one hand, and the desire for public service on the other, always formed a diatomic unity. In some periods, however, one of the components exceeded the other in importance ; at other times there was a more even balance between the two. Moreover, it seems to us that the public service side of nationalization never eclipsed the immediate benefits which would accrue out of the new order ; though there may have been certain sections of the Labour Party of which this is not true.

Thus originated two distinct movements in the miners' group, which also to a great extent influenced the Labour Party in general. The first considered nationalization as a social necessity and was prepared to gain it even at the price of certain sacrifices on the part of the miners ; the second had more immediate and economic ends in view, aiming rather at obtaining better working conditions, wages, and standard of life for the workers. Even in the nationalization schemes this difference is easily noticeable. Those who desired direct advantages for the miners refused to let them endure hardship and privation for the sole purpose of a struggle for nationalization. Again, the leaders of the nationalization camp were ready even to give up certain advantages in order to secure the principle in which they believed.

Dualism of ideas on the development of their movement, described by Mr. Keynes [1] as " the two hearts and two heads of Socialism ", existed to a certain extent in the miners' lodges also before the War. In 1912 the controversy was already well defined and carried on energetically on both sides. The non-political trade unionists, who were then vigorously endeavouring to create a militant spirit in the lodges and " to keep up steam ", refused to endorse any sort of nationalization which would not hand over the industry to the miners. [2]

At the time, in view of the economic difficulties the " trade unionists pure and simple " were a much more extreme party than the wing advocating nationalization. The difference between the believers in some kind of economic short-term policy, who aimed at gripping immediate and large advantages, and the believers in a premeditated long-term reconstructional programme which, remote though it might seem, would yet solve finally and for ever the existing troubles, was very much accentuated during the period immediately after decontrol. At that time, the miners, who had been going from strength to strength, were compelled owing to the economic slump of 1921, and the subsequent decontrol, to bring their advance to a complete halt, especially so in the exporting districts. [3] The majority of

[1] J. M. Keynes: An address delivered in the Transport House, London, on the 13th December, 1931.

[2] *The Miner's Next Step ; being a suggested scheme for the Reorganization of the Federation*, issued by the Unofficial Reform Committee, Tonypandy, 1912. Its authorship is ascribed to Noah Ablett and A. J. Cook, and it forms a protest against the official draft of proposals prepared by the Executive of the South Wales Miners' Federation and submitted to the Federation's " Reform " Conference in March, 1911. This anonymous scheme claimed immediate benefits for the miners. It is not astonishing therefore that they disapproved of the highly bureaucratic scheme propagated at this time ; on the ground that it " does not lead in this direction, but simply makes a ' National Trust ', with all the force of the Government behind it, whose one concern will be to see that the industry is run in such a way as to pay the interest on the bonds with which the coal owners are paid out, and to extract as much more profit as possible in order to relieve the taxation of other landlords and capitalists ". Hence, the policy of this section of the miners was to oppose any sort of nationalization which would not bring them better wages and better conditions. " Our only concern is to see to it that those who create the value receive it." Through the " irritation strike " and " ca'canny " it was proposed to reduce the profitability of the industry to nil, and, in this way, to eliminate the shareholders.

[3] Cf. Appendix A.

the miners and the chief leaders were then prophesying nationalization and endorsing the radical but, in their opinion, the only solution. They were prepared to pay a very high price for it, since one of the generals of the movement, Vernon Hartshorn, said during the Federation Conference on 22nd April, 1921 : " Whether we get a reduction [in wages] of 3s., 4s., or 5s. a day is a mere bagatelle in comparison with the principles we are aiming at."

The trade unionists, desiring more immediate welfare for labour, were as a whole passive, so long as the price of nationalization did not necessitate any extra sacrifices on their part. As soon, however, as it became clear that the trend of events did not favour nationalization, and that it would be very expensive to engage in a fight for such a drastic change, they turned exclusively to the short-term policy which, from the point of view of the others, appeared opportunist. A survey written by Mr. W. Livesey,[1] late chief clerk of the Miners' Federation, gives us a full account of the stubborn controversies which existed in the Federation. Mr. Livesey, opposing the " extremists' " section, deplored this " boring from within " of the rank and file by the doctrinaires of socialization, and thought that the industrial side ought to have the first call.[2] Professor Tawney [3] well reproduces the atmosphere then prevailing in the following sentence : " ' Nationalization,' ' public ownership,' ' individual enterprise,' ' workers' control,' ' industrial democracy '—these are phases out of which controversialists appear able to construct either heaven, or hell."

The purely industrial wing was not strong enough on the eve of the 1921 struggle to carry through its ideas, and therefore the official Miners' and Labour movement were forced to unite the political and economic aspects. It was

[1] W. Livesay, *The Mining Crisis, its History and Meaning to all Workers*, London, 1921, p. 55.

[2] W. Livesay, loc. cit., p. 83 : ". . . The first essential principle which must underlie any real reform, reconstruction, and reorganization of the industrial wing . . . is that trade unions as organizations must drop all political aims, and must discountenance any political activities by their officials as such."

[3] R. H. Tawney, " The British Coal Industry and the Question of Nationalization, *The Quarterly Journal of Economics*, vol. xxxv, 1920, p. 63.

not then a question of how to secure better conditions and wages from the owners, but of how to destroy them altogether as a class. Direct claims for shorter hours, better wages, housing, working conditions, etc., eventually gave place to political demands. The industrial wing, which always considered that the chief aim of Labour policy was to secure a higher degree of welfare among the miners, was nevertheless steadily striving for its own ends by opposing in 1920, during the general rise of prices, any further increases in the prices of coal, as in their view this would force up the cost of living quicker than wages could be raised.[1]

After this brief reference to the existence of a dual programme in the miners' lodges it will be relevant here to sketch the evolution of the industrial wing, which led to the creation of the positive Labour coal policy. Since after 1921 both nationalization and any return of economic prosperity became more and more unattainable, the official Labour policy-makers began to incorporate one by one different points of reform which would in their view alleviate the situation of the men and would set the whole structure of the industry on a sounder basis. The trade decline put the miners' Unions on the defensive against deflation and unemployment, and has really kept them so ever since, in contrast to their previous aggressive policy. Now discussions of the Labour Party became concerned less with political and more with economic problems. And thus, in devising the necessary future changes in the architecture of the coal industry, the leaders had direct recourse to what they conceived would be the remedial effects of nationalization. What in the nationalization regime were only taken as results (i.e. all the economic effects of socialization grouped round the chief feature, concentration), we find now slowly becoming aims in themselves.[2] " Concentration," " unification," " centralization," " control "—all these capital accessories of nationalization begin to possess an independent existence.

[1] Cf. G. D. H. Cole, *Labour in the Coal Mining Industry* (1914–1921), Oxford, 1923, chap. vii.
[2] See *Unification in the Coal Mining Industry*, published by Philip Gee, London, 1924 (?).

This was already the case in the scheme outlined in *Labour and the Nation*, where nationalization was proposed in order to secure unification. Other more recent official publications carry the idea even further. A scheme called *Coal and Commonsense*,[1] dealing with the Labour Party's solution of the coal question, while endorsing unification, clearly indicates that national ownership has been degraded from a factor of industrial reconstruction to a safety valve, protecting the community from the eventual evils which might arise under a private system of unified control. In view of the exceedingly difficult economic position of 1927 and 1928, the realization that the miners could not improve their status until the industry stood on a sound basis became general. It was now admitted by the Labour Party that the process of integration could be carried out in exactly the same way under private as under public ownership; but they still insisted that nationalization was the best means of securing public control over this basic industry. In the meantime more attention was being paid to the question of economic reconstruction, and to interpreting more fully the meaning of unification. The importance of this was also beginning to be realized among the coal-owners. In the early labour schemes, unification was conceived as a huge national system of more or less undefined consistency. Later on, a much more precise significance became attached to it. It was no longer thought of only on a national scale, and the value of much smaller degrees of concentration was realized. Local co-ordination schemes, or district organizations, gradually found approbation in certain Labour quarters. This was clearly expressed in the Miners' Report of the Lewis Committee [2] on Co-operative Coal Organization and also by the late Vernon Hartshorn,[3] who in 1926 approved of the integration movement on a district basis. He believed district unification to be a useful preliminary to a larger degree of concentration on a national and later

[1] *Coal and Commonsense*, Labour's scheme for the future of the coal industry, p. 13.
[2] Reports of the Departmental Committee on Co-operative Selling in the Coal Mining Industry, Cmd. 2770, 1926.
[3] *Vide*, the Rt. Hon. Vernon Hartshorn, *Mr. Baldwin attacks Miners' Hours and Wages*, London, 1926, p. 10.

on an international scale. Thus he enriched the general notion by a closer definition. For though the schemes and the Parliamentary Bills for nationalization of mines elaborated details of the national mining administration, they did not sufficiently explain what they meant economically by unification. In a later passage [1] Hartshorn simply suggested the adoption of some sort of artificial restriction scheme, which would prevent the fall of prices, and thus indirectly affect the miners' wages.

The legislation already in force, passed with the object of fostering amalgamation, was regarded as inadequate, and the miners asked for a further enlargement of State authority in this respect. At this point we must bear in mind that the existing provisions of the Mining Industry Act, 1926, dealing with compulsory amalgamations, were probably in a large measure due to the Socialists' pressure on the Government. In a letter sent to the Prime Minister on the 30th April, 1926, the Miners' Federation had presented a declaration containing the basis for the settlement of the pending labour dispute. This included the details of the suggested solution of difficulties within the industry. It asked for the institution by the State of compulsory amalgamation, after the expiration of the date assigned for the completion of voluntary amalgamation.[2] The necessary capital for the reorganization of districts and undertakings was to be provided by the Government. The acceptance of a trial period before the application of compulsion bears some resemblance to the attitude of the Labour members in the Lewis Committee on the question of obligatory marketing schemes.

A few days after the submission of the Miners' Memorandum to the Prime Minister, the General Council of the Trade Union Congress drafted on the 3rd of May, 1926, in agreement with the Miners' Federation, a " scheme for the adjustment of the coal industry, with a view to establishing the industry upon an economic footing ". However, in this, the demand for amalgamation is formulated in a different way, i.e. the proposed National Mining Board,

[1] Loc. cit.
[2] Statement of the General Council and Miners' Federation to the Conference of Trade Union Executives, 29th April, 1926. *Vide* § 13.

which would deal with amalgamation, is given the duty of undertaking inquiries as to the best methods of forming amalgamations and selling agencies.

Strong pressure from the Labour Party in favour of concentration bore immediate fruit in the form of the Prime Minister's pledge [1] that " the Government shall introduce and endeavour to pass this Session (1926) a Bill to give effect to the proposals of the Commission regarding amalgamations ". A few months later the pledge was fulfilled and provisions dealing with amalgamations found their way into the Statute Book. But, as we have seen, mere legislation concerning integration did not satisfy the demands of Labour; they required a more speedy amalgamation, asking that the State should be entitled to acquire any firm which opposed concentration. As an interim measure before public ownership, the newly amalgamated company should be entitled to " acquire the firm in question on terms decided by arbitration ". *The Mining Situation—an Immediate Programme* stated the opinion that partial and small-scale amalgamation would not provide an adequate solution of the existing difficulties.

As already pointed out, the Socialists considered that, apart from nationalization, settlement of economic ills was to be found by means of (a) reducing costs, and (b) securing the best possible prices. Thus while amalgamation of mines dealt with the first, improved marketing was to meet the second. The Miners' Federation began after 1926 to pay still more attention to selling agencies as a means of reducing the undercutting of prices. In their Memorandum containing the proposals for the settlement of the pending dispute, the importance of such agencies was much stressed.[2] And again, as the result of these requests,

[1] Proposals of the Prime Minister presented to the parties to the Mining Disputes on the 14th May, 1926.
[2] Loc. cit., § 12: " It is impossible to measure the exact degree of economies which would be effected by the use of selling agencies and prevention of overlapping in the export trade and underselling in the home market, but such economies would materially help the position. Similarly the power of municipalities to sell coal by retail while allowing for an increase in the pit-head price would not necessarily increase the price to the consumer."
Vide also the Rt. Hon. Vernon Hartshorn, M.P., *Mr. Baldwin attacks*

the Government promised to appoint a committee to investigate the question of selling syndicates. This was realized by the nomination of the Lewis Committee on Co-operative Selling but the Socialists did not consider the Committee's Report as sufficiently exhaustive. According to their immediate programme, a selling monopoly would have to be instituted in each coal-field, together with a co-ordinating body for the whole country. The selling monopolies were to be conducted either by the State, or by a public utility company. Such a solution of the problem of competition stands in close relation to later views of the Miners' Federation expressed in the Memorandum on the marketing clauses of the Act of 1930.[1]

The Labour scheme for immediate action [2] did not stop at the national solution of the coal problem. It went much further, recommending some sort of international way out of the difficulties, and foreshadowing the necessity for an understanding between coal exporting countries ; as indeed had been emphasized a long time ago in international coal miners' circles by Émile Lewy.

The expediency of co-operation between coal-producing countries or at least between coal-exporting nations, was brought forward on all occasions in official Labour quarters. Mr. A. J. Cook,[3] the Peter Pan of the Miners' Federation, gave to it the following explanation :—

"We all fully realize that work, wages, and hours are an economic trinity, and that the problems relating thereto

Miners' Hours and Wages, London, p. 10. He wrote : "The next thing that has to be done is to adopt the necessary machinery to prevent the undercutting and underselling that have been going on, which are a characteristic of the industry, and which are producing such ruinous results all through the country." And also *The Mining Situation : an Immediate Programme*, London, by The Labour Publications Department, p. 17 : "There is only one satisfactory way of dealing with the wholesale distribution of coal. There should be a selling monopoly on each coal-field conducted either by the State or by a public utility company, with some co-ordinating body, and there should be broad general plans for distributing both industrial and domestic coal with a minimum of transport . . ."

[1] Miners' Federation of Great Britain, Memorandum on Part I of the Coal Mines Act, 1930, *The Case for Coal Trade Regulation*, 25th February, 1932.

[2] See, *The Mining Situation : an Immediate Programme*, London, p. 18.

[3] A. J. Cook, "The Real Coal Problem," *Labour Magazine*, vol. x, July, 1931, p. 104, see also E. Shinwell, "Coal and the Future—A Socialist Plan," *The Nineteenth Century*, vol. cxiv, August, 1933, p. 182.

cannot be completely solved by national action, hence our desire for international regulation on hours, production, and prices. We were the first to recognize this and to make provisions for same."

In addition to amalgamations and better organization of marketing, the miners proposed a general reorganization of the industry. For this purpose a survey of individual collieries should be held, and all the collieries should be divided into three groups, according to their physical efficiency and wage-paying capacity. The capital needed for the reorganization should be provided with the aid of the Government. Apart, however, from this classification into three groups, there is little information as to how they proposed to effect the reform. More material about reconstruction was comprised in the proposals of the General Council and Miners' Joint Sub-Committee, 3rd May, 1926, according to which a National Mining Board should be established, composed of : persons appointed by the Government, representatives of mine-owners, and representatives of miners. Among other things it would be the objective of the Board to :—

> "investigate and decide the steps to be taken forthwith in the matter of reorganization and conduct of the industry (§ 3) . . . they shall determine the steps necessary for dealing with those matters of reorganization for which a longer period is necessary for giving effect to the recommendations of the Commission (1925), S. 4."

As we see, the Labour plans of organization in the coal industry referred to several aspects of its structure. Starting from the general conception of unification, they created a programme of amalgamations of mines, of co-ordination of marketing, and of general reconstruction. They also had methods of financing the schemes they preferred. Finally they claimed the establishment of a mixed National Mining Board which, besides its important activities in reconstructing the industry and in fixing an " economic price ", was to perform weighty duties more directly affecting the relations between capital and labour. It was to be the wage-fixing body ; in case of disputes " all parties represented . . .

shall accept its findings, including the Government ". The National Board was conceived in their proposals on a very large scale.   In their hands was to rest not only the treatment of labour questions but practically the whole initiative for reorganizing the fabric of the coal industry.   In this way the functions, which in a regime of national ownership would have to be vested in the national and district coal committees, were left to the Board, which included the owners of mines.   In the latest scheme, promulgated in 1933, the National Mining Board was to be made responsible for the subordinate regional amalgamations or trusts which would operate the socialized industry.[1]   As to the financing of the reforms, the Labour Party proposed in its latest publication to appoint a National Investment Board, which would direct the stream of long term capital into such industries as coal.[2]

Simultaneously with the demand for nationalization, expressed in successive Labour Party conferences at Margate in 1926, and at Blackpool in 1927, an immediate policy for dealing with the industry originated in Labour circles.   The economic depression and the ravages of foreign competition caused the leaders to form a direct programme to cope with its problems, and above all with unemployment among mine-workers.   The miners understood that the chief evil of the existing depression was due to the undercutting of prices and to the ensuing competition.   They knew that their wages were to a large extent dependent on the price obtained for coal, and they often thought that the control of prices could secure for them a better standard of life.   This explains the importance attached by the miners to the price-fixing arrangements which would be achieved by unification, and to the amalgamation of mines, although this was indeed the reverse of their policy of low prices in 1920.

In 1928, when internal competition was at its height and the voluntary district schemes began to work, the claim

[1] *Problems of a Socialist Government*—A symposium by eminent members of the Labour Party.   London, 1933, p. 177.
[2] *Vide*, the Labour Party, Policy Report, Currency, Banking, Finance, July, 1932.

for price-control was general. Under the joint ægis of the
Trades Union Congress, Labour Party, and Miners' Federation a mining programme appeared to meet immediately
the existing situation.[1] Constructive elements were involved
in the scheme, and they went far beyond empty phrases
about unification. The meaning of this term was explained
and suggestions were brought forward as to how to tackle
the existing state of affairs, without referring to nationalization. This scheme undoubtedly influenced to a very considerable extent the actual development of the industrial
structure. It assumed that the root of the coal evil was to be
found in excessive costs of production and in the bad working
of the price apparatus. Hence attention should be chiefly
focused on (a) reducing costs and (b) securing the best
possible prices. Both these ends could be achieved only by
changes in the existing organization. Two main alterations
were necessary, unification and better marketing. By
unification the pamphlet probably meant amalgamation of
collieries, since in one of the paragraphs we find :—

"It is generally admitted that a greater measure of
unification is desirable in the mining industry, though there
may be a difference of opinion as to how far amalgamation
should proceed."

The latest views in the Miners' Federation are all in
favour of keeping the prices of coal high by means of
artificial control. They even go as far as to suggest the
introduction of a system of zones for the fixation of home
prices.[2] By-product industries are also included.[3]

We have given a very short survey of the development of
prevailing opinions in the Labour Party on the subject of
reorganization of the coal industry, and have pointed out
the co-existence in the movement of the two wings, which
were merged into one after the disappearance of the
immediate prospect of public ownership. But though it

[1] *The Mining Situation : an Immediate Programme*, London, 1928.
[2] *Vide* Miners' Federation of Great Britain, Memorandum on Part I
of the Coal Mines Act, 1930, the Case for Coal Trade Regulation, 25th
February, 1932, and cf. George Hall, " More Waste in the Coalfields,"
The Labour Magazine, vol. xi, No. 3, p. 105, July, 1932, speaking for the
renunciation of the policy of cheap prices.
[3] *Vide* T.U.C. Congress, 1932.

pushed on with its immediate policy, the Labour movement remained on the whole [1] faithful to its ideas of unification and nationalization, emphasizing their importance on every possible occasion,[2] and as the industrial and financial crises developed after 1930 they demanded a wider application of a nationalization policy, not excluding even the Bank of England.

Constructive proposals, however, which could assist the reorganization of the industry under the existing order of private ownership, were all involved in the short-term policy. Many of the proposals found approval even among the other parties, and from some of the coal-owners themselves, as being the sound way of bringing the industry back to its traditional position and prosperity.

In appraising the Labour schemes we must note, however, that in all of them one extremely important factor has been deliberately passed over in silence. They do not try to solve the question of over-capacity. This omission of one of the burning problems is explicable to a great extent by the fact that Labour knew that the reduction of output would most certainly add to the number of unemployed. The proposed shortening of the working time, the restriction of entry of fresh miners' recruits, the raising of the school age, and all other devices were insufficient to absorb the unemployment already existing, to say nothing of that which would be created by eventual restriction of output, as well as by the introduction of better methods of mining.

In framing its short-term programme the Labour Party had always in mind the enormous unemployment among the mining population. Hence all reforms involving labour-saving devices were carefully omitted in the plan for reconstruction. Amalgamation was treated rather vaguely,

[1] There were, however, now certain divergencies of opinion on this subject : Mr. T. T. W. Newbold (Lab.) wrote on nationalization in connection with the rationalization of the forms of property to conform with the evolution of productive technique: " But it makes obsolete the whole notion of nationalization of mines. Actually, that panacea of the propagandists of the last twenty years has been as dead as mutton for half a decade." (*The Miner*, 17th August, 1929.)

[2] Cf. the election manifesto, *Labour's Call to Action*, 9th October, 1931. E. Shinwell, *Coal and the Future—A Socialist Plan*, loc. cit. and *Problems of A Socialist Government*, London, 1933.

and sufficient weight was not given to the possible effect on the output per worker. Efficiency hardly occupied any room in vast Socialist schemes, and all the effects of static rationalization for a non-expanding market obtainable under amalgamations and mergers were ignored. Neither was there, for the same reason, any word of mechanization of production. The Royal Commission on the Coal Industry (1925) emphatically recommended the introduction of better mechanical equipment,[1] especially of coal cutters and conveyors ; they also realized the need for closing a number of inefficient collieries and concentrating on the best.[2] But when the Labour Party quote the recommendations of the Commission, they cautiously avoid alluding to those which aim at higher efficiency and at securing the working of large units at full capacity.

In this way better mechanization, rationalization, the working at full capacity, scrapping of inefficient mines, and other labour-saving reforms were excluded from the remedies suggested by the Labour group.

§ 2.   COAL POLICY OF THE LIBERALS

The attitude of the Liberals towards the coal dilemma has undergone an evolution, both shorter and more continuous

[1] Cf. *Report of the Royal Commission on the Coal Industry* (1925), vol. i, p. 123 : " It is not sufficient to possess, as we believe this country does possess, a body of mining engineers second to none in skill, experience, training, and ingenuity. It is essential to secure that these qualities are applied, and that the system of mineral ownership and the organization of the mining industry are such as to give them unfettered scope. It is not sufficient that the best of our mines should be, as we think they are, unsurpassed in efficiency by those of any other country in the world. It is necessary that *all* our mines should be brought as nearly as possible to the level of the best."

[2] Cf. ibid., p. 230 : " Whatever the course that may be taken in these and other matters, it seems to be inevitable that a certain number of collieries must be closed in the immediate future. In view of the state of demand at home and abroad, together with the developments in South Yorkshire and Nottinghamshire, it is plain that the industry, in the other districts, is too large in size for the requirements it has to fulfil. Under nationalization precisely the same situation would present itself."

than that of the Labour Party.   The basic assumption underlying the modern Liberal outlook is the belief that the State
should take a part in the struggle between Labour and
Capital,[1] and in the coal industry it should pay special
attention to some of the industrial activities of coal-mining
with a view to "maintaining a far-sighted and co-ordinated
national mining policy".   It must be noted, however, that
even before the War many Liberals adhered to the view
formulated by Professor Hobhouse [2] that "the function of
State coercion is to override individual coercion, and, of
course, coercion exercised by any association of individuals
within the State".   In this way, while rejecting the
extreme solution of nationalization of mines, they
nevertheless strongly advocated some degree of State
interference in the staple national industry.   Already during
the discussion on the Eight Hours Bill, mining royalties
were not regarded by the Liberals as "taboo" and were
freely criticized as constituting a very heavy item in costs
weighing against the share of labour.   However, the pre-War
Liberal reforms in the coal industry were only pursued in the
field of labour.   The Eight Hours Act of 1908, and the
Minimum Wage Act, 1912, were the achievements of Liberal
policy.

In the post-War period the Liberals urged the State to
interfere in coal affairs in spite of the resistance of the
coal-owners.   After the publication of "Coal and Power"
in 1924, Mr. Lloyd George was blamed by the Mining
Association [3] (Central Organization of the Coal-owners) for
giving ear to the propagandists' teaching that "something
ought to be done" about industry.

The functions of the Government in relation to the
Coal Industry had by this time been explained more fully

[1] *Coal and Power*, the Report of an inquiry presided over by the Rt. Hon.
D. Lloyd George, London, 1924, p. 31 : "Our conception of the function
of the State in a modern industrial society is not that it should undertake
creative and productive functions, but that it should see to it that the
necessary conditions shall exist in which the creative enterprise and
energy of its citizens can most effectively operate."

[2] L. T. Hobhouse, *Liberalism*, London, p. 146.

[3] *Politics and Coal*, an answer to *Coal and Power*, which contained
Mr. Lloyd George's proposals for the reorganization of the mining
industry.   Issued officially by the Mining Association of Great Britain.

by other Liberal utterances. To all those who wanted to learn how the Party leaders proposed to use this authority, what was their programme for the organization of the coal industry, how Governmental action could reconcile private administration with interventionism, how the old doctrines of Liberalism such as those of John Bright, Richard Cobden and others on the function of the State could be made compatible with Governmental interference—a forcible answer was given by Mr. McNair.[1] He thought that just as the State succeeded in the past in changing terrible industrial conditions, so now it ought to bring a better order into the coal industry. A few years later Sir Herbert Samuel strongly condemned the lack of initiative of the Government in coal matters.[2] The so-called Liberals' Yellow Book,[3] which referred to the whole of national industry including coal, maintains that while hostility is exchanged between organized bodies of the community engaged in production, the duty of the State is energetic action and settlement of difficulties. Thus, notwithstanding the opposition of the coal-owners on the one side and the claims of the miners for nationalization on the other, the Liberal Party succeeded in building up an independent coal policy of its own, which, at the time when the Coal Mines Bill, 1930, was before Parliament, played a dominating part.

After the War the first indication of the Liberal attitude to coal organization may be found in *The Proposals and Decisions of the Government*, issued by Mr. Lloyd George on the 22nd August, 1919, which contained several very important sections on the reorganization of coal-mining. Two of them especially are of singular significance. One pertained to the need of reducing expenses of management and the other to State purchase of mineral rights. Both these formed the rudiments of the later Liberal schemes for mining organization.

In dealing with the reduction of expenses, the Liberals

---

[1] Arnold McNair, *The Problem of the Coal Mines*, London, 1924.
[2] The Rt. Hon. Sir Herbert Samuel, *The Problem of the Coal Mines*, London, 1927, pp. 4 and 16.
[3] *Britain's Industrial Future*, being the Report of the Liberal Industrial Inquiry, London, 1928, book iii, p. 166.

had in mind amalgamations of neighbouring mines within the area, which if necessary could be made subject to State supervision as a preventive against exploitation of consumers. In the relevant part of the proposals (Clause 7) it was, however, not quite clear how they would have to be created, whether by compulsion or voluntarily. The idea of amalgamation was only vague in the Government's proposal. It originated out of the desire to reduce costs, which were highly inflated at the end of the War, by means of economies obtainable under a higher degree of concentration of neighbouring mines.

The other important point in the early Liberal policy was the acceptance, under the influence of the Sankey Commission, of the principle of State acquisition of mineral rights with compensation, part of which should be retained as a levy towards a fund for amelioration of the miners' social conditions. The last mentioned proposal formed part of the Liberal programme of social reorganization in coal-mining. Nationalization of royalties was advocated as a way of securing some authoritative control over the whole industry.

Another suggestion [1] involved in this early scheme referred to the participation of Labour in the mixed Area Board controlling the policy of the Area Group of mines. This was the first of a long series of Liberal suggestions for co-operative apparatus between Labour and Capital in industry, and in coal affairs especially. Wages were the chief item which it was proposed should be fixed by the Board.

In the course of time many fresh ideas were added to the first foundations of the scheme. The basic policy of the Liberals remained the same, however ; they always attempted to combine private ownership with better social relations in the mines and with more economical methods of production. This last point which was strictly bound up with problems

---

[1] Section 8. Representation of Labour on Area Boards : " The Government propose that all workers in and about the mines should have a direct voice on the Board controlling the policy of the Area Group of coal mines. Further, the status of each representative of the workers on the Board shall be in all respects equal to that of the other members."

of industrial efficiency, already found great sympathy long before the War. One of the chief arguments of the Liberal promoters of the Eight Hour Day was that the costs of shorter hours could be made up by economies from greater efficiency.[1]

After the War the prevailing conditions required the Party to adopt a definite attitude towards the Labour nationalization schemes of the day. The Liberals pronounced themselves in favour of State ownership of mineral rights, but strongly opposed the nationalization of mines. As early as the 28th November, 1919, the National Liberal Federation at its annual meeting at Birmingham [2] passed a resolution, saying that " this Council approves of the acquisition of all mineral rights by the State ". This request, however, had no class foundation. The resolutions of the Nottingham [3] Assembly of 1921 are the best proof that the Liberals wanted to secure a considerable amount of State control through the royalties but did not consider it as an end in itself. Section 6 of the Industrial Policy Resolutions adopted in February, 1921, in Nottingham, declared that " the owners of mining royalties should be required to make a return of their respective interests, and that these returns should be checked by a Valuation Department ". Then followed the suggestion of two further moves which would secure a better organization of the industry :—

(a) That mining royalties should be subject to site-value rates and taxes ; and

(b) if the " minerals are afterwards purchased by the State, the price should be the capital value fixed for rating and taxation ".

The royalty rates contributed to the State were conceived according to some later Liberal schemes as gradually rising, so that after a prescribed time the Government would be the

[1] Cf. the Rt. Hon Winston Spencer Churchill, *Liberalism and the Social Problem*, London, 1909, p. 173 et seq. : " We on this side are great admirers of cheapness of production " (p. 185).
[2] *Vide The Coal Mining Industry : Recent History, Causes of Unrest, and the Liberal Remedy*, London, p. 8.
[3] Ibid.

exclusive owner of royalties. In this way, after a period of from thirty to sixty years all the royalties would be received by the State. In the meantime, however, the Government could effect a large degree of control over all mining operations. In later schemes the Liberal Party insisted that control should be secured without delay.

The urgent need of reorganization and growing trust in the State as an organ of rationalization quickly persuaded the Liberals to reject any indirect means of State control, such as gradual taxation, which work too slowly to secure an immediate effect. In more recent schemes we do not find any more suggestions for taxing the royalties, such as those in the Nottingham declaration of 1921. By 1924 they were already making a direct claim for nationalization of minerals with fair compensation.

Mr. A. McNair, late Secretary of the Sankey Commission, whose scheme [1] greatly influenced the official inquiry of the Liberal Party, pleaded for the purchase of royalties " The effect of the step recommended would be to substitute the State for the royalty-owner on payment of adequate compensation, and thus place the State in the strategic position of being able to deal to the best advantage with what is admittedly one of our principal national assets—our coal ". Organization, he considered, must be first of all modernized and at the same time a part in the administration assured to the workers. In order to secure better results from the mines, amalgamations should be carried out in all the coal-fields. These schemes of amalgamation, which already played an important part in Mr. Lloyd George's scheme of 1919, were now much enlarged and elaborated. They were not to be mechanical, nor were they to follow a general uniform plan ; economic considerations would in the first place determine which mines should be combined together. Automatism was thus excluded.[2] Amalgamations of mines were to be carried out by way of granting State Leases for mining coal.

[1] Arnold McNair, *The Problems of the Coal Mines*, " The New Way " Series, 1924, p. 7.
[2] Ibid., p. 16.

Mr. McNair distinguished six classes of probable applicants for leases to the Royalty Commissioners :—

(1) Owners whose mines were of adequate size and well administered. In this case they would have their leases renewed.

(2) Owners of one or more small collieries which were considered too small to be worked economically.

In these cases the whole apparatus would be put in motion to force amalgamations upon the parties. The Commissioners would be entitled to refuse any individual colliery the lease unless it amalgamated with others.

(3) The next group consisted of large district mergers, somewhat on the lines of Sir Arthur Duckham's scheme laid before the Sankey Commission. In this case the power of effecting amalgamation should be left to Parliament.

(4) The Public Authorities were in the fourth group of lessees, which would admit throughout a large degree of joint control of management and labour. This group was not embraced by State Administration.

(5) In his fifth group was the Admiralty, which potentially could be made responsible for a number of mines producing bunker coal for the Navy.

(6) In the last group he placed the co-operatives' and miners' guilds as eventual lessees of the mines.

Since the author was on the whole a believer in private enterprise, and would like to preserve for the industry " the large fund of experience and initiative which is represented by the colliery owners ", he advised that public bodies should be treated by the royalty authorities on exactly the same footing as private lessees.

A few months after the appearance of this scheme, the Liberal Party published, in July, 1924, a special report on Coal and Power,[1] which forms the first official codification of the Liberal views on the coal and power questions. It

[1] *Coal and Power*, the Report of an Inquiry presided over by the Rt. Hon. D. Lloyd George, London, 1924.

does not, however, add many new points to the beliefs hitherto expressed. Socialization as a suitable solution of the problem was rejected in the Report. In its place the Liberals proposed to introduce the co-operation of the four elements primarily interested in mining. (1) The miners, (2) the owner, (3) the consumer, and (4) the national interests. Like the project of Mr. McNair, the Report advocated nationalization of royalties and the entrusting of their administration to the Royalty Commissioners. A whole scheme for collaboration between Labour and Capital was included. The Report provided for the creation of a system of Pit Committees and District Boards subordinated in the last resort to a National Mining Council. In this way the workers would be given a chance to participate in the conduct of the industry and to benefit it by concentrating their efforts on increasing efficiency and raising its status. Among other functions, the National Mining Council would be called upon also to " make recommendations affecting the hours and conditions of labour, the safety of the workers, and amenity of their surroundings, having regard to the financial conditions of the industry ". Further duties of the Council included the administration of the National Welfare Fund created by the Mining Industry Act, 1920, which imposed a levy of 1d. per ton of coal upon the royalty-owners for a period of five years, afterwards prolonged. Wage-fixing was not among the duties of the Council, but in the case of a deadlock between the directly negotiating parties it was to act as a conciliating body, to which the question should be referred, and before the publication of the reports neither party would start direct action.[1] Other suggestions put forward to meet the claims of the miners comprised the raising of their status in the industry, improved housing conditions, the introduction of better educational facilities, paid holidays, and many secondary items.

Among difficulties encountered by the progressive mine-owners, the Report mentioned, apart from Royalty owners, the recalcitrant fellow-owner, who by his behaviour or extortionate demands might hinder the progress of a

[1] Loc. cit., pp. 60–6.

colliery group. This referred especially to the advancement
of amalgamations, which were regarded as necessary for
the well-being of the industry. Such an obstinacy should
be overcome by the leasing power of the Royal
Commissioners.[1] Besides dealing with amalgamation, the
Commissioners would be entitled to institute inquiries and
subsequently to introduce changes in mineral leases at
the request of the representatives of the owners or of the
miners. As a guiding principle in the granting of leases, the
Commissioners would have to consider the possibility of
developing the more productive areas, keeping in view their
gradual concentration and the transfer of labour towards
more productive districts. They would also have to consider
the size of undertakings [2] in each case. The Liberals realized
that efficient working was not in simple proportion to the
size of collieries, but it depended also on other determinants
which varied from district to district. The tendency of
this publication is to favour larger units.

The question of costs of production and the low price
of coal underlies the whole Liberal structure. Realizing the
importance of having a cheap supply of power and fuel they
made this their guiding aim. At the time of the publication
of the Report, when the extraordinarily favourable
conditions in the export market had just disappeared, the
industry was forced to contemplate a reduction of prices,
in order to stave off the danger to exports. Efficiency
therefore emerged very soon in the Liberals' programme
as a counter-action to high costs. *Coal and Power*
recognized that though small units secure better personal
relations, nevertheless this advantage would have to be
abandoned in favour of cheapness of the product and
better yield both from capital and labour.

Thus lower costs and better yields became the two main
objectives of the Liberal schemes ; it was with these in
view that all their remedies were suggested. The demand
for working full capacity, which is heard in later years,
arose from the same cause. But besides amalgamations the

---

[1] Loc. cit., p. 34.
[2] Loc. cit., p. 57.

Report advised a progressive development of new mines in place of old. Some of the districts were not worth working, owing to natural difficulties, or to exhaustion of coal, resulting in a very low output per man employed. Old and inefficient collieries depress the whole industry and tend to lower the wages paid to the miners. The proposed Royalty Authorities ought thus to stimulate the transition from the old to the new. The Liberals were aware, however, that this movement would have to be set on foot gradually, and consequently it could not achieve its full effect in the immediate future. For this reason amalgamation had to be carried on as a direct means of securing more economic production during the period of elimination of poor pits.

The " New mines for old " campaign was severely criticized by the coal-owners,[1] who rightly maintained that unless capital could be freely attracted no development of new mines could ever take place. In their opinion any sort of imposed scheme would be likely to hamper the flow of capital towards coal investment and to increase the process of capital consumption.

The Liberal plan regarded amalgamation and modernization as the surest channels for determined effort towards reduction of costs. Cheap coal was the *sine qua non* of successful competition abroad. In reference to the home market, the scheme recommended more economical use of coal in order to avoid the enormous waste of fuel, which occurred under the existing conditions. It also advised the generation of lower qualities of coal into electricity. In this way cheap power could be secured for national industries.

From the standpoint of organization of the industry, this first official Liberal coal programme introduced four important principles, which will be found more fully developed in the later schemes. They are :—

(1) Amalgamation of existing units,

(2) Concentration on better mines and development of new mines for old,

[1] *Politics and Coal*, an answer to *Coal and Power*, by the Mining Association of Great Britain, London, 1924.

(3) Securing a large degree of control for the employees by the creation in the industry of a network of joint co-operative bodies,

(4) State purchase of royalties, which would facilitate the execution of the whole coal reform.

Whereas in 1924 the dearness of coal had received merely a passing reference, in the later Liberal pronouncements it figured in the forefront of the whole problem. It became the crucial question of 1925, when the process of price deflation was advancing.[1] " Why is our coal so costly ? " asked a Liberal publication, " Clearly not because of high wages or exorbitant profits," and it sought the reply in a wrong organization of the industry. Increase in working hours from seven to eight would not help the case ; much more essential reform was needed. In addition to difficulties due to causes beyond its control, the industry also suffered from internal troubles resulting in high prices of the product. High prices were the direct result of excessive costs. In this way amalgamation of mines, substitution of new methods for old, and gradual replacement of old mines by new, strongly advocated in *Coal and Power*, became the essence of coal reform as bringing a reduction of costs. By the term " new methods ", one is inclined to understand here the desire to introduce more rational working and the latest equipment into the pits. This point, however, has never been elucidated in any of the Liberal schemes.

Passing allusion is made to the volume of production and its relation to costs. " In order to pay, the mines must produce increased quantities of coal at a lower cost." [2] Thus the cost of mining must be linked with the quantity of coal extracted. Though this essential economic point has not been fully elaborated and forms only a sort of digression, nevertheless its significance is great. From this rough scheme emerged the whole idea of working at full capacity and thus reducing the overhead charges. It is very

[1] *The Coal Mining Industry : Recent History, Causes of Unrest, and Liberal Remedy*, London, 1925.
[2] Ibid., p. 7.

interesting to notice that the scheme provided cheaper working by increasing the quantity of coal produced. It was believed that at low prices the industry could find an outlet for the additional flow of coal. There is no idea of securing work at full capacity for the better units by scrapping the inefficient, nor is there any thought of restriction of output. Where transfer from old to new mines is mentioned it signifies merely the conveying of the increased productive capacity from the former to the latter.

But in addition to this the Liberals also believed that the demand for coal in the long run is of a considerable elasticity for a rise, sufficient to absorb the fresh supplies offered.[1] Such a view was expressed in 1927 by Sir Herbert Samuel,[2] who was of opinion that " in course of time no doubt a considerable reduction of price may so stimulate the consuming industries that the market may improve ". Clearly, to take full advantage of the elasticity of demand for a rise in coal in the long run, he required a stream of cheap fuel. Hence, infers Sir Herbert, one must adopt a course of policy which will facilitate the introduction of lower prices. But as these are only the repercussion of the general costs of production and of transport, therefore the whole problem centres upon the lowering of the expenses on those two items. The miners' standard of life should not be lowered.

The Liberal author enumerated five possible courses which might be followed to deliver the industry from its troubles :—

(1) A revival of industrial activity at home and abroad, a larger volume of commerce on the sea resulting in a greater demand for coal. State activity could help this revival only to a limited extent.

(2) An increased demand for coal through a reduction of prices. This could be made possible by adopting more economical methods of production and transport. An analagous effect could be obtained by extracting a greater value from coal by means of its more rational treatment and more scientific use.

[1] Cf. Section on the Demand for Coal in Pt. I, Chap. II.
[2] Sir Herbert Samuel, *The Problem of the Coal Mines*, Liberal Publication Department, London, 1927.

(3) " A diminution of supply through the closing of the pits or the seams where the natural conditions are the least favourable."

(4) Organized resistance of Labour, by national and international action, against the tendency to link the downward movement of prices with reductions in miners' wages ; coupled with a general agreement of all the coal-owners to fix minimum scales below which wages should not be reduced.

(5) Prices could be controlled by combinations of sellers so as to prevent them from falling below a remunerative level.

Sir Herbert, after making this enumeration, observes that " all, or most, of these methods may operate together ". It seems to us, however, that it would in practice be scarcely possible to combine, for instance, the maintenance of coal prices by artificial control, as suggested in point (5) with increasing at the same time the demand for fuel, by making it cheaper through more economical production and transport, as projected in point (2). Among all these suggested remedies the writer seems most to favour this second course.

With this aim in view he suggested that the number of mines is excessive, while their size on the whole is not sufficient to obtain the best working results.[1] The State, when granting leases, should carefully discriminate between the individual features of the companies and localities where coal is mined. Idle time in British mines, which was then equal to 25 per cent, should be removed, and everything possible done to avoid the faults in transport which are chiefly responsible for days lost by the collieries. All this points to a better use of labour in the industry. Apart from economies, the author also tackles the wasteful methods of production and distribution. The need for working full capacity for more than one shift is imperative.[2] Emphasis has been laid on concentration of undertakings, but little has been said about the ways of scrapping the excessive capacity.

[1] *Vide* ibid., p. 10.
[2] Ibid., p. 8.

On the question of curtailing extravagance in the processes of production and distribution, Sir Herbert Samuel calls attention to the findings of the Royal Commission, of which he was the Chairman, and also to the recommendation of the Lewis Committee. He regrets that co-operative selling agencies had not been established by the collieries. Pursuing the Liberal policy of cheap fuel for the consumer, the distinguished author urges bringing down the cost of retail distribution in the towns by empowering the municipalities to undertake this service. In order to raise the utility of every unit of coal produced and to check the lavish waste of by-products, extensive research work has been strongly recommended. Already in *Coal and Power* references had been made to the significance of research, and the suggestion put forward that after the nationalization of royalties, the Royal Commissioners should charge the mine-owners with " a contribution to mining research ".

Three recommendations were devised to meet the chief social problems. They were :—

(1) A further ascertainment of the real value of coal sold in the composite concerns and the basing of the wages' computation only on the true market value of coal, and not on book entries of the collieries.

(2) The introduction of profit-sharing schemes for the miners ; and

(3) Closer co-operation between labour and management by the establishment of Joint Pit Committees. Such Committees should be instituted on the basis of a legal provision of 1926.

The Liberal publication of 1928, *Britain's Industrial Future*, makes a very strong case for rationalization and lays stress upon the need for enabling the collieries to work at full capacity.[1] The Liberals conceived that the abnormal

[1] *Britain's Industrial Future*, being the Report of the Liberal Industrial Inquiry, London, 1928 : " If the worst collieries could be shut down and the remainder worked full-time there would be a double saving, firstly a saving owing to the elimination of these collieries, and secondly a further saving by working the remaining collieries at full or about full capacity " (p. 128).

position of the coal industry arose from productive over-capacity accompanied by a very slack rise in consumption. That situation would need re-adjustment on the part of the colliery owners. But " they have been reluctant to face the necessity for reorganizing ".[1] While amalgamation would secure a higher degree of efficiency and economy, selling combinations would help to stabilize prices and enable exporters better to meet foreign competition. But *Britain's Industrial Future* did not concentrate only on production. It aimed at securing also more rational methods in transport, marketing, and in the utilization of coal.

Since only through amalgamation could all these benefits be obtained, the Liberals wanted to secure this preliminary provision as soon as possible. Apart from the activity of Royalty Commissioners, the Liberals now supported the proposal of the Samuel Commission to exclude the bad mines in the districts from wage ascertainments. In this ingenious way wages would have to be paid in the future according to the capacity of the most efficient mines. Bad mines were always a depressing influence on the general financial results of the area. Wages rates, which since 1921 were based on proceeds in every area, would be therefore considerably affected. By excluding the bad units from wage ascertainment a better general result would be obtained and wages would rise, forcing the marginal collieries to close.[2] This recommendation tended to abolish the artificial minimizing of differences existing between the efficient and the inefficient mines. It may be perhaps appropriate here to remember that *Coal and Power*[3] defended a converse policy in requesting the Royalty Commissioners to differentiate between the rich and the poor mines. As the logical outcome of the rationalization policy the Liberals advocated the closing of a number of poor and inefficient mines. They realized that this expedient involved the danger of releasing a certain number of workers, but they boldly stated that the reform would have to be executed, notwithstanding the sacrifice involved. Consequently it was

[1] Ibid., p. 343.
[2] Ibid., p. 353.
[3] *Coal and Power*, p. 56, para. 76 b.

necessary to frame a scheme for dealing with the displaced miners,[1] and thus the Report contained a complex plan for meeting the whole unemployment problem. The main suggestions for remedying unemployment fell under three heads : (a) Limitation of recruiting ; (b) Pensioning of workers ; and (c) Transfer of existing workers into other industries. The first of these measures provided that a compulsory scheme of limitation of new recruits should be instituted. The second suggested the elaboration of a special pension scheme for workers over sixty years of age. The third proposed to encourage workers to take up other occupations. All necessary expenses should be paid out of the taxes on royalties.

The Liberals realized that the length of the working day was also a determining factor in the state of employment, since shorter hours resulted in an additional demand for labour. Nevertheless they were most careful not to express any definite opinion on hours of work. Hence the paragraph of their Report relating to this subject is most perplexing.[2] However, they held that the British Government would be well advised to give active support to international agreements for reduction of working hours.

Following very closely the findings of the Samuel Commission, the Liberals' suggestions included the institution of a National Wages Board with a neutral element, as in the case of the National Wages Board for the railway service. The Liberal scheme went, however, one step further than that of the Royal Commission, for it entrusted this Board with the powers of a Trade Board for the fixation of minimum rates. Such a Board would supplement the whole machinery for co-operation between Labour and Capital already outlined in *Coal and Power*.

The findings dealing with transport and sale were in

[1] Loc. cit., p. 345.
[2] Loc. cit., p. 365 : " It is, of course, the miners themselves who are most affected by the choice to be made. Although it is to the general interest that they should enjoy the fullest leisure that is practicable, if they found that the restoration of the pre-stoppage hours involved a further reduction of their earnings they might themselves prefer further to postpone that measure until the industry had been brought to a more prosperous position."

favour of restricting excessive competition by the introduction of co-operative selling agencies.   Compulsory
restriction of output had not, however, been included among
the Liberal proposals ;   though in referring to selling agencies
they favoured a certain degree of compulsion.   Moreover,
in order to reduce the price of coal to consumers, it was found
desirable that municipalities should be empowered to engage
in retail trade.   Likewise in Sir Herbert Samuel's scheme,
attention was devoted to State assistance for research work
in the utilization of coal.

We may summarize this short outline of the different
demands brought forward in *Britain's Industrial Future*
by observing that nearly all the points in the Liberal
programme aimed at increase of efficiency.   Cheap coal was
the *leit-motiv* of the whole scheme.   In their opinion the
demand for coal, especially if spread over a long period,
was not inelastic, and they purposely omitted, therefore, any
forms of restriction.   The plan also laid much weight on
good wages and full employment for the miners.

Britain's Industrial Future codified the whole of the
Liberal   programme.   Theoretical   considerations   were
supplanted at this juncture by more practical discussions
closely connected with the realization of their programme.
On numerous occasions the Liberals have urged both in the
Press and in Parliament the possibility of reconstruction of
the coal industry along the lines described.[1]

Some ideas contained in the Yellow Book were repeated
in later Liberal publications.   Rationalization and the need
for lowering the costs of production occupy a very prominent
place.   A later work [2] laid before the Government in 1930
by Messrs. D. Lloyd George, B. Seebohm Rowntree, and the
Marquess of Lothian calls attention to these two processes
as means of conquering unemployment.

Summing up the Liberal coal programme as it was fully

[1] On the eve of 1929 Sir Herbert Samuel, in his Newcastle speech,
severely blamed the Government for their neglect of the proposals of the
Royal Commission, especially those which were devised to raise efficiency.
(Reported in the *Liberal Magazine*, vol. xxxvii, No. 425, p. 95.)

[2] *How to Tackle Unemployment*, the Liberal Plans as laid before the
Government and the Nation, by the Rt. Hon D. Lloyd George, the
Marquess of Lothian, and B. Seebohm Rowntree, London, 1930, p. 98.

developed on the eve of the Coal Mines Bill, 1930, we must put in the first place the pursuit of efficiency : more rational methods in all the processes through which coal is passed from the face to the ultimate consumer. Working at full capacity became one of the chief requisites, since it secured cheaper products and a better utilization of invested capital goods. Amalgamations with all their consequences, and the effects arising out of large scale production were strongly advocated. All other reforms which might reduce the price of coal and raise its value to the consumer in terms of fuel or power found strong support from the Party.

One very important point, however, was not entirely solved. It was the question of excessive capacity of British coal-mining in comparison with actual demand. The Liberals suggested the closing of a number of pits and the replacing of old mines by new. But we must remember that even if the smallest undertakings were scrapped the capacity of the industry would prove too large to meet the demand.

Table No. 33 shows at the first glance that the group of the smallest undertakings was responsible for only 12·7 per cent of the output, notwithstanding the fact that about 900 of the Lilliputian undertakings, with a cumulative output of 5 per cent of the whole production, have been excluded from the Table altogether. All this group of collieries produced about 27 million tons, and presumably they constituted a class of collieries working at a much higher rate of capacity than the average for the whole industry. The potential unused capacity is concentrated in the larger mines and is several times larger than the total output of the first group. Now even assuming, as the Liberals did, that their plans could succeed in closing down the mines in the smallest category, the problem of excessive capacity would still be left open.[1] The Report of the Royal Commission, 1925,[2] contains some more figures which throw light on the production of small mines. These refer to the year 1923, which has been taken as representative. More than 98 per cent of the output was produced by 715 undertakings, each

[1] On the question of excess capacity consult Pt. I, Chap. I, § 1.
[2] Report, p. 47.

TABLE No. 33

OUTPUT OF COLLIERY UNDERTAKINGS OF VARIOUS SIZES IN GREAT BRITAIN

Based on January to June, 1925

Yearly Output of Undertaking. 1,000 tons.		Number of Undertakings.	Tonnage raised.	
			Total 1,000 tons.	Percentage of Total.
(1)		(2)	(3)	(4)
Less than 5		10	32	—
5 and under 200		307	27,360	12·7
200 ,, ,, 400		126	36,394	16·9
400 ,, ,, 600		72	35,118	16·3
600 ,, ,, 800		28	19,132	8·9
800 ,, ,, 1,000		20	17,992	8·4
1,000 ,, ,, 2,000		42	56,280	26·2
2,000 and over		8	22,744	10·6
All		613	215,052	100·0

Note.—The tonnage referred to throughout is tonnage commercially disposable. The total tonnage of commercially disposable coal raised by all mines in the period of six months was 113,250,000, so that the mines included in the table cover about 95 per cent of the whole.

The total number of undertakings in Great Britain in 1925 was about 1,400. More than 880 undertakings not comprised by the Table produced about 5 per cent of the whole output of the country.

From *The Report of the Royal Coal Commission on the Coal Industry* (1925, vol. i, Cmd. 2600).

employing over 100 persons ; over 93 per cent by 467 undertakings, each employing over 500 miners ; and over 84 per cent by 323 undertakings, with over 1,000 workers each. The whole number of undertakings was at that time about 1,400, producing coal from more than 2,400 separate mines.

Nowadays the contrast between the small units and the large undertakings is even more conspicuous than at the time when the Royal Commission were presenting their Report. A certain number of amalgamations were carried through in the coal-fields, especially in 1929 and 1930. During the single year 1929, according to the Report of the Secretary for Mines,[1] collieries with 61 pits, employing about 44,000 persons, were amalgamated. In 1930, 88 pits normally employing 46,500 workers were involved.[2] This concentration has had the effect of increasing the percentage of

[1] Ninth Annual Report of the Secretary for Mines for the year ended 31st December, 1929, and the Annual Report of H.M. Chief Inspector for Mines for the same period, 41–26–0–29.
[2] Ditto for the year ending 31st December, 1930.

the small units in the total number, and at the same time of diminishing their share in the whole production, shifting in this way the bulk of the weight on to the largest collieries.

Even assuming the closing, urged by the Liberals, of this multitude of small units, the industry would only derive a very slight benefit because these mines, though very numerous, produce only a minute fraction of the whole output. Excessive capacity would still remain, even if the industry could get rid of the smallest collieries. Consequently, in order to remove all the excess capacity it would be necessary to extend the shutting down to the groups of undertakings yielding between 200 and 400 thousand tons of yearly output, and perhaps even to those between 400 and 600 thousand tons. But this was probably not the course the Liberals were advocating. Neither did they succeed in solving the dilemma of financing this reform, which involved a large degree of capital consumption, nor did they state satisfactorily the relationship between mere size of the units and efficiency, especially in the various districts. Similarly, the amount of excess capacity remained undisclosed.

However, on account of the economic situation, it slowly became realized that the surplus capacity could not be absorbed by the market. In July, 1929, soon after the King's Speech in Parliament announcing the repeal of the Eight Hours Act and other matters of reorganization of coal mining, the Liberal weekly, *The Commercial*,[1] published an article expressing disbelief in the possibilities of expansion of the industry and discussing the need for correlating production with demand.

The Liberals understood that many of the coal difficulties originated in the excess capacity of the industry. But at the same time they strongly disapproved of anything approaching the quota system, or the rationing of production by a central body. Even after the Coal Mines Act, 1930, was passed, the quota system was regarded as undesirable and harmful. Though they voted for the marketing clauses of the Act, nevertheless they considered that in doing so

[1] *The Commercial*, vol. xix, No. 472, p. 4, " Coal : A World Problem."

they were choosing the lesser of two evils. It was argued
that the Party found itself between the devil and the deep
sea, and it had to decide between the " bad Coal Bill " or
the defeating of the Labour Government at the time when,
according to the words of Mr. Lloyd George,[1] they were :—

> " invited to go into the Tory lobby to defeat the Government
> and to have a dissolution when trade was slumping down,
> and they knew that at the end of that lobby the scaffold of
> Free Trade had been erected and that Mr. Baldwin had his
> hand at the lever."

§3. THE CONSERVATIVES AND THE COAL PROBLEM

The Conservative Party, as rightly described by the late
Lord Melchett, adhered always to the fundamental principle
of individualism.[2] Hence general planning in industry from
outside as well as any heteronomous action was strongly
disliked by the Party. For this reason its policy excluded
reorganization, and no official coal programme has been
found requisite to meet the situation. If any reform were
necessary it ought to come from the industry itself :
Parliamentary action could not be very helpful, because
economic difficulties themselves were not controllable
by the State, and no Government could ever ameliorate
the conditions of the coal industry by penetrating into its
fabric. Even those sound reforms which were the result of
natural evolution should not be forced on the recalcitrant
section of the industry.

It can be gathered from the words of Sir Philip Cunliffe
Lister, late President of the Board of Trade, how strongly
the Conservatives disapproved of compulsory methods in
the realm of private management of the industry. In his

---

[1] Mr. Lloyd George's speech during the Annual Conference of the
National Liberal Federation at Buxton on 15th May, 1931. (*The Times*,
16th May, 1931.)
[2] Sir Alfred Mond, *Industry and Politics*, London, 1927, p. 304.

reply for the Government to a Socialist resolution moved in the House of Commons on 22nd February, 1927, to introduce a system of compulsory co-operative agencies for the sale of coal,[1] he said that by compelling reorganization, the State becomes responsible for the success or failure of the industry.   This refers especially to amalgamation, where separate undertakings are forced to enter into new financial obligations.   In 1929 the Conservative Party issued a great number of publications which in plain words condemned State intervention.   They even went so far as to say that the small amount of progress already being achieved would be completely obliterated if the industry were not left alone.   If a coal programme may be credited to them, opposition to any sort of external pressure might be quoted as the most prominent point.   This resistance does not, however, refer exclusively to coal, but extends to the whole sphere of industrial activity.

Broadly speaking then, they left the formation of any long-term policy to the industry alone, but they did not refrain from dealing with problems immediately affecting the prosperity of the industry.   When the Conservative Government was in power they were obliged to express their opinion on the fundamental question of organization.   We must, however, remember that there is a great difference between a party's programme and the same party's Government policy.   Government action, by its very nature, is to a great extent eclectic and must consider all possible phenomena of economic life.   We may easily conceive an instance where the Government has to deal with certain problems which were never before comprehended in the party's policy.   The Conservatives, however, in their propagandist literature very often confused the actual achievements of their Government in the field of industrial structure with the coal policy of their Party.   In this way they associated themselves with certain individual moves of their ministers, but failed to produce a programme of reconstruction for coal-mining.   They trusted so much in the natural, unaided

[1] *Gleanings and Memoranda*, published by the National Union of Conservative and Unionist Association, vol. lxv, January–June, 1927, p. 481.

power of recovery in the industry that they rejected any artificial cures. Reorganization could only be salutary if it were not thrust upon the industry. The Conservative Prime Minister [1] objected to the over-straining of the term, and his Party did not include official reorganization among current problems to be dealt with.

Much more was done by the Conservatives in the way of direct assistance in order to enable the coal industry to resist the depressing conditions after the War. The Conservatives were also inclined to think that the State should cope with the difficulties immediately, rather than by indirect influence through pressure on reorganization. So the Conservative Government used various methods of State assistance calculated to meet the emergency. It must be emphasized here that in the days previous to the coal stoppage of 1926, the Conservatives' coal policy existed only during the time when they were in power. A short Conservative publication, *Mines and Miners*,[2] is the narrative of the history of coal legislation passed by the Conservatives and of those laws advocated by the Party, which aimed at the betterment of the conditions of the miners. These Acts, dealing with various questions, constituted only fragmentary regulations

[1] Mr. Baldwin warned the House of Commons in his speech on the 15th of June, 1926, not to expect too much from reorganization (see *Gleanings and Memoranda*, vol. lxiv, pp. 85 and 86).

[2] *Mines and Miners*, Social Reform Series, published by the National Unionist Association of Conservative and Liberal Unionist Organizations, No. 1630.

The list begins with the Act passed by Sir Robert Peel in 1842, preventing employment underground of women and of boys under ten years of age. Various Royal Commissions on the coal industry are mentioned, in which the Conservatives took part. Reference is made to the Mines Regulation Act, 1887, carried by the effort of Lord Cross, supported by the Conservatives. The Act, as a matter of fact, merely collected all the different regulations for the safety of miners and put them in one. The pamphlet goes further, enumerating more Conservative Government Acts which had a good effect on miners' conditions, among them the Coal Mines Regulation Act, 1896, which was an amendment to the Act of 1887, and dealt chiefly with safety ; the Workmen's Compensation Act, 1897, is also mentioned, and called the " great and far-reaching measure . . . of the Conservative and Unionist Party ". Some few more Acts of secondary importance are added to the record of the Party. It is nevertheless difficult to infer from these legislative ventures of the Conservatives anything whatsoever about their coal policy. Nor can we agree to call them a planned action which followed lines drawn in advance.

which sprang up in the great field of industrial activity during the term of office of the Conservatives. It may be noted, in addition, that these measures introduced little that was new in principle into the existing state of affairs, as they did not usually proceed beyond amending or enlarging the provisions already in force. Such a line of action, however, is in agreement with the Conservative doctrine of non-interference. They hardly admitted that the State should interfere even in disputes between Labour and Capital. We must not, therefore, be surprised to find so little that is positive in the industrial policy of the Unionists.

Energetic diatribes were raised on numerous occasions by the Conservatives against some of the bolder attempts of other political groups to reorganize the industry. After the War, simultaneously with the growth of the extremist movements, the Conservatives were unwilling to agree on any reorganization which did not originate from the industry itself. Slowly, however, concomitantly with the dissipation of the prospects of State ownership of mines, they apprehended clearly that certain sections of the coal industry would not be able to keep their heads above water unless material help were given to them by the State. Evidently, a critical attitude towards the schemes of other parties, or towards the recommendations of the Royal Commission, 1925, would not prove sufficient, especially as the Conservatives were at that time in office. Even the longer hours favoured by them, and introduced after the stoppage of 1926 were not sufficient to assist the industry in this time of hardship, and further action was expected. Mere opposition to interference could no longer remain the keystone of the Party's coal policy. At this juncture they began to conceive a definite programme, which has gradually assumed its present form. A Unionist Coal Committee was nominated at the end of June, 1927, on lines similar to those of the other Party committees already in existence, to deal with coal-mining matters.

We may now observe two distinct aspects in the Government coal policy. The first concerned the industry itself, the second dealt with the assistance scheme for men thrown out of employment.[1] The starting point of the Conservative arguments was that the industry could not be set on a sound basis unless it was able to work in normal conditions free from intervention. Further, they assumed that provided the coal industry received some assistance it would spontaneously tend to put its house in order. How was this to be carried out ? The industry was too much exhausted to adjust itself to the new conditions. Export markets were lost to a large degree, costs of production were much too high, a surplus productive capacity depressed prices at home. The Conservatives first paid attention to the declining export figures. In their mind Great Britain's export should be maintained at any price. The main reason justifying this opinion was that the smaller the amount of coal which could find outlet abroad, the more this additional flow at home would depress internal prices and force mines to close,[2] so displacing vast numbers of men from employment. But it was practically impossible to recapture the international coal trade and to dispose of more coal abroad, unless a low competitive price were secured. Thus again the whole difficulty lay in the question of costs. Round this problem centred nearly all the different schemes for reorganization of the industry.

The Conservatives now argued that the industry could not override its hardships alone. Additional elements had to be taken into account. Coal was too closely bound up with the destiny of other industries for those responsible to be able to act without considering the development of the latter.

The Conservatives believed that revival of coal-mining would come from increased demand for fuel, which was the pivot of the whole situation, and that every attempt should be made by the Government to push forward the industrial consumption of coal at home. This, of course, was dependent

[1] Cf. Sir P. Cunliffe-Lister, The President of the Board of Trade, in the House of Commons, 7th December, 1927.
[2] *The Real Facts about the Coal Industry*, published by the National Union of Conservative and Unionist Associations, No. 2802/8/28, p. 8.

entirely on the speeding up of production in the country. But, as the Unionists observed, those industries which consumed a large quantity of British coal had to meet the unfair competition and dumping of goods made in foreign countries.[1] Hence protection of home industries would result in their revival, would assist progressive development and thus raise the demand for coal. Ultimately, therefore, tariffs became a master-key for all possible difficulties.

In addition to this indirect policy of increasing the demand for coal, the Conservative Party advocated and passed in Parliament, measures which were intended to assist the industry in a more direct way. New uses for coal formed part of the Conservative policy in connection with the mining crisis in England. This has been strongly emphasized in several instances. Discussion dealt especially with the practicability of producing oil from British coal. Both the de-rating scheme and the railway rebates were included in the Budget introduced by the Conservative Government. In case of emergency the Conservatives preferred subsidies in some form to any method of restoring industrial prosperity through forced reorganization. Hence originated the subsidy paid to the industry during the 1925–6 period. But the granting of direct monetary subsidies could hardly be considered a purely Conservative measure, as they had already been paid by the Government in 1921. The fact that the Government made over to the industry a certain amount of money, or that the Prime Minister offered financial assistance in order to facilitate a settlement, does not in itself prove that this stop-gap policy was specifically Unionist. On the contrary, different prominent representatives of the Party [2] spoke of subsidies rather as an unavoidable evil which should not be tolerated too long. Not that they were flatly opposed to paying grants in aid to coal-mining, but

[1] *The Truth about the Coal Industry*, published by the National Union of Conservative and Unionist Associations, London, No. 3210, November, 1930, p. 28.

[2] *Vide Gleanings and Memoranda*, vol. lxiv, July–December, 1926, p. 380.

they sought for more fundamental solutions, especially on the questions of costs of production and costs of manual labour.

Furthermore, the attitude of the Unionists towards different subsidies was subject to alteration, depending on whether they were in power or in opposition. On certain occasions the same measures which were approved as useful and good so long as the Conservatives sat on the Government benches, became detrimental and undesirable as soon as they crossed the floor of the House. As a very representative instance of this change of opinion we may take their attitude towards subsidizing coal for export. After the introduction of rebates on transport, the Conservative Government was asked in the House of Commons if a railway rebate on exported coal acts as a subsidy for foreign industry against British. These fears, however, were dissipated by a Governmental statement,[1] which in four points explained them to be groundless, saying clearly that the subsidy on exported coal does not act as an assistance to foreign industry. But as soon as the Conservatives formed the opposition, a subsidy on the export of coal became in their opinion most decidedly injurious to British production. In 1929 the Conservatives violently criticized the Coal Mines'

[1] In the House of Commons, 1st February, 1929, Sir Philip Cunliffe-Lister, President of the Board of Trade, gave four arguments on behalf of the Government, proving that there is no rebate on British coal consumed abroad. His points were :—

(1) " A very small fraction of coal exported from this country goes into foreign industry which is competing with this country. It does not go to competing foreign consumers. It does not go to the Ruhr, France, and Belgium."

(2) ". . . the great foreign steel works are supplied with coal from their own coal-fields, and that coal which our foreign competitors are using is not British coal, but coal they buy on the spot out of their own coal mines."

(3) " Where our coal goes to is into the shipping of the whole of the World, that is all the ships that burn coal. It goes to the railways of all the World . . . I am perfectly certain there is no divorce of interest in this matter between the mining industry and the general industries of this country."

(4) " When we increase our exports of coal we are not in the least helping foreign competitors, but supply very largely non-competitive industries and railways. We are helping our shipping trade, and not injuring the industries of this country in the least." House of Commons Debates, 1st February, 1929 (cols. 1304–7).

Bill for just the reason—amongst others—that it taxed the home consumer in favour of foreigners.[1]

The Conservative politicians nevertheless realized very clearly that these were only ephemeral expedients unable permanently to meet the situation. So long as the grants operated, it was practicable to maintain the volume of trade and foreign exports, but after the removal of assistance, high costs of production would immediately hamper all development. Emphasis was thus laid on the necessity for maintaining low prices of coal and proportionately low costs, not only for the export markets, but also for home purposes. During the debate on the co-operative agencies for the sale of coal, on the 22nd February, 1927, the President of the Board of Trade gave in Parliament strong reasons against any attempts to bolster up prices.[2] This view was closely bound up with the claim to protect the consumers of coal. Similarly a campaign for cheap coal was fought truculently during the debates on the Coal Mines Act, 1930, which was termed " a Christmas present from Lossiemouth for the coal owners ".

Coal problems were forced into special prominence when prices for certain grades of coal became actually lower than costs. In such circumstances the Conservatives regarded Government subsidies as a half measure, appropriate only in a transitory period of readjustment of costs to prices, and operating only as an anæsthetic to induce insensibility during the transition to changed conditions. Reduction of costs, in their opinion could not be effectively secured otherwise than by reduction of costs of labour, i.e. either by increasing the number of hours without a proportional rise in the wages, or by reduction of wages, or finally by both. Wages versus hours formed the dilemma of the costs of production, and the Conservatives had to choose one or the other. After consideration, the lot fell on the length of the working day. This decision expressed the view that it was better to

---

[1] *Vide Your Coal will Cost you More*, published by the National Union of Conservatives and Unionist Associations, No. 3093 ; and Debates, House of Commons, 19th December, 1929 (col. 1677), speech of Commodore Douglas King.

[2] Debates, House of Commons, 22nd February, 1927.

preserve the existing standard of wages as far as they thought it possible and to lengthen the hours of employment. In so doing they entirely neglected the recommendation of the Royal Commission,[1] which advised :—

> " If a reduction of wages is necessary to enable the industry to surmount its immediate difficulties, this reduction should be made directly, and not indirectly, by a lengthening of working hours for the same remuneration."

The Government had already passed a law in 1926 allowing for the extension of the working day. In this way the cost of labour per man per hour was substantially reduced, and was finally reflected in the cost of a ton of coal.

In connection with the problem of reducing average costs, the Conservatives' attention was often called to the urgent question of organization. But if we examine their opinion on amalgamations, we are bound to realize that the Party never accepted the view that any one amalgamation in the industry is desirable ; they were rather sceptical as to the real value of concentration, and wanted to prevent all artificial combining of undertakings. On the problem of wholesale rationalization and amalgamation the Conservative Government [2] was careful not to generalize as they realized that the utmost discrimination was the only criterion of successful results. And how in such conditions could compulsion be applied ? " Above all, the Government must not embark on a policy which would force the efficient units to take in against their will all the most inefficient mines." The whole initiative to combination should be left unreservedly to the owners of the mines, whose judgment in the matter of integration was the most authoritative.

Opposition to State intervention into matters of organization led the Party also to reject all attempts by the Government to promote the co-operative selling of coal, which was strongly recommended by the

[1] *Report of the Royal Commission on the Coal Industry* (1925), vol. i, p. 175.
[2] *Vide* Debates, House of Commons, 7th December, 1927, speech of the President of the Board of Trade.

majority of the Lewis Committee. The convictions underlying this hostile attitude towards compulsory schemes
were two : in the first place, any obligatory scheme would
limit the freedom of action of the different economic subjects,
and secondly, Conservatives distrusted the selling agencies
on account of their price policy. They thought that
obligatory organizations for the distribution of coal were
bound sooner or later to infringe the rights of home
consumers, about which they always claimed to care so
much. When the Coal Mines Bill, 1930, was shaped in
Parliament, the Conservatives on many occasions proved
themselves protagonists of the consumers' privileges.
The imminent danger to the freedom of the consumer to
carry out unhampered purchases of coal, and to that of
the producer to act according to his best interest,
led the Unionist Party to resist compulsory selling
organizations. Likewise on the 22nd February, 1927, soon
after the appearance of the Committee's Report on the
subject, when Mr. A. Parkinson, M.P., proposed the Labour
motion providing for the speedy institution by the Mines
Department of a network of selling agencies, the Unionists
moved a sweeping amendment against it.

The Conservatives, however, were not always inimical
to selling agencies. In this respect we may notice changes,
even very sudden changes. Not more than three years after
the motion for non-interference with trade, Sir Philip
Cunliffe-Lister was to be found making a statement in the
House—based on the familiar ground of protection of users
of coal—in which he voiced opposite views and blamed the
Government then in power for omitting pooling agencies
from the Bill.[1]

Nationalization of royalties, propagated both by the
Labour and Liberal Parties and by the Samuel Commission, was rejected by the Conservatives on the grounds

[1] Debates, House of Commons, 17th December, 1929, col. 1294.
Dealing with cheap distribution, Sir Philip said : " Will the Right Hon.
Gentleman (President of the Board of Trade) tell me one part of the Bill
which will ensure that coal is distributed cheaply ?   There is not one.
There is no pooling of agencies or depots. Every colliery is still left
perfectly free to sell coal in competition with its neighbour in any way,
provided that it does not sell it below the minimum price."

x

that the Act of 1923 and the amendments in the Act of 1926 [1] gave enough support to amalgamation, and that they sufficiently secured the rights of the colliery owners against abuses or obstructions by the landlords.

In summarizing the Conservative attitude towards the industrial problems of coal, we notice that the dominant ideas behind it have been the protection of consumers, on the one hand, and the abolition of any kind of interference on the other. The State could give useful assistance directly by means of rebates and other bounties; it could also co-operate with the industry in reducing the costs of manual labour. But where organization and internal management problems were concerned, the leaders of the industry should be left free. Under no conditions should the State enter this field.

Now, after having glanced at the Party's attitude towards economic questions, we may add a few words on the social programme of the Unionists with reference to coal. The re-absorption of displaced labour was one of the most difficult problems to solve. The Government, therefore, laid down the principle of reserving the mining occupation in the first place to miners by putting a ban on the entry of new workers to the mines. In the case of new vacancies, miners had the preference before any other outside workers. Such a policy, which closely corresponded to the short-term Labour policy, was designed to restrict the supply of labour in the mining districts only to miners. Alone it would do very little to meet the situation; but the Government had a second remedy in the transference of unemployed mine workers. Strongly pressed by the Socialists, and many times challenged for its inaction, the Conservative Government formed in January, 1928, an Industrial Transference Board to stimulate and assist the transference of workers from distressed areas to openings in other industries both at home and overseas. The Minister of Labour, under

[1] The President of the Board of Trade (Sir P. Cunliffe Lister) discussed in Parliament, on 1st March, 1928, the futility of nationalization of royalties. " The action taken under the Coal Mines (Working Facilities) Act did far more than any nationalization of royalties could possibly do " (House of Commons Debates).

whose supervision the Board was to operate, appointed three of its members to act as a link between various existing departmental activities with the object of effecting their closer co-operation in matters dealing with the transfer of the displaced miners.   In order to give the workers a certain training beforehand in the industry to which they were to be transferred, the Government established a few training centres for miners, where they were taught their new professions, as well as special training schools for emigrants at Claydon and Brandon.   Juvenile training centres through-out South Wales, Northumberland, and Durham gave instruction to a certain number of boys in various professions, and had also to help the pupils to get employment in different trades at the end of their course.   A Socialist suggestion of pensioning all the miners over 60 years of age in order to make room for the other displaced workers, and the raising of the school age were also rejected.   In judging the practical effect of all the steps taken by the Government in the matter of unemployment, we must observe that this effect was very meagre and the plan, as could be anticipated, was not able to stem the rising tide of unemployment, though some of the Conservative leaders considered it very efficient.

Strong support was given by the Conservative Government to a vast philanthropic plan for the distressed miners.   Many different funds were at the time in operation with the object of giving them additional help.   The Lord Mayor's Fund was supported by the Unionists.   In December, 1928, the Government [1] proposed therefore to pay £1 for every £1 paid in voluntary subscription.   It also decided to contribute a sum of £150,000 as the equivalent of the money already subscribed.   The total of voluntary subscriptions to the Lord Mayor's Fund stood in 1929 at £752,000.   In March, 1929, assistance was given through the Coal-fields Distress Funds in various forms in kind and by special grants.   Scotland possessed her own funds, such as the Oustram Distress Fund, which stood at about £80,000, the Lord Provost of Edinburgh Fund £30,000, and other small funds.   The Government contributed 11/80 of the amount of

[1] *Gleanings and Memoranda*, January, 1929, p. 59.

any voluntary subscription and furnished in addition a sum of £82,000.

In conclusion, we wish to emphasize the fact that the Conservative coal policy was expressed rather as a critical opposition to existing schemes than as a creative force. In contrast with the other political groups, the Unionists did not advocate any elaborate coal organization, they left much more room to the initiative of industrialists. They were not preoccupied with building a new industrial order, or with wholesale rationalization, so that their references to coal were *ipso facto* bound to be rather of a critical than of a creative character.

§ 4. CONTRIBUTION OF THE POLITICAL PARTIES TO THE IDEA OF REORGANIZATION

Now that we have acquainted ourselves with the outlines of political reasoning on the coal question we must compare the views of the main political parties on the problem, and judge their significance for the reorganization movement. Here it must be remembered that the programmes dealt with in the previous sections formed the official views of the leading political groups in this country, and that apart from them a multitude of other ideas can be traced in various branches of society, which of course did not entirely match with the official views of the parties. Notwithstanding the differences, however, they could always be classified with some reservation into one of the three groups already dealt with. Hence a description of these programmes gives a fair idea of the ways by which the *political outlook* affected the *economic outlook* in the sphere of organization in Britain's basic industry.

Naturally in any political programme, even pertaining to industry, the main emphasis is always laid on the political aspect of the question. The leading political issue here is the question as to what proportion of economic life should be submitted to State authority, regulation, and control— how much should the State interfere with national economic development. For this reason the coal programmes of the political parties differ perhaps not so much in their economic demands, such as efficiency, mechanization, unification of control, etc., as in the degree of compulsion and State intervention they would like to apply. In this way the intensity of the political coal programme must be measured, not by the economic reorganization it advocates, but by the degree in which it affects the will of individuals and the private ownership of coal mines and minerals.

Taking the coal programmes as they were evolved historically, the Labour Party possessed politically the most radical plan of reconstruction, and it was also the first to postulate reorganization in the coal industry. But the emphasis was laid exclusively on the problem of ownership and control of mines and minerals. The whole reform was conceived through changes in property. On the other hand, the economic reconstruction desired by the Labour Party did not go very far beyond abstractions, oscillating round the chief point of unification. In fact, however, there existed always in the Party a dualism of opinion on the matters of organization : while some extremists were for the whole programme, or nothing, others, reckoning with the existing economic and political possibilities, wanted to achieve something at least. They would be temporarily satisfied if even a small part of the programme could be put into force. In general the attitude of the Labour group was a desire to bring about a change in the industry, first merely through changes in ownership, and later through the policy of making the market bear the costs imposed by the new organization.

In the Liberals' programme we observe a lesser degree of authoritarian alteration of the existing forms of organization, while great stress is laid on the economic problem of efficiency and amalgamation. This demand for the elimination of the weak from the industry is reminiscent of the old-time Liberalism of the middle of the nineteenth

century, but the difference is that now this elimination of
the weak units would not be spontaneous, but compulsory,
and so would result in a considerable consumption of capital.
The criteria on which the reform was to be based were in
fact not elaborated and the whole programme moved in a
world of pure generalizations.

Whereas the Liberals and the Labour Party created
schemes for a thorough reconstruction of the coal industry,
the Conservatives regarded the whole question from an
entirely different angle. They left complete freedom to the
economic aspect of organization and refused to modify
it by political action. But while abstaining from
intervention the Conservative Party favoured a scheme of
short-term assistance to the industry to aid the transition
to new equilibrium. As this could not be carried on
indefinitely its only effect was to retard the process of
adjustment of costs to demand.

In all these discussions where the attitude of the State
towards the coal industry was in question, purely political
thought had contributed its share. During the time of
Control, and especially after 1919, schemes dealing with
the whole organization of the British coal industry began
to crystallize in the rank and file of all the parties. When
ten years later the electoral campaign of 1929 began, which
led eventually to the victory of Labour, all the parties
entering the polls were provided with definite proposals
for the coal mines. By then all the suggested remedies
had either already had time to prove their value in practical
though partial application, as, for instance, the amalgamation
of mines, or they were already extensively ventilated in
public discussion and analysis.

Evaluating now the views of all the parties on the
organization of the coal industry, it must be said that on the
whole they followed closely the natural developments of the
industry. While the original political ideas brought forward
by the parties were only figments of the human brain—
economic thought always emanated from actual life, it was
taken directly from experience. Only when economic
reforms were already spontaneously evolved or tried did

similar measures find free entry to the political programmes. On the whole, political thought has not proved capable of bringing forward any practical idea which has not been already produced by the industry itself. Those proposals which were either premature or impractical, even if they succeeded in entering the Statute Book, actually bore no fruit whatever. By this we do not intend to minimize the enormous importance of political activity in other spheres of the coal industry and the indirect effect of such action on the forms of organization. What is contended here is that those attempts of *politics* which were aimed directly at organization in the face of opposing *economic* considerations were always bound to fail.

PART III

NEW FORMS OF ORGANIZATION

(Politics meet Economic Reality)

CHAPTER I

THE SECOND LABOUR GOVERNMENT AND COAL

§ 1. THE COAL PLEDGES OF THE GOVERNMENT

We have seen how forces affecting the organization of the coal industry were developing from two sides—the economic and the political. Though on several occasions politics affected the industry in various ways, previously there had been no sign of intervention in organization and control.

During the General Election campaign of May, 1929, the political parties made large use of their various schemes, and among other pledges given to the electors was included a vast programme for reorganization of the coal industry. This was especially important in the policy of the Labour Party. To possess the thorough support of the rank and file of the mining population was for them a vital matter, upon which the issue of the election depended. To judge *a posteriori* by the results obtained, it seems that the Labour Party must have rightly estimated the value of the mining constituencies, since these succeeded in giving them forty-three seats in the House of Commons. The electors in the coal districts have always been taught to regard the Labour Government as " their Government ", whose goal should be to bring better conditions, employment, and wages to the miners. Vague pledges were not enough, they wanted special care and attention from " their Government ". As the Labour Party, in the event of its coming into power, was very anxious to have this invaluable support from the well-disciplined ranks of mine-workers, they paid particular heed to propaganda in the coal basins. Promises were freely distributed, pledging radical changes both for the alleviation of working conditions and for the thorough reorganization of the whole structure of the industry in conformity with the interests of the miners.[1]

Since all the other promises given were of a vague character, the more emphatic became the statement that the working day in the mines was too long and needed reduction. In the opinion of the miner there was no necessity to postpone the shortening of the working day. Just as the additional hour was imposed by law after the Strike in 1926, similarly, it was generally argued, this burden could be removed by law whenever Labour should come to power. One must note that an average miner elector, when giving his voice for the Labour Party, greatly discounted other remote and rather vague promises which he had heard so many times before, e.g. the nationalization of mines; but the pledge to reduce the working time was the magnet for him, and formed a tangible expectation for the immediate future.

Mr. Ramsay MacDonald, in his election speech broadcast from Newcastle on 28th May, 1929, referred to the coal-mining industry as follows: "The coal industry is in a special position, and will be dealt with specially in accordance with our election manifesto."

Authoritative pledges both social and political were

[1] In its General Election number *The Labour Magazine*, official journal of the Labour movement, speaks to the miners as follows: "By our industrial Babylons we children of industry, the outcast and disinherited of the pits, lift our eyes out from our years of travail and captivity to the Dawn of Deliverance. . . . But the hope of the dream is near realization. To those unbelievers the coming of toil to power in the land seems a miracle; to those who have toiled and looked with longing eyes over the desert places of material and ethical need, the miracle is to be found in the long delay of the ascendance of humanity and justice." And further, the article goes on to describe the new epoch which would begin in the coal industry when the Socialists came to power: "Our Labour Government, having taken over ownership and control of the coal resources of the nation, will humanize the industry first. Material wastage and life wastage will be at once removed. When we go down the pits to our shift it will be in the strength of knowing that we leave behind us a kindly and friendly Government. Economic costs will not be given precedence over human welfare and justice." A pledge to bring in the immediate reduction of the working day was included. The author of the article, however, did not promise a prompt realization of the Nationalization programme. "We miners will do well not to expect the great liberation of our dream in the twinkling of an eye. Patience and sympathetic understanding between the Labour Government and ourselves will make sure, and lead us the speediest way. If we fail together, then the God of pits and tragedy help us all. (Edward Hunter, "Mining Life under a Labour Government," *The Labour Magazine*, May, 1929.)

contained in the manifesto *Labour and the Nation*.[1] This manifesto, after dealing at some length with the question of nationalization of mines, turned to the more immediate needs of the industry and discussed the social reforms which Labour would introduce in the coal-fields :—

> " The disastrous Act by which the Tory Government added an hour to the working day of the miners must be at once repealed. The pressure of unemployment on the coal-fields must be relieved by providing superannuation allowance for the veterans of the industry (towards which the royalties received by mineral owners may properly be required to make a substantial contribution), by a general measure raising the school-leaving age with the provision of the necessary maintenance grants, by the regulation of recruitment into the industry and by assisting the migration of miners into other districts and other suitable occupations. The improvement of the Unemployment Insurance Scheme, which Labour contemplates, its proposals for relieving the heavy burden of rates, and its general attack on the trade situations would go far to assist both the miners and the coal industry itself."

Far the most important of all these pledges commanding the general sympathy of the workers, was the obligation undertaken by the Party to cut down hours in the mines. Socialist leaders declared *urbi et orbi* that it would be amongst the first actions of the Government to introduce at the earliest opportunity a measure to provide for reduction of hours from eight to seven. This was promised to the miners on several occasions, but especially during the meeting between the Executive Committee of the Parliamentary Labour Party and the delegates of the Miners' Federation on 26th March, 1929. On that day, the Socialist Party assured the miners' leaders that out of the five burning questions awaiting solution, " one of the first things to be done in the first session of the Labour Government will be the introduction of a Bill to deal with the working hours of the miner." Thus the Labour Party acquired the firm support of the miners for a definite pledge and the late Mr. A. J. Cook could announce that " he had the pledge sealed and signed and in his office desk ".

---

[1] The Labour Party, *Labour and the Nation*, London, pp. 25–6.

In this way the Labour Government bound itself directly to the coal-mining industry from the very outset, and in the event of a successful election would be obliged to introduce immediate legislation on hours of work. But as it was quite obvious that such a change could not be carried through without causing far-reaching disturbances in the whole industry, the Government would be forced to initiate measures which would enable it to endure the considerable adverse effect upon costs per ton of coal involved in such an alteration of working hours. The proposed political and social reform gave rise to a whole superstructure which was designed to meet the economic requirements of the industry. Actually it only underlined and gave official expression to those natural tendencies which were already noticeable and had been growing for some time in numerous home sections of the coal industry. Shortening of hours created the necessity for introducing far-reaching economic reforms, affecting the whole fabric of the industry.

After a protracted Party campaign, the General Election came at the end of May, 1929. In the first days of June the results were announced. Labour received the largest number of votes, and returned to Parliament with a strength of 289 seats, while the Unionists obtained 260 seats, the Liberals 58, and Independents 8. Under these conditions the Labour Party won the Election, but did not succeed in securing a clear majority which would have allowed them to pass any legislation they pleased. Hence more radical changes in the structure of the coal industry, with which a section of the Opposition would undoubtedly disagree, had no chance of being carried through. As a result, the coal scheme which emerged out of this situation bore the stigma of political compromise and was an agglomeration of various social ideas. The Government was obliged to defer to the other parties' programmes in steering the Bill through the House, and had to compromise with the Liberals in order to make any progress at all. When the Act finally appeared in its definite shape the only really Labour elements which it contained were the provision shortening working hours in the mines, and to some extent the National Wages Board. The initial plans of the Labour Government had undergone such a substantial alteration that one could hardly recognize the original features in the final shape of the Coal Mines Act, 1930.

Coal affairs very soon occupied the attention of the new Government. On the 5th June, 1929, the King received Mr. MacDonald at Windsor Castle and invited him to form an administration. Three days later the Cabinet was already appointed and its members received their seals of office. Seeing a Labour Government established, the rank and file of the miners grew impatient to have all the pledges fulfilled and they pressed vigorously for their execution. Thus on the 8th June, the late Mr. A. J. Cook wrote in *The Miner* :—

> " Miners voted solidly for a repeal of the Eight Hours Act, a new Compensation Bill, Minimum Wage Act, and nationalization of the mines, minerals, and by-products. I feel sure that the Labour Government will not betray their trust. . . . Our members are aware that the Labour Party has pledged to move in the first session for a repeal of the Eight Hours Act."

A week after the Government was officially installed, the Executive Committee of the Miners' Federation decided to put pressure upon the Ministers for the immediate carrying out of their obligations during the first session of Parliament. Having regard, however, to the fact that the majority in the House of Commons was only relative, the miners brought the question of working hours to the fore-front of all reforms as being the most urgent.   As most of the working collective agreements in the districts terminated by the end of 1929,[1] the miners wanted to see new conditions already based on statutory limitation of working hours before negotiating for new contracts. The trend of the miners' policy towards the new Government was

[1] The district working agreements in Yorkshire, Lancashire and Cheshire, Scotland, South Wales, Forest of Dean, Cumberland and North Wales were concluded for three years, and the period expired in December, 1929. Nottingham and Derby had agreements for five years, while Northumberland and Durham only for twelve months, terminable at a month's notice.

clearly defined on the 16th June, at Hinckley, by Mr. Cook, who said that the first intention of the miners was to approach the Government in a friendly spirit and to discuss the whole situation of the industry in relation to the repeal of the Eight Hours Act.   Further reforms dealing with nationalization and reorganization were not less important, but they were less urgent than the question of hours, which ought to be handled immediately.   Thus the problem of reduction of hours was brought to the forefront right at the beginning of the Labour administration.

As a counter-measure to the announcement of the miners, Mr. Evan Williams, President of the Mining Association, emphatically condemned such proposals, in the name of the South Wales coal-owners, as being utterly impracticable and a sheer blunder.   But the miners, under the leadership of Mr. Herbert Smith and Mr. A. J. Cook, reminded the Government on all possible occasions of the pledges given before the election.   The latter was especially active, and though he showed a much more conciliatory spirit than a few years before, he stood firm on the necessity for shortening the working day.   All through the coal-fields, high hopes were entertained that the Government would quickly fulfil its promises.   Mr. A. J. Cook rejected any sort of " safety first " policy which would bring down the present Government, as it brought down the Government of Mr. Baldwin.   A bold attack was required.

In the face of the extremely energetic bearing of the miners, the Government resolved to begin to redeem its pledges.   On the 27th June, 1929, officials of the Miners' Federation of Great Britain were invited by the Prime Minister to a conference.   After this first meeting, in which other Ministers besides Mr. MacDonald also participated, a brief *communiqué* was issued from No. 10 Downing Street, stating that the situation of the coal industry had been fully reviewed with the miners and that the Government intended to confer also with the mine-owners.   On the 1st July the Central Committee of the Mining Association representing the owners of mines gave the Ministers their views on the critical position of the industry and pointed out the consequences of reducing hours of work.   At this meeting the owners learned the definite resolution of the Government to fulfil the electoral pledges, and were asked to give their views on the question of reorganization.

Next day the King's Speech was read in both Houses at the opening of Parliament.   It contained a short but prominent reference to the Government's coal policy which read in full as follows :   " My Government have under consideration the question of the reorganization of the coal industry, including the hours and other factors and of the ownership of the minerals.   Proposals to this end will be submitted in due course."   On the same evening the Prime Minister divulged in the Commons the intentions of the Government to act in close connection with both the owners and the workers.   He announced that the reorganization would mean a thorough reconstruction of the coal industry, including co-ordination of pits, selling agencies, ownership and control of the mineral and the length of the working day.   The Ministers would avoid measures which would merely prove " temporary and patchwork " and they would attempt to pass a durable reform.

§ 2.   HOURS OF WORK AND COSTS OF PRODUCTION [1]

In the time of depression in the coal industry, the most far reaching of all the changes proposed by the Government was the reduction in hours of work.   Provided that the wages were to remain the same, a heavy burden was to be imposed upon the already flagging industry, at a time when deepening economic depression meant operation at lower and lower capacity.   Consequently, the economies which are normally derived in well equipped collieries were cancelled to a great extent owing to high overheads, which were not sufficiently employed to yield

[1] Those readers who would not like to read through this more theoretical section should consult only the conclusions on p. 341.

a quasi-rent over the antiquated mines. Hence the proposed alteration in the total calculation of costs of production caused by additional labour costs became the crucial issue of the whole discussion raised by the Labour proposals.

Even among the Labour Party [1] many apprehended that abolition of the Eight Hours Act would greatly add to the difficulties of the coal industry. They therefore wished to combine the reform of working time with a better organization and with international regulation, enforcing an all round reduction of working hours in the European mines. The main difficulty arose, assuming an unchanged level of wages, from the incompatibility between reduction of hours and such reduction of costs as was required at that moment in order to remain competitive in the international markets and in order to prevent the home demand contracting.

We must note, however, at this point that the proposed flat reduction of hours in the mines would not have the same economic effect in all the coal-fields because they were not all working the same length of time. While Yorkshire, Nottinghamshire, Derbyshire, and Kent were working $7\frac{1}{2}$ hours, in all other districts the eight-hour day prevailed, except for the hewers in Northumberland and Durham, who were employed $7\frac{1}{4}$ hours. The reduction, therefore, would be less resented in the areas working a shorter time. As we have already explained in previous discussions,[2] the effect of the shorter hours in the districts could not be proportionate to the actual reduction of the length of the shift, but could only move in sympathy with the actual time spent at work. From our formula $y = \dfrac{(X - Z)\ (X - Q)}{X\ [(X - Z) - Q]}$, we see that a reduction of one hour does not mean a twice as big fall in output as a reduction of half-an-hour, but actually means a proportionately larger

[1] Mr. J. Strachey, M.P. (Lab.), wrote in *The New Leader*, on 21st June, 1929 : ". . . it is possible for our opponents to allege that the repeal of the Eight Hours Act would at once precipitate an economic crisis . . . Therefore it behoves us to give to the mining problem the most careful, serious, and patient consideration . . ."

[2] *Vide* footnote (p. 29), Part I, Chap. I, § 1.

fall because the value of the formula does not directly and simply depend on the value of Q. Hence the districts working eight hours, were bound to feel a one hour reduction of the shift proportionately more than the districts already working $7\frac{1}{2}$ hours.

The shortening of hours was not to be paid for by a consequent reduction of wages; assuming, therefore, an unchanged rate of capacity at which the industry was employed, *ceteris paribus*, the costs of production were bound to rise heavily. We shall make an approximate calculation of the increase of cost of labour per ton of coal. This can be arrived at in several ways, first by comparison of the conditions prior to the stoppage of 1926 with those after 1926, when the Eight Hours Act was in force. In order to be able to proceed along these lines, we append below a table which provides us with comparative figures selected for the first quarters of seven successive years. A special percentage computation has been made in the case of labour costs per ton and other costs per ton, facilitating comparison with the corresponding items in 1926 as well as with the total costs per ton in each year.

It is obvious from Table 34 that after 1926 the wages costs per ton substantially decreased, while at the same time the output per man-shift has risen very considerably. These two features are chiefly, though not entirely, due to the additional hour of work introduced in the mines after the stoppage in 1926. The reversion, therefore, to the seven-hour day, without effecting at the same time necessary economies in the costs of production and distribution, would mean an additional burden upon the industry, and so would lead to more expensive coal at pit. Moreover, between 1926 and 1930 many new investments had been made in the collieries throughout the coal-fields.[1] In the case of a reduced working time these investments must increase the costs of overhead above the 1926 level.

Various computations circulated in the coal-fields estimated the probable additional costs of shortening the working day at between 1s. 6d. per ton commercially

[1] *Vide* Pt. I, Chap. I, Statistical Addendum.

TABLE 34

Wages and Other Costs per ton of Coal Produced and Output per man-shift in Great Britain in March Quarters from 1926 to 1933

	Quarter ending 31st March							
	1926.[1]	1927.[2]	1928.[2]	1929.[2]	1930.[2]	1931.[3]	1932.[3]	1933.[3]
	s. d.	s. d.	s. d.	s. d.	s. d.	s. d.	s. d.	s. d.
Wages costs per ton* . .	12 3¾	11 1¾	9 7¾	9 0¼	9 1½	9 2¼	9 0¾	8 9
Per cent of 1926 . . .	100·0	90·5	78·3	72·97	73·9	74·3	73·6	70·9
Per cent of total costs . .	72·2	69·0	68·2	67·9	68·7	67·9	66·9	66·8
	s. d.	s. d.	s. d.	s. d.	s. d.	s. d.	s. d.	s. d.
All other costs per ton* . .	4 10¼	5 0¾	4 6¾	4 2¾	4 2½	4 4	4 5½	4 4½
Per cent of 1926 . . .	100·0	104·6	94·4	87·9	86·8	89·6	92·2	89·7
Per cent of total costs . .	28·8	31·0	31·8	32·1	31·3	32·1	33·1	33·2
	cwts.	*cwts.*	*cwts.*	*cwts.*	*cwts.*	*cwts.*	*cwts.*	*cwts.*
Output per man-shift . .	18·46	20·66	21·24	22·13	21·94	21·78	21·98	22·67
Per cent of 1926 . . .	100·0	112·5	115·2	120·1	119·0	118·0	119·2	122·6

(*) The figures include subvention. [1] Seven hours' working day. [2] Eight hours' working day. [3] Seven and a half hours' working day.

Based upon the *Quarterly Statistical Summaries of Output* and of the Costs of Production, Proceeds, and Profits of the Coal Mining Industry.

Page 324.]

disposable in Northumberland, to 3s. in South Wales. Sir D. Llewellyn reckoned for South Wales that the reduced hour would necessarily mean a 20 per cent reduction of wages.[1] The estimate adopted by the Royal Commission, 1925, gave the value of the hour of work in question as equal on the average to 2s. per ton of coal, a calculation more " probably under than over the mark ".[2]

In our view, a convenient way of arriving at an estimate of the cost of one hour's work is by comparing the results in 1928 with those in 1925. We shall see that during the eight-hour day, the cost of a ton of coal has diminished by 2s. $11\frac{1}{2}d.$; of this, labour cost accounted for 2s. 8d. This is nearly 1s. more than the estimate of the Royal Commission, which seems to be more optimistic and depends upon the maintenance of a fairly high degree of capacity employed. But at the rate of capacity operated in 1925, it is safer to assume for the whole country a figure from 2s. 8d. to 2s. 10d., subject to wide variations from district to district.

Similar results can be arrived at also in a different way, viz., by a computation of the percentage reduction in the actual working time underground in the case of an all-round reduction of shifts by one hour. As we show a little later, this would amount to a 17·3 per cent rise in costs of labour. Now, the 1925 [3] wages cost per ton is equal to 12s. 10d., so we can roughly calculate the rise in wages cost as equal to 17·3 per cent on this sum, i.e. 2s. $2\frac{3}{4}d.$, to which must be added a proportionate rise in other costs, equal approximately to 4d., to 5d. Adding the two items we shall obtain the figure of 2s. $6\frac{3}{4}d.$ or 2s. $7\frac{3}{4}d.$, which closely resembles our first computation.

Taking as a basis the figures of 1930 from the Fourth Census of Production we can arrive at the value of one hour of work in a different way by computing it from the net output per person employed. The Census [4] shows that the

[1] Information from *The Commercial (Manchester Guardian)*, 4th July, 1929, p. 5.
[2] *Report of the Royal Commission on the Coal Industry* (1925), vol. i, Cmd. 2600, p. 173.
[3] This computation is based on 1925 figures taken from *The Quarterly Summary of Output*.
[4] Fourth Census of Production, 1930. Preliminary Report No. 26.

net output per person equalled £148. On the other hand the average length of time spent at the coal face amounted to about 6½ hours. Hence we can easily deduce the cost of one hour's work per man by dividing his net output by the average time, and further, knowing that the output per man was in 1930 equal to 262 tons, we can compute easily the cost of one hour's work per ton of coal. This will actually be $\dfrac{£148 : 6\frac{1}{2}}{262}$ or 1s. 8¾d. To that we must add a sum of about 5d., representing the rise in costs other than wages ; so altogether the rise will be equal to about 2s. 2d.

Comparing the results of the March quarter, 1926, which is the only normal quarter in that year, with those of the succeeding years, we notice from Table No. 34 that the wages costs per ton of coal produced at first fell rather rapidly by 22 per cent, and afterwards fluctuated, reaching the greatest reduction in 1929, which amounted to slightly more than 27 per cent. In the last two years the wages costs per ton went up to 74·3 per cent of the 1926 level. All other costs per ton revealed a similar tendency, with variations in the time of occurrence and in intensity. The percentage decrease of costs other than wages per ton of coal was considerably lower than that of labour. On the other hand, output per man-shift, owing to longer hours of work, increased in 1929 by more than 20 per cent and, though it dropped somewhat in 1930, it still remained above the 1926 figures by 19 per cent.

In making any inference, however, *a posteriori* from our figures concerning the value for the industry of the one hour of work, one must always bear in mind, especially when a fall in wages is represented as a percentage (or relative cost), that the amount of wages paid to the miners for a ton of coal was not necessarily an invariable figure. According to trade conditions which determine the rate of capacity at which the mines are working, and according to the optimum employment of the collieries,[1] the proportion of

[1] An interesting study on the effects of optimum employment on costs in the coal industry can be found in a publication in Polish and English by G. S. Brooks, A. W. Kwieciński, S. B. Walsh, T. H. Wiewiórski. (*Critical Social-Economic Problems in the Silesian Coal Industry*, Katowice, 1932, chap. iii.)

wages costs in the costs sheet might, as actually happened, substantially fluctuate, even if no alteration of hours or of rates of pay took place. So we concentrate here on the problem of capacity.

The proportion of wages to total costs depends to a large extent on the rate of capacity at which the industry is working. We may apply here the useful formula contained in the Report [1] of the International Labour Office, which extends our formula used above. This formula, though serving in the Report for another purpose, can satisfactorily be brought in to prove our statement. Adopting symbols : the time spent in the mine is denoted by X, the time at the face by Y, the winding and travelling time by a, and breaks by b. Hence we can write the following equation :—

$$Y = X - (a + b) \qquad (1)$$

But now in order to calculate the real number of hours actually spent in the industry, Y will have to be reduced by a period Z, which represents the losses of time occurring from not exploiting the pits at full capacity and thus preventing the individual miner from working at his best. We may, therefore, calculate the exact time spent by the miners at work or A.

$$A = Y - Z = X - (a + b + Z) \qquad (2)$$

In this formula our Z is not exactly the same Z as in the I.L.O. Report, where it denotes the losses due to unforseen irregularities in workings. In our example, however, Z has a larger significance, for it represents in addition those factors which cause a reduction of time actually spent at work, as the result of under-employment of the mines. Generally the management of the collieries tries to keep the value of Z as low as possible. By working some mines or some sections of the mines at fullest possible capacity, the value of Z is scaled down as far as the labour of hewers is concerned, but the further the worker operates from the coal-face

[1] International Labour Office, Studies and Reports, Series D (Wages and Hours of Work), No. 18, *Wages and Hours of Work in the Coal-Mining Industry*, Geneva, 1928, pp. 18–19.

the larger is the item Z if the mine is not in full operation. Now it should become clear that the output per-man-per-hour is dependent to a large extent on the rate of capacity at which the mine is worked.[1] Therefore, the production per man-shift, though the shifts were of identical length, has varied in different years according to the rate of capacity at which the mines worked. (See Table 34.) Technical improvements and rationalization have had in certain coal-fields—especially in Scotland and in the Midlands—some beneficial influence on results per man employed, but chiefly in the case of hewers. The full result of rationalization, however, cannot be visualized, owing to the working under capacity, which concealed its effects by emphasizing the overhead costs.

[1] Dr. E. C. Rhodes in a paper, " Labour and Output in the Coal Mining Industry in Great Britain," read on 19th May, 1931, before the Royal Statistical Society, clearly demonstrated on statistical data relating to Great Britain the connection between the output per man and the rate of employment of the mines. Thus he rejects, e.g. the explanation of seasonal fluctuations in the ratio between the number of workers and the output representing the man-shift per output on the ground of higher expenditure of human energy in winter than in summer. He goes on to prove that the nature of the demand and the consequent fluctuations in the rate of employment in the industry provide the real causes of changes. Hence the exporting districts show smaller fluctuations in the ratio man-shift per output than the home districts, where the demand is more subordinated to seasonal changes. " When changes," says Dr. Rhodes, " are made from winter to summer and vice versa, some or all of these variables may be changed, and in summer some or all mines are working below capacity. Herein lies the explanation of the up-and-down movements observed in the ratios C/O, E/O, S/O (manshift per output at the face ; elsewhere below ground ; and on the surface)." Besides the relation between the working of the mines at full capacity and the output, Dr. Rhodes calculated also that there exists an important correlation between the rate at which individual workers are employed and the output. He summarizes this connection as follows :—
" The most important fact which emerges from a study of the formulæ connecting C/O, E/O, S/O with D (number of days worked), W (number of workers), and t (time element) is that the signs of the multipliers of log. D are mostly negative, and those of the multipliers of log. W are mostly positive. This means that, when we consider the possibility of W and t remaining the same and increasing D in order to increase the output, C/O, E/O, S/O decrease ; that is, there is improvement in working results." Thus keeping all the miners fully employed gives the optimum of output per man-shift. On the other hand, similar computations by Dr. Rhodes for varying W and constant D and t gave the reverse result, i.e. a rise of the ratios C/O, E/O, S/O simultaneously with the rise of W, which means falling output *pari passu* with the growth of working at less than actual capacity of labour. (See *Journal of the Royal Statistical Society*, vol. xciv, pt. iv.)

From what has been said it is evident that the rate of employment of men and mines has great and even compound influence upon the relative shares in the volume of production. Theoretically, therefore, if we want to ascertain the value of a working shift, or of a fraction of it, we must clearly define at the different periods the rates of employment of capital and labour which determine the size of A, in order to assure ourselves that we are dealing with equal values. After having done that, we shall be entitled to infer the significance of a unit of labour-time in the whole shift by dividing the daily output per man-shift P by the ratio between the size A and the specified unit of time q, by which we increase or reduce the length of the working day. Hence in terms of output the unit q brings about the following result :—

$$P : \frac{A}{q} = \frac{Pq}{A} \qquad (2a)$$

thus in the case of reduction of the working day by q, the theoretical output per man-shift equals :—

$$P - \frac{Pq}{A} \quad or \quad P\left(1 - \frac{q}{A}\right) \qquad (2b)$$

If we substitute the value of A expressed in our previous equation (2) we shall finally obtain the theoretical output per man-shift :—

$$P\left(1 - \frac{q}{A}\right) = P\left(1 - \frac{q}{X - (a + b + Z)}\right) \qquad (3)$$

Since Z is the item which varies according to the rate of working of the industry, it is impossible to ascertain its value without knowing what production will be in the future. For this reason any computation of the significance of an hour's reduction of working time can only be of a very approximate nature. In our case, the proportion between Pq and A where $q = 1$ hour cannot be definitely stated beforehand. Hence, if we possess the average time of actual work, we may calculate only with some degree of probability the significance of one unit of work, provided that the rate of employment of the industry does not alter considerably. But when the general trend of trade is definitely downwards, the presupposition is quite well founded that the theoretical output per man-shift will greatly diminish. Moreover, apart from the reservations already made, we must remember that the computation does not refer equally to all classes of underground workers and that it is designed in the first place to apply to hewers.

Now after having examined the significance of our data we can compare the actual values of A before and after 1926, during the 7-hours' shift and the 8-hours' shift. In 1925, the average time spent at the coal face in the British coal mines,[1] less breaks, amounted to 5 hours 45 minutes ; after 1926 the time spent went up to from 6 hours 15 minutes to 6 hours 45 minutes. For the whole country the weighted average amounted to 6 hours 34 minutes. The transition, therefore, to the new conditions added 49 minutes of actual work in the mines, which amounted then to 14·2 per cent of the former time. Actually, not all the coal-fields took their chance to increase work hours by the total time allowed in the Act of 1926, but if they had done so the difference would have amounted to 17·3 per cent. Considering the two periods from the point of view of costs, we may note that in 1929 costs decreased by 22·8 per cent compared with the first four months of 1926. In 1930 and 1931, which were not such good years for the coal industry as 1929, the difference was smaller ; however, it was substantially more than 14·2 per cent (representing longer hours). This was due, in the first place, to some reductions in wages, and in the second to a more economical distribution of costs other than wages per ton of coal ; and to a certain extent also to rationalization and mechanical methods of production.

During the whole of 1932 the fall of costs equalled 2·7 per cent, but this was partly due to reductions of wages which took place in the second quarter of 1931. Part of the fall should be explained by the increased physical productivity

[1] Information from International Labour Conference, Fourteenth Session, Geneva, 1930, *Hours of Work in Coal Mines*, Report 111, p. 89. For 1924, the Report of the Royal Commission on the Coal Industry, 1925, Annex-Sect. 4, gives the amount of net working time at the coal face as equal to 5 hours and 53 minutes.

due to the concentration of production on the best seams and best mines, and on the most efficient workers who were left in employment ; thus in the March quarter of 1933 the costs were the lowest on record in the whole post-War period.

The length of the shift, however, had a considerable influence over the costs through the output per man-shift worked. As we have noted, in 1929 the costs per ton of coal decreased in comparison with 1926 by 22·8 per cent, while the tonnage of coal raised per man-shift worked rose by 20·1 per cent, thus showing a high degree of correlation between costs and output per man, on the one hand, and between output per man-shift and the time worked in the mines, on the other.

We may note now from Table 34 that after the lengthening of the working day the costs of wages per ton of coal show a proportionately larger decrease than the other costs. This observation raises the question : do longer working hours in the mines for the same absolute remuneration alter the proportion of costs of labour to other costs ? And is this proportion affected in the same way in all districts ? In order to reply to the first part of this question, let us imagine that before longer hours were introduced, each worker produced K tons of coal per shift, and the wage bill of the worker amounted to a. Afterwards the workers produced $K + \Delta K$ tons of coal per shift for the same remuneration. How will this affect the proportion of other costs to labour costs ? By assumption

$$K < K + \Delta K ; \quad a = \text{const.}$$

All costs other than wages during longer hours equal D, while during shorter hours of work they equal C. The proportion of $\dfrac{C}{a}$ and $\dfrac{D}{a}$ expresses the ratio between all other costs than labour costs during shorter and longer hours, that is, the proportion of other costs to work costs per unit of labour. We may telescope our inquiry to the question : is $\dfrac{C}{a} = \dfrac{D}{a} = \text{const.}$, when $K < K + \Delta K$?

In order to reply to this question one must clearly investigate the nature of magnitudes C and D (costs other than wages). For our purpose they can be easily split into two groups of costs, which behave in a different manner in association with labour costs. On the one hand, one may distinguish between such items as are used directly in fixed proportion and always simultaneously with the application of labour, and on the other such overhead costs as do not move in fixed relation with the number of labour units applied in the productive processes. Hence, while the former items closely follow changes in the amount of labour applied, the latter tend to be more or less constant. Now C and D may be represented as composed of two items each, of which one is common to both and constant, i.e. the relatively non-variable costs per ton which will be represented by v, while the costs varying in proportion and changing in relation to the average costs of labour can be represented by b, b', b'', etc., respectively, hence :—

$$C = b + v \text{ and } D = b' + v ;$$

the ratio $\dfrac{b + v}{a}$ and $\dfrac{b' + v}{a}$ represents the relation between other costs and labour costs when the worker produces K and $K + \Delta K$ tons. By its nature v, being technically fixed to labour in a definite proportion, moves proportionately with labour, allowance being made as time goes on for the gradual change in the productivity of labour. When the amount of labour increases, the expenditure on v increases equally ; since v is a quasi-complementary item to labour costs. On the contrary b and b' proportionately fall simultaneously with a rise in total labour costs. When a larger amount of coal is mined, the overhead fixed charges per ton of output tend, as a matter of course, to fall. Thus, with the absolute increase of labour costs, the costs of fixed charges gradually decrease. Graphically, we can represent the relative position of the values for v and the amount of labour engaged in production of a ton of coal in the form of a straight line sloping upwards from the origin.

The abscissa denotes the total technically fixed costs, and the ordinate the costs of labour. In the case of the coal industry, the line slopes rapidly upwards and inclines more to the labour axis because the amount of wages per ton produced is several times larger than those items which move directly in fixed proportion with labour. The proportion of wages to the

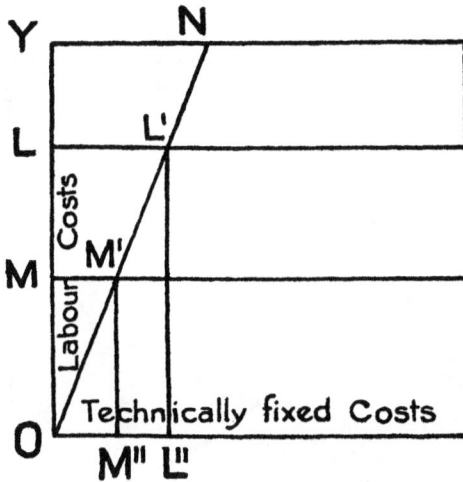

FIG. 4.

aforesaid costs is always the same, so long as wages remain constant. Therefore in Fig. 4 the ratios

$$\frac{LL'}{L'L'} = \frac{MM'}{M''M'} = d$$

where d is the coefficient determining the proportion in which v is technically fixed to labour. Hence the equation for the line of relative participation of labour and technically fixed items is $v = d(a)$. This symbol can be compared to the concept of Walras' technological coefficient of production.

Let us pass now to our second item in the costs other than wages, i.e. to those of which the total sum is fixed, and which resemble the Marshallian notion of supplementary costs.[1] We may remember that as it is a fixed total capital investment independent of the application of labour, its relative cost per unit of product decreases in reverse proportion to the growth of the labour units applied. Indeed, if we measure the relative cost of those supplementary costs per unit of labour applied, i.e. roughly speaking, per unit of product extracted, we shall observe as labour increases a fall in the ratio between those

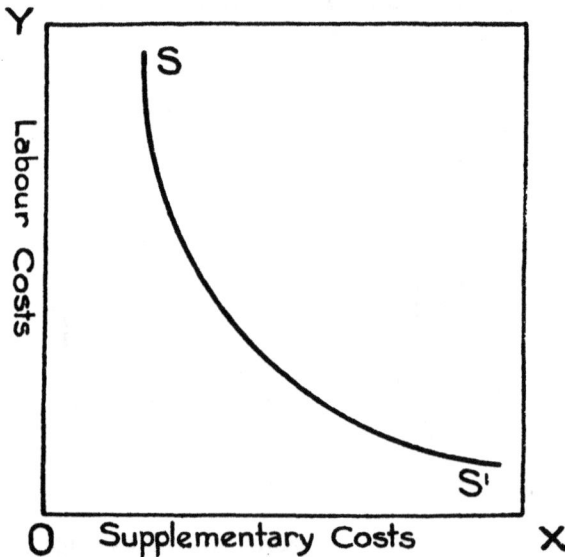

FIG. 5.

costs and labour costs. Thus our b's, representing the relatively variable costs per ton produced, will tend downward concomitantly with the increase of labour costs.

Above we draw a curve showing the fall of relative costs of invariable overhead costs per ton of coal produced.

In Fig. 5 the abscissa measures the changes in the relative values of supplementary costs per unit of labour costs in a ton

[1] Marshall distinguishes between special, direct, or prime costs, and the supplementary or general costs " that is one which will . . . also bear its proper share of the general expenses of the business." (*Principles of Economics*, 8th ed., p. 359.)

of coal, while the ordinate, as on the previous graph, shows the amount of labour costs proportionately as labour increases in absolute volume.[1] Both of these graphs could be represented in a three-dimensional diagram. For the sake of simplicity, however, we avoid such a method of representation and restrict ourselves to two-dimensional graphs, where the addition in the labour expended gradually rises from K to $K + \Delta K$; $K + 2\Delta K$; $K + 3\Delta K$; etc. Analogously, Professor G. C. Evans [2] shows in a mathematical form the relative decrease of supplementary costs, which he calls " overhead expenses ", in reverse proportion to the increase of the number of commodity units produced, which on our assumption are linked with the amount of total labour used.

Finally we must put all the component parts of our costs together in order to construct a joint curve denoting the relation between labour costs and all other costs per ton of coal produced, to which we gave the symbols C, D, etc. Our inquiry is now telescoped to the question : Does the

[1] Professor Aftalion calls the production more capitalistic if it uses a larger fixed capital ; the proportion of fixed costs to other costs determines in his opinion the degree of capitalistic production (*Crises*, vol. ii, p. 163).

[2] Professor G. C. Evans investigates the influence of changes in the size of the average unit cost $\frac{q(u)}{u}$ in relation with the variations of u (number of units produced). The function $q(u)$ denotes the cost of manufacturing and getting to market u units of this commodity per unit of time. The author analyses the quadratic function determining the whole, or a portion of the relative costs curve. Such a function reads then :—

$$q(u) = Au^2 + Bu + C \qquad (1)$$

" The overhead cost per unit time is obtained by putting $u = 0$ in the equation. The overhead cost has, therefore, the value C. We shall want to assume C to be some positive quantity. The average unit cost is given from (1) by :—

$$\frac{q(u)}{u} = Au + B + \frac{C}{u} \qquad (2)$$

which becomes large when u is small." Indeed the average unit cost decreases with the rise of units produced. C moves also in reverted proportion to u. (Professor Griffith C. Evans, *Mathematical Introduction to Economics*, New York, 1930, p. 3.)

Professor Jacob Viner maintains that not only the " fixed costs " which are "fixed only in their aggregate amounts" can vary in connection with output per unit, but that "the direct costs " are variable in the aggregate amount as output varies, as well as, ordinarily at least, in their amount per unit. (" Cost Curves and Supply Curves," *Zeitschrift für Nationalökonomie*, Wien, 1931, vol. iii, p. 26.) Of course, on our diagram the latter are represented by ON as a straight line inclined to the ordinate, because labour costs are not included in it.

proportion of labour costs to all other costs remain constant ? But such a presupposition would mean that the combined line determining the required proportions is straight. If the line were not straight, or even not straight along all its length, it would mean that the proportion varied. From what has already been said we may expect that the combined

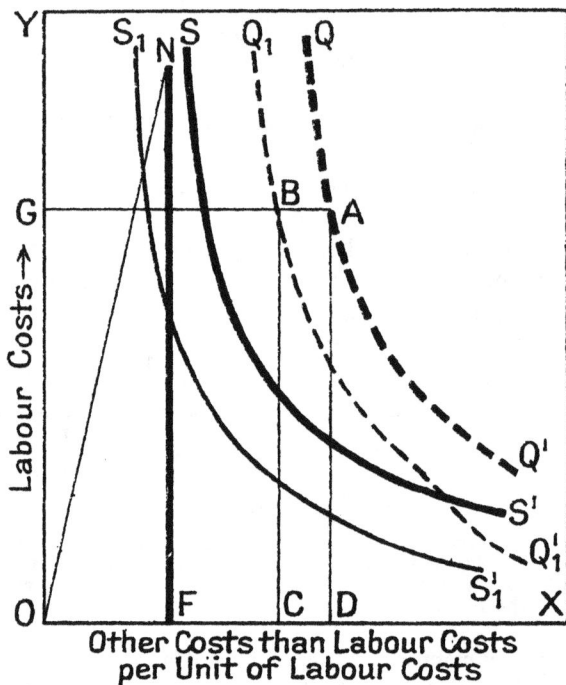

Fig. 6.

line cannot be straight, but that it must be concave, since one of its components is a curve. Let us now add the lines together and see the shape of the curve so obtained.

Before, however, doing so, we must change our diagram of the technically fixed costs in such a way that it could show the relation of the technically fixed costs to the labour costs when total labour costs increase. This condition will be satisfied by drawing from point N a straight line NF parallel to the ordinate. After this simple transformation we can add the lines together by drawing the figure as on p. 336.

The curve QQ' on Fig. 6 is the result of the addition of $FN + SS'$. It denotes the dependence of all costs other than labour (technically fixed costs + supplementary costs) on the changes in the labour costs.[1] Our curve QQ' bears some resemblance to Professor Viner's [2] curve for the trend

[1] The equation for the QQ' curve is represented by :—

$$x = \frac{\frac{\text{Const.}}{y} + dy}{y} = \frac{\text{Const.}}{y^2} + d$$

or by a similar equation.

[2] This curve is shown by Professor Viner on his familiar graph, reproduced below, in the shape of $ATUC$, which is the result of addition of the curve AFC representing the trend of the average fixed costs (our supplementary costs) and of the curve ADC showing the trend of average direct costs per unit as output increases, corresponding in our example to the technically fixed costs curve + cost of labour curve.

By MC Professor Viner denotes the trend of marginal costs as output is increased. " Any point on it represents the increase in aggregate costs as output at that point is increased by one unit."

Short-run Cost Curve

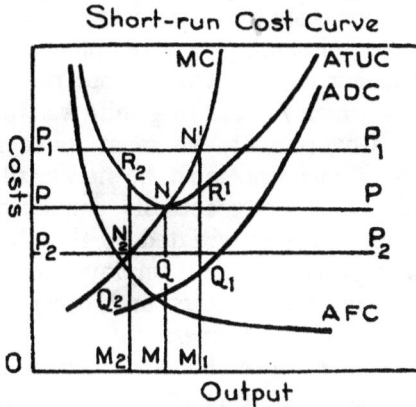

FIG. 7.

Professor Viner formulated the equations for his curves, denoting by Ya = average fixed cost per unit, by Yb = average direct cost per unit, and by X = output, then the curve $ATUC = Ya + Yb$, and $MC = \frac{d\,[(Ya + Yb)\,X]}{dX}$. " It is important to note that no consideration need be given to the fixed costs, if they really are absolutely fixed, in computing the marginal since $XYa = C$, and

$$\frac{dc}{dX} = 0 \ldots$$

$$\frac{d[(Ya + Yb)\,X]}{dX} = \frac{d(XYb)}{dX} \text{,,}$$

(*Zeitschrift für Nationalökonomie*, loc. cit.)

of average total (fixed + direct) unit costs as output increases. The chief difference is that we measure the costs in terms of labour costs, thus dealing with relation of all costs to the costs of labour. Our technically fixed curve does not, therefore, contain labour costs. The curve QQ' representing all costs other than labour, tends gradually, as total labour costs increase, to run parallel to FN, which means that, as the costs of machinery and other fixed costs tend to diminish, QQ' is gradually more and more dependent on technically fixed costs.

At this stage, we are already in the position to draw certain practical conclusions from our discussion. Our QQ' curve is obviously not a rectangular hyperbola, but we have proved that it tends to become assymptotic to the line FN. Hence, as y or the total amount of labour cost increases, or otherwise when the industry is better employed, the proportion of labour costs to other costs per unit of product tends to increase (assuming full employment). Hence, reverting now to our computations about the value of one hour of work by which the existing shift was to be reduced by the Labour Government, we must make it perfectly clear that such calculations must be necessarily based on the existing rate of capacity actually employed, and that they are liable to be largely vitiated by the changes in this rate. A fuller capacity of employment alters the proportion between labour costs and other costs nearly always in favour of the former.[1]

Assuming now that, since the beginning of 1931, owing to shorter hours, the labour factor of production becomes more expensive, so that, instead of paying, as in the previous

---

[1] It is a common mistake in comparing the coal output in cwts. per man-shift not to take into account the rate of capacity at which the industry was actually employed. Such a mistake, for instance, was committed in the *Industrial Survey of South Wales*, 1932, p. 39. Especially where the changes are only fractional, all inferences can be vitiated if we do not account for the alterations caused by the rate of employment. Having discovered the change in the proportion of our cost-items caused by alteration of the rate of employment, or otherwise in the amount of labour used, we are entitled now to carry on one step further and see what will be the effect of a change in the cost of one of our factors in which we are interested, viz. labour.

example a, we have to pay $a + \Delta a$ for the same amount of work done, or, otherwise expressed, we still pay a but the working day is shorter, which eventually means that labour becomes dearer—the fixed costs curve SS' will have to shift to the left, in our Figure 6 to $S_1 S'_1$, hence the total costs curve (other than labour) QQ' will be also shifted to $Q_1 Q'_1$, so that after the introduction of shorter hours of work both curves are shifted to the left-hand side. Simultaneously with the rise of the price of a unit of labour (long-term adjustment and effects of rationalization excluded), the proportion between labour and other costs has changed.

Now using our former symbols C, D, and a (for wages), we can show on Fig. 6 the changes which would take place if hours of work were reduced without revisions in wages. We can choose any point (A) on the curve QQ'. The distance GA between the ordinate and A corresponds in our example to D, while GB corresponds to C, AD corresponds to the total wage bill which is proportionate to a.

The proportions $\dfrac{GA}{AD}$ and $\dfrac{GB}{BC} = \dfrac{GB}{AD}$, represent our ratios $\dfrac{D}{a}$ and $\dfrac{C}{a}$ divided by the number of labour units employed.

From Fig. 6 it is obvious that $GA > GB$, hence also $\dfrac{GA}{AD} > \dfrac{GB}{AD}$, or else that $\dfrac{D}{a} > \dfrac{C}{a}$. A rise in the cost of labour, or what is tantamount to it, a shortening in working time, is connected with an alteration in the proportionate participation of various factors of production in the costs per unit of product, and tends to increase the share of labour in a unit.

In a greatly simplified form all this discussion can be shown on a diagram which measures the percentage participation of various factors in a unit of product. This method, however, being simple and merely explicative, does not prove very suitable for the causal-genetic analysis.

On Fig. 8 the abscissa measures the participation of various items of cost in the total average cost as output gradually increases. The total cost line forms the extreme case where the cost of any one factor is the only cost of production, other factors being delivered free. The curve representing other costs is derived as the residual between this line and the sum of all other costs curves. Its shape is the reverse shape of the $(LC + RFC)$ curve. The sum of $[OC + (LC + RFC)]$ for any value of X always equals 100 per cent.

Now that we have replied at some length to the first part of the question put above and have noticed that the

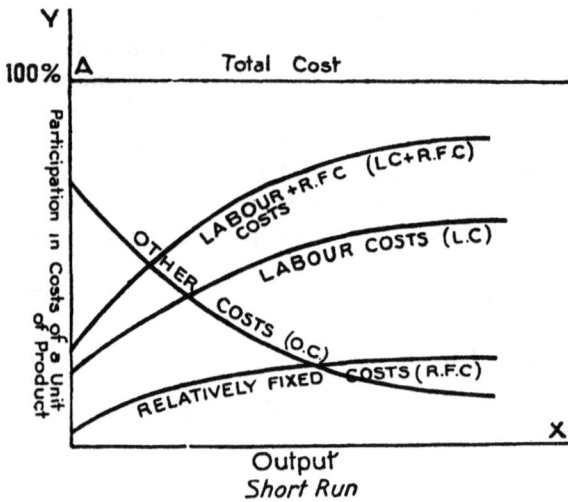

FIG. 8.

proportional costs are highly dependent on the rate of capacity at which the industry is employed, let us deduce the implications affecting the second part of the question. Does the change in relative costs affect all the districts in the same way ? The reply is obviously in the negative. Since the different coal-fields in the country have widely different degrees of equipment and different distribution of overheads to other costs, therefore the effect of under-employment of the industry is different for them. Obviously the heavier the average overhead costs the greater the pressure on the part of the industry to keep as fully employed as possible.[1]

This theoretical discussion, in our view, helps to show the uncertainty with which all computations of the value of the working time can be undertaken. In the abstract world of *ceteris paribus* it looks quite simple, but in actual life, where data are changing, it is extremely difficult. But in 1930, the proposed reform of working hours made some estimate essential.

Now, however, we can draw final conclusions from this part of our discussion and throw an adequate light on our previous computation of the value of one hour of labour on the basis of 1926 costs. It will be remembered that we estimated this figure at something between 2s. 6d. and 2s. 10d., which the industry would have to earn somehow or other to cover the extra costs. Now, in view of our remarks, it is clear that such an estimate holds good only if the production is maintained at an unchanged rate of capacity. Moreover, it must be added that the proportion of labour costs to all other costs remains constant only when the rate of employment does not alter, and when the price of the factors remains constant. In the computation, however, which circulated in the districts on the eve of the Coal Mines Act, 1930, only the alteration of the price of factors of production was made known, while the other variables such as, e.g., the future rate of capacity, could not be determined accurately, hence all computations were made to some extent in the dark.

We have already investigated the behaviour of the ratio between other costs and labour costs when the total volume of production increases, we have analysed the alteration of these ratios when the price of labour increases, but our investigation has purposely excluded the alteration which occurred over a very long period in the relation between labour and capital in the coal industry of this country. If we may be allowed a short digression on this subject, we should like to note in this respect a few important

[1] This wide difference in the distribution of costs between the districts, which is to a great extent the result of technical considerations, is one of the disintegrating factors in the industry which have been analysed in Pt. I, Chap. II.

points. The necessary data on costs of production are very scarce. Till the early pre-War years there are only very rough figures giving the various items of costs, and even those very often provide information only over the

TABLE No. 35

LABOUR COSTS AND OTHER COSTS PER TON OF COAL PRODUCED IN THE UNITED KINGDOM EXPRESSED AS PERCENTAGES OF TOTAL COSTS OF PRODUCTION FROM 1874 TO 1932

Year.	Labour costs. %	Other Costs. %
1874 [1]	62·8	37·2
1876 [2]	72·7	27·3
1879 [3][9]	61·7	38·3
Average 1875–9	66·3	33·7
,, 1889–1893	70·0	30·0
,, 1897 [1]	78·0	22·0
,, 1899–1903 [9]	73·3	26·7
,, 1900–4	72·7	27·3
,, 1900 [1][10]	81·7	18·3
,, 1909–1913	70·9	29·1
1913	73·7	26·3
1918	73·3	26·7
1919 [4]	76·7	23·3
1920	74·8	25·2
1921 [5]	70·3	29·7
1922	66·5	33·5
1923	69·7	30·3
1924	70·2	29·8
1925	70·7	29·3
1926 [6]	71·1	28·9
1927	67·6	32·4
1928	67·1	32·9
1929	66·4	33·6
1930	67·9	32·1
1931 [7]	66·9	33·1
1932 [8]	66·1	33·9

[1] Based on cost sheets of three different collieries.
[2] Based on the cost sheet of one newly erected colliery.
[3] Based on the cost sheets of two old collieries.
[4] Seven hours day introduced.
[5] Strike from March till July.
[6] Strike; eight hours' day restored.
[7] The Coal Mines Act, 1930, in force; the 7½ hours' day.
[8] First months.
[9] Based on the figures of Henry Bramall, a well-known Lancashire mining engineer.
[10] Based on the figures of D. A. Thomas (later Lord Rhondda).
Computed from the following: Sir R. Redmayne's *The British Coal Mining, Colliery Year Book and Coal Trades Directory, Quarterly Statistical Summaries of Output,* and of *The Costs of Production, Proceeds and Profits of the Coal Mining Industry,* Allan Greenwell—*Economic Position of the Coal Industry in the United Kingdom.*

average of five years, thus rendering more accurate computations hardly possible. Table No. 35 gives some idea of the participation of various costs in the British coal industry in the past.

The above Table shows that on the whole in the very long run labour costs tend to occupy a fairly definite position in the cost sheet [1] per ton of coal produced. The main variations depend either on the changes of the price of labour, usually through reduction of working time, but still more on the falling of the rate of employment of the industry, which, as has already been demonstrated, largely affects the proportion of labour costs to other costs.

After these few remarks on the significance of the rate of employment in the industry and of the costs of labour per unit of time, we return to the position with which the coal industry as a whole was faced when the Government announced their intention of reducing the working time in the mines. This announcement was tantamount to a declaration of an increase in the costs of labour, a burden which the industry could ill bear at that time, when all prospects pointed towards a further reduction of the rate of employment. In these circumstances, the difference between costs of production before and after the reduction of hours, equal to nearly 3s., had to be bridged by any, or all, of the three following ways :—

  1. By reducing the rate of wages for the workers paid by time, and preserving the existing scales for the miners paid on piece work ;
  2. By raising the prices of coal ; and finally
  3. By a reduction of the costs of production through

---

[1] In discussing the cost sheets of the colliery companies, one must bear in mind that the methods of computing various items of costs differ. To quote an instance, we will say that some of the collieries, in computing their costs per ton of coal produced, divide their costs by the actual pithead tonnage, while some others divide them only by the quantity of coal commercially disposable. Thus, with a smaller divisor than the others, they arrive naturally at higher costs, though in fact their costs may be equal to, or smaller than, those of collieries adopting a larger divisor. Various difficulties, and the lack of standard methods for calculating costs in the coal industry, have been indicated by Mr. W. G. Grace in an address to the North of England Branch of the National Association of Colliery Managers (May, 1929).

better methods of working and through extensive industrial concentration.

One thing was certain, that to keep the industry going with relatively increased labour costs was not possible at the time without incurring heavy losses.

In fact, the colliery owners took the necessary precautions to meet the situation immediately after they were notified of the reduction of hours. From motives of expediency they safeguarded themselves on both sides, i.e. they announced that the price of coal could not be maintained at the existing level, that they would be forced to reduce wages according to the fall in hours of work, and at the same time they must consider the possibilities of reorganizing the industry on a better foundation in order to achieve economies and avoid competition. As a result of these precautions many colliery owners all over the country inserted new clauses in their sales contracts, providing that in the event of statutory alterations in the length of the working day during the period of contract they should be entitled to revise the prices by agreement between the parties. These clauses presumably did not appear in any foreign contracts.

However, these steps were not sufficient to pay for the higher costs and the colliery owners announced their determination to compensate the reduction in hours of employment by a sweeping cut in wages. Hence the whole controversy raged round this dilemma ; namely, who was to pay the bill for a shorter working day : the owners, the workers, or the consumers ? The most spectacular struggle arose between the owners and the workers. The former pressed for a lower wages scale, the latter demanded the minimum wage. Other courses, including the raising of prices of coal and economies to be obtained from reorganization, did not come into such prominence as the question of labour costs, for the following reasons. The general trend of prices was continually downwards ; in 1928 the price index of all articles as measured by *The Times* decreased by 3·1 per cent, in 1929 by 6·3 per cent. There was but little hope that it would be possible in such circumstances to raise the prices of coal to a level which would counterbalance the increased costs of labour. Moreover, the structure of the British coal industry was not adapted to a deliberate increase of prices, owing to the unregulated competition of all the districts. The pressure of the owners for reduction of costs was therefore all the more obstinate since prices had no upward flexibility and were likely to be met by the elasticity of demand for a fall.

But the Government, on the other hand, though fully informed by the Mining Association of the economic significance of a reduction of hours, was strongly urged by the miners not to yield to the demand for reduction of wages. The miners argued that the moral significance of the whole reform would be frustrated if it were the miners who ultimately paid for it. They emphatically discarded any suggestion of wage-reduction, and proposed to establish a national agreement and regulation of their pay by a National Wages Board to protect the workers from eventual cuts. But the owners objected to anything of the sort. The protest came most forcibly from South Wales, which, with her enormous volume of foreign trade, equal to about 50 per cent of her output and nearly 40 per cent of total capacity, was more likely than the other districts to be affected by the rise of labour costs.

Most of the other districts also protested against the rise of the cost of labour. In such conditions the Government was driven to expect large advantages from the co-operation scheme which was the industry's own product, and which now entered Parliament to cross swords with politics.

§ 3. FRAMING A NEW ORDER IN THE COAL INDUSTRY

The shortening of the working day became the kernel of a broad reform in the coal industry. By introducing all possible economies involved in co-ordination on a national scale, the Government hoped to make it feasible for the industry to bear increased costs of labour. The political views of the Liberals also favoured reorganization in this way. Moreover, both the miners and some of the owners urged the Government to take special measures to bring about co-operation in the industry on a national scale. During the annual conference of the miners at Blackpool in July, 1929, Mr. Herbert Smith, in his Presidential address, expressed the view that regional organizations such as the Scottish Scheme, the Five Counties Scheme, or the South Wales Marketing Scheme, were insufficient to meet the emergency and that national organization was imperative.

Similar views were laid before the Cabinet by many influential coal-owners on the eve of the announcement of the Cabinet's coal policy. The recommendations of the Samuel Report dealing with organization, especially those that concerned co-operation and marketing, thus revived again as the result of the proposal to reduce working hours. The economic reality expressed in the shape of higher costs of production, of an excess of supply over demand, of the competition of foreign coal producing countries, of the depressed state of other industries depending on a cheap supply of coal and many other problems forced the politicians to devise a workable scheme which would allow the industry to continue its operation. It was often said that by reorganization the industry could be better equipped both for the national and international markets, the competitive struggle could be straightened out, and new order introduced. In this way when the late Mr. William Graham announced the coal scheme on behalf of the Government the public for the first time learned from his answer in the House of Commons that the question of hours would be linked up with organization reforms.[1]

[1] Parliamentary Debates, House of Commons, 23rd July, 1929, col. 1085 : ". . . the Government," said the President of the Board of Trade, " desired the owners to develop the organization of district marketing arrangements and a central scheme for co-ordinating the activities of the district organizations. In the legislation to be introduced in autumn, the Government will take powers to enable them, if necessary, to compel colliery owners to conform to the rules of a district organization inaugurated with the approval of owners of collieries producing the majority of the

In Mr. Graham's statement some leading principles of organization were laid down, of which perhaps the most important enjoined that the whole reform should be left for execution to the owners themselves. They would carry out the reorganization along the lines initiated by the Central Marketing Committee in 1928. Further, the whole structure should be based on national and district schemes covering the coal industry throughout the country. One of the most essential points was the intimation that no colliery owner should be allowed to remain outside the co-ordinating system. Government's precise attitude as to the question of hours was not yet disclosed by the Ministers, and the project for the nationalization of minerals, sponsored by the miners and advocated by some Liberals, still remained undecided.

It was, however, apparent from the outlines of Government policy, that the Ministers desired to include in the Bill a large range of organization proposals combined with the shortening of working hours. The original preparatory work of the Coal Marketing Committee on national co-operation proved a good background for Governmental schemes which left the whole initiative to the owners. At this stage, the coal-owners began to show active interest, and the sphere of discussion widened.

After the exposition of their plans by the Government, the Mining Association took the lead. Under its auspices the coal-owners met to lay down the provisional lines for their own organization. The already existing district schemes greatly assisted the preparatory work, as only Northumberland and Durham had never possessed anything more than loose price agreements. These two had consequently to devise some kind of organization. This difficulty was, of course, stressed during the first representative meeting of colliery owners from all over the country, held in the summer of 1929. During the meeting it

output of the district. The Government will also take power to enable them to initiate a scheme in any district which fails to constitute an organization having the approval of the majority, and will take similar power to set up a central co-ordinating authority, if one is not constituted voluntarily."

soon became clear that the schemes would necessarily have to embrace not only restriction of production, but also regulation of prices. This meeting of the coal-owners, after the announcement of the Government's design to reorganize the industry, is of great significance, because the main lines of the future schemes were then sketched for the first time. In spite of some pressure, especially from certain economists and coal experts,[1] the plausible principle of completely closing down the so-called inefficient and moribund pits in order to enable the modern and developing mines to work at full capacity, gave way to the previous idea of an all round restriction of production.

In view both of the Government's desire to bring in reforms and of the increasing demand from the miners for reduction of hours, the coal-owners set to work to frame a draft scheme for a national organization. In order to keep in permanent contact with the industry, the Government had during the recess appointed a Cabinet Coal Committee to hold discussions with the representatives of the Mining Association and of the Miners' Federation concerning the proposed legislation. Such discussions covered a wide range of matters intended for inclusion in the Government Bill. At this juncture it was already discernible that the superstructure raised over the provisions concerning hours would be a vast one and would include several different provisions in order to satisfy Liberal opinion and to win its support in the reading of the Bill. Mr. Lloyd George definitely stated in the House on the 3rd July, 1929, that his Party agreed to purchase of royalties, grouping and co-ordination of mines, and reduction of hours.

After a busy summer crowned with success in the international field, the Labour Government again devoted their attention to home affairs, and in the first place to the coal industry. Among the important international

[1] e.g. R. C. Smart, *The Economics of the Coal Industry*, London, 1930. On p. 79 the author puts his views on the subject as follows : " What is most necessary is that output should be centralized at our best-equipped and most modern collieries. They should work full time—100 per cent capacity —to give us the necessary supply of a competitive, low-priced fuel. That is, the supply of coal should be regulated by controlling the number of the producers, not the scale of their production."

events which occurred in summer, 1929, affecting British coal mining, was the acceptance of the Young Plan, with the British modification forbidding the Governments which received coal on account of reparation to re-sell it in the world markets.[1]

In addition to the provision in The Hague Agreement regulating reparations in kind, the Italian Government had undertaken to buy yearly on behalf of Italian State Railways one million tons of British coal during a period of three years, and also " to abstain from importing Reparation coal via sea over and above the maximum quantity of 1,500,000 tons per annum during the said three-year period ".[2] Some reapportionment of the quantities to be delivered in the

[1] The deliveries of coal by Germany on account of reparations to Italy had somewhat risen since 1925. Under the Dawes Plan the amount was fixed at 200,000 tons per month, which rose to 375,000 tons towards the end of 1926, and reached, by the beginning of 1928, 420,000 tons per month, thus representing a yearly delivery of approximately 5 million tons. In order to distribute the Reparation coal supplies a company had been formed under the name of Societa Nazionale Consumatori di Carbone S.A. The company is a joint-stock company with a capital of Lira 5,000,000 subject to State control, and works in co-operation with the main coal consumers of the country.

On the other hand, according to official Italian statistics, though imports of coal on Reparations' account have increased since 1924, the total volume of coal imported from Germany has remained stable. Below we append a Table showing the coal imports from Germany :—

TABLE No. 36

COAL IMPORTS FROM GERMANY TO ITALY, 1924-7

Year.	On Private account. Tons metric.	On Repara-account. Tons metric.	Total. Tons metric.
1924 . . .	749,197	3,608,710	4,357,907
1925 . . .	527,557	1,727,861	2,255,418
1926 . . .	1,614,440	2,886,008	4,500,448
1927 (on the basis of the 1st 10 months) .	1,614,931	3,094,202	4,709,133

Between 1913 and 1928, the coal consumption of Italy was increased by more than 4 million tons, whereas at the same time the British coal export to that country decreased by nearly 3 million tons to about 6·8 million tons. Thus it would be scarcely possible to sustain the thesis that the deliveries in kind were the main cause of the losses in the Italian market.

[2] See Protocol of the Hague Conference (Cmd. 3392), 1929. Annex II, Appendix II. The third million was not actually purchased owing to the decision of the Italian authorities to suspend purchases of coal under The Hague Agreement as from 1st May, 1932.

immediate future and in later periods was also made with the object of assisting the British coal industry.

In the first days of August the Mines Department circulated to all collieries in the country official formulas requesting them to submit by the middle of October final suggestions for the organization of district marketing schemes and for the central co-ordinating body, so that they might be put into action by the 1st January, 1930. Consequently, the representatives of the coal-owners met in London to discuss the draft schemes laid before them. Some difficulties were raised by Northumberland and Durham, where progress in framing the district scheme was very slow. Lanarkshire also was reluctant to abide by the proposed marketing plan for Scotland, which she found inadequate for her large inland sales because it did not include a single selling agency. The sword of Damocles, however, hung over the industry, in the shape of the Government's announcement that, should the owners fail to launch a scheme of their own, one would be imposed by compulsion. Slowly, but nevertheless steadily, a scheme of organization emerged.

The most advanced proposals at that time came from South Wales, and these included both the regulation of production by means of quotas and the control of prices. A scheme along these lines was actually in working order, so South Wales served as a standard example for a district scheme. The Welsh organization was the result of experience acquired during its two years of existence. It is not surprising that the framers of the district schemes looked towards the Welsh organization as a model for their own, since South Wales was the only district in the country which hitherto had accepted price control. The majority demanded that both the national and district schemes should be based on regulation of output and prices such as had been accepted by South Wales. Also the President of the Board of Trade requested the owners to include these two provisions in their schemes.

By August the preparation for a marketing network over the whole country had substantially advanced under the influence of the Government, and a meeting of representatives of the district coal marketing committees was held, at which the outlines of co-ordination of the district schemes were discussed. A fortnight later a report on co-ordination of district schemes was nearly ready for submission. In framing that part of the national scheme which dealt with restriction of output, the drafting sub-committee found the well-moulded provisions of the Five Counties Scheme of great help. But serious difficulties were encountered in settling the question of prices. The Sub-Committee, therefore, provided for special central machinery solely to handle the objections of one district against another in the matter of prices, but left the actual fixing of minimum price schedules to individual districts.

At that time the Midland Coal-field and South Wales had already complex organizations for marketing.[1] Northumberland and Durham, though very reluctantly, made some progress in bringing about organizations of their own. The former asked, amongst other things, that a levy of 3d. per ton produced should be raised to compensate those pits that might be idle owing to the working of the quota. Only in Scotland was there practically no progress in drawing up a scheme, notwithstanding the request of the Government.

In September the national drafting Sub-Committee submitted to the Central Marketing Committee[2] representing all the owners in the country a vast plan including both national and district schemes. The whole plan was to be administered by a Central Marketing Committee and by District Committees. But only the general lines common to all the schemes were elaborated, while the details were to be left to the districts. On the whole, the draft provided more fully for the central body but rather neglected the remainder.

While the owners were engaged in drafting the scheme,

---

[1] A Shipping Committee of the Central Collieries Commercial Association took charge of the export's assistance, and entered into agreements with the Humber and Mersey exporters whereby the latter sold coal on the basis of fixed percentage commission.

[2] The Central Marketing Committee was independent of the Mining Association of Great Britain, and was composed of fourteen representatives of the districts.

the miners' leaders were becoming increasingly active in their efforts to secure national co-ordination. Mr. H. Smith, in particular, gave special consideration to this point in his presidential address to the miners' conference at Blackpool. But the miners at the same time adhered with tenacity to the principle that their wages must not be affected by the proposed shortening of the working day. Therefore, as district wage agreements were coming to an end, they demanded a national agreement and a general minimum wage as armour against attempted reduction in pay.   In September, as the result of the resolutions of the annual conference, the Miners' Federation embarked upon the policy of forcing a national working agreement.   With this purpose the officials of the Miners' Federation sent an invitation to the organization of the owners (Mining Association) requesting them to open negotiations for the establishment of national machinery to deal with wages. The Prime Minister openly favoured national regulation of wages. Only a small section of the miners, having the best minimum wages in the country, represented by the so-called Miners' Industrial non-Political Union in Nottingham and District, headed by Mr. G. A. Spencer, did not favour national agreement, and so was not willing to strengthen the power of the Miners' Federation. On the other hand the owners were adamant on this point, and steadily refused to allow any consideration of wages on a national basis. When, at the beginning of November, the Government suggested a round-table conference between the mine-owners, the miners, and the Ministers, the owners refused to accept such an invitation. The Government found itself between the devil and the deep sea. On the one side the miners urged that a shortening of hours was useless if they were to pay for it out of their wages. Miners' leaders argued that, since all the owners would possess a large central co-ordinating apparatus, " this logically involves a properly defined national relationship between the coal-owners and the mine-workers." [1]   The owners,   on   the   other   hand, throughout   sweepingly   rejected   the   possibility   of

[1] The *Miner*, 19th October, 1929.

co-operating for the settlement of wages, and other labour questions, on national lines.

In such circumstances the Government were obliged to mould the provisions of the coal reform in such a way as to combine the redemption of their pledges with conformity to economic considerations and the practical functions of the State.   On the one hand they had to regard the requirements of the industry, which, on the whole, desired to strengthen its position in face of the consumers by eliminating the vicious competitive fight through some voluntary regulation of output and prices ;   on the other hand they were obliged to countenance the insistence of the rank and file of Labour on a definite arrangement concerning wages and methods of negotiation between capital and labour.   One could perceive at this stage that all the problems which might be attacked in future legislation fall into two types : i.e. those which must enter the Statute Book at the same time as the provisions for the reduction of hours, being created to make that reduction of hours possible ; and those which had remoter ends in view.   The first may be described as relating to the fulfilment of the short-term plan, the latter to the execution of the long-term plan.

Immediately connected with the hours of work were the problems of organization of marketing, which it was hoped the owners themselves would solve, and questions of wages. The Government could not take full responsibility for guaranteeing a stabilized wage on the previous basis, but they considered the possibility of creating a Board to regulate wages.   Finally, since the national organization of producers might by its very existence threaten the interests of the consumers, measures to protect the public were included, and were brought forward at the same time as the marketing scheme.   All these matters formed the immediate legislative programme.

Other problems connected with the structure of the coal industry, especially amalgamations of mines and the nationalization of royalties, seemed to have retired to a deferred programme of the Labour Government.

A a

They constituted very important reforms from the Government's point of view, but as they were not necessarily connected with the shortening of the working hours, they did not require such prompt treatment as the others. Both the nationalization of royalties and the promotion of forced amalgamations were proposals meant to satisfy the desires of certain political detachments rather than to bring immediate alleviation to the industry itself. Necessary safety-valves to make the royalties work smoothly were already included in the Mines (Working Facilities) Act of 1923,[1] and in the Mining Industry Act, 1926,[2] so the accusation that private ownership was hampering the development of the industry no longer applied.

Thus in the forefront came the problems of hours, marketing, protection of consumers, and safe-guarding of wages through a National Board, and, in the second rank, nationalization of royalties and amalgamations. The Government intended to handle these questions in separate Bills, but they were pressed by the miners' leaders to redeem their election pledge to shorten working hours. So Ministers were especially anxious to have the marketing schemes prepared by the mine-owners ready on the date fixed, the 15th October.

The Coal-owners' Central Marketing Committee was working on the schemes. The Coal Committee of the Cabinet, composed of the Prime Minister, the Lord Privy Seal, the President of the Board of Trade, and the Secretary of Mines were in permanent contact with the representatives of the owners and of the miners, hearing the views of both parties. During the conversations with the owners, the matter of costs was fully thrashed out, and the Government yielded to some extent to their demands. The Government asked the owners to consider the possibilities of securing for both miners and consumers some representation on the administration of the proposed marketing schemes, which in Conservative quarters were simply regarded as letters of marque given to the colliery-owners to exploit the public.

[1] This Act gave to the Railway and Canal Commission the right to decide questions of the rights of mineral owners. See Pt. II, Chap. I, § 3.
[2] *Vide* Pt. II, Chap. I, § 3.

During the first weeks of October the scheme was presented by the coal-owners to the President of the Board of Trade. But still the Government did not disclose their intentions. They allowed things to order themselves as far as possible. Even the burning question of hours had not been decided at this time. Nor did the Government bind themselves in any way to guarantee wages, or to enforce national agreement between the industry and the workmen, in spite of the constant pressure of the miners' officials. Moreover, it was apparent that miners from those districts which already worked seven hours and a half would not agree to any half measure reduction of hours, as they would gain no advantages whatsoever therefrom. On the other hand, those districts which would benefit even from a partial reform of working time, provided it did not bring reduction in wages, were more inclined to be satisfied with less than the electoral pledges. The opinion of the miners of different areas was thus divided. Some, including the London headquarters of the Federation, did not want to cause additional trouble to the Government, nor to produce stagnation in trade ; the others, especially Yorkshire, held to their original demands.

Mr. Philip Snowden (later Lord Snowden), then Chancellor of the Exchequer, was the first to make an official pronouncement on the Government's plans on the hours problem [1] ; he warned the miners that a whole hour less of work might mean ruin to the industry. For this reason, according to his view, the reduction of time must not be hasty. The actual suggestions for Government legislation, as communicated to the miners and owners by the end of October, included a reduction of working time by stages, beginning with half-an-hour a day from the 7th of April, 1930. As things then stood, the Government offered to deal with the following three questions :—

1. Time of work below ground ;
2. The nationalization of coal royalties ;
3. The regulation of production and marketing.

[1] The *Iron and Coal Trades Review*, 25th October, 1929, p. 647.

Nationalization was to be carried out by paying a compensation calculated at the market value for all present coal property. The marketing proposals, based on the scheme devised by the owners themselves, included the control of output and prices by one central co-ordinating body, and several district committees. Output was to be regulated by the central administration which should from time to time allocate production quotas to the districts, distinguishing between coal produced for home and foreign consumption. In turn, the district committees had to allot to each colliery in the area a percentage of the district basic tonnage called quota, in such a manner as not to exceed the total district allocation. It was permitted to transfer quotas from one colliery to another.

The Government proposals left the regulation of prices to the district schemes. Some degree of co-ordination of district price schedules was to be obtained through the action of the central scheme. This scheme could also provide for a levy on the whole output of coal in order to subsidize exports. Full machinery for arbitration was provided. The arbitrator, or arbitrators, would judge all appeals brought before them by the coal-owners against the decision of district committees. Also the individual districts could seek arbitration against any enactment of the central committee. For contravening the provisions of the scheme penalties might be imposed. In order to represent the consumers and the work-people, the scheme provided in each district for a mixed committee to watch its working. Similar provisions referred to the inter-district mixed committees.

Such in brief were the legislative proposals of the Cabinet Coal Committee. They seemed, indeed, to be of the nature of a *ballon d'essai*, which was attempting at the same time to bring together the divergent views of capital and labour and to serve as a basis for further negotiations, in which both the Prime Minister and Mr. A. Henderson now personally collaborated. Henceforward the work of the Committee proceeded at a much quicker pace, and gradually many points began to crystallize definitely.

The Miners' Federation, though claiming a national basis for wage negotiation, in fact agreed to the principles of the Government proposals, and recommended their acceptance to the districts.   This decision was accompanied by some scenes of trenchant protest from the miners in Yorkshire and the Forest of Dean, which localities bluntly refused to approve of a half-way reduction of working time by half-an-hour only.   Apart from this, the Yorkshire miners also disagreed with the suggestions of raising a levy on the output of the whole country for the purpose of assisting the export trade. In such critical situation Mr. Herbert Smith, President of the Miners' Federation, tendered his resignation on the ground that he had no mandate from the electors of Yorkshire to accept the decision of the Federation. Nevertheless, in the absence of the Yorkshire delegates the Miners' Federation endorsed the terms of the Government policy.

On the other hand, the colliery owners rejected the possibility of negotiating a national agreement with the miners about wages and they declined even to take part in any conference with the Miners' Federation.   Mr. Evan Williams,[1] President of the Mining Association, gave the following explanation for this refusal :—

> " The coal industry is not one unit, but a series of units, each of which has its own problems, which can only be dealt with in the district by those who know the situation.   There is no item of a national agreement which can justly be made uniform for the country as a whole.   One of the arguments which has been put forward, and the only argument perhaps that had any strength in it, in favour of a national agreement was that it would prevent to some extent competition between one district paying lower wages and another paying higher wages.   The fallacy of that argument is that the national agreement would not determine the actual wages to be paid in the districts, and even if it did, now that inter-district marketing arrangements are to be entered into and made effective, unfair competition of that kind between districts—if it existed at all—will be made impossible in the future."

[1] *Iron and Coal Trades Review*, 8th November, 1929, p. 732.

The Government, however, succeeded in securing support for their proposals amongst some of the coal-owners. Thus the South and West Yorkshire Coal Owners' Associations, representing together about 20 per cent of the whole national output, voted for a resolution in which they dissented from the policy of the Mining Association and endorsed both the reduction of the working time by half-an-hour and the provisions for the marketing of coal.

In this way the Government had the support of the majority of the miners (except Yorkshire and Forest of Dean) and a strong backing from the Yorkshire owners. They could proceed at once to bring the Coal Bill into its ultimate shape. But one problem of the utmost importance still awaited solution—the question whether there would be any adjustment of wages to offset the half-hour reduction in working time. The miners' leaders rejected this possibility and urged a national minimum wage. The Chancellor of the Exchequer [1] emphatically proclaimed that "there must not be any reduction of wages". But in fact the Government felt unable to assume an obligation to maintain the existing level of wages. A compromise was therefore devised in the form of a National Wages Board, to be entrusted with the settlement of wages. Only a very general description of the Board was supplied, from which one gathered that it would operate on similar lines to the Board for the railwaymen under the Railways Act of 1921. Presumably the Government intended to make the Board a mixed institution, including representatives of various interests. By proposing the creation of the National Wages Board, the ministers relieved themselves of the responsible task of either guaranteeing wages, or of fixing the legal minimum wage. The idea of a Board, while likely to be more acceptable to the owners, at the same time conceded something to the miners. The owners, however, were very much opposed to the idea of a national board and boycotted it from its very conception. Even the Yorkshire owners, who backed the Government plans, did not express any opinion on the proposed institution.

[1] Mr. P. Snowden's speech at Leicester, 23rd October, 1929.

By the end of November, 1929, a Government Bill gradually emerged from the combined views of the Cabinet Coal Committee. A large section of the owners still strongly opposed the Government proposals, the South Wales Coal Marketing Association protested to the Board of Trade against the interference of the Government, and a body of independent Midland colliery owners not associated with the C.C.C.A. also objected vigorously to the proposals. Scotland, again, adopted the tactics of passive resistance to the marketing provisions. The South Staffordshire and East Worcestershire Coal Masters' Association lodged their objections against any attempt to curtail their output, especially in view of the peculiar physical conditions of the Black Country's coal-fields. The chief objections raised by the coal-owners against the Government scheme were :—

1. That it introduced a large measure of State control and empowered the representatives of the consumers to deal with matters they were not competent to handle.

2. Some owners strongly resented the provision that the standard tonnage was to be fixed on the basis of the years 1928–9, in which year many district schemes for regulation of output were already operating. In other words, they would be handicapped by those areas which were then free to produce coal without restriction.

3. The proposals as to arbitration did not altogether satisfy the owners, who in some instances desired to lay their case before an arbitrating body rather than before a single individual.

Many owners, especially in the exporting districts, objected to the idea of regulation of production altogether. In spite, however, of the cleavage between the main body of the owners and the Government on the important problems of marketing, arbitration, and the Wages Board, the Cabinet hurried on the introduction of the Bill before the Christmas recess in order not to arouse further discontent among the miners.

Desiring to obtain Liberal support beforehand, they

invited three prominent Liberals, Mr. Lloyd George, Sir Herbert Samuel, and Sir John Simon, to meet the Cabinet Coal Committee and to explain their attitude towards the intended legislation.   While these Liberal leaders agreed to the reduction of hours, and to the creation of a Wages Board, they objected to the marketing scheme on the grounds that it would raise the prices of coal to the consumers and that it was creating fresh obstacles to amalgamation. Furthermore, they condemned the proposals referring to a levy for the subsidy of exports as being fundamentally inconsistent with their principles.   So, though the Government succeeded in securing their support. for certain items, in fact it did not obtain any guarantee for the backing of the Bill.   Nevertheless much effort was expended by different sections in the attempt to reconcile the Liberals with the main provisions of the Government scheme.

We can see that a number of factors have contributed to bring about the proposed statutory reorganization of the coal industry.   The Coal Mines Bill was brought into being partly by economic forces working in the industry itself, partly by the sudden increase in the costs of labour, and partly by political ideas of the Labour and the Liberal Parties.   Of all these factors, the strongest was the action of forces in the industry itself and additions were made later from the political side to satisfy current political thought. But, as we shall see, all these later additions proved weak, and unable to withstand economic realities.   They were unable to affect in any way the natural development of the industry.   The Coal Mines Bill, which was the combined result of all these factors, soon entered into Parliament and emerged from the struggle between the parties much battered from different political contacts.

CHAPTER II

The most spectacular part of the whole controversy over the organization of the British coal industry came during the debates in Parliament. After a long series of negotiations between the Cabinet Coal Committee, the miners, the owners, and finally the Liberals, the Government issued the text of the Coal Mines' Bill. In spite of the stout opposition of various sections of the trade, they intended to have the Bill read and passed on the soonest possible date. Also, in consideration of the temporary improvement of the trade, they considered that the time was favourable for the swift carrying out of the reform.

The Bill introduced by the Government was in four parts :—

Part I dealt with production, supply, and sale of coal, that is with the marketing scheme ;

Part II shortened the time of work below ground by half-an-hour ;

Part III instituted a Coal Mines National Industrial Board ;

Part IV contained general provisions, including an interpretation clause.

In addition to these followed a schedule giving the list of twenty-one districts approved for the purposes of Part I of the Bill, and provisions dealing with amalgamation and adjustment of districts.

State acquisition of royalties and other problems of organization were not included in this Bill, as they were to be in a second Bill to be introduced later. As we have already pointed out, the Coal Mines Bill contained only those reforms which the Government believed would allow the industry to stand the immediate return to shorter hours. The argument was that benefits from reorganization would be secured at once, and so after a few months the working day could be reduced without placing an undue burden on the industry from the alteration in the labour costs of production.   The whole marketing scheme was therefore designed to strengthen the fabric of the British coal trade.   A few words must be now devoted to this scheme.

According to the *marketing provisions* contained in Part I of the Bill the production, supply, and sale of coal were henceforward to be regulated by a central co-ordinating scheme (Central Council) and by district schemes (Executive Boards) all administered by the coal-owners themselves. All schemes were subject to approval by the Board of Trade, which was entitled to authorize them (with or without modification) in the form proposed by the majority of the owners, i.e. those producing more than half of the national or district output respectively by the end of the year 1929. The Bill gave the owners three months, from 1st January, 1930, to submit their schemes and put them into operation.

The Central Council was to be composed of representatives of the owners in the several districts, elected by them, or, in case of refusal by the owners to co-operate with the scheme, they were to be nominated by the Board of Trade.   The main functions of the Central Council were the allocation to all the districts of a maximum output for a definite future period ;   the advising and co-ordinating of operation in the districts ;   the setting up of machinery for arbitration in order to secure to any Executive Board the right of appeal against any act or omission of the Council ;   and the collection of penalties from districts for contravening or failing to comply with the Central Scheme.   Among the optional functions in the Scheme was the provision for the collection from the districts of levies imposed upon them in proportion to the output or allocation, " for the purpose of facilitating the sale of any class of coal ".   This clause was chiefly designed to subsidize exports by taxing the home consumers.

The Bill provided that the district schemes were to be administered by Executive Boards elected by all the owners of the district, or in cases where the scheme was imposed they were to be appointed by the Board of Trade, after consultation with the representative associations of the owners. The Executive Boards had the duty of classifying the coal produced in the district ; of determining a standard tonnage for every mine in the area for each class of coal produced ; of fixing the quotas or percentages of the standard tonnage, i.e. the proportion of the total district allocation allowed to each mine. Each class of coal would receive a separate quota, to be the same for all the mines producing this particular class. The sum of individual quotas was not to exceed the district allocation. Transference of quotas for coal in general or any special class from one enterprise in the district to another was allowed. An important function of the Executive Board was the determination of the minimum prices for each class of coal. Moreover, the Board was entitled to examine the books and accounts of the mines in the district. Arbitration was to be left to arbitrators specially appointed ; and fines were fixed for the contravention of the provisions. Similarly to the national levy collected from the districts, individual districts could institute subsidies to be paid from levies collected in the district on any class of coal. They were also allowed to provide for deductions from quotas for any period of any amount of coal produced by the collieries in excess of the previous quota. A special provision made it possible to introduce alterations in the district schemes on the request of the Executive Boards.

In order to investigate any complaint on the operation of the scheme, the Bill was to bring into existence a National Committee of Investigation and several District Committees. The National Committee was to be composed of nine members, the District Committees of five, all of whom would be appointed by the Board of Trade. Half of the members other than the chairman were to represent the interests of consumers, and the others, the mine-owners and mine-workers in equal proportion. The Bill gave the Committees of Investigation access to all accounts and sources of information necessary for the fulfilment of their duties.

If the Committees found that any provisions of the scheme were contrary to the public interest, it was their duty to report the matter to the Board of Trade, which would in turn, after investigation, make recommendations to the Council, or to the Executive Board in question. If the district scheme was not rectified to the satisfaction of the Board of Trade, they could direct that it should cease to have effect under the Act and impose a new one upon the district ; but if any voluntary association of owners carried out the functions of a district scheme successfully and complied with the Central Scheme, the Board should not, except at the request of the Central Council, enforce a new scheme. Further the Bill provided for the furnishing of confidential information by the Central Council and by the Executive Boards, to the Board of Trade, which in turn was requested to lay before Parliament every year a report upon the operation of all the schemes. So much for the marketing clauses.

The whole of Part II of the Bill, which dealt with the question of reduction of hours by half an hour from 6th April, 1930, was contained in six lines only.

Part III of the Bill treated questions connected with the institution of a Coal Mines National Industrial Board, to be composed of a Chairman and sixteen members appointed by the Board of Trade after consultation with the Mining Association of Great Britain (six members), with the Miners' Federation of Great Britain (six members), with the Federation of British Industries and Association of British Chambers of Commerce jointly (one member), and with the General Council of the Trade Union Congress, the Co-operative Union, and the National Confederation of Employers' Organizations (one member each). The Board had the duty of recording all agreements between the owners and mineworkers regulating the wages and conditions of labour. In case of dispute between labour and capital in any district, each side was authorized to refer the case to the National Industrial Board for inquiry and to receive the Board's report. The Bill left much freedom to the Board to make rules of procedure.

Finally, Part IV of the Bill contained general provisions and an explanation of the terms used.

The Bill, which we have described at some length, combined several proposals of quite a different nature. Besides smaller points it contained two main alterations, first in the structure of the industry and second in the length of the working day. It was calculated that the economic effects of these two measures would balance each other, that is to say, that the rise in costs caused by the rise in the price of labour per unit of product would be counteracted by increased proceeds due to the general cartellization of the industry.   In criticizing this assumption we must point out, however, that whereas the rise in costs was an immediate fact, the economies (if any) and increased proceeds could naturally only accrue in time and constituted a long-term reform. The only possible way open to the compulsory cartel for the increase of proceeds was to have recourse to a rise of prices at home, and in all markets where the conditions of demand [1] allowed such action.

Immediately on the publication of the Bill an enormous number of protests were raised from different quarters, directed both against the measure as a whole and against individual parts. The only two important bodies to approve the Bill as proposed by the Government were the Miners' Federation, who regarded the whole as the first instalment of a comprehensive scheme, and the Yorkshire coal-owners, whom the Bill affected in a much less degree than those in the other districts, and who were particularly keen to bring their own dissentient owners under the framework of a compulsory organization of producers.   Practically all other sections of opinion opposed at least one of the main parts of the Bill.

The coal-owners and other critics of the Bill turned their attacks in the first place upon the shortening of hours of work in the mines.   Furthermore, the marketing provisions gave rise to anxious warnings from several persons intimately connected with the industry against possible harmful results.   Thus a few weeks before the publication of the

---

[1] *Vide* Part I, Chap. II, § 2.

Bill, Sir William Beveridge [1] cautioned the Government against the imitation of the cartellization methods of South Wales in constructing the Central Scheme, and against the perpetuation of old and inefficient collieries. " A colliery," he wrote in referring to quotas, " which cannot produce profitably, even at the prescribed minimum prices, will be given a valuable right of standing in the way of others which can. An efficient colliery, which is in the position to produce cheaply and expand its production, will not (beyond narrow limits) be allowed to do so, except under penalties, or by first loading itself with the cost of buying up rights of production. On the other hand, the scheme, so far as can be seen, contains nothing whatever that will tend to closer co-operation between collieries in the actual business of marketing or of transporting and distributing coal." The same view led Mr. R. C. Smart [2] to fear that the National Coal Marketing scheme would create " an industrial monopoly that perpetuates the existence of the uneconomic pits ", and that the taxpayer and the consumer would have to foot the bill. He would prefer to see all the best mines working at full capacity and the others closed down for a compensation. [3] In his opinion, the allotted quotas should conform to actual capacity but not, as in the Scottish Coal Marketing Scheme, to achievement in the past. [4] Mr. G. D. H. Cole [5] also criticized the quota system on the ground that it would increase the costs of production and that a well-equipped colliery would work under the law of increasing returns (i.e. within limits, which are not likely to be exceeded, its costs of production are likely to fall with every addition to its weekly or monthly output), while the quota restriction, applied equally to good and bad collieries, will compel them all to reduce output and will bolster up prices of coal from good collieries, without securing any reduction of prices from the others. Even the sales of

[1] *The Times*, 21st October, 1929.
[2] R. C. Smart, *The Economics of the Coal Industry*, London, 1930, p. 220.
[3] Op. cit., p. 56.
[4] Op. cit., p. 75.
[5] G. D. H. Cole, " The Problem of Mines," *The Political Quarterly*, January, 1930, p. 55.

quotas would not cure the evil, because the price paid for them would have to come out of the price of coal. Mr. Cole calculated that the difference between the costs per ton produced from a mine working at full capacity and from one working under the scheme would amount to 3s. 6d.; therefore, it would pay to buy quotas at any rate lower than this.

A similar view was expressed in an article in the Mining Journal [1] on the quotas, which were described as merely a subsidy to the out-of-date units. The article suggested that " what the Government should do, is to say whatever they consider is right about hours, wages, and other conditions of working and leave the pits to meet these conditions ". Sir Richard Redmayne criticized the Government proposals on account of increased prices. He always maintained that coal should be cheap and he admitted the existence of a large degree of elasticity of demand, both for a fall and for a rise. In a letter to *The Times* Sir Richard [2] alludes to the address of Mr. C. H. Merz read to the British Association on " The National Scheme of Electricity Supply in Great Britain ", which expounds the view that the requirements for coal will rise owing to a higher standard of life. Referring to the old collieries, Sir Richard says : " If the determining factor in regard to this quota is the productive capacity of a district or colliery, as demonstrated by its past or present attainment in this respect, then the old and dying districts and collieries, where the cost of production is high, will be supported at the expense of the modern and expanding districts where the cost of production is low." Further in a rejoinder to Lord Joicey,[3] he added that he would like to simplify the distribution and that " the question of distribution of coal is inseparable from that of amalgamation ".

Although the Liberals disagreed with much in the Bill, their support of the Government ultimately enabled the measure to pass. So we shall refer here to our section on the Liberal

---

[1] " The Government's Coal Proposals—the Dear Coal Bill," the *Mining Journal*, 4th January, 1930, p. 7.
[2] 23rd October, 1929, *The Times*.
[3] 30th October, 1929, ibid.

coal policy,[1] in order to recall the Party's chief demands. While they advocated the reorganization of the industry by amalgamating the smaller units, at the same time they were opposed to the increase of costs of production and to higher prices of coal. On the principle of free-trade they objected to a national levy imposed on the home consumer for subsidizing exports of coal. They did not, however, object to the reduction of hours of work. On the whole, they disliked the idea of a compulsory marketing scheme. The establishment of a National Wages Board was one of those provisions which the Liberals could easily accept, since it was already involved in the Samuel Report as an appropriate measure for approaching the labour question in the coal industry. The main body of the Liberals, with Mr. Lloyd George, expressed themselves reluctant to accept the Bill, for the reason that it would create a heavy burden on the coal consumers and that owing to the quota system and to the increase of prices the worst collieries would hamper the development of the best and thus diminish general efficiency. Some Liberals wanted only to force certain amendments to the Bill, which would improve the marketing clauses and provide machinery for compulsory amalgamation and lower costs of production. In contrast to the Liberals, the Conservative Party strongly objected to the whole Bill and presented against it a united and intransigent front.

We see that the chief economic arguments against the Bill were objections to the prospect of the rise of prices and to the impeding influence of quotas on the process of elimination by the industry of its weaker units.

In such conditions, on the 17th December, 1929, only a few days after its introduction, the Bill had to come up for the second reading. The Conservatives decided to propose a straightforward motion for its rejection, whereas the Liberals moved an amendment, opposing the Bill, on the ground that it did nothing towards reduction of costs, hampered efficiency, and gave a vested interest to the inefficient pits. The Liberals, however, admitted that it contained certain good points with which they entirely

[1] Cf. Part II, Chap. II, § 2.

agreed, and for that reason some of them (Mr. Runciman and Sir Donald Maclean) advocated that the Bill should be improved, rather than rejected outright. Voting was somewhat complicated by the fact that a direct rejection of the Bill would lead to a Government crisis, and the Liberals did not want to take the responsibility for causing another general election at that time.

It thus came about that the late Mr. Graham, President of the Board of Trade, had the exacting task of persuading and conciliating Liberal opinion. He had, at the same time, to show himself ready to consider possible future amendments in return for which Liberal assistance could be acquired. The terms of the Liberals were presented in the Commons during the second reading, by Sir Herbert Samuel, who subjected the whole Bill to a very searching scrutiny. He severely condemned the marketing clauses, especially the provisions giving statutory rights to moribund collieries, which would inflate the actual value of those concerns and thus render the progress of amalgamation much more complicated. The idea of a national levy is " an inverted form of protection, which taxed the Briton for the benefit of the foreigner " was also clearly not acceptable to the Party. In the course of his speech Sir Herbert Samuel specified the main conditions of the Liberal support ; they were :—

1. The inclusion in the Bill of compulsory amalgamation ;
2. A provision which would make the marketing scheme only temporary ;
3. Effective control of prices by the Board of Trade ;
4. A fair valuation of moribund mines not based on monopolist computation.

In spite, however, of the extreme opposition of both Conservatives and Liberals, the Bill passed the second reading by a narrow majority of eight votes, due to the abstention of a few Liberal members. This division saved both the Bill and the Government. Henceforward it was clear that the final form of the measure would depend on

B b

Labour-Liberal collaboration. The question raised by the Liberals during the second reading of the Bill did not wait long for a reply, the Government decided to satisfy some of their demands at once as the price of their assistance. Thus, a few days after the division, the Government announced their intention of carrying the Bill further, and agreed to insert clauses dealing with amalgamation of mines, the proper ascertainment of values of undertakings and with a time limit on the operation of the marketing clauses. Moreover, they agreed to take further steps to protect the public from a rise of pit prices, while they proposed that the retail prices should be controlled by the Consumers' Council covering the necessaries of life. This body the Government intended to create in a special Bill independently of the coal legislation.

In this way the path to compromise was very well smoothed out, and the Bill proceeded safely to the Committee stage in the year 1929, notwithstanding the numerous protests from different organizations.[1]

The Government, however, was firmly determined to see the Bill through the Committee stage. In January, 1930, during the recess, international coal affairs in Geneva once again occupied much attention. A few days after the termination of the Geneva coal conference, the Government tabulated their amendments to the coal Bill, which were the outcome of the debate during the second reading, and which met to a large degree the postulates of the Liberal Party :—

[1] Those protests came from such organizations as the Coal Consumers' Committee, representing a certain number of small consumers and trades-men, especially ex-Service men ; the Council of the London Chamber of Commerce, which registered an emphatic remonstrance against the Bill, as well as many coal-consuming industries, which protested against the preposterous attempt to raise the prices of coal. This refers in the first place to the gas and electricity undertakings ; while the Council of the British Engineers' Association objected to the Bill on the ground of State intervention. A strong disapproval of practically all the provisions of the Bill came also from the Association of British Chambers of Commerce. Many of the colliery owners also joined in the chorus of protest. Thus South Wales, Yorkshire, and the Midlands formed temporary *ad hoc* com-mittees of independent coal-owners to rouse public opinion against the Bill. These Committees were chiefly composed of owners who remained outside the district cartel systems, and who presumably would lose their freedom under the new régime.

(I) The first of these strengthened the power of the Committees of investigation, who were now entrusted with making direct representations in the proper quarter when the working of the scheme ran contrary to public interest.

(II) A further amendment created a time limit of three years for the operation of the compulsory marketing arrangements, which had to be concluded by the end of 1933.

(III) But the most important of all the amendments was the formation of the Coal Mines Reorganization Commission, composed of three commissioners, whose duty it would be " to further the reorganization of the coal industry with a view to facilitating the production, supply, and sale, of coal by owners of coal-mines, and for that purpose to promote and assist, by the preparation of schemes and otherwise, their amalgamation ".

The Commission was entitled to prepare and submit to the appropriate bodies schemes of amalgamation or absorption of undertakings, without the consent even of a section of the owners, as had been required by the provisions on amalgamations of the Mining Industry Act, 1926. Moreover, the amendment ordered that a reasonable value should be taken for the purpose of amalgamations.

From this point matters developed very quickly, especially as the Liberal-Labour co-operation was almost established. With the greatest ease the Government succeeded in passing in the Commons the resolution providing financial means for carrying out the work of the Coal Mines Reorganization Commission and of the Committees of Investigation.[1]

The Liberals arranged with the Labour Party that in the procedure of the Committee the marketing clauses, being the most controversial part of the Bill, should be dealt with at the end, after the discussion on the other parts, arguing " first, let the Committee decide whether it is going to put

[1] Coal Mines Bill, 1929, Memorandum on Additional Expenditure likely to be incurred if the Bill is altered in the manner proposed by the Government Amendments of which notice was given on 21st January, 1930 (Cmd. 1476).

fresh burdens upon the mines by the curtailment of hours ; secondly, let it consider how this is to be met ". After securing this order of debate, the Government easily put through the reduction of hours, the Coal Mines National Industrial Board, as well as the Coal Mines Reorganization Committee with a special new clause to make amalgamations compulsory in certain cases. All the measures passed with very few alterations. A significant change accepted by the Government was the provision that in compulsory amalgamation schemes there should be no separation of collieries from their ancillary works, e.g. coke ovens, etc.

The crucial debate came, however, over the question of regulation of output and the marketing scheme. A Liberal amendment proposed to omit the regulation of production. The Government stubbornly opposed this change, which went deep into the root of the whole Bill. After a very energetic defence of the provision by the President of the Board of Trade, the Government won in a critical division by the very small majority of nine. This narrow victory was followed by rapid progress of the Bill in the Committee stage. In spite of a plethora of amendments, chiefly designed to restrict the operation of the marketing scheme, and to exclude from it the vertical combinations, or mixed concerns deriving coal from their own collieries, the Bill passed without important mutilation. There were amendments designed to exempt coal used for iron and steel industries in this country from the working of the quota system, and to exclude export coal from the operation of the Bill. None of them, however, succeeded in commanding a sufficient majority. The only major change in the Bill was the deletion of the central levy scheme for the assistance of the export of coal.

During the last stages of the Committee, a truculent fight arose over the provisions for the compulsory regulation of prices. This last attack on the marketing scheme was well prepared by a fierce campaign on the part of a large section of colliery-owners supported by coal merchants opposing the entire Bill. The majorities of colliery-owners in the districts for and against the Bill were now divided as follows :—

Against the Bill	*For the Bill*
Scotland.	South Yorkshire.
Northumberland.	West Yorkshire.
Durham.	Lancashire and Cheshire.
South Wales.	Derbyshire.
South Staffordshire.	Nottinghamshire.
Warwickshire (part of).	North Staffordshire.
Shropshire.	South Derbyshire.
Somerset.	Leicestershire.
Bristol.	Cannock Chase.
Kent.	Warwickshire (part of).
Cumberland.	Notts and Evewash Valley.
Flintshire.	North Wales.

This division roughly corresponds to the exporting and home-producing districts. The Government, however, made it sufficiently plain that the regulation of prices was essential for the satisfactory working of the marketing scheme. The amendment was defeated, thanks to the Liberals, who abstained from voting owing to their alleged desire not to harass the Government further during the International Naval Conference then in progress. After that division, with a few minor changes in the third reading on the 3rd April, 1930, the Bill was passed by a majority of forty-three.

In the House of Lords, some essential alterations were voted. Besides several drafting amendments, which were accepted by the Government, the Lords brought forward some significant innovations. Notwithstanding the resistance of the Government, they decided that each district was entitled to a minimum allocation, to be fixed after taking into consideration the last ascertained consumption in that district of coal produced therein. This provision was especially important for those areas which possessed a " passive balance of trade in coal " and which consumed actually even more than they could produce, such as South Staffordshire or Lancashire, where practically all the output of the district is consumed on the spot and coal from outside is required in addition. The proposed amendment would mean that these districts would receive a relatively larger proportion of the total allocation than under the original proposals of the Government. The

Lords also added a provision by which any district might make a request to the Central Council for the changing of its allocation in order to meet an increased demand for coal or any class of coal. Another amendment was concerned with the problem of quotas in the vertical combination. This question, so well known in the German cartels, was raised during the committee stage in the Lords by Lord Melchett, who succeeded in excluding coal supplied to associated undertakings from the quota provisions. We may recall that the same question of mixed concerns was, after discussion, voted in the opposite sense by the House of Commons. Furthermore, the Lords deleted the provisions relating to the district levy and the clauses which provided for the nomination of a Coal Mines Reorganization Commission composed of " peripatetic commissioners going round the country and earning their salaries by effecting compulsory amalgamations, whether desirable or not ". The duties of the Reorganization Commission were transferred by the House of Lords to the Board of Trade, with the reservation that the Railway and Canal Commissioners should not sanction a scheme unless they were satisfied that it was in the national interest, that amalgamation would result in lowering the costs of production or disposal of coal, that it would not be financially injurious to any of the undertakings, and that the terms were fair and equitable to all persons affected.

One of the most important amendments voted by the House of Lords dealt with the question of hours. After the passing by the Commons of the fixed reduction of working time by half an hour, the Mining Association invited the officials of the Miners' Federation to discuss the possibility of substituting for the daily curtailment of hours a weekly, or fortnightly method. They proposed to adopt a 90 hour fortnight instead of a rigid $7\frac{1}{2}$ hour day, with the alternative of working either 11 days with one free Saturday every fortnight, or 5 long shifts of 8 hours and one short shift of 5 hours on Saturday. But the owners refrained from giving a definite undertaking that the level of wages would be preserved. In such circumstances the miners refused even to consider these "spread-over" proposals. Nevertheless, in spite of this breakdown of negotiations between the mine-owners and the workers, the Lords carried the amendment facilitating the spread-over of hours. This significant amendment closes the list of changes introduced by the House of Lords. The Bill received its third reading without more alteration, and soon returned to the Commons for further consideration.

The Government, however, resolved to fight to the last ditch and to defend the Bill with determination against any attempt at mutilation. When the measure returned in June to the House of Commons, they restored it to its former state with some minor changes ; the most important being the adoption of the amendment to provide a possibility of revising the district allocations in the case of a suddenly increased demand for coal. All other alterations were rejected by the House. The Bill now entered its final stages before reaching the Statute Book. It had already taken nearly half a year to bring it to this advanced point.

The Lords, however, were not inclined to resign their rights to change the Bill, and in spite of the opinion of the House of Commons they reiterated some of their former amendments. While not rejecting conciliatory measures, they gave way only on the question of amalgamations, but insisted, none the less, that only those schemes should be approved which lowered costs and were not injurious to any undertaking concerned. Moreover, by a great majority, the Lords deleted district levies from the marketing provisions, and finally retained the principle of the spread-over of hours, but in a modified form. Instead of requiring an agreement between owners and men, the amendment now provided that the spread-over would operate by an order of the Board of Trade substituting it for the $7\frac{1}{2}$ hour day. This order could be made only on the application of the parties concerned in any district and its purpose was to guarantee to the miners that the spread-over would be wholly optional and that there would be no coercion by the owners to force the arrangement.

At this juncture only two questions remained to be

finally settled :   the district levy and the spread-over.
Already by their amendment the Lords had greatly eased
the whole position, and they allowed the pendulum to swing
by thus inviting further discussion on the question.   The
position, however, was very delicate.   The Government
had to manœuvre very carefully in order not to wreck the
whole Bill, which as it then stood was of great significance
to the industry.   Compromise was indispensable if the Bill
was to be brought to a successful end.   But, while the miners
refused to concede anything from their half-hour reduction
of working-time, the Upper House was similarly stubborn
on the points of the spread-over and district levy.

When the Bill came back again on the 9th of July, 1930,
to the House of Commons, they rejected the spread-over
proposals once more.   But they showed a more conciliatory
spirit on the district levy and voted a new amendment by
which the district levy proposals did not appear in the
standard scheme designed for a district, and any
Executive Board was only permitted to draft a district
levy scheme with the approval of the Central Council.
Moreover, the consent of the Board of Trade was requisite,
and, as an ultimate measure of control, the two Houses
of Parliament could pronounce their judgment on such
schemes within twenty-five days after any draft order was
laid on the table of either House.

After this decision, the cleavage between the two houses
was only upon the question of hours.   On all other questions
a large measure of agreement had been secured.   But the
Lords, where the coal-owners' interests were represented
very strongly, obstinately insisted on the permissive
spread-over of hours and overwhelmingly voted for
this measure when the Bill came again to the Upper
House.   This strong attitude of the Lords put the
Government in the dilemma of having either to renounce
the Bill altogether, or to give way and come to terms
with the Lords.   In such conditions the Government had
naturally to take account of the opinion of that strong-
hold of obstinacy—the Miners' Federation.   Finally, a face-
saving formula was found, which permitted the reconciliation

of the two conflicting views. The miners agreed to the permissive spread-over of working hours provided that such an arrangement in any district would be subject to approval by the Miners' Federation and the Mining Association. Thus, while the initiative for making such an arrangement would remain with the districts, the Miners' Federation would obtain the legal power to veto any spread-over, in order to guarantee to the miners that their decision would be completely free from coercion. This solution was easily accepted by the House of Commons and the amendment commanded general approval and passed without division in both Houses.

Looking back and summarizing the main changes made in the Bill by Parliament, we notice that most of them were the outcome of the Labour-Liberal coalition and so show a strong Liberal influence. The four chief changes brought about by the House of Commons were :—

1. The creation of the Coal Mines Reorganization Commission ;

2. The imposition of a time limit on the operation of the compulsory marketing provisions ;

3. The strengthening of the Committees of Investigation to control prices ;

4. The exclusion from the Act of provision for a central levy to subsidize exports.

To those changes the House of Lords added two further amendments :—

5. The permissive spread-over of working hours, and

6. The deletion of the provision for district levies from district schemes. If the districts so desired they were allowed, however, to produce schemes for the collection of a levy, after obtaining the consent of official bodies, including Parliament.

On the first day of August, 1930, the Bill received the Royal Assent and thus, after a protracted struggle both between the Government and the House of Commons, and between the two Houses—a struggle which lasted more than half a year and took eighty-eight divisions—the Coal Mines Act, 1930, finally became law.

CHAPTER III

COAL INDUSTRY UNDER THE COAL MINES ACT, 1930

§ 1. CHARACTERISTICS OF THE NEW COAL ORGANIZATION

The new organization of the British coal industry brought about by the Coal Mines Act, 1930, is of primary importance to the development of the industry. All the structural changes which the Act initiated may be divided into two groups, viz. : those which concern the *organization* of production, marketing, and selling of coal, and those which deal with *amalgamations* of mines. The former group is far more important than the latter since it asserts a new principle for the whole industry. The latter only gave legal authorization to already existing tendencies.

The whole scheme regulated production and marketing of coal under Government authority and was based on certain principles which we must now analyse.

The administration of the Central and District Schemes was left to the coal-owners. Both the District and the Central Schemes were to be framed by the industrialists themselves. In fact, all the district cartels but one have been prepared by them, the only exception being Scotland, for which a scheme of district organization had to be imposed by statute at the end of 1930, owing to the unwillingness of the owners to omit from their original project provisions for a compulsory levy scheme, designed to subsidize exports.[1]

[1] The proposed subsidy scheme was constructed in a very ingenious manner, and looked as if it could operate both ways, to benefit exports as well as to benefit the home trade. It was a dual system of subsidies, in which the home market was assisting exports and vice versa. The scheme proposed " to stabilize the difference between export prices and home market prices in such a way that the average price for all coal sold on the home market was always to be 20 per cent above the average price for all coal exported. This is the actual difference in price between home and export coal, which has been found to exist over a long period of time, and it was proposed to make it permanent by means of a price pool. Thus, if the home price proved to be more than 20 per cent above the

Furthermore, all the functions connected with the administration of the new organization were left to the owners themselves, forming a kind of self-government, and the Act provided that the Central Council should be composed of representatives of all the owners of coal-mines in the several districts.[1] This, however, as the High Court of Justice decided, does not amount to saying that the Executive Committee of any district is prevented from electing its representatives to the Central Council. The power of election to that body should be directly open to all coal-owners or their representatives.[2]

It is characteristic of the new coal organization that all authorities controlling and supervising the working of the marketing schemes are located outside their administration and have no direct influence upon their trade policy. This principle is diametrically opposite to the way in which the German coal cartels have been organized. In Germany, the representatives of all interests : owners, miners, consumers, the States, scientists, etc., have seats on the Coal Council and the Coal Union (corresponding to the Central Council in this country), and representatives of the workers sit on the councils of all the eleven district coal syndicates and of the coke syndicate. Professor Macgregor[3] calls attention to this important point of difference :—

> "These [British] Cartels were to be purely owners' administrations. The control of the consumers' and workers' representatives was to come from outside the administrative system by a parallel system of investigating Committees. Any complaint, and therefore any complaint about prices, could by this method reach the Board of Trade. There had to be some system of arbitration as between owners, and a number of details were not filled in, such as the exact relation

export price, owners who had sold coal for land sale would pay the difference (over and above 20 per cent) into the pool, and the funds would be used to make good the deficit to those owners who had sold coal for export. If the difference between inland and export prices was less than 20 per cent those who had sold for export would be required to make good the difference to the owners who had sold on the home market."

[1] Section 2 (1).

[2] High Court of Justice, King's Bench Division, Rex v. President of the Board of Trade, *ex parte* Walton, 13th February, 1931.

[3] Professor D. H. Macgregor, "The Coal Bill and the Cartel," *The Economic Journal*, vol. xl, March, 1930, p. 39.

of the Central Council to the Local Boards. But a great deal was notably omitted in the Bill, which belongs to what in Germany is considered to be an adequate substitute for nationalization, in the way of including within a single system of interlocked administration all the interests which may claim to be represented in the public regulation of an industry."

In appraising this fact one may recall here that the German law regulating the administration of the coal industry [1] originated from the decree concerning nationalization,[2] and was meant to be in some degree a substitute for it. The principle, adopted by the English coal schemes, of pure self-government by the owners resembles the provisions of the Polish Coal Convention,[3] a semi-compulsory organization administered by the representatives of all the three Polish coal basins. The Convention has for its purpose the regulation of output and the control of minimum prices, but does not contain at present any selling syndicate. Both in Great Britain and in Poland the principle of keeping the other interests outside the cartels proper has been consequently preserved. The British system seems to be more efficient than the German, where in theory vast room is reserved to laymen's influence, although in practice all these mixed bodies are merely insignificant accessories and completely superfluous. The best proof of this is that in April, 1933, the membership of the Coal Council in Germany has been reduced from 60 to 32.

One of the striking features of the new organization in the British coal industry is the element of State authority and supervision standing behind all the schemes. The notion of compulsion, and the right to impose penalties upon those who refuse to comply with the new economic order which sometimes is responsible for grotesque situations,[4] forms an essential *novum* in the structure of the industry.

[1] Gesetz über die Regelung der Kohlenwirtschaft.

[2] *Sozialisierungsgesetz*, both decrees of the same date, 23rd March, 1919, published in the Reichsgesetzblatt, 1919, p. 341.

[3] Polska Konwencja Węglowa.

[4] Cf. Case of South Wales District Coal Mines Scheme *v.* Wenallt Colliery, Ltd. before Mr. Justice du Parcq in the King's Bench Division 29th March, 1933, in which a colliery capable of producing more than a thousand tons quarterly was allowed to produce only four tons and was penalized for the excess at the rate of 2s. 6d. per ton.

Though, as we have already noted, the Government remains outside the operation of the schemes, nevertheless it retains an important function. All schemes made by the coal-owners are subject to approval by the Board of Trade, which can also make schemes of its own in certain cases ; all amendments to schemes already in force must also receive its sanction. In addition, the Board of Trade may also appoint members of Central and District Boards if the owners fail to do so[1] ; they may dissolve any scheme which they think prejudicial to the public interest ; they may hold inquiries for the purpose of verifying complaints made by the National or District Committees of Investigation, whose duty it is to examine any complaint made with respect to the operation of the Central and District schemes. The obligatory character of the membership of the owners in all the schemes is emphasized by the fact that subscriptions to the district organizations are regarded as taxation and can therefore be deducted from the assessable profits for income-tax purposes.[2] Under the new regime compulsion has the effect of directing certain economic forces into fresh channels and of creating a certain degree of planned economy, though this is planned by the majority of the owners themselves.

Among other features which distinguish the new coal organization, one notices that it embraces all the enterprises as well as all coal produced in the country. Henceforward nobody will be allowed to remain outside the operation of the marketing scheme. Every coal producer is obliged to comply with the provision of the cartels both in reference to production and to prices. This principle of extending restrictions is consistently carried very far by the Coal

[1] In the Scottish District (Coal Mines) Scheme, 1930, the Executive Board is directly nominated by the Board of Trade. Clause 5 of the Scheme reads : 5 (1) " The Scheme shall be administered by an Executive Board composed of twenty persons nominated from time to time by the Board of Trade in accordance with the provisions of Sub-section (1) of Section (4) of the Act, and the Board of Trade, after consultation with the Associations of Coal Owners for the several areas in Scotland hereby nominate the following persons to be the members of the Board in the first instance that is to say " : (twenty names follow).

[2] *Vide* Case Thomas Merthyr Colliery Co., Ltd. *v.* Davis (Inspector of Taxes) Court of Appeal.

Mines Act, 1930, since it applies to all coal-owners in an equal degree. It is a very " democratic feeling " that the marketing scheme introduces into the industry. All the collieries, in principle, are allowed to work a certain fixed percentage of their actual capacity, and they have, therefore, to be employed at an equal percentage, without further consideration of any economic factors. Otherwise expressed, this means that they are legally prevented from operating full capacity at their discretion.[1] But some mines can easily work comparatively efficiently below capacity and some cannot. The more modern and highly equipped the colliery is the more it operates under the law of decreasing costs and the more prejudicial to its development is work at reduced capacity ; moreover, as we have already noted, the conditions of demand determine the various rates of employment. Such a " democratization " putting these concerns on an equal level with the technically out-of-date collieries, will prove most injurious to them. In fact, however, the Act provides a certain alleviation of this burden upon the better collieries, and introduces a slight departure from the principle of rigid equality by allowing for the transfer of allotted quotas within the districts. The quotas are thus made negotiable commodities within the boundaries of one area, but this can be effected only by adding the price of the quotas to the costs of production.

We have pointed out that all producers are covered by the schemes : similarly the schemes apply also to all coal produced in the country. No description of coal, whatever its destiny, quality, or origin, is exempted from the provisions of compulsory organization. On this principle, coal produced in mixed concerns or for subsidiaries, or for the " mother " undertakings, cannot be excluded from the operation of the general restrictions or given any special preferential treatment. By this provision, the Act has removed one of the chief incentives to vertical combination of undertakings. Hence the mixed concerns severely criticized the Coal Mines Act, 1930, and complained that it rendered their own supplies of coal unduly expensive. We may remember that when the

---

[1] Cf. Part I, Chap. I, and Part II, Chap. II, § 2.

Bill was being discussed in Parliament, the amendment to exclude such coal from restrictions failed to command a majority.

The methods of regulating output and prices distinguish the British coal schemes from several foreign cartels of a compulsory nature. While the control of output has been highly unified, at the same time there may be as many price policies as districts. Actually each Executive Board, which is charged with administering the district scheme, is free to adopt a price policy of its own without regard to the others. The districts are not subject to any central authority in their capacity of price controlling agents. The only requirement which the scheme makes concerning prices is that each district has to fix minimum prices below which the firms will not be allowed to quote. But there is no provision fixing these minimum price schedules and no definite date for their introduction. Thus, for instance, in the first quarters of its operation, the Scottish Executive Board had not imposed minimum price schedules.[1] And again, when in August, 1931, under the pressure of the Central Council, Scotland fixed her minimum prices they were alleged to be so low that the actual dealings were transacted in fact much above those prices. But even then the Midland coal-owners complained strongly against the low minimum prices of sea-borne coal coming from the north.[2]

In this way the minima were in reality without any practical value as real safeguards against inter-district competition. Moreover, the schemes were framed in such a way that it was not necessary to fix prices simultaneously with the restriction of output.[3]

[1] See Report by the Board of Trade under Section 7 of the Act on the Working of Schemes under Part I of the Act during the June and September Quarters, 1931 ; Cmd. 3982.

[2] Cf. Report by the Board of Trade under Section 7 of the Coal Mines Act, 1930, on the Working of Schemes under Part I of the Act during the year 1932. Cmd. 4224, 1932, p. 11.

[3] This principle has been established in the appeal case by the Carriden Coal Co., Ltd., v. the Scottish (Coal Mines) Scheme, 1930. It has been decided by the Sheriff Principal of Lanarkshire, Mr. A. O. M Mackenzie, K.C., that the control of production is the main purpose of the marketing schemes, while the fixation of minimum prices is only its corollary, and therefore must not necessarily be contemporaneous with the former.

The district basis for fixing minima, if carried out, would have one effect only : that of shifting the competitive struggle from individual concerns to district organizations. We agree on this point with the Memorandum [1] of the Miners' Federation, which says :—

" It was felt that, in the absence of an effective co-ordination of prices, the mere fixing of minimum prices on a district basis would tend only to substitute interdistrict competition for individual competition, and in such an event competition within the industry would be more severe than before."

This is the more true if one considers the great ease with which coal from all the districts can reach the competitive Southern area of England either from the North-Eastern or from the Western coal-fields, by sea, by canal, or by rail. Thus, for instance, the Great Western Railway gives a special rebate of 1s. per ton of coal shipped from South Wales by barges through the Brentford and Chelsea Basins for premises on the River Thames.[2] A considerable tonnage of sea-borne coal from the North-East coast enters the port of London for the use of public utility companies, many of which possess their own collier fleets.[3]

In 1923, when coal was demanded for foreign export, 7,225,000 tons or 42·3 per cent was water-borne to London, while 9,855,000 tons or 57·7 per cent was rail-borne ; whereas in 1931 the proportions were almost exactly reversed 10,704,000 tons or 57·21 per cent was water-borne and 8,006,000 tons rail-borne. This acute competition of water-borne with rail-borne coal began first in 1927 and developed under the regime of the voluntary cartel in the Midlands, the Central Collieries Commercial Association. At present, this competition of the districts can only arise under the working of the marketing schemes if the district allocations were not correctly ascertained, and if they greatly exceeded the actual requirements of their own natural markets. Thus we consider that a careful allocation of district maximum tonnages would never lead to a very acute competitive struggle in

[1] Miners' Federation of Great Britain, *Memorandum on Part I of the Coal Mines Act*, 1930, 25th February, 1932, p. 13.
[2] *Vide Collieries and the G.W.R.*, London, 1932, p. 62.
[3] The *Observer*, 16th October, 1932.

the contested areas, but the difficulties of such allocation are practically insurmountable, and very harmful if the long-term aspect is being considered.

On the other hand, it must obviously be admitted that district regulation of prices has two positive advantages over a central regulation of prices : First of all, it allows the efficient and cheaper coals in the long run to establish themselves in the market, thus gradually eliminating the inefficient districts and, secondly, it constitutes a sort of safety valve for the consumer in the short run, if prices are fixed too high, irrespective of comparative costs of production in other districts and other countries. This latter consideration has special bearing as the districts cannot charge differential prices. Otherwise prices in some areas would probably be much higher than in others. In the short history of the new coal organization a case of this sort has already arisen and reached its epilogue before the Courts. The Midland (Amalgamated) District Scheme actually charged higher prices for the Western ports of England than for those on the Eastern coast. Instead of charging one pit-head price for all consumers they fixed differential f.o.b. prices for the same class of coal loaded at different ports ; by doing so they were accused of prejudicing the business of the port of Liverpool.[1] The judgment was definitely against the zoning of prices. But it seems to us that, although the formal zoning system is not allowed by law, nothing should stand in the way of the districts in quoting prices different from pit-head prices, if these are more competitive with the prices of other districts. Moreover, we do not see any reason why the districts should be prohibited from taking into account in their pricing the various features of the demand for coal, which—as already has been shown—are extremely uneven. The scheme generally has not introduced any co-ordination of prices as between the districts, and on this ground it is much criticized in various quarters.

In the whole structure of the marketing scheme, this

[1] Case of the Ocean Steamship Company, Ltd., Liverpool v. the Executive Board and the Central Sale Committee under the Midland (Amalgamated) District (Coal Mines) Scheme, 1930 (*Iron and Coal Trades Review*, 21st October, 1931).

two-deck system of controlling output and prices on different planes emphasizes particularly national regulation, while the district arrangements seem rather to be a safeguard against possible abuse by monopolistic tendencies on the part of coal-owners. The scheme did not even provide the length of the period of district allocation of output, but it soon became the practice of the Central Council to fix a quarterly basis.

This point brings us to the next characteristic of the marketing scheme, which is the large degree of economic planning introduced into the whole administration of the industry. It was now necessary to prepare quarterly plans of production for the future output of coal, and considerable foresight was required from the Committees. A great amount of grading and classification was required in order to prepare district schedules of prices. Some districts had to distinguish a considerable number of grades, sub-grades, and descriptions of coal. Durham alone distinguished fifty-three main classes of coal divided into many sub-classes. Lancashire is alleged to possess a still higher number.

However, though the classification of coal and fixing of minimum prices thereof was left to the discretion of the district boards, no zoning of coal was allowed in the scheme. Coal could be classified either according to its quality or its destination, but not according to the geographical situation of the home market.[1] The real effect of abolishing the zone system of prices was greatly to reduce the power of any efficient or cheap coal-field to sell coal far from its centre, and so to force it to carry on business in its own " natural "

----

[1] Clause 3 (2) f. of the Coal Mines Act, 1930, decided that every district scheme has to provide " for the determination, at such times and for such periods as may be decided in accordance with the provisions of the scheme, of the price below which every class of coal produced in the district may not be sold or supplied by owners of coal mines in the district, and for securing that the actual consideration obtained by the sale or supply of the several classes of coal, exclusive of coal supplied free or at reduced rates for the use of persons who are or have been employed in or about the mine and the dependents of persons who have been so employed, shall not be less in value than the price so determined " : The Board of Trade interpreted this clause in the sense that it did not permit the introduction of zone-prices for the home consumers.

geographical market; for now the price could not vary, according to destination and the distance from the pit, in such a way as to minimize heavy transport charges. Lancashire and several other districts were particularly anxious to preserve the zone system of prices, while Kent was against it, fearing the potential competition of the distant coal-fields.[1]

The Memorandum of the Miners' Federation on the marketing scheme appears to favour the fixing of minimum delivered prices for various classes of coal in pre-arranged zones, but this would require a larger measure of national co-ordination of prices.[2]

A developed system of zoning was also included in the proposals for changing the marketing schemes, and for tightening the whole price regulation which were elaborated by the Central Council and circulated in the districts during the whole of 1932 and the first half of 1933. All this zoning of prices can be compared with the Coal Transport Scheme introduced during the War in July, 1917, which divided the country into areas for the purpose of economy and better organization of rail deliveries.[3]

The quarterly plans of production have not been, however, completely inflexible, nor were they prepared afresh every quarter. We have already referred to the quota selling arrangement which could operate within the boundaries of any one district. By these arrangements the rigidity of individual quotas was to some extent diminished. But as the quotas could not be shifted from one district to another, transfers did prevent the passing of production from one area to another more rapidly developing, e.g. to

[1] See Cmd. 3982, 1931, p. 11.
[2] Loc. cit., p. 14, § 58 : " The Federation feels that in the inland trade, minimum delivered prices should be fixed for various classes of coal in pre-arranged zones, so as to ensure that coal is not sold in any zone below the price fixed for the particular class of coal in that zone. If properly co-ordinated and carried out, this would ensure that, as far as possible, each zone would supply its natural market, and that collieries outside a particular zone would supply that zone only with coal which could not be produced from collieries within the zone. Such a policy would eliminate internal competition, raise the price level of the industry, and retain within the industry large sums which are now paid away in transport charges."
[3] See Sir R. A. S. Redmayne, *The British Coal-Mining Industry during the War*, Oxford, 1923, p. 101.

the Midlands. If transfers of quotas were allowed between district and district, presumably the exporting areas would attempt to buy all home quotas available in order to secure for themselves a better foothold in the home market, which at present is more remunerative than the World market, also the new coal-fields would purchase quotas from those not so efficient. In fact, under the Five Counties Scheme which paid to the exporting collieries a subsidy up to 4s. a ton exported, these collieries proceeded to purchase all available quotas in order to work at a fuller capacity and thus reduce prices.[1]

In addition to the quota-transfer provisions, the scheme contains other means of rendering the restrictions of output less rigid. First, provisions for application to cartel authorities for increase of the allocation, and secondly, the clause [2] of the Central Scheme by which each district is entitled, whenever the period of allocation is less than twelve months, to obtain a figure of output below which the allocation in respect of the remainder of the period of twelve months shall not be fixed, and which shall be lower than the expected output for the period aforesaid. The latter arrangement gave to the districts a sort of guarantee for some continuity of planning, and thus rendered the quarterly plans not entirely independent of one another. Finally there exists a very important provision which helps to render the whole organization more elastic, i.e. amalgamation and adjustment of districts contained in Part II of the Schedule. By the amalgamation of districts, the inconvenience arising out of the prohibition of quota transference from one district to another can be to some extent overcome. At first, comparatively little use was made of all these safety valves in consequence of the falling demand due to the deepening of the economic depression, but several transfers of quotas were effected during 1932. On the whole, though the scheme contains a vast quantity of planning, nevertheless in numerous fields it fails to

---

[1] Information from a paper, " Reorganization of the Coal Industry," by Mr. A. W. Archer, kindly sent to us by the author.
[2] Clause x (2).

bring about a higher degree of co-operation between the component parts which it has created.

Such a lack of closer organization between the districts or between individual colliery undertakings must be explained by the very nature of the marketing scheme as it stands at present. It is chiefly a restrictive scheme. Hence it allows the owners to make constructive arrangements on their own initiative, while it attempts to limit output and maintain prices, enforcing these provisions by means of penalties upon producers. In the scheme there is much room for individual enterprise. Thus, for instance, the owners are entitled to divide any district scheme into sectional blocks, as is the case in the Midlands,[1] where each section receives an aggregate annual sectional standard tonnage, which in turn is divided among members of those sections. The owners may pool their unraised quotas in a " pool tonnage ", from which those desiring to buy additional quotas can do so, and such proceeds are distributed among those who resigned their quotas. Such a clearing house arrangement was successfully introduced in the Midland scheme. In South Wales, even the basic tonnages given to collieries can be sold. This provision was undoubtedly framed with the aim of facilitating amalgamation, and the permanent basic tonnage of a colliery does not cease with the closing of the pits. Similarly, compensation for " compensatable deficiencies ", or unraised quotas of output, worked to induce the mines of South Wales to close (Clause 54 of the Scheme).

The whole marketing scheme leaves ample room for special arrangements enlarging the scope of the statutory organization. Thus private cartels have still plenty of scope beyond the scheme. In the first place they can extend the district minimum prices over the whole country or over a large competing territory. A common arrangement for

---

[1] The London Gazette, published by Authority, No. 33657, p. 6829. The division of a district into sections is admissible by the Act, and falls under the purview of Section 3 (3) (b) which stipulates that a district scheme might provide " for such matters as appear to the Board of Trade to be incidental to, or consequential on ", the provisions of the marketing scheme, " or to be necessary for giving effect to those provisions " (see the case Rex v. President of the Board of Trade, ex parte Walton).

the regulation of home prices made important progress during May, 1931, when ten of the districts, including all those entering into the Midland (Amalgamated) Scheme, adopted a common price basis for all coals except locomotive coal, coal for export, bunker, and coastwise shipments.[1] The arrangement was terminated in 1932 owing to strong competition of other districts.[2]   Another scheme, proposed in West Yorkshire in September, 1933, provided not only for the co-ordination of prices and for the determination of standard conditions of sale, but also for the introduction of a selling agency when agreed by an 85 per cent majority.

The marketing scheme also leaves much scope to enterprises for setting up voluntary arrangements, e.g. levy schemes for subsidizing voluntarily the exports of coal, or to the establishment of closer relations between the producer and the consumer through the institution by the collieries of unified selling and distribution at home and abroad.   Such a plea was recently put in the form of a booklet by Mr. Merrett, a well-known Welsh coal agent, in which he advocated the complete elimination of the " speculative middlemen " on the ground of their alleged inefficiency and action which was contrary to the interests of the industry.[3]   The coal exporters were not long in giving a determined reply [4] to such accusations, clearly demonstrating that Mr. Merrett himself participated in the same practices of selling oil and foreign coal as

[1] The arrangement was entered into by the following districts : Midland (Amalgamated), Cannock Chase, Forest of Dean, Shropshire, Lancashire and Cheshire, North Staffordshire, South Staffordshire, Somerset, Warwickshire, North Wales.   The minimum price adopted was the basic price on 30th April, 1931, fixed at 90 per cent of the average price obtained by each coal-owner for his various classes of coal in the period of twelve months ending 30th June, 1930, plus a flat rate increase of 1s. per ton for all classes of coal to which the agreement applied (with the exception of coking slack for metallurgical purposes, the basic price of which is subject to a deduction of 1s. per ton) and the following further increase for :—
(a) Coal for gas making and Public Utility undertakings, 1s. 6d. per ton.
(b) Coal for other industrial purposes, 1s. per ton.
See : Mines Department, Coal Mines Act, 1930.   The working of Schemes under Part I of the Act during the March quarter, 1931, Cmd. 3905, p. 11.
[2] *Vide* Cmd. 4224, 1932, p. 10.
[3] *I Fight for Coal*, London, 1932.
[4] *We Fight for Facts*, a reply to Mr. Merrett's book *I Fight for Coal*, issued by the British Coal Exporters' Federation, London, 1932.

themselves. Moreover, they refused to take any responsibility for the diminution in the coal exports which are due to a falling demand. In this latter argument we consider the exporters to be fully justified, since in fact it is the economic and financial depression which is the real cause of the fall in exports, while Mr. Merrett seems to concede it as a rather secondary cause of the decrease in demand.[1] Attempts to eliminate or to limit the freedom of the exporters and middlemen to play one colliery against another, when the supplies are very abundant, have already been undertaken by the coal-owner in the past. Thus, the Central Commercial Collieries Association made an agreement with the Humber and Mersey exporters to sell their coal on fixed percentage commission. This agreement was observed so long as the export subsidy was paid and thus it prevented the exporters from absorbing the amount of the subsidy into their profits. But soon in view of the falling prices the exporters demanded the power to sell coal at their own risk, without fixed profits. So we see that the commission base of selling coal is not novel in the practice of the industry and in the past has not proved able to withstand the all-powerful economic force of falling prices. Either prices or sales were bound to collapse.

To pass now to other arguments raised against the new compulsory organization of the British coal industry, it has been very often attacked on the ground that it does not secure a sufficient measure of co-operation, and that it does not contain enough positive injunctions. The lack of co-ordination of prices between the districts which were thus still free to undersell each other has evoked many protests against district regulation of prices. Some critics would like to see the industry completely controlling distribution with a syndicate on the model of the Westphalian Coal Syndicate and thus removing every vestige of competition. " Syndication on the lines of the Westphalian Coal Syndicate," says Mr. Smart,[2] is the soundest method of securing a fair proportion of the fruits of

[1] Loc. cit., p. 17.
[2] R. C. Smart, " The State and the Mining Industry," *Fortnightly Review*, 2nd March, 1931, p. 392.

the industry to the producer, etc . . . " He also urges the creation of a united front in the export trade, in order to avoid unnecessary and ruinous competition. A similar scheme of district selling with a central co-ordination of prices was recently suggested by Mr. Nicholson,[1] and a specially strong plea for the co-ordination of prices on a national basis was put forward by the Miners in their Memoranda,[2] and by Mr. Archer in *The Times*.[3] Some writers wanted to create, behind the compulsory schemes, spheres of influence confined to individual districts and undertakings. Mr. G. D. H. Cole [4] discussing the Coal Mines Bill in the *Political Quarterly*, like Mr. Smart, would favour an "organization whose business it will be actually to sell coal", and he would wish to see an application of State authority in that direction as close as possible to nationalization. Professor Macgregor, who regretted that the Coal Mines Act, 1930, did not create an administrative unity in the coal industry such as exists in Germany but instead "doubled the organization by putting watching Committees outside ",[5] goes even further and wants to institute a "managed coal industry" and other industries, which, like the "managed" currency, should be used to abate and prevent the recurrence of . . . . . the trade cycle.[6]

[1] Godfrey Nicholson, " Coal : the Immediate Future," in the *Nineteenth Century*, vol. cxii, p. 438.

[2] Memorandum on Part I of the Coal Mines Act, 1930, *The Case for Coal Trade Regulation*, issued in February, 1932, and *The Plea for Unity in the Coal Trade*, November, 1932.

[3] A. W. Archer, " The Mining Code in U.S.A." *The Times*, 8th August, 1933.

[4] G. D. H. Cole, " The Problem of the Mines," the *Political Quarterly*, January, 1930, p. 60 : " Personally, I should strongly urge reorganization broadly along the lines advocated by Sir Arthur Duckham in 1919—that is to say complete amalgamation of all the collieries in each coalfield, subject to certain very special exceptions, into a single unified concern embracing good and bad pits alike. These amalgamated concerns would clearly need to be subject to some measure of public control, as Sir Arthur Duckham himself suggested. Their position would be broadly analogous to that of the railway companies since their compulsory amalgamation into groups under the Railway Act of 1921."

[5] Professor D. H. Macgregor, " Problems of Rationalization : A Discussion," *Economic Journal*, vol. xl, No. 59, Sept., 1930.

[6] *Idem*, " Salvage of the Slump—Moving Towards Control of the Trade Cycle," Annual Review the *Manchester Guardian Commercial*, 29th January, 1931, pp. 22-3.

Among those who favour closer co-operation for better marketing of coal is Professor J. H. Jones,[1] who maintains that in reorganizing the industry too much stress has been laid on the cheapening of the processes of production, while the revenue side was ignored. He thinks that authorities ought to concentrate on the revenue side and create machinery for the purpose of improving the revenue of the industry, and so they would facilitate the introduction of better methods of production and distribution, and reduction of costs. Some of the active industrialists advanced even more comprehensive proposals for co-ordination, which ultimately result in the scrapping of a good number of inefficient units. Thus Mr. Merrett, in his publication,[2] repeating the plea for unified selling, advocated compulsory scrapping of inefficient mines by buying up and closing down. Roughly speaking, all these various plans wished to base co-operation on a central fund collected out of a small levy on all output. The central fund would be used for buying out and closing down for ever the most inefficient mines. Similar co-operative organizations created by a wide branch of industry to eliminate the moribund units were already operating in several industries : shipbuilding (National Shipbuilders Security, Ltd.),[3] flour-milling (Millers' Mutual

---

[1] Professor J. H. Jones, " The Coal Problem," the *Accountant*, 14th September, 1929, p. 323.

[2] H. H. Merrett, *I Fight for Coal*, London, 1932. We read there : " I thus definitely advocate the creation of a compensation fund within the South Wales Coalfield, believing that by central selling and distribution this fund can be raised by increased realization upon our products. I would deduct from the price obtained for all coals sold a fixed amount per ton, and for the purpose of giving a clearer view of my ideas I would fix this amount at 1s. per ton upon all coal sent inland and 6d. per ton upon coal exported . . ." (p. 64) : " I would . . . adopt the same lines as are laid down by Act of Parliament in connection with amalgamation. To a colliery able to prove it was handicapped by a neighbouring mine producing similar coal at higher cost I would give an opportunity of appealing to the Tribunal for the closing down of this adjacent mine, and compel its owners to accept such compensation as expert examination found to be equitable to all interested parties " (p. 67).

[3] The National Shipbuilders Security, Ltd., was formed in 1930 by the shipbuilding companies in order to eliminate the redundant yards. In the course of its activity the company purchased and closed down a number of shipyards. This institution was greatly assisted financially by the Bankers' Industrial Development Company. In January, 1931, the N.S.S.L. issued 5 per cent obligations to the total amount of £1 million

Association) [1] ; the compensating arrangements for the reduction of the excessive number of licensed houses ; the recently-formed organization for closing down of redundant plants in the woolcombing industry (The Woolcombers' Mutual Association, Ltd.) [2] ; and others. In the American section of the Lancashire cotton-spinning industry, also, a detailed scheme for dealing with redundant machinery was being debated by a joint committee of cotton trade organizations. In the coal industry, however, enormous difficulties would block the way to such a reform. As we have already shown it is nearly impossible to define what is to be regarded as excessive capacity and what constitutes normal capacity ; furthermore, neither the size alone, nor the age of the colliery alone, are sufficient criteria for determining the degree of efficiency. Moreover, the proportion of inefficient collieries, though greatly diminished since the War, is still very high, and hence their buying up, if possible, as suggested, out of the levy collected by the industry would greatly add to the price of coal just in times when cheap supply is most desirable. A scheme like this has been initiated in September, 1933, by the West Yorkshire coal-owners. Special levies had to be collected for the purpose of (1) closing down any selected coal mines temporarily or permanently, (2) purchasing mines by the members of the scheme. This scheme which required the approval of the Railway and Canal Commission

for furthering the scrapping of superfluous plants. From its foundation up to May, 1932, the company has dismantled a total of 82 building berths with a total annual capacity of nearly 600,000 tons, spread equally over England and Scotland.

[1] The Millers' Mutual Association was formed in 1929 by a large number of flour millers, with the object of purchasing and dismantling the inefficient, or badly situated mills. The surplus capacity of the milling industry was estimated to be about 20 per cent. During its existence the M.M.A. bought up and closed a large number of undertakings.

[2] The Association was incorporated on 21st February, 1933, as a public company for the main purpose of assisting the Lancashire woolcombing industry by the purchase and dismantling of redundant and obsolete mills and plants, the disposal of the same, and the resale of the mills or the sites thereof under condition against further use for woolcombing. The company does not work for profit. Altogether twenty-six firms representing 90 per cent of the industry, took part in the formation of the Association the share capital of which amounts to £10,000. Early in April the Association issued £346,000 of 5 per cent debenture placed privately, and began its operation at once.

failed to command a sufficient majority required by the Act. The same scheme proposed a co-ordination of marketing; and a central purchase of stores and supplies.

Among other characteristics of the organization of the British coal industry under the statute we noted its very great complexity. The Coal Mines Act, 1930, was the result of such a multitude of divergent political and economic views that they all not unnaturally left their marks on it; indeed, the organization created by the Act has to serve a great variety of ends and combine them all. It regulates the production, sale, and marketing of coal; it interferes with the working time; it calls into existence consumers' protection; it gives power to the Mining Association of Great Britain and to the Miners' Federation to perform the purely official duties of approving the fortnightly schemes of the distribution of hours of work, and reserves an official veto to those bodies, as well as a statutory sanction without which the arrangement is legally void; it establishes a machinery for joint inquiry into the disputes between labour and capital. Throughout the whole structure it is easy to observe the distinct influences of politics, economics, social reform, and technical rationalization.

Further, we must note a remarkable feature of the new coal organization in the introduction, alongside of State supervision, of another system of control by mixed committees of investigation, half of the membership of which is composed of consumers. Their purpose is to notify the Board of Trade of anything which, from the point of view of the community, might be undesirable. Since the coal cartel is enforced, and since it is guarded against the working of certain economic forces which otherwise provide natural safety valves, the Board of Trade needs such a channel of information. The committees of investigation are formed parallel to those bodies which regulate production and price, i.e. together they compose a double organization of which one section concerns itself with national problems, and all others are related to particular areas. There is, however, little connection between the committees of investigation; they all act in absolute independence of one another and they communicate only with the Board of Trade. The national investigation committee deals only with the Central Council.

The new regime was initially introduced as a compulsory measure for a limited time only, to operate for little more than two years. Part I of the Coal Mines Act, 1930, was to continue in force until the end of 1932, unless Parliament otherwise determined. After the expiration of the appointed time, it has already been renewed for a further period of five years by the Coal Mines Act, 1932. This temporary nature of the organization gives it also the significance of a protective measure, since it safeguards the public against possible exploitation, and reminds the undertakings to improve their position so as to be in readiness should the State remove compulsory membership of the Schemes.

Finally, in describing the new structure of the coal-mining industry, it is impossible to pass over in silence the complete lack of any regulations referring to distribution. The Labour Government then (1930) in power had clearly in view the enormous disparity between the rise in retail coal prices to about 100 per cent above the pre-War level, and the rise of pit-head prices equal to about 27 per cent. Nevertheless there were no provisions for the reorganization of this section of the trade in the marketing scheme. The measure was a purely industrial reform. The President of the Board of Trade announced during the third reading of the Bill that this question, urgent though it was, must be treated separately.

Epitomizing the review of the new marketing organization introduced by the Coal Mines Act, 1930, we perceive the following features :—

1. The whole administration of the scheme is left to the colliery owners, and in principle no outside element is made responsible for the conduct of the industry ;

2. The element of State authority and compulsion, however, enters on several occasions into this organization ;

3. The system is extended to cover all the enterprises producing coal in Great Britain, as well as all coals extracted ;

4. Production is controlled on a national scale, while prices are regulated only on a district basis ;

5. A large amount of economic planning has been introduced, though in several respects the Act fails to achieve a high degree of co-ordination.

6. Apart from its restrictive nature, the new organization does not provide for any special institutions or settlements facilitating the production, or marketing, of coal ; all such are left to the optional decision of the coal-owners. Wide room for individual arrangements is thus reserved to their initiative.

7. The system created by the Act is a medley of politics, economics, social theory, etc.

8. A safeguard is provided in the interest of consumers.

9. The new organization of the industry introduced by the Act is limited in time. It is to be enforced only for a definite period.

10. The problem of organizing the distribution of coal has not been included.

The Coal Mines Act, 1930, was not only responsible for creating a compulsory marketing scheme in the form of a national cartel, but it provided also potential machinery for the rationalization of the industry through *amalgamation* and reduction of costs.

Those provisions of the Act dealing with the reconstruction of the industry are not *sensu stricto* actual reorganization : they only prepare an instrument for carrying it out. Practice has shown, however, that the enormous steam-hammer erected by the Act for the purpose of refashioning the whole industry has in reality not even succeeded in breaking a nut. Part II of the Act, engendered from purely political demand, and foreign to the industry, called into being a permanent Coal Mines Reorganization Commission, with the duty of promoting and assisting, by the preparation and launching of schemes and by other means, reorganizations and amalgamations within the industry. The chief difference, therefore, between reorganization as proposed under the Coal Mines Act, 1930, and as instituted by the

Mining Industry Act, 1926,[1] is that the later Act provided a special body for the promotion of reconstruction, while the earlier consistently left the first initiative to the coal-owners. The liberty to produce reconstruction schemes, without considering the opinion of the industrial leaders themselves as to their desirability and soundness, may easily result in somewhat fantastic plans of amalgamating the units on the basis of purely accidental criteria, such as mere geographical distribution of mining resources. This was enforced without deeper consideration of all economic factors, in the case of Leicestershire, even without a *prima facie* case showing the advantage accruing from amalgamation and the satisfaction of the four conditions prescribed by law [2] under which amalgamations can be enforced. Those conditions are that the amalgamation must (1) be in the national interest; (2) lower costs; (3) be fair to all; (4) not be financially injurious to anybody. Artificially created units, as foreign practice shows, in the long run usually do not survive ; in order to do so they require permanent assistance from outside.

At this moment it is difficult to predict the real effects of the activity of the costly Coal Mines Reorganization Commission, especially in view of the fact that their work continues without visible progress and can under the circumstances hardly be expected to advance. We may, however, say definitely that the less there is of artificial combination, the less of the doctrinaire and the more of the purely commercial and economic calculation,[3] the

---

[1] See Part II, Chap. I, § 3.

[2] *Vide* the protest by Leicestershire colliery owners in the *Iron and Coal Trades Review*, 7th July, 1933, p. 4.

[3] Professor Dron called attention to this point after quoting the advantages which may accrue to the companies from the grouping of their undertakings, he warns us that : " Undoubtedly there may be advantages obtained in certain circumstances by the amalgamation of colliery interests. On the other hand, instances might be quoted where decentralization of ownership and control have been advantageous. In each instance the whole facts of the case must be reviewed in detail, and a decision come to on these facts and not on generalizations. . . . One conclusion which may be stated with safety is that the most economic output for any given unit of production is the largest output which may be obtained subject to the limitations imposed by physical and marketing conditions. Any attempt to go beyond these limitations leads to irregularity of output, with a resulting increase of costs and possibly a decrease in average selling

surer and quicker will be the process of recovery in the industry. A similar opinion was authoritatively pronounced by the venerable Professor Henry Louis, who expressed the most positive view that " it must be emphasized that both the laying-in and the amalgamation should be left to the industry itself, and not placed in the hands of a Parliamentary Commission on which political considerations would prevail, possibly to the entire exclusion of economic realities ".[1]

In spite, however, of all these sagacious warnings the Reorganization Commission, in their zest for amalgamation, have gone so far as to devise units on an enormous scale. After a visit to the districts and a superficial study of the intricacies of the various undertakings, the myrmidons of reorganization came to the conclusion, in spite of the view of all experienced industrialists, that vast amalgamations should be enforced. *Ut aliquid fecisse videatur*, they issued in summer, 1931, a memorandum on colliery amalgamations [2] in which, after having expatiated

price of coal " (Robert W. Dron, the *Economics of Coal Mining*, London, 1928, p. 118).

[1] Professor Henry Louis, " The Coal Industry : the Reconstruction," published with *The Times Trade and Engineering Supplement*, 7th May, 1932.

[2] Coal Mines Reorganization Commission, *Memorandum on Colliery Amalgamation*, July, 1931. The relevant passage on page 5 reads : " If the advantages of amalgamation are what the Commission thinks them to be, it follows that, other things being equal, the larger the size of the unit the greater will be the benefits that amalgamation can bring. There is, too, to be remembered that the fewer the hands that control the industry, the better will it be placed for competing with foreign rivals or for negotiating agreements with them, if that should prove the wiser course. It will perhaps be said that other things are not all equal, and that beyond a certain size a unit becomes unmanageable. That may be so, but the functions that would properly be performed by the directorate of a great amalgamated concern must not be confused with the functions of technical management. Unless those in control realize what can be centralized and what must be decentralized, amalgamations are likely to lead to a last state that is worse than the first. In technical management there is, no doubt, a very definite limit to the practicable size of a single unit. But that has nothing to do with the size of the unit of direction. This latter may, for the purposes of technical management, contain many units, each practically autonomous. The task of the central directorate would be to determine where the coal for which there is a demand can be produced, what further development of the coalfield is required, and how and where it shall be undertaken—to control sales and any other activity that conveniently admits of centralization (as, for instance, wagons, research, and the treatment of coal), and to regulate the financial position

on the advantages accruing from amalgamation, they explained their views on the subject, and mentioned large natural groupings within the boundaries of the six coal districts as their ultimate goal.   In view, however, of a very strong criticism of such a stereotyped organization, the Commission issued, in June, 1932, another supplementary memorandum in which they carefully deny having any desire of making " a fetish of mere size " and in which they express the view that voluntary amalgamation on a valuation of profits basis is the ideal aim.[1]

As it could easily be foreseen, the crop reaped by the Commission so far is very small.   During the first year of their activity only one small amalgamation was completed and two more were discussed before the Railway and Canal Commission.[2]   During 1932 no more had been achieved. Three collieries in North Staffordshire, the Chatterley-Whitfield Collieries, Ltd., the Norton and Biddulph Collieries, Ltd., and the Sneyd Collieries, Ltd., controlling together

and policy of the undertaking. The Vereinigte Stahlwerke A.-G. in Germany controls an annual output of 35,000,000 tons.

The Commission therefore contemplates, as the ultimate goal of a policy of amalgamation, that the country should be divided up into geographical units, in each of which there should be only one colliery undertaking.   It is not supposed that this can everywhere be reached in one stride.   It may well be, for instance, that certain undertakings now in existence are not worth bringing into any amalgamated concern.   Again, it might sometimes prove wise to begin with amalgamation in smaller units as a step towards the combination of these into larger ones.   And it is recognized that, if the policy of amalgamation is to reap its full advantages and the proposal to nationalize royalties is not carried out, it may eventually be found necessary to impose some statutory restraint on the freedom of royalty owners to dispose of their property as they please.

If the industry be looked at in its largest possible national groupings, it is found to consist of the following :—

Scotland—(Ayr, Lanark, Fife, Lothians).
North-east (Northumberland, Durham).
North-west—(Lancashire and Cheshire).
East Midlands —(West Yorkshire, South Yorkshire, Nottinghamshire, Derbyshire).
Central Midlands—(North Staffordshire, South Staffordshire and Cannock Chase, Shropshire, Warwickshire, South Derbyshire, Leicester-shire).
South Wales and Monmouth.
Outside these are six small coalfields that do not fall so naturally within any grouping.   They are the Forest of Dean, Bristol, Somerset, Kent, Cumberland, and North Wales."   (*Vide* Appendix D.)

[1] Coal Mines Reorganization Commission, Suppl. Notes on the application of Part II of the Coal Mines Act, 1930, 9th June, 1932.
[2] *Hansard*, 1st December, 1931.

about 1·5 million tons, formed an organization for the joint selling of their fuel.[1] The largest effort, however, namely an attempt to bring about complete amalgamation of all collieries in Lancashire, which are more homogeneous than in any other district, failed dismally owing to the opposition of the better concerns, which refused to run the risk of jeopardizing their position by taking over and financing the less prosperous collieries.

Towards the close of 1932 the Reorganization Commission determined to keep "the weapon of compulsion in its sheath no longer",[2] and decided to break down the isolation of the coal-owners. At the end of November they urged the Eastern district and the Midlothian, the Forest of Dean, the St. Helens area of Lancashire and the North Wales coal-owners to have their undertakings valued by independent accountants for the purpose of providing necessary data forming the basis for future amalgamations. At the same time they requested all Fife coal-owners to submit a scheme for general amalgamation and only a few days later the same request was sent to the owners of Cannock Chase, while early in January, 1933, South Derby and Leicestershire were asked to prepare schemes for their districts. All these requests, however, met immediately with adamant opposition and no district submitted a scheme. In Fifeshire the Wemyss Coal Co., Ltd., issued a circular strongly protesting against the action of the Coal Reorganization Commission.[3] In Cannock Chase, eleven collieries out of the thirteen which had to be amalgamated opposed it tooth and nail.[4] Despite this hostile reception, in June, 1933, the Commission began to valuate the mines on their own account, but in this work they had to meet a terrific opposition from the coal-owners. The coal-owners contended that any shareholder of forcibly amalgamated units has the right to ask to be paid out and so in this way they jeopardized the whole action.[5] In Leicestershire the owners of six companies

[1] *The Times*, 4th August, 1932.
[2] Pronouncement by Sir Ernest Gowers, Chairman of the Coal Reorganization Commission to the Cardiff Business Club on 24th February, 1933.
[3] *Vide Iron and Coal Trades Review*, 16th December, 1932.
[4] *Vide* Parliamentary Debates, House of Commons, 29th June, 1933.
[5] Cf. the *Manchester Guardian Commercial*, 11th February, 1933, vol. xxvi, No. 660, p. 102.

went even so far as to refuse outright to provide the Commission with the necessary information. The President of the Commission threatened to report the matter to the High Court [1] and only after long persuasion was information supplied. No more successful were the attempts of wholesale reorganization in Warwickshire where the Commission met again with flat refusal. No result was achieved in Nottingham and North Derbyshire, nor in Durham where partial " amalgamation " of the whole district was pressed by the Commission. All these defeats did not discourage the Commission and in December, 1933, they decided to take steps for a " new deal " in enforcing in West Yorkshire a partial amalgamation on the lines of the unsuccessful West Yorkshire scheme. The Commission requested also the owners from Durham, South Yorkshire and Nottingham and North Derbyshire to prepare schemes of partial amalgamation.

In summing up the real significance of this attempt to force purely artificial reorganization from political considerations, one cannot refrain from admitting that it has proved a dismal failure. The two years of experience since the institution of the whole machinery have proved clearly enough that compulsory experiments must fail unless they are the spontaneous product of the industry itself.[2]

Having thus outlined the chief characteristics of the new coal organization in the light of the first three years of its existence, we pass now to discuss the operation of the marketing scheme in practice.

§2. THE NEW COAL ORGANIZATION ON TRIAL

The changes brought about by the Coal Mines Act, 1930, called for a great deal of readjustment in the industry. Not all the districts had had experience of conducting their

---

[1] *Vide* the *Iron and Coal Trades Review*, 7th July, 1933, vol. cxxvii.

[2] How far this proposition holds good can be easily judged by the fate of another institution imposed upon the industry by politics—the Coal Mines National Industrial Board, which since the very start was incapable of successful operation owing to the refusal of the coal-owners to co-operate in it.

economic activities under regulation of prices and output, and for those districts the new coal organization meant a transition to completely unfamiliar conditions. They had to work out afresh the framework in which to carry on production henceforward. Even for those districts which previously had restricted and regulated output, the scheme meant the adaptation of their methods to the new requirements of the Act.

As we know, it was intended that the reorganization of marketing should be carried out some months before the cutting down of the working time in the mines, so as to consolidate the industry beforehand and thus prepare it to endure the increase of costs of production caused by the change in labour costs. The Board of Trade, which was in charge of the preparation of the central and district schemes, invited the owners to submit their draft schemes for approval in the middle of September, 1930. But by that time, though two months had already elapsed since the Act was signed, no scheme has yet been presented, nor was any scheme anything like ready for submission. Moreover, some districts obstinately insisted on the introduction of provisions which were clearly incompatible with the positive ruling of the Act. Not until the end of October, 1930, were the schemes for the national and district administration completed by the districts and approved by the Board of Trade. The only district which did not elaborate its own scheme was Scotland, where the owners could not agree upon the controversial question of a levy for subsidizing exports of coal. For that reason, the Scottish District Coal Mines Scheme was not yet ready when all others came into operation and the Board of Trade found itself finally obliged to make a scheme of its own.[1]

Immediately after the formal adoption of the general framework for the whole organization, the industry began work on the individual provisions of the central and district regulations. This, however, took so long, that before the new machinery was set in motion the date [2] arrived for the half-hour reduction in working time. This brought

---

[1] The Scheme was published on 24th November, 1930.
[2] 1st December, 1930.

further serious complications ; and Scotland, South Wales, and Bristol, suffered from severe strikes.

The Coal Mines National Industrial Board, created by the Act expressly to inquire into disputes as to wages and other conditions of labour between owners and workers and to report thereon, encountered ill-success from the very beginning. It was not able to remove the imminent danger of labour troubles. Failure was chiefly due to the refusal of employers to appoint their representatives to the Board. All the coal-owners declined to acknowledge the Board as a National body with the right to intervene in the district regulation of labour problems on the ground that the situation could not be met adequately from any central organization owing to the vast disparity of conditions between one district and another.

Owing to the boycott of this institution by the Mining Association, the Federation of British Industries, the Association of British Chambers of Commerce, and the National Confederation of Employers' Organizations, all of which were entitled by the Act to send their own delegates to the Board, its potential conciliatory merit could not be revealed. Confronted with such a flat refusal of co-operation, the President of the Board of Trade was obliged to chose other suitable members to fill the employers' posts on the Board. But this unexpected torpedoing by the owners greatly retarded the functioning of the National Industrial Board, which held its first meeting only a few days before the date of the reduction of working hours. The insufficient time did not allow the Board to investigate individual grievances in full, and they limited themselves to issuing some few general recommendations which failed to persuade the disputing parties or to stop the strike. The owners formally refused to acknowledge the ruling of the Board and its capacity to interfere with wages. On the other hand, the miners exerted all possible pressure on the Government to strengthen the Board and to bring about some kind of national negotiation. The principle of national regulation of wages was partially achieved by the miners in the Coal Mines Act, 1931, which was passed hurriedly by Parliament in July to prolong the $7\frac{1}{2}$ hours day for one more year, and at the same time to stabilize the existing minimum wages all over the country for a period of one year.

The question of national regulation, and consequently of the National Industrial Board, soon came up again however. Long discussions between the owners and the miners were held in the spring of 1932 with the hope of finding a *modus vivendi* when the Act regulating wages and hours should come to an end on the 8th July, 1932, but they brought no practical result. In June, a labour crisis was barely averted on the definite promise of the coal-owners to the Board of Trade that the existing wages would not be altered for a period of twelve months, and on the assurance of Mr. Runciman and Mr. Foot (President of the Board of Trade and the Secretary for Mines) that they would attempt to persuade the coal-owners to collaborate with the National Industrial Board and that the British Government should try to secure the ratification of the International Draft Convention reducing the hours of work in the mines by fifteen minutes. The last two points, however, were never realized and the miners a few months later again came forward with a strong claim for a national system of negotiation in the industry. In an appeal issued by the Miners' Federation [1] at the end of October, 1932, the miners argued that as " the level of wages in any district is not the concern of that district alone, but vitally affects the other districts " and since the industry is nationally organized " the natural corollary of the arrangements under Part I of the Coal Mines Act " should be a machinery for national negotiation of wages. Similar demands were made several times during 1933. The owners, however, refused to acknowledge this line of reasoning and continued to oppose it strongly.

On the other hand the colliery owners, while refusing in labour matters to give their assistance in fulfilling Part IV of the Coal Mines Act, 1930, on the whole collaborated very loyally with the Board of Trade in setting in motion the complicated and heavy mechanism of the national cartel. With a few exceptions or additions all the schemes were their genuine product. We shall now try to

[1] *The Times*, 29th October, 1932.

sketch in brief the chief features of the whole contrivance for regulating output and prices of British coal as it worked in practice.

Only a very extensive administrative apparatus could evolve such colossal machinery. At the head of the whole system stands the *Central Council*,[1] which is responsible for the national regulation of production. This body consists of representatives of colliery owners from all the districts, who are also members of their respective District Executive Boards. They can be either elected by all the owners, or appointed by the district Executive Boards.[2] Each district has a minimum of one representative, but is also entitled to one additional delegate for every $7\frac{1}{2}$ million tons of annual output (Cl. IV, 1). Membership of the Central Council thus proceeds on a combined principle : representation of the districts and of the proportion of annual tonnage produced in each district. In this way certain anomalies which would otherwise have occurred are eliminated, e.g. Cumberland with its annual output of about 600,000 tons would have been equally represented in the Council with South Wales having approximately seventy times as large a production. The rules applying to voting at the meetings of the Council allot to each member one voice ; in the case of a poll, however, each district is entitled to one vote for every ton of its annual output.

The chief duty of the Council is the allocation from time to time of fixed amounts of district maximum output ("district allocations"). Before fixing the maximum output the Council is obliged to request each district to submit its own estimate of the tonnage which its members can reasonably expect to dispose of during the coming period. When determining the district allocations, the Council must have regard to all relevant circumstances affecting the several districts, not excluding their relative position before the War (Cl. X, 7). Among the chief facts which the Council must certainly take into account is whether the district is a young

---

[1] *Vide* the *London Gazette*, 24th October, 1930, No. 3655.

[2] *Vide* decision of the High Court of Justice, King's Bench Division, Rex *v*. President of the Board of Trade, *ex parte* Walton, 13th February, 1931.

and developing one, or whether its production is already tending to diminish. Mere rule of thumb cannot be applied in either of these cases and, apart from the present position, the time element and the dynamic factor must both be introduced into the economics of regulation of production. Further, we must remember that certain districts, especially those associated in the Central Collieries Commercial Association voluntarily reduced their output during 1928 and 1929, in order to diminish competition. It would thus be prejudicial to them if they were treated on equal terms with those districts which continued to work without any restrictions whatever. As a general rule, however, the Central Council based its allocation policy on applying a fixed percentage ratio to output in a past period.[1]

In any period of allocation the districts may apply to the Central Council to have their allocations raised if they can prove that the demand for coal or for any special description of coal has increased (Cl. X, 10). During the first three years of the scheme relatively few applications were made under this clause. The most important was an early application of the Midland district, which, however, was refused by the Central Council because of the opposition of other districts, which suffered from the price cutting policy of the Midlands.[2] When in September, 1931, Great Britain abandoned the Gold Standard, and the exporting districts expected to increase their sales, the Central Council immediately granted additional allocations to South Wales, Durham, and Northumberland. During the June quarter of 1932 several districts, chiefly producing for home trade, received higher allocations, the majority of which were not utilized.

Considerable additional allocations were made in December quarter of 1932, but only in five cases was the decision of the Central Council referred to arbitration.

This larger number of additional allocations was due to the new practice of the Central Council, introduced towards the end of 1932. In order to prevent complaints of the

[1] Cf. Coal Mines Act, 1930, the Working of the Schemes under Part I of the Act during the year 1932, Cmd. 4224, 1932, p. 6.
[2] *Vide* Coal Mines Act, 1930, the Working of the Schemes under Part I of the Act during the March quarter, 1931, Cmd. 3905, p. 5.

districts against the allocations to Scotland and Northumberland, which were alleged to be too generous, the Central Council allocated to each district a certain minimum tonnage based on the results during the corresponding period in the preceding year. Under this system the district had to apply for the supplementary allocation in the course of the period of allocation. Needless to say this correction of the methods of allocation was a further hindrance to the reduction of costs of production and to the supply of cheap coal in the South of England.

In the June quarter of 1933, some of the exporting districts received larger allocations in anticipation of better foreign trade following the conclusion of commercial agreements with the Scandinavian and Baltic countries.

Similarly, considerable additional allocations were made in the September quarter of 1933. In Scotland the output quota was raised in July by 500,000 tons, i.e. by 6 per cent. bringing the total amount to 75 per cent of " standard ", and again in September by 325,000 tons to 80 per cent of standard. In Northumberland and Durham output quotas were increased in the September period by 300,000 tons and 250,000 respectively, and later by a further 300,000 tons for Northumberland and 350,000 tons for Durham. The Midland quota was also raised from $50\frac{1}{2}$ per cent to 55 per cent for the September quarter 1933. All these increases were necessitated by an acute shortage of certain brands of coal, especially of steam coal of smaller description, and bunker coal, which was the result of the operation of the marketing clauses of the Act, which had disequilibrated the balance between supplies of different types of coal.

In only a few cases did the districts appeal to arbitration against the allocation by the Central Council. During 1932, North Staffordshire, which in the September quarter produced 25,000 tons in excess of its allocation, demanded an additional allocation of 35,000 tons. However, this was not granted. Another case is that of Kent, which received an increased tonnage for the March quarter of 1932, but demanded a still larger allocation on account of its development. Half of this, amounting to 20,000 tons, was granted by arbitration.   Kent often had to appeal against the decisions of the Central Council.[1]

In order to facilitate the conclusion of contracts in advance the Council will, whenever the period of allocation is less than a year, fix a minimum figure of output below which the district allocation will not sink (Cl. X, 2). Such an arrangement permits a large degree of continuity in production and greatly facilitates planning ahead. The districts are not allowed, however, under any circumstances to transfer their allocations to other districts (Cl. XI, 2), to carry them over to the next period (Cl. XI, 3), nor to exceed their allocations, in which case they are fined at the rate of 2s. 6d. per ton of such excess output. Such fines are paid into the central fund (Cl. XI, 1) instituted to receive all payments made to the Central Council (Cl. VIII, 2). If there is an excess of money over current expenditure in the fund which is derived from the above-mentioned penalties and other contributions, then the outstanding credit may be distributed among the districts in proportions decided by the Council (Cl. VIII, 3).

Among its secondary duties the Council has to consider the operation of the schemes in the districts and to advise them with a view to co-ordinating their activities (Cl. XIV) ; but in this respect it has no power to enforce its decisions. So far little has been achieved in this field.

The most difficult task in the new organization is left to the *district cartels*, which have to re-distribute among the colliery undertakings the district allocations obtained from the Central Council, and further to classify all coals extracted, and to fix minimum prices for each variety. Originally the Coal Mines Act, 1930, created 21 districts,[2] but gave them the right to amalgamate for the purpose of making common schemes.   Thus five districts, those

[1] Cf. Cmd. 4224, 1932.

[2] Those districts were: Northumberland, Durham, Cumberland, Lancashire and Cheshire, Yorkshire, Derbyshire (exclusive of South Derbyshire), South Derbyshire, Nottinghamshire, Leicestershire, Shropshire, North Staffordshire, South Staffordshire (exclusive of Cannock Chase) and Worcestershire, Cannock Chase, Warwickshire, Forest of Dean, Bristol, Somerset, Kent, North Wales, South Wales (excluding Monmouthshire), Scotland.

of Yorkshire, Derbyshire (exclusive of South Derbyshire), South Derbyshire, Nottinghamshire, and Leicestershire, amalgamated into one called the Midland (Amalgamated) District (Coal Mines) Scheme, 1930. Those five districts formerly belonged to the Central Collieries Commercial Association together with Lancashire and Cheshire, North Staffordshire, Cannock Chase, and Warwickshire. But the last four found it more convenient to form separate schemes than to join the Midlands. Owing to the dovetailing of five districts and to the covering of such a vast area, the Midland Scheme obtained the power to manipulate the quotas on a very wide scale, and consequently to transfer them within a vast territory and over a large tonnage. This is an important advantage for the district in view of the fact that the Coal Mines Act, 1930, does not allow the transfer of quotas from one district into another. Hence the Midlands arrangement allows a more liberal disposal of the " unraised shortages " quotas. Through the formation of the Midland Amalgamated Scheme the total number of twenty-one districts prescribed by the Act has been in fact reduced to seventeen.

All the district schemes closely resemble one another in their constitution, probably because they were all modelled chiefly on the South Wales pattern. Indeed only the Midland and South Wales districts have made somewhat more complex statutes, apparently for the reason that they were already fully conversant with regulation of production some time before compulsory cartelization was inaugurated by the Government.

The chief characteristics of the district schemes are to be found in :—

(1) The classification of coal produced ;

(2) The determination of standard tonnages for every mine in the district ;

(3) Fixing of the proportion of the standard tonnage (or quota) above which no mine is entitled to raise its production.

(4) The determination of mimimum prices for various

kinds of coal below which no undertaking is permitted to sell its coal ;

(5) The penal provisions for breaking any of the restrictive regulations ;

(6) Machinery for arbitration in case of conflicts ;

(7) The executive mechanism which runs the various schemes.

(1) In most of the districts coal is classified by the Executive Boards, which have in this respect full authority to act according to their discretion.[1]

In a few districts it can also be classified by some special *ad hoc* body, the decisions of which are afterwards approved by the Executive Board. This method has been adopted by Lancashire and Cheshire (Cl. 30, 31), where a special Sales Committee appointed by the Board carries out the classification, which thereafter must be approved by the Board. The Sales Committee is entitled to appoint sub-committees to deal with any class of coal, or with any other matters within the province of the Sales Committee. So far all classification must be approved by the Board.

Only in the Midland district, which is constructed on a federal basis and comprises five distinct territorial sections, corresponding to the five amalgamated districts, is the classification carried on by the Central Sales Committee (Cl. 3), advised by the Sectional Sales Committee. The latter recommend to the former the class to which any coal produced in their section should belong for any purpose. The Sectional Committees are composed of representatives of all owners in any Section, and each Committee appoints one representative and one additional representative for every 5 million tons of total output to the Central Sales Committee (Schd. 4, 6).

In no district are the coal classifying authorities bound as to the method by which they carry out their work. Only the South Wales and Midland districts have inserted in their

[1] Thus in Cannock Chase, Scotland, North Staffordshire, Durham, Bristol, Somerset, Northumberland, Cumberland, North Wales, Warwickshire, Shropshire, Forest of Dean (Cl. 36), South Staffordshire and Worcestershire, Kent (Cl. 28), and South Wales (Cl. 8), coal is classified only by the Executive Boards.

schemes provisions, embracing certain types of coal which in any case must be treated separately. Thus, in South Wales, anthracite, Swansea steam coal, and all other classes of coal must be treated separately and have their own standard tonnages (Cl. 10, 11), while the Midland Scheme distinguishes a separate coking standard tonnage and a general standard tonnage. These two tonnages together, form the monthly standard tonnage (Cl. 15, (7)).

Gradually, however, a general principle for classifying coal met with wide approval as the schemes came into full operation. This principle permitted differentiation according to the following criteria, first the values of the coal ; secondly the trade, industry, or other category of consumer supplied ; and finally the home demand and the foreign shipments.[1] Such a division excluded any differential treatment according to the location of the consumer, i.e. the zoning of the markets, which was also opposed by the policy of the Board of Trade in their capacity of supervisory body over the scheme. In certain cases differential treatment was allowed even between the different industries, for instance the arbitrators' award in North Staffordshire permitted the distinction between potters' fuel and industrial fuel. Some of the more ardent protagonists of compulsory marketing schemes would like to see a complete division of the market, coupled with a full system of zoning. Among the chief advocates of this plan is the Miners' Federation, which has expressed its view on the future working of the Coal Mines Act, 1930, in a special Memorandum.[2]

(2) Like the method of classification, determination of the standard tonnage of each mine for all or any special kind

[1] See judgment of Mr. Justice Maugham, Chancery Division, Attorney General v. Wright.

The Court decided that it is not permissible to " classify coal except according to the nature or kind of coal, the trade, industry, or other category of consumer for whom coal is supplied, or whether it is supplied for use in this country or for export abroad, to treat as different categories of consumers persons of the same trade or industry merely by reason of their being situated, or taking delivery of coal, at different places " (Cmd. 4224, 1932).

[2] Memorandum on Part I of the Coal Mines Act, 1930. The case for Coal Trade Regulation, 25th February, 1932, p. 58.

of coal is also carried out in most districts by the Executive Boards. Lancashire, which in this respect resembles the Midlands district and for some years co-operated with it in a voluntary arrangement, adopted in its scheme a Standard Tonnage Committee appointed by the Executive Board to advise it on all points arising in relation to the determination of a standard tonnage. This acts, however, purely in an advisory capacity and the Board ultimately decides the standard tonnages. Contrary to all other schemes the Midland, which alone is built on a federal basis, leaves little room for the Executive Board in fixing the standard tonnages, both sectional and individual. It entrusts the duty of settling the standard tonnages to a Standard Tonnage Committee consisting of one representative from each section and one additional representative in respect of every 10 million tons of the annual standard tonnage of the section (Cl. 15, (1) (c)). We may point out in this connection that the Midlands scheme, as a consequence of its federal principle, has a two-decked standard ; an aggregate annual sectional standard tonnage for the sections, and an individual one for each mine. The existence of separate sectional standard tonnages for each of the five associated districts caused some friction during the first year of their operation, which had to be settled by arbitration. The developing district of South Yorkshire put out a claim for a revised sectional tonnage. But under the scheme the owners in any section could not obtain any increase of their individual standard tonnage without injuring other owners at the same time, since the general sectional standard was fixed and could not be freely increased. All such difficulties prejudicial to modern undertakings led to an amendment of the scheme providing that each year the adjustment of the section standard tonnage can be decided by arbitration.[1]

But even with this improvement the scheme did not work quite smoothly and two further difficulties soon emerged. First the question whether the annual standard tonnage might be freely changed at any time, or whether

[1] Eleventh Annual Report of the Secretary for Mines and the Annual Report of H.M. Chief Inspector of Mines.

once fixed the tonnage should remain unchanged in the future. This question came before the Court and a middle course was adopted, namely that " until circumstances changed or other circumstances warranted a change, a mine was to have the standard tonnage as awarded ".[1] The second question was whether all increase in the aggregate annual sectional standard tonnage should be divided among all the non-special coal mines in the section. This important question arose in Derbyshire and Nottinghamshire, when these sections received in 1932 an additional tonnage of 335,000 tons from the Midland Board and refused to divide it among all collieries in the section. The Court, however, decided that the scheme (Cl. 15, 8 (c)) was clear on this point and all mines should participate in the increase, but not necessarily in equal proportions.[2]

Different plans have been adopted by other districts for arriving at the standard tonnage. First, some districts possess fixed and others variable standards. Secondly, the districts differ as to the basis of computation. Some of them allow the owners to choose a relatively long time on which to base their standard, some permit only a short period, and some others do not leave any choice but simply prescribe which period is to be taken.

The majority of the districts, however, assess the standard tonnage as an invariable quantity, but Scotland has a changeable standard fixed from time to time by the Executive Board. (Cl. 28). Most of the central districts have taken a long period as the basis of the computation. Thus Cannock Chase, Lancashire, and Cheshire, and the Midland Scheme have adopted the average production of the years 1923, 1924, 1925, and 1927, as their standard tonnages. Apparently the traditions of the Five Counties Scheme, that the choice of the " basic tonnage " out of the fifteen years ending the 31st December, 1927, should be left to each member were still very strong and influenced them considerably.

---

[1] *Vide* King's Bench Division, New Hucknall Colliery Co., Ltd. *v.* Standard Tonnage Committee and Midland Executive Board (8th May, 1933).
[2] Ibid.

Some districts base their calculation on the result of a single year or even on shorter periods.[1]

In many districts, besides a yearly standard tonnage a monthly standard is also provided.

In fixing the annual standard, however, all districts have regard both to the past circumstances determining a certain output of coal during the prescribed period and also to the special circumstances of each mine, including the efficiency, the degree to which it has been developed for working coal, and the extent to which production is increasing or declining.

Recent practice in the working of the district cartels has proved that, in some cases, it is advantageous to divide the yearly standard tonnages into unequal parts during the different seasons of the year. And thus under the amended Warwick District Scheme [2] every owner may choose how he may desire the monthly or quarterly proportion of his standard tonnage to be distributed in the forthcoming year, subject to adjustment by the Executive Board (Cl. 8/VIII). This new provision permits the colliery undertakings to avoid rigidity by spreading their output over a whole year. After the end of the year the owners are free to divide the standard differently, but they are not allowed to introduce alterations during the current year.

In some districts the standard can be reviewed either at undefined times—as in Cannock Chase, Cumberland (Cl. 29) ; North Wales, Warwickshire (Cl. 8), Midland (Cl. 15 (b))—or they are officially revised at determined periods as in South

---

[1] Somerset, North Staffordshire, North Wales, and Warwick based their calculations on 1927 ; Shropshire on the year ending June, 1930 ; Forest of Dean on the year 1929. South Staffordshire permits the choice of any twelve successive months between the beginning of 1927 and July, 1930, or of the months of March, 1929 or 1930, in which case it takes the multiplier $\frac{300}{26}$ (Cl. 40 (a) b). South Wales bases the calculation on any one quarter between the 1st January, 1927, and June 30th, 1928, or on the month of March, 1929. In the former case the result must be reduced by 10 per cent, while in the latter it has to be multiplied by $\frac{75}{26}$ (Cl. 9). Durham and Cumberland ground their calculation only on a particular half-year, while Durham goes still further and takes only the last quarter of 1929 as its basis.

[2] In force since 1st November, 1932.

Wales, where this takes place every two years, and in the meantime they remain fixed. In South Staffordshire and Worcestershire, and in the Midlands, in principle, the standard is invariable, but can be revised for every developing or decaying mine. Most of the schemes contain a provision which assists amalgamation and permits the aggregate tonnage of the two or more merged undertakings to be treated in the same way as if the standard tonnage so constituted were the standard of the combined undertakings ; the same applies in the case where an undertaking absorbs only a part of another one. The Midland Scheme carries this principle still further and, in the case of the purchase of a colliery situated in another section, allows the standard tonnage to be transferred to the disposal of the purchasing undertaking, the approval of the Standard Committee being necessary (Cl. 15 (8) (*d*)). In the South Wales scheme there is a very interesting clause allowing, under certain conditions, the transfer of the standard tonnage of a coal mine which permanently closes down (Cl. 15). This measure was designed to assist the scrapping of redundant collieries.

(3) In all districts, the quotas of production, or the permitted percentages of the standard tonnages, are decided by the Executive Boards. The Midland is the only exception where a Special Quota Committee, constituted in the manner of the Standard Tonnage Committee, is entrusted with the duty of fixing the quotas. In most cases the quotas are determined for a period of three months in advance [1] ; the South Staffordshire and Worcestershire Scheme does not prescribe the length of the quota period, but leaves the decision to the Board (Cl. 46 (3)) ; Northumberland (Cl. 42 (2)) and South Wales (Cl. 19) have yearly quotas ; with the reservation in the latter district that the quota should be divided between each quarter of the year as equally as possible with regard to the number of working days in each. The Midland Scheme has separate monthly quotas (Cl. 16 (*d*)) for coking coal and other coals

---

[1] Cf. the case Executive Board of the Midland (Amalgamated) District (Coal Mines) Scheme, 1930, *v.* Shipley Collieries, Ltd., before the Court of Appeal, 24th May, 1933.

and such other kinds of coal as may be decided by the Quota Committee. Certain districts provide that provisional quotas may be fixed whenever the period of allocation is less than twelve months ; such provisions, whose purpose is to facilitate long-term contracts, are found in Bristol (Cl. 30 (2)), Somerset (Cl. 33 (3)), North Wales (Cl. 41 (3)), and other schemes. Under the new Warwickshire Scheme the Executive Board can withhold a part of the district allocation in its determination of quota according to immediate prospects of trade ; a similar policy has been also followed in the Midland scheme, where considerable tonnage has been withheld by the District Executive Board.

As to intertemporal transfer, some schemes do not allow the carrying forward of quotas.[1] Other districts allow the carry forward of quotas unconditionally within a quarter of allocation from month to month up to 50 per cent of the whole amount of unraised shortage.[2]

All the schemes possess clauses which permit the owners to transfer their quotas to other coal-owners, provided that the Board is notified of such transfers. A permanent acquisition of quotas is, however, not allowed ; nor can there be any transfer from one class of coal to another for which separate quotas are fixed. During the working of the schemes some use has been made of the provision allowing for the transfer of quotas. Several such transfers took place either without charge or at charges ranging from a few pence per ton up to 1s. 6d. (in Scotland). Such transactions chiefly occurred in the exporting districts, where the general allocation was in excess of the demand and some of the collieries had free quotas to sell, while at the same time the exporting collieries desired to get a share in

---

[1] Cannock Chase (Cl. 48) : Lancashire and Cheshire (Cl. 50), Bristol (Cl. 32) ; Somerset (Cl. 35), Somerset (Cl. 35) ; Cumberland, North Wales (Cl. 43) ; South Staffordshire and Worcestershire (Cl. 48).

[2] Northumberland Cl. 48, Cumberland Cl. 33 ; North Wales Cl. 43 ; Shropshire, Forest of Dean, Cl. 48. In Durham (Cl. 46 (2)) and South Wales (Cl. 21) the carrying forward can be affected only after communication with the Executive Boards ; in the Midland Scheme 50 per cent of unraised shortages can be carried forward after notification to the Quota Committee (Cl. 16 (h)). In the amended Warwick Scheme any owner is entitled to carry forward his shortage within a quota period which may not exceed three months (Cl. 9 (ix)).

the home sales.   Thus in South Wales in the December quarter, 1931, when the collieries had sold their allowed output, 108 transfers were executed, involving a tonnage of 700,000 tons.   In Fifeshire, where many collieries exhausted their quotas in the winter of 1931, a certain number of purchases were reported at 1s. 6d. per ton.   A certain number of transfers also took place in Northumberland in the autumn of 1931.

While in several export districts (Northumberland, Durham, Warwickshire, Cannock Chase, Bristol, South Wales, and Scotland) the transfers of quota were arranged directly between owners, sometimes at a price touching 1s. 6d. per ton ; in other districts they were carried on by the Executive Boards.   In Lancashire a special voluntary scheme was set up in March, 1931, whereby, on or about the 21st of each month, any owner who anticipated that owing to breakdown, short time, or other reasons, he would have surplus unworked quotas at the end of the month should notify the Executive Board.   This surplus quota is then distributed *pro rata* before the end of the month in question among those firms who apply for additional quotas, the recipients paying 6d. per ton to those who have surrendered their quota.

In Shropshire, Somerset, North Staffordshire, and Kent, somewhat similar arrangements have been introduced. In South Staffordshire the maximum price for the quota has been fixed at 9d. per ton.   The Midland Scheme created in its area a special pool for unraised shortages to co-operate with buyers and sellers of quotas in the district.[1]

All these transfers, however, have had very little effect in concentrating production on the best mines and their significance should not be overrated.   In July, 1933, a private Bill was introduced with a view to fixing the maximum price for transfers at 6d. a ton.[2]

(4) Turning to the fixing of minimum prices, below which the owners are not allowed to sell coal, we see that in the majority of the districts this duty has been reserved

[1] For more details see Parliamentary Debates, House of Commons, 1932–3, vol. 278, pp. 204–6.
[2] Bill 158, 20th July, 1933.   Coal Mines Act, 1930 (Amendment).

to the Executive Boards alone.   In some districts, however, though the Boards actually fix the minima, these are previously submitted by advisory bodies such as the Group Committees in South Wales, whose business it is to advise the Board as to the minimum prices for the class of coal produced by the particular group (Cl. 26 and 29) ; or the Sales Committee in the Lancashire and Cheshire district (Cl. 30 (1) (*b*)), which is charged with the preparation of all the minimum price schedules.   In the Midlands, as in Lancashire, the same body which classifies the coal also prepares the price list. Thus the Central Sales Committee decides the minimum prices after the Sectional Committees have submitted their proposals.   In practically all the schemes the prices for shipment are calculated f.o.b., while other prices are either pithead prices, or delivered prices, etc.

It must, however, be remembered that the price fixing authorities in the districts can be, to some extent, restricted by voluntary arrangements entered into with a view to co-ordinating prices co-operatively between several districts. In fact in May, 1931, ten of the central districts accepted for some time a common price basis for certain types of coal. A further restriction on the freedom of fixing minimum prices is the fact that there must be only one price for the same kind of coal.   In this connection an interesting case arose in Northumberland and Durham, where there exists a disparity of $1\frac{1}{2}d$. between the Tyne export dues and the Wear export dues, and consequently trade was diverted from the Tyne to the Wear.   After a long discussion and investigation the Durham Executive Committee ordered in July, 1932, an extra compensatory charge of $1\frac{1}{2}d$. per ton at pit on all coal shipped at Sunderland.   This charge, however, which infringed the principle of one price for one kind of coal had to be abandoned in October, 1932, as the result of the decision of Mr. Justice Maugham.[1]   The same decision, however, left to the Executive Boards the right of quoting minimum prices at pithead, or f.o.b. at their own discretion.   In September, 1933, a final agreement was reached by which the collieries shipping from the Tyne

[1] Cf. Case **Attorney General** *v.* **Wright.**

were allowed to pay Tyne export dues out of their minimum prices and the Durham scheme amended respectively.

The fixation of minimum prices in the districts was probably the most restrictive element of all introduced by the compulsory cartelization. Thus, it is not astonishing that considerable evasion of the minimum prices must have taken place. Some of these evasions are enumerated by official reports on the working of the Coal Mines Act, 1930.[1] All of them can be divided into two groups : those infringing the letter of the Act and those infringing the spirit. The former includes the fixing of a deliberately low level in order to undercut another district, this being done with the approval of the local Executive Board ; the latter includes operation through selling agencies connected with the collieries. Several such agencies, called trading companies, have been formed especially in the Midlands, where they often buy coal from their associated collieries above the fixed minimum prices, enter it in their books and then sell coal below their own fictitious costs much cheaper to the consumers, or coal factors, and thus they evade the Act and show fictitious book losses. Very often under these arrangements large coal factors now buy their coal from these trading companies, which are especially helpful to collieries wherever the interdistrict competition is keen. Other methods of evading the minimum prices which occurred from time to time, especially in Durham, Northumberland, and Scotland, include the sale of coal at the price of a lower quality, selling coal for export, which is resold after some time in Britain, or selling coal at fixed price but charging a fictitious freight and so on.

(5) All the district schemes imposed heavy penalization for trespassing the main provisions. For exceeding the maximum allowed output, or for selling below the minimum district prices, the coal owners are liable to pay a fine which in most cases amounts to 2s. 6d. or 3s. per ton. In the Warwickshire district scheme, the lowering of prices has been

[1] *Vide* Cmd. 4224, 1932.

as heavily penalized as 4s. per ton. On the other hand, the Midland Scheme grants immunity to those who exceed the permitted tonnage by no more than 1 per cent. Besides these penalties, however, the schemes contain others to be exacted from those who fail to observe the administrative provisions, such as orders for furnishing returns or information, etc., to the Board. The first case of this sort was tried in November, 1932, at Cardiff, where the owner of a small mine was punished for failing to make returns for one quarter.[1] In some districts, in addition to the monetary penalty, any owner exceeding his quota may, at the discretion of the Board, be punished by a reduction of his quota for the next period of allocation by the amount of his excess.[2]

In the Durham district where the evasion of price regulations was practised very extensively, an amendment to the scheme stated explicitly that the Board can prescribe conditions of sale, whether coal is supplied directly by the owners, through agents, or through any subsidiary company. Moreover different illicit practices have been enumerated explicitly and each subjected to a penalty of 2s. 6d. per ton so disposed.[3]

All penalties go to the district fund. Out of the credit outstanding in the district fund compensation is usually distributed periodically between the members of the scheme in two ways ; it is divided either in proportion to the standard tonnage of each of them, or according to the payments made by each owner to the fund. This latter method, however, is less common ; it is practised in Lancashire and Cheshire, in Shropshire (Cl. 84) and in Cumberland—but only in reference to those credits arising out of the revenues from levies paid by each member for the purpose of defraying the costs of the administration of the scheme—while the

---

[1] Executive Board of the South Wales District Coal Mines Scheme v. Thompson.

[2] Bristol (Cl. 56), Somerset, Northumberland (Cl. 78), North Wales, Forest of Dean (Cl. 77), South Staffordshire and Worcestershire (Cl. 76), South Wales (Cl. 43 (1)), Warwickshire (Cl. 21 (l)).

[3] The Durham District (Coal Mines) Scheme, 1930. Amendment, 1st August, 1933.

credit balance accruing from penalties paid is distributed *pro rata* to the standard tonnages (Cl. 56). South Wales has invented a very ingenious plan by which it compensates out of the credits those owners who had a deficiency in production below the allotted quota (compensatable deficiency), provided however that such a compensation should not be higher in any circumstances than 2s. for every ton (Cl. 54) and that the deficiency was not caused by strikes, accidents, or breakage of machinery, and that it did not exceed 10 per cent of the total allocation.

(6) Provisions appertaining to arbitration in the case of differences were included in all the district schemes. The Midland Scheme makes several allusions to arbitration.

(7) All the schemes provide for the creation of an executive to administer the district cartels. This work is done by the Executive Boards acting on behalf of the coal-owners in the districts. All members of the Boards are either elected by the majority of the coal-owners, or in some smaller districts, appointed by each of them separately. The number of members varies from district to district,[1] from five in Shropshire to thirty-six in South Wales. In the Shropshire district all the owners with an output of less than 20,000 tons a year have a right to elect together one member, while the larger producers send four representatives to the Board (Cl. 5 (1)). In those district cartels where the members of the Board are appointed, each owner can appoint either one or more delegates.[2]

Not all the schemes admit representatives only on the basis of tonnage, but also on the number of shafts, or in proportion to the number of votes obtained. Geographical considerations play a great part in some schemes. Thus

[1] Lancashire and Cheshire has 21 members on the Executive Board, Cannock Chase 16, Durham 20, North Staffordshire 18, Northumberland 15, North Wales 15, Shropshire 5, Forest of Dean 15, South Staffordshire and Worcestershire 9, South Wales 36, Scotland 20.

[2] In Cumberland and Warwickshire each owner has a single representative, while in Kent and Bristol he has more than one. But in Somerset each owner has the right to send one representative for each shaft from which coal is being raised.

Scotland [1] has an arrangement in the Board which keeps the proportion between the four areas represented, viz. Lanarkshire, Fife, the Lothians, and Ayrshire, equal to $9:5:3:3$. The Midland Scheme, which is a federation between five territorial sections, possesses a system of indirect elections to the Executive Board through sectional organizations. Each section is entitled to one member and one additional member for each 5 million tons of output, and in any case to not less than two representatives. This sectional principle is also clearly present in the Midland Scheme in connection with the election of representatives of the District to the Central Council, who are elected at sectional meetings. Each section has the right to elect a number of representatives for the area from the members of the Executive Board or its officers (Cl. 9 (g)). Apart from district authorities the Midland Scheme has also sectional secretaries, who keep records of proceedings at sectional meetings of the owners.

This Scheme has also erected complicated machinery to assist its members in all commercial functions connected with the compulsory cartel. For the exporting interests it has called into being an Export Committee whose duties shall be : to confer with British coal exporters, representatives of other districts, and other bodies about export affairs, also to discuss with foreign coal producers and importers matters connected with overseas trade, to circulate to the coal-owners reliable information and statistics referring to export trade, and to establish a Shipping Bureau to act on behalf of coal-owners in the export markets, etc. (Cl. 17 (i)).

The District Boards can perform all their duties in their own capacity or they may appoint special committees

---

[1] Section 6 of the Scottish District (Coal Mines) Scheme, 1930, Statutory Rules and Orders, 1930, No. $\frac{921}{\text{S.52}}$ says: " Any casual vacancy occurring on the Board may be filled by a person nominated by the Board of Trade, after consultation with the Association of Coal-owners concerned, in such manner as shall maintain the proportionate representation of areas as aforesaid, and the Board of Trade may from time to time recall the nomination of any member or substitute member of the Board and nominate after consultation as aforesaid another person in his place."

and sub-committees (Kent, South Wales, Bristol). At the general meetings, in nearly all the schemes, besides voting by show of hands, there is a poll, at which each member is entitled to one vote plus an additional vote for a fixed number of tons of his standard tonnage. In Warwickshire and in Kent each ton of coal entitles the owner to one vote.

The machinery controlling the operation of the schemes in the districts, especially the control of prices, is extremely simple. Some of the districts have appointed auditors to examine the books of the coal-owners, inspectors to visit colliery sidings, or other supervisory measures. Thus, for instance, in Shropshire " since the commencement of minimum prices, the Executive Board made an arrangement whereby the accountants made periodical visits to all owners for the purpose of verifying the prices fixed." [1] In the amended Durham Scheme special inspectors are appointed by the Board to inspect the sales of coal and the ships or wagons used for coal transport.

We have now completed a short review of the way in which coal mining has adapted its architecture to the requirements of the Statute. While the readjustment of labour problems to fit the Act has caused some trouble, the cartelization of the industry has proceeded on the whole without great friction. The passing from one regime to another has taken place on the whole very smoothly, which goes to prove that a great part of the industry was already ripe for a national reform of some kind.

The regulation of prices, however, has caused a certain amount of difficulty, chiefly owing to lack of co-ordination and simultaneous action in all the districts, and in view of the fact that prices during 1930–33 in the exporting districts were generally lower than in 1929, while prices for home coal were either higher or remained the same. Hence the exporting districts all the time tended to undercut the home areas. In fact, as is officially stated,[2] " the determination of minimum prices proved to be an even longer process [than the regulation of output],[3] and only in a few

---

[1] Cmd. 4224, 1932, p. 11.
[2] Mines Department, Coal Mines Act, 1930, the working of Schemes under Part I of the Act during the March quarter, 1931, Cmd. 3905, 1931.
[3] The words in brackets are added by the Author.

districts were minimum price schedules operative during the first quarter of this year [1931]." Price cutting went on still, even under the regulation of output, which in practice did not prove a very restrictive measure since nearly all the district allocations were in excess of the actual output; in some districts as much as 12 per cent (Durham) in 1931, and 10 per cent for the whole country during 1932.[1] As we have already pointed out elsewhere, certain districts fixed their minimum prices much below the actual prices, thus leaving for their members a wide margin for reducing prices. By this method Scotland succeeded in taking a certain proportion of business from the Midlands by sending coal to Lancashire and to the South Coast. This interdistrict rivalry, which in our view was vitally necessary in order to keep up the level of efficiency between the various enterprises, caused many people to ask for a statutory co-ordination of prices and for other measures which would reduce still further the freedom of determining prices by the colliery units, and which would be guilty of further divorcing costs of production and efficiency from the price quotations.

During nearly the whole of 1932 and 1933, the Central Council discussed a scheme for co-ordination of minimum prices, as well as the various schemes for zoning of prices demanded by the miners. Moreover the question of a levy on coal to subsidize export was widely ventilated and strongly supported by the Yorkshire coal exporters who were competing with Polish coal in Scandinavia; but great opposition was raised by the home producing districts. Owing to a diversity of views, no amendments dealing with the fixation of minimum prices have been included in the Coal Mines Act, 1932, which prolongs for five more years the compulsory marketing scheme. The initiative in this matter was left to the districts. In October and November, 1932, an elaborate scheme for the co-ordination of prices was circulated in the coal-fields, but no agreement was

[1] Cf. Report by the Board of Trade under Section 7 of the Act (1930) on the Working of Schemes under Part I of the Act during the year 1932, Cmd. 4224, p. 5. "Indeed, in the March and September quarters it would appear that many districts were virtually freed from regulation of output by the Central Council."

reached on this subject, owing to the great importance which some districts, especially those exporting, attached to freedom of price determination. Moreover, some districts like Scotland and South Wales were, by large majorities, altogether against any compulsory regulation of production. In this they were supported by a considerable number of coal-owners from other districts. Again, in October, 1933, another scheme for export pools and for the co-ordination of prices was put forward by the Central Council. Its chief aim was to give additional export allocations to the exporting districts but exclusively for foreign shipments. The scheme was rejected by those producers who could not compete with the cheaper districts which would be thus left free to expand. On the whole home districts objected to the idea of export pools and suggested complete separation of home and foreign allocations.

In appraising the general effect of the " unco-ordination " of district prices on a national scale, we must note that in this way the competition between the districts as a whole has been preserved and the more efficient areas were given a fair chance gradually to eliminate the less efficient. The framework however did not allow the individual collieries to prove their efficiency since minimum prices were fixed on a district basis. The importance of inter-district competition only became acute through the too optimistic allocation of district tonnages. In order to produce the whole of the permitted allocation, districts had recourse to price reductions which came as a corollary of the deepening economic depression ; export pools would increase this competition still more. One must, however, realize that if the permitted tonnages of output were tightly trimmed to the demand there would be in fact no room for interdistrict competition.

This brings us back to a short investigation of the tonnage restriction policy of the Central Council and to a comparison of the allocated output with the actual demand. During the first years of the operation of the marketing scheme the Central Council on the whole overrated the prospective foreign demand, which fell substantially below expectations, owing to the foreign restrictions on imports, to various import duties, or to differential railway rates operating in France, Germany, Belgium, Poland, Spain, Portugal, and Italy,[1] as well as to other causes such as severe foreign competition in the free markets and the general fall of demand for coal.

For the first year of the operation of the schemes the Central Council fixed the total country allocation as below :

1st quarter $= \dfrac{90}{100}$ of 1st quarter of 1930.

2nd quarter $= \dfrac{\text{2nd and 3rd}}{2}$ quarter of 1930.

3rd quarter $= \dfrac{96}{100}$ of 2nd quarter of 1931.

4th quarter $= \dfrac{90}{100} \dfrac{\text{4th quarter of 1927} + \text{4th quarter 1928} + \text{4th quarter of 1929} + \text{4th quarter 1930.}}{3}$

For the year 1932, the allocations were :—

1st quarter (1932) = 1st quarter (1931) + 15% of 1st quarter 1931.
2nd quarter   = 2nd quarter (1931).
3rd quarter   = 3rd quarter (1931).
4th quarter   = 95% of 4th quarter 1931.

All these allocations, however, proved in general much too optimistic for the whole country, though for certain districts they were inadequate and caused some shortage. The figures below (see Table 37) serve as an illustration showing to what extent the quarterly allocations were reached in various districts. During 1932, total output fell nearly 10 per cent short of the allocation made by the Central Council, while for the year finishing March, 1933, the output proved to be about 6 per cent short of the allocation. And again for the June quarter, 1933, the allocation had exceeded the output by 9 per cent, and in September quarter by 2 per cent.

As one can see from Table 37, the Central Council took great care in determining the country's consumption and did not attempt to bring about a scarcity of fuel. In nearly

[1] For further details see the written reply by Mr. Colville, Secretary of the Overseas Trade Department, House of Commons, 13th May, 1932.

TABLE No. 37

COMPARISON OF THE OUTPUTS OF COAL WITH THE CORRESPONDING QUANTITIES OF COAL ALLOCATED BY THE CENTRAL COUNCIL TO THE DISTRICTS UNDER THE PROVISIONS OF PART I OF THE COAL MINES ACT, 1930 (DURING THE YEARS 1931 AND 1932).

District	MARCH QUARTER, 1931.				JUNE QUARTER, 1931.			
	Allocation by Central Council.	Output as returned by Executive Board to Central Council.	Tonnage and Percentage by which output exceeded or fell short of Allocation.		Allocation by Central Council.	Output as returned by Executive Board to Central Council.	Tonnage and Percentage by which output exceeded or fell short of Allocation.	
	Tons.	Tons.[1]	Tons.	%	Tons.	Tons.[1]	Tons.	%
Northumberland	3,368,150	3,397,100	+ 27,950	+ 0·77	3,178,154	3,129,900	− 48,254	− 1·52
Lancashire and Cheshire	3,093,900	3,094,500	+ 600	+ 0·01	3,545,445	3,477,700	− 67,745	− 1·91
Cannock Chase	1,300,190	1,301,100	+ 910	+ 0·02	1,091,492	1,097,700	+ 6,208	+ 0·57
North Staffordshire	1,521,810	1,509,700	− 12,110	− 0·79	1,308,881	1,335,600	+ 26,719	+ 2·04
Kent	400,000	392,000	− 8,000	− 2·0	400,000	398,000	− 2,000	− 0·50
Shropshire	166,820	165,700	− 1,120	− 0·67	157,125	152,600	− 4,525	− 2·88
Midland Amalgamated	19,056,060	19,078,200	+ 22,140	+ 0·11	17,250,000	17,003,300	− 246,700	− 1·43
Warwick	1,190,950	1,195,500	− 4,550	− 0·38	1,151,579	1,151,300	− 279	− 0·02
North Wales	882,740	848,100	− 34,640	− 3·90	794,871	794,700	− 171	− 0·02
South Staffordshire	431,930	391,400	− 40,530	− 9·37	375,854	341,200	− 34,654	− 9·22
Somerset	232,430	228,600	− 3,880	− 1·64	199,616	198,000	− 1,616	− 0·81
Scotland	7,937,010	7,726,700	− 210,310	− 3·0	7,927,152	7,336,700	− 590,452	− 7·45
Forest of Dean	344,610	319,600	− 25,010	− 7·2	304,223	261,500	− 42,723	− 14·04
Bristol	52,180	39,800	− 12,380	− 24·0	50,200	34,300	− 15,900	− 31·67
Cumberland	599,160	528,800	− 70,360	− 12·0	586,357	503,000	− 82,757	− 14·11
Durham	9,306,810	8,542,000	− 764,810	− 8·0	8,755,577	7,618,100	− 1,137,477	− 12·99
South Wales	11,859,840	8,779,000	− 3,080,840	− 26·0	11,139,474	10,043,300	− 1,096,174	− 9·84
Great Britain	62,585,590	58,377,800	− 4,207,790	− 6·75	58,216,000	54,878,100	− 3,337,900	− 5·73

[1] To nearest 100 tons.

TABLE No. 37 (continued)

District	SEPTEMBER QUARTER, 1931.[1]				DECEMBER QUARTER, 1931.[1]			
	Allocation by Central Council.	Output as returned by Executive Board to Central Council.	Tonnage and Percentage by which output exceeded or fell short of Allocation.		Allocation by Central Council.	Output as returned by Executive Board to Central Council.	Tonnage and Percentage by which output exceeded or fell short of Allocation.	
	Tons.	Tons.	Tons.	%	Tons.	Tons.	Tons.	%
Northumberland	2,860,534	2,871,600	+ 11,066	+ 0·39	3,681,344	3,469,600	− 212,344	− 5·77
Lancashire and Cheshire	3,162,786	3,160,000	− 2,786	− 0·09	3,808,000	3,724,600 [2]	− 83,400 [2]	− 2·19 [2]
Cannock Chase	1,086,415	1,089,900	+ 3,485	+ 0·32	1,250,000	1,233,700	− 12,300	− 1·30
North Staffordshire	1,196,133	1,216,700	+ 20,567	+ 1·72	1,452,000	1,449,500	− 2,500	− 0·17
Kent	410,000	433,900	+ 23,900	+ 5·83	461,600	461,900	+ 300	+ 0·06
Shropshire	147,763	149,100	+ 1,337	+ 0·90	160,163	161,200	+ 1,037	+ 0·66
Midland Amalgamated	17,264,084	17,173,900	− 90,184	− 0·52	19,500,000	18,741,900	− 738,100	− 3·89
Warwick	1,143,195	1,143,600	+ 405	+ 0·04	1,230,000	1,229,900	− 100	− 0·00
North Wales	770,905	770,800	− 105	− 0·01	817,000	807,500	− 9,500	− 1·16
South Staffordshire	360,089	349,700	− 10,389	− 2·89	392,000	365,000	− 27,000	− 7·06
Somerset	195,000	187,800	− 7,200	− 3·69	219,000	193,300	− 25,700	− 11·74
Scotland	6,999,345	6,411,200	− 589,145	− 8·40	7,999,745	7,855,000	− 144,745	− 1·81
Forest of Dean	293,317	266,200	− 27,117	− 9·24	290,120	280,600	− 9,520	− 3·28
Bristol	47,365	40,700	− 6,665	− 14·07 [2]	53,000	48,300	− 4,700	− 8·93
Cumberland	536,098	224,200	− 311,898	− 58·18 [2]	560,049	483,200	− 76,849	− 13·72
Durham	8,149,650	7,113,500	− 1,036,150	− 12·71	8,540,803	8,231,200	− 309,603	− 3·62
South Wales	10,509,441	9,566,200	− 943,241	− 8·98	11,102,185	10,070,800	− 1,081,385	− 9·29
Great Britain	55,132,120	52,169,000	− 2,963,120	− 5·37	61,518,309	58,807,200 [3]	− 2,711,109 [3]	− 4·41 [3]

[1] To nearest 100 tons.
[2] The low output was due to labour difficulties.
[3] Cmd. 3905, 1931 ; Cmd. 3982, 1931 ; Cmd. 4076, 1932.

TABLE No. 37 (continued)

District.	MARCH QUARTER, 1932.[1] Allocation by Central Council. Tons.	Output as returned by Executive Board to Central Council. Tons.	Tonnage and Percentage by which output exceeded or fell short of Allocation. Tons.	%	JUNE QUARTER, 1932.[1] Allocation by Central Council. Tons.	Output as returned by Executive Board to Central Council. Tons.	Tonnage and Percentage by which output exceeded or fell short of Allocation. Tons.	%
Northumberland	3,743,000	3,383,000	− 360,000	9·63	3,300,000	3,051,000	− 249,000	7·54
Lancashire and Cheshire	4,371,000	3,639,000	− 732,000	16·73	3,728,000	3,436,000	− 292,000	7·82
Cannock Chase	1,450,000	1,199,000	− 251,000	17·30	1,137,000	1,120,000	− 17,000	1·57
North Staffordshire	1,631,000	1,506,000	− 125,000	7·6	1,407,000	1,417,000	+ 10,000	+ 0·69
Kent	490,000	481,000	− 9,000	1·71	490,000	491,000	+ 1,000	+ 0·02
Shropshire	175,000	163,000	− 12,000	6·80	163,000	160,000	− 3,000	1·66
Midland Amalgamated	21,000,000	18,254,000	− 2,746,000	13·08	17,250,000	16,802,000	− 448,000	2·60
Warwick	1,295,000	1,242,000	− 53,000	4·06	1,151,000	1,136,000	− 15,000	1·31
North Wales	914,000	816,000	− 98,000	10·77	805,000	767,000	− 38,000	4·71
South Staffordshire	416,000	373,000	− 43,000	13·23	370,000	361,000	− 9,000	2·45
Somerset	230,000	192,000	− 38,000	16·39	197,000	171,000	− 26,000	13·47
Scotland	8,500,000	7,714,000	− 786,000	9·25	7,500,000	7,083,000	− 417,000	5·56
Forest of Dean	319,000	285,000	− 34,000	10·63	269,000	252,000	− 17,000	6·21
Bristol	53,090	47,000	− 7,000	11·40	47,000	44,000	− 3,000	6·88
Cumberland	610,000	475,000	− 135,000	22·05	503,000	463,000	− 40,000	7·94
Durham	9,651,000	7,814,000	− 1,837,000	19·03	7,850,000	7,217,000	− 633,000	8·06
South Wales	12,250,000	9,400,000	− 2,850,000	23·26	10,400,000	9,453,000	− 947,000	9·10
Great Britain	67,100,000	56,998,000	− 10,112,000	15·07	56,569,000	53,424,000	− 3,145,000	5·56

[1] To nearest 1,000 tons.
Cmd. 4224, 1932.

TABLE No. 37 (continued)

District.	September Quarter, 1932.				December Quarter, 1932.[1]			
	Allocation by Central Council.	Output as returned by Executive Board to Central Council.	Tonnage and Percentage by which output exceeded or fell short of Allocation.		Allocation by Central Council.	Output as returned by Executive Board to Central Council.	Tonnage and Percentage by which output exceeded or fell short of Allocation.	
	Tons.	Tons.	Tons.	%	Tons.	Tons.	Tons.	%
Northumberland	3,000,000	2,761,000	− 239,000	− 7·95	3,546,000	3,487,000	− 59,000	− 1·38
Lancashire and Cheshire	3,160,000	2,762,000	− 398,000	− 12·60	3,618,000	3,507,000	− 111,000	− 3·07
Cannock Chase	1,090,000	981,000	− 109,000	− 9·94	1,234,000	1,206,000	− 28,000	− 2·22
North Staffordshire	1,216,000	1,241,000	+ 25,000	+ 2·05	1,530,000	1,524,000	− 6,000	− 0·39
Kent	490,000	493,000	+ 3,000	+ 0·63	503,000	503,500	+ 500	+ 0·10
Shropshire	163,000	159,000	− 4,000	− 2·64	165,000	165,000	0	0·00
Midland Amalgamated	17,500,000	14,404,000	− 3,094,000	− 17·69	18,055,000	17,892,000	− 163,000	− 0·90
Warwick	1,143,000	1,139,000	− 4,000	− 0·41	1,188,000	1,188,000	0	0·00
North Wales	802,000	652,000	− 150,000	− 18·72	777,000	747,000	− 30,000	− 3·88
South Staffordshire	370,000	341,000	− 29,000	− 7·83	380,000	375,000	− 5,000	− 1·31
Somerset	187,000	161,000	− 26,000	− 13·83	197,000	197,500	+ 500	+ 0·25
Scotland	7,285,000	6,502,000	− 793,000	− 10·74	7,912,000	7,816,000	− 96,000	− 1·23
Forest of Dean	266,000	227,000	− 39,000	− 14·72	281,000	279,000	− 2,000	− 0·49
Bristol	47,000	38,000	− 9,000	− 18·64	47,000	44,000	− 3,000	− 6·38
Cumberland	530,000	372,000	− 158,000	− 29·73	459,000	403,000	− 56,000	− 12·20
Durham	7,750,000	6,492,000	− 1,258,000	− 16·23	7,820,000	7,424,000	− 396,000	− 5·06
South Wales	10,000,000	8,557,000	− 1,443,000	− 14·43	9,802,000	9,047,000	− 755,000	− 7·70
Great Britain	55,002,000	47,285,000	− 7,717,000	− 14·03	57,515,000	55,807,000	− 1,708,000	− 2·97

[1] Provisional figures. To nearest 1,000 tons.

all the most important districts the allocation did not correspond with the actual output. Taking the country as a whole, one could even say that the restriction of output failed altogether, since the majority of the districts had to keep their output below the restricted maximum output owing to the diminished demand.

Obviously the actual fall of the volume of production did not affect all the areas proportionately. It chiefly hit Durham, South Wales, and Scotland, while such districts as Yorkshire were comparatively untouched. Actually, South Yorkshire felt very keenly the restrictions of output, which caused the big pits to consider the possibility of closing down temporarily. This position became so acute in June, 1933, that the Yorkshire quota for June has been increased from $62\frac{1}{2}$ to $67\frac{1}{2}$.

However, under the quota, all districts were requested to share proportionately in output restriction. In the first quarter of 1931 the total allocation was based on the results of the first quarter of the previous year, and afterwards was reduced by something more than 10 per cent, which meant a fall of $7\frac{1}{2}$ million tons as compared with the same period of 1930, and about 1 million less than in the quarter preceding the allocation. The only exception from the principle of equal distribution of the allocation among the districts was a small extra-quota of 250,000 tons which the Central Council reserved at their disposal in order to compensate some of the smaller and rapidly developing districts like Kent, whose allocation for the first quarter was raised from 332,000 tons up to 400,000 tons.

For the first quarter of 1932 the allocations were substantially increased in anticipation of larger export trade facilitated by the depreciation of the £. Trade, however, was disappointing, and the allocations remained well above the output. On the other hand, in the June quarter ten of the districts chiefly producing for home trade applied for increased allocations, which were granted by the Central Council. But only a fraction of these allocations was actually utilized.

At the end of the second year of the operation of the

compulsory cartel, the Central Council substantially curtailed the permitted output, chiefly in view of the debit balances which had appeared in the summers of 1931 and 1932. In South Wales, where the output-quota was already reduced by 34¼ per cent of the standard tonnage, the December allocation in 1932 was further cut down by 10 per cent. South Wales is one of the districts which has suffered most from the depression. On the whole, this policy caused fresh trouble by upsetting the balance between the supplies of different kinds of coal. In this way it brought about a shortage of certain kinds of coal, especially of small descriptions and sized coal, which, since they constitute a joint product with other coals, cannot be supplied indiscriminately from those other kinds of coal.[1] Thus while large coal was being piled in stocks, other kinds of coal were difficult to obtain. At Hull cases were reported in September, 1933, where shippers had considerable difficulty in obtaining suitable burden. Collieries had to resort to the uneconomical breakage of coal. Moreover, in view of the fact that Poland supplied the Northern market with very cheap large coal, the foreign demand for British coal was concentrated on small and sized. This further intensified the existing shortage. In Fifeshire and the Lothians, a shortage of supplies was so noticeable that the Scottish Executive Board raised the production quota by 1½ per cent up to 73½ per cent of the standard tonnage allowed by the Central Council.

Having regard to the expected increase in foreign trade in connection with the commercial agreements negotiated with the Scandinavian and Baltic Countries [2] the Central Council gave extra allocations to Scotland— 150,000 tons thus bringing the permitted output to 78½ per cent of the standard tonnages, to Northumberland 100,000 tons, to the Midland District 250,000 tons, and to South Wales 15,000 tons for anthracite.[3] But even these

---

[1] *Vide* Part I, Chap. II, § 2.
[2] *Vide* Part II, Chap. I, § 3.
[3] The total increase in allocation for the July–September quarter, 1933, was equal to a million tons. The principal increases were : Scotland, 825,000 tons ; South Wales, 760,000 tons ; Northumberland, 875,000 tons ; Durham, 600,000 tons ; North Staffordshire, 180,000 tons, Lancashire and Cheshire, 150,000 tons.

increased allocations did not solve the problem of the famine for small coal, and great shortage of small and sized classes was noticeable in South Wales, and other exporting districts, throughout 1933.

But while failing in their chief objective, that of fitting the whole supply to demand, the restrictions of output were successful in bringing all these detrimental effects upon the production of the individual owners which arise from rigid regulations. Hence *pari passu* with the growing depression, more and more complaints were heard from the most efficient colliery companies of the country, and while on the one hand many industrialists demanded a complete abolition of compulsory cartelization, the other wing of critics, equally unsatisfied, asked for the tightening of the restriction and for the introduction of some kind of selling syndicate. Few were satisfied with the scheme as is stood, and scarcely anybody expected that it could help substantially in the chief cause of all troubles—the economic depression in the higher stages of production.

It has sometimes been argued that cartellization is a stimulus to the combination movement and that it fosters amalgamation. This argument is perfectly legitimate in respect of voluntary cartels, but is very doubtful in the case of compulsory cartels, where the relation to economic forces is artificial. The very fact that some undertakings are forced into the framework of the whole machinery goes to prove *a priori* that their interest might be better satisfied in a free economic system. Moreover the vested interest in the form of a quota works in the majority of cases to swell the value of inefficient undertakings, and has the effect of retarding amalgamation. In a compulsory cartel, the units not only represent the value of their actual assets, but they also represent the value of a certain vested tonnage, which they unrestrictedly command under the protection of law.

A strong case against compulsory regulation of output was brought by some of the developing companies, which under the operation of the scheme were not given a chance to develop any further since the quotas did not take sufficiently into account the fact that past output was an unsuitable base for determining the present production of such units.   Besides being prejudicial to the modern and growing collieries, the compulsory scheme forced some units to operate at a loss by restricting working below potential capacity.   Generally speaking, the more up-to-date a mine is, the greater are its overheads, and hence they must be spread over a large tonnage of output, in order to bring a low average fixed cost, and in this way to maximize the profit of the firm.[1]   Among the many attacks on the marketing scheme which were especially numerous at the close of 1932, Sir Samuel Instone, chairman of the Askern Coal and Iron Co., Ltd., in South Yorkshire, quoted [2] a convincing example where a colliery capable of working profitably with a weekly output of 16,000 tons, was compelled to produce not more than 12,000 tons and consequently to bear losses and dismiss workers.   Many more such cases could be cited against the operation of the schemes.   Among them a prominent place is occupied by a resolution passed in September, 1933, by the Association of British Chambers of Commerce against the regulation of output and prices, which act prejudicially to the export trade.

We would like before closing our review of the first two and a half years of the working of the cartel to say a few words about the voluntary achievements of the industry designed to meet the depression and to revive the coal trade.

How greatly the havoc of the depression was felt by the industry can be judged best from the following comparison

[1] Mrs. Joan Robinson, in her otherwise admirable book on imperfect competition, seems to deny the importance of spreading the overhead costs over the optimum output. She calls it an " overhead costs fallacy " when a business man considers " that as output has fallen off, each unit has to bear a higher share of the overhead cost than before ".   And she holds that only the consideration of the rate of profit can determine the price of commodities.   But surely in the majority of cases profits are largest (or losses are smallest) when the price covers in the best way all costs, including the overheads ; and this can happen best when the latter are at minimum. *The Economics of Imperfect Competition*, London, 1933, pp. 48, 73 n.
[2] *The Times*, 10th November, 1932.

TABLE No. 38

Profits and Losses of Some of the Leading Collieries in 1930, 1931, and 1932

Name of Company.	*Net Profit,* 1930.	*Ord. Div.*	*Net Profit,* 1931.	*Ord. Div.*	*Price in July,* 1932.	*Yield* %.	*Net Profit,* 1932.	*Ord. Div.*	*Price in July,* 1932.	*Yield* %.
	£	%	£	%		£ *s. d.*	£	%		£ *s. d.*
Amalgamated Anthracite £1	446,153	*Nil.*	289,478	*Nil.*	3*s.* 3*d.*	*Nil.*	256,736	*Nil.*	6*s.*	*Nil.*
Bolsover Colliery £1	163,654	2½	302,409	7	$\frac{15}{16}$	7 11 0	323,694	7½	29*s.* 4*d.*	5 1 3
Edinburgh Collieries £1	Dr. 28,815	*Nil.*	Dr. 27,085	*Nil.*	1*s.* 6*d.*	*Nil.*	Dr. 12,309	*Nil.*	1*s.* 3*d.*	*Nil.*
Fife Coal	99,837	6 [1]	43,548	3 [1]	15*s.* 0*d.*	8 0 0	42,987	3 [1]	22*s.* 6*d.*	2 13 3 [1]
Glass, Houghton, & Castleford	4,497	*Nil.*	2,542	*Nil.*	—	*Nil.*	—	—	—	—
Hickleton Main £1	62,685	5 [1]	61,624	5 [1]	13*s.* 9*d.*	7 5 0 [2]	60,167	4 [1]	—	—
Madeley Collieries £1	—	—	11,958	*Nil.*	—	—	13,579	2½	12*s.* 0*d.*	4 3 3
Manchester Collieries £1	148,306	*Nil.*	177,503	2	—	—	177,810	2½	—	—
Niddrie and Benhar Coal £1	—	—	Dr. 5,135	2½	—	—	—	—	—	—
North's Navigation Collieries 5*s.*	2,180	*Nil.*	Dr. 23,255	*Nil.*	6*d.*	*Nil.*	6,089	5	17*s.* 0*d.*	5 18 0
Ocean Coal & Wilsons £1	277,829	4	170,035	2	6*s.* 3*d.*	6 8 0	70,147	*Nil.*	8*s.* 1½*d.*	*Nil.*
Penrikyber Navigation £1	4,741	*Nil.*	Dr. 22,549	*Nil.*	—	*Nil.*	Dr. 50,199	*Nil.*	—	—
Powell Duffryn £1	12,308	*Nil.*	970	*Nil.*	5*s.* 7½*d.*	*Nil.*	53,108	*Nil.*	13*s.* 6*d.*	*Nil.*
Shipley Collieries £1	6,838	*Nil.*	29,877	*Nil.*	7*s.* 6*d.*	—	—	—	—	—
Tredegar Iron & Coal	—	—	87,589	5 [1]	—	—	53,304	3 [1]	$\frac{23}{32}$	4 2 0 [1]
Welsh Associated [2]	208,711	*Nil.*	44,232	*Nil.*	—	*Nil.*	19,492	*Nil.*	—	—
Welsh Navigation 5*s.*	—	—	954	*Nil.*	—	*Nil.*	84	*Nil.*	9*d.*	*Nil.*
Wigan Coal £1	5,441	*Nil.*	4,461	*Nil.*	—	*Nil.*	3,690	*Nil.*	1*s.* 3*d.*	*Nil.*
Wilson's & Clyde Coal £1	Dr. 28,301	*Nil.*	11,405	*Nil.*	4*s.* 0*d.*	*Nil.*	14,377	*Nil.*	7*s.* 6*d.*	*Nil.*
United Collieries 2*s.* 6*d.*	Dr. 25,434	*Nil.*	Dr. 23,674 [3]	*Nil.*	1½*d.*	*Nil.*	—	—	—	—
Yorkshire Amalgamated	54,332	2½	8,460	*Nil.*	—	*Nil.*	1,924	*Nil.*	6*s.* 6*d.*	*Nil.*

Source: *The Economist*, 9th July, 1932, and 24th June, 1933; and *The Times* Company Reports.

[1] Tax free.
[2] 11 months.
[3] Before Sinking Fund.

of profits in some of the country's leading collieries, representing together in normal times about 40 million tons of output.

As we can see from the example of these few companies, the financial results during 1931 and 1932 were hardly better under the working of the compulsory scheme than before, while in several cases they substantially deteriorated. In the second quarter of 1933, the proceeds per ton were the lowest since the introduction of the schemes with a debit of $4\frac{1}{2}$d. per ton and fell even lower to 5d. per ton in the third quarter. Obviously this was due to the world economic depression.

The compulsory scheme, as might be expected from the very beginning, could not provide any cure whatever against the depression. On the other hand, if it appears that it has worked so far fairly successfully, this is only owing to the fact that all the restrictive clauses were applied on the whole extremely liberally leaving an all-round substantial margin for output and price reductions. Partly was it also due to evasions of the schemes.[1] In other words, this is equivalent to saying that *de facto* it had no influence whatsoever and that the course of economic development was independent.

The industry, however, did not remain passive in face of the depression, and attention was paid both to increasing home consumption and to export trade. The latter received assistance for a short period from the external depreciation of the £, which from 21st September, 1931, was temporarily disconnected from gold. But the deflationary effect of the fall in the £ on the price level of other countries soon wiped off the whole benefit in the export markets.

Another stimulus to export was found later in 1933, in the various arrangements with Britain's chief importers who were keen to use more British coal in order to bring their

---

[1] *The Times Trade and Engineering Supplement* prints a short catalogue of different types of evasions which were practised in the districts. These included : (1) Bogus agencies, (2) subsidiary companies to facilitate sales below the minimum, (3) bonus payments to customers, (4) systematic overweight, (5) excessive allowance for short weight, (6) contra-purchases, (7) juggling with transport charges, (8) misdescription of coals and their destination. [August 19, 1933.]

favourable balances of trade with this country more closely into equilibrium by importing more British goods altogether. While pointing out these circumstances favouring the enlargement of British coal exports, we must not forget the counterbalancing effect of coal quotas, embargoes, etc. on the leading purchasers of coal from this country. But in the free markets of the Baltic and in Scandinavia British coal has succeeded in recapturing a substantial tonnage, which, since 1927, had gone mostly to the Polish exporters.[1] This export was chiefly secured by Durham, Scotland, and Yorkshire.

The Welsh coal exporters had to overcome formidable difficulties in import-restricting countries.   On many occasions they had recourse to diplomatic intervention, since obviously State interference can only be met by another State's intervention.   The Welsh coal-owners, who were mutually competing in Italy, France, and other countries, decided in August, 1932, to form a loose marketing organization eliminating price-cutting and regulating to some extent the physical conditions of coal delivered in such a way as best to meet the demand. This arrangement, called the Associated Welsh Mines, was entered into by some of the leading Welsh concerns, controlling 75 per cent of the Welsh production : The Welsh Associated Collieries, Ltd., the Powell, Duffryn Steam Coal Co., Ltd., the Ocean Coal Co., Ltd., the Tredegar Iron and Coal Co., the Ebb Vale Steel, Iron and Coal Co., Ltd., Cory Bros. and Co., Ltd., and the Amalgamated Anthracite Collieries Co., Ltd. The undertakings composing this new marketing arrangement will not lose their personality, since no syndicate has been established.

[1] The following table shows the improvement in British export of coal in the Scandinavian and Baltic markets during the first half year of 1931, 1932, and 1933 :—

TABLE No. 39

Country.	1931 000 *tons.*	1932 000 *tons.*	1933 000 *tons.*
Finland	58	136	187
Sweden	425	556	741
Norway	309	449	500
Denmark	711	902	1,248
Total	1,503	2,043	2,676

Cf. also the *Board of Trade Journal*, 16th February, 1933.

One of the chief aims of the newly established scheme is to strengthen the competing power of South Wales in Italy against other countries and other districts shipping coal. Among the other functions of the new organization will be the ungrateful task " of stimulating new uses of coal " against oil and other substitutes, or fostering the use of oil produced from British coal.

In pursuance of this policy one of the greatest coal exporting firms in South Wales decided in the middle of May, 1933, not to charter any motor or oil-burning vessels for their business in spite of cheaper operating costs. As the result of this economic nonsense about a couple of hundred vessels, mostly belonging to Cardiff, have been forced to lay up and pay off their crews.

A comprehensive scheme for co-operation was initiated in West Yorkshire in autumn, 1933, under the name of West Yorkshire Collieries Federation. This scheme, which, as we know, failed to command a sufficient majority, had among other purposes to close a certain number of mines considered as uneconomical, and to regulate the distribution of coal on a standardized basis for the whole district.[1]

Besides stimulating the export of coal the coal-owners attempted in different ways (although not by reduction of prices) to increase the volume of consumption. Various movements such as " back to coal ", were launched with the object of fighting cheaper substitutes. In October, 1932, the coal-owners and traders established a Coal Utilization Council whose duty should be to educate the public in ways of using coal and to study the best uses and appliances for generating heat and power from coal. The Council have nominated their director, and are now studying how best to fulfil the difficult duties with which they are charged. Moreover, they must not interlock with the purely scientific research carried on successfully by the Fuel Research Board, an organization partially financed by the Government.

A series of publications showing the advantages of using coal instead of oil have been initiated, the first of which

[1] For further details see A. W. Archer, " Reorganizing Industry by Co-operation," in the *Manchester Guardian Commercial*, 23rd September, 1933, and *Iron and Coal Trades Review*, 15th September, 1933, p. 432.

deals with suggestions for meeting competition from oil for central heating.   The Coal Utilization Council has undertaken a small inquiry into the coal market and it received a fair sample of cases. In many respects the results of this inquiry corroborate our general conclusions referring to the demand for coal.[1]

The results achieved during the first year of the Coal Utilization Council are remarkable, although it still has a thankless task to perform.   The machinery which it had erected includes, besides the Central Coal Utilization Council, regional committees composed on the same lines as head-quarters.

This terminates our brief account of the voluntary organizations which have arisen under the marketing scheme.   From the outset, results were bound to be small, as the only effective weapon—price reduction—had been removed.   Instead of letting the price of coal fall, where necessary and thus recapturing the British and foreign market for British fuel, the Government forced the industry on the one hand to bolster up prices, and on the other hand to begin a desperate policy of artificially restoring the market to the coal industry, thus raising the price of fuel still higher.

Under the existing marketing schemes the situation gradually became so complicated, especially in respect to the division between coal for home and coal for foreign use, that in November, 1933, the Government announced its desire to introduce a new Bill containing a strong injection of Government intervention further restricting the freedom of enterprise in matter of prices and of regulation of home and foreign trade.[2]

§ 3. THE ESSENTIAL CHANGE

The new principles on which the whole structure has been laid differ in several respects from those ruling

---

[1] *Vide Survey and Recommendations*, The Coal Utilization Council, London, 1933.

[2] *The Times Trade and Engineering Supplement*, vol. xxxiii, p. 203, 11th November, 1933, " Future of the Coal Quota."

previously and have caused far-reaching changes. Especially is this the case in the relations between the State and the industry, and in the lines along which the commercial policy of the coal industry was henceforward to proceed.   We shall now analyse these two aspects of the change.

The Coal Mines Act, 1930, gave a general and final recognition to the necessity of using the State as a weapon of reorganization.   As we know, the State was already connected with the industry in many ways and was regulating the industry in manifold directions, but hitherto it had not meddled in organization questions.   Now it also took under its control, on a national scale, the organization of the producing units and their mutual relations.   Formally speaking, the unlimited commercial freedom of movement of different producing districts and that of individual producing units has been taken away—the autonomous authority being now the national body.

If comparison may be allowed, the only similar case of the organizing of a whole industry on a national scale known to British practice before 1930, was the Stevenson Rubber Scheme—that lamentable failure of 1928.[1]   It was, however,

[1] The Stevenson Restriction Scheme was imposed on British rubber growers and became effective from 1st November, 1922.   The idea of controlling the production of rubber had already been mooted in 1918. In that year a Commission under the presidency of Sir George Maxwell, after a study of the existing difficulties, prepared a scheme for the restriction of output in Malaya and the Dutch East Indies.   This scheme, which never came into force, was only the seedling of future control, which was introduced four years later as the result of the Stevenson Committee.   This Committee was appointed in October, 1921, by the Colonial Secretary, who was urged by producers in Malaya and Ceylon to introduce compulsory restriction.   The Netherlands Government was officially invited to participate.   After its refusal the Committee still recommended the imposition of a scheme of restriction on a compulsory basis, and upon this the Government took their decision.   Legislation concerning Ceylon, the Malay States, and the Straits Settlements came into force on 1st November, 1922.   The scheme provided for the introduction of moving export quotas, dependent on the price of rubber.   It was a sort of sliding scale linking the amount which was to be exported with the market price. In the case of falling prices the exportable tonnage of rubber had to be reduced by a certain definite percentage.   The whole machinery was more or less automatic, one shilling and threepence per pound being accepted as the basic price.   All exports exceeding the allowed quota had to pay a prohibitive duty, while those within the quota were subject to the minimum rate of duty ($\frac{1}{4}d$. per lb.).   By this method of export taxes, all shipments

then the only example of the legislative imposition of national compulsory control on industry.

However, the details of the rubber scheme and the coal scheme are very different. Rubber was restricted by means of control of exports, while the coal scheme regulates output directly. The Stevenson Scheme failed because the Dutch and other producers, sheltered by the British restriction, greatly increased their output and share of world commerce. In the coal scheme all producers are being restricted, both efficient and inefficient alike. This equality of treatment must lead one day to the failure of the present scheme.

But the Stevenson Rubber Restriction Plan was of great importance in the development of British opinion on the question of artificial control of industries. During the discussions on the Coal Mines Bill reference was made to it in Parliament and in the Press on numerous occasions. Mr. de Rothschild,[1] pleading for the rejection of the Bill

were regulated and, as practically all the output of rubber was exported, this was equivalent to the restriction of production.

The scheme was in force for six years, but finally broke down owing to extension of the activity of foreign producers, who, being completely free in action, in the meantime greatly increased their share in the international market at the expense of British producers. In the first quarter of 1928 prices fell sharply below the basic price, and in April, 1928, the Government decided to remove all compulsory restriction on the export of rubber. This decision came into force in August, 1928. Such was the fate of the first British compulsory industrial scheme.

Cf. J. W. F. Rowe, " Studies in the Artificial Control of Raw Material Supplies " No. 2, *Rubber*, Memorandum No. 29 by the Royal Economic Society, April, 1931, and Charles R. Whittlesey, *Governmental Control of Crude Rubber and Stevenson Plan*, Princeton, 1931. See also J. H. Jones, " Coal and Rubber," the *Accountant*, 14th December, 1929, and J. C. Macedo Soares, *Rubber : An Economic and Statistical Study*, London, 1930, p. 36.

[1] Parliamentary Debates, House of Commons, Official Reports, vol. 233, No. 58, 17th December, 1929. Mr. de Rothschild : " The recovering of the coal industry by statutory organized restrictions is, indeed, surprising after the terrible failure which occurred both in the cotton and rubber industries. The Stevenson Rubber Scheme failed lamentably because those countries where the output and the price were unrestricted improved their production and reduced their costs in such a manner that they were able to compete, and oust to a great extent our own rubber-growers, who were secure and asleep behind the barricade of restricted output and fixed prices. The same will happen about the coal trade. Our coal-owners will go to sleep and the miners will think themselves secure, but the Germans will keep up their watch in the Ruhr " (Col. 1338).

during the second reading debate in the House of Commons, compared the probable effect of the Bill with that of restriction in the rubber industry. The Stevenson Scheme was cited to prove the undesirability of direct State interference in the management of industry.

Here we may perhaps mention the reorganization of the railway system by the Railway Act, 1921, which compulsorily merged all existing railways into four companies, to which the monopoly of rail transport has been granted; also some of the public utility institutions such as the British Broadcasting Corporation, being a public corporation possessing the monopoly of broadcasting under a Royal Charter of 1927, or the Central Electricity Board, which was given in 1926 [1] the monopoly of concentrating the generation of electricity at standard frequency in the most efficient stations and of supplying electricity in bulk for further distribution. All these schemes, however, merely involve the transference of monopoly rights to certain private or public institutions and do not constitute any novelty in the history of British industry. In all these cases the Government entitled selected bodies to perform certain industrial activities. In principle such action does not direct the industry, but merely excludes others from the field. Direct State intervention goes one step further, and this is the type of Governmental activity which has gradually developed in the coal industry. For a long time already the idea of direct interference by the State in the mining industry had been growing in Great Britain and was continually gaining supporters. It was, however, an innovation to appoint the Government as an organizer and guide of industry, and it could not, therefore, be accepted easily without opposition. At first all Statutory regulation of the management of the industry was emphatically condemned by the owners. We must recall that the movement for nationalization of mines reached its climax after the War, and that the political reformers always had State management of the industry in mind. Hence, not

[1] Under the Electricity (Supply) Act, 1926.

only the representatives of the colliery owners, but also all those for whom nationalization was taboo, interpreted direct Governmental interference as a preliminary to nationalization, and were, therefore, reluctant to countenance anything of the kind.

In the structure created under the Coal Mines Act, 1930, the function of State action is quite different from that which had been prophesied by the sponsors of the nationalization of mines. We have to do here not with the State-entrepreneur, or State-colliery-owners, but with governmental action of a purely regulative character.[1]

Concomitantly with the change of public opinion the intensification of State power was more widely demanded, even beyond the rank and file of the miners' group. The Coal Mines Act, 1930, sanctioned this new function of the State—the assistance of co-operation in coal mining. This does not imply that the progress of organization in industry has since been virtually completed, but it means that such changes cannot henceforward be effected without State sanction and collaboration. Indeed, the essence of the organization can and probably will change, but the ways in which changes can be brought about are now definite, unless, as we have already pointed out, international forms of control are imposed.

State management of the industry or a system of State dictatorship under some of the variants of the suggested nationalization have given way in the Act to the use of Parliamentary power as a rationalization factor. Both in the case of nationalization and compulsory schemes, as Dr. Thoenes points out in an investigation into the nature of compulsory coal cartels, the State brings into existence a monopoly for the industry. This monopoly may be under public administration, in which case we have nationalization, or its administration may be left in the hands of the previous owners, forming thus a compulsory cartel.[2] The Coal Mines

[1] Cf. Part II, Ch. I, § 2.
[2] Dr. Walter Thoenes, *Die Zwangssyndikate im Kohlenbergbau und ihre Vorgeschichte*, Jena, 1921, p. 11.

Act, 1930, has originated a private monopoly, compelling all members of the mining community, however reluctant, to abide by its decision. Formerly the State always steadily resisted the monopolistic tendencies of the industry and attempted to preserve free competition—but this Act has finally reversed its policy. Our sketch[1] of the increase of State activity in the coal industry clearly reveals the development of political ideas and a complete shifting of Parliamentary authority from one extreme to another.

The degree of compulsion involved in the Coal Mines Act, 1930, obliges all the owners of mines to submit their decision on certain questions of production and sales policy to the will of a collective self-governing body—a compulsory cartel. The essence of a cartel of this sort has been expressed in an able definition by Dr. Thoenes,[2] drawing attention to the element of restraint. He says: " A compulsory cartel is a union enforced by the State (often under State supervision) upon all otherwise independent undertakings of the same kind, with the object of common regulation of production and marketing." The element of compulsion involved in the definition of an obligatory association of this kind consists in the necessity for every owner to join the cartel and to follow both its general lines and the recommendations of its committees.

This definition stresses the creation by the State of definite common commercial conditions for the whole industry. In a compulsory cartel the parties are constrained to conform to these conditions. Private initiative has been supplanted by an official decree. It follows from the definition that a compulsory scheme embodies all under-takings of the same kind. By applying the law to all units equally, the State compels them to move within a certain concerted formation. The definition points out that the units are of the same kind and remain independent. We do not entirely agree with the element of kinship of

---

[1] *Vide* Part II, Chap. I, § 3, and Appendix C on the Rise of State Interference in the Coal Industry before the War.
[2] Op. cit., p. 13.

units which is involved in the definition, but in the case of the coal-marketing scheme it holds good in so far as we can regard, e.g., the anthracite-producing units as being of the same kind as the coking coal-producing undertakings. The feature of independence of the units entering the compulsory scheme has been rightly stressed in order to distinguish it from compulsory amalgamation, where they lose their personality and independence. Evidently in a compulsory association of this sort there is no room for dissentients and competition from non-associated units cannot take place, since one of the chief features of the association is that it covers all the producers. The real significance of compulsion is that it forces such outside units which find the restrictive policy non-profitable to take part in the scheme. Moreover, it involves a large degree of political control and Parliamentary intervention in the basic industry of the country and this is perhaps the most essential feature of all.

Besides the political part to be played by the State in the coal industry henceforward, another interesting change of economic nature took place after the passing of the Coal Mines Act, 1930. It referred to the price policy of the whole industry. True, it was not a sudden change, but the Act finally did away with the policy of lowering prices in order to increase sales. The new marketing scheme based the trade policy on the supposition that neither elasticity of demand for a rise or fall existed in the market. Hitherto a large section of the coal-owners had always considered that the best remedy against the prevailing depression and lack of demand was to embark upon a policy of reducing prices, and through this means to extend their sales. Many believed equally in the working of elasticity of demand for a fall, which tends to contract the demand whenever the price is too high. "Dear coal," wrote Sir R. Redmayne, "means a diminishing demand, restricted output, and enhancement of cost of production, necessitating still further increase in price and consequential further curtailment of demand and so on . . . "

Before 1928 this attitude governed price determination in the industry. Practically all coal-owners were working on the theory that cheaper production would allow them to obtain larger sales and to reap greater profits. But the whole difficulty lay always in producing cheaply enough to be able to reduce prices and enlarge the market sufficiently to combat external substitution. In order to achieve these ends the owners embarked upon increasing output, and the cost of a ton wrought became cheaper.

However, a certain check upon this tendency to reduce prices to the ultimate consumer was given by the distributing section, which always acted in the direction of stiffening prices and to some extent inflexibly impeded the process of getting a wider market by means of cheaper coal at the pit-head.[1]

In spite of all such objections, however, the captains of the coal industry always pleaded for a low price level.[2] A representative opinion on this matter can be found in a leading article in the *Iron and Coal Trades Review*,[3] the official organ of the National Association of Colliery Managers, the writer of which answers the proposal of the Labour ex-Minister of Mines to raise the price of coal with a suggestion for cheap coal and an increase of production. The most important part of the article reads :

" The remedy for the ills of the coal industry is not to be found in price increases. It will be discovered rather in a

----

[1] Professor Jones called attention in the *Economic Journal* to this phenomenon, saying : " A comparatively slight fall in demand, for example, produces substantial reduction in the pit-head price of coal. It was this characteristic of coal that made the mining industry highly speculative before the outbreak of the War. The pit-head price quickly reflected the relations of demand to supply, but the lack of competition on the distributive side of the coal industry prevented the consumer from enjoying a proportionate benefit" (" Organized Marketing in the Coal Industry," *Economic Journal*, June, 1929, vol. xxxix).

Mr. Alfred Morgan was opposing the policy based on assumption of the elasticity of demand for a rise or fall (" The Coal Problem as seen by a Colliery Official," *Economic Journal*, December, 1926, vol. xxxvi).

[2] Cf. on this question, Albert Aftalion, *Les Crises Périodiques de Surproduction*, Paris, vol. ii, p. 159.

[3] The *Iron and Coal Trades Review*, 13th July, 1928, " Mr. Shinwell's Remedy."

greater output which will reduce production costs and secure to the colliery owner a fair margin of profits, and at the same time allow coal to be sold at reasonably low prices. The first essential for attaining this end is to revive the heavy industries which automatically will increase their demand for coal; incidentally railway traffic will grow, and the companies' present unsatisfactory position undergo a decided improvement.''

Before the War, especially, sagacious arguments had been brought forward in favour of cheap coal. It had been rightly said that '' in England especially, cheap coal is an article of faith; it is always the same story; coal must be cheap, so that the coal-consuming industries may prosper''.[1]

Later, even after the publication of the Samuel Report, after the General Strike and after the appearance of the recommendation of the Lewis' Committee on co-operative selling of coal, such opinions reigned among the great majority of the coal industrialists, especially among the more efficient. Any measures aiming at the restriction of production and at the increase of prices were flatly condemned by most of the unfettered owners and considered impracticable. They adhered to large sales and low prices. Though some of the progressive coal owners, mostly of South Wales, who participated in the investigations of the Lewis Committee, candidly accepted the view that certain forms of restriction were incumbent and, though they quoted *exempli modo* the smooth working of the Rhenish-Westphalian Coal Syndicate, nevertheless the majority was obstinate and in strong disagreement with any authoritarian action.

One could easily cite many parallel utterances by the representatives of the coal-owners censuring the high price policy. The Minority Report of the Committee on Co-operative Selling in the Coal Mining Industry, signed by Sir David R. Llewellyn, Messrs. J. R. D. Bell and A. K. MacCosh, furnishes another instance of this opinion.[2]

---

[1] George R. Carter, *The Tendency Towards Industrial Combination*, London, 1913, p. 235.
[2] Report of the Departmental Committee on Co-operative Selling in

To-day we must agree retrospectively that all those views which planned to meet the situation merely by a reduction of prices without readjustment of the size of the industry seem now to be over-optimistic and not to have faced sufficiently clearly the development of the post-War crisis. All the passages quoted above, to illustrate the prevailing opinions of the majority of the industry, appear to have overlooked the fact that a mere economy in costs per ton of coal produced, resulting from operating the mines at full capacity, would be in the short run not sufficient to make use of the elasticity of demand for a rise, which operated at too low a level to be attained by all producers. But rightly enough all these people were aware of the dangers of reaching the region of elasticity for a fall. Moreover, price-raising policy ignored the very essential truism that an inefficient mine, even working at full capacity, will always remain inefficient, although it may be making profits under artificial conditions. Further, the differences in the costs will be much greater when all the up-to-date and the obsolete units work at full capacity, especially if rationalization is lacking. This raises the problem of static and dynamic rationalization which is of great importance to the coal industry.[1]

It has been noticed in this country that better methods of mining and new developments in the pits were usually introduced in times of rising demand. Generally, when the market expanded, the owners carried out vast schemes of dynamic rationalization, which allowed them to increase the total volume of output and to introduce at the same time improved methods of production. Such dynamic rationalization was like a new suit ordered for a quickly growing boy : it always

the Coal Mining Industry, 1926, Cmd. 2770, p. 41. We read in Sections 3 and 4 of the Report as follows : " This policy of increase of prices by way of limitation of output is diametrically opposed to the real need of the country and of its coal industry to-day ; namely, a high rate of production at a low cost. The principles underlying the idea of co-operative selling are fundamentally unsound. The point of view involved must always be limitation rather than expansion of output, and the tendency must be to sterilize the development of the coal industry, hamper the expansion of industrial activity, and depress the standard of living all round."

[1] Cf. Part I, Chap. I.

left some space for growth.   But in the case of a stationary, or even a declining market, the coal-owners were very reluctant to invest and to introduce better methods of production.   This was so because the new overhead costs required to be distributed over a large and increasing tonnage, in order to effect economies in production and to render the costs per ton of coal produced lower.   In addition, static rationalization was alleged to produce a proportionately larger volume of unemployment in the coal industry than in other industries, and was viewed unfavourably by the miners.   Hence any tendency to rationalization implies an expansionist policy.

When the industry was growing, dynamic rationalization was carried out on a large scale ; on the other hand static rationalization found little support.   In the few cases of a shrinking market, the coal-owners tried first of all to reduce their costs by working their mines at full capacity, and it was only afterwards, when they failed by this means to obtain a desirable result through insufficient reduction of price, that they gradually resorted to static rationalization devices, first of all through concentrating production on their best units.   We have already demonstrated elsewhere how important is full-capacity production for the coal industry, and how it affects all the items in the costs sheet both absolutely and relatively.[1]   Hence, before the coal industry, which in this country requires more overhead charges per ton of coal than in most of the competing coal-fields, embarked upon the static rationalization policy, it attempted first to reduce costs by producing more coal. This again led to a greater supply of coal than could be absorbed and, further (and not before), to a reduction of prices below costs.   But in times of acute depression, like the one which began in 1928, this method of belated reduction of prices has scarcely ever proved successful ; partly because the static rationalization came too late, partly because the reduction of prices came too late, and primarily because of the general fall of demand for

[1] See Part III, Chap. I, § 2.

industrial and bunker coal. Unlike other industries, where the law of supply and demand appears in the short run to work more rigidly, the coal industry showed many decreases in demand for coal unaccompanied by corresponding falls in prices, though these falls always affected the demand in the long run.

Moreover, we notice, studying the prices of coal and those of other goods, that the swing of the price of British coal usually lags behind that of all other prices. In this industry the highest prices were obtained in times when most of the remaining industries, especially those of the higher stages of production already found themselves plunged in acute depression. In the British coal industry, it is usually one year after the economic conjuncture curve has turned downward that the prices of coal begin to fall, or to follow the pace of the general fall. To quote an instance : while between June, 1929, and June, 1930, the wholesale price index of all articles declined by 11 per cent the index for coal shows a decline of only 3·6 per cent.[1]

This tendency of the prices of coal to lag behind the general movements of prices has often been emphasized by different writers. G. Carter refers in his book to one period only, namely that of the revival of trade, when he says :—

> " It has been rightly stated that the coal trade is the last to participate in a general revival of trade, and also the trade that suffers longest from any general depression. The coal trade is also considerably influenced by the fluctuations of particular industries and trade generally."[2]

This statement correctly emphasized the fact of a late response of the price of coal to the trade cycle, as the coal industry feels the depression first through a fall in quantities sold. This, however, is also true in times when the general price

[1] This fact was used by certain economists to prove the alleged effectiveness of the minimum price arrangements under the voluntary marketing plan then in force in some districts. But these have usually chosen the unsuitable base of 1923 or 1924 for their computations, and thus got wrong results. Others, like Professor Aftalion, used these figures to prove that coal depends chiefly on the industries of the later stages of production.

[2] George R. Carter, op. cit., 1913, p. 223.

level is falling. Coal has the tendency to follow the general trend with a time-lag, but the tonnage rises first together with the revival of the higher stages of production.

The explanation of this phenomenon in the price of coal is quite simple. One must remember that, in Great Britain, more than anywhere else, the costs of production of coal are largely determined by the cost of labour, which accounts for roughly 70 per cent of all costs, subject to variation according to the rate of capacity at which the industry is employed.[1] The price of coal therefore cannot be easily reduced from one day to another without a corresponding reduction of wages. But wages, on the other hand, are determined, partly at least, by the cost of living index, which ultimately depends on the retail prices of consumers' goods. A certain time must always elapse before the retail prices will follow the general fall in the price level of the raw materials or goods of the higher stages of production. This dependence has been stated by Professor Bowley [2] as follows :—

> " Any substantial reduction in retail prices, to correspond with one in wholesale prices, is dependent on a fall in wages and other intermediate costs. Wages, however, cannot generally be reduced till after a fall in the cost of living, and consequently some time elapses before wages begin to fall, and a considerable time before equilibrium is again reached."

Hence we obtain the following chain of causes and effects. The prices of raw materials are falling ; these affect the retail prices after some time ; the fall in retail prices of consumers' goods affects the cost of living index ; the changes in the cost of living index have an important bearing upon wages ; and finally, the new level of wages is reflected in the price of coal. But between the first of these processes and the last there must be a margin of time —and this is the explanation of retarded fall in prices of coal.

Hitherto we have been discussing the question of the

---

[1] See Part III, Chap. I, § 2.
[2] Professor A. L. Bowley, " The Relation between Wholesale and Retail Prices," *Lloyds Bank Limited Monthly Review*, June, 1930, p. 110.

price of coal and those elements which are its chief determinants. Now let us shortly analyse the quantitative problem of sales (if it may be so called) expressed in the tonnage of coal disposed of in the market. This has quite an opposite direction. As the fall of prices during the slump starts in those industries which are the main users of coal (iron, steel shipbuilding, sea and rail transport, etc.) and which nearly all belong to higher stages of production, they at once adversely affect the demand for coal. The sales of coal fall immediately with the beginning of depression. And the coal industry at the beginning of each crisis confronts a situation where, in spite of diminishing sales, the prices for the time being are unduly high, owing to costs. This accounts for the fact that the colliery owners then consider a general reduction in prices as their first act of defiance against the falling demand. Such reduction is a weapon commonly used to stimulate sales, and though usually it does not prove quite sufficient, because it comes too late, and because elasticity of demand for a rise for industrial coals works in the short run only at a very low level, nevertheless it does prove adequate in the longer period.[1]

In the post-War period the situation on the productive side in the British coal industry has completely altered. Such reduction of prices as could previously be effected by lowering the margin of profits, or working for a time without any profit at all, could hardly be achieved nowadays, when the industry generally works with a very lean profit, and sometimes even with a loss. There is much less freedom in determining prices in the post-War period in Great Britain than there used to be, when the normal rate of profits taking year by year was about 6–8 per cent on all assets of the companies, or approximately $1s.$ $6d.$ per ton produced. Nowadays, a fresh risk is involved. As there is no margin of profits to adjust the price policy, when the regulation of prices in a downward direction is sought with a view to stimulating demand, it can only be achieved from the very

[1] Compare with Part I, Chap. II, § 2.

TABLE No. 40

A Sample of Profits in the Coal Industry before the War

Name of Firm.	Annual Output. Tons.	Paid-up Capital and Properties, Plants, etc., Reserve Fund. £	Profits. Sums. £	Profits. Period of Ascertainment. No. of years.	Date.	Average Weekly Rate of Profit. £	Average Yearly Rate of Profit per cent on Capital, etc. %	Profits per ton of Coal produced. £ s. d.
LANCASHIRE.								
Astley & Tyldesley Collieries, Ltd.	⁵	200,000¹	⁵	6	1904-9	⁵	23⁴	5 0 0
Pearson, Knowles Coal & Iron Co., Ltd.	⁵	2,700,000	470,000	6	1905-1910	78,000	3	⁵
Wigan Coal & Iron Co., Ltd.	⁵	1,800,000	700,000	5	1906-1910	140,000	8	⁵
YORKSHIRE.								
John Brown & Co.	3,000,000	9,600,000	1,456,000	6	1905-1910	242,000	2½	1 6¼
Henry Briggs, Son & Co., Ltd.	950,000	1,100,000	315,000	5	1906-1910	63,000	6	1 4
Lofthouse Colliery, Ltd.	⁵	60,000³	31,000	4	1907-1910	8,000	19½	⁵
Manvers Main Collieries, Ltd.	1,250,000	800,000³	⁵	—	1907 & 1908	⁵	21⁴	⁵
New Sharlston Collieries Co., Ltd.	⁵	550,000³	130,000	6	1905-1910	21,000	4	⁵
Wath Main Colliery Co., Ltd.	⁵	230,000¹	⁵	5	1904-9	⁵	13¾	⁵
DERBYSHIRE.								
Staveley Coal & Iron Co.	2,500,000	2,600,000³	910,000	6	1905-1910	150,000	6	1 3
Sheepbridge Coal & Iron Co., Ltd.	1,200,000	1,900,000³	170,000	2	1909-1910	85,000	4½	1 5¾
SOUTH WALES.								
Brunyeat, Brown & Co., Ltd.	1,100,000	860,000³	320,000	7	1904-1910	47,000	5	10¼
Cambrian Collieries, Ltd.	1,200,000	1,250,000	890,000	12	1899-1910	74,000	6	1 2¾
Cardiff Collieries, Ltd.	⁵	900,000	280,000	5	1908-1910	57,000	6¼	⁵

1 Includes only the paid-up capital.
2 Paid-up capital and reserves.
3 Paid-up capital and properties, plants, and other assets.
4 Dividend paid.
5 Figures not available.

Computed from the figures collected together by Mr. Tom Myers in a pamphlet "The State and the Coal Supply".

TABLE No. 40 (*continued*)

Name of Firm.	*Annual Output.*	*Paid-up Capital and Properties, Plants, etc. Reserve Fund.*	PROFITS. *Sums.*	PROFITS. *Period of Ascertainment.*	*Date.*	*Average Weekly Rate of Profit.*	*Average Yearly Rate of Profit per cent on Capital, etc.*	*Profits per ton of Coal produced.*
	Tons.		£	No. of years.		£	%	£ s. d.
			SOUTH WALES.					
D. Davis & Sons, Ltd.	1,700,000	1,600,000 [3]	1,500,000	12	1899–1910	125,000	7½	1 5½
Glamorgan Coal Co., Ltd.	1,100,000	520,000 [2]	570,000	11	1900–1910	52,000	10	11
Great Western Colliery Co., Ltd.	1,000,000	1,140,000 [3]	710,000	12	1899–1910	59,000	5	1 2½
Guest, Keen & Nettlefolds, Ltd.	2,000,000	10,900,000 [3]	4,100,000	10	1901–1910	410,000	4	4 1½
International Coal Co., Ltd.	[4]	230,000 [3]	200,000	12	1899–1910	17,000	7	[4]
Main Colliery Co., Ltd.	450,000	480,000 [2]	426,000	12	1899–1910	35,000	7½	1 7
Locket, Merthyr Collieries, Ltd.	750,000	300,000 [1]	350,000	12	1899–1910	29,000	9½	8
Newport Abercarn Steam Coal Co., Ltd.	500,000	400,000 [3]	360,000	12	1899–1910	30,000	7½	1 3
North Navigation Collieries, Ltd.	1,000,000	1,520,000 [3]	1,000,000	12	1899–1910	83,000	5½	1 8
Partridge, Jones & Co., Ltd.	1,250,000	1,400,000	1,000,000	12	1899–1910	83,000	6	1 4
Powell, Duffryn Steam Coal Co., Ltd.	3,200,000	3,300,000 [3]	2,000,000	7	1904–1910	285,000	8½	1 9½
Tredegar Iron & Coal Co., Ltd.	[4]	2,300,000	1,200,000	12	1899–1910	100,000	4½	[4]
			DURHAM.					
Bolckow, Vaughan & Co., Ltd.	3,000,000	9,400,000	2,500,000	6	1905–1910	417,000	4½	2 8½
Horden Collieries, Ltd.	1,200,000	2,000,000 [3]	280,000	6	1905–1910	47,000	2½	—
Pease & Partners, Ltd.	3,000,000	3,900,000	1,700,000	6	1905–1910	283,000	7	1 10½
Bearpark Coal & Coke Co., Ltd.	[4]	410,000 [3]	220,000	6	1905–1910	36,000	8½	[4]
Weardale Steam Coal & Coke Co., Ltd.	1,500,000	2,900,000 [3]	540,000	5	1906–1910	108,000	4	1 5

[1] Includes only the paid-up capital.
[2] Paid-up capital and reserves.
[3] Paid-up capital and properties, plants, and other assets.
[4] Figures not available.

Computed from the figures collected together by Mr. Tom Myers in a pamphlet "The State and the Coal Supply".

start by a process of capital consumption, or by reducing costs.   Hence the policy of enlarging the sales of coal by reducing price schedules is now subject to much greater rigidity than before the War, when the margin of profits [1] could serve as a buffer.

After the War this possibility almost disappeared.   The only feasible way of reducing prices was by curtailing costs, but these were largely determined by wages.   As wages to a great extent were sensible to and connected with retail prices, and as, on the other hand, the sales of coal were largely dependent on wholesale prices of raw materials for production, the whole situation became very difficult.

But besides the lack of profit-margin, which would help a policy of price reduction, there was another cause which made for a further complication.   We refer here to a complete alteration in the linking of the prices of coal and the level of wages.   So long as wages were more or less dependent on and determined by the price of coal on the market, there was obviously less rigidity in reducing the prices, since wages also automatically went down.[2]

How enormous were the fluctuations in wages occurring under this system is clearly presented on the table on p. 457, which we reprint from Professor H. Jevons.[3]

Table 41 shows how flexible the wages were, and to what extent they varied in the districts.   The miners disliked this sliding-scale system and they turned all their energy to overthrowing it.   Already during the strike in July, 1893, the workers emphatically asked for the abolition of the sliding-scale system and for the introduction of a more stable method of computing wages.   The principle of relating wages to prices was steadily undermined by the

---

[1] See Table 40.

[2] " Wages," says Mr. J. W. F. Rowe, " have, in fact, been formally regulated almost solely by the selling price of coal, either directly, as under a sliding scale, or indirectly, by joint negotiation conducted on well-established principles.   The ordinary factors of labour supply and demand, as affecting wages, are quite subordinated to the controlling influence of price movement : the price of labour is not fixed by the condition of the labour market, but by the condition of the market for the product " (*Wages in the Coal Industry*, London, 1923, p. 120).

[3] H. Stanley Jevons, *The British Coal Trade*, London, 1915, p. 497.

TABLE 41

PERCENTAGE ABOVE STANDARD OF COAL HEWERS' WAGES BETWEEN 1890–1912

Percentage above Standard of Hewers' Wages at end of—	*Northumberland.*	*Durham.*	*Cumberland.*	*Federated Districts.*	*Forest of Dean.*	*Somerset.*	*S. Wales and Monmouthshire.*	*West Scotland.*	*Mid & East Lothian.*	*Fife and Clackmananshire.*
	%	%	%	%	%	%	%	%	%	%
1890 . . .	31¼	30	40	40	30	30	52¼	50	50	50
1896 . . .	3¾	15	30	30	15	15	10	12½	10	[1]
1900 . . .	61¼	65	60	50	50	42½	73¾	100	100	97¼
1912 . . .	38¾	46¼	52½	55	40	45	57½	68¾	68¾	68¾
Net percentage increase between October, 1896, and 31st December, 1911 . . .	38¾	42½	50	55	37½	45	50	75	73¾	68¾

[1] At Standard.

Taken from Fifteenth Abstract of Labour Statistics (Cmd. 6228, 1912), p. 71, and Sixteenth ditto. (Cmd. 7131, 1913), p. 86.

Page 457.]

workers, and finally, after the 1921 strike, a completely new system was substituted by which wages were rendered much less flexible, being made dependent on profits earned in the districts. This system, which lasted till 1926, automatically rendered all the costs of production much more rigid, and in consequence greatly hampered attempts to lower prices.

Thus it gradually came about that the policy of reducing prices could not be applied so freely owing to the combination of the factors already discussed :—

(1) The inflexibility of labour costs ;

(2) The lack of static rationalization accompanied by the impossibility of reducing prices without considerable consumption of capital ; and

(3) The diminishing demand for industrial coal.

When in the critical year 1928, the last-mentioned factor made itself felt acutely for the first time, the coal-owners' policy of making use of the elasticity of demand for a rise approached its limit. Several coal producing districts began to apprehend that the cutting down of prices did not at once lead to sufficient enlargement of markets and to the absorption of the plethora of coal, but merely to a suicidal competition between districts and individuals. It was at this moment that the voluntary schemes of control of output or prices began to spring up and to cover certain areas where the demand was of a pronounced inelasticity both for a rise and a fall. But not until the passing of the Coal Mines Act, 1930, did this method of regulating sales gain an official recognition.

The great economic significance of the Act is that by the introduction of compulsory regulation of prices and by the restriction of output it finally did away with any attempt at influencing sales by means of prices. Rather the opposite henceforward became the practice of the industry forced to operate under the marketing clauses. It was now compelled to regulate prices according to sales. The minimum price schedules and the maximum output provisions had the effect of discouraging the industry from continuing to employ those methods of marketing which it had used on the whole successfully in the past. The whole marketing policy was by the Act, 1930, shunted into a new track. Low prices and increased sales have thus been given up completely, and the Act confirmed for the whole industry the process which began early in 1928 in certain districts.

To turn now from retrospect to prospect, it is not easy at this stage to appraise the full merits and demerits of the new compulsory organization, which doubtless will have a colossal influence not only on the future of the coal industry, but also on the development of the methods of administering economic activities in general. The Coal Mines Act, 1930, imposing this organization, belongs to a type of legislation marking a complete turning point in the history of national economic development. This is not perhaps so much because of its direct influence on the evolution of the industry, as because of the introduction of certain entirely new principles. To express it in a more precise way, this piece of legislation put an end to the free play of economic forces in the whole field of one of the country's staple industries. This statutory regulation, temporary though it was intended to be, and supposed only to accelerate certain already existing and well defined tendencies, nevertheless without any doubt did away with freedom of trade and enterprise by introducing a strong political factor into economics. It had very often to be administered in the face of resistance from many owners of mines, who consider the regulations unfair, burdensome, and contrary to their own welfare.

The Act is the more important as coal mining is to be the first experimental field in this country for the working of a compulsory marketing scheme—a scheme which had its origin inside certain brains a long time ago, though in a very different form.

Coal mining has always been a laboratory for economic and social experiments, and it is so to-day ; but hitherto the basis of its structure has not differed much from that of the other industries. Its fabric has been refashioned willy-nilly by State compulsion and political interference. One is inclined here to recall the Continental political idea of the eighteenth century Rationalism, of a " Police State ", the aim of which was to render the people happy by any means, even against their will, since they were considered to be ignorant of the basis of real happiness.

At this point, coal mining is faced with two alternatives only ; it can either revert to some previous form of organization and thus re-open questions which are now past history, or it can look forward to a further remodelling on international lines. Perhaps, indeed, the Coal Mines Act, 1930, will prove only an introduction to some new system in the mining industry, possibly based on inter-national co-operation and control. An impasse has now been reached, where the more progressive and most economic units are forced to bear the havoc of the economic depression equally with the most retrograde and most backward. This must mark the final stage of national organization, and future development must be along other lines. We do not suggest, of course, that the Coal Mines Act, 1930, is responsible for the present situation in the industry. But, on the other hand, considering especially the economic position of the British coal industry, an Act of this sort can do little good and may do a lot of harm.

In appraising the influence of the Coal Mines Act, 1930, account should be taken not only of the changes which it introduced directly into the coal industry, but perhaps still more of the extent to which it has indirectly accelerated the development of various forms of organization in other branches of national economy.   It ought to be considered from the point of view of the changes which it has wrought in the opinion of society concerning the conduct of industry, and in the establishment of direct contact between the State and the management, a contact which has constantly progressed in other industries with the deepening of the economic depression. This entrance of the Government into the current affairs of an industry and the sharing of responsibility with its leaders is perhaps the most out-standing and the most dangerous feature of the new coal legislation. It is an experiment worked out on an immense scale in which all responsibility is not equally distributed. The only way out of the difficulty is to return the whole management of coal affairs without political intervention to those who have in the past successfully steered the fate of Britain's basic industry through many difficulties and many troubles.

APPENDICES

APPENDIX A

HISTORICAL REVIEW OF THE COAL INDUSTRY SINCE THE WAR

This section is not essential to the main argument of the book, nor does it bear directly on the economic aspect of reorganization as we are discussing it here. But it was felt that a brief recapitulation of the history of the coal industry since the War would help the reader to connect the forces at work with the actual events of the past fourteen years.

Year 1919. The industry was working under State control, and prices for home consumers, as well as those quoted for France, Belgium, and Italy, remained under the restriction of maximum schedules. Both costs of production and prices soared high, export prices being particularly excessive. The whole world was badly in need of coal and had to pay whatever price asked. During this period exports increased by nearly 8 million tons compared with 1918, while home demand was 4 million tons less. Coal production was on the whole below the demand and coal consumers had to compete for coal supplies at rising prices. At the same time, however, the cost of living indices were quickly moving upwards. The miners demanded substantial increase of wages, and in February they threatened to go on strike. The miners also demanded an increase in the reinstatement from the Army of demobilized miners, the introduction of a six hour working day instead of the existing eight hour day in order to make room for the demobilized, and finally the nationalization of mines and minerals. In order to avoid labour troubles in such time of general disorganization in the industry, Parliament passed a Bill setting up a Coal Industry Commission, under the Chairmanship of Mr. Justice Sankey (now Lord Sankey). This Commission, which was the central event in the coal industry for years to come, was composed of thirteen members (including the Chairman), representing the miners, the owners, and the employers. After two weeks work, they issued three interim reports—a Chairman's Report, a Labour Report, and a Coal-owners' Report. The Chairman's

Report, which reconciled the extremes of the other two Reports, advocated the introduction of a seven hour shift, and some increase in wages of all classes of miners. After the issue of the Report the danger of a strike was temporarily averted, and the Government introduced a Bill reducing the time of work to seven hours. During spring the Commission again began to hear evidence on the reorganization of the industry. There was much talk of nationalization and unification of mines, and elaborate proposals were laid before the Commission recommending drastic changes in administration of the industry. On the 23rd June four final reports were issued, none of which constituted the views of the majority of the Commission ; three of them were in favour of different forms of nationalization, the fourth recommended only the establishment of a Government Mines Department, but rejected all compulsory reorganization. So the recommendations pointed in several directions, while the Commission itself proved to be a very useful buffer between divergent opinions. The nationalization controversy was widely ventilated and received greater publicity than ever before. This was especially due to the " Mines for the Nation " campaign, inaugurated at the end of the year by the miners. The second half of the year was less rich in events owing to the still greater demand of the market and the rising prospects of prosperity. The only important event was a wage dispute in Yorkshire, which led to a three weeks' strike.

The Year 1920 was one of those years when the coal industry of this country had no necessity to look for consumers. It was a year of unprecedented coal hunger, probably on a scale unknown in the annals of coal history. Both at home and in the export section coal was in permanent demand. At all British ports ships were waiting in queues for their turn to coal. All countries looked to Britain to provide supplies. Europe yearned for coal. Many of the chief European basins were producing at a reduced rate or had been destroyed by the War. French and Belgian collieries were still in process of reconstruction. The Upper Silesian coal-field was disorganized owing to the uncertainty of the future of that country, which then strongly desired to be united with Poland. In Milan, Signor Luzatti wrote on 9th March desperately asking for coal : " Italy looks at present to England alone for the greater part of that coal supply of which she is in dreadful need, and England should not refuse it, not only for the sake of old friendship and alliance in

the war, but also in order to enable Italy to pay her debts. . . .
We know the difficulties of the coal industry in England, but
they should not bar the possibility of devising a scheme for
supplying Italy with 100,000 tons monthly and giving her
some help in her urgent economic reconstruction."

But England herself was in bad need of coal, not being able,
in spite of all pressure, to increase her output above the level
of the preceding year. Hence the foreigners had to satisfy their
requirements with a restricted supply, which was, in fact, about
$7\frac{1}{2}$ million tons smaller than in 1919, this corresponding exactly
to the increased consumption at home. As the prices of coal
for export were not restricted they soared very high, in some
cases reaching over ten times the pre-war quotations, which,
even allowing for the depreciation of the pound, meant a six-
fold rise in terms of gold. Home prices, being under strict control,
did not soar to such an extent. Under the Coal Mines Control
Agreement (Confirmation) Act, 1918, and the Coal Mines
(Emergency) Act, 1919, all profits were pooled and divided
between the districts, and the State was obliged to make up all
losses. In such circumstances the miners were sagaciously
demanding that the prices should be reduced, arguing that would
lead to a general reduction of prices and consequently in the
cost of living. At the same time they continued the " Mines
for the Nation " campaign, which they desired to enforce by
means of direct action with the help of the Trades Unions.
The latter, however, declined to lend their support to violent
action. When political aims failed, the miners began to press
for an increase of wages. Special pressure came from exporting
districts, where prices and profits soared. The Welsh miners,
with their motto " Let's share the Swag," demanded participation in the profits.

The whole of the year 1920 is one of permanent demand for
higher wages, threats, strikes, rising prices, and rising costs.
The miners went from strength to strength in putting forward
their demands, but in the quickly changing conditions they could
not press both for higher wages and nationalization, hence we
can perceive waves of political demands, which soon give way to
economic demands.[1] The wise policy noticeable at the beginning
of the year to oppose any rise in the price of coal soon gave way
to the demand for an increase in wages. In practice, all increases
demanded were granted. In November, the granting of the last

[1] For details see G. D. H. Cole, *Labour in the Coal-mining Industry*
(1914–1921), Oxford, 1923, p. 120, and *The Times*, 13th March, 1920.

rise after a short strike was specially important, since it created a scale combining the increases with an additional premium depending on the tonnage of the total national output.

In the field of organization certain important changes took place during this year. The Mining Association of Great Britain, the redresentative body of the coal-owners, was changed into a Federation of district associations, so that henceforward individual owners could not become members as before. The ceaseless demand by the miners for public ownership and joint control led the Government to make them certain offers in the field of organization, but anything short of nationalization was not acceptable. In August, the Mining Industry Act, 1920, was passed, creating, in Part I, a Mines Department attached to the Board of Trade. Part II was intended to give some form of joint control in management of the industry by creating Joint Pit Committees, Joint District Committees, Area Boards, and the Joint National Board, but the miners boycotted this part of the Act. Part III, among other provisions, instituted a levy of 1*d.* per ton on output, which was to build up a Miners' Welfare Fund. The year finished with renewed demands for effective joint control and for a National Wages Board.

The chief event *in 1921* was a sudden cessation of State control on 1st April, and the return of the normal reign of private ownership. This sudden decontrol came in tragic commercial conditions, and for some time threw the industry into turmoil. Already, from the beginning of the year, it had become obvious that the hunger for coal was satiated and that the short spell of industrial activity was giving way to depression. Both at home and abroad the demand greatly decreased. The home consumption figures showed a much greater fall, probably due to the fact that British export was previously restricted and unable to satisfy all the demand abroad, which had, in consequence, attracted large consignments of U.S. coal to Europe. Prices fell rapidly, especially the uncontrolled quotations for export, and debit balances appeared throughout the whole industry, with the result that the Government had to pay out of the Exchequer a sum of approximately £34,000,000 to make good the losses and guaranteed profits. With the end of State control the owners had now again to become responsible for the whole management and to face the economic realities of the moment. Thus it became quite obvious that drastic reduction of costs was essential and, in the first place, that high wages would have to come down. The miners, reinforced now by the so-called Triple Alliance with the railwaymen and transport workers, passed from the offensive attitude of 1920 to the defensive, protecting first their wages and the principle of national wage regulation. With the ebbing tide of prosperity in the industry, the owners announced a reduction of wages from 1st of April, which was followed by a severe and prolonged stoppage lasting through the whole June quarter. During the negotiations the miners aimed at the principle of enforcing National regulation of wages and a National pool, by which richer mines and more prosperous districts would subsidize the less prosperous. This, however, was not accepted by the owners. After protracted negotiations the Government offered a subsidy of £10,000,000, and an agreement was finally reached. National and District Wages Boards were to be established and all the proceeds of the industry were to be divided on district bases between labour and capital in an agreed proportion, with the provision that wages should never fall below a minimum, which was fixed as equal to a standard wage in each district plus 20 per cent. The proceeds of the industry had to be ascertained in each district by accountants appointed by the owners and miners. The agreement was to last to the end of September, 1922.

This new agreement, though it preserved the principle of regulating wages which existed before the War, nevertheless introduced the novelty of general division of all proceeds between labour and capital in a proportion adopted for the whole country.

In the September quarter immediately following the stoppage, the reduction of wages was not much felt by the miners, owing to the State subsidy, but in the last quarter the actual reductions were severe. The average earnings in the quarter ending March, 1921, were £58 per man, in the September quarter they amounted to £48, while in the December quarter they fell to £28. Equally drastic were the reductions in employment, especially in view of the fact that during 1920 the number of miners was rising quickly, reaching in January, 1921, the figure of 1,224,000. This figure was in the course of one year reduced to about 1,045,000.

The Year 1922 can be called a year of consolidation of the industry. It was the first " normal " year since the return of the mines to private administration. New colliery developments took place on a wide scale and the reconstruction of the industry

for the first time since the War [1] became visible, especially in
the exporting divisions of the Midlands and in Kent. Output
per man was rising.

In the first half of the year production was slack, but towards
the end demand substantially increased and good profits were
reaped.   The industry was again reviving and full of hopes.
Export was greatly stimulated by a coal stoppage in the U.S.A.
which lasted nearly four months and allowed Britain to make
up some of her lost markets. For the first time 4,000,000 tons
of British coal went to Canada and Central America. Exports
reached the high figure of 87,000,000 tons, which compares
favourably with pre-War shipments. Home demand for coal,
though greater than in 1921, was not very large however,
remaining at 162,000,000 tons. *Pari passu* with the improvement
of trade towards the end of the year unemployment decreased
by 68,000 men, i.e. from $10 \cdot 4$ per cent in January to $4 \cdot 6$ per
cent in December, while the average figures for all trades were
$16 \cdot 2$ per cent and $12 \cdot 2$ per cent, respectively.   In September
the wage agreement was tacitly prolonged for another year.

In 1923, as in the previous year, the chief feature in the
situation was an excellent demand from foreign countries, caused
by the occupation of the Ruhr coalfield by the Allies and the
consequent stoppage in that district, which cut out practically
70 per cent of its normal production. British exports, including
bunkers, rose to 104,500,000 tons, constituting a record never
attained before, while the country's total output of 276,000,000
tons had only been surpassed on one occasion, in 1913, when it
had reached 287,000,000 tons.   Home consumption, however, did
not display such a brisk improvement as the foreign section,
but it was considerably better than in the previous two years.
The prices, which had been falling all the time, now began to go
up, chiefly in the exporting areas. The industry earned a total net
profit of about £27,500,000.   Average profit per ton for the year
amounted to 2s. 2d., but wages did not rise more than 1d. per
ton, owing to the working of minimum scales in 1922 which had
then the effect of bolstering up wages above the ratio of division
between profits and wages adopted in the agreement of 1921.
But as more shifts were worked, the yearly earnings were actually
£9 higher than in 1922.   Taking the individual districts, some
were working at minimum scales, and some showed substantial

[1] For details see the Second Annual Report of the Secretary for Mines,
and the Annual Report of H.M. Chief Inspector of Mines.

increase in wages per shift (Scotland 1s. per shift, South Wales 4d. per shift, Northumberland 1s. 3d., Durham 10d. per shift). The Midlands paid about 10d. per shift less than in 1922. Prosperous undertakings in the exporting districts carried out extensive development works and sinkings and the Mines (Working Facilities and Support) Act, 1923, gave large privileges to the owners for developing their mines. Of the two parts of the Act, Part I is by far the more important. Its aim is to overcome certain difficulties in the working of minerals which cannot be arranged privately with the Royalty owners. Part II amended an old Act of 1845 dealing with minerals under or near railways.

The Year 1924 is a transition period from excellent market conditions to a position considerably more difficult. During the first five months of the year, the prosperity which prevailed during the whole of the preceding year continued. Weekly output substantially exceeded 5,500,000 tons, reaching nearly 6,000,000 tons in April. Home and export prices were rising. This high pitch of production was due not only to the continued demand of foreign countries, but also to the increasing needs of home consumption, which for the whole year absorbed nearly 12,000,000 tons more than in 1923. This growing home demand produced a rise in the proceeds of those areas producing for home use ; but the output of exporting districts in the later part of the year decreased very substantially. There was no external event to assist the exporting section, like the American coal strike in 1922, or the occupation of the Ruhr area in 1923. On the contrary, all competing districts started to work with increasing regularity and to intensify their sales. Hence the whole balance rested now more on home demand than on foreign exports. This situation remains practically the same to-day. In spite, however, of the great fall in foreign demand, which amounted to nearly 12,000,000 tons, thanks to the improved demand for industrial, transport, and all other internal uses, the total output did not fall by more than 8,500,000 tons. Improving demand for home consumption gave a fillip to fresh developments in the home areas, chiefly in South and East Yorkshire and in Kent, but in South Wales, Scotland, and the North-East Coast important schemes were also carried out.

In the second half of the year, both home and export prices were on the downward trend, and profits were greatly reduced. For the whole year profits went down to 3d. per ton, as against 2s. 11d. for the previous year. In many districts losses were

recorded.   These losses were not only due to falling revenue,
but also to greater costs, since the miners, who wanted to have
a larger share in the proceeds, succeeded in enforcing better
terms for themselves in the new wage agreement which became
effective from May.   This new agreement was preceded by the
Report of a Court of Inquiry on the Question of Wages, under
the chairmanship of Lord Buckmaster.   After a short investigation the Report recommended a speedy resumption of negotiations
between owners and miners.   These negotiations gave to the
miners a greater minimum wage and a larger share in the proceeds
than before.   As a result of these advances the minimum wage
rates went up to approximately 10 per cent above the 1921
level.   Unfortunately this advance in wages synchronized with
the turn of the prosperity tide, and occurred indeed when the
most difficult period was about to come.   With increased cost
of labour and with a reduced working day the industry had
now to strive against the coming hardships.

The year 1925 was a year of grave events in the industry.
It was perhaps, together with 1928, the most difficult year since
the War.   While in the previous year there had already been
signs of falling demand and prices in the foreign market, yet
home demand was well maintained owing to the good condition of
industry as a whole.   During this year, however, both markets
were greatly depressed and prices continued to fall.   The revenues
of the industry were everywhere reduced, and losses were common,
especially at the beginning of the year.   On the whole those
districts which had carried out recent development works were
relatively less affected than the others.   The depressed state of
the industry was reflected immediately in the volume of unemployment which rose from 7·9 per cent at the end of 1924
to 25 per cent in June, 1925, when conditions were at their
worst.
Important developments were also taking place in the
international markets, which in the immediate future were to
affect British exports.   On 15th June, Germany suddenly
prohibited the import of coal from Poland, who at that time had
been sending about 550,000 tons monthly.   This drove Polish
coal north towards the Baltic, where it met and competed with
British coal.   We must also add the return of Britain to the gold
standard during the year, which arrested to some extent conditions in the export markets, especially in France, where
the franc was then depreciating.   Meanwhile, the discouraging

result of the first months of 1925 led the British coal-owners [1] to realize the acuteness of the depression. June especially was a bad month, showing a mean loss of 2s. per ton.[2] This deplorable condition brought the owners and miners together to discover some way out of the impasse, but the joint negotiations gave no result ; the miners rejected the proposal for longer hours and for the discontinuation of minimum district percentages. In such critical conditions the Government appointed a Court of Inquiry,[3] under the chairmanship of the Right Hon. H. P. Macmillan, whose report however failed to give any solution of the deadlock. In view of imminent labour difficulties the Government decided to grant a nine months' subsidy to the industry which would make it possible for the minimum wages to be continued, and which allowed for small profits [4] up to the maximum of 1s. 3d. per ton in each district. Meanwhile a Royal Commission was set up to investigate the whole economic position of the Coal Industry and report before the end of April, i.e. when the subsidy expired. The Royal Commission was composed of four members, all outside the coal industry, under the chairmanship of Sir Herbert Samuel. By the end of the year the Mining Industry (Welfare Fund) Act, 1925, was carried through, providing for the continuation of the Miners' Welfare Fund for a further period of five years.

Owing to the depressed state of the industry there was no important event during the year in the field of technical development. The direct result of State assistance was a very bad one, since pits which were closed owing to losses were re-opened again, and some 44,000 men were added to the colliery books. The subsidy created an artificial reduction of wage costs which in fact was not effected.

The Year 1926 was abnormal, not only for the British but for the whole world's coal industry, owing to the consequences of the great British stoppage in the last two quarters. Only the first four months of the year and the last three weeks can be considered as normal ; during the rest of the year the industry was in a state of turmoil. During the period of the subsidy,

[1] During the June quarter the owners were losing, on the average, 1s. per ton. The exporting districts were considerably worse off than that.
[2] *Vide* Cmd. 2478, Report of Enquiry concerning the Coal Mining Industry Dispute, 1925.
[3] Court appointed under Industrial Courts Act.
[4] The profits were paid on the average district basis, and did not allow each individual marginal colliery to make profits. Thus the principle of district average was maintained.

which lasted to the 1st May, production was on the level of the previous year, i.e. about 22,000,000 tons monthly, and owing to the subsidies the industry could show, on the average, a profit of more than 9d. per ton, in spite of the slightly downward trend of prices. Employment actually increased up to that date by about 25,000 wage earners. During the pre-stoppage period, there was a slight improvement in the output per man-shift of about $\frac{1}{2}$ cwt., and costs of production fell by 6d. per ton. The fall in prices was greater than that, and affected chiefly the profits of exporting districts, which actually absorbed £16,000,000 out of the total subsidy of £23,000,000. So much for the first part of the year.

The second period, which revolutionized the whole nation's industrial life and had consequences in all spheres of world economic life, started with the publication on 10th March of the Report of the Royal Commission on the Coal Industry. The Commission, which had been sitting continuously since August, 1925, and had heard evidence from all possible parties, had before them the difficult choice between a drastic reconstruction of the industry along the lines proposed by the miners, leading eventually to nationalization, or a reduction of costs along more conservative lines. The Report took the middle course, and while recommending preliminary changes in the structure of the industry, such as the nationalization of royalties, the hastening of amalgamation, some steps toward co-operative selling agencies, the establishment of profit-sharing schemes and Joint Pit Committees, it retained the chief outlines of the existing organization. But all the recommendations referred to long period reconstruction, which would take months and years to carry through ; and they did not solve the burning, imminent problem of costs of production after the period of subsidy came to an end. So, though it was a document of value, particularly as a mine of information about the industry, it did not succeed in smoothing out the accumulating difficulties, nor did it provide any way of averting the coming storm. Even the promise of a further Government subsidy did not induce the owners and miners to come to a permanent settlement. The great and thorny problem of adjustment of costs of production to the possibilities of the market was destined not to be solved by peaceful methods. The gap was too wide to bridge by concessions. Matters of principle were involved ; the most important being national versus district regulation of wages. After painstaking negotiations and mediation by the Government, no settlement had been reached, and on 4th May the General Strike began and lasted eight days; the miners, however, remained out of work until December. We shall not describe the well-known and tragic developments during the stoppage. We may only add that it finshed with the complete loss and surrender of the miners. Gradually more and more miners returned to work, accepting the terms on a district basis, with the result that by the end of the year nearly 950,000 were back in employment and about 90 per cent of the industry, covering the larger basins, had concluded district agreements. These agreements contained an extension of the working day ranging from $\frac{1}{2}$ to 1 hour and a reduction of all wage contracts. Such an extension of hours was made permissible by the Coal Mines Act, 1926, which was passed in July.

While the main struggle over immediate reduction of the cost of production was left to the owners and miners, the Government decided nevertheless to give effect to some of the recommendations of the Samuel Report. In July they appointed a Departmental Committee headed by Sir Frederick W. Lewis, to study the practicability of developing co-operative selling in the industry. The Committee issued in December two reports. The majority report recommended the establishment of co-operative selling and the application of very moderate pressure on dissenting owners, while the minority report was opposed definitely to the whole principle. The recommendations of the Samuel Commission on amalgamations were carried through in the Mining Industry Act, 1926, which received the Royal Assent on the 4th of August. The Act was divided into six parts. Part I was the most important—its aim was to facilitate the amalgamation or absorption of undertakings in spite of objecting parties. Part II amended the existing provisions facilitating the working of mineral rights. Part III imposed a levy on the royalty owners. The money was to be spent on pit-head baths in connection with the Welfare Fund. Part IV regulated certain questions connected with recruitment of new miners. The remaining two parts dealt with minor matters, *inter alia*, with permissive profit-sharing schemes and with joint committees at pits. Towards the end of the year the industry resumed its normal working on new principles. Thus the tragic conflict was settled with great losses to the miners, the owners, and the whole nation. During 1926 it had been necessary to import 20,000,000 tons of coal and 1,000,000 tons of coke and manufactured fuel. Most of the districts made arrangements on the basis of an eight hours' working day ; only Yorkshire, Nottinghamshire, Derby-shire, and Kent agreed on a 7½ hour basis, whilst the North-east coast introduced 7¼ for hewers only. Wages had been reduced in most districts.

In the first part of 1927 the industry was healing its wounds after the longest and most acute stoppage in its history. The depleted stocks required replenishing and this alone provided a good demand at the beginning of the year. This demand secured to the industry during the first quarter a mean profit of over 1s. per ton. But when the first rush for coal was satisfied, it soon became clear that trade was not as easy as it looked in the first quarter, and that prices could not be maintained. This was especially true of the export section, as ominous congestion of coal was apparent in many markets. New competitors appeared. Polish and German coal was competing against British coal, whilst the notorious import restrictions to protect native coal industries had already begun in France and Spain. Prices were falling all the year, both at home and still more abroad. Not having any subsidy to rely on, the industry had to bear the heavy losses which occurred during the last three quarters of the year itself. Quantitatively the results were not as bad as they appeared from a survey of profits. Output amounted to 251,000,000 tons, which was about 8,000,000 more than in 1925. Exports were on the level of 1925, while home demand rose by 10,000,000 tons, which actually exceeded the average of 1909–1913.

The lengthening of the working day, however, with consequent rise of output per man-shift, as well as the slackening of trade in the second half of the year, caused a reduction of employment by nearly 62,000 workers. Some 500 pits, chiefly of exporting districts, were closed down and one-fifth of the men employed in those districts prior to the stoppage in 1926 were now out of work. Of all the exporting areas, the Humber ports displayed the greatest fall. Wages, which were regulated now on a district basis, had been arranged on similar principles to the agreement of 1921, but reductions were effected everywhere. The heavy debit balances, which in the last quarter surpassed 1s. for the whole country, drove the owners to take steps towards co-operative action designed to stem the tide of losses. The result of these only became apparent early in the next year, but they originated from 1927 conditions. For the advancement of new organization in the industry the schemes in South Wales, Scotland, and in the Midlands are of the most importance. Apart from these, a certain number of amalgamations took place in an attempt to reduce costs. During the year the industry took full advantage of the clauses of the Mining Industry Act, 1926, facilitating amalgamations and making freer the use of minerals.

With the exception of the last few months, the trade *during 1928* was still more gloomy than in 1925 or 1927. Total output shrank to the very low level of 237,000,000 tons, i.e. 14,000,000 tons less than in the preceding year. This time the whole decrease was in the home trade ; iron, steel, and other industries were chiefly responsible for this fall in demand. With the sole exceptions of Durham and Kent, all districts shared in the decrease of output. The extremely keen competition abroad and the small demand at home depressed all prices, but when comparison is made with the previous year, it must be remembered that in the first months of 1927 prices were very high and afterwards fell considerably. The fall in home prices was sharper than in exporting sections, where the volume of shipments was maintained at the previous level of 71,500,000 tons. During the year the coal industry secured further economies in costs and Durham, Northumberland, and Shropshire reduced the minimum percentage addition to basic rates of wages. A marked improvement took place in the output per man-shift amounting to 3·3 per cent more than in 1927. Regularity of work also improved, but unemployment rose by 76,000 men. Marked progress was evident in the advance of mining technique, but wages in all districts remained at the minimum level. All the year the industry worked at a loss, which for the whole country amounted to 11d. per ton, 5d. more than in 1927. Some improvement came at the end of the year and the debit balance of 1s. 4d. in the summer and autumn months was reduced to a debit of only 3d. per ton in winter. In order to relieve the industry of its heavy burdens the Government passed the de-rating scheme, which abolished three-quarters of the ordinary payable local rates. Moreover, a rebate of 7d. per ton on railway transport was granted as from 1st December, 1928. The most important changes, however, took place in the sphere of organization, where co-operative schemes for coping with the excess capacity and ensuing losses were put into operation in South Wales, the Midlands, Scotland, and in a loose form on the North-East Coast. Moreover, the amalgamation of colliery undertakings made great strides. From August, 1926, to the end of 1928, 172 pits employing normally 126,000 workers[1] were included in amalgamation schemes.

The *Year 1929* was one of general improvement, both at home and abroad. For certain foreign nations this year brought the highest record in their yearly output.[2] Great Britain was not so fortunate as to beat her previous record, or even her post-War record, but nevertheless she increased her output by $20\frac{1}{2}$ million tons, of which $10\frac{1}{4}$ million went to home consumption and the rest to enlarge exports. This general revival of trade was partly stimulated by an excessively hard winter and partly by an intensified demand from other industries, chiefly iron and steel. On the whole, the revival of demand was much greater in the exporting sections than at home, with the result that Northumberland and Durham experienced their highest production since the war. On account of the slow trade in the cotton industry Lancashire alone was in a relatively bad position. Prices in all sections were on the upward swing. From the average of 12s. 10d. in 1928 they moved to 13s. 5d. in 1929 ; while the average declared prices f.o.b. for export had risen from 15s. 7d. to 16s. 2d. Employment was better than in the previous year ; more than 50,000 additional workpeople were reabsorbed by the industry.

Wages in most of the districts did not display great changes in comparison with 1928, though in a few minor districts they rose above the minima. In South Wales a reduction of subsistence-wage took place as a result of an award by the independent chairman of the conciliation board. Profits were well maintained throughout the whole year, owing both to an increase in proceeds and to a general diminution of costs. For the whole country profits of $4\frac{1}{2}d.$ were secured. In the field of organization we must record certain events both at home and abroad. In the League of Nations' Report which followed an inquiry by the Economic Committee, an international arrangement between coal-owners was very strongly recommended, thus giving an incentive to achieve national organization. Another important international event was the Hague Agreement of August, 1929, settling the problem of German reparations, and

[1] *Vide* Report by the Board of Trade under Section 12 on the working of Part I of the Mining Industry Act, 1926, H.M. Stationery Office, 1928. Cmd. 3214.

[2] In France, output amounted to $66\frac{1}{4}$ million tons, in Poland $45\frac{1}{4}$ million, in Germany to $160\frac{3}{4}$ million tons, exclusive of brown coal.

in which the Italian Government undertook to purchase during three years British coal for the State railways. Equally important events happened at home, the chief of which was the coming into power of the Labour Government, with its proposed reforms in the industry. In fact, in December, the Government introduced into Parliament the famous Coal Mines Bill, 1929, which was only to become law in July, 1930.

The co-operative marketing schemes which had their origin in 1927–8 were now developing reluctantly and displayed certain difficulties. The Scottish scheme for closing down inefficient mines was not renewed after the 31st March, 1929 ; the Midland scheme which succeeded in expanding the Humber exports by 54 per cent lost its partners in Lancashire and Cheshire, as these counties withheld from the scheme. South Wales modified its statute to include both the regulation of output and prices. Conversations on the centralization of all schemes were conducted, but without great progress. Yet the amalgamations proceeded further, affecting during the year sixty-one pits with 44,000 men. By the end of the year a report was published by the Standing Committee on Mineral Transport,[1] in which was recommended, among other things, a speedy introduction of wagons of not smaller capacity than 20 tons, a more efficient conveyance of coal, and the pooling of mineral wagons.

The Year 1930 marked a striking contrast to the propitious year 1929. Owing to the advance of the industrial and financial depression the demand for coal greatly diminished. All the chief exporting countries curtailed their production. British exports declined by 8·5 per cent, compared with a 12·7 per cent decline in Germany and 19 per cent in Poland. Home demand and foreign exports each declined by 7 million tons, making the total amount of coal consumed at home equal to 166½ million tons in 1930, against 173½ million tons in 1929. In the exporting districts this diminution of exports was felt relatively more strongly than in the home areas, the only exception being the first months of the year. Though the tonnage of coal fell considerably, prices on the contrary went slightly up, noticeably in the exporting sections. For the whole year this rise over the average of 1929 in coal shipped abroad amounted to 6*d*. per ton, while at home to only 2*d*. per ton. This compensation for the fall in tonnage should probably be explained by the operation of the co-operative schemes and by the price arrangement among the

[1] *Vide* Cmd. 3420, 1929.

coal-owners. A subsidy on exports payed by the Midland collieries concealed the reduction of prices, which actually had a marked downward inclination from the very high level of 17s. 2d. in January to 16s. 4d. in December. Generally the fall of prices was greater in coal exported from the Eastern ports than from the South and West, owing to the keen determination of cheap Polish coal to defend the new position acquired since 1925 in the Baltic area.

A special delegation of British coal-owners and experts, under the leadership of the Secretary for Mines visited Sweden, Norway, and Denmark to investigate the possibilities of enlarging British sales in those countries. The delegation found certain inadequacies in the methods of marketing British coal in Scandinavia, they also advised the paying of more attention to actual treatment and transportation of the coal. Moreover, they recommended the industry to come to some satisfactory agreement with other competing countries. In fact, soon afterwards, in October, the Secretary for Mines (Mr. Shinwell) held separate conversations with the delegates of the Polish and German Governments with a view to concluding some form of understanding. These conversations, were, however, only of a preliminary nature. Other important events in the international field took place at Geneva during the International Labour Conference in June, where the question of a reduction of hours by a quarter of an hour in spite of strong pressure from the delegates of the British Government was defeated by a narrow majority. Only in the following year was sufficient support found to carry it through. By the reduction of hours of work it was intended to attain two objectives; first to restrict the supply of coal, and secondly to make room for more miners in the industry. During the year the number of employees had diminished from 950,000 in the first quarter to about 890,000 in the last.

Owing to sluggish trade, wages remained at their minima throughout the whole period with a few exceptions in the first quarter, which was relatively more prosperous than the others. Some alterations were made in wages in December owing to the introduction of a uniform $7\frac{1}{2}$ hours' shift for the whole country, in accordance with the Coal Mines Act, 1930. They took place in Northumberland, Durham, and South Derby, but in the last district they lasted only four weeks, up to the introduction of the " spread-over " of hours over a week. In the last month of the year important changes in time of work were effected in the majority of the districts in connection

with new legislation, which prescribed a statutory limit of
$7\frac{1}{2}$ hours underground, spread-over, if desired, on a weekly
basis. While most of the districts worked provisionally on
the spread-over, Scottish miners refused to follow, and they
went on strike for a week. In the meantime a general strike
threatened, but this proposal failed to command a majority
among the miners. The Miners' Federation on the suggestion
of the Prime Minister raised the ban on the spread-over of hours,
thus allowing the conclusion of temporary agreements on this
principle in most of the districts. Wage costs in the whole
period measured per ton of coal commercially disposable increased
by $3\frac{1}{4}d.$, other coal by $\frac{1}{2}d.$ Small profits in nearly all districts
had been secured, the country average being $4\frac{1}{2}d.$

The passing of the Coal Mines Act, 1930, which came into
force on 1st August, constituted the chief event in the province
of organization, not only during the year 1930, but probably
during the last decade. This Act instituted a compulsory
regulation of production and prices by the coal-owners ; as
already mentioned it reduced the time worked underground by
half an hour with a permissive spread over an hour ; finally it
set up a National Industrial Board for wages questions and a
Coal Mines Re-organization Commission entrusted with the duty
of fostering the amalgamation of collieries. During the second
part of the year both the Government and the coal-owners were
busy setting up the bodies necessary to administer the schemes
called into being by the Act, especially the Central Council and
the District Boards. In the Midlands, five districts were merged
together forming one Midland (Amalgamated) District Scheme,
covering roughly the area of the old cartel known as the Five
Counties Scheme. But the schemes did not operate until the
beginning of the next year. Hence we can safely conclude that
this year 1930 was free from compulsory regulation other than
that coming from voluntary agreement amongst the owners.
It was the last year of *laissez-faire* in the British coal industry.

During 1931 the production of British mines was the lowest
on record since 1901 (excluding the years 1921 and 1926 of
abnormal stoppage). The world-wide financial and industrial
crisis was responsible for this position in the coal industry. Demand, falling to a very low ebb, caused a drop in production of
more than $23\frac{1}{2}$ million tons from the previous year and of nearly
38 million tons from 1929. Throughout, the industry was under
strict control of both output and prices. But the former

was virtually without any practical effect on the industry since
during the whole period the allowed allocations were much in
excess of actual output, which amounted only to 220,100,000
tons.   Home demand absorbed $10\frac{1}{4}$ millions less than in 1930,
exports were responsible for a relatively much higher decrease
of $13\frac{1}{2}$ million tons.   The fall in value of exports amounted to
£12,500,000.   Even the abandonment of the gold standard on
21st September did not stimulate foreign trade to any visible
extent, owing to the network of restrictions operating in most
of the European markets.   The regulation of prices by the
District Boards prevented a substantial fall, with the result that
the average selling price recorded at pit decreased only by 1d.,
i.e. to 13s. 5d., while export prices, not subject to such a degree
of control, declined by 5d.   The greatest decline in foreign
shipments was noticeable at the Humber ports, where it amounted
to more than 30 per cent.   Of all markets the Scandinavian and
the Baltic show the greatest decline.   At home the decrease in
tonnage sold was due to a decline in industrial demand, chiefly
from iron and steel plants.

In the second half of the year certain events operated to assist
British export of coal,—The war debts moratorium,—the so-called
President Hoover Moratorium,—suspended German payments in
kind chiefly composed of coal exports.   Further assistance came
from the abandonment of the gold standard by this country,
to which reference was already made ; and from the passing
at Geneva of the draft International Convention shortening
hours all round by a quarter of an hour.   All benefits which
might have arisen from these measures have since been thwarted.
The labour convention has not been ratified, while the import
restrictions in Europe have prevented all expansion.   Discussions
between coal-owners of the chief producing counties took place
in London towards the end of September, soon after the departure
from the gold standard, when British owners expected easily to
recapture the foreign markets.   They, however, yielded no
practical result.

During the year the state of employment in the industry
deteriorated, the number of workpeople declined from 883,000 at
the outset of the year to 840,000 at the end.   Wages, with two
small exceptions, remained at the minima agreed in the districts.
Some of the districts reduced their minimum percentage additions
to standard rates as the result of shorter of hours work (South
Wales, Bristol, Scotland). In South Wales and Bristol stoppages
occurred as a result of the reductions at the beginning of the

year.   With the exception of Scotland and Durham, all
districts worked with credit balances ranging from 1s. 4½d. in
South Derby, Leicestershire, Cannock Chase, and Warwick to
¼d. in South Wales. The average proceeds were 3½d. There
was very little progress during this period in the concentration
of undertakings ; only three amalgamations were carried through.
All schemes for the regulation of production and prices worked
smoothly.   Except for some minor shortages of special brands of
coal in the Midland area there were no great frictions.   Price
regulation, however, which was throughout the whole year
unco-ordinated between the districts, caused a certain amount
of difficulty.   The maximum length of the working day—
7½ hours—was maintained for another year by the Coal Mines
Act, 1931, which postponed the reversion to the 7 hour day
to the next year and preserved the existing minimum additions
on basic rates.   The Mining Industry (Welfare Fund) Act, 1931,
maintained the levy of 1d. per ton to the Miners' Welfare Fund.

In 1932 the position was even worse than a year before.
Output fell to 209 million tons, that is 10 million tons less than
the year before.   This was the lowest output in Great Britain
during the whole twentieth century, excluding, of course, the
two years of strike, 1921 and 1926.   Exports also fell compared
with 1931, reaching 57 million tons.   This fall, however, was
much less rapid than in the two previous years.   These results
were exceedingly bad, and were, of course, accompanied by
exceedingly depressing unemployment figures.   Employment
averaged only about 800,000, hence unemployment among the
insured workers reached about 20 per cent.   The highest point
recorded was in October, when it rose to 23·1 per cent.   Comparing the fall in output in the exporting and in the home
districts, we notice that for the first time for several years the
home districts were as badly affected as those exporting.   This
was due to the falling industrial consumption of coal at
home.   Compared with other coal-producing countries, Great
Britain was even in a relatively favourable position.   Her exports
were partly assisted for a few months by the depreciation of
the £, but as the corollary to this came a further deflation
abroad and other countries soon brought down their costs to
competitive levels.   In this brief period, whenever coal could be
traded freely without quotas and restrictions, British exporters
recaptured a part of their trade.   Thus, in the Baltic and
Scandinavian markets, British coal exports rose from   3·6

million tons in 1931 to 4·8 million in 1932. Similarly, in the same period, an increase in exports took place to U.S.A., Canada, and South America from 4·2 to 4·8 million tons. In nearly all the remaining markets greater or smaller losses must be noted, owing to the appalling state of depression, and in consequence of restrictions on imports. Total British exports actually fell by 4·5 million tons. The political dispute between this country and the Irish Free State, which imposed a duty of 5s. a ton on all British coal imported, was partly the cause of a fall in exports of ½ million tons. About 140,000 tons of coal was supplied to Ireland from Poland and a large quantity from Germany. Export prices were, on the average, well maintained, though in the best qualities and in anthracite the quotations were downwards. The average prices of coal at pit fell by 3d. to 13s. 3d., while the tonnage exported fell by 7·5 per cent and revenue declined by 7·8 per cent, which expressed in gold pounds shows an enormous fall. This happened in spite of the operation of the compulsory marketing schemes for the regulation output and fixing of prices. The low prices prevented the industry from reaping high profits, proving once more the well-established maxim that coal can only be prosperous when it is sold in large quantities and relatively cheaply. Profits were secured only by the home districts, while the exporting areas went on making losses.

No important Government action took place during the whole year, except the statutory prolongation of the 7½ hour working day until the ratification of the International Convention on Hours of Labour adopted at Geneva in June, 1931. Moreover, by the same Act, Part I of the Coal Mines Act, 1930, was prolonged for another period of five years. A working agreement was concluded between owners and workers, becoming for one year the *status quo ante* for wages. The Coal Mines Re-organization commission was busy framing proposals for large amalgamations of mines ; by the end of the year the owners of Fifeshire, Cannock Chase, and North Wales were officially requested to submit voluntary schemes for complete amalgamation of their undertakings. A large part of the industry proved adamant to these proposals. The owners, however, formed a Coal Utilization Council to foster the uses of coal at home by propaganda and research. Spontaneous amalgamations did not increase to any significant extent. Some small progress was made in the treatment of coal for the market. During the year a Departmental Committee of Inquiry on the Miners' Welfare Fund was in session ; it issued a majority report [1] recommending a reduction of the levy on output paid to the fund to $\frac{1}{2}d$. per ton and its continuation for twenty more years ; moreover, they suggested the discontinuation of the sharp division between general and district funds.

Such a quick film of the developments in the coal industry will clarify the advancement of the organization movement with which we are dealing in this work and project sidelights on the struggle between the economic and political conceptions of re-organization.

[1] *Vide* Miners' Welfare Fund, Departmental Committee of Inquiry (1931), Report to the Secretary for Mines. Cmd. 4236, 1933.

APPENDIX B

A COAL CARTEL OF THE EIGHTEENTH AND NINETEENTH
CENTURIES

Report of the Select Committee on the State of the Coal Trade,
1836, vol. xi.

The Select Committee appointed " to inquire into the State
of the Coal Trade, as respects the Supply of coal to the Port
of London and the adjacent counties, from the Rivers Tyne,
Wear, Tees, and other places ; and into the Charges added to
the Price of Coal " ; and to whom two Petitions, one from the
County of Middlesex, and the other from the Inhabitants of
Westminster, were referred ; and who were empowered to
Report their Opinion, together with the MINUTES OF EVIDENCE
taken before them, to The House ;—Have examined the Matters
referred to them and have agreed to the following Report :—

MINUTES OF EVIDENCE.

Tuesday, 14th June, 1836.

Members Present :

Mr. Hume	Mr. Wason
Mr. Pusey	Mr. Aaron Chapman
Mr. William Crawford	Mr. Ingham
Mr. Lambton	Major Beauclerk
Mr. Hector	Mr. Edward Curteis
Mr. Pease	Mr. Humphery

Mr. Hume in the Chair.

Robert William Brandling, Esq., called in, and examined.

Q. 1. Chairman : Are you chairman of the committee of coal-
owners at Newcastle ?—I am.

Q. 2. Are you also an owner of any collieries ?—I am part
owner in three collieries, two in the County of Durham,
and one in the County of Northumberland.

Q. 66. Chairman : You stated you were chairman of a meeting
of coal-owners in July, 1833 ?—Yes.

Q. 67. Were not resolutions come to at that meeting ?—If

there was a meeting I have no doubt there were resolutions.

Q. 68. Have you any doubt about being Chairman in July, 1833 ?—I cannot speak as to the time, or what the resolutions were.

Q. 69. Look at that paper, and say if you believe those are the resolutions that were come to [handing a paper] ?—I will read them.

Coal Trade Office, Newcastle-upon-Tyne, 13th July, 1833. General Meeting of the Coal-owners, held this day, Robert William Brandling, Esquire in the Chair.

1st. Resolved, that this meeting entirely concurs, in the opinion expressed by the meeting, held at Chester-le-Street, on the 26th June last, that the prosperity of the coal trade, and consequently of this district can only be permanently secured by some equitable arrangement amongst the parties concerned, whereby the *supply should be proportioned to the demand at a fair and remunerative price* ; and also in the recommendation, that a general regulation of the coal trade should be entered into, and in the principles to be adopted in apportioning the quantities to the respective collieries ; viz. 1st, Powers of working and leading. 2nd, Proportion of the different sorts of coal and their respective selling prices. 3rd, Facilities of shipment.

2nd. Resolved, That an unrestricted, full and impartial reference of all matters in dispute is the only general principle upon which an equitable and permanent regulation can be carried into effect.

3rd. Resolved, That the following rules and regulations would accomplish the object in view, provided they are signed by all the collieries shipping coals from the Tyne, Wear, Tees, and the ports of Seaham, Hartley, and Blyth.

Rules

1st. A representative to be nominated by the proprietors of each colliery, with full power to act for that colliery, until the 31st day of December, 1834.

2nd. The owners of each colliery to be allowed to change their representative, upon giving notice in writing of their intention to do so.

3rd. That district committees be chosen by the representatives within their respective districts.

4th. The united committee to be composed of the local or district committees.

5th. The united committee to settle the quantity to be vended by the separate districts, having regard to powers of working and leading, proportion of the different sorts of coal, their respective selling prices and facilities of shipment. If any dispute should arise between the committees respecting the quantity to be allotted to a district, two referees to be appointed, one by the dissatisfied district, and the other by the united committee, and an umpire by such referees before they proceed to business, the decision of such umpire to be final.

6th. The district committees to settle the quantities to be vended by collieries in their respective districts, having like regard to quality, power of working, and vending, and if any party or parties should be dissatisfied, referees and an umpire to be appointed, as provided for in rule the 5th.

7th. The united committee to fix the monthly quantities to be vended by each district.

8th. The district committees to fix the monthly quantities to be vended by each colliery within that district ; no colliery to exceed the quantity so given out, without the express leave obtained from the committee in writing ; if any colliery, upon application, shall think itself aggrieved by the refusal of such leave, the question to be decided by referees, and an umpire to be appointed as directed in rule 5th.

9th. Any colliery where particular difficulties may be reasonably apprehended at particular seasons of the year, to be allowed such quantity from time to time in anticipation thereof, as the committee shall deem proper.

10th. That giving over-measure or over-weight, or any other mode of evading or departing from the spirit of these rules, shall be punishable by fines, which shall be fixed by the general committee, and paid monthly.

11th. That each party shall deposit in the hands of the chairman, a promissory note payable on demand, to the amount of £20 per 1,000 on the basis, as a security for the payment of such fines.

12th. This agreement to continue until the 31st day of December, 1834.

I am convinced that is a correct copy of the resolution of the meeting of which I was chairman.

Q. 70.   Were the resolutions at this meeting the basis on which
         the present vend is established ?—They were the basis
         of the agreement which was prepared and executed by
         the parties.

Q. 71.   Was there an agreement entered into by each of the
         coal-owners according to those resolutions ?—There
         was a printed agreement.

Q. 72.   Look and see if that is the nature of the agreement
         entered into ?—I have no doubt this is a correct copy
         of it.

[It was handed in, and was as follows :—]

Articles of agreement made this   day of   , 1835,
between the several persons whose names are subscribed, being
owners or lessees of certain collieries within the counties of
Northumberland and Durham.

1st.   The owners or lessees of each of the undermentioned
       collieries, will by a written document appoint a repre-
       sentative with full powers to act for such colliery, and to
       bind the owners during the continuance of this agreement.

2nd.   That the representative shall have such an acquaintance
       with the general management of the concerns, and the
       money transactions of the colliery he represents, as to be
       able at all times to state correctly the quantity of coals
       sold, and the price actually received for the chaldron or
       ton, of both round coals and small, and shall be responsible
       for any irregular allowance or other deduction from the
       price at which his coals ought to be sold, or for any other
       violation of either the letter or spirit of this agreement.

3rd.   That the owners or lessees shall have the power of
       changing their representative, upon giving notice in
       writing to the chairman.

4th.   That a committee for the Tyne, consisting of nine members
       (selected from the representatives), shall be appointed by
       lists to be sent from each colliery to act for one year,
       subject to re-election at the expiration of every 12 months ;
       but though it is desirable that the committee should
       consist of the number above stated, for the purpose of
       settling the basis for the respective ports and collieries,
       the committee shall nevertheless be competent to form
       among themselves a sub or execute one for the purpose
       of carrying the provisions of this agreement into effect,

so that such committee shall not consist of less than three for the Tyne.

5th. That five constitute a quorum, that the votes be taken by ballot, and that the decision of the majority shall bind the parties to this agreement in all cases, except where an appeal is allowed.

6th. That the parties to this agreement will adopt the existing basis for the collieries, whose quantities are now fixed, till such quantity shall have been objected to by the committee or the representatives, and finally settled by the referees, and, in settling the quantity to be allowed to any colliery, the committee or referees to be guided by the powers of working and leading proportion of the different sorts of coal, their respective selling prices and facilities of shipment. But that in estimating the powers of the respective collieries for the purpose of fixing the basis, such proportions of their respective powers as are applied to the producing of coals sold, foreign or land-sale, shall not be taken into account.

7th. That impartial reference shall continue to be the great leading principle on which the arrangements of the trade must be governed, and that it must be applied to settle the quantities between the different ports or rivers, forming parties to this agreement, as well as between individual collieries.

8th. That before an appeal be entertained from a river or district, a majority of the representatives of the collieries of such river or district must have declared their conviction of the propriety of it, and have made such request in writing to the united committee.

9th. That the dissatisfied river or district shall name their referee, and that the united committee shall do the same, and that those two gentlemen shall name a third as umpire, previous to their entering upon the inquiry.

10th. That the whole expense shall be equally divided between the appealing part and the trade at large.

11th. That the referee shall have power to reduce or to augment the quantity of such appealing river or district, and such decision shall be final.

12th. That the above principles which are to guide the reference in the case of rivers or districts, shall be applied to individual collieries appealing from the decision of the respective committees in the district to which they belong, except that it shall not be necessary for any individual colliery to obtain leave of the committee of the river to which it belongs, to make an appeal from their decision.

13th. That as soon as this agreement shall be signed, the rivers and districts shall be at liberty to appeal to the present united committee, but in case no appeal is made previous to the commencement of 1836, that then no change of basis as between the rivers or districts shall take place, except at the commencement of each year, and then only in case the river or district shall have given four months' notice to the then existing united committee of their intention to make such appeal.

14th. That in the case of individual collieries, they shall be at liberty to appeal also as soon as the agreement shall have been signed ; but in case no appeal is made previous to the commencement of 1836, then no change of basis shall be made except at the termination of any six months, and then only on the representative of such colliery giving three months' notice previous to the 1st day of January and the 1st day of July in any year to the respective committees of his intention to make appeal.

15th. That the decision of the referees shall take effect in the case of rivers or districts from the commencement of the year, in the case of individual collieries from the commencement of the six months succeeding the period when he shall have given such notice.

16th. That the committee or referees shall have power to summon the parties to this agreement, or their agents, to answer any interrogatories, and to produce any documents necessary to enable them to give full effect to this agreement, but such power not to justify calling for the private accounts of the colliery.

17th. That the parties so summoned shall, for non-attendance or refusal to answer or produce such documents, forfeit £20 to be returned only in cases where on appeal to a general meeting of representatives the majority shall decide in favour of the party appealing, the Committee at such meeting not to vote upon the appeal against their decision ; the votes at such meeting to be taken by ballot.

18th. That the relative prices of every description of coal be fixed by the committee and the representatives of each colliery, subject to an appeal to referees.

19th. That no colliery, without leave of the committee, shall vary the fixed price agreed on between such colliery and the committee as the selling price of that colliery, under a penalty of 5s. for every chaldron so sold, subject to an appeal to referees in case of dispute.

20th. The committee in concert with the committee of the Wear and Tees, and the other parties to this agreement, shall make such issues of round coal from time to time, as may be necessary to meet the demand.

21st. Any colliery where particular difficulties of shipment may be reasonably apprehended at particular seasons of the year, or other causes, may be allowed such quantity, from time to time, in anticipation thereof, as the committee shall deem proper ; and colliery thinking itself aggrieved by the refusal of such leave, the claim to be decided by reference.

22nd. All coal to be sold by weight, either by the ton of 20 cwt. or the chaldron of 53 cwt. ; any colliery found by the inspector giving over-weight to be fined 2s. 6d. for each and every cwt. of excess on an average of 10 wagons ; every colliery to have a weighing machine, in proper order, in a convenient situation, under a penalty of £20.

23rd. Any colliery exceeding the issue beyond 100 chaldrons, or 2 per cent. upon the basis, to finish a ship, shall forfeit for every chaldron so exceeding 5s., and such excess shall also be deducted from the issue to the colliery for the next month.

24th. That each party shall deposit, in the hands of trustees, a promissory note, payable on demand, to the amount of £20 per 1,000 on its respective basis, as a security for the payment of fines and the general performance of this agreement, the committee to fix the amount of fines in every case not specially provided for ; the trustees to consist of the chairman and the committee.

25th. That the inspectors of the Tyne, Wear, and Tees shall, as often as the committee of either river may deem it expedient, examine together the measure of all the collieries of the different ports comprehended under this agreement, that the weight per chaldron may be kept moderate and uniform, as provided in rule 22nd.

26th. No freighting or upholding freights or prices to be permitted with permission from the committee of the river or district in which the respective collieries are situated under a penalty of 5s. per chaldron on the quantity of coals so vended, subject to reference.

27th. That all the parties to this agreement shall strictly adhere to such regulations as to the sale of coals in London by the coal-factors as the united committees shall, from time to time, agree upon.

28th. That if, at any time, during the continuance of this agreement, the united committees shall deem it expedient for any temporary purpose to grant an additional issue of coals to the markets upon the coast, they shall have power to do so under such modifications and upon such terms as they may consider expedient.

29th. That it be imperative on the committee to enforce the penalties incurred under this agreement, and collect the same once a month, and pay the same to the Newcastle secretary for the general purpose of the trade.

30th. This agreement to commence on the 30th day of January, 1836, and to continue from year to year, during the pleasure of the parties hereto, any of whom may withdraw, on giving six months' notice, in writing, to the united committee previous to the end of any year after the first year, and thus terminate this agreement.

31st. If circumstances should arise to render it expedient that this agreement should terminate otherwise than before provided for, and that, at a meeting of representatives of the three rivers, and the other parties to this agreement, called for that purpose, four-fifths of the parties hereto shall so think it expedient, then this agreement shall terminate.

32nd. No party to be bound by signing these rules until they shall have been agreed to and signed by the proprietors of every colliery upon the Tyne, and until the coal-owners of the Wear, Seaham, Tees, Hartley, Cowpen, and Netherton, shall have signified their willingness to act in concert with the Tyne committee upon the general principles of this agreement.

33rd. That in case any difference of opinion should arise between the respective committees, or any individual coal-owner and the committee of the district to which he belongs, upon the construction of any of the above articles, or upon any other point not herein provided for, that the same shall be submitted to reference.

APPENDIX C

RISE OF STATE INTERFERENCE IN THE COAL INDUSTRY BEFORE
THE WAR

It is a common fallacy that State interference in the British
Coal Industry is only a very recent product.   This is only true
of direct intervention, indirect interference dates back very far.
We shall trace in this Appendix some of the phases of the
development of Government activity and the gradual rise of
interference, actually by peeping into retrospect and by gleaning
some facts from the long history of the coal industry.

The first dealings between the Government and the coal-mining
industry concerned two points—the *price* policy of the industry
and the *taxations*, and other payments made to the Crown for
privileges permitting the imposition of special monopolistic
prices.   We shall deal with financial relations between the
State and the industry first.

The earliest known licence to dig coal was given by King
Henry III to the good men of Newcastle in 1234 for a fee-farm
rent of £100 per annum.[1]   In 1404 a Society of Hoastmen was
established in Newcastle by the 5th Statute of King Henry IV
to provide for and entertain " merchants and alliens ".   During
the reign of King Henry V, Parliament granted to him in 1422
as a custom 2*d*. per chaldron produced by the corporation.

---

[1] Robert Edington refers to this licence in the following words : " King
Henry III being earnestly supplicated by the good men of Newcastle to
confirm King John's Charters, this was done upon the 2nd day of July,
in the year of our Lord 1234. King Henry did not enlarge their jurisdictions,
but granted them the charter in the very same words as King John has
his charter. King Henry III, by his letters patent under the great seal of
England dated at Westminster the 1st day of December in the 23rd year
of his reign upon the good men of Newcastle's supplication, thought fit to
give them licence to dig coals and stones in the common soil of that town,
without the walls thereof, in the place called the Frith, and from thence
to draw and convert them to their own profit, in aid of their fee-farm rent
of £100 per annum, and the same as often as it shall seem good unto
them, the same to endure during his pleasure ; which said letters patent
were granted upon payment of 20*s*. into the hamper. Nothing more was
given, neither lands, etc., but only to work the coals during pleasure for
their own use." (Robert Edington, *A Treatise on the Coal Trade with
Strictures on its Abuses and Hints for Amelioration, etc.*, London, 1814, p. 5.)

But the Hoastmen were long in arrear and did not pay any duty. Only during the reign of Queen Elizabeth were the payments again resumed,[1] when in 1600 the Fraternity of Hoastmen obtained the great monopoly of coal trade against an increased payment of 12d. per chaldron.

During the reign of Charles I, who was notoriously in need of money and was looking continuously for fresh sources of revenue, new corporations of free-hoastmen and monopolies of coal trade were established in 1638 and 1639.[2] Against these monopolies the Commons raised a very strong diatribe. In 1641 a committee of the House of Commons presented to the King a " Common's Petition and Their Declaration of the State of the Kingdom ". The remonstrance contained an emphatic

[1] In 1600 Queen Elizabeth granted a monopoly of selling coal to a Society of Hoastmen in Newcastle. This monopoly was granted by the Queen to William Jennison the elder, and forty-four persons belonging to an ancient fraternity known as the Governor and Stewards and Brethren of the Fraternity of Hoastmen, " and by that name to have a perpetual succession, to purchase receive and hold land and tenements, and to make and use a seal of the Fraternity, and to hold and enjoy all such liberties, privileges, etc., concerning the loading, unloading, shipping or unshipping of stone-coal, pit-coal, grinstone, milstones and whetstones, in or out of any ships and vessels within the river and port of Tyne." (Hylton B. Dale, *Coal and the London Coal Trade*, London.)

Edington described the conditions in which the Hoastman's monopoly was granted: " Queen Elizabeth requires the great arrear of 2d. per chaldron, which was granted to King Henry V, as custom, by the Parliament, as appears by that statute, Chap. 10, the 9th year, which was neglected to be paid unto the Crown, by the mayor and burgesses for many years together, insomuch that they were not able to pay the same, but humbly beseeched those arrears may be forgiven by reason of their inability: and to grant them a Charter to incorporate a new fraternity or brotherhood, to be called Free-hostmen, for the selling and vending of all coals to shipping ; and in consideration thereof, they would pay to Her Majesty and her successors 12d. for every chaldron exported from thenceforth to the free people of this nation."

" The Queen, conceiving that 12d. upon every chaldron would be better for the future, and being well paid, would be raised to a greater revenue than the 2d. so long in arrear could produce, this was granted, on the condition specified in the grant remaining in the Exchequer, with many seals to it, that they should sell all coals to masters of ships. At this day the fitters reckon with the masters for 11s. a chaldron, for so many as are conceived to be on board the ship, and when he goeth with the master to reckon, the said masters pay the 1s. per chaldron custom, being allowed in his hand, the master conceives he doth not pay it further than being left in his hand by the fitter ; but if the masters will look upon that lease, they will find they are to have the best coals for 10s. and the worse for 9s. the chaldron at most, and now they pay 11s. by which means the 1s. per chaldron is paid by the master and not by the hostmen, and so falls upon the whole nation's back ; for if the master buy dear, he must needs sell dear." (Robert Edington, op. cit., pp. 10–11.)

[2] Consult J. V. Nef, *The Rise of the British Coal Industry*, London, 1932, vol. ii, chap. iv (i), pp. 267–284.

condemnation of diverse monopolies, including, of course, coal.[1] After the execution of Charles I, the system of monopolies gave way to the rise of a series of taxes, which were often imposed upon the coal trade. Whenever funds were needed for some special national purpose coal was the surest source to get revenues. An early Act of 1651 imposed a duty on coals to meet the expenses connected with the building of war-ships.[2] A few years later a special levy on sea-borne coal greatly assisted the reconstruction of the City of London, destroyed by the Great Fire.[3] On various occasions coal duties reappeared in the history of the coal trade. As Mr. Hawkes justly noted in the preface to the *Catalogue of Early Mining Literature*, " New churches are required : coal dues are increased ; war funds are needed : coal dues go up again ; and so it went on till in 1793 it is stated that the duty on coals at London is upwards of one hundred per cent. of the prime cost." [4]

All these special taxes, however, dating back to 1379,[5] were far from being systematic or permanent—they appeared when special needs arose, and they were withdrawn when the necessity vanished. These duties latterly took two forms : the duty imposed on sea-borne coal and the export tax. Export taxes were imposed twice on the industry, operating from the beginning of the nineteenth century till August, 1850, when they were finally repealed, and for six years in the twentieth, from 1901–7.

Besides taxation, the *protection of consumers* of coal was

[1] *Vide : The Parliamentary or Constitutional History of England* ; being a faithful Account of all the most remarkable Transactions in Parliament, from the earliest times to the Restoration of King Charles II. Collected. Vol. x, London, 1753, p. 67.

[2] An Act for laying an imposition upon coals, towards the Building and Maintaining Ships for Guarding the Sea. *Die Veneris*, 28 Martii, 1651.

[3] John Holland thus describes the history of that special levy : " Duties were laid upon sea-borne coal, to assist in building St. Paul's church, and fifty parish churches in London, after the great fire in that city and in 1677, Charles the Second granted to his natural son, Charles Lennox, Duke of Richmond, and his heirs a duty of 1s. a chaldron on coals, which continued in the family till it was purchased by Government. This impost, so troublesome to the Tyne coal merchants, and long known as the ' Richmond shilling ', produced, soon after it came into the hands of Government, £25,000 a year." (*The History and Description of Fossil Fuel, the Collieries and Coal Trade of Great Britain*, London, 1835, p. 317.)

[4] Arthur J. Hawkes, *Annotated Catalogue of the Jubilee Exhibition of Early Mining Literature*, Wigan, 1928, p. xi.

[5] The first Government tax on coal was laid in 1379 : " In 1379, a duty of 6d. per ton every quarter of a year was imposed upon ships coming from Newcastle with coals." (See Matthias Dunn, *An Historical, Geological, and Descriptive View of the Coal Trade of the North of England, Comprehending its Rise, Progress, Present State, and Future Prospects, etc.*, Newcastle-upon-Tyne, 1844, p. 12.)

among the earliest functions of the Government in relation to the coal industry. This kind of interference came, however, later, when coal was already well established as an article of general consumption. In this capacity the State was a guardian of prices. State regulation of prices related only to the upper margin, that is to the maximum price, which the owners were allowed to receive for their coal. Already in 1595, following numerous complaints against cornering of coal, a special Commission was appointed in order to inquire into the abuses [1] which then existed. The legislative regulation of coal prices usually referred only to certain parts of the country, and was only in force from time to time when prices soared unduly high. In this case, the State sometimes resorted to prohibitions of export, as for instance in 1563 in Scotland.[2]

In 1642, a law [3] directly to protect the consumers was issued forbidding unduly high quotations for coal in the cities of London and Westminster. This ordinance, however, did not apply to the whole country.

But as a rule the price mechanism was free from State interference. Very often, thus, in the course of the coal trade's history, the citizens or deputations of different organizations

---

[1] We quote here an extract from the correspondence between the Council and the Bishop of Durham dated 27th October, 1595,which reads: " Whereas we are informed that the prices of sea coles are of late rysen to very highe rates within the City of London and elsewhere . . . since divers of the richer sorts of the towne of Newcastle havinge a lease from your lordship of xii cole pittes . . . do forbeare to set the same a worke upon a covetous desire of excessive gayne to themselves and do worke in certain cole pittes of their own in other places which yelde a far worse sort of cole and less quantity . . . " (Reprinted from the Council Register by M. Dorothy George, in " The London Coal-heavers : Attempts to Regulate Waterside Labour in the 18th and 19th Centuries," *Economic Journal*, Hist. Suppl., May, 1927.)

[2] *Vide* Robert Bald, *A General View of the Coal Trade of Scotland, chiefly that of River Forth and Midlothian, etc.*, Edinburgh, 1812, p. 87.

[3] An Ordinance of the Lords and Commons assembled in Parliament, " that no Wharfinger,Woodmonger, or other seller of Newcastle coals, within the Cities of London and Westminster or the suburbes thereof shall after the making hereof sell any Newcastle coales, above the rate of 23s. the chaldron, and after the first of April next, above 20s. at the most, 23rd February, 1642."

The price of coal in those days was excessively high owing to the Ordinance of 16th January, 1642, prohibiting that any vessel " shall make voyage to Newcastle for the fetching of coales . . . until that Towne shall be reduced into such hands as shall declare themselves for King and Parliament ". As the fuel became scarce in London and the price rose to £4 per chaldron, the necessity for statutory regulation arose. This Ordinance is supposed to be the earliest regulation of prices in the coal industry by the State.

asked the Government to regulate the upper limit of prices.
In 1801, Henry Gray Macnab asked the Government to intervene
on account of the high prices of coal.[1] The Limitation of Vend,
an organization of the owners from the Tyne and Wear, was one
of the Government's tasks which brought it into close relation
with the coal industry. A committee on the coal trade was
appointed in 1800 to investigate and present criticisms upon
the practices of the Vend.

A further field where intercourse between the State and the
coal industry was progressing appertained to the Royal Orders
which periodically regulated the *measures* adopted for selling
coal. John Holland pointed out that already in 1327 the
importance of measuring sea-coal was a matter of consideration ;
in 1357, Edward III made several orders referring to the
measuring of coal,[2] while in the XVth century it was regulated
by an Act of Parliament.[3] In 1638, Charles I, in the lease
granted to a corporation presided over by Sir Thomas Tempest
Knight, rigorously prescribed the observance of due measure of
twenty-one bowls to the chaldron, under penalty of confiscation

---

[1] *Vide* " Observation on the probable consequence of even attempting
by legislative authority to obtain a large supply of coal from Staffordshire
to the Metropolis ; on the price of coal to the inhabitants of London
and Westminster ; on the collieries in the North, etc."—Macnab, Henry
Gray, M.D.

There were, however, earlier claims on behalf of the citizens to regulate
the prices of coal by statutory means. But such petitions did not find the
approval of the deciding authorities. Professor Herman Levy quotes one
of such complaints. In his *Monopolies, Cartels, and Trusts in British
Industry*, p. 25, we read : " . . . concentration of the coal trade in a few
hands much disturbed the London buyers, the more so as the price of
coal rose greatly between 1582 and 1590. Rumours of a monopolist ring
among northern coal miners were in the air, and in 1590 the Lord Mayor
of London made complaint to the Treasurer Burleigh that the hostmen
had engrossed the mines, and petitioned that all mines should be worked
and a maximum of 7s. a chaldron fixed." The current price at this time
was 9s. Cf. Matthias Dunn, *A General View on the Coal Trade of the North
of England, etc.*, Newcastle-upon-Tyne, 1844, p. 13.

Cf. J. V. Nef, op. cit., vol. ii, chap. iii.

[2] *Vide* Dunn, op. cit., p. 12.

[3] The Act prescribed " that whereas there is a custom payable to the
King of 2d. per chaldron on all coals sold to persons not franchised in the
port of Newcastle, and whereas the keels which carry the coals from the
land to the ships in that port ought to be of the just portage of twenty
chaldron, according to which burden the custom aforesaid is paid ; yet
many are now making their keels to hold twenty-two, or twenty-three
chaldrons, the King is thereby defrauded of his due : Wherefore it is now
(2nd May, 1421) enacted that all keels be measured by Commissioners
to be appointed by the King, and to be marked of what portage they be
under pain of forfeiting all the said keels which shall be found not marked ".
(See the *History and Description of Fossil Fuel, the Collieries, and Coal
Trade of Great Britain*, London, 1835, p. 313.)

of the cargo in case of abuse.[1] In 1664 an Act was issued regulating prices and measures of coal in London.[2]

While all the earlier regulations of measures prescribed the maximum limits and had fiscal ends in view, viz. the taxation of coal, later Acts aimed at the protection of the consumer against fraudulent practices.[3] Besides protection of consumers by the control of measures and prices, the *quality* of coal delivered was from time to time the subject of State supervision. Cunningham[4] says that there was a considerable interest in the institution of a royal surveyor of coal appointed by King James I to survey " against such as shall offend in such mingling or uttering of unmerchantable coales ".

On the whole, however, all these early regulations only slightly affected either the actual conduct of the industry or its general organization.

Further development of coal-mining brought about a much closer relation with the State. Legislation penetrated slowly

[1] *Vide* Robert Edington, *A Treatise on the Coal Trade, with Strictures on its Abuses and Hints for Amelioration*, London, 1814, p. 18.

[2] Cf. Roman Piotrowski, *Cartels and Trusts : Their Origin and Historical Development from the Economic and Legal Aspects*, London, 1933, p. 293.

[3] To the latter category belongs an Act for reviving a former Act (1665) for regulating the measures and prices of coals (20th December, 1690).

[4] W. Cunningham, "The Growth of English Industry and Commerce in Modern Times," part i, *Mercantile System*, Cambridge, 1925, p. 300, etc. " The King's Most Excellent Majestie . . . having beene very credibly informed of the great abuses and wrongs daily committed in mingling, amongst coales, commonly called Newcastle coales, much Blacke Earth, Dirt, Slate, and other bad stuffe not fit to burne, or serve for firing, and so mingled, are brought and uttered within the Realme of England and thereby for the most part the same Newcastle coales are made unmerchantable to the great hurt and prejudice of the buyers thereof, as well Noblemen, Knights, Gentlemen, and other his Majestie's loving subjects who partly for the preservation of woods, and partly for the scarcitie of woods, doe for the most part burne of the same. With a view to prohibit and suppresse such wrongs and abuses aforesaid a surveyor is appointed to be Surveyor of the said coales who or his Deputie or deputies are to be attending and attendant in and about the searching, viewing, seeing, and surveying of the said coales. And are appointed to informe and complaine against such as shall offend in such mingling or uttering of unmerchantable coales as aforesaid. And to have a seal of office under which to certify what coales and of what sort of goodness of coales any Master, Owner, of Shipper, doe or shall take in, fraight or lade into their Ships or Barkes at the places abovesaid to be brought to the Citie of London or otherwise to be spent within this Realme of England, to the end that the buyers of the same coales may the better know and be informed of the goodnesse or badnesse of them. Anyone having cause or complaint is to go to Andrew Boyde Esquier, his Majestie's Surveyor and then in writing without charge to such as shall so complaine to leave his complaint when the matter shall be attended to." 26th February, 1616.

into the various fields of the industry, progressively regulating more and more of its functions.   When one follows the later history of coal-mining legislation, it is convenient to divide it into that concerned with *safety measures*, and that dealing with the *economic development* of the industry.   This division has been successfully adopted by Mr. D. Morrah [1] in his historical outline of coal mining legislation.   The laws regulating safety, as the author rightly points out, develop *pari passu* with mining technique and belong more strictly to the history of mines as such.   The greater the advance of knowledge, the more complex became safety precautions, and legislation " appeals mainly to the technical expert, e.g. the Act of 1887 [2] compared with that of 1872 discloses a development not of legislative policy, but of the science of mining ".

While technical legislation depended on the development of mining technique and growth of knowledge in preventing accidents, social and economic legislation grew at the same time as the penetration of new ideas concerning the duties of the State in the industry.   This latter form of legislation exerted a dominating influence upon the actual organization of the industry in spite of the resistance of the coal-owners, who derided it as " mixing politics with economics ".[3]

This legislation, which in the early days was haphazard, and regulated fragmentarily or temporarily certain questions in the industry, and so very often tended to disappear or degenerate after a few years of operation, gradually became more systematic and permanent.   The executive element was strengthened and the compulsory features came also more clearly into view.   The conditions created by the State for the coal industry could no longer be evaded ; their observance was subject to strict control.   On the other hand, the position of the coal industry gradually became a subject of detailed

---

[1] Dermont Morrah, *A Historical Outline of Coal Mining Legislation—Historical Review of Coal Mining*, 1924, London.

[2] 50 and 51 Vict. cap. 58.

[3] Mr. Smart reminds us that they were always emphatically opposed to the extension of State influence over the industry, saying : " The feeling against legislation as regards health, compensation, working hours, wages, Government inspection, legislative enactments of 1886 and 1911, etc., have all provoked the use of the same intellectual weapons and remarks in the past, as now in the present. It was stated when children could not be allowed to work underground, ' that the mines must close,' etc." (R. C. Smart, *The Economics of the Coal Industry*, London, 1930, p. 203.)

investigations by means of Select Committees of Parliament. In the nineteenth century social questions and the problem of the reserve of coal, besides technical matters such as safety in mines, etc., were essentially the topics of State investigation.[1] The well-known results and investigations of the Committees provided material for the legislative cure of the evils brought to light. The deplorable *labour conditions* were the first to receive special attention, and it was in that direction that State interference was first directed.

Already in the eighteenth century Acts of Parliament had attacked labour problems by abolishing in 1778 the system of bondage or life serfdom of Scotch miners. A great development of State regulations of social status came in the first half of the nineteenth century. Initially, the miners benefited from general labour legislation, but later there was a necessity for further legislation more particularly on their behalf. After an investigation in which Lord Ashley (afterwards Earl of Shaftesbury) took a leading part, the Ashley Act of 1842 [2] found its way into the Statute Book, prohibiting the employment underground of women and boys under the age of ten. This Act [3] also established inspection of the mines in its embryonic form. But it was only the beginning, and the workpeople were clamouring for an enlargement of the system of inspection and for an increase in safety measures. Several petitions to the House of Commons, inquiries by official and unofficial bodies, the growing organization among the rank and file of the miners, led the Government to introduce a Bill which enlarged the degree of State interference in the working of mines with a view to securing greater safety. This became law and was promulgated in 1850.[4]

The *safety* apparatus created by this Act was temporary, to continue only for a period of five years, and it came nowhere near modern ideas concerning State inspection of mines; none the less it was an important step along the path of State interference in the management of the industry. The new inspectors of mines obtained the right to enforce the clauses

[1] The objects of the Select Committees of both Houses of Parliament (1829, 1830) on the state of the Coal Trade were economic, and referred to the repeal of the duties on sea-borne coal, but they took also a large interest in the question of safety in mines in connection with the use of the Davy lamp. The criticisms brought forward before the Committees were analysed in 1835 by a Select Committee of the House of Commons appointed to investigate and report on the question of accidents in mines.
[2] 5 and 6 Vict. cap. 99.
[3] For further details, see D. Morrah, loc. cit., p. 309, etc.
[4] 13 and 14 Vict. cap. 100.

of the Act relating to safety by legal proceedings against the owners. On the other hand, they could not yet exert any direct influence on the management of the industry.

It was thus only a question of time until the expansion of coal mining caused an elaborate system of State inspection of mines and extensive safety legislation to be evolved, developing side by side with mining technique. Two further legal enactments helped to complete the system of State inspection and to bring the safety regulations to a high pitch. The temporary Act of 1855 [1] created a table of seven " general rules of safety ", which were to be observed by each mine, and opened the way for the permanent law of 1860.[2] This law finally and permanently strengthened the inspectorate, laying the foundations of the modern system of safety regulation in the collieries.

The subsequent mining acts covered an ever larger variety of problems and some of them dealt with several mining questions simultaneously. Thus the law of 1860 gave to the miners the right to appoint checkweighers at every shaft, whose duty was to ensure accuracy in the weighing of coal hewed by miners at the face. In addition to this, Sections I, II, and IV of the same Act raised the required age for certain categories of underground workers.

Legislation henceforth tended clearly towards enlarging the field of State interference by placing more matters under its supervision through a series of enactments of a social character, consolidating the whole into a system of more ordered unity, Thus the Act of 1872 [3] contained orders referring to a variety of questions ; it codified the safety system, which then remained in force for fifteen years and it introduced regulations concerning qualifications required by the managers of mines. Further regulatory Acts appeared successively in 1887, 1894, 1905, 1908. In 1910 came the Mines Accident (Rescue and Award) Act, and finally the Coal Mines Act, 1911, supplemented in 1914.

Owing to the growing Governmental interference in the social, technical, and economic affairs of the coal industry, the authorities appointed to deal with these questions became larger and more complex. The State system of inspection of mines had greatly enlarged its scope and had itself been reconstructed and reinforced by the institution of a Chief Inspector of Mines in 1911. What we have said so far about State interference refers broadly

[1] 18 and 19 Vict. cap. 108.
[2] 23 and 24 Vict. cap. 11.
[3] 35 and 36 Vict. cap. 76.

to the regulation of social questions in the mines, but more strictly to the conditions of work and health.

Government action in recent times, however, has not stopped at this point. Further problems standing on the border-line between the social and the economic provinces of the industry have been embraced. These include the limitation of the working day, the determination of minimum rates of wages, fixing of statutory relations between capital and labour employed in the industry, and other important problems inherent in the industry. The principle of reducing the *hours of work* was already introduced in the Act of 1872, but it referred then only to boys, for whom the ten hours' maximum day was instituted.

Such a limitation of hours marked a new departure in State interference in the social affairs of the industry. It comprised the exclusion of certain categories of the working population from underground work, the methods of paying and ascertaining wages, etc. It opened the gate to State interference in a new field. This limitation of hours was fully made use of in 1908 through the Eight Hours Act,[1] when all underground work was limited to eight hours, including one winding time.

A few years later the Coal Mines (Minimum Wage) Act, 1912, marked a fresh penetration of the State into the industry. It established the principle of a *minimum wage*, but left the actual fixing of the minima for all grades of miners to the *ad hoc* created bodies—District Boards. These Boards consisted of representatives from both sides of the industry together with independent chairmen, who, where the parties failed to agree, very often themselves fixed the amount of the *minimum wage*.[2] Leaving out of consideration the War period when wages were controlled completely from Whitehall, this principle of State regulation of wages was varied even further in 1931—when an Act of Parliament stabilized precisely the amount of the minimum for one year. While the 1912 Act left the fixing of the rates to the District Board, the Act of 1931[3] contained

---

[1] 8 Edw. 7, Ch. 57.

[2] For further particulars see J. W. F. Rowe, *Wages in the Coal Industry*, p. 102, and H. Stanley Jevons, *The British Coal Trade*, p. 520, etc.

[3] 21 and 22 Geo. 5, Chap. 27, An Act to remove for a period not exceeding one year the limitation upon the number of days on which the hours of employment below ground in coal mines may be extended under Section 3 of the Coal Mines Regulation Act, 1908 ; to restrict the duration of such extensions to half an hour on any day, and to provide

provisions for the maintenance during the "period aforesaid of the minimum percentage additions to basic rates of wages and subsistence rates of wages". The difference between the two legislative enactments is that while the former recognized the necessity for the enforcement of minimum rates and left the decision to the district bodies without determining the amounts, the latter decreed the amount of minimum rates. Though the last fixation was only temporary and its main purpose was to avert a pending labour crisis in the mining industry, nevertheless this "stop-gap Act" put Parliament in 1931 for the first time in the position of a direct wage-fixing body.

All these regulations which we have already mentioned referred to the coal industry especially, but a good deal of State interference came also as the result of general industrial legislation applicable also to other industries. Most of these regulations referred to the relation between employers and employees. Acts such as the Truck Act, 1831, the Trade Disputes Act, 1906, the National Insurance Act, 1911, Workmen's Compensation Act, 1905, Employers' Liability Act, 1880, a whole series of Factory and Workshop Acts, which we quote merely as examples and not as an exhaustive list, all had their repercussions on the structure of the coal industry. The Acts dealing with traffic and transport, e.g. the Railway and Canal Traffic Act,[1] which regulated charges and conditions for carrying coal, had a similar influence.

In summarizing the development of State interference in the coal industry, we perceive that up to the War it was reserved to the regulation of social problems and to the provision of multifarious conditions making up the industry's environment. All these measures affected the running of the industry and were indirectly responsible for certain evolutionary changes in its technical and structural formation. But there was not as yet any legislation actually compelling the parties in the industry to adopt fresh forms of organization. Except for the Wage Boards, no other bodies created by the State existed within the coal industry.

for the maintenance during the period aforesaid of minimum percentage additions to basic rates of wages and of subsistence rates of wages (8th July, 1931).
[1] 51 and 52 Vict. Ch. 25.

APPENDIX D

Coal Mines Reorganization Commission

Extracts from Memorandum on Colliery Amalgamations,
August, **1931**

The Coal Mines Reorganization Commission, appointed under the Coal Mines Act, 1930, to further the reorganization of the coal-mining industry, has issued (in 1931) a Memorandum of preliminary notes on the application of Part II of the Coal Mines Act, 1930.

In the course of some introductory remarks, it is pointed out that the object of the memorandum is to make a preliminary survey of the ground and to put forward certain views, not dogmatically but tentatively, as an indication of the lines on which the Commission approaches the subject, and as a basis of discussion with those engaged in the industry. The troubles of the coal-mining industry are much the same as those of the other heavy industries. The days of easy supremacy are gone ; supply exceeds demand ; costs are swollen by part-time working ; unrestricted competition of many hundreds of independent units, which served well enough when we had things all our own way, is positively self-destructive in the altered conditions of to-day. The policy recommended for all these industries by the Balfour Committee on Industry and Trade is one of combination.

Manufacturing industry has an advantage over the coal-mining industry in that rationalization enables it to reduce costs by specialization and concentration on particular processes at particular places. The coal industry cannot do this, but combination is not without analogous advantages on the productive side. Sometimes, for instance, it enables coal to be worked to more convenient shafts, water problems and power supply to be dealt with more rationally, economy to be secured by centralizing the coking and other treatment of coal, the supply, design, and use of wagons, analysis and grading of coal, and so forth. It is true that advocates of amalgamation in the coal-mining industry are often tempted to overstate the possibilities of benefits of this sort. But the opportunities for them vary greatly; and it is not here that the chief importance of amalgamation lies. The vital need of the industry to-day is that costs should be reduced by concentration of productive effort. More pits ought to work to fuller capacity; some ought to stop work altogether, at least temporarily if not permanently. The Commission does not overlook the possibility that this process of shutting down what is often called the " uneconomic " mine may be complicated by obligations to royalty owners. But, speaking generally, this should only mean that the economy is less than it would otherwise be ; it should not mean that no economy is there. The Commission is convinced that nothing can be a satisfactory cure for the ills of the industry unless it has this as its main object. It knows of no sure way of bringing about the necessary concentration of output in the coal-mining industry except consolidation ; and believes that it is precisely because large-scale amalgamations alone can do it that large-scale amalgamations are essential. Central sales organizations are sometimes suggested as an alternative to amalgamation. No doubt they would be useful to the industry. But they cannot do all that is needed, for they do nothing to concentrate productive effort. An attempt to maintain prices is not an adequate substitute for tackling the problem of lowering costs by reorganization.

If the advantages of amalgamation are what the Commission thinks them to be, it follows that, other things being equal, the larger the size of the unit the greater will be the benefits that amalgamation can bring. There is this, too, to be remembered : that the fewer the hands that control the industry the better will it be placed for competing with foreign rivals, or for negotiating agreements with them if that should prove the wiser course. It will perhaps be said that other things are not at all equal, and that beyond a certain size a unit becomes unmanageable. That may be so. But the functions that would properly be performed by the directorate of a great amalgamated concern must not be confused with the functions of technical management. Unless those in control realize what can be centralized and what must be decentralized, amalgamations are likely to lead to a last state that is worse than the first. In technical management there is no doubt a very definite limit to the practicable size of a single unit. But that has nothing to do with the size of the unit of direction. This latter may, for purposes of technical management, contain many units, each practically autonomous. The task of the central directorate would be to determine where the coal for which there is a demand can best be produced, what further development of the coal-field is required, and how and where it shall be undertaken ; to control sales and any other activity that conveniently admits of centralization (as, for instance, wagons, research and the treatment of coal) ; and to regulate the financial position and policy of the undertaking. The Vereinigte Stahlwerke A.-G. in Germany controls an annual output of 35 million tons.

The Commission therefore contemplates, as the ultimate goal of a policy of amalgamation, that the country should be divided up into geographical [1] units, in each of which there should be only one undertaking. It is not supposed that this can everywhere be reached in one stride. It may well be, for instance, that certain undertakings now in existence are not worth bringing into any amalgamated concern. Again it might sometimes prove wise to begin with amalgamation into smaller units as a step towards the combination of these into larger ones. And it is recognized that, if the policy of amalgamation is to reap its full advantages, and the proposal to nationalize royalties is not carried out, it may eventually be found necessary to impose some statutory restraint on the freedom of royalty owners to dispose of their property as they please.

If the industry be looked at in its largest possible natural groupings, it is found to consist of the following :—

Scotland (Ayr, Lanark, Fife, Lothians).
North East (Northumberland, Durham).
North West (Lancashire and Cheshire).
East Midlands (West Yorkshire, South Yorkshire, Nottingham-shire, Derbyshire).
Central Midlands (North Staffordshire, South Staffordshire and Cannock Chase, Shropshire, Warwickshire, South Derby-shire, Leicestershire).
South Wales and Monmouth.—Outside these are six small coal-fields that do not fall so naturally within any grouping. They are in the Forest of Dean, Bristol, Somerset, Kent, Cumberland, and North Wales.

[1] The Commission does not mean to rule out the alternative of grouping according to product, which may in some places temper geographical division. But obviously geography must be, in the main, the determining factor.

SCOTLAND

The Scottish coal-field is well defined, and is sufficiently distant from any other coal-field to be regarded as a separate and single geological unit. It covers approximately 2,400 square miles. Except in the East Lothians, the field is much cut up by faults. Water is prevalent, many of the seams are thin, and the inclination of the strata is often steep and varied. Mining is, therefore, difficult.

The great bulk of the coal is bituminous and, generally speaking, is of a lower grade than English coal. The West Fife area, however, produces high-class dry steam coal, and about 700,000 tons of anthracite are raised annually, chiefly in Stirlingshire. In Lanarkshire, Stirlingshire, and Fifeshire good navigation coals are produced, and in Lanarkshire, Stirlingshire, and Dumbartonshire there are coking coal seams. During 1930 nearly 500,000 tons of coke were produced by 480 coke ovens. The reserves of the field were estimated in 1925 to be 16,500 million tons, about 70 per cent of it in seams over 24 inches thick, and all at a depth less than 4,000 feet. The tendency has been for the production from the eastern and western parts of the field to increase at the expense of the central or Lanark area, some of which is now either nearing exhaustion or working very thin seams in difficult areas rendered more difficult by water problems and the depressed state of industry.

The output in 1930 was nearly 32 million tons, and was produced by 161 undertakings from 373 separate mines. About fifty undertakings, however, were responsible for 95 per cent of the output, nearly 74 per cent was produced from mines owned or controlled by less than twenty undertakings, and over 40 per cent from six undertakings.

Ayr.—The Ayrshire area stretches from the borders of Renfrew in the north to Ayr in the south, about 25 miles, with a width of about 14 miles, with extensions beyond Muirkirk, the detached basins at New Cumrock and Dalmellington, the isolated area of limestone coals near Girvan, and another small area, about 7 by 3 miles, in Dumfrieshire. The output in 1930 was 4 million tons. Nine concerns had an output of 100,000 tons or more, but Messrs. William Baird & Company, Limited, largely dominate the area. Including the three mines in Dumfriesshire of the Sanquhar & Kirkconnel Company, which belongs to them, Messrs. Baird produced over 52 per cent of the 1930 output ; and of the remainder, nearly one-half was produced by the

Dalmellington Iron Company, Limited, and the New Cumrock Collieries, Limited.

Fife and Clackmannan.—In Fife, on the east, the coal-field stretches along the northern shores of the Firth of Forth from the village of Culross in the west to Leven in the east, a distance of 32 miles, with an average width of 6 or 7 miles, and covering an area of about 170 square miles. Westward from Cowdenbeath are the "outer" coal-fields of Saline, Oakley, Blairhall, and Valleyfield, measuring about 6 by 4 miles. The output is about eight million tons a year, and the bulk of it is produced by nine companies, with the Fife Coal Company, Limited; Wemyss Coal Company, Limited, and Lochgelly Iron & Coal Company, Limited, as the largest units. The Fife Coal Company, Limited, produces approximately half the output, and nearly two-thirds of the remainder is produced by the other two. Clackmannan, in which the Alloa Coal Company, Limited, is the chief operator, is possibly more akin to the Central Area.

Lothians.—The Lothian coal-field extends along the southern shores of the Firth of Forth for about 8 miles between Portobello and Port Seaton, and stretches inland for a distance of almost 20 miles. The coal measures dip beneath the Forth, and are presumed to continue into the Dysart-Wemyss field on the north side. The output in 1930 was about five million tons, four-fifths of which was produced by seven different concerns. Three of these, namely, the Lothian Coal Company, Limited; the Edinburgh Collieries Company, Limited; and the Niddrie & Benhar Coal Company, Limited, accounted for over one-half.

Lanark.—The Central Area is roughly bounded by Glasgow and Paisley on the west, by Linlithgow and Bathgate on the east, by Stirling and Carron on the north, and Hamilton, Wishaw, and Shotts on the south, and covers about 1,700 square miles. There are, in addition, two detached basins on the south, at Douglas and Coalburn. Lanarkshire is by far the most productive part of the area, but in its central districts, comprising Glasgow, Hamilton, Airdrie and Wishaw, the bulk of the coal is being got from deep and thin seams, and the output has fallen progressively over a number of years. Future production in this area is likely to gravitate towards the limestone coals to the east and south-east. The Mid-Lanarkshire coal-field is being rapidly exhausted, and the county output as a whole will probably go down.

The total output in 1930 was rather over 15 million tons, of which 10¾ came from Lanarkshire, 2 from Linlithgow, 2 from

Stirling, and something over half a million from Dumbarton. Over 70 per cent of it was produced by fourteen different concerns, of which four, namely, William Baird & Company, Limited, Coltness Iron Company, Limited ; United Collieries, Limited ; and Archibald Russell, Limited, accounted for over one-third. This area depends in the main upon its proximity to local industries. Many of the collieries are practically in vertical combination with iron and steel, but, owing to the present state of those industries, a very small proportion of the coal produced by the vertical combination coal companies is being used by themselves. The position in this respect is entirely changed from 1913.

Such are the four divisions of the Scottish coal-field. They are not isolated and self-contained. Fife and the Lothians are exporting districts. So also is Ayrshire, which sends nearly a third of its output to Ireland. But all the main exporting undertakings have also a large interest in the inland trade. Moreover, several of the larger concerns own pits in more than one of the areas. Nor, again, is any of these areas sufficiently isolated to make it commercially independent of any other. Each of these districts has, from its geographical position, a certain preference in immediately local trade. But, apart from this, there is no practical commercial boundary between the Central Area and Ayrshire on its west, or Fife and the Lothians on its east ; nor is there one between Fife and the Lothians.

It does not appear likely that the full advantage of a policy of amalgamation could ultimately be obtained by any unit smaller than one which comprised the whole of the Scottish coal-field. As has already been mentioned, three-quarters of it is already controlled by under twenty concerns. But practical considerations may point to a less ambitious initial programme of amalgamation by districts.

SOUTH WALES

The South Wales coal-field consists of a single basin, oval in shape, its major axis running almost due east and west. Its extreme length is about 90 miles and its greatest width about 20 miles. The total superficial area, including the undersea extensions in Swansea, and Carmarthen Bays, is a little under 1,000 square miles. The estimated reserves in seams 12 inches thick and over are 26,000 million tons, of which 48 per cent is classified as steam coal, 30 per cent as bituminous, and

22 per cent anthracite. At the present rate of production this is equivalent to a life of over 500 years. The output in 1930 slightly exceeded 45 million tons, equivalent to about 18½ per cent of the total British output. In 1930 the output was produced by 224 undertakings from 464 separate mines, but 24 undertakings were responsible for 92 per cent of the output, and nearly 75 per cent was produced from mines owned or controlled by seven undertakings. More than half the output in 1930 consisted of steam coal, much of it of a high-grade smokeless variety. About one-third was bituminous, 14 per cent of which was converted into coke at 996 coke ovens. The remainder, about 12 per cent of the total output, consisted of anthracite.

The policy of amalgamation has been pursued in South Wales to a far greater extent than in any other coal-field. The land-locked areas created by the deep longitudinal valleys in the eastern and central part of the coal-field are obvious units for single control. It has accordingly been the policy for large concerns to seek to secure domination over the particular district in which they operate. The Ebbw Valley, for example, is dominated by the Ebbw Vale Steel, Iron & Coal Company, Limited; the Tredegar Valley by the Tredegar Iron & Coal Company, Limited; the Rhymney Valley by the Powell Duffryn Steam Coal Company, Limited. But these unifications have gone still further. Already there exist in South Wales seven great undertakings, of which the smallest has an output of 2 million tons and the two largest an output exceeding 8 million tons each. As already stated, they account for nearly 75 per cent of the total production.

One concern—namely, the Amalgamated Anthracite Collieries, Limited—now controls approximately 80 per cent of the Welsh Anthracite output. Five more—namely, Welsh Associated Collieries, Limited; Messrs. Powell Duffryn Steam Coal Company, Limited; Ocean Coal & Wilsons, Limited; Cory Bros. & Company, Limited; and Tredegar Iron & Coal Company, Limited—among them control approximately 70 per cent. of the steam-coal output. Each of these organizations either disposes of its coal to the buyer direct, or has associated with it a selling agency by whom the whole output is dealt with.

There has not been the same concentration of bituminous-coal production. The Ebbw Vale Steel, Iron & Coal Company, Limited, is the largest single producer, but generally speaking, the working of bituminous coal is in the hands of small concerns, of which there is a great number.

Northumberland and Durham

The coal-field of Northumberland and Durham forms a single geological unit, roughly triangular in shape, with its apex at Amble and its base, about 25 miles long, in the latitude of West Hartlepool. The area of the main coal-field amounts to approximately 200 square miles, and is estimated to contain about 10,000 million tons of workable coal, of which about one-fifth lies beneath the sea. It is to the working of undersea coal that modern mining development in the area has been directed. An immense fault, known as the Ninety-fathom Dyke, running along almost the same line as the Tyne, separates the coal-mining areas of the two counties, and brings about a marked physical difference in the seams on each side of it. Those to the north of the fault consist largely of hard, dry steam coals. Those to the south of it are more soft and friable, have admirable coking qualities and are eminently suitable for gas making. Elsewhere faults are relatively rare, inclination is moderate and physical conditions permit working by multiple shifts. But in many other respects there is considerable dissimilarity between the coal-mining areas of Northumberland and Durham.

Northumberland.—The Northumberland coal-field is little more than a third the size of that of Durham and produced just over 13 million tons in 1930. Northumberland is essentially an exporting district in the sense that the bulk of its coal is consumed outside its own borders. There is practically no industry of any size north of Newcastle, and therefore no local industrial market. The district is, therefore, compelled, in order to dispose of its output, either abroad or at home, to do so at highly competitive prices. The output in 1930 was produced by fifty-six undertakings from ninety-nine separate mines. Seventeen undertakings were, however, responsible for over 92 per cent of the output, and four—namely, Ashington Coal Company, Limited ; Mickley & Associated Collieries, Limited ; Hartley Main Collieries, Limited ; and Bodlington Coal Company, Limited—accounted among them for 52 per cent. The royalties of these four undertakings adjoin, extending for a distance of 16 miles from north to south, and occupying practically the whole of the central region of the coal-field. Both the Mickley and Hartley Main groups are the result of recent amalgamations of colliery undertakings.

Durham.—Durham is the third largest coal-field in Great

Britain. The output of 1930 was nearly 36 million tons produced by 97 undertakings from 237 separate mines. About
21 undertakings, however, were responsible for 92 per cent
of the output and over 52 per cent was produced from mines
owned or controlled by 7 undertakings. The bulk of the coal
is coking coal, and a considerable proportion is converted into
metallurgical coke. In 1929, $6\frac{1}{2}$ million tons of coal were
carbonized in 2,860 local coke ovens. In 1930, however,
owing to the depressed condition of the iron and steel trade,
the tonnage of coal treated fell to little over 5 million tons
in 2,504 ovens. The field is an old one, development having
proceeded from west to east, until in recent years the working
of undersea coals, at considerable depths, has been undertaken.
Many of the older pits were intimately associated with the
manufacture of iron and steel. Some are exhausted and have
closed down. Others are approaching exhaustion.

The closing of mines near the outcrop and the percolation
of water into their old workings is constituting a serious menace
to adjacent collieries situated to the deep. The problem of
mine drainage promises to become progressively more acute
as collieries to the rise close down, but so far no scheme for
co-operative pumping has materialized. Nor, apart from a
few isolated cases, has there been any recent movement towards
amalgamation of colliery interests in any form. Yet Durham
is essentially a district of small amalgamations in the sense
that many concerns operate a number of collieries. Eleven
undertakings control five or more collieries. Four of them have
ten or more. One concern has twenty. No less than 81 per cent
of the total output is produced by 15 undertakings, each with
an output of over one million tons per annum.

In spite of their contiguity, therefore, the coal-fields of
Northumberland and Durham show marked differences in
conditions and circumstances. Whatever developments there
might ultimately be, it seems enough, at present, to consider
the question of amalgamation in each separately ; and
Northumberland, at any rate, seems to afford a *prima facie*
case for a single undertaking.

EAST MIDLAND COAL-FIELD

The East Midland coal-field is the largest single coal-producing
area in Great Britain. It extends from Leeds to Nottingham,
a distance of about 68 miles, and its total area is about 2,100

square miles.   The developed part of the coal-field is contained
in three counties, namely, Yorkshire, Nottinghamshire, and
Derbyshire (north of the river Trent).   It contains three series
of coal measures, most of the best seams occurring in the middle
and lower series.   The western part of the field works the
lower coals at shallow levels, but in the east these seams are
below the limits of practical mining and it is the middle measures
that are worked.   The prize of this series is the Barnsley Bed,
which is known to exist over an area of 600 square miles.   In
Nottinghamshire a change in the inclination of the seams enables
both middle and lower series to be worked.   The estimated
reserves of a field whose limits have not yet been defined can
only be conjectured.   They were estimated by the Royal
Commission of 1905 at 26,500 million tons.   The output in 1930
was nearly 73 million tons, which is equivalent to over 30 per cent
of the total British output.

It is only for certain special and limited purposes that the
whole of this area has been treated as a single unit or as part
of a single unit.   For most purposes it is divided into four
districts, viz., West Yorkshire, South Yorkshire, Nottinghamshire,   and   North   Derbyshire.   The   division   between
Nottinghamshire and Derbyshire, however, is almost entirely
an arbitrary one.   It is true that the Nottinghamshire field is
newer and deeper than that of North Derbyshire and produces
steam coals as well as the softer coals of the lower series, but
it is essentially a development of the North Derbyshire field.
Several large concerns have colliery properties in both districts,
and a single association represents owners in both.

West Yorkshire.—The output of coal in 1930 was about 12$\frac{1}{4}$
million tons from 113 mines in 71 different ownerships.   Ninety
per cent was, however, produced by 18 concerns operating 41
mines, and 48 per cent by 4 concerns and their subsidiaries.

Owing to the comparative shallowness of the seams the field
is more fully developed than South Yorkshire, and the suitability
of its products for manufacturing purposes has led to the growth
about it of a densely populated industrial area, which absorbs
the greater part of the output.   West Yorkshire is notably
a district of intermixed ownerships.   There are many places
in which different seams in the same lands are being worked by
different concerns.

South Yorkshire.—The South Yorkshire coal-field is a newer
development.   The output in 1930 was 32$\frac{1}{4}$ million tons from
104 mines owned by 72 different undertakings.   Ninety-one

per cent was, however, produced from 54 mines in 28 ownerships. Eleven of these concerns had an output of over one million tons each and seven more approached that figure.

The eastern extension of the field, in which most of the new pits are situated, is still rural. No town of any size exists, save Doncaster, and there are practically no local manufacturing industries. Accordingly the greater part of the output is consumed outside the district. Much goes to Lancashire, and a considerable quantity is exported either as cargo or as bunkers for foreign-going vessels. Coal shipments from the Humber ports in 1930 were nearly nine million tons. A special feature of the area is the uniformity with which the seams persist at a convenient thickness over large areas, and the pits are generally of the newest type and equipment.

The surface over a great part of the coal-field is flat and but a few feet above sea-level. The question of subsidence is therefore of special importance, and the problem of surface drainage is both serious and difficult. For purposes of mines drainage the community of interests of the collieries has already been recognized in an Order under Section 18 of the Mining Industry Act, 1920, which, shortly stated, has put the control and the cost of mines drainage upon a co-operative basis. There have been several amalgamations of colliery undertakings in South Yorkshire in recent years. Four large concerns, namely, Denaby & Cadeby Main Collieries, Limited; Dinnington Main Coal Company, Limited; Maltby Main Colliery Company, Limited; and Rossington Main Colliery Company, Limited; are combined under the title of Yorkshire Amalgamated Collieries, Limited. The amalgamated concern is linked up with the Sheepbridge Coal & Iron Company, Limited, which has extensive colliery interests in Derbyshire. The Carlton Main Colliery Company, Limited; Hatfield Main Colliery Company, Limited; and the Hodroyd Coal Company, Limited, are also under single control, which, too, has interests in another coal-field. Several smaller unifications have taken place. Moreover, groups of undertakings, though maintaining their legal individuality, have joined together for common selling of their products and other purposes. The largest of these organizations is the Doncaster Collieries Association, which disposes of the output of six of the largest collieries in the East Midlands, five of which are in South Yorkshire. Another is the Rotherham and District Collieries Association.

Nottinghamshire and North Derbyshire.—The coal-field of

Nottinghamshire and North Derbyshire is similar to that of Yorkshire in that development has proceeded from west to east, and has resulted in adding the steam coals of the middle series to the softer coals of the lower series worked in the west.

Nottinghamshire is not, however, so essentially a steam-coal area as is South Yorkshire.   The Barnsley Bed (or the Top Hard, as it is locally known) is neither so persistent nor of such uniform quality in Nottingham as in Yorkshire.   On the other hand, lower seams which, owing to their depth, are incapable of being worked at present throughout the greater part of South Yorkshire, are worked in Nottinghamshire.   Nottinghamshire, therefore, has developed a house-coal trade, particularly with London and the South of England.   The output of the Nottinghamshire and North Derbyshire coal-field in 1930 was $28\frac{1}{2}$ million tons from 143 mines in 78 different ownerships. Ninety-one per cent of the output was, however, produced by 26 undertakings operating 82 mines.   Nine of these concerns had an output of over one million tons each and four others approached that figure.   Several of them have substantial interests in colliery properties in other districts, mainly South Yorkshire.

The natural division of the East Midlands coal-field appears to be into three.   Between Nottinghamshire and North Derbyshire no logical line seems to exist.   Between Nottinghamshire and South Yorkshire (subject always to the precise location of the boundary line) a clearer demarcation can be found.   Apart from the fact that much Nottinghamshire coal is of a different kind from that of South Yorkshire, it appears, broadly speaking, that in practice the markets which it serves are rather different from those of South Yorkshire.   Much of the coal of which South Yorkshire disposes outside its own area goes abroad or into Lancashire.   The coals of Nottinghamshire and Derbyshire tend rather to gravitate southwards.

Between West and South Yorkshire again, a distinction can be drawn as regards both the mining and the commercial conditions of the older and shallower field in the west of the country and the newer and deeper pits of South Yorkshire. The precise line of the boundary between the two divisions might require some rectification to bring it more into keeping with the circumstances of to-day, but, subject to this, it may be said, broadly, that West Yorkshire produces in the main a different class of coal from that produced in South Yorkshire and sells it in a more restricted market.   There may be grounds, therefore, for regarding this coal-field as comprising three distinguishable districts : (1) West Yorkshire, (2) South Yorkshire, and (3) Nottinghamshire and North Derbyshire, and for the view that the problem of amalgamation should be considered separately in each of them.

LANCASHIRE AND CHESHIRE

The Lancashire coal-field is triangular in shape with its apex 4 miles north of Burnley and its base between Prescot on the west and Stalybridge on the east. The most productive part of the field is, however, confined to a belt about 8 miles wide at the base of the triangle. The resources of the proved coal-field are estimated at about 4,000 million tons. The output in 1930 amounted to 15 million tons, produced by approximately 74,200 workpeople. During the present year (1931) the output has been at a level equivalent to 15¼ million tons a year with an average number of workpeople employed of 72,100. Production has gradually declined since 1907 (when it was in the region of 26 million tons per annum) mainly owing to the exhaustion of some of the richer seams. Many of the older collieries are now working less productive seams at great depths.

The highly industrialized and thickly populated area of South Lancashire absorbs practically the whole of the local output. Lancashire is, indeed, a heavy importer of coal, particularly small steam coal for industrial purposes, from other districts. Much of the deficiency is supplied by South Yorkshire. The output in 1930 was produced from 190 collieries in 101 different ownerships, but 33 undertakings were responsible for 75 per cent of the total, and 37 per cent was produced from mines controlled by two undertakings.

Lancashire is faced with heavy costs of production, particularly wages costs, and though proceeds are about 3s. a ton higher than the average, the net result is to leave Lancashire worse off than any other large district.

Before 1929 Lancashire contained no large amalgamation of colliery undertakings, although several concerns each operated a number of pits. Of these, the Wigan Coal & Iron Company, Limited, was the largest. In 1929 six colliery companies and their subsidiaries operating 22 mines combined to form the Manchester Collieries, Limited, which brought under a single control practically the whole of the collieries in the south-eastern portion of the coal-field. Three other amalgamation schemes have since come into operation. The Garswood Hall Collieries Company, Limited, and the Garswood Coal & Iron Company, Limited, who operate six pits between Wigan and St. Helens, are now a single company. Messrs. John Hargreaves and Company, Limited; George Hargreaves & Company, Limited; and the Altham Colliery Company, Limited, who among them own 20 small mines in the Burnley district, have centralized the treatment and disposed of their products in a new company under the name of the Lancashire Foundry Coke Company, Limited. Four other concerns—namely, the Wigan Coal & Iron Company, Limited; Pearson & Knowles Coal & Iron Company, Limited; Moss Hall Coal Company, Limited; and the Wigan Junction Colliery Company, Limited, have combined their colliery assets, consisting of 17 pits, in an amalgamated undertaking known as the Wigan Coal Corporation, Limited. The new concern is controlled by the Lancashire Steel Corporation, Limited, which is a combination of the iron and steel interests of two of the constituent companies and of their subsidiaries. These four groups among them produce over 46 per cent of the total Lancashire output. Proposals for further amalgamation of the Lancashire coal industry are now being canvassed.

Apart from the small northern extension around Burnley, the Lancashire coal-field is highly concentrated, and its products are absorbed in the thickly populated industrial area which has developed about it. Lancashire collieries not only compete among themselves in a purely local market, but must also compete with the more cheaply produced coal from other districts. Yet, notwithstanding the excess of local demand over local supply, short-time working is more prevalent in Lancashire than in almost every other district. Lancashire is, therefore, faced with the necessity for reducing costs to maintain her own market, and it appears unlikely that this can ultimately be accomplished by anything short of a district amalgamation.

CENTRAL MIDLAND COAL-FIELDS

In the central part of England are five small coal-fields. They are known as the coal-fields of (1) Shropshire, (2) North Staffordshire, (3) South Staffordshire (including Cannock Chase) and Worcestershire, (4) Warwickshire, (5) South Derbyshire and Leicestershire. The combined output of the five coal-fields in 1930 was 21¼ million tons, which is equivalent to nearly 9 per cent

of the total British production. This is less than the output
of any of the five large districts, Lancashire excepted.

Shropshire.—The county of Shropshire contains a number
of small coal-producing areas, only one of which is of relative
importance. This, known as the Coalbrookdale coal-field,
extends from Lilleshall in the north to Linley in the south
and covers an area of about 18 square miles. It is estimated
to contain about 150 million tons of workable coal. Its output
in 1930 was less than 700,000 tons from 37 mines in 27 different
ownerships. Ninety-three per cent, however, was produced
by four separate undertakings operating seven mines, and
75 per cent by two concerns which, between them, work five
collieries. Most of the coal is of the household and manufacturing variety and is consumed in the locality.

North Staffordshire.—The North Staffordshire coal-field consists
of a triangular-shaped area, about 100 square miles in extent,
situated around the pottery towns. It contains an available
quantity of coal estimated at about 4,000 million tons. A
small extension of the main field to the east in the neighbourhood
of Cheadle covers an area of about 18 square miles. The total
output in 1930 amounted to about $5\frac{1}{2}$ million tons, which was
produced by 49 separate undertakings operating 60 collieries.
Ninety-seven per cent was, however, produced by 16 undertakings from 34 mines.

Practically the whole of the output is consumed inland, the
greater part of it locally.

South Staffordshire and Cannock Chase.—The South Staffordshire and Cannock Chase coal-field extends from Rugeley in the
north to Bromsgrove-Lickey in the south, a distance of about 26
miles. Its greatest width in the latitude of Wolverhampton is
about 9 miles. The total area is about 149 square miles and the
field is estimated to contain about 1,400 million tons of workable
coal. An immense faulting system north of Wolverhampton,
known as the Bentley Fault, divides the coal-field into two
distinct portions, each of which has definite characteristics of
its own. In the southern part certain seams have converged
to form a single seam, known as the South Staffordshire Thick
Coal or Ten Yard seam. This seam, owing to its easy accessibility,
has been worked for centuries past, and is now nearly exhausted.
Its extraction has resulted in disastrous consequences, both to
the surface and mine workings. The whole district is becoming
more and more waterlogged and decreasing in importance as
a coal-producing unit The northern part of the field, known

as Cannock Chase, is a more modern development, and has now assumed the importance previously enjoyed by its southerly neighbour.

South Staffordshire.—The output in 1930 was 1·6 million tons produced by 55 different undertakings from 74 mines. The great majority are very small concerns working isolated remnants of the Thick Coal, and are of no practical importance. Many of the larger undertakings, too, have but a short life before them. Nearly 59 per cent of the total output was produced by three undertakings. Most of the output is consumed locally.

Cannock Chase.—The Cannock Chase coal-mining area is compact, and possesses fairly uniform conditions throughout. There are eight seams of economic importance at present being worked, which yield house, manufacturing, and locomotive coals. The output in 1930 was nearly 5 million tons from 38 mines in 23 separate ownerships, 99 per cent of which, however, was produced by 13 separate concerns from 24 mines. The size and capacity of the more important colliery undertakings in Cannock Chase are fairly uniform. Each employs over 1,000 workpeople, and practically all have outputs ranging from a quarter to half a million tons per annum. A large proportion of their products is house coal. Most of it is disposed of in markets outside the district, particularly London and the South of England.

Warwickshire.—A deep geological trough separates the South Staffordshire coal-field from the Warwickshire coal-field. The latter extends from Tamworth in the north to Warwick in the south, has a maximum breadth of about 8 miles, and occupies slightly under 150 square miles. The estimated quantity of coal remaining unworked is about 1,000 million tons. The output in 1930 of 4·92 million tons was produced by 16 different undertakings from 18 mines, but 82 per cent of it was produced by 9 undertakings from 10 mines. The curious feature of the South Staffordshire coal-field represented by the Ten Yard seam is reproduced in Warwickshire, where towards the centre of the coal-field five seams converge into a single seam 24 feet thick. Unlike South Staffordshire, however, this coal is found at much lower levels, and requires not only a high degree of skill, but also heavy maintenance costs in working it. There is, too, a considerable diminution in the workable resources towards the northern part of the field. These physical changes have placed certain collieries at a disadvantage compared with their neighbours, and for a time special wage rates, at a lower level than those generally prevailing in the district, were applicable to them.

The remainder of the collieries are relatively successful undertakings. The Warwickshire coal-field is nearer to London than any other coal-producing district, except Kent, and it is to London and the south that most of the output is sent. The district, therefore, enjoys an easily accessible inland market, and commands uniformly high pithead prices. Costs, on the other hand, are little above the average. Apart from the Warwickshire Coal Company, Limited, and Merry & Cuninghame, Limited, which are subsidiaries of colliery undertakings in another district, the larger Warwickshire concerns have neither any close associations one with another nor with coal interests elsewhere. But, like Cannock Chase, there is a good deal of similarity among them both as regards their size, their products, and their markets.

South Derbyshire and Leicestershire.—Five miles north-east of the Warwickshire coal-field is situated the most easterly of the Central Midland coal-fields. It occupies an area of about 76 square miles, 60 of which are in the county of Leicester, and 16 in South Derbyshire. The available reserves are estimated at 1,800 million tons. The output in 1930 was 3·6 million tons, which was produced by 27 collieries in 20 separate ownerships. Ninety-nine per cent was, however, produced by 21 mines operated by 14 completely independent undertakings. Like most of the Central Midland districts, the pits are of a moderate uniform size. The output is almost wholly consumed inland, either locally or in the South of England.

As to the proper application of a policy of amalgamation, this much at least is obvious, that each of these small self-contained and compact coal-fields ought to be under single control. And the question whether any two or more of them ought to be combined is clearly one for consideration.

COAL-FIELDS IN THE FOREST OF DEAN, BRISTOL, SOMERSET, KENT, CUMBERLAND, AND NORTH WALES

There now remain only the six small coal-fields which need separate consideration.

Forest of Dean.—The Forest coal-field is reputed to be the oldest in the country. It is situated on the northern bank of the Severn estuary, and occupies an area of about 34 square miles. The ownership of minerals is in the Crown, but the right to work them is governed by curious statutes and customs, the application of which has confined mining operations to comparatively shallow levels until recent years. The output in 1930 was 1·30 million tons from 45 mines in 38 separate ownerships. Eighty-six per cent of the output was, however, produced by four concerns operating seven mines. Each of these four undertakings is working the Coleford High Delf, but, apart from friendly co-operation in selling arrangements, they have no connection with each other. Their product is eminently suitable for manufacturing purposes, particularly the tinplate trade, and finds a ready market in the near locality.

Bristol and Somerset.—Situated on the southern bank of the Severn estuary, partly in the county of Gloucester and partly in Somerset, are six detached areas of coal measures. These constitute what are commonly known as the Bristol and Somersetshire coal-fields. Their total area is estimated at 240 square miles, and the net available resources at 4,000 million tons. There is considerable variation both in quantity and quality of the deposit of the various areas, but, on the whole, the seams are thin and furnish coal of inferior quality. Only a few of the seams are worked. The total output of the two fields in 1930 was slightly over one million tons, of which about 200,000 tons were produced in the Bristol coal-field and 800,000 tons in Somerset. It was produced from 19 mines in 9 separate ownerships. Nearly 50 per cent, however, was raised by two concerns, one of which has colliery interests in both districts. The bulk of the coal is consumed locally.

Kent.—The coal-field of Kent is the newest development in Great Britain. It now contains four working collieries, whose combined output in 1930 was 1·29 million tons. All the collieries are in process of development, and have not yet reached their maximum potential capacity. Two are in common ownership. Most of the output is consumed by local industries, particularly paper and cement works situated along the Thames estuary, and by the Southern Railway. A little is exported.

Cumberland.—The Cumberland coal-field extends from White-haven to Maryport, a distance of 14 miles with an average width of $4\frac{1}{2}$ miles. An estimate of the reserves is problematical, but it is assumed to be about 1,500 million tons. The bulk of the coal is bituminous, and much of it is capable of being converted into metallurgical coke. In 1930 about one-third of the total production was carbonized locally in 302 ovens. The output in 1930 was slightly over two million tons. It was raised by 17 separate undertakings from 32 mines. Ninety-eight per cent, however, was produced by 8 separate undertakings operating 21 mines. The Cumberland coal industry is closely allied to the local iron and steel industry. The United Steel Companies, Limited, consume nearly 50 per cent of the coal produced in the county, and a further 20 per cent is sold in neighbouring industrial and domestic markets. Of the remainder, most goes to Ireland.

North Wales.—The developed portion of the North Wales coal-field is situated in the counties of Denbigh and Flint. The coal-producing areas of the two counties are practically detached from each other, and are sometimes regarded as constituting separate districts. The Denbighshire district occupies an area of approximately 47 square miles, and is estimated to contain about 950 million tons of working coal. That of Flintshire occupies an area of about 35 square miles, with 750 million tons of unworked coal. The field is much disturbed and heavily faulted. Water is encountered in large quantities. The bulk of the coal produced is classified as steam-raising, but some seams yield house and gas coals. The output in 1930 was just over $3\frac{1}{4}$ million tons, produced by 25 mines in 23 different ownerships. Ninety-one per cent was obtained from 11 mines belonging to 9 different undertakings. One mine, Llay Main, is by far the largest single unit, and is owned by the Carlton Main Colliery Company, Limited, a South Yorkshire undertaking.

The internal circumstances to be found in each of these districts, coupled with the smallness of their outputs, suggest that in none of them can there be room for more than a single control. The districts of Bristol and Somerset, too, being so nearly contiguous and so similar in their conditions, must be regarded for this purpose as one. Whether any others of them should ultimately be combined with any of the larger districts is one of the matters which requires closer examination.

INDEX

Names of books and reports are not included in the index.—A (Appendix).

Printed in Great Britain by Stephen Austin & Sons, Limited, Hertford.

For Product Safety Concerns and Information please contact our EU
representative GPSR@taylorandfrancis.com
Taylor & Francis Verlag GmbH, Kaufingerstraße 24, 80331 München, Germany

www.ingramcontent.com/pod-product-compliance
Lightning Source LLC
Chambersburg PA
CBHW031348210326
41599CB00019B/2686